The
BOOKER T. WASHINGTON
Papers

The
BOOKER T. WASHINGTON
Papers

VOLUME 8

1904–6

Louis R. Harlan
and
Raymond W. Smock
EDITORS

Geraldine McTigue
ASSISTANT EDITOR

University of Illinois Press
URBANA · CHICAGO · LONDON

The Booker T. Washington *Papers*
is supported by
The National Endowment for the Humanities
The National Historical Publications and Records Commission
The University of Maryland

Library of Congress Cataloging in Publication Data

Washington, Booker Taliaferro, 1856–1915.
The Booker T. Washington papers.

Includes bibliographies.
CONTENTS: v. 1. The autobiographical writings.
—v. 2. 1860–89.—v. 3. 1889–95.—v. 4. 1895–98.—v. 5. 1899–1900.
—v. 6. 1901–2.—v. 7. 1903–4.—v. 8. 1904–6.
Vol. 8 edited by L. R. Harlan and R. W.
Smock; G. McTigue, assistant editor.
1. Washington, Booker Taliaferro, 1856–1915.
2. Afro-Americans—Biography. 3. Afro-Americans—
History. 4. Afro-Americans—History—Sources.
I. Harlan, Louis R. II. Smock, Raymond W.
E185.97.W274 301.45'19'6073024 75–186345
ISBN 0–252–00728–X (v. 8)

To the Memory of
Timothy Thomas Fortune

CONTENTS

ILLUSTRATIONS

TUSKEGEE INSTITUTE IN 1906
Photographs by Frances Benjamin Johnston

INTRODUCTION

IN THE NEARLY TWO YEARS covered by this volume, Washington rode the crest of the wave of fame and influence that followed *Up from Slavery* and the dinner at the White House three years earlier. Despite Washington's unrivaled position, however, much of his energy in these years went into putting out the fires of black opposition to his leadership.

The volume begins with Washington's instructions to one of the black newspaper editors he subsidized. J. Max Barber's gradual movement out of Washington's orbit and into direct criticism is treated in detail, as well as Washington's efforts to silence Barber. The volume includes the complete text and enclosures of W. E. B. Du Bois's letter to Oswald Garrison Villard charging that Washington used "hush money" to control the black press.

In politics Washington consolidated his position as presidential adviser and patronage broker, while seeking publicly to understate his role. Roosevelt's renomination and re-election in 1904 with Washington's help and advice allowed Washington the opportunity to reward and punish. His lieutenant Charles W. Anderson became internal revenue collector for the Wall Street district. Judson W. Lyons of Georgia, on the other hand, was removed as register of the treasury after Washington learned that he had written a letter of sympathy to William Monroe Trotter after the Boston Riot. Washington pushed his Chicago lieutenant S. Laing Williams as Lyons's replacement, but when Williams could not get the backing of his state's congressional delegation Washington had to acquiesce in this political plum going to William T. Vernon, who was not really a member of the Tuskegee Machine.

As the Committee of Twelve for the Advancement of the Negro

Race died aborning because Washington packed its membership, Du Bois in 1905 launched the Niagara Movement to promote civil rights and black advancement. Washington's response was to spy on and infiltrate its meetings, and to use his power and influence to thwart both the organization and its individual members. Washington and Emmett Scott became so busy managing the Tuskegee Machine that Washington employed a ghostwriter, the white journalist and later University of Chicago professor Robert E. Park, to write the more general books and articles signed by Washington.

The story of Tuskegee Institute figures less prominently in this volume even though important events in the school's history such as the celebration of its twenty-fifth anniversary are documented. Washington lost a close friend and adviser with the death of William H. Baldwin, Jr., a Tuskegee Institute board member. After Baldwin's death, however, Oswald Garrison Villard raised a Baldwin Memorial Fund for Tuskegee and aided Washington's secret civil rights efforts, thus preserving the neo-abolitionist connection with Tuskegee. The school easily weathered the furor caused by a scurrilous booklet written by a local white man charging sexual misconduct on the campus. Ex-students continued to go into the South as teachers and workers, and four went to the Sudan to take part in a cotton-growing experiment.

Washington's influence on philanthropic aid to black schools was enhanced in 1905 by the first gifts to southern rural black schools by Anna T. Jeanes. He also was instrumental in the securing of Carnegie libraries by Fisk, Livingstone, and Wiley universities.

Among the honors that came to Washington in this period were the vice-presidency of the American Peace Society and election as an honorary member of Phi Beta Kappa at Harvard. A different sort of notoriety, however, followed his entertainment at dinner in a Saratoga, New York, hotel by the millionaire John Wanamaker and his daughter. The Wanamaker dinner revived memories of the White House dinner and produced similar denunciations. These were so vehement that Washington hired a Pinkerton detective to guard him on his return to Tuskegee and a few weeks later on the occasion of President Roosevelt's visit to the institute. Washington was also criticized by blacks and liberal whites for unnecessarily explaining that he did not escort Wanamaker's daughter into the dining room.

The staff of the Booker T. Washington Papers has maintained its cheerful efficiency through this volume, and the editors warmly thank Patricia A. Cooper, Sadie M. Harlan, Janet E. Hartman, Denise P. Moore, Susan M. Valenza, and Richard B. Wilkof.

We thank John F. Marszalek of Mississippi State University and Ralph E. Luker of Allegheny College for calling to our attention the errors corrected on the errata page of this volume.

We are grateful to the National Endowment for the Humanities, the National Historical Publications and Records Commission, and the University of Maryland for their generous support of this project.

ERRATA

Volume 3, p. 43, n. 11. The man wrongly identified as John William De Forest was actually Henry Swift De Forest (1833–96), president of Talladega College from 1879 until his death.

Volume 4, p. 309, n. 1. The man wrongly identified as Robert Brown Elliott was actually William Elliott, a white man. The letter to BTW, Apr. 25, 1898, was from Rev. G. M. Elliott of Beaufort, S.C.

Volume 4, p. 436. J. C. Ladevize should be John Carrie Ladeveze, a light-skinned black man of Haitian origin who conducted an art store in Augusta established by his father, with a largely white clientele, but owned real estate in the black sections and was a deacon in the upper-class black Union Baptist Church. Biographical information on Ladeveze and an analysis of the Cumming case may be found in J. Morgan Kousser, "Separate but *Not* Equal: The Supreme Court's First Decision on Discrimination in Schools," Social Science Working Paper No. 204, California Institute of Technology, March 1978.

Volume 4, p. 510. The full name of J. S. Harper was James Snowden Harper. He was a first cousin of John Carrie Ladeveze, a railway mail clerk for three decades, an officer of Paine Institute, and from 1885 to 1912 president of a black bank, the Workingman's Loan and Building Association of Augusta.

SYMBOLS AND ABBREVIATIONS

STANDARD ABBREVIATIONS for dates, months, and states are used by the editors only in footnotes and endnotes; textual abbreviations are reproduced as found.

DOCUMENT SYMBOLS

1. A — autograph; written in author's hand
   H — handwritten by other than signator
   P — printed
   T — typed

2. C — postcard
   D — document
   E — endorsement
   L — letter
   M — manuscript
   W — wire (telegram)

3. c — carbon
   d — draft
   f — fragment
   p — letterpress
   t — transcript or copy made at much later date

4. I — initialed by author
   r — representation; signed or initialed in author's name
   S — signed by author

Among the more common endnote abbreviations are: ALS — autograph letter, signed by author; TLpI — typed letter, letterpress copy, initialed by author.

REPOSITORY SYMBOLS

Symbols used for repositories are the standard ones used in *Symbols of American Libraries Used in the National Union Catalog of the Library of Congress*, 10th ed. (Washington, D.C., 1969).

ATT	Tuskegee Institute, Tuskegee, Ala.
CtY	Yale University, New Haven, Conn.
DHU	Howard University, Washington, D.C.
DLC	Library of Congress, Washington, D.C.
MH	Harvard University, Cambridge, Mass.
NN-Sc	Schomburg Collection, New York Public Library, NYC.
ViHaI	Hampton Institute, Hampton, Va.
NNC	Columbia University, NYC.

OTHER ABBREVIATIONS

BTW	Booker T. Washington
Con.	Container
NNBL	National Negro Business League
RG	Record Group

Documents, 1904–6

To Charles Alexander

South Weymouth, Mass. July 4, 1904

Dear Mr. Alexander: Enclosed I am sending considerable matter, but I am very anxious that all of it appear in this week's paper. I will see you about it Tuesday.

You will note that my name is mentioned twice in the correspondence and I hope you will see that it does not appear anywhere else in your paper this week.

The editorial on John F. Cook I think you will find will increase your circulation in Washington; it will certainly attract some attention there. Yours very truly,

[Booker T. Washington]

TLc Con. 19 BTW Papers DLC.

To William Harvey Goler[1]

South Weymouth, Mass. July 4, 1904

My dear Sir: I wonder if you have ever made an application to Mr. Andrew Carnegie for a library building for your college? If you have not, perhaps I can help you to secure one. I do not want to make the attempt, however, if you have plans under way that will secure the same result. I am very anxious that while Mr. Carnegie is giving away his money that our race be benefited as much as possible. Yours truly,

[Booker T. Washington]

TLc Con. 288 BTW Papers DLC.

[1] William Harvey Goler was born in Nova Scotia in 1846. He was pastor of St. Matthew's Church (A.M.E. Zion) in Greensboro, N.C., from 1881 to 1884. He joined the faculty of Livingstone College, Salisbury, N.C., in 1884 and was president of the school from 1894 to 1917.

To Joseph Oswalt Thompson

South Weymouth, Mass. July 4, 1904

Personal

My dear Mr. Thompson: I am in receipt of your letter of June 27th which I have been delayed in answering owing to being continually on the railroad.

I heard most excellent reports when I was in Chicago a few days ago about the manly stand that the Alabama delegation took in regard to all matters affecting our race and the party. We won a great victory.

I fear I shall not see you until you come North to go to Oyster Bay. I will try to be in New York at that time.

In regard to the Mexican mission, I would state that I have some question as to whether Captain Scott[1] would accept the mission owing to his important business connections. Would it not also be a better plan to try to push Mr. Hundley for that position in case Captain Scott could not for any reason take it? I will be willing to cooperate with you in any way that I can.

I saw the President for an hour and a half last week and went over matters very thoroughly with him. I asked him to appoint Judge Kyle to the Panama Judgeship and he agreed to do so at once and in my presence wrote the order to Secretary Taft. I hope that he has acted all right regarding the clerkship. Yours truly,

[Booker T. Washington]

TLc Con. 25 BTW Papers DLC.

[1] Charles Herrington Scott.

To George Washington Taylor[1]

South Weymouth, Mass. July 5, 1904

Dear Sir: I am in receipt of your letter of June 27th[2] which has been forwarded to me here, which will be my address during the summer.

I thank you very much for your full and frank letter. It is always to me a matter of the deepest satisfaction to have correspondence with a man who uses his reason instead of his feelings.

Doubtless since your letter was written you have seen the census figures which contain an answer I think to the main point raised in your letter, and that is, the proportion of Negroes with mixed blood in this country. If you have not seen these figures I will send them to you as soon as I can put my hands on them; I take for granted, however, that you have seen them as they were evidently sent out in the Associated Press and published rather widely only three days ago.

On one point raised in your letter I cannot bring myself to the point of agreeing with you. You are evidently of the opinion that persons with mixed blood have been those who have exhibited the most strength of mind. Let me give one example: From the organization of our institution at Tuskegee we have made it the plan to give the highest honor — the valedictory — to the student who stood best in his academic and industrial work as well as in his moral character. In voting to select the valedictorian our teachers do not have even the name of the students before them, they simply deal with the marks and do not know who is selected until they know the results of the four years' record. I have watched with some care, and I find that about half the honors have been given to students with no white blood in their veins. You are mistaken regarding Dunbar; he is absolutely black with no trace of white blood. Isaiah T. Montgomery, the most prominent colored man in Mississippi, is purely black. Dr. J. W. E. Bowen, of Atlanta, Ga., who received a very high vote for bishop in the Northern M. E. Church at its recent General Conference at Los Angeles, is black with no white blood. The late J. C. Price, who was perhaps the greatest orator save Douglass that the race has produced, had no white blood. When it comes to the matter of executive or organizing ability and tenacity of purpose, I agree with you that those with mixed blood have shown superiority, in a word, in those matters where the feeling or imagination plays a large part I do not believe that there is any difference; in the application, however, of education or mind development I think I have the feeling that there is a difference.

This to me is a very interesting and serious question, and I shall be glad to hear from you at any time regarding it.

I agree with you again on the point that it will prove harmful to all concerned to merely stir up the South on the question of reducing representation for political purposes only without anything being done that will prove of lasting benefit to either race.

I wonder if you have read Mr. Edgar Gardner Murphy's book, "The Present South"? If not, I think you will find it worth reading. It is published by the Macmillan Co. Mr. Thomas Nelson Page[3] has an article in the July Scribner's which is also pregnant with suggestions.[4] Yours truly,

[Booker T. Washington]

TLc Con. 872 BTW Papers DLC.

[1] George Washington Taylor (1849–1932), Alabama congressman from 1897 to 1915.

[2] Taylor wrote BTW: "I am interested in securing data on the percentage of mixed and pure blooded negroes in the United States." After looking at a photograph of the Tuskegee faculty council, Taylor concluded that there was "but one full-blood" on BTW's staff. He also remarked that the mixture of white and African had "produced the Afro-American, a decided improvement upon the African." (June 27, 1904, Con. 872, BTW Papers, DLC.)

[3] Thomas Nelson Page (1853–1922), a well-known southern novelist residing in Washington, D.C., was later U.S. ambassador to Italy from 1913 to 1919.

[4] Thomas Nelson Page, "The Disfranchisement of the Negro: One Factor in the South's Standing Problem," *Scribner's Magazine*, 36 (July 1904), 15–24. Page praised the suffrage restrictions imposed by southern states as a positive step toward ending the abuses of black suffrage since Reconstruction. The restrictions, Page thought, would help blacks fit into the mainstream of American life, and would allow those blacks who met property and educational qualifications for suffrage to free themselves of the ignorant masses. He criticized BTW's black critics in Boston (without giving names) and stated that race consciousness, fueled by northern white radicals and their black counterparts, would only retard black progress in America.

To Theodore Roosevelt

South Weymouth, Mass. July 5, 1904

Personal

My dear Mr. President: I understand that Mr. Behan,[1] the acting Postmaster in New Orleans, is seeking permanent appointment at your hands rather urgently. The information which I have in hand leads me to say that I am quite sure that the appointment of Behan at this time, or any time soon, would hurt matters very much during the campaign. Behan, of all the people in Louisiana, is considered the most violent of what is known as the "Lily Whites."[2] He has been most outspoken against the colored people, and to make his appointment permanent at the present time would be interpreted on the part of the colored people of the country as an endorsement of "Lily Whiteism" on your part. Yours very truly,

[Booker T. Washington]

TLc BTW Papers ATT.

[1] William J. Behan (1840–1928?) was a militia general, merchant, sugar planter, and former mayor of New Orleans. A Democrat who switched to the Republican party after Cleveland attempted to remove the tariff on sugar, Behan attended the Republican national conventions from 1896 to 1912 and was chairman of the Republican state executive committee in Louisiana. In 1904 he ran for governor of Louisiana but captured only 10 percent of the vote. Behan had been postmaster of New Orleans in the 1880s, was acting postmaster in 1905, and was postmaster again in 1911.

[2] A few days later, BTW asked William Loeb, Jr., to show Roosevelt a letter to the New Orleans *Picayune* by Behan's wife opposing teaching the children of the South about the life of Abraham Lincoln. (BTW to William Loeb, Jr., July 8, 1904, BTW Papers, ATT.)

From Emmett Jay Scott

Tuskegee, Alabama July 5, 04

My Dear Mr. Washington: I am at Tuskegee again! After the first breath I want to let you know how sincerely grateful I am for the opportunity of serving at Chicago and at St. Louis. There was much work to do at Chicago. I spent myself as unsparingly as I could and I believe to some good effect. I am not vain gloriously proud, but on the contrary am deeply sensible of the responsibility attendant; of the tremendous cost if a frightful blunder sh'd be made. Every moment I had only your own interests at heart, acting as I thought you w'd & as discreetly as I could. I feel that the President owes you a debt of real gratitude for saving him & the party from the consequences of the blunder contemplated. He, nor his friends, will ever properly repay you for all that you have done for him since his incumbency & before! As for the race — it is pitiable that it sh'd be weak, so pathetically unable to help itself. Without what you have done to sustain it in its death struggles it w'd be absolutely without standing; absolutely without position in the councils of the party. I am sure you must get sorely tried that in spite of all you do there sh'd be so much ingratitude & meanness rampant, but the really sensible men are knowing of your influence and appreciating it at its full value. I am deeply grateful then for the opportunity to serve you in these momentous efforts. It is all history-making and you will certainly have every reason in the end to feel that you have done your part toward helping a helpless people to sustain interests it cannot sustain for itself.

I am also glad to tell you that the being away helped me very greatly. I feel better in every way & yet am glad to be at work again. I find everything in satisfactory shape and am bringing up the work & getting in fighting trim for a hard summer's campaign.

I hope the meeting of the Committee of Twelve was all that you c'd wish. I hope our friends will stick close by you & do what you w'd have them do. Yours very truly

Emmett J. Scott

ALS Con. 24 BTW Papers DLC.

Emmett Jay Scott to Charles William Anderson

[Tuskegee, Ala.] July 5, 1904

Personal

My dear Charlie: I wish to suggest that you keep in mind, as soon as our arrangement is effected, to write to Mr. W. H. Steward, publisher the American Baptist, Louisville, Kentucky, a communication which will enlist both his sympathy and interest, in carrying out our plans.

Mr. Steward is the President of the Afro American Council, succeeding Mr. Fortune, and it would be most satisfactory for us to work with him as President of the Council, rather than with the Bishop,[1] who plans, if possible, to use the Council in promoting his own ends.

The Bishop as you know, is only Chairman of the Executive Committee.

Steward is a strong, resourceful man, and will resist any encroachments which may be made by the Bishop.

I wish to assure you of the sincere pleasure I have found in our intimate association of the past two weeks. It has been very pleasant to work with you in carrying out these plans, which are near and dear to both of us.

With kindest regards to Mrs. Anderson, I am, Very truly,

Emmett J. Scott

TLpS Con. 283 BTW Papers DLC.

[1] Alexander Walters.

To Archibald Henry Grimké

South Weymouth, Mass. July 8, 1904

Dear Mr. Grimke: Since our meeting I have been thinking a good deal of your suggestion that we ought to have in our general directions to the secretary something bearing more directly upon the franchise, and the more I think of it the more I agree with your view, and if you approve of it I should like to submit by letter to each member of the Committee of Twelve the following addition to one of the paragraphs agreed to in New York:

"And to keep constantly before the people through the medium of the press, pulpit and platform &c the importance of registering and voting at all elections, both municipal state and national, and the prompt and regular payment of all taxes, especially that class of taxes that are a condition for voting." Yours very truly,

Booker T. Washington

TLS Archibald Henry Grimké Papers DHU. A carbon is in Con. 288, BTW Papers, DLC.

To Walter L. Cohen

South Weymouth, Mass. July 8, 1904

Personal

My dear Mr. Cohen: The more I think of it the more I am convinced that it will be a good plan if you can get one or two or three of the most substantial and wealthy white men who supported you at Chicago to visit the President and lay the case before him. This would impress the President with the fact that you have with you and behind you white men of respectability and prominence. I shall be glad to undertake to attempt to arrange for an audience any time you think it wise for these gentlemen to visit the President. Yours very truly,

[Booker T. Washington]

TLc Con. 19 BTW Papers DLC.

To Emmett Jay Scott

South Weymouth, Mass. July 8, 1904

Dear Mr. Scott: Doubleday, Page & Co. are planning to get out a subscription edition of "Working with the Hands" and are anxious to put into it about a dozen additional cuts. I wish you would take the matter up with a good deal of care and see that the cuts are selected that will illustrate in a better manner the higher forms of work being done at Tuskegee. In the other illustrations the academic work, electrical engineering, architectural drawing, etc., are very largely omitted. See that they get illustrations very soon.

While in New York City yesterday I learned that Mr. Battey[1] had taken both the outside and inside views of Mr. Nail's[2] bar room with a view of using these illustrations being used in the book which I am preparing. I do not know where Mr. Battey got his authority to do this. I do not remember that Mr. Nail was among the names which I gave you. Of course we cannot afford to put pictures [of] bar room fixtures neither the outside view of a bar room in a book of this kind, and I fear we shall have to let Mr. Nail down very gradually. Some of these pictures might be used at the Business League. Mr. Nail is a good strong man and I do not want to offend him in this matter. Mr. Moore told me that Mr. Battey told him he had authority from some one to take the pictures. Yours truly,

Booker T. Washington

TLS Con. 255 BTW Papers DLC.

[1] Cornelius M. Battey (1873–1927) was born in Georgia and later became a prominent black photographer in New York City, where he was superintendent of the Bradley Studio. Battey was best known for his photographs of blacks which occasionally appeared in *Crisis* and *Opportunity* magazines. In 1916 he moved to Tuskegee, where he headed the photographic division in the department of mechanical industries until his death.

[2] John B. Nail was a saloonkeeper in New York's Tenderloin district beginning in the 1880s. Later he sold the Tenderloin property and bought several apartment houses in Harlem. He also owned hotels with his brother Edward in Washington, D.C., and New York City. John B. Nail's son, John E. Nail, was a successful realtor and businessman in Harlem.

To Theodore Roosevelt

South Weymouth, Mass. July 9, 1904

My dear Mr. President: According to your request, I enclose you the figures bearing upon the population of Mr. John Sharp Williams'[1] congressional district in Mississippi. You will note that he was elected to congress in 1902, by a vote of 1493, and that there are twelve thousand white voters in his district and thirty thousand colored voters. Yours very truly,

[Booker T. Washington]

TLc BTW Papers ATT.

[1] John Sharp Williams (1854–1932) of Mississippi served in the U.S. House of Representatives from 1893 to 1907 and the U.S. Senate from 1911 to 1923.

To William H. Steward

South Weymouth, Mass. July 9, 1904

Personal

My dear Mr. Steward: If possible, I am very anxious to have a conversation with you sometime during the summer, although I do not know whether this will be practicable. I am to be in New England most of the summer except when I go to Indianapolis for the Business League the last week in August.

I think it very important that you have a full understanding regarding the Afro-American Council otherwise I fear the organization will disappear and that some other organization that will not be so helpful to the race will take its place. I understand that you are now the acting president of that organization. I think it very important that you take active measures at once to see that the Council and its work is kept constantly before the people through the medium of the Negro press and otherwise. I think it also important that you get a good, sensible program for St. Louis. My experience is that the only way to keep down folly at a public meeting is to have a full program and have the time so occupied in connection with the program that there will be little time for foolish speaking. There is going to be a strong effort made to use the Council to further the political ends of individuals; that ought to be prevented as far as possible. I also think it was a mistake for the executive committee to have turned the Council into a political organization. I do not think the executive committee had any such power; I think it weakens the influence of the Council for it to be known as a political organization. It would be much more helpful to the race and to the President for that matter, as standing as an independent body than to be allied with any political organization. I think it would be a good plan for the executive committee to have an early meeting and rescind that action rather than let it go before the whole body, which would prove in the long run harmful.

I think you as president, should take strong, vigorous hold of the work of the Council and let the country understand that you are at the head of it and not somebody else.

This will be my address for the summer.

[Booker T. Washington]

TLc Con. 5 BTW Papers DLC.

To Emmett Jay Scott

[South Weymouth, Mass.] July 9, 1904

Dear Mr. Scott: The leading editorial in the Indianapolis Freeman for July 2d,[1] which I send you, is an unusual and hurtful editorial. It was evidently written by somebody not connected with the paper. One weakness with Knox's paper is that it seems to have no editorial policy. If Trotter sees this editorial he will make a great ado over it as an endorsement of his policy. While there are many things in connection with Mr. Ogden's work with which I cannot agree, at the same time on the whole I think it is helpful and it is certainly better than no work, and we have nothing to gain by going to the other side. I wonder if you could not get Thompson[2] to either see Mr. Knox or write him rather strongly and get him to change his policy in regard to Mr. Ogden? Yours truly,

Booker T. Washington

TLS Con. 24 BTW Papers DLC.

[1] The editorial attacked the northern liberals of the Ogden Movement for being swayed by southern rhetoric into accepting racial discrimination in the South. It also stated that the Ogden junkets amounted to little more than several days of banqueting followed by viewing blacks in the worst possible circumstances. (Indianapolis *Freeman*, July 2, 1904, 4.)

[2] Richard W. Thompson.

To the Editor of the New York *Daily News*

South Weymouth, Mass. July 9, 1904

Personal and Confidential

Dear Sir: So far as the enclosed editorial clipping has reference to my distributing patronage in Alabama or elsewhere it is wholly without foundation. The President has his political advisers in Alabama, as I believe he has in other states, who make recommendations to him as to persons to fill offices, and I would not consent under any consideration to attempt to distribute patronage in any state and the President so understands it. He does consult with me, however, from time [to] time on vital matters pertaining to the welfare of the Negro race, and on such occasions I feel it to be my duty to advise with him, but as being one of his political office distributors, I would not for a minute consider such a proposition, neither would the President, I am sure, ask me to serve in such capacity. Yours truly,

[Booker T. Washington]

TLc Con. 870 BTW Papers DLC.

A Draft of a Press Release[1]

South Weymouth, Mass. July 10, 1904

Booker T. Washington, while in Boston today, said that he was surprised to see that Captain R. P. Hobson[2] had made the statement in a speech delivered before the St. Louis Democratic Convention to the effect that he (Washington), in a recent address before the National Educational Association in St. Louis, had suggested that colored people and white people attend the same schools and churches in the South. Principal Washington said that he was quite sure Captain Hobson must have made a mistake in reading his speech, or had been misinformed, as he had never suggested such a matter ~~North or South either in a speech or in any of his writings,~~ and that the subject was not even referred to in his address. ~~He further stated that he was quite sure the colored people in the South preferred to attend their own schools and churches.~~

TMd Con. 870 BTW Papers DLC.

1 Attached is a letter transmitting the statement to the Associated Press.

2 Richmond Pearson Hobson (1870–1937), a graduate of the U.S. Naval Academy and a hero of the Spanish-American War, was an Alabama Democratic congressman from 1907 to 1915. He moved to Los Angeles and later to New York City. In the 1920s he was an active promoter of alcohol and narcotics education.

From Joseph Oswalt Thompson

Birmingham, Ala., July 11, 1904

Dear Doctor: The enclosed clipping explains itself.

It seems that Capt. Hobson was accused by his opponent, Mr. Bankhead,[1] with having cooperated with and had the support of the republicans in his recent race for Congress, and acting the part of a demagogue, in order to refute the charges he felt that he must make some thrust at the President in order to redeem himself with the democratic party.

The more I see of democratic appointees by republicans the more I am convinced that it is bad policy. We gain no recruits for the party by doing so and the man so appointed more often than otherwise feels that it was on account of his great personality that he got consideration, rather than the influence of republican friends.

Our friend Judge Jones is making himself very disgusting to the people of Montgomery and everywhere else he goes by his criticisms of Scott and myself, saying that the President will not be controlled in Alabama appointments by those two young men. The whole truth is that he is disappointed that the President does not make him the sole referee for Alabama. I hope you will take the first opportunity you have to let the President know the disappointment Judge Jones has been to his friends. If it was not for losing the opportunity of having one of our friends to succeed him as Judge in this State I would withdraw my endorsement of him for the appointment on the Circuit Bench.

The President, in order to show his appreciation for the Naval hero, and in his broad and liberal spirit appointed old man Hobson, only to receive as his reward for it the unjust criticism that he did by young Hobson at St. Louis.

Kyle's letter as you will see is not at all satisfactory and I hope you will write him a letter in care of the Commission in Washington (where he will be until July 19th), if you feel that you can afford to do so, requesting him to give consideration to Alabama republicans in his appointments. Your friend,

Jos. O. Thompson

TLS Con. 25 BTW Papers DLC.

[1] John Hollis Bankhead (1842–1920), Democratic congressman from Alabama (1887–1907) and U.S. senator (1907–20).

From Emmett Jay Scott

Tuskegee, Alabama. July 12, 1904

Dear Mr. Washington: I call your attention to the letter of Mr. S. Laing Williams, forwarded to you on yesterday.

Mr. Williams is not easily frightened, as you know, and there can be no doubt on my part, as there seems to be none on his part, that the Morris gang is making a desperate effort to control the Western end of the situation. The only satisfactory thing in the Morris movement, is the effort to block Barnett[1] and his wife.[2]

Mr. Cortelyou has semi-officially, announced that Coolidge,[3] President of the Gridiron Club, is to be in charge of the Eastern end of the campaign as press agent and Elmer Dover and Harry S. New, of the Western end. There seems no very good reason then, why he should not announce Anderson's appointment at once.

I hope the matter can be settled soon for obvious reasons. This is especially desirable because of the Bishop's desperate efforts. Very truly,

Emmett J. Scott

TLS Con. 20 BTW Papers DLC. A press copy is in Con. 881, BTW Papers, DLC.

1 Ferdinand Lee Barnett was a prominent black Chicagoan for decades after founding the city's first black newspaper, the Chicago *Conservator*, in 1878. Leaving the newspaper, he became a lawyer, politician, and civil rights advocate. For years he was assistant state's attorney, and in 1904 was head of the Chicago branch of the Republican party's Negro Bureau. He opposed BTW and was a member of the Equal Opportunity League of Chicago and the Niagara Movement.

2 Ida B. Wells-Barnett.

3 Louis Arthur Coolidge (b. 1861), the Washington correspondent of a succession of leading newspapers since 1891, was president of the Gridiron Club in 1904 and in the same year director of the Literary Bureau of the Republican National Committee. He was assistant secretary of the treasury in 1908–9.

From Archibald Henry Grimké

Washington, July 13/04

My dear Mr. Washington: I am in receipt of your letter from South Weymouth, & think the additional directions to the Secy of the

Committee of Twelve very good as far as they go. But as I sent Mr. Browne last week my resignation as a member of the Committee & also as its treasurer, I am not now in a position to cooperate officially with the Committee.

With kind regards & best wishes, I am   Cordially yours,

Archibald H. Grimké

ALS Con. 288 BTW Papers DLC.

From Emmett Jay Scott

Tuskegee, Alabama. July 13, 1904

Dear Mr. Washington: In a recent editorial which appears in the Guardian July 2nd, is the following sentence: "We do not wish to misrepresent the views of any one, much less of so good a friend as Register Lyons, whose repugnance to our being jailed by the *Tuskegeean,* we shall ever appreciate."

Little by little, the names of the persons who have stood behind Trotter, are being revealed. I have marked this editorial and shall keep it for future use. Very truly,

Emmett J. Scott

TLS Con. 20 BTW Papers DLC. A press copy is in Con. 881, BTW Papers, DLC.

To Emmett Jay Scott

South Weymouth, Mass. July 15, 1904

Dear Mr. Scott: I spent yesterday and the day before in New York and saw Mr. Cortelyou twice. I think we have matters arranged as well as they can be at this date. He has definitely promised to put Anderson in charge of the whole colored work, Chicago as well as New York. He will have a deputy in Chicago. Last night Anderson and I saw him together and went over matters in general. He hesitated a little about anouncing Anderson's appointment at the same time he announces the executive or working committee for the reason that he does not want to give the Democrats at present too much of an idea what his plans are.

He also told me that he would not do anything about the Cohen case that is not satisfactory to Cohen, nor would he make any move in the matter before consulting with me. Mr. Cortelyou seems to lean toward Cohen's side. He is anxious, however, to get the campaign started and get rid of more weighty matters before taking up the Louisiana matter. Yours very truly,

Booker T. Washington

TLS Con. 881 BTW Papers DLC.

To Emmett Jay Scott

South Weymouth, Mass. July 15, 1904

Dear Mr. Scott: Regarding what Manly[1] says about The Record, I would state that I have heard very little of the paper recently and do not know what influence it has one way or the other. I agree with Manly, however, that if he cannot control it, it will be just as well to let the paper die. In some way, however, I very much wish that Cooper's paper might live. I very much fear that if he loses control of it or it dies, some other parties will revive it and make it a power for good or for evil. I have not seen the paper for several weeks and do not know whether it is now published or not. Yours truly,

Booker T. Washington

TLS Con. 550 BTW Papers DLC.

1 Frank G. Manly taught printing at Tuskegee Institute from 1903 to 1907. He was a co-owner of the Washington, D.C., *Record*, a black weekly founded in 1899. In July 1904 Manly wrote to Emmett J. Scott that he thought the Record Publishing Co. was going under and that he was seeking to dissolve the partnership. (July 12, 1904, Con. 553, BTW Papers, DLC.)

To Emmett Jay Scott

South Weymouth, Mass. July 16, 1904

Mr. Scott: I wish you would get into several of the white papers, such as the Evening Post, etc., the fact that I have been elected an honorary member of the Harvard chapter, Phi Beta Kappa.[1]

I am also very anxious that the enclosed two editorials from the Record Herald be published in several of the most important colored papers. Yours truly,

B. T. W.

TLI Con. 550 BTW Papers DLC.

[1] William C. Lane of Cambridge on July 15, 1904, notified BTW of his election on June 30. (Con. 291, BTW Papers, DLC.)

To W. Allison Sweeney

South Weymouth, Mass. July 16, 1904

Personal and Confidential

My dear Mr. Sweeney: I want to congratulate you upon the new position which you are occupying as editor of the Conservator. I am sure that under your charge the paper will be clean, conservative and strong. At the present crisis in the history of the race the policy of division and of personal abuse should be gotten rid of. It seems to me that what we need just now more than anything else is a policy of construction, calling the attention of the country to the progress that the race is making and not altogether to the weak points that may exist, to let the world know that we unite as a race and are not dismembered. Under your wise guidance I am sure that the Conservator will be made a power in this direction. Yours very truly,

[Booker T. Washington]

TLc Con. 871 BTW Papers DLC.

To the Editor of the Birmingham *Ledger*

South Weymouth, Mass. July 16, 1904

Personal and Confidential

Dear Sir: I thank you for your editorial in the issue of July 7th. I think I ought to say further that the impression given out from certain quarters to the effect that I am one of the dispensers of patronage in Alabama for the President is wholly a mistake. The President would not offer me any such position, neither would I accept it if it were offered. I have however, from time to time advised regarding important matters just as any other citizen of the state would have done when requested, but no amount of pressure could induce me to become an office distributor for any one. Yours truly,

[Booker T. Washington]

TLc Con. 284 BTW Papers DLC.

A News Item in the St. Louis *Palladium*

St. Louis, Missouri, July 16, 1904

MRS. BOOKER T. WASHINGTON CLAIMS COLORED WOMEN ARE DISCRIMINATED AGAINST

At the opening of the National Association of Colored Women yesterday morning Mrs. Booker T. Washington created a sensation by opposing the proposition to participate in the Colored women's day exercises at the World's fair to-day. Mrs. Washington was vehement in her stand, maintaining that the exposition directors had discriminated against Colored women in the matter of securing employment on the grounds and against the race in general. In support of her position she introduced a resolution to abandon the plan of holding Wednesday's session on the fair grounds. The St. Louis delegates tried hard to stem the tide of opposition, but the resolution was adopted by a large majority.[1]

The session of the association was held at St. Paul's M. E. church, Leffingwell and Lawton avenues. Mrs. M. L. Harrison[2] of St. Louis welcomed the delegates. The president, Mrs. J. Silone Yates,[3] responded. She quoted census reports showing progress made by the Colored race. She declared that in forty years the Colored people had acquired 1,500,000 farms and homes valued at $750,000,000; that their personal property was worth $170,000,000 and church property $40,000,000.

In support of Mrs. Washington's stand Mrs. Hallie Q. Brown reported that she had sought employment on The Pike Monday as a test of the report that Colored women were not wanted there, and had been refused.

St. Louis *Palladium*, July 16, 1904, 1. Reprinted from the St. Louis *Globe-Democrat*, July 13, 1904.

1 The resolution gave as the reason for withdrawal that "certain of our race have been refused refreshments and other privileges at the World's Fair accorded to every other people, simply on the ground of color." (St. Louis *Palladium*, July 16, 1904, 1.)

2 President of the St. Louis federation of twenty-four black women's clubs.

3 Josephine A. Silone Yates (1859–1912) was the first president of the Kansas City Woman's League in 1893. Later she served as treasurer and president of the National Association of Colored Women, presiding over the conventions in St. Louis (1904) and Detroit (1906).

To Timothy Thomas Fortune

South Weymouth, Mass. July 18, 1904

Dear Mr. Fortune: On further consideration of the Nail matter, I wonder if it would not be possible to give him a certain amount of space in the book regarding his hotel and restaurant business, leaving out his bar? In that case we would be treating him exactly as we would be treating a white hotel keeper who runs a bar in connection with his hotel. Yours truly,

[Booker T. Washington]

TLc Con. 21 BTW Papers DLC.

From Hugh Mason Browne

Cheyney, Penna., July 18th, 1904

Dear Sir: In compliance with the resolution unanimously adopted by the New York Conference of January 1904 of which you were a member the Committee of Three has selected the following nine gentlemen to complete the Committee of Twelve:

Dr. I. B. Scott	Charles W. Anderson
H. T. Kealing	Dr. E. C. Morris
Bishop George W. Clinton	Prof. Kelly Miller
T. Thomas Fortune	Archibald H. Grimke
Dr. C. E. Bentley	

The Committee of Twelve has met, effected a permanent organization by electing Dr. B. T. Washington, Chairman; Hugh M. Browne, Secretary; and Archibald H. Grimke, Treasurer, and approved the following suggestions as a basis for a modest beginning of the work which it was the sense of the Conference should be prosecuted in the interest of our people.

Suggestions for Committee of Twelve

I. That the chairman, secretary, treasurer and two other members constitute an executive committee who shall have authority to act between meetings.

II. That the secretary be authorized to open and conduct an office for a year that shall be considered the center of operations.

III. That for the present the work of the office shall be mainly directed in the following channels:

Turning the attention of the race to the importance of constructive, progressive effort, and the attention of the country to Negro successes.

Emphasizing and keeping before the public points of agreement rather than points of difference amongst us. Example — substance of matter agreed upon in New York conference document.

Correcting errors and misstatements concerning the progress and activities of the race, as well as making known the truth regarding the acts of the white race affecting us.

That the central office, under the direction of the executive committee, have power to bring and bear its influence upon emergency conditions that may arise from time to time in any state, county or municipality.

That the central office shall utilize as a medium of doing this work the press, North and South, black and white, the pulpit, platform, printed circulars, private correspondence, and any other means that may be deemed wise.

That as far as possible, the central office shall collect and tabulate data bearing upon the condition and progress of the race, as well as the relation of other races to our own.

That the foregoing suggestions to [shall] be carried out with a view of perfecting a larger and more systematic effort in the unification of the race.

May we not expect from you from time to time any authentic data you may possess which will assist the Committee in its efforts to carry out these suggestions? It is believed that if you will in a quiet way direct the thought and action of those in your community whom you may influence along the lines of these suggestions very profitable and lasting results will follow.

Hugh M. Browne

TLSr BTW Papers ATT.

From Charles William Anderson

New York, July 20th, 1904

Confidential

My dear Doctor: I called at the Custom House to see General Clarkson, and found James H. Hayes and Melvin Chisum standing on the corner in front of the Custom House. They stopped me for a moment, and during that time, Bishop Walters and Rev. Granville Hunt[1] came up. Walters had been in to see the General, and reported to Hayes that the General had refused to take any interest in their matter, and had advised them to lay it before Mr. Cortelyou. The Bishop took me aside and told me he had been to Oyster Bay and had learned from Mr. Loeb that I was in good odor with the President, and then advised me, confidentially, to look out for myself and not to make any alliance with *any other leading Colored man.* He said he wished he was at liberty to tell me some things that he knew, and was quite confident that if I was in possession of this information, I would not go around fighting other people's battles, but would "look out for Charlie Anderson," as he put it. He also said that he had a matter before "the friends" at Oyster Bay, and if I happened to call there, he would like to have me endorse the same. I told him pretty plainly that I was not in the endorsing business just now, and that he could expect me to stand by my friends to the last ditch, all advice to the contrary notwithstanding. He did not seem to like this reply very well, but finally asked me to name a day when he could see me. I told him I could name no day, but that I was to be seen almost any day "at the old stand." With this, the good Bishop wrapped his official robes about him, and made for the Elevated Railway station, in company with Hayes, Hunt & Chisum. To-day, I received a circular from Hayes, calling a private conference of Negro citizens of New York, New Jersey, Connecticut and Rhode Island, to be held Wednesday, July 27th in Abyssinia Baptist Church, this City. "The object of this conference," so goes the circular, will be "to take into consideration how the political power of the Negroes of these States can best be put into operation to break up Southern disfranchisement." The circular is signed by James H. Hayes, Bishop W. B. Derrick, Bishop Walters, Rev. Charles S. Morris, Rev'd M. W. Gilbert,[2] Rev. S. W. Timms,[3] Rev. J. L. Birchet,[4] Rev. E. N. McDaniels.[5] Thus you see, the "hold-up men" are hard at work. Do you think I had better attend this conference and find out their plans? If so, kindly wire me on receipt of this letter.

After leaving the aforesaid group of gentlemen, I saw General Clarkson, and learned from him that he had absolutely refused to confer with Walters. He told me that he had advised Mr. Cortelyou in Washington to have nothing to do with Walters, as he could not be trusted. The General informed me that he saw Mr. C., in Washington on Monday, about two hours after I left him, but did not seem to know what Mr. C.'s views were with reference to myself and the Bureau matter. I gave him no information. He seems to think that the matter is still open, and suggested that I take some steps to see that the right man was placed in charge. From this, you will see that it is evident that the General has been "dropped" out of this work. I am afraid he is a little unhappy about it, too.

I saw Moore on yesterday, and told him that I thought he and I ought to get together about the printing matter. I have said nothing to Fortune about it, and will not until I find out definitely what can be done for Moore's magazine. Will advise with you before I take any further steps in the matter. Yours respectfully,

Charles W. Anderson

TLS Con. 261 BTW Papers DLC.

1 Granville Hunt was a Baptist minister from Mt. Vernon, N.Y.

2 Matthew William Gilbert (1862–1917) was minister of the Mt. Olivet Baptist Church in New York City from 1904 to 1910. He became president of Selma University in 1910.

3 Stith W. Timms, born in Virginia in 1863, was a Baptist minister residing in Brooklyn, N.Y.

4 John L. Birchett, born in Virginia in 1866, was a Baptist minister in New Jersey.

5 E. N. McDaniels was a Baptist minister in Buffalo, N.Y.

To Charles William Anderson

South Weymouth, Mass. July 21, 1904

Personal

My dear Mr. Anderson: I am in receipt of your kind letter of the 19th and thank you for it; I find it very satisfactory. I have written Mr. Williams as you have suggested.[1]

There is one thing which perhaps you omitted to inform Mr. Cortelyou about, and that is the fact that Barnett during the first part of McKinley's term did all he could to prejudice the colored people against the administration and only came around to support him and his policy toward the end of his administration when he wanted to get hold of the campaign. He did the same thing in regard to Mr. Roosevelt. He and his wife were most bitter during the first year of Mr. Roosevelt's administration. At some time, in the proper manner, Mr. Cortelyou should know all this.

Enclosed I send you a copy of a letter which I am sending Mr. Cortelyou.[2]

I shall hope to be in New York next week and plan to see you.

Could you possibly find employment in one of the headquarters for the wife of Charles Alexander, who is publishing a good Republican paper here? It would help forward the interest of the paper very much if this could be done. Fror the present perhaps she would not object to taking a rather menial position with the understanding that she could get something better later. Yours very truly,

[Booker T. Washington]

TLc Con. 1 BTW Papers DLC.

[1] BTW wrote to S. Laing Williams on July 21, 1904, urging him to make himself known to Charles G. Dawes before the Republican national convention, for "his word is going to go a long ways in regard to matters in Chicago." (Con. 26, BTW Papers, DLC.) Comptroller of the currency from 1897 to 1902, Dawes was president of the Central Trust Co. of Illinois in Chicago and was for decades a powerful figure in Republican affairs.

[2] See BTW to Cortelyou, July 22, 1904, below.

To George Bruce Cortelyou

South Weymouth, Mass. July 22, 1904

Personal

Dear Mr. Cortelyou: In looking over the field I find that in various parts of the country, especially in the doubtful states, there are at least a half dozen pretty respectable and reliable colored men who are Democrats, that is they have voted and supported the Democratic ticket in municipal and state elections. I have found out from several of these men that notwithstanding they are Democrats, they mean to support President Roosevelt. In my opinion, it would be a strong point gained if through Mr. Anderson at the proper time, or in any other way you may deem wise, several of these men could be secured for campaign work. The fact that they are Democrats and would come out and support the President because of his interest in the colored people would carry great weight with the colored vote. I mention the matter now so that you may have them in mind before the Democrats secure them. Yours very truly,

[Booker T. Washington]

TLc Con. 2 BTW Papers DLC.

To John Elmer Milholland

South Weymouth, Mass. July 22, 1904

My dear Mr. Milholland: I am in receipt of your letter of recent date enclosing copy of an article which you have sent to the Post. I thank you very much for both.

Matters are getting very warm just now politically in this country. The Republicans are going to have a hard stiff fight, but I believe President Roosevelt is going to win. The Democrats expressed themselves very mildly on the question of the Negro in their platform; it is evident that they mean to make a bid for the Negro vote in the doubtful states.[1]

The Evening Post has decided to support Parker.[2] I had an hour's interview with the editors last week trying to show them their error, but I fear without good results.

I have many things to talk to you about when you return.

I shall see that the manuscript is put where it will accomplish good. Yours very truly,

[Booker T. Washington]

TLc Con. 4 BTW Papers DLC.

1 Milholland replied that it was a sad commentary on Republican leadership that, though the party had been right on the slavery issue, saved the republic, and put the country on "a sound financial basis regarding silver," it faced the possibility of defeat every four years. "And why? Because [through disfranchisement] it has allowed one of the strongest wings of its army to be disarmed by the enemy without raising anything but a feeble protest." (Aug. 2, 1904, Con. 4, BTW Papers, DLC.)

2 Alton Brooks Parker (1852–1926).

From Wilford H. Smith

New York City, July 22nd, 1904

Dear Mr. Washington: Our friend, Chisum, is very much in need of help but I am in no condition to serve him. He is a good worker in politics, and I think he could be of service to Mr. Anderson. I have written Mr. Anderson, asking him to put Chisum to work in some position where he can earn his support. I am sure Mr. Anderson can do so if he will.

If I am not requesting too much, it will be a favor to me if you would make a similar request for Mr. Anderson in Chisum's behalf. Very truly yours,

Wilford H. Smith

TLSr Con. 25 BTW Papers DLC.

To Jane E. Clark

[South Weymouth, Mass.] July 24, 1904

Mr. Baldwin is very sick. Not expected to live. I go to New York today to see him.

Booker T. Washington

TWSr Con. 555 BTW Papers DLC.

From Charles William Anderson

New York, July 28th, 1904

Confidential

My dear Doctor: I attended the meeting yesterday at Abyssinia Baptist Church, as per your advice. I also had a letter from Mr.

Cortelyou advising me to be sure and attend. The meeting was called to order at about twelve o'clock, and among those present were James H. Hayes, Bishop Walters, Bishop Derrick, Reverend Gilbert, Reverend Churchman, Reverend Granville Hunt, Reverend McMullen, Reverend Jacobs[1] from Brooklyn, Melvin J. Chisum, Reverend Parks, Mr. Samuel Scottron,[2] Reverend Lawton,[3] two men by the name of Gaines from South Carolina, and several other Reverend gentlemen whose names I do not recall. Bishop Walters made the first set speech and indulged in many sharp criticisms of the Republican party. He said that the Negro plank in the National platform was unsatisfactory to him, and to all other thinking men of the race. He also said, that such as it was, it was insincere and would never be enforced. He criticised the Senate for its failure to confirm Doctor Crum, and then admonished the conference that it was time to fight all along the line. Bishop Derrick made a very volcanic speech and referred to Hayes as another Nat Turner. He told of his own war record, and described how he had stood ankle deep in blood, to help free the race, and asserted with all the strength of language he could command, that he was *ready to fight.* He said he was tired of being led by weaklings of the race, and men who believed in [the] white man, and would sacrifice the race at any time if they were asked to do so by the whites. Much more of this sort of thing was said by the Bishop, and he was warmly applauded at the conclusion of the speech. Walters then took the floor, and made another red-hot speech in favor of fight. At this point, I had someone inquire what they intended to do, whereupon Hayes outlined the program and assured them that the Suffrage League desired to defeat "Joe" Gaines[4] of West Virginia, for the nomination for Congress. Failing in this, the League intended to defeat him at the polls, and intended to carry the fight into New York, New Jersey and Connecticut. He was very careful however, to refrain from openly stating that his plan was to attempt to defeat all Republican Congressmen whose districts were close, and contained a number of colored voters. A resolution was presented, endorsing President Roosevelt, and calling upon him, Mr. Cortelyou and Chairman Babcock[5] to advise that Joe Gaines be dropped as a candidate in West Virginia. Before taking the vote on this resolution, I gained the floor, and in [a] long speech, pointed out to them the advisability of caution. I described to them the condition we would be in if President Roosevelt was defeated, and the plight we should certainly find ourselves in, if Parker should be elected and die, and old man Davis[6] succeed him in the White House. I explained the danger of attempting to elect one man, and defeat another on the same ticket. I showed them the number of defective ballots cast in one election in this city through unsuccessful attempts to cut the ticket. I then opposed very strongly the sending of this complaint to the President. I tried to show them that it was not his province to ask that any candidate be withdrawn, and if a committee called upon him for this purpose, and he should refuse to act, the committee would then go away with fresh ground for complaint. Mr. Scottron and Reverend McMullen took the same view of the case that I did, and finally Doctor Parks came around. The result was that the resolution endorsing the President was passed separately from the one asking for the withdrawal of Gaines as a candidate. A committee was appointed to take the President's resolution to him, and to take the Gaines protest to Chairman Cortelyou and Chairman Babcock. This did not please Hayes or Derrick. Thus, you see, we succeeded in preventing them from annoying the President with their kick. I forgot to say that when I entered the room Bishop Derrick seemed to be very much disturbed. He came to me and insinuated that I was not invited, but I told him that I was invited, and intended to remain. Before leaving the Church, Derrick drew me aside, and tried to "sweeten" me a little. I saw that he was anxious that I should not tell the leaders of the part he played in stirring up the trouble, but should, on the contrary, advise them to "see" him to have the differences composed. In short, it was very plain that he was helping to make trouble in order to be bought off. This was also the course of Walters. He finally supported my resolution to endorse the President, and my resolution directing that the complaint should not be sent to the President, although he indulged in more criticism of the administration, and by inference, of the President, than any other man in the conference, save Derrick. The whole movement is a "graft" scheme. They now mean to go into Connecticut. Will write you more of this anon. The Age was endorsed in the matter of state printing by Chairman Barnes.[7] I am now on the look-out for something for the Colored American Magazine.

The magazine could not be designated to print the concurrent resolutions. Only daily and weekly papers are permitted to print these under law. I shall, however, visit all of the State Departments next week, when I am in Albany, and see if I cannot possibly find something for the magazine. The State Comptroller and the Superintendent of Insurance both have at times some printing. I will look them both up, and see if something cannot be secured for the Colored American Magazine. My plan is to leave here for Saratoga tomorrow night, or Saturday morning. I will live at the Thompson Cottage, 61 Hamilton Street, Saratoga. Of course, I shall spend three or four days of each week in this city, and run up to Saratoga from Friday until Monday. You can keep these facts in mind when you desire to communicate with me. I shall leave here tomorrow afternoon if I can definitely arrange with Mr. Ward[8] for the placing of the men about the headquarters. If not, I will stay here until I do arrange it. Perhaps I ought to quote to you Mr. Cortelyou's letter. He says, "I quite agree that it would be well for you to attend the meeting to which you refer, and hope to hear from you in regard to anything that you think should be brought to my attention." Yours truly,

Charles W. Anderson

TLS Con. 261 BTW Papers DLC.

[1] Frederick H. Jacobs was a black Baptist clergyman in Brooklyn, N.Y., born in South Carolina in 1865.

[2] Samuel R. Scottron, born in Philadelphia in 1843, resided in Brooklyn until the Civil War, when his father sent him into the South as a sutler for a black regiment. After two years in Florida, where he attempted unsuccessfully to run a grocery business, Scottron moved to Springfield, Mass., where he opened a barbershop. He invented and patented Scottron's Adjustable Mirror and formed a partnership in New York to sell it. He eventually invented several more household items including an extension cornice. During the 1870s Scottron was active in the anti-slavery movement and was a founder of the Cuban Anti-Slavery Society.

In 1882, as cornices were replaced by curtain rods, Scottron invented an extension curtain rod. In 1894 he invented an onyx-like glass which was used in brass lamps and candlesticks, and that same year he was appointed to the Brooklyn Board of Education, a position he held for many years.

Scottron wrote articles on race matters in many newspapers and magazines. He was especially concerned with the displacement of blacks by whites in certain occupations such as barbers and caterers.

[3] W. E. Lawton was a black Baptist minister in Barryville, N.Y.

[4] Joseph Holt Gaines (1864–1951), a Republican from West Virginia, was in the U.S. House of Representatives from 1901 to 1911.

[5] Joseph Weeks Babcock (1850–1909), a Wisconsin congressman from 1893 to 1907,

was chairman of the National Republican Congressional Committee from 1894 to 1904. A wealthy lumberman, he at first supported but later opposed Robert M. La Follette, who brought about his political defeat in 1908.

6 Henry Gassaway Davis (1823–1916), the Democratic vice-presidential candidate in 1904.

7 Probably William Barnes (b. 1866), publisher of the Albany *Journal* beginning in 1889, and member of the Republican state committee from 1892 to 1914.

8 William Lukens Ward (1856–1933), a manufacturer and former congressman (1897–99), was a member of the Republican National Committee from 1904 to 1912. He worked closely with Charles W. Anderson in efforts to organize the black Republican clubs in New York.

From Walter Moran Farmer[1] and David E. Gordon[2]

St. Louis, July 28th, 1904

Dear Sir: Sometime ago you were advised by the local Committee that August 1st had been set apart as "Negro Day" at the World's Fair. You were invited to participate in the programme and kindly consented to do so.

We regret very much that since your acceptance, a chain of circumstances seemed to have conspired to make a success of the "Day," we had hoped to make.[3]

We suppose it is well known to you that the sentiment throughout the country is to the effect that "the Negro is not wanted at the World's Fair." Although this sentiment is not correct and is not based upon facts, the World's Fair Management has been exceedingly unfortunate in the fact that from time to time unfavorable articles have appeared in some of the leading daily newspapers in the country.

The one that appeared on the 2nd day of June in the St. Louis Globe-Democrat, presented the probable treatment of the Negro at the World's Fair in a very unfavorable light. This article was copied by various papers throughout the country.

The Committee however, set to work to undo the unfavorable impression made by this article and to adjust all cases of discrimination as they arose from time to time at the Fair Ground.

Among the features that we hoped to have on "Negro Day" was a military parade. One military organization counted on to render this feature a success was the Eighth Illinois Regiment. On the 25th day of June, Col. Marshall[4] of said Regiment received a letter from Lieut. Haight,[5] a military attaché at the World's Fair, in which Col. Marshall was informed that inasmuch as his Regiment was a Colored one, special arrangements would have to made and that they would have to bring their own outfit, etc. Col. Marshall on receipt of this letter informed the World's Fair Management that his Company would not go in camp at the World's Fair.

The local Committee in company with other gentlemen who chanced to be in the City at that time held a conference and it was the unanimous opinion of those present that the "Negro Day" be abandoned.

We wish to add however, that while there are a few cases of discrimination on account of Race the conditions at the Fair have been highly colored and greatly overdrawn.

It is the opinion of the Committee that more places will accommodate our people than will refuse them.

We wish to express our regret for having to abandon "Negro Day" because we felt that it was the best opportunity that the Negro had had since freedom to present a comparative object lesson as well as to tell of the wonderful progress the Race has made in the last forty (40) years.

Appreciating the encouragement you have given us in this move, we are, Yours for the Race,

W. M. Farmer
D. E. Gordon

TLS Con. 288 BTW Papers DLC.

1 Walter Moran Farmer (b. 1865) was chairman of the Committee on Negro Day of the St. Louis Exposition. He was a St. Louis lawyer and was active in national Republican politics. In 1905 he moved to Chicago, where he continued his law practice.

2 David E. Gordon, principal of the L'Ouverture School in St. Louis, was secretary of the Committee on Negro Day.

3 Sentence thus garbled in original.

4 John R. Marshall (b. 1859), active in Cook County, Ill., politics, was a colonel in the black 8th Illinois Infantry beginning in 1898.

5 Charles Sidney Haight (b. 1877).

To Charles William Anderson

South Weymouth, Mass. July 29, 1904

Personal

My dear Mr. Anderson: I have received your long and interesting letter and have read every word of it with the deepest interest. There are two motives which actuate the leaders in such a meeting as was held this week: One is an uncontrollable desire to be prominent. Second: A consuming desire to get hold of money. I am sure that your presence balked the plan, however, that they meant to carry out in a very large measure. I am also quite sure that you will have to keep an eye on these men all through the campaign.

I may be in New York again next week, in that case I will write or telegraph you.

I am very glad that you let Mr. Cortelyou know about your plan for attending the meeting. Yours truly,

[Booker T. Washington]

TLc Con. 20 BTW Papers DLC.

To Theodore Roosevelt

South Weymouth, [Mass.] July 29, 1904

Personal and Confidential

My dear Mr. President: I want to congratulate you heartily upon your address at Oyster Bay. I write, however, especially to say that I am glad that you did not touch upon the Southern question. Waiving for the moment the matter of right and justice, as a matter of political expediency, at this time in my opinion, it will be wise for you to make no reference to that subject in your formal letter of acceptance. My business takes me among all classes of people in the North, and I have perhaps unusual opportunities for getting hold of their views and feelings. There are two considerations which must not be overlooked just now, as I said, as a matter of expediency:

First. There is a large amount of Northern capital invested in Southern enterprises, and this makes a large element in the North sensitive about anything that stirs up the South.

Second. If the labor strikes[1] continue and the effort is kept up to have colored laborers take the place of the strikers, I very much fear that the Democrats will make an effort to connect your interest in the colored people with the efforts of the operators to have Negro laborers take the place of white laborers, and in that way turn the labor unions against you.

As a matter of rights and wrongs at the South you of course know that I have never felt that reduction of representation was a remedy. I have felt that the thing for Congress to do is to take up each individual case of fraud and punish that individual case whether it relates to a single congressman or to those from a whole state.

These, of course, are mere suggestions. Yours very truly,

[Booker T. Washington]

TLc BTW Papers ATT.

1 The Chicago meat-packers' strike of July-September 1904. See BTW to Theodore Roosevelt, Aug. 27, 1904, below.

From Ruth Standish Bowles Baldwin

[New York City] July 31, 1904

My dear Mr. Washington: I thank you for your letter.

I knew you were in New York last week & I wanted to see you, but I was not sure enough of my self-control to risk seeing any one who has held so large a part in Mr. Baldwin's life and affections for so many years.

Alas, in waiting & hoping & praying you are doing for us all the only thing which can be done at present, but it [is] a vast help to me to feel that so many hearts are hoping & praying with us. It buoys up and sustains me and makes me feel that we shall win in the end. My love to you both. Mr. Baldwin has spoken of you several times, but he does not talk much.[1] Sincerely yours

Ruth S. Baldwin

ALS Con. 18 BTW Papers DLC.

[1] Robert C. Baldwin wrote to BTW on Aug. 2, 1904, that William H. Baldwin had said: "I have been thinking of him [BTW] so often as I have been lying here. *He* is one of the *chief* reasons for my struggling to get well." (Con. 18, BTW Papers, DLC.)

From Theodore Roosevelt

White House, Washington. Aug. 2, 1904

Personal.

My dear Mr. Washington: I had a most satisfactory talk with Durham and thanked him most heartily for the suggestion.[1] You and he, of course, will talk to Chairman Cortelyou about the matter.

The Evening Post is showing even more than its usual hypocrisy and mendacity about the colored question. Last year Rollo Ogden, on behalf of the Evening Post, pledged the support of his paper to us on this issue in the presence of John Hay.[2] I paid no heed to it, for I do not believe that either Ogden or Villard have any idea of truthfulness or of keeping a promise, so I was not in the least surprised at their attacking me. The plank which was put in the National platform calls for Congressional action, and not action by the President. It is in intention morally all right, but the question is one of such importance that I should not be willing to discuss it without going over the whole subject with you and best men I could get at, white and black, in the South. So I think I shall follow your suggestion, at any rate for the time being, and let it alone.

With great regard, Sincerely yours,

Theodore Roosevelt

TLSr Copy Con. 294 BTW Papers DLC. Marked "Copy for Mr. Scott."

[1] BTW had written Roosevelt a letter to be handed to him by John S. Durham suggesting that two black men, presumably including Durham, be employed to try to win over Tammany black workers to the Republican party. (Aug. 1, 1904, BTW Papers, ATT.)

[2] John Milton Hay (1838–1905), McKinley's and Roosevelt's Secretary of State (1898–1905).

To William Loeb, Jr.

South Weymouth, Mass. August 3, 1904

Personal

My dear Mr. Loeb: Several white Republicans of some standing from Louisiana very much desire to have a short interview with the President sometime between the 15th and 18th of August. I do not like to seem to add a single burden to the President at this time, but I think it would be really worth while to spare these men a few minutes if he possibly can. Will you be kind enough to inform me here, and I will communicate with the men referred to. I would not trouble the President with the matter except I have the feeling that these are a high type of men whom it would be worth while for the President to see. Yours very truly,

[Booker T. Washington]

TLc BTW Papers ATT.

To Sumner Alexander Furniss

South Weymouth, Mass. August 3, 1904

Personal

My dear Dr. Furniss: I have your letter of July 30th in which you make inquiry as to where I prefer to stay when in Indianapolis. Ordinarily I very much prefer the accommodations of a hotel, but I have the feeling that if I stay at a hotel that a great many colored people would be constantly calling to see me and that might prove objectionable on the part of the hotel proprietors and might stir up some trouble. I think it just as well to face all these matters in a frank manner. Please let me have your opinion on this point.

Please regard this letter as private. Yours very truly,

[Booker T. Washington]

TLc BTW Papers ATT.

To Timothy Thomas Fortune

South Weymouth, Mass. August 3, 1904

Dear Mr. Fortune: I have your letter taking up several very important matters, and I write to say that I am planning to be in New York on next Wednesday and Thursday and shall try to see both you and Mr. Moore and go over matters as thoroughly as possible. I want to be of whatever service I can. As I have told you, however, I have no financial interest in the magazine.[1] Yours very truly,

[Booker T. Washington]

TLc Con. 21 BTW Papers DLC.

[1] *The Colored American Magazine.*

Emmett Jay Scott to Hertel, Jenkins and Company

[Tuskegee, Ala.] 4 August, 1904

Gentlemen: As you have doubtless been advised, I have severed my relations with "The Voice of the Negro," – your monthly publication. I take it that this separation will not wound the tender sensibilities of the young man[1] hired by you, to write you as the publishers of the magazine, in this manner.

I have no quarrel with the policy of the magazine or with the publishers. The first, under Dr. Bowen's spirited direction and management, is in accord with my own inclinations; and the publishers have been praised by me repeatedly for their enterprise, etc.; but the malevolent spirit of Barber, his nagging propensities, his studied affectation of superiority; the man's overweening egotism and acceptance of everything as an insult, have made my relations with him unbearable. Further, his gratuitous statement that I am connected, directly or indirectly, with a competitor of "The Voice of the Negro," is without foundation – is false absolutely and completely; and is offered to insinuate some disloyalty to my understanding with your firm. I should wish properly to characterize such flagrant unfairness, but I understand that the attack is only covert, and is meant to reach another than myself. I have striven — I would wish you to know — earnestly, to advance the interest of the publication, and my severance of relations is due entirely to incompatibility of temperament in dealing with your self-sufficient, arrogant and mischievous representative. As you know, however, I became connected with the publication because of Dr. Bowen's relations as *Editor-in-Chief*, but his primacy has been disputed and disowned, and under all the circumstances it is more satisfactory to me, as it will be to your Mr. Barber, to sever my relations. For the magazine I shall continue to hope abundant prosperity.

With sentiments of appreciation for you and your generous enterprise in starting the publication, I am, Very truly yours,

E J S

TLI Copy Con. 21 BTW Papers DLC. Marked "Copy, Dr. Washington."

[1] Jesse Max Barber.

Austin N. Jenkins[1] to Emmett Jay Scott

Atlanta, Ga., Aug. 5, 1904

Dear Mr. Scott: Your welcome favor of the 4th at hand. I am certainly glad that you have written me first. I was thinking of writing and expressing a regret for the recent unpleasantness referred to.

Let me say that there is certainly no malice in my heart toward you, your institution, nor its president. We have, in a round-about way, through Mr. Hertel and Naperville, been working together for some time. We have learned to think well of one another & the works that we engaged in.

Let me say to you that I have taken no part in this quarrel. I requested Barber to modify his business letter to you, and did all I could to keep things moving sweetly.

Of course, I do not know what he has written you in private, personal letters, but know that he has exchanged three or four letters with you.

We received *quite definite* information that Doubleday-Page and Prof. Booker Washington practically own The Colored American,[2]

and since you are Prof. Washington's private secretary (although you might be perfectly honest and loyal to our publication), it did not seem to me that it was just the proper thing for you to continue as associate editor of our publication.

You see, every business firm have their private consultations. We expect to have monthly meetings of the editors, and, knowing the position, we would not feel, I fear, perfectly free to discuss all business propositions in an editorial meeting if you were present.

Let me again say that I do not doubt your honesty in the matter, yet, since we were in possession of the knowledge that your employer was running a similar publication, we could not — it would not be our nature — to feel perfectly free and easy in discussing all important questions; therefore, I was perfectly willing to sign the check when I was asked to do so. Let me again say that I suggested that the letter to you be modified.

I want to again call your attention to the fact that we have considerable money tied up in race publications. I want to say to you that I am not in this wholly for the money there is in it; I feel only too glad of the privilege of doing something to help the race. I would therefore request you, if you can possibly do so, to drop the little matter, and then whenever it is convenient for you to say a good word for the magazine, would be glad to have you do so.

I should like very much, indeed, for you to get the magazine regularly, without cost to yourself, so I will try and remember to mail you a copy each month.

Perhaps things would have been different had Dr. Bowen been with the paper for the last three months. No doubt you are aware of the fact that he was away in the West for a time on a lecturing tour. Finally he returned on a very sad mission. Yours very truly,

A. N. Jenkins

TLS Con. 21 BTW Papers DLC.

[1] Austin N. Jenkins (b. 1865) was manager of J. L. Nichols and Co. until he became a partner in the firm of Hertel, Jenkins and Co., successors of the Nichols firm.

[2] On Aug. 10, 1904, Jenkins sent to BTW a copy of a letter from an unnamed informant, stating that BTW, C. W. Anderson, and Doubleday, Page and Co. were the real owners of the *Colored American Magazine*, and that the New York white journalist John C. Freund advised Moore on magazine editing. (Con. 21, BTW Papers, DLC.) For a fuller account of BTW's interest in the magazine, see Meier, "BTW and the Negro Press."

To Emmett Jay Scott

South Weymouth, Mass. August 9, 1904

Dear Mr. Scott: I have your letter of recent date, and wish to assure you that what you did in connection with the Hobson matter was entirely satisfactory and met my full approval, and I thank you for your action in the matter.

In regard to Barber, I think it would have been wiser for you to have ignored the man altogether and have dealt with the heads of the firm. I do not think it ever pays to deal with a little man. I am determined to find a way, however, very soon to show him his place. Enclosed I send you a copy of a letter which I am sending to both Mr. Jenkins and Mr. Hertel. I think this will serve in a small degree to bring them to their senses. You will note that I have ignored Barber altogether. Let me know what you think of this letter. Yours truly,

Booker T. Washington

TLS Con. 24 BTW Papers DLC.

To Cora Lina Cherry White

South Weymouth, Mass. August 9, 1904

Dear Mrs. White: I hope you have not gotten the idea by reason of my delay in writing you that I have not been giving attention to the matter of your daughter getting into school. There are several schools that I had to give attention to. First, I wanted to be very sure to get your daughter into a school where the teachers and all would be sympathetic and kind. Some of the best schools are willing to take one or two colored students but do not care to have more. There is the Cushing Academy at Ashburnham, Mass., that has the reputation of being a very good institution, but they admit both boys and girls and Mrs. Washington has the idea that you might not like that on account of its being a mixed school, but if you feel satisfied with it I feel quite sure I could gain admission for her there. My own feeling is in this direction – According to present plans Portia will graduate from Bradford Academy next June, and if you would care to have your daughter to do so, I think I could arrange definitely to get her into that school. At Bradford she would receive every consideration and would be kindly and sympathetically treated by all. That is a school which I can recommend without reservation. I was wondering if you would not take the catalogue and have your daughter study privately or somewhere there in Washington for a year and then be all the better prepared for work at Bradford. If you decide to follow this plan I could arrange definitely now for her admission so there would be no question about it. I should like to have an answer to this just as soon as possible. By this mail I am sending you some printed matter bearing upon Bradford, also Cushing Academy.

A letter sent here will reach me. Yours truly,

[Booker T. Washington]

TLc Con. 872 BTW Papers DLC.

To Robert Curtis Ogden

South Weymouth, Mass. August 9, 1904

My dear Mr. Ogden: I have yours of August 2d regarding Mr. Moore and his magazine. Permit me to say that I appreciate the advice which you have given him, but I do not think you know all the circumstances.

In the first place, the magazine has been kept alive for six or seven years and already has a circulation of between four and five thousand. I think perhaps unconsciously, you are likely to compare the cost of such a magazine as Mr. Moore is publishing with the white magazines. It would surprise you to know how cheaply many of the publications are published and kept alive; just how it is done in all cases I confess I do not know, but in Mr. Moore's case he already has a printing establishment and the cost of getting out the magazine is much less in other directions than is true in the case of white magazines. For example, it is very seldom I think, that he pays for contributions. If he were starting an entirely new venture with nothing in the way of plant or circulation I think that your view of the case would be a correct one, but he has gone over with me very carefully the whole matter, and I am of the opinion that the figure which he gives would put the magazine upon its feet. For example, the New York Age, published by Mr. Fortune, was started years ago with practically no capital behind it. At the present time that paper clears above expenses about $50 a week. The fact that in the case of many of the colored publications there is not as severe competition as among the whites may have something to do with their opportunities of succeeding.

Lastly, I wish very much that something might be done to help Mr. Moore upon his feet for the reason that it is very important that here in the North the colored people be kept in touch with and in sympathy with such work as you and others are doing in connection with the General and Southern Education Boards. This is an influence that in the long run will prove very helpful.

Please forgive me for troubling you with this long letter. Yours very truly,

[Booker T. Washington]

TLc Con. 550 BTW Papers DLC.

To Doubleday, Page and Company

South Weymouth, Mass. August 9, 1904

Dear Sirs: It has been stated by a certain publishing firm that you and I own the Colored American Magazine now being published in New York. Will you be kind enough to write me a letter on this point which I may show to other persons if necessary. For myself, I do not own a dollar's worth of interest in a single Negro publication in the country. Whether or not you have such interest I do not know. Yours truly,

[Booker T. Washington]

TLc Con. 255 BTW Papers DLC.

Emmett Jay Scott to Austin N. Jenkins

Tuskegee Institute, Alabama. August 9, 1904

Dear Mr. Jenkins, I have your letter and thank you for it. It is quite satisfactory to learn from you that you were, and are, wholly in disaccord with your Mr. Barber's malevolence and unfairness. I have no desire to continue a profitless correspondence, but lest my silence be misjudged I am hazarding an additional letter. You are entirely — absolutely — completely off in your statement that you have "definite information that Dr. Washington has purchased the Colored American Magazine." Now here is a case where "definite information" is positive misinformation. Dr. Washington (nor I) has no more interest in that publication than you have. He has no interest in any publication of any kind — never has had and has no such thing in contemplation, and your definite information has doubtless come from the malicious newspapers which abuse, slander and misrepresent Dr. Washington on every possible occasion. Will you permit me to say that I am greatly surprised that you should have (in forming your opinions) trusted unauthorized and prejudiced sources of information when you could have been advised correctly at the only place to secure the information straight. As I say — I send you this information and this letter solely and only that you not be controlled by misrepresentation in a matter touching my personal integrity and loyalty (if I had continued with the magazine) — a thing all but impossible however dealing with a man of Barber's peculiar temperament. Yours very truly,

E J S

TLI Copy Con. 21 BTW Papers DLC.

To Theodore Roosevelt

South Weymouth, Mass. August 10, 1904

Personal

My dear Mr. President: Your kind letter received. I confess that I am very much disappointed in the attitude of the Evening Post. Last winter I spent a night with Mr. Rollo Ogden and went over the whole situation with him, and later did the same thing with Mr. Villard, and I understood both of them to say that they were going to support you because of your attitude towards the colored people. Of course while I have noted that they have criticized you adversely from time to time before your nomination, I took for granted that they, however, meant to stand by their promise and would be on your side after the campaign opened, hence I was hardly prepared to have Mr. Villard tell me what he did when I saw him a few days ago. I am going to New York again today and may see Mr. Ogden again but I confess I have little hope of accomplishing any good. I am also going to see Mr. Cortelyou and take up some matters which I think are of importance.

On the subject of your discussing the Southern question in your formal letter of acceptance, I am still of the opinion that it will be wise to say nothing about it unless it is forced upon you by something Mr. Parker may say.

I have recently had a talk with Dr. Lyman Abbott, and I am going to prepare some matter for him to use editorially, showing what you have done in the way of purifying official life in the South. The matter will be submitted to you before it is published. The Outlook I find is willing to do anything that it reasonably can in your favor. Yours very truly,

Booker T. Washington

TLS Theodore Roosevelt Papers DLC.

To Austin N. Jenkins

South Weymouth, Mass. August 10, 1904

My dear Sir: My secretary, Mr. Emmett J. Scott, has brought to my attention a letter of yours dated August 5th, 1904. In that letter you make certain statements which I confess I am surprised to see coming from a reputable business concern. The particular statement in mind is as follows: "We received quite definite information that Doubleday, Page, and Professor Booker T. Washington practically own the Colored American." I never give any attention to ordinary street corner gossip, but for a concern of the reputation of yours to make such a statement, it seems to me rather extraordinary unless you have definite information upon which to base your assertion and your consequent action. I do not know anything about what concerns Doubleday, Page & Co. are interested in, but I do know that so far as I am concerned the statement has no basis and is untrue, and it seems to me that you ought to have gotten direct information from me before making the assertion. I have had long and satisfactory dealings with the head of your firm, Mr. Hertel, and on all occasions whenever he wished information he has written me in a direct and frank manner, and as a result, our business relations have been of a most satisfactory nature. Aside from not having the money to invest in such publications, as a matter of public policy I think you will agree with me that it would be highly improper for me to own an interest in any publication. I do not own one cent's worth of financial interest in any colored magazine or newspaper in this country, and have always consistently and persistently refused to have any such investment.

Permit me to state that I hope hereafter that if you wish any information concerning any matters bearing upon our relations I shall be very glad to furnish you with it if you will communicate directly with me. I have tried to promote the interest of the Colored American Magazine just as I have tried to promote the interest of your magazine. I hope that you do not and will not take the narrow and short-sighted view that your magazine will prosper in proportion as there is no other similar publication. Taking the broader view, I am quite sure you will find that if there were three or four reputable magazines circulated among the race it would not hurt but help your own magazine. The more magazines the race gets in the habit of reading, the more such publications it will desire. The existence of other educational institutions does not hurt the Tuskegee Institute, but rather helps its work. The same is true of a magazine, in my opinion. Only a few weeks ago I manifested my interest in your magazine by sending a copy of it in a sealed envelope to the President of the United States in order that he might see what was being done by the race, and I expect in the future, as I have tried to do in the past, to promote the success of your publication in any way that I can. I have not failed to keep in mind the large amount of money which your firm is investing in a book which I am now preparing on the business development of the Negro in this country; with the hope of stimulating the sale of that book and bringing together our own interests as well as advancing the interests of our race, I invited Dr. J. W. E. Bowen, your editor in chief, a man whom I consider to be one of the wisest and most helpful members of our race, to deliver the principal address at the meeting of our National Negro Business League in Indianapolis. With the same idea of stimulating the interest in this publication and in the organization upon which the book is to be based, I had a carefully prepared article on the Negro Business League sent to you for publication. I believe that you will find, as a firm, that it is to your interest to cooperate in the way I have suggested. I believe that such cooperation would lead to our mutual business advantage as well as in the direction of helping the race in the maner in which both of us are so much interested.

I am sending a letter direct to Doubleday, Page & Co., to inquire of them whether or not there is any truth in your assertion that they own any part in the Colored American Magazine. Permit me to state further, that if you wish facts concerning the ownership of the magazine I think if you will address a letter directly to Mr. Fred R. Moore, 181 Pearl St., New York, he will be glad to give you such information.

Under all the circumstances, I think you will agree with me that your firm has wronged Mr. Scott in acting upon a mere rumor. Yours truly,

[Booker T. Washington]

TLc Con. 261 BTW Papers DLC.

To Charles William Anderson

South Weymouth, Mass. August 14, 1904

Personal

My dear Mr. Anderson: I tried to reach you as I came through New York Saturday, but I presume you had left town.

First, I believe that it would be a good plan for us to try to get some of the icicles off of that chairman by a new move which I think would kind of open his eyes and at the same time help the cause of our friend Roosevelt. My suggestion is this, that we collect a sum of money ourselves and place it in your hands to be presented directly to Cortelyou as our contribution towards the campaign. They are so in the habit of thinking that every colored man that presents himself is seeking money that I think it would create a surprise to know that there are a class of colored men who were willing to contribute money instead of seeking it. I shall be willing to contribute, say $100 at any time you may call for it. I think we could get together quite a little sum by calling upon other of our friends. Please let me know what you think about the plan.

Second. I hope you have already written to Durham about the work to be done in New York. His address is Crozer Bldg., Philadelphia. I merely suggested Cohen to you. If you know of anybody else you prefer to Cohen and could do the work just as well why of course feel free to correspond with him instead of Cohen.

What do you think of my writing to Cortelyou direct calling his attention to the importance of consulting you about putting one or two of our good colored men on the advisory committee in case he appoints one?

I have had another letter from the President today, and I am quite sure he thinks Cortelyou is doing things which he is not.

One other suggestion. Since thinking the matter over more carefully I think it would produce rather a bad impression for Mr. Fortune to make an application to Mr. Cortelyou for money with which to use in the paper as we have suggested; it would appear as though Fortune was seeking to feather his own nest in the way the average colored man is seeking to do. If you think well of the suggestion, I shall be willing to write a letter to you suggesting very strongly that 20,000 copies of Mr. Fortune's paper be used during the campaign and that he has sufficient funds to enable him to employ additional force and that he be put in a position to do this work in a satisfactory way. You could use my letter as the basis with which to make your application. I feel more and more that we must bring these people to the test as soon as possible. We must find out whether they mean business or whether they mean to play.

Mr. Moore is very anxious that you see him about the Age matter before you see Mr. Fortune.

[Booker T. Washington]

TLc Con. 550 BTW Papers DLC.

To Emmett Jay Scott

South Weymouth, Mass. August 15, 1904

Dear Mr. Scott: I have your letter regarding Morris's work in Chicago. Mr. Cortelyou has decided that there are to be no separate bureaus of any kind during the campaign, the work, however, is to be looked after by individual colored men in some way, Anderson being in charge so far as the East is concerned. I do not know the details of how it is to be done in the West, but it is very probable that Barnett will be a prominent factor owing to the fact the Dover friend, has such a strong position in Chicago. I really think that Mr. Cortelyou is going to pursue the policy of doing most of his work through the state committees rather than directly.

I have several matters that I will explain to you when I see you. Yours truly,

Booker T. Washington

TLS Con. 881 BTW Papers DLC.

To Charles William Anderson

South Weymouth, Mass. August 15, 1904

Personal

My dear Sir: In your relation to the work to be done among the colored voters, I wish to place a matter before you which I have carefully thought out. If you think it wise you might put the suggestion before the Executive Committee.

(1) The colored voters are so largely segregated from the rest of the voters in the United States in their industrial and social life that special efforts are needed to reach and influence them and keep them interested.

(2) I suggest that arrangements be made with the publishers of the New York Age in New York whereby twenty thousand or twenty-five thousand extra copies of this paper can be circulated among

the colored voters in such states as New York, New Jersey, Connecticut, Delaware, and West Virginia.

(3) I suggest the Age for the reasons, that it is our ablest and most influential paper, and that the other colored papers reproduce what appears in it more than from any other Negro paper, and further, the mere fact that Fortune, the editor, has assumed from time to time a more or less independent attitude, will make what he says carry all the more weight with those who would be inclined to fly the track.

(4) If this is done, there should be some arrangement made by which the editorial force could be strengthened a little, and a thorough understanding [of] what you desire is to appear in the paper, and it shall be conducted during the campaign in harmony with the views of the Executive Committee.

(5) This, in my opinion, is one of the cheapest and most effective ways of reaching our voters.

I have not mentioned such doubtful states as Indiana, etc., for the reason that they will perhaps be looked after from the Chicago end, and through colored papers in that section, but there is no colored paper as you know, so ably edited as the Age. Yours truly,

[Booker T. Washington]

TLc Con. 283 BTW Papers DLC.

To Theodore Roosevelt

South Weymouth, Mass. August 15, 1904

My dear Mr. President: I have just written Mr. Cortelyou to say that within a few days I shall be going to Indiana and West Virginia, and shall want to spend some time looking quietly into the situation among the colored voters. I want to discover, if possible, what means Mr. Taggart,[1] who is very popular in Indiana, is employing or is likely to employ to get hold of the colored people. I used to live in

West Virginia and know the situation there pretty well. I have said to Mr. Cortelyou I would be glad to follow any suggestions that he cares to make. Yours very truly,

[Booker T. Washington]

TLc BTW Papers ATT.

1 Thomas Taggart, an Irish-born Democratic politician from Indiana, was chairman of the Democratic National Committee from 1904 to 1908.

From Theodore Roosevelt

[White House, Washington, D.C.] August 18, 1904

Personal.

Dear Mr. Washington: I am very glad to hear that you are going to Indiana and West Virginia, and shall await the result of your visit with interest.

You may have seen that the Evening Post has been sneering at me for saying nothing about the fourteenth amendment, or rather the colored question. I do not know that I shall say anything, but the enclosed seems to me to put our position straight. I do not limit what I have to say by the fourteenth amendment. I simply make a plea for fair treatment, and hold up Taft and an ex-Confederate, Wright,[1] as giving the kind of treatment to the Filipinos that I should like to have given to our colored citizens here at home. Let me know if you think this is all right. I may not put it in anyhow, but I should like to have your views on it. Sincerely yours,

Theodore Roosevelt

TLpS Theodore Roosevelt Papers DLC.

1 Luke E. Wright (1846–1922), a Memphis lawyer, was a member of the U.S. Philippine Commission (1900–1904) and succeeded William H. Taft as governor-general of the Philippines (1904–6). After serving as ambassador to Japan (1906–7), Wright followed Taft as Theodore Roosevelt's Secretary of War (1908–9).

An Article by Max Bennett Thrasher

Phila., Pa. Aug. 20, 1904

Booker Washington's First Sunday-School Teacher

One Sunday noon I happened to stand beside Booker T. Washington in the great and beautiful chapel which the Tuskegee students have built to accommodate their devotional exercises, and watched the young negro men and women — nearly a thousand of them — file out to their respective Sunday-school class rooms.

"When did you first begin to go to Sunday-school, Mr. Washington?" I asked. "Do you remember anything about the Sunday-schools of your boyhood?"

The principal of Tuskegee stopped to think a moment, and then said: "One sunny Sunday forenoon, not very long after my mother and her family had moved to Malden, in the coal-mining country of West Virginia, I was playing marbles in the road with some other boys when a colored man came along — he seemed old to me then, but he could not have been, for he is still living — and asked us if we did not want to go to Sunday-school. I did not know what a Sunday-school was, but he told us something about it. I went with him, and had my introduction that day to a Sunday-school service."

The "old man" to whom Mr. Washington referred is "Father" Rice, the retired pastor of the little colored Baptist church in Malden, West Virginia, which Mr. Washington joined when he was fourteen years old, and of which he is still a member. For more than half a century Father Rice has preached the gospel in the Kanawha valley — preached it so simply, so earnestly, and so honestly — and lived it so sincerely — that he has gained the respect of every one, and has been enabled to go up and down the river valley preaching and organizing churches as perhaps no other man would have been able to do.

One day in the autumn of 1901 I was in Malden with Mr. Washington, and went with him to call on his old pastor. It was just coming on evening of a perfect September day, and I can imagine few scenes more beautiful than the Kanawha valley at such a time. On each side of the valley the West Virginia hills rose steep, green-wooded, and near at hand, leaving between them barely room for the river and the railroad, with here and there a settlement strung up and down the river-bank. As we walked down to the old minister's house we faced the west, and the river valley opening before us showed a wonderful vista of golden sunset sky, across which wreaths of black smoke drifted from a passing railway train. In one place, sharply outlined against the sky, was the huge old stone chimney of a salt furnace at which Mr. Washington as a boy had worked. The tanks and vats and pump-house have been gone for years; only the chimney remains, standing now in a corn-field.

As we went along, Mr. Washington pointed out other familiar scenes of his childhood to me — the site of the first school he went to; the site of the old church in which was held the Sunday-school he had told me of; the mouth of the coal mine in which as a boy he had been a mule driver and miner's helper; the house which was the home of that Mrs. Viola Ruffner, whose thorough training of him in neatness and honesty he has always felt so grateful for; and the building in which he taught school for three years after he had graduated from Hampton.

"When I was a boy," said Mr. Washington, "I used to look up at these hills here, and wonder what was behind them. I used to wish that I could climb up to the top of the highest one, so that I could see what was in the great world on the other side." I thought to myself, as he said this, that if ever a man had got his wish it was he.

Father Rice lives by the side of the river, in a little house so old and weather-beaten that it looks as if one strong gust of wind would blow it into the Kanawha. The old minister and "Mary," his wife, who is blind now, have lived there for forty years. The place is home to them, and they love it as they do no other place in the world. They have a son living in a city not far away who would be glad to furnish them a comfortable home there, but no amount of urging has been sufficient to induce them to leave the old house.

Just as we were nearing the house, a neatly-dressed young colored woman rode up on a bicycle. She was the old man's granddaughter, at that time teaching the regular term of public school for colored pupils in the village. The schoolhouse was not far away, a comfortable and convenient building.

And yet easily within the memory of Mr. Washington — and he

is a man still young — the first imperfect attempt at a colored school which had ever been known of in that vicinity was made in that same village. Truly, times have changed.

The old preacher saw us coming, and met us in the yard. He had not expected us — did not even know that Mr. Washington was in town — but there was nothing of embarrassment in his manner, and no apologies for the every-day working clothes which he was wearing. We went into the living room of the old house so that "Mary" might enjoy the visit also.

The attitude of the two men toward each other was extremely interesting to me, and I studied them closely all the time they were together. Father Rice is evidently very proud of Mr. Washington, and of the fact that the early religious life of so famous a man developed under his training; but with all his deference to Mr. Washington's fame and ability there showed an unconscious — for no one could see the old preacher and not realize that he is a thoroughly modest man — touch of authority, the authority which a lifetime of honest Christian labor gives to every good minister, be he ever so unlearned and unknown, toward any person whose life he has influenced, and who is still a member of his flock, be that person ever so learned or famous.

On the other hand, Mr. Washington's manner toward the old man was singularly beautiful. I have seen him the honored guest of distinguished doctors of divinity more than once, but I never saw one of them to whom he listened with more interest, or to whom he showed more deference, than to this old colored minister in his cabin home.

After Mr. Washington went away, I stayed for some time longer to have the old man tell me something about the early life of both of them. Asked if he had been a slave, the old man said: "Yes, I was a slave in Virginia. I seem, as a very small child, to remember a short, dark woman who, I imagine, was my mother, but if so, I never knew anything of her at any later date. I grew up on a small plantation, and was kindly treated. When I was a young man I was sold. The reason for this sale was that the family had got into debt in some way, and it was decided to sell one of the slaves to pay this debt. The man who bought me was a dealer in slaves, who bought and sold them as a speculation, and I was taken by him to Richmond to be sold again. I was kept in Richmond for some time, one of a considerable number gathered there for that purpose. We were kindly enough treated, and not closely confined. I remember that when a customer came a negro rang a bell to summon us together to be looked over. If we liked the looks of a man, we used to try to get him to buy us. I was finally bought by a man from this place. He was a good man, who always treated me well. I liked his looks from the first, and was glad when he bought me. He was a man who did not own many slaves, and he bought me as an investment. Most of the time he worked me in the mines or about the town. I never was hard worked. I had such a "stunt" to do, and when that was done for the day, I could do as I pleased.

"This owner died, and I was sold again. This last time I sold myself. The estate of the man who had died was to be settled. I went to a man whom I knew, and told him I wanted him to buy me, and he did. That was not long before the War, and in time, of course, I was free."

I asked the old man if he ever had thought of running away into Ohio or Canada. "Sometimes at night," he said, "I would look up at the north star, and think that, if I was sure of getting off all right, I might like to go; but I always got along pretty well here, and after I was married I didn't want to leave. Besides that, I thought I could see how things were going, even before the War broke out, and I made up my mind that if I stayed right along here, and did as I ought to do, I would be all right."

It will delight the hearts of Tuskegee students to know that their much-loved and respected principal, as a boy, was not altogether letter-perfect in deportment himself. Father Rice reports him — although one of the best-intentioned boys possible at heart — as being decidedly lively at times; and told of one particular instance when "Booker" substituted a reading-book for a Testament as his seatmate rose to read one day in Sunday-school, to the surprise of the school and the confusion of the boy.

"I baptized Mr. Washington myself, right down there," the old man said, leading me to the door of the cabin and pointing to where the Kanawha river slipped silently by in the starlight. "He was about fourteen years old, but he was old for his years. He was so reliable, and was able to read and write so much better than most of our people, that not long after that he was made the clerk of the church. The old records of the church still show the entries which he made then."

This church, organized by Father Rice, has had a continuous existence for many years. It has a younger pastor now, but the old minister still preaches occasionally. The colored Baptist churches of the district, many of which Father Rice organized, contribute regularly for his support — not as a matter of necessity, but as a duty and a pleasure. I talked with the Rev. Dr. C. H. Payne of Huntington — probably the best-known colored Baptist clergyman in the state, and one of the most prominent in the denomination — about Father Rice, and he spoke of him in the highest terms, both of his character as a man and of his simplicity and power as a preacher, free almost entirely, as he said he was, from the artificial mannerisms of so many of the preachers of his race. "He has gone up and down the Kanawha valley," said Dr. Payne, "often when no one else could or would have gone, preaching Christ and a godly life, and living what he has preached."

When I rose to go, the old man came out with me. "Let me lead you to the road," he said; and I was glad to have him, for it was dark, coming out from the cabin, and there were obstacles — there usually are — in Southern cabin yards.

When I was safely started in the highway, I turned to look back. The sky was cloudless, and above the hills back of the cabin the north star shone bright and steady. I thought of the times when the old man had looked at this star, so many years before, and that perhaps it was providential that he did not heed its invitation, so that Mr. Washington's early life might have the influence of his character and teaching.

"Good-night!" I cried.

"Good-night!" the old man's voice came back through the darkness. "God bless you, and keep you, and cause his face to shine upon you."

I bowed my head in the starlight to add, "Amen!"

PD Clipping Con. 1038 BTW Papers DLC.

To Sumner Alexander Furniss

South Weymouth, Mass. August 24, 1904

Personal

My dear Dr. Furniss: Let me caution you on one point. In the present sensitive condition of the country on the Negro question, and especially in view of the fact that there is a campaign in operation and the Democratic party is looking in every direction for campaign material, it would be a mistake to have too many colored people stop at any one white hotel in Indianapolis. This is merely a personal suggestion for your own eye only. Yours very truly,

[Booker T. Washington]

TLc BTW Papers ATT.

To Theodore Roosevelt

South Weymouth, Mass. August 24, 1904

Personal

My dear Mr. President: I have read with care the enclosed statement, which you are thinking of putting in your forthcoming letter of acceptance. I have also taken the liberty of discussing the matter with one or two colored persons in whose judgment I have a good deal of faith.

If you are to say anything upon the color question or Southern matters, this statement will meet the case in a very strong manner. You will note that I have inserted a single word.

I, however, am still of the opinion that it will be wiser to leave the whole subject untouched. The minute you mention the "Fourteenth Amendment," the whole Southern question looms up in the eyes of many timid people in the North and West. I am speaking of course purely from the point of political expediency at the present time. You have said and done so many brave things as bearing upon the race question that the colored vote is with you almost as unanimously as it could possibly be with any one. I do not think that these statements will win any white votes in the North, and they may drive some away. Of course I may be wrong in my opinion, and I should feel safe to be guided by your better judgment. Yours very truly,

Booker T. Washington

TLS Theodore Roosevelt Papers DLC.

To Theodore Roosevelt

South Weymouth, Mass. August 27, 1904

Personal

My dear Mr. President: Enclosed I send you a copy of a telegram which I have just received from members of the Labor Union in Chicago.[1] Of course I shall not go to Chicago for any such purpose and shall keep clear of the whole business, but, as I have stated to you in a former letter, it is very important that this movement be watched in order that the Democrats do not use it in a way to turn the labor people against you on account of the fact that the colored people are being used in a measure to break the strike. I shall keep an eye on the situation as far as I can.

In case you decide to make a comparison between the treatment of the Negro and that of the Philippinos, would it not be effective to call attention to the fact that the leader of the Democratic party in the House of Representatives is elected by only 1400 votes out of a total population of about 190,000 in his district, which means of course that there is less self-government in that district than there is in the Philippine Islands. What is true of Mr. Williams' district is true of the average congressional district in the Black Belt of the South. Yours truly,

[Booker T. Washington]

TLc BTW Papers ATT.

[1] The strike of the meat-packing industry in Chicago from July to September 1904 was the first in which large numbers of blacks acted as strikebreakers. As the packing companies resumed production after the walkout, few local blacks took jobs, but

southern blacks by the trainload were brought into the plants under police escort. In the most serious outbreak of violence, a crowd of several thousand stoned black strikebreakers on their way to the plants. On Aug. 23, John J. Fitzpatrick and William Roselle, leaders of the strike, sent a telegram to BTW, copies of which also appeared in the newspapers. They asked BTW to address a mass meeting of Chicago blacks on the subject, "Should Negroes Become Strikebreakers?" (Con. 802, BTW Papers, DLC.) Meanwhile, at the NNBL meeting in New York in mid-August, S. Laing Williams attacked the racial bias and violence of the Chicago packers' unions and praised the courage of the strikebreakers. (New York *Evening Post*, Aug. 18, 1905, Clipping, Con. 1041, BTW Papers, DLC.)

From Charles Hilton Weir[1]

Haineville, Ala., Aug. 28, '04

Dear Mr Washington: I left school in the afternoon of May, 29, and arrived at Montgomery, in the evening of the same date.

Shortly after reaching there, I learned that there was a good deal of brick work going on in that place. The next day Mr Wm Randall[2] (of the class of '04) and I started out in search of work. Very soon after leaving our room, we reached a building that was being erected by union men; and was refused employment because we were not members of the bricklayers' union.

After learning upon what terms it was possible for us to become members we decided to do so. But met with another difficulty by the foreman being in need of pressed bricklayers.

We could not afford to wait on a union job, as these same obstacles stood in the way: so on June 1, we went to work on an oil mill, for Mr J Stanley & Co, where we worked until the third week in July, having completed the brickwork.

Since then, I have been working here at Haineville, Ala, on a brick store for Mr. Russell. He has been quite satisfied with my work and has promised to employ me until the building is completed.

While at Montgomery, I went to Sunday school every Sunday morning, and visited a large number of the Churches. On more occasions than one I remember counting more than a half dozen young men from Tuskegee, who were in the same Sunday school class with me at the Rev Holly's[3] Church on Dexter Ave. I assisted in singing in the choir of Rev Brooks'[4] Church at Montgomery, and taught a Sunday school class every Sunday since I have been here.

I have been receiving from $2.25 to $3.50 per day, which I considered pretty fair wages for not being a union man.

I took no holidays, save those caused by rains, and the scarcity of brick.

Despite the inducements to stay away from school, I shall return early in September D.V, as I realized how much better fitted I shall be to do the tasks of life creditably, I am yours Respectfully

Chas Weir

ALS Con. 288 BTW Papers DLC.

[1] Charles Hilton Weir of New Providence, Bahamas, B.W.I., was a senior at Tuskegee Institute in 1904.

[2] William Walter Randall of Macon, Miss.

[3] Possibly Watt Holly, a railroad brakeman.

[4] J. R. Brooks was pastor of the Colored Episcopal Church of the Good Shepherd.

From Robert Curtis Ogden

Kennebunkport Maine August 28th/04

My Dear Mr Washington Herewith I return the Presidents letter and memo of proposed paragraph in his letter of acceptance. I sincerely hope that all allusion to the representation plank will be omitted from the letter. And this hope does not arise from any timidity. Perhaps the course I prefer demands the larger courage.

Few Northern men understand the South — especially the rural South. Long patience and sympathy will be required in bringing up the arrested development of the white civilization to the level with the rest of the country.

The action of the Republican Convention has already tied the hands of the Negro's friends and will probably raise again the issue that has once been fought and won concerning the division of the school funds. Only harm can come to the Negro from discussion — action by Congress, there will probably be none in any event. It is the worst sort of philanthropy. Politically it is worse. The door is thrown wide open to Southern democratic demagoguery to stump the North upon the issues that the Republicans are stimulating sectionalism by waving the bloody shirt and the conflict between the Negro (as a rival) and the labor union. These things involve a real danger and with no compensatory possibility either moral or material.

In the last analysis what will become of the Southern Negro if the states of the South are left free by paying the penalty to deal with him as they may please.

The Evening Post: It is true to its own nature. Excuse me for writing what, to you, can be only platitudes. Very Sincerely

Robert C Ogden

ALS Con. 550 BTW Papers DLC.

To Harry Stewart New

Indianapolis, Ind. September 2, 1904

My dear Mr. New, This note will be handed you by my Secretary, Mr. E. J. Scott, whom you can trust absolutely. He has some matters to put before you which he will verbally state. Mr. Scott is continually serving me in many important matters in connection with President Roosevelt, and is thoroughly acquainted with all of my views and interests, and you can talk to him freely. He will let you know among other things something about what I have done regarding Mr. Knox, and what I am planning to do. Yours truly,

Booker T. Washington

TLSr Copy Con. 24 BTW Papers DLC. Signed in E. J. Scott's hand.

From Isaiah T. Montgomery

Mound Bayou, Miss. September 6th., 1904

My Dear Sir: When at our late business meeting I made slight mention of a species of lawlessness known as white-capping,[1] which had effected our people very unfavorably in some portions of this state, but hardly deemed the matter sufficiently pronounced to be mentioned in our Resolutions; on my return home however, I found two letters on my desk, which clearly indicate my unpreparedness to appreciate the depths to which Mississippi has descended, and I seriously wonder if other southern states are as bad: The letter of Mr. Collins with copy of reply and correspondence relative thereto explains itself.

The case of Rev. C. A. Buchanan, see his general letter and my reply[2] attached with Newspaper clippings; Rev. Jernagan happened to be here and favored me with fuller particulars; Rev. Buchanan has the best appointed printing establishment of any colored man in the State, and conducts a Baptist Newspaper (The Preacher and Teacher's Safeguard) at West Point in Clay County, a junction of the Mobile and Ohio and Southern Railways, and reached by a branch of the Ill. Central Ry., and was no doubt prospering, his daughter was his cashier and Book-keeper, they kept a Horse and Buggy, which the young woman used frequently in going to and from work; they kept a decent house and a Piano; a mass meeting of whites decided that the mode of living practiced by the Buchanan family had a bad effect on the cooks and washerwomen, who aspired to do likewise, and became less disposed to work for the whites.

Rev. Buchanan's letter is dated at Meridian the sheriff of Clay County and the Banker of West Point met him there, and together they are trying to arrange some plans for the removal of his business, many of the mob agree that he ought to be allowed to return and wind up his affairs properly, but no one cares to call a meeting to rescind their former action. Previous to Rev Buchanan's difficulty several other happenings took place which show the moving spirit in the play, viz:

Thomas Harvey runs a neat little Grocery, he kept a Buggy and frequently rode to his place of business, he was warned to sell his Buggy and walk. Mr. Chandler keeps a Grocery, he was ordered to leave, but was finally allowed to remain on good behavior. Mr. Meacham ran a business and had a Pool Table in connection therewith, he was ordered to close up and don overalls for manual labor. Mr. Cook conducted a Hack business between the Depots and about town, using two Vehicles, he was notified that he would be allowed to run only one and was ordered to sell the other. Mr. Meacham is a member of the state Committee, I was in hopes of securing the interest of that body in gathering reports of conditions throughout the state, and occasionally bringing them to the notice of the public by petition to the Governor, or other constituted authorities, through the press and other means, but it seems impossible to get that body out of the Machine groove. Possibly you may be able to find judicious ways in which the information imparted may be gotten into the pending campaign to advantage; enclosed find clipping from Memphis Scimitar of this date touching our League resolutions. With warmest regards for you and yours. I am sincerely yours,

Isaiah T. Montgomery

TLS Con. 292 BTW Papers DLC.

1 A detailed account of this white terrorist activity is Holmes, "Whitecapping," 165–85.

2 In an attached letter, Buchanan wrote that a mob of eighty to a hundred white men came to his office on a Saturday and ordered his office closed and him and his family and possessions out of town by Tuesday. Since he was 200 miles away in Natchez at the time, the mob notified him by wire and threatened him with death if he returned. His wife, children, and employees had to leave his and their possessions behind them, and he wrote begging to be allowed to return to pack his belongings. Montgomery's reply, Sept. 6, 1904, could only urge Buchanan to "by all means stand up against discouragement." The whole episode challenged the optimistic assurances of BTW, Montgomery, and the NNBL that the South offered an open field for black business enterprise.

To Charles William Anderson

South Weymouth, Mass. September 7, 1904

Personal

My dear Mr. Anderson: Trotter is making an effort to get the Guardian helped by the Republican State Committee of Connecticut. I hope you will take measures to thwart his plans at once. I understand that the member of the National Committee from Connecticut[1] is connected directly with the New York bureau; perhaps you can do it through him.

Mr. Scott, who has been in Chicago lately, has just communicated to me the fact that Barnett occupies a very subordinate and unimportant position, his duties being mainly local. Mr. New has agreed to take care of Williams on the stump during the campaign. Yours truly,

[Booker T. Washington]

TLc Con. 283 BTW Papers DLC.

1 Charles Frederick Brooker (1847–1927).

To Theodore Roosevelt

South Weymouth, Mass. Sept. 8, 1904

Personal

My dear Mr. President: I have just returned from Indiana where I spent four days. I found matters in that state so far as the colored people are concerned in reasonably good condition, except some dissatisfaction among some of the colored leaders which I think can be allayed within a few days. I have put the details of this matter before Mr. Harry S. New who understands conditions pretty well and is going to take the matter up at once. I shall also speak to Mr. Cortelyou about the same matter. My only fear so far as the Negro vote in Indiana is concerned is that the Democrats are going to make a systematic effort to pay them to remain away from the polls on election day, sending them off on an excursion or something of that kind. This plan has been followed in the past, and I am told by colored people who know that it has worked in a great many cases successfully.

While there I had a conference also with several of the colored leaders from West Virginia, and I find in West Virginia that matters are in as good shape as possible at the present time. Mr. Henry G. Davis's utterances on the race question seem to have solidified the race in that state. I shall, however, expect to go there personally in a few weeks and shall look closely into conditions.

I shall see Mr. Cortelyou tomorrow on my way South. Yours very truly,

[Booker T. Washington]

TLS Theodore Roosevelt Papers DLC.

To Julius Robert Cox[1]

[Tuskegee, Ala.] September 13, 1904

My dear Mr. Cox: There are one or two points which I think it well to make clear to you in writing, so that there can be no misunderstanding.

In the first place, I think it well, as I stated to you, that you not give up your work in Indianapolis until you have remained with me a suitable length of time to find out whether you would like to serve here as a permanent occupation. Secondly, while the work which I wish you to do will be of a secretarial nature, it would not be in the capacity of my principal secretary. Mr. Scott occupies that position, as you perhaps know.

The work that I desire you to perform would be perhaps in the nature of a personal secretary, more than anything else, and as I have stated, a large portion of your time would be occupied in traveling with me.

Whether you are at the school or away from the school, I should desire you to make a careful study of methods by which you could help and relieve me from the detail worries and responsibilities. I think I ought to add further that when I am away from the school, it is often necessary for my personal secretary or stenographer, to work regardless of hours.

He is sometimes occupied until midnight, and it is often necessary to work on Sunday. While this is true, on the one hand, on the other, there will be days when he would have almost nothing to do.

For the work, we can allow you the equivalent of a salary of Eight Hundred Dollars per year, for practically twelve months work, of course allowing reasonable vacation and also furnish you with a house. During the time you might be absent from the school with me, all of your expenses including board, would be paid.

All this of course, is based on the understanding that the preliminary trial will prove that you are thoroughly fitted for the permanent position. Very truly yours,

Booker T. Washington

TLpS Con. 284 BTW Papers DLC.

[1] Julius Robert Cox (1867–1907) was BTW's traveling secretary from 1904 until his

death following an operation for appendicitis. Born in Louisville, Ky., Cox moved to Indianapolis in 1891 as a bookkeeper and then a postal employee. His wife, Gertrude L. Caldwell Cox, taught the fifth grade in the Children's House at Tuskegee Institute.

From Fredrick L. McGhee

Saint Paul, Minnesota. September 14, 1904

My Dear Mr. Washington: On my return last Monday I found your letter of August 26th inquiring if it was still my intention as announced while in New York last June to support Mr. Roosevelt for re-election. I delayed answering that I might give you in some measure what my position is.

I am very anxious for the re-election of Mr. Roosevelt and am still of the opinion then expressed, "that every Negro owes it to the race to see to it that Mr. Roosevelt is re-elected." Since then I have discussed the matter at great length with the strong men of the Democratic party in our State, and so have had the question much under consideration and am very much bothered yet concerning what attitude I shall take: Whether I should not go out and take the stump and bend my every effort to that end, or remain in the ranks of the Democratic party doing what I can to assist them to win a victory in the State and County this fall. That I could do anything to effect good results by pursuing the former course, I might be presuming. I might state that I am certain that the Negro vote in my own State is solid for the President, and if they were not our vote would not nor could effect the result. I must also consider my own interest. I know what my Democratic friends would say should I take that course. The Democratic party show me every consideration I have asked for – more than any Negro now enjoys at the hands of the Republican party of this State or will for many a year to come, unless there be a radical change of men who have control of that party. For ten years I have worked and been associated with the Democracy. Could I at all influence the Negro vote in other parts of the country, they would be justified in charging me with desertion when every influence was needed most. I have had the experience of opposition because of change of politics

— from Republicanism when I first championed Democracy. Since then I have made many attachments and alliances, and I can less afford now to break off and form new ones than I could then. I have urged in justification of my position then, though Democracy be wrong in some questions of politics, yet that much would [be] counted for the race did we not solidly support one party. Experience in my home city has convinced me that I am right.

The Democratic party as a whole seems to be committed against the race, but there is no thinking man but will admit that there are strong elements in the party that are not incurred with the anti-Negro sentiment that seems to dominate it. This, too, troubles me: I find myself unable to say that those who have heretofore stood with the party do not owe it to themselves and the race as a duty to stay now, that their staying may strengthen and encourage that right element in the party to stand out against the other and press further on.

I entertain, absolutely, no fear of adverse legislation should the Democratic party succeed in the Nation in the coming election. This, therefore, brings us to a consideration of the two men — President Roosevelt and Judge Parker. That we know where the President stands with respects to the Negro, his rights, etc., I grant it; that we do not know precisely where Judge Parker stands, I grant it. But we must remember that nearly all great reforms that have benefited humanity have come through men of the profession and walk in life in which Judge Parker is and has been — able lawyers; besides that I have good and reasonable assurances that Judge Parker does not share the anti-Negro sentiment that is in his party. As between men, I would chose Mr. Roosevelt; indeed I yield to no man in admiration of and faith in the President. I am not prepared to say that Judge Parker will do wholly as well; I am, however, of the opinion that he can be relied upon to promote a healthy sentiment in the interest of the race, and, mindful of the precept, 'make thou friends of thy enemy' is it not, then, to be concluded that some of the race — especially those who have been conspicuously associated with the Democratic party — owe it a duty not to do that which might alienate or tend to weaken the ardor of those who entertain good intentions toward us and who are of the enemies' camp, by deserting them now. Thus instance: The Democracy of New York and Massachusetts have done well by their colored constituents; should not that constituency stand now when the Democratic party believes they have a reasonable chance of winning a National victory? If they go over now, will it not weaken our friends and thereby the race sustain a positive loss; a loss which it will take years to regain, for shattered faith is welded only by the slow process of time.

I believe you will agree that should Judge Parker win, it would be to the good of the race that there be somewhere in the country Negroes who had the confidence and respect of the Democrats of their State; who could do a little service towards securing their good office in urging those things that would make for our uplift and check against radical action. I say it, though it smacks of conceit, one of the great drawbacks in reaching Democratic leaders and affecting good in the party is that there are but few men of respect of any standing among its Negro constituents. Should those few drop away now? I fear it must need be harmful to the race. I am reminded that there is a principle at stake and because the President has stood for them, and on that account alone, certain sections of the country would bend every effort to accomplish his defeat, and that the people of this class are largely, though not altogether, Democrats. Therefore, the Negro being the bone of contention he must choose on which side he will stand — for the race or against it. But concerning this I am also mindful of the fact that there is very serious doubt that the party will in the coming four years school its acts with respect to the Negro with the policy that the President has pursued.

I would not hesitate to tender my services to the Republican National Committee did I not more than doubt that could the President be elected and the party defeated — lose the Lower House — in which case my way would be equally clear. This is altogether unlikely and to take such a stand would render me an undesirable ally. So that amid these perplexities I am not prepared to say that I am in a position to go out as a champion of the election of Mr. Roosevelt, however much I desire it. Your field of observation, your experience, your knowledge of men and affairs, is so much broader and riper than mine, I feel to ask that you give me the benefit of your views and suggestions on the premises I have here set forth, and I assure you that I will give to any matters you may have to communicate my best consideration, and I need not say keep them inviolate.

With sincerest regards, I am Yours sincerely,

Fredrick L McGhee

TLS Con. 4 BTW Papers DLC.

To Isaiah T. Montgomery

[Tuskegee, Ala.] September 16, 1904

Personal

My dear Sir: I wish to thank you for your courtesy in sending me a letter from the several men who are suffering from whitecapping disturbances in that section.

For your personal information only, I write to say that I am planning to use this information in a way that I think will be helpful to the cause.[1] The conditions certainly do seem all but unbearable.

Thanking you very sincerely for these various clippings and other information communicated, I am, Very truly yours,

Booker T. Washington

TLpS Con. 4 BTW Papers DLC.

[1] See BTW to E. H. Clement, Sept. 21, 1904, below. BTW sent similar letters to the editors of the Springfield *Republican* and the New York *Evening Post.* Clement printed in the Boston *Transcript* Montgomery's letter and its enclosures without using Montgomery's or BTW's name.

To William W. Bryant[1]

[Tuskegee, Ala.] Sept. 21, 1904

Personal and Confidential

Dear Mr. Bryant: You will have to perfect your plans very carefully so as to be sure that none of the men that have promised to attend the banquet will be drawn off on that night. I think you will find the opposition gang will attempt to have a large political meeting in Cambridge on that same night. Do not let any one know that this information has come through me, but it is pretty reliable. The best way to head off the meeting will be for you to get Dr. Courtney and Mr. W. H. Lewis to see the proper Republican authorities in Boston and Cambridge and prevent their giving aid or consideration to a rally that night in Cambridge. Yours very truly,

Booker T. Washington

TLpS Con. 19 BTW Papers DLC.

[1] William W. Byrant, born in Virginia in 1858, was a hotel waiter in Cambridge according to the 1900 census.

To Edward Henry Clement

[Tuskegee, Ala.] September 21, 1904

Private and Confidential

My dear Sir: I send you herewith, three exhibits, being first, a letter from a representative colored man from Mississippi to me, with enclosures of letters to him, from two men who have been compelled to leave their homes in Mississippi, apparently for no reason other than the fact that they were sufficiently prosperous to earn the envy of their white neighbors.

This condition of affairs is so terrible that I have thought that you would care to bring to the attention of your readers, something of the particulars now wide-spread in Mississippi, largely I believe as a result of Governor Vardaman's excitement. It has been necessary to leave off, except in the case of Rev. Mr. Buchanan, the names of the various parties to the correspondence, for obvious reasons. Very truly yours,

Booker T. Washington

TLpS Con. 869 BTW Papers DLC.

To the Editor of the Chattanooga *Times*[1]

[Tuskegee, Ala.] Sept. 21, 1904

Personal and Confidential

Dear Sir:[2] Referring to the attached editorial,[3] please permit me to say that my action has been in no manner different during the last year from what it has been during the last fifteen years in attending any such functions as you speak of in this editorial note. The fact is where I accept an invitation to one such affair I refuse ten and whenever I do accept it is purely a matter of business. I have to follow the wishes of the people who support this institution as to the time and method of meeting them; sometimes it suits their convenience for me to meet them at their office, at another time at lunch, dinner or a banquet. For example, on the occasion referred to in this editorial, one of the gentlemen whom I had never met before gave $500: but for my meeting him in this way the institution would have received nothing. I received frequent invitations to attend weddings of distinguished and wealthy people, but in every case I have refused to accept such invitations on the ground that there would be no excuse for my doing so, nor would it be in the line of furthering the business interests of this institution. The fact is, I have attended fewer such functions within the last year than I have during the previous ten or fifteen years of the existence of this institution. No colored man has been more careful to try to regard the feelings of the Southern people than I have while in the South, but I believe you will agree with me that when I am out of the South, in the North or in Europe, I cannot be expected to conform to the same rules of living as when in the Southern States.

I have taken the liberty of making this rather lengthy explanation for your personal information only, because of the interest which your paper has always manifested in this institution and in myself personally. Yours truly,

Booker T. Washington

TLpS Con. 869 BTW Papers DLC.

1 BTW sent similar letters to the editors of the Charleston *News and Courier*, Washington *Post*, Nashville *American*, and Atlanta *Constitution*.

[2] Lapsley Greene Walker (1854–1939) was editor-in-chief of the Chattanooga *Times* beginning in 1903.

[3] On Sept. 10, 1904, the Chattanooga *Times* ran a brief editorial note criticizing BTW for "cultivating race equality" by dining with whites in the North.

From Charles William Anderson

New York, Sept 21 1904

My dear Doctor: I have this day learned that Clarkson is to have an interview with Trotter of Boston tomorrow (Thursday) at his office in the Custom house. I mean to drop in, quite by accident, and see what it means. I learned of this tonight, on my return from the Adirondacks. Why does Clarkson play with these fellows? It is very strange. I will report tomorrow. Yours Hastily,

Charles W. Anderson

ALS Con. 283 BTW Papers DLC.

To Clifford H. Plummer

[Tuskegee, Ala.] September 23, 1904

Personal

My dear Friend: Enclosed, I send you Ten Dollars, which I wish you to use in paying your expenses to New York. I shall be at 27 Broadway, Stevens House, on September 27th and I wish to have a consultation with you there.[1] Be very careful to see that no one knows of the fact that you are to make a trip to New York, nor that any one knows that you are to be out of Boston. I will let you have the money for the return trip when I see you.

I shall hope that you will be in possession of full information concerning all the matters by the time we meet in New York. Very truly yours,

Booker T. Washington

TLpS Con. 870 BTW Papers DLC.

[1] BTW later changed the date of the meeting to Sept. 29. (BTW to Plummer, Sept. 24, 1904, Con. 870, BTW Papers, DLC.)

From Charles William Anderson

New York Sept 23rd [1904]

When are you coming here general had two hours conference with Trotter will unearth details & report.

C. W. A.

TWIr Con. 18 BTW Papers DLC.

From Harry Stewart New

Chicago, Ill., Sept. 24, 1904

My dear Mr. Washington: I just now have your favor of the 22nd, and hasten to reply. With reference to the matter of taking Mr. Dancey into the campaign in Indiana, I beg to say that arrangements have already been made for a number of colored orators of note to canvass that state, and my impression is that the State Central Committee is as well supplied as need be at present. However, I will take up this matter with them and see if they can use Mr. Dancey. While on that subject, I may say that I have seen some pretty savage growls from some of the Indianapolis colored people in the papers recently over *any* colored men being brought into the state from the outside. The man who has objected most vigorously is J. H. Lott, who is probably well known to you. There is no more reason why a distinguished colored man from outside the state need not be taken into Indiana than that a distinguished white man should not be and the weakness of Brother Lott's case individually lies in the fact that he has himself made application to me to send him into *other* states as the representative of the National Committee.

With reference to Brother Knox, I regret to say that I believe that gentleman is going to become an independent candidate, and I notice by the papers this morning that he has about completed a petition containing sufficient names to get his name on the ballot. I may say to you confidentially that Brother Knox shows up with this same purpose as regularly as the campaign comes around, and speaking for myself at least, I have grown so tired of it that in my judgment the end might as well be reached one time as another, and I have advised against making any concession to him. The Republican party has been very good to Knox in various ways and I am afraid, Mr. Washington, that he is one of the members of it that represents the colored race to its disadvantage.

I will be very glad to see Major F. A. Denison,[1] of Chicago, and talk to him with reference to campaign matters. I will get word to him at once.

With assurances of my personal regard and high esteem, believe me, Very sincerely yours,

Harry S. New

TLS Con. 4 BTW Papers DLC.

[1] Franklin A. Denison (1862–1932), a black lawyer and politician in Chicago, was chief assistant prosecuting attorney from 1895 to 1898 and assistant corporation counsel for Chicago from 1907 to 1911. In 1915 he became commander of the 8th Illinois Infantry and led black troops in the Mexican expedition in 1916 and to France during World War I.

To Charles William Anderson

[Tuskegee, Ala.] September 26, 1904

PERSONAL

Dear Mr. Anderson: I do not know whether it is possible or practicable to do anything about it, but I wish that in some way, Cooper's paper, The Colored American, could be helped. Cooper is in a bad way just now, and I do not know to what extent he is getting out his paper regularly. I have not seen any recent issue, but up until the last six months Cooper's paper has been doing fine work and I am sure is an assistance to the Party and is standing by President Roosevelt.

I have not said anything to Cooper directly or incidentally about our doing anything, but in my opinion with a little help every week, he could get his paper out regularly. While he has many weak points he has some strong points and one is that he always stands by his friends. Very truly yours,

[Booker T. Washington]

TLp Con. 20 BTW Papers DLC.

From William W. Bryant

Cambridge Mass Sept 26 1904

Plot uncovered mass indignation meeting through white party taken options Halls miller[1] traitor to them must stop them mayor says disgrace City aid me by telegraph order dare not ask financial help here looks like success.

Bryant

AWSr Con. 19 BTW Papers DLC.

1 Charles A. Miller, president of the Men's Forum of Cambridge, sponsors of the banquet in honor of BTW.

To Clifford H. Plummer

New York N.Y. Sept 29 1904

Wire me definite and precise information final plans of enemy as developed to present Are you sure of control?

W.

TWIr Con. 293 BTW Papers DLC.

From William W. Bryant

Cambridge, [Mass.] Sept. 29th/04

Dear Sir: Your informant is giving you a little late news. I did not think that matters of detail in that respect would interest you, plans of the halls have been drawn, and distributed to those who will be in attendance, and the difficulty as near as we can in regard to coat-rooms obviated. There are larger problems more vital confronting us and myself especially, that if I could see my way clear would make the affair a success. Last evening was a stormy meeting, Newsome,[1] Trotter & Co. getting in their work to create among the men bad blood, it is what I have feared, and if they have the proposed meeting, it will not in point of numbers be a failure.

I most respectfully suggest that instead of your informant sending what I consider small suggestions to you, they come and help me work; or if they want to take up the work right here, they can because it is something that I did not bargain for, the abuse, villification, and filth that has been poured upon me, my business affairs disarranged, anon. letters to my family, and to people I work for, and 30 or 40 men to be pacified, furniture ruined etc, and some small fellow, writing about coat rooms, when the Banquet is over I am sure it will be a success, and many men will have contributed to make it so, but they will not be any of your correspondents, but the plain people, who are not looking for anything, but who love you for the work you are doing, and the enemies you have made. Yours Truly,

W. W. Bryant

ALS Con. 19 BTW Papers DLC.

[1] Moses Newsome, born in Virginia in 1863, was reported as a day laborer in the 1900 census.

From Melvin Jack Chisum

New York, N.Y. Oct. 1st, 1904

Dear Dr. Washington: Last night I read your wise and prophetic speech — made at Indianapolis Ind., before the N.N.B.L. convention. Having been very busy I laid the paper aside that I might read it carefully which I have done, since I was not there to applaud my quota of appreciation I take occasion to express my self upon paper.

I have read somewhere these lines;

"Dear friend, I pray thee, if thou wouldst be proving
    Thy strong regard for me,
Make me no vows. Lip-service is not loving;
    Let thy faith speak for thee."

— and I have ever tried to observe them, I have been tempted often to write you upon subjects good and otherwise and have desisted upon each occasion because I feared I might *say*, things, that I would rather *do*.

This much I beg you, if ever you *need* a real genuine piece of steel send for me, *I am not a recent convert to the principles of the Wizard of Tuskegee*, I am an original Booker Washingtonite; was born reared and raised in *Texas*, and may I be pardoned for saying, that nature in putting me together forgot to put in fear.

I have accomplished a long line of failures for my self, but *never once*, have I *failed* in an undertaking for a friend.

You have proven to be the only man the race has, who is actually working for the race, and millions of us love you, worship your name and accept your counsel in the fullest measure.

The few unfortunates who do not are weaklings, half crazy or something, and we pitty them. This great speech, may I be pardoned for saying it, ought to be put in pamphlet form, and circulated among all the people of this country, black and white.

From your obedient humble servant,

Melvin J. Chisum

ALS Con. 286 BTW Papers DLC.

To William W. Bryant

New York Oct 3/04

See that the officers who are present tonight are in citizens dress as far as possible.

W.

HWIr Con. 19 BTW Papers DLC.

A Handbill by Moses Newsome

Cambridge, Mass. Oct. 3, '04

TO THOSE MEMBERS OF THE NEGRO RACE who value their political privileges and manhood rights as of the first importance, who believe that under our form of government these privileges and rights can be best secured through an intelligent and proper use of the ballot — to such we make this address.

Our fathers and mothers suffered all manner of pain, even death, that we might enjoy what privileges we have: cannot this generation make some sacrifices that our children's lot may be even better than our own? The liberties of a people have never been purchased over a Banquet table, but history's pages are filled with instances where, in their revelry, the powerful have taken from a people every vestige of liberty. Let us not, for a seeming present gain, be misled by these glittering shows. Let us trust those self-sacrificing ones who are trying to point out the danger, or else yet a little while and our lot shall be worse than the dreaded days of slavery. Think over this matter, and in the quietness of your closet between yourself and God, ask yourself the question — what benefit does the race derive from the coming Banquet? In that solution, decide for yourself and your children's children.

It is proper to honor any respected member of our race, but we should at the same time take care that in so doing we are not giving approval of their honest, yet misguided efforts. If a banquet to any race leader tends to aid and abet the South in her endeavor to keep us down, then every race lover should frown upon it. If the Negro's fealty to the Republican Party is to be judged by his unqualified acceptance of Dr. Booker T. Washington's policy, better we hasten to take the advice of Rev. J. Henry Duckrey and make friends with the Democracy and the South.

We believe that because of the criticism of Dr. Washington's policy, to-night he will give an address on race rights far in advance of anything he has yet said or done. Let us honor Dr. Washington as an educator and a respected citizen, but condemn his pernicious policy of subordination to Southern prejudices. For the future of my children and yours

MOSES NEWSOME

PDSr Con. 1103 BTW Papers DLC.

OCTOBER · 1904

A News Item in the Boston *Globe*

Boston, Oct. 4, 1904

PRES ELIOT AND DR WASHINGTON

THEY SHARE HONORS AT THE DINNER OF MEN'S FORUM AT CAMBRIDGE

Pres Eliot of Harvard university divided the honors with Dr Booker T. Washington at a banquet given by colored men in honor of the negro leader and educator last evening in Cambridge.

The toastmaster gave the company the impression that dining with colored men was a new departure for the president of Harvard, but the latter soon assured them that it was not. He remained till the close of the program, at about 11:30.

The banquet and its arrangements were of a character to reflect credit upon the organization which gave it — the Men's forum of Cambridge — and the occasion will be long remembered by the colored population of the university city. Prospect hall was filled. Beside invited guests, who included Mayor Augustine J. Daly[1] and most of the clergymen of Cambridge, also Hon A. E. Pillsbury, Hon J. H. H. McNamee, Prof Hart of Harvard and William Lloyd Garrison, many other white men, who had bought tickets, were scattered about at the dinner tables. The balcony was filled with colored women.

Mayor Daly was obliged to leave early, so he was presented between courses and spoke as follows:

"A score of years ago that great poet of humanity, John Boyle O'Reilly, prayed that God might send the negro race wise guides. If he were here tonight in the presence of the distinguished guest of the evening, he would thank God that his prayer had been answered. Among the world-famous men who have favored our city with their presence we welcome Booker T. Washington.

"At the critical period in the development of every race, great men are sent by the Almighty — men trained in this special way to best serve their people. So has it been with him. Through slavery, sacrifice and scorn his great soul has enabled him to view life with sympathy and tenderness. To feel a pride in his manhood, a faith in his power to overcome obstacles, a hope in the ultimate triumph of justice.

"It is eminently fitting that our city should welcome Booker T. Washington because he is destined to help to finish the work for the negro which was hastened forward a generation ago by the pens of Longfellow and Lowell, by the magnificent daring of Higginson, by that first company of volunteers, by that great university which has raised a fitting memorial to the young men who went forth from her halls to lay down their lives for the negro.

"Courage, steadfastness, patience and faith win every true victory. Those are the qualities which should grow stronger in the negro with every added year of freedom."

Pres Eliot Introduced

After dinner Pres Charles A. Miller welcomed the guests and the company and called upon William W. Bryant to act as toastmaster. Mr Bryant first asked all to arise for a moment in honor of Senator Hoar, which was done. The toastmaster then read a letter in which Gov Bates sent cordial greetings and spoke of the funeral of "the great Massachusetts senator" preventing his attendance. Mr Bryant also read letters from E. H. Clement, Hon Levi S. Gould, chairman of the commissioners of Middlesex county, Minister Powell of Hayti and others.

Dr Henderson, pastor of the Charles St A. M. E. church, Boston, spoke for the colored clergy.

The toastmaster said: "For the first time in history a president of Harvard puts his feet under the mahogany with black men." Here the orchestra played a strain of "Fair Harvard," then the toastmaster added: "Without more words — for you all know him — I will present Pres Eliot." The whole company arose with Pres Eliot, who, after they were seated, smilingly began his speech by saying:

"I have sat at table with colored men many times in my life. I began when a boy in my father's house at the top of Beacon Hill. In my boyhood home I ate with an old colored man who had been a slave and had crossed the Canadian line more than once. Then I have had the honor to sit with Dr Washington at the college table on commencement day. There's nothing new in this association. So, gentlemen, your toastmaster was a bit in error in thinking the conditions of this meeting had any novelty to me."

Education of the Physician

After laughter and applause had subsided, Pres Eliot continued: "We have heard tonight that this race should have equality with others. Who led the first colored companies in the civil war? Wentworth Higginson, Robert Gould Shaw and Hallowell, all graduates of Harvard."

This declaration was the signal for three rousing cheers for Pres Eliot and Harvard. "Have you ever had anything but equal opportunity at Harvard?" asked the president. (More cheers.)

"But it is a very solemn truth," said Dr Eliot, "that the negro in this country needs equal opportunity. He needs freedom and without equal opportunity freedom is imperfect. What your people need is: First, just legislation, and next, just administration. But then you need education. Your race is not the only one to which the opportunities of education are not equal.

"There is one here of that race who has done more than any other in the world to open the way of equal education to this race. This is an immense service which Dr Washington has rendered to your people and to our country. I see one particular form of higher education which seems to be the next demanded for the colored people of the country, and that is the education of the physician. The death rate of the race is disproportionately high. It is so because of ignorance of the people of the conditions for healthy living."

In closing Pres Eliot impressively gave his hearers two quotations from Scripture for their guidance and encouragement. They were: "Ye shall know the truth, and the truth shall make you free," and "Where the spirit of the Lord is, there is liberty."

Dr Washington's Address

Asst U S Dist Atty W. H. Lewis said he liked Mr Washington first because he was a hopeless optimist, and that was necessary in leading an educational movement, especially a movement for the education of a downtrodden people.

When Dr Washington was presented all arose and the orchestra struck up "Fair Harvard," to which all joined in singing the Tuskegee song, written by Paul Laurence Dunbar. Three cheers for the speaker followed; then Dr Washington said:

"Before I utter one word upon the subject immediately in hand

I must let you know how deeply I share with the people of Massachusetts their sorrow in the death of George Frisbie Hoar, who, in addition to being a great statesman, was a friend tried and true to the American black man in every part of the country. Had I not accepted an invitation to this meeting nearly a year ago, I should not attend a meeting of this nature on the day his body lies in state.

"In the presence of the president of Harvard college I feel almost ashamed to utter the word education. I was born a slave, and my opportunities for education have been very limited."

Regarding the colored race in America he said in part:

"I believe that in the fullness of time we shall demonstrate to the world that we can become a potential and helpful part of the highest and best civilization. Because of this progress in the present and my faith in the future, I was never prouder than I am today of being a negro and of being identified in some slight degree with the struggles and triumphs of a race in which I have such confidence. As regards the black man in America, and as you well know, I would set no limits upon his development, whether of body, mind or soul.

Should Have the Ballot

"We need not only the industrial school, but the college and professional school as well, for a people so largely segregated, as we are, from the main body of our people must have its own professional leaders who shall be able to measure with others in all forms of intellectual life. It is well to remember, however, that our teachers, ministers, lawyers and doctors will prosper just in proportion as they have about them an intelligent and skillful producing class.

"I believe thoroughly in the work which the college, the university and the industrial school can do at the present time for the advancement of my race at the south. In a very large measure the negro has in his hands, at the present time, a large proportion of the trades and the skilled and common labor of the south. We must see to it that while the head is being educated that the hand is also trained, so we may hold on to the fundamental occupations that are represented in agriculture, mechanics and the domestic sciences. No race can advance very far in education, morals, religion or politics that does not have an economic or industrial foundation. It is because of this fact that the Tuskegee institute years ago began to lay its foundation in economic or industrial directions, that we are now able to give employment to 32 negro college graduates — a larger number than is employed by any other one institution in the world. This takes no account of the 110 other officers, teachers, etc. of the various kinds.

"In regard to the ballot I repeat here what I often said in the south. As to my position on this subject, I do not approve of the negro's giving up anything that is fundamental and that is guaranteed by the constitution of the United States. It is not best for him to relinquish any rights, nor would his doing so be best even for the southern white man. Every law placed in the constitution of the United States was placed there to encourage and stimulate the highest citizenship. If the negro is not stimulated and encouraged by just national and state laws to become the highest type of citizen, the result will be worse for the southern white man than for the negro. Unless these negroes are encouraged by just election laws to become taxpayers and intelligent producers, the white people will have an eternal millstone about their necks.

"Any subterfuge, any makeshift in the form of a law that gives the ignorant white man a right to express his wants at the ballot box and withholds the same right from the ignorant negro is an injustice to both races. In most cases such laws give the negro the incentive to become a voter by getting property and intelligence, but say to the white man in so many words, 'Remain in ignorance and poverty and a way will be found for you to exercise the franchise.' No question is settled until it is settled right; till it is settled in accordance with the absolute, immutable laws of justice.

"No race of people, whether white or black, can depend solely upon political activity or the chance of office holding for permanent success. There must always be an intelligent and economical foundation, otherwise political activity is a mockery.

PROGRESS REGARDING LYNCHING

"Regarding lynching, I also repeat what I have said many times in the south: That the taking of human life without due process of law, whether in Georgia or Ohio, is a blot upon civilization. Further, that we should for all times stand ready as a race to join hands with all people to see that the crime is not committed by our people, and to see that legal punishment follows such crimes.

"No happenings within the last 10 years have given me more encouragement than the frank, brave manner in which lynching has been condemned in the south within the last few days by the daily press, the white pulpit, by grand juries, governors, and, in several cases, by confederate camps.

"The present commendable sentiment regarding the disgraceful habit of lynching never could have been brought about except through the cooperation between the better class of whites and the same class of blacks. It is through such sympathetic cooperation between the races that our difficulties are finally to disappear.

"Let us never become discouraged regarding our future. We are making progress in moral directions, where it is most questioned. This progress is proven by the fact that almost no negro who holds a diploma from one of our recognized colleges, universities or industrial schools, can be found within the walls of the penitentiary.

"In the business world you can find the negro making advancement, making progress as bankers, as merchants, as real estate dealers, as well as operating thousands of valuable and successful farms.

"Slavery presented a problem of destruction; freedom presents a problem of construction. The latter requires patience, time, courage and toil, but in the end we shall reach our goal. Of this we have no doubt whatever."

The committee was W. W. Bryant, James Epps, Minor Hamlin, Samuel E. Wilson, S. P. Clark, Robert A. Dixon, Nathan Bullock.

Boston *Globe,* Oct. 4, 1904, 7.

1 Augustine J. Daly (1861–1938) was mayor of Cambridge from 1902 to 1906.

From George Washington Albert Johnston

[Birmingham, Ala.] Oct-7-1904

Dear Uncle: Perhaps what I am writing you is well known to you and yet, because I do not know that it is I am writing you.

It is needless for me to say that I wish my part in the matter kept quiet because my stating these facts to you, were it known by the parties, would cause me some trouble.

Mr. Albert Davis, an old Graduate of Tuskegee is as unworthy the respect of ever having been a student of Tuskegee as a person can be. Because of your refusal to help him in his matter concerning his recent trouble,[1] he has written the Boston people who are continually *knocking* you and your actions, a long article denouncing you, Mr Logan and every thing else. Whether they will use this or not remains to be seen. Anyway I know that he mailed them a long letter just after hearing from you this week & one of the graduates here saw the whole letter.

Davis is simply a Drinking Worthless Character, talked about by all the whites who know him & most of the colored.

Messrs R. L. & Chas Mabry's[2] Tailor Shop is a Pure & Simple Gambling House & Mr. Robt. Mabry never misses a game in it. The wonder is that it has not long ago been raided by police. You can hardly ever enter the back room unless some kind of game is in progress. A teacher from Tuskegee here last week ran in on a game in full swing. I have heard that you would be here on the 20th & would like to know if it is true & exactly what time you will reach here & how long remain.

We are well & have no cause for complaint.

Love for Aunt Jacobum & yourself. Sincerely,

Albert

ALS Con. 22 BTW Papers DLC.

[1] The state superintendent of education accused Davis of speculating in teachers' certificates. See above, 3:15.

[2] Charles Taylor Mabry, a Tuskegee graduate of 1901 trained in tailoring.

An Article in *Outlook*[1]

8 October 1904

Cruelty in the Congo Country

My interest in the race to which I belong, and in the advancement of the cause of humanity regardless of race, is my excuse for discussing a subject which I have not hitherto called attention to in public print.

The oppression of the colored race in any one part of the world means, sooner or later, the oppression of the same race elsewhere. Not only this, but what is equally important and equally true is the fact that the degradation and weakening of the oppressors always follow any wrong done to a defenseless people.

No one who has followed conditions as they have been developing in what is called the Congo Free State in Africa during the last few years can fail to reach the conclusion that there is something wrong — a wrong so widespread that civilized nations cannot escape their duty nor evade their responsibility. I am sure that I state the case very mildly when I say that while in this article I can call attention to only a few of the cruelties practiced in that country upon my race, there was never anything in American slavery that could be compared to the barbarous conditions existing to-day in the Congo Free State. But let me be more specific.

When the United States, in April, 1884, recognized the King of Belgium's government in the basin of the Congo, it did so because of "the humane and noble object" which that government represented. These are the words of the declaration.

It was understood that "an independent confederation of free negroes" was being formed in equatorial Africa, under the benevolent patronage of the King and the association of scientists and explorers that he had gathered about him. Not many years before, the negro State of Liberia had been established in Africa, as a result of the efforts of the philanthropic people of the United States. This movement to erect in the heart of Africa an independent negro State seemed to be an effort to realize on a grander scale the same philanthropic purpose. It was this, no doubt, that led our Government to intervene in what seemed to some people at that time a purely European affair. It is, moreover, to this timely intervention that the Congo State owes in large measure its existence. These are facts which we should bear in mind.

One of the first things the King did as ruler of the Congo was to declare all vacant lands to be the property of the State. This decree did not seem at first either extraordinary or peculiarly important. But that was because the King had not yet succeeded in establishing his authority in the interior of the continent. As fast as he did so, however, the social status of the native and his relation to the soil changed. It became a crime for him to gather on his own account the rubber and ivory in which the forests abounded; and the white trader, to whom he had been accustomed to sell these things, was treated as a receiver of stolen property.

This decree worked great injustice to the natives. It took from them at one stroke all the natural wealth of the country, with which they might have been able to purchase the products of civilization, as soon as they learned to value them. At the same time it took from them every incentive that they might otherwise have had to work, and to learn from the white man the use and value of the great natural resources of the land on which they lived. So far from making the native free and independent, this method of dealing with him took away what little natural ambition and desire for a higher and better life he may have had.

But that is not all. This first false step led, naturally enough, to the second. Having taken from the negro his right to trade, to which the West African has a native bent and a peculiar aptitude, it became necessary to find other means to induce him to work. If the natives could not in some way be made to gather the rubber and the ivory in the forests, the reason for the white man's presence in equatorial Africa would no longer exist. From this time on we hear the complaint that the West African will not work. This great obstacle to his advancement the Government has sought to remove by the imposition of taxes and the introduction of forced labor. So it has come about that, instead of making the negro free and independent, King Leopold has been led to set up a system in the Congo which, from all that I can learn about it, is harsher and more evil in its consequences than any form of slavery that has ever existed on African soil.

Suppose we ask ourselves, before we go any farther, why it is that the African in the Congo will not work. Before the white man came to Africa it was not necessary for the negro to work. The soil supplied, almost without effort of his own, all that he needed for his existence. After the white man arrived, however — at least this seems to have been the case in the Congo State — there was no longer any inducement to labor, since the white man took from him the only means by which he might, if he chose to do so, have been enabled to raise himself to a higher and happier plane of existence. At the same time his new master, under legal forms and with ceremonies that were new and strange to him, has imposed tasks so heavy and heartbreaking that men die under them as if stricken by a pestilence. During the building of the railway from Matadi to Stanley Pool, which cost so many hundreds of lives, thousands of natives, I am told, crossed the Portuguese border, preferring the virtual slavery that prevails there to the sort of freedom they were given in the Free State.

One of the most unfortunate results of this method of dealing with the African is the heritage of misunderstanding, mutual distrust, and race hatred that it inevitably leaves behind it. This alone, in my opinion, will render fruitless for many years to come every effort to bring the great mass of the natives under the better and higher influences of our Christian civilization.

I have thus far simply sought to point out the consequences of what it is charitable to call a mistaken policy. I now wish to refer to certain actions of the King's government that cannot be attributed to an error of judgment, but only to a rash expediency and a desire to pay dividends on the money invested in a so-called philanthropic experiment.

It is said that King Leopold owes his success in the Congo to the fact that he has known how to turn the forces of savagery against itself. He conquered one after another the different parts of his vast domain by arming one tribe of savages and pitting it against the others. In this way he has not only subdued pretty nearly the whole of the territory assigned to him by the Belgian Conference, but has compelled the conquered tribes, by employing one tribe as a policeman to control the others, to bring in under the title of taxes large quantities of tribute. The consequences of this method of collecting tribute have sometimes been horrible. I shall quote only one short passage from the report of the Rev. W. H. Sheppard,[2] a colored missionary, whom I knew slightly as a fellow-student at Hampton Institute. This is a report written on the spot by an eye-witness. Mr. Sheppard had been sent out by the mission to investigate what is called a "rubber raid." The raiders in this case were a tribe of cannibals known as the Zapo-zaps. After a day's journey he came up with the chief of the band, and, as he was acquainted with him, talked with him about the raid. According to the report, the following conversation ensued:

"How many did you kill?" I asked.

"We killed plenty; will you see some of them?"

"Oh, I don't mind," I said, reluctantly; but that was just what I wanted.

He said, "I think we have killed between eighty and ninety, and those in the other villages I don't know. I did not go, but sent my people."

The chief and I walked out on the plain just near the camp. There were three people with the flesh carved off from the waist down.

"Why are the people carved so, leaving only the bones?" I asked.

"My people ate them," he promptly answered. He then explained. "The men who have young children do not eat people, but all the rest ate them." On the left was a great big man shot in the back and without a head. (All these people were nude.)

"Where is the man's head?" I asked.

"Oh, they made a bowl of the forehead to rub up tobacco and diamba in."

We continued to walk and examine until late in the afternoon, and counted forty-one bodies. The rest were eaten up by the people.

On returning to the camp we crossed a young woman, shot in the back of the head; one hand was cut away. I asked why, and Mulumba N'Cusa explained that they always cut off the right hand to give to the State on their return.

"Can you not show me some of the hands?" I asked. So he conducted us to a framework of sticks, under which was burning a slow fire, and there they were, the right hands – I counted them, eighty-one in all.

There are not less than five hundred guns all told, and sixty women (Bena Pianga) prisoners. I saw them. Some of his followers or principal men are Lualaba, Kabunga, Kasenda, and Zapo Kingonda.

The chief of the band told Mr. Sheppard that he had been sent out to do this wild work by the State officers. It was intended as a punishment to certain of the neighboring villages for failure to bring in the required amount of rubber. I might add that Mr. Sheppard, who has been eleven years in that region and knew the methods of the Government, believed this statement of the native and holds the Government entirely responsible for the crimes this band of raiders committed. The whole truth about this matter will probably never be known.

I wish to point out, however, that whether the Congo Government is directly or only indirectly responsible for this hideous piece of savagery, it cannot escape responsibility for the conditions which made it possible. Having armed these savage black men and incited them to make war on one another, it cannot avoid responsibility for the consequences of its policy.

And what is the result of it all? Not the improvement and uplifting of the black men, since wherever the white man has put his foot in the Congo State the black man has been degraded into a mere tool in the great business of getting rubber. And what is the effect upon the white men who are condemned to perform this degrading work? All reports agree that these men almost invariably give themselves over to the worst vices, if for no other reason than to escape from the melancholy which their isolation breeds. Some of these men, it is said, condemned on account of their crimes for long terms of service in the interior, give themselves up to despair and kill themselves or commit horrible crimes. It is clear that the native is not the only victim of this system. What a comment on the whole situation is the single fact that only a few months ago an officer of the Government was condemned to fifteen years' imprisonment, after he had been convicted of killing one hundred and twenty-two persons!

If anything that I have said will serve to call the attention of civilized nations, and especially that of our own country, to the conditions existing in the Congo Free State, and will further serve to bring about such action as will in any manner modify or improve the present status of affairs, I shall feel that I have not written in vain. Certainly the whole subject demands careful investigation and swift action.

Outlook, 78 (Oct. 8, 1904), 375–77.

1 Robert E. Park ghost-wrote the article. BTW sent him the $30 that the *Outlook* had paid him for it, writing: "I cannot feel I should accept this money since this article was so largely prepared by you." (Oct. 11, 1904, Con. 293, BTW Papers, DLC.)

2 William Henry Sheppard (b. 1865), a Presbyterian minister and missionary.

To Oswald Garrison Villard

Tuskegee, Alabama. October 10, 1904

Personal

My dear Mr. Villard: I hope that you will not think that we are becoming a burden upon you, but you do not know what a relief it is to know that there is a paper of respectability and wide influence through which matters that ought to be known can get before the public.

Enclosed I send you a letter from a reliable colored man in Selma, Dallas County, Alabama, regarding the registration of Negro voters. You will perhaps recall that in this state the temporary clause has expired and if the provisions of the permanent plan are carried out honestly, any colored man who owns $300 worth of property or who can read and write is entitled to registration for voting without question. In a good many of the counties I think the Board of Registrars has made an honest effort to deal fairly with the colored voters, but in some of the counties, notably Dallas, they have been outrageously unfair.

The name of the writer of this letter is Mr. R. B. Hudson, but I have taken his name from the copy of the letter as it will injure him for his name to get in print.

It will interest you further to know that so far as I have seen, without exception the Southern daily press that has discussed the matter at all has sat down on Heflin[1] good and strong. Some of the papers that I thought would support him, or at least be silent, have spoken out most strongly. Yours very truly,

Booker T. Washington

TLS Oswald Garrison Villard Papers MH.

[1] James Thomas Heflin (1869–1951), an Alabama lawyer, served in the U.S. House of Representatives from 1904 to 1920 and in the U.S. Senate from 1920 to 1931. A persistent race-baiter, he was rumored to be an active ally of the Ku Klux Klan in the 1920s.

To Bradley Gilman[1]

[Tuskegee, Ala.] October 14, 1904

My dear Mr. Gilman: I thank you very much for your kind letter of recent date and for the suggestions which it contains.[2] It is very kind of you to think of me and the interests of the school in the way that you have done.

I would say, in the first place, that while there are a few cases here and there throughout the country of colored people who oppose me and my views, this opposition centers almost wholly in Boston and to a small extent in Washington City. Outside of these centers, no man could have more loyal and constant support from all classes of people than I am constantly receiving. The Boston situation is a rather peculiar one. The opposition there centers in and is led by about a dozen colored men, the leaders being a man by the name of Trotter, Clement G. Morgan and Butler Wilson.[3] What their ground of opposition is, is very difficult for me to understand. I think it is largely jealousy or personal ill-will, because on every occasion where I have spoken in Boston and given them an opportunity to come and hear me express my views on all public questions, they have failed to be present. In dealing with these three men mentioned especially, I do not believe that you or anyone else could go very far in changing their views or at least their attitude toward me, and the question is, whether any attention given them in this direction would not make them receive an exaggerated idea of their own importance and influence and thus make them more foolish than they otherwise would be. These represent one class. There is still another class, how large I am not able to say, which does not understand me because I have never been thrown enough in contact with it to enable me to state my views fully, but I have taken definite means of finding out how the masses of the colored people in Boston and Cambridge stand, and I find that they understand my position and approve it.

All this has little, however, to do with your direct question. I would state that I am quite sure you could accomplish much good by pursuing the course which you suggest, and I am sending you letters of introduction to a number of the very best colored people in Boston and Cambridge. I am also sending you some printed matter containing some of my recent speeches which state my position on public questions pretty fully. Yours very truly,

Booker T. Washington

TLpS Con. 288 BTW Papers DLC.

1 Bradley Gilman (1857–1932), a Unitarian clergyman, served several pastorates in New England including the First Congregational Parish of Canton, Mass., from 1903 to 1917. He was the author of several books and edited the *Christian Register* in 1915 and 1916. In 1917 he moved to Palo Alto, Calif. BTW considered Gilman a loyal supporter and a friend of the race.

2 Gilman wrote to BTW on Oct. 10, 1904, asking for the names of black persons in Boston to whom he could speak on the Negro problem and BTW's work. "I have, many a time, told *individuals* that they must stand by you, as their great leader," but he hoped to promote the same cause before larger audiences of blacks.

3 Butler Roland Wilson (1860–1939), the son of a black Atlanta physician, was a graduate of Atlanta University and Boston University Law School. Establishing himself as a Boston lawyer, first with Archibald H. Grimké and George L. Ruffin and then independently, he developed a clientele that included more whites than blacks. Early in his career Wilson developed a special interest in civil rights cases, and he was a close ally of W. M. Trotter in the opposition to BTW in Boston.

Wilson was a signer of the call for the Niagara Movement in 1905 and was an early member of the NAACP. He helped found the Boston branch of the NAACP in 1912 and continued for decades as an active member locally and nationally. In 1915 he was a leading opponent of the showing of *The Birth of a Nation* in Boston. A regular Republican, Wilson took no interest in officeholding. (Contee, "Wilson and the Boston NAACP Branch," 346–48.)

To Thomas Goode Jones

[Tuskegee, Ala.] October 14, 1904

Personal

My dear Sir: Will you permit me to extend to you my most sincere thanks and gratitude for your very able, wise, and courageous charge to the Grand Jury in Huntsville,[1] a few days ago. I have heard your words spoken of in the highest terms by numbers of people, and the whole country is your debtor for what you have done. Very truly yours,

Booker T. Washington

TLpS Con. 22 BTW Papers DLC.

1 Jones charged the federal grand jury with investigation of a white mob's lynch-

ing of a black federal prisoner in Huntsville, on the ground that the mob violated the victim's civil rights under the Thirteenth Amendment by denying him trial by jury. His charge was quoted in full in the Montgomery *Advertiser*, Oct. 12, 1904, 3.

To Robert Curtis Ogden

[Tuskegee, Ala.] October 14, 1904

My dear Mr. Ogden: When I see you, which I hope will be next month, I will talk with you more fully about conditions in the Congo. I think it pretty safe to discount in a very large measure what anyone who is connected with King Leopold's government may say regarding conditions in the Congo. While in my article I mentioned Mr. Sheppard's name, I would state that I got perhaps more information from Rev. Dr. Morrison,[1] a Southern white man who is engaged in missionary work in the Congo under the auspices of the Southern Presbyterian Church. It seems that King Leopold has a systematic method of pulling the wool over the eyes of most people who go to Brussels to protest about conditions, but Mr. Morrison has been one of the few men who has been able to stand up and look the king in the face and tell him frankly what the conditions are. Perhaps you know that the king has a number of agents at work in this country for the purpose of putting his side of the case before the American public. I was very careful to see that all the statements which I made in my article could be proved before I made them. Yours very truly,

Booker T. Washington

TLpS Con. 23 BTW Papers DLC.

[1] William McCutchon Morrison (b. 1867) was a missionary in Africa beginning in 1896. He was a leader in the movement to expose Belgian atrocities in the Congo. From 1903 to 1906 he appeared before officials in the United States, Belgium, and England to describe Congo conditions. He returned to the Congo in 1906 to edit a newspaper and carry on the struggle to end Belgian misrule.

From George Washington Carver

[Tuskegee, Ala.] Oct. 14–'04

My dear Mr. Washington; I beg to acknowledge receipt of your note[1] and come now to the most painful experience of my life.

For sixte[e]n years I have labored with you; have built up one of the best Agrl. laboratories in the South so much so that the people of your own town recognize its value.

Only yesterday the Tuskegee Cotton Oil Co. submitted samples of cotton seed meal, and cake for analysis, and have arranged to bring in samples every week.

The museum is the best of its kind in the south and constantly growing. The Experiment Station, in the nature of the problems chosen and the results obtained I am sure has no equal south. Now to be branded as a liar and party to such hellish deception it is more than I can bear, and if your committee feel that I have willfully lied or [was] party to such lies as were told my resignation is at your disposal.[2]

I deeply regret to take this step but it seems to me the only manly thing to do.

I shall always feel kindly to your work and shall continue to be loyal to Tuskegee and its interests. Yours Very truly,

Geo. W. Carver

ALS Con. 551 BTW Papers DLC.

[1] After a committee of Tuskegee faculty members had reported adversely on the management of the poultry yard, BTW wrote criticizing Carver and accusing him of exaggerated reports of the efficiency of the poultry yard. (Oct. 13, 1904, ViHaI.)

[2] BTW mollified Carver with a reply: "Your devotion and loyalty to the school is unquestioned, and I very much fear that it was because of your great devotion and ambition you were led perhaps, into the error of permitting exaggerated statements to come from your department." (Oct. 14, 1904, ViHaI.)

To Theodore Roosevelt

Tuskegee, Alabama. October 17, 1904

Personal

My dear Mr. President: Your telegram was received. I am glad you like the editorial.[1] I am sending it to Dr. Lyman Abbott today with the request that he use it just as soon as possible. I have added the name of Mr. Wilson[2] and have also inserted the attached paragraph.[3]

I am surprised to find, on investigating the subject through the records kept by the Chicago Tribune that there have been fewer lynchings in the country during the two years you have been President than for any similar period since 1885. With the exception of one year under Mr. Harrison, the largest number of lynchings occurred during the two years when Mr. Cleveland was President. Yours very truly,

Booker T. Washington

TLS Theodore Roosevelt Papers DLC.

1 See An Editorial by Washington in *Outlook*, Oct. 29, 1904, below.

2 Edgar Stewart Wilson.

3 The attachment, with a few minor variations, is the next to the last paragraph of the *Outlook* editorial of Oct. 29.

To Lloyd G. Wheeler

[Tuskegee, Ala.] Oct. 17, 1904

Mr. L. G. Wheeler: There are one or two suggestions which I wish to make for your consideration.

1st. I think it very important you keep in mind the matter of anticipating as far ahead as possible all the needs of the school. For example, if it has not already been done, you should now be preparing to place orders for goods to be used in the winter and spring. You will find that you cannot depend to any large extent upon the heads of departments and divisions to anticipate their needs, you will have to do this for them. Whenever we are crowded in time for getting goods I am afraid we suffer in not getting the best prices because of lack of time to investigate prices and get up competition.

2d. In looking over our bills from Montgomery, I very much fear that we are getting our trade too much centered in the hands of a few Jews. Wherever we can get equally fair treatment in prices and quality of goods from persons other than Jews, I prefer to have our trade scattered among them. In creating public sentiment in favor of the institution the Jews cannot be of much service. I mean not nearly so much as is true of native Southern white men like Hobbie & Teague and Vandiver & Co.

3d. Where all things are equal with our giving trade to Jews, I hope you will bear in mind Mr. J. Loeb.[1] Quite a number of years ago when other wholesale merchants refused absolutely to deal with us and were threatened by boycott by the town merchants in case they did deal with us, Loeb paid no attention to our want of money and threatened boycott in town and stood by us and sold us goods at wholesale prices. Of course, after he was brave enough to stem the tide for some months, others fell in line, but we owe him a great deal for helping us out in this way in our earlier days.

4th. All that I have said is mainly in the way of suggestions. I understand thoroughly how very difficult it is to satisfy all parties concerned in buying goods.

B. T. W.

TLpI Con. 551 BTW Papers DLC.

[1] Jacques Loeb (1855–1912) immigrated to the United States from France in 1872, settling in Montgomery. He was president of Winter Loeb Grocery Co., vice-president of the Montgomery Chamber of Commerce, a bank director, and secretary of the United Hebrew Charities of Montgomery.

To George L. Knox

[Tuskegee, Ala.] October 17, 1904

Personal and Confidential

My dear Mr. Knox: I am very sorry to hear that after I left Indianapolis you came out as a full-fledged candidate for Congress. I had hoped that you would be willing to take my advice and not do so. I think that you are making a mistake on two grounds. I think your reasons will be misunderstood and misinterpreted, and in the long run it will not help your paper in its influence throughout the country. Secondly, I very much fear your candidacy will hurt that of our friend, the President, as it is very hard to get people on election day to draw the line. Perhaps you may be at the point now where you are willing to make a change.

I shall be very glad to hear from you at any time. Yours very truly,

Booker T. Washington

TLpS Con. 21 BTW Papers DLC.

To Charles William Anderson

[Tuskegee, Ala.] October 17, 1904

Personal

My dear Mr. Anderson: I have received your letter of recent date, and I thank you very much for what you have done regarding that Indiana man.[1] When I was in Indianapolis during the summer, the colored people there told me that he was a very small and bigoted individual and had no liking for colored people, but notwithstanding that, for the sake of the President they were going to support him. Since I have heard from you I am satisfied that the colored people's opinion of him is entirely correct. He certainly must be a very small fellow. No one aside from an inexperienced little man would have made charges or taken all these matters for granted without first having put the matter before me in a manly, straightforward manner and heard my side of the case. I have not reached the point yet where I feel it necessary to do his bidding or carry out his suggestions for the purpose of establishing my own reputation as to loyalty to the party or probity in money matters. No man understands better than Dr. Furniss how I stand in this matter. I did not know until your letter came that this individual contributed any money toward the expenses of the Business League, and certainly it is a gross error for any one to state that I made any suggestion regarding keeping his contribution quiet. I could not have done so because I did not know that he had contributed one cent, and the National Negro Business League never handles one cent of money that is contributed for local expenses, and I never handle anybody's money except my own and pursue the same plan in that respect that you do. When I got to Indianapolis and saw the unsatisfactory state of affairs there so far as Knox was concerned, I urged upon Mr. New through the telephone and others the suggestion of helping Knox's paper as a means of pacifying him in the same way that I urged upon you the wisdom of helping Fortune's paper to keep him in line, the two cases being almost wholly identical; that was as far as I went in the matter except, as I told you before, I saw Knox two or three times and urged upon him the importance of not standing for Congress, trying to let him see the injury that he would likely do the President and our race as well as the harm he would do himself and his paper, but I found there was a stronger influence at work upon him than mine and I could not do anything; the fact is, I fear at the time that he had somebody's money in sight. I am sure that the Indiana man need give himself no trouble about the opinion of Mr. H. H. Hanna.[2] I have known Mr. Hanna for years, not only as a trustee of this institution but as a friend. He is man enough to come to me directly whenever he has anything to say.

I want to thank you again for your great kindness in this matter. I think you will agree that I am pursuing the proper course. If you have any suggestions to make, however, I shall be very glad to follow them. Yours very truly,

Booker T. Washington

TLpS Con. 5 BTW Papers DLC.

1 Anderson to BTW, Oct. 14, 1904, Con. 261, BTW Papers, DLC. Anderson reported his conversation with Jesse Overstreet, Republican congressman from Indiana, who was irate over the possible candidacy for Congress of George L. Knox, and accused BTW of being behind the Knox candidacy. Anderson told BTW that he had managed to mollify the congressman.

2 Hugh Henry Hanna (1848–1920) was a financier and an advocate of the gold standard. From 1880 to 1912 he was president of the Atlas Engine Works in Indianapolis. In the late 1890s Hanna was active in promoting legislation for a reformed gold standard which was included in the federal currency act of 1900. In 1903 he was appointed chairman of the Commission on International Exchange. He was active in the General Education Board and Southern Education Board and was a trustee of Tuskegee Institute from 1900 to 1910 and a trustee of Hampton Institute.

From George Washington Carver

[Tuskegee, Ala.] Oct. 17, 1904

Mr. B. T. Washington: For two years the Experiment Station has been making a pretty thorough test of the Spanish peanut. I have just completed digging them for this year and they have produced 50 bushels to the acre – that is to say, 5 bushels were taken from a one tenth-acre plot. Quite as many were produced last year.

The peanut is one of the most valuable foods for hogs, and there is no doubt – to my mind – that we can produce them at the rate of 50 bushels to the acre, which would pay us handsomely in the matter of feeding our hogs. Yours very truly,

Geo. W. Carver

TLS Con. 286 BTW Papers DLC.

To Edgar Gardner Murphy

[Tuskegee, Ala.] October 19, 1904

Personal

My dear Mr. Murphy: I have received your kind letter,[1] for which I thank you very much. I was very much disappointed that I did not have an opportunity of meeting you at Mr. Ogden's office or at your own rooms, as I had planned the day so as not to be so hurried in talking with you as I usually am. I shall be very glad, however, the very first time I can find another spare hour when in New York to have you talk with me fully and frankly about the matters that are in your mind.

However we may differ in our views regarding certain matters, there is no man in the country whose frankness, earnestness and sincere disinterestedness I respect more than yours, and whatever you say always has great weight with me.

Your letter emphasizes the tremendous difficulty of the work at the South. In most cases and in most countries where a large section of the people are down and are to be helped up, those attempting to do the work have before them a straight, simple problem of elevating the unfortunate people without the entanglement of racial prejudice to be grappled with. I think I do not exaggerate that perhaps a third or half the thought and energy of those engaged in the elevation of the colored people is given in the direction of trying to do the thing or not doing the thing which would enhance racial prejudice. This feature of the situation I believe very few people at the North or at the South appreciate. What is true of the Negro educator is true in a smaller degree of the white educator at the South. I am constantly trying as best I can, to study the situation as it is right here on the grounds, and I may be mistaken, but aside from the wild and demagogical talk on the part of a few I am unable to discover much or any change in the attitude of the best white people towards the best colored people. So far as my own individual experience and observation are concerned, I am treated about the same as I have always been. I was in Athens, Ga., a few days ago, to deliver an address before the colored people at the state fair, and the meeting was attended by the best class of whites and the best class of colored who seemed to be enthusiastic over what I said. Mr. Heflin just now is making a good deal of noise, but you will recall that Mr. Heflin spoke just as bitterly against me before Mr. Roosevelt became President as he has since. I do not want to permit myself to be misled, but I repeat that I cannot see or feel that a great alienation has taken place between the two classes of people that you refer to.

For the sake of argument I want to grant for the moment a thing which I have never done before, even in a private letter, and which is very distasteful to me, and that is, I am the leader of the colored people. Do you think it will ever be possible for one man to be set up as the leader of ten millions of people, meaning a population nearly twice as large as that of the Dominion of Canada and nearly equal to that of the republic of Mexico without the actions of that individual being carefully watched and commented upon and what he does being exaggerated either in one direction or the other? Again, if I am the leader and therefore the mouthpiece for ten millions of colored people, is it possible for such a leader to avoid coming into contact with the representatives of the ruling class of white people upon many occasions, and is it not to be expected that when questions that are racial and national and international in their character are to be discussed, that such a representative of the Negro race would be sought out both by individuals and by conventions? If, as you kindly suggest, I am the leader, I hardly see how such notoriety and prominence as will naturally come can be wholly or in any large degree avoided.

Judging by some of the criticisms that have appeared recently, mainly from the class of people to whom I have referred, it seems to me that some of the white people at the South are making an attempt to control my actions when I am in the North and in Europe. Heretofore, no man has been more careful to regard the feelings of the Southern people in actions and words than I have been, and this policy I shall continue to pursue but I have never attempted to hide or to minimize the fact that when I am out of the South I do not conform to the same customs and rules that I do in the South. I say I have not attempted to hide it because everything that I have done in this respect was published four years ago in my book, "Up from Slavery," which has been read widely throughout the South, and I did not hear a word of adverse criticism passed upon what I had done. For fifteen years I have been doing in the North just what I have been doing during the past year. I have never attended a purely social function given by white people anywhere in the country. Nearly every week I receive invitations to weddings of rich people but these I always refuse. Mrs. Washington almost never accompanies me on any occasion where there can be the least sign of purely social intercourse. Whenever I meet white people in the North at their offices, in their parlors or at their dinner tables or at banquets, it is with me purely a matter of business either in the interest of our institution or in the interest of my race; no other thought ever enters my mind. For me to say now after fifteen years of creating interest in my race and in this institution in that manner, that I must stop would simply mean that I must cease to get money in a large measure for this institution. In meeting the people in this way, I am simply doing what the head of practically every school, black and white, in the South is constantly doing. For purely social pleasure I have always found all my ambitions satisfied among my own people, and you will find that in proportion as the colored race becomes educated and prosperous, in the same proportion is this true of all colored people.

I said a minute ago that I had tried to be careful in regard to the feelings of the Southern people. It has been urged upon me time and time again to employ a number of white teachers at this institution. I have not done so and do not intend to do so, largely for the reason that they would be constantly mingling with each other at the table. For thirty years and more, in every one of our Southern states white and colored people have sat down to the table three times a day nearly throughout the year, and I have heard very little criticism passed upon them. This kind of thing, however, at Tuskegee I have always tried to avoid so far as our regular teaching force is concerned. But I repeat, if I begin to yield in the performance of my duty when out of the South in one respect, I do not know where the end would be. If I yield to people in one regard, there will come a class who will criticise me for going to visit people in their parlors or in their drawing rooms. It is very difficult for you or any other person who is not in my place to understand the difficulty and embarrassment that I am often confronted with. You have no idea how many invitations of various kinds I am constantly refusing or trying to get away from because I want to avoid embarrassing situations. For example, over a year ago Mr. Sedgwick[2] invited me to go to Stockbridge, Mass., near Lenox, to deliver an address on General Armstrong's life and work. When I reached Stockbridge an hour or so before the time of delivering the address, I found that Mr. Sedgwick who had invited me, had also invited five or six other gentlemen to meet me at luncheon. The luncheon I knew nothing about until I reached the town. Under such circumstances I am at a loss to know how I could have avoided accepting the invitation. A few days afterward I filled a long standing engagement to lecture at Amherst College. I reached the town a few hours before dinner and found that a number of people, including several college presidents, had been invited to meet me at dinner. Taking still another case; over a year ago I promised a colored club in Cambridge, Mass., that I would be their guest at a banquet in October. The banquet was held on the 3d of the month, and when I reached Cambridge I found that in addition to the members of the colored club, the mayor of the city and a number of Harvard professors, including President Eliot, had been invited, and I could go on and state case after case. Of course if I wanted to make a martyr of myself and draw especial attention to me and to the institution, I could easily do so by simply writing whenever I receive an invitation to a dinner or banquet that I could not accept on account of the color of my skin.

Six years ago at the Peace Jubilee in Chicago where I spoke at a meeting at which President McKinley was present, I took both luncheon and dinner in the same dining room with President McKinley and was the guest of the same club that he was a guest of. There were Southern men present, and the fact that I was present and spoke was widely heralded throughout the South, and so far as I know not a word of adverse comment was made. For nearly fifteen years the addresses which I have been constantly making at dinners and banquets in the North have been published throughout the South and no adverse comment has been made regarding my presence on these occasions.

I wish very much that my Northern friends to whom you refer would speak with me frankly. Practically all of the invitations to functions that are of even a semi-social character are urged upon me by Northern people, and very often after I have refused to accept invitations pressure is brought to bear on special friends of mine in order to get me to accept. Notwithstanding all this, where I accept one invitation I refuse ten, in fact you have no idea how many invitations to dinner I refuse while I am in the North. I not only do so for the reason that I do not care to excite undue criticism, but for the further reason that if I were to accept any large proportion of such invitations I would have little time left for my legitimate work. In many cases the invitations come from people who do not give money but simply want to secure a notoriety or satisfy their curiosity.

I have stated the case as I see it, and with a view of having you think over these matters by the time that we meet.

In conclusion, permit me to repeat that I am most grateful to you for your interest, friendship and frankness. Either through letter, or by the time we meet, I wish very much you would tell me, however, definitely just in what way you and others think I have changed my policy or am putting emphasis upon points that I have not heretofore done. Yours very truly,

Booker T. Washington

TLpS Con. 292 BTW Papers DLC.

1 Murphy wrote BTW expressing agreement with a suggestion for an interracial

conference at Hampton to stem "the growing estrangement between the best people of the South and the best negroes of the South." He said the estrangement resulted from "the instinctive feeling among the masses of our white population that there has been in your own leadership a distinct change of emphasis, if not of direction." Murphy said that he himself thought this feeling was "not wholly unreasonable," and that BTW's truest friends in both sections had expressed this feeling, "not in bitterness but often in sadness, and sometimes in despair." (Oct. 14, 1904, Con. 292, BTW Papers, DLC.)

2 Alexander Sedgwick of The Old House, Stockbridge, Mass.

An Item in the New York *World*[1]

[Oct. 23, 1904]

LEAVING BOOKER T. WASHINGTON

GROWING OPPOSITION TO HIM AMONG THOSE WHO WERE HIS SUREST FRIENDS

ASSERT HE DOES NOT LIVE UP TO HIS PREACHING

SCHOOL HE ADVOCATES NOT GOOD ENOUGH FOR HIS CHILDREN — EDUCATED WITH WHITES

Montgomery, Oct. 22 — For some time there has been growing an opposition to BookerWashington from among the very men and classes which have been his surest friends, this being a result of his meddling, or it may be more politely said, being drawn into politics by the request of Mr. Roosevelt and because of the fact that he not only sends his own children to schools outside of the State and South, but to schools for white students. His daughter in Wellesley and his son in Phillips-Exeter are poor support for the policy he has preached of patronizing negro schools, it is pointed out, and the assertions he has repeatedly made that negro schools in the South and other sections are capable of giving the negro youth and maidens all they can get elsewhere. The negroes say that if his school is not good enough for his own family there must be something wrong. His son is now captain of the football team at Phillips-Exeter and on equal social footing presumably with the sons of leading white men of the country. While it is not said that his daughter made any great impression one way or the other at Wellesley, it is so that she was the cause of dissatisfaction among those white girls who did not feel that they should be placed upon social equality with a negro, no matter whose daughter she was.

The management of the school at Tuskegee has been questioned more than ever recently, and some comparisons made that do not look as well as they might. The Negro Normal and Industrial School at Montgomery, with a white man, W. B. Paterson, as President, had last year within 100 pupils as many as Tuskegee, with an income of $13,000, compared to the stated income of $71,933 and actual receipts of $155,000 of the Washington school, yet it has never been said that the students of the former were not well equipped to take care of themselves.

The two schools illustrate the argument as to management for some time prominent, i.e., that the negro cannot manage successfully where great executive ability is required. If Paterson can do good work with $13 a pupil, why does it take $155 for Washington?

The Tuskegee Normal and Industrial Institute was established as the Tuskegee State Normal School by act of the Legislature in 1880, and given an appropriation of $2,000 a year. It opened for work the following July in a rented shanty with thirty pupils and one teacher. The appropriation was increased in 1893 to $3,000, and later $1,400 more was given, and the school incorporated as the Tuskegee Normal and Industrial Institute. At the last reckoning the following is given as the property holdings of the school: 123 buildings, 2,300 acres of land, 903 head of live stock, 58 carriages and vehicles. These buildings are valued by the trustees at $719,000. The last session of Congress gave to the school 25,000 acres of mineral lands worth at least $100,000. This gives a total endowment of $1,043,905, and a total valuation, all told, of $1,862,905.

The school teaches all branches of literary studies and gives diplomas of college grades. In addition all lines of industry are practically taught, and with every known appliance in each department. Full courses are given in cooking, dairying, shoemaking, farming and general agricultural work, carpentering, and in fact all lines of service where skill is required.

Some idea of the impression of the conduct of the school may be gained from the following extract from the report of State Examiner J. T. Gorman, made to the Governor:

"The Treasurer (Warren Logan) has a most excellent and methodical system of bookkeeping. The institute is in a flourishing and successful condition. Last year there was an enrollment of 1,501 students, with 151 instructors and assistants. There were students in attendance from thirty-six States and nine foreign countries. The endowment fund now amounts to $1,020,553.28, and the total valuation of real and personal property $686,379.29, making a total valuation of $1,716,932.57. The total receipts for last year were $71,933, and the annual current expenses are about $155,000. The deficit is met principally by donations and contributions, through the personal efforts of Principal Booker T. Washington."

New York *World*, Oct. 23, 1904, Clipping Con. 290 BTW Papers DLC.

[1] Hervey W. Laird, Montgomery correspondent of the Birmingham *Age-Herald*, wrote BTW acknowledging authorship of the story and apologizing for the misinformation he had gathered as the basis for the account. (Nov. 10, 1904, Con. 550, BTW Papers, DLC.)

From Portia Marshall Washington

Bradford, Mass. Oct–23–04

My dearest Papa: I was so glad to get your letter and the music. I suppose you are very tired after the busy time you had North. I kept up with you.

I read Mamma's address in the Transcript[1] — & also saw that a man in Iowa has left Tuskegee $100,000. This is splendid.

School is going nicely. We keep busy every single minute and while I really love Bradford I shall not be sorry when I graduate because of the nervous strain I feel nearly all the time.

Last Saturday night, we had a mock campaign and Mr. Roosevelt was elected 81 to 12. We Republicans had a long procession with Parker in effigy borne on poll [pole] — it was surely fun.

One of the teachers here is getting up a party to go abroad, next summer, and is very anxious to have me in her party — it is to cost about four hundred dollars – what do you think of this? I hope that Miss Clark can go too. I have written her about it.

I hope that you and Booker are both well – I had a letter from Dave. He seems happy.

With lots of love – I am your daughter

Portia

ALS Con. 17 BTW Papers DLC.

[1] The Boston *Transcript*, Oct. 19, 1904, 13, contained an excerpt from Margaret M. Washington's speech before the National Congregational Council in Des Moines, Iowa. She spoke on "The Advancement of Colored Women."

To N. P. T. Finch

[Tuskegee, Ala.] October 24, 1904

Personal

Dear Mr. Finch: You do not know how very grateful I am to you for your kind and thoughtful letter. I appreciate most deeply all that you say and understand thoroughly your position. I am hoping to be in Birmingham sometime in November and shall plan to have a talk with you if possible. My race is constantly grateful to you for the help you render in connection with putting down the mob. In that direction I am enclosing to you a copy of an address which I delivered in Athens, Ga., last week; you will note that I refer pretty pointedly to the work of the mob, and I was pleased to see that the white people in the audience applauded heartily what I said in that direction.

Mr. Heflin's attacks are so bitter and unreasonable that in a very large measure they nullify themselves. Of course there is a class of ignorant and prejudiced people with whom these attacks will have influence, but I do not believe they will amount to much with the thinking and intelligent. I am taking no more part in Captain Walker's campaign for congress than you are. In fact, perhaps you know that Mr. Walker was named before my friend, Hon. C. W. Thompson died. I had no warmer or more helpful friend in the South than Mr. Thompson, and should have been the last person to have taken a part in nominating anyone to oppose him.

Now that I am writing you, I am going to take the liberty of enclosing a copy of a letter which I have just written to a friend of mine. This letter outlined my whole position. Of course you will regard it as personal.

Thanking you for your thoughtfulness and kindness, I am, Yours truly,

Booker T. Washington

TLpS Con. 288 BTW Papers DLC.

To Edwin Doak Mead

[Tuskegee, Ala.] October 24th, 1904

Personal & Confidential

Dear Mr. Mead: Replying to your kind letter of recent date, I would say that in my opinion, the election of Mr. Parker would turn loose in the most rampant manner, the very worst element in the South. The Tillmans, Vardamans etc., would feel that their attitude regarding the Negro, in a way, had been endorsed by the nation, and there would be no limit to the extent to which they would go in attempting to harass the black man. On the other hand, if President Roosevelt is elected by an overwhelming majority, this same element would feel that the country has strongly disapproved of Tillmanism, Vardamanism etc., and that the President has been sustained in his policy of dealing justly with all citizens of the country, regardless of race or color. I have no doubt that the election of Mr. Roosevelt will help the whole country, as far as the Negro is concerned. This of course, is for your private information.

I thank you very much for the generous words you were kind enough to send me regarding the little talk which I gave at The Peace Congress banquet.

I shall hope to see both you and Mrs. Mead when I am in Boston later on during the Fall or Winter.

Enclosed, I am sending you my check, payable to Dr. Benjamin F. Trueblood,[1] for a membership in The American Peace Society.

You will be glad to know that we are making commendable

progress in showing to the world the true condition of matters in the Congo Free State. Very truly yours,

Booker T. Washington

TLpS Con. 292 BTW Papers DLC.

[1] Benjamin Franklin Trueblood (1847–1916), Society of Friends minister, educator, and general secretary of the American Peace Society from 1892 to 1915.

From Clifford H. Plummer

Boston, October 24, 1904

Dear sir: I herewith enclose a card of an important meeting held by the sub-committee of the New England Suffrage League, which I received about the same time I received the telegram from Mr. Scott (on the 17 inst).

The business of the meeting was to form plans for the conference which took place on the 19th at Providence, R.I. This committee meeting was hot and interesting, for the suggestion of resolutions, which I naturally know was going to arise, was brought up. The suggestions in the resolutions did not by any means, please me, but I am satisfied that in my objections I did not uncover myself. The ostensible purpose of the resolution was to ask Congress to appropriate $120,000,000 a year for ten years, for educational purposes in the south. In some portion of the preamble, however, in referring to the numerous "beggars who come from the South" your name was mentioned. This I defeated by objecting to the whole of the paragraph referring to that, stating to the Committee that I was opposed to any personal reference, or to helping anybody to carry out their personal spite by unhorsing others whom they imagined had the call. I told them, that while I opposed Mr. Washington in Boston, and his adherents here, I was perfectly willing to work with the committee on a line whereby we could derive the best good to the race but would not allow myself to be used by this committee, or Mr. Washington's adherents, in any other way than for the best interests of the race, and if the committee took opposite views from mine in this respect I should do all I could to be heard at the conference. Our committee finally dropped all reference to Washington; but the temptation to strike at him was too great, so by a vote of 4 to 3 in our committee it was decided that the portion of the resolution referring to "beggars coming from the South" should be presented at the conference.

When a permanent organization had been effected with the Chairman of the conference an anti-Washington man, Mr. Trotter was appointed on the Committee on Resolutions with his friend Rev. Gunner,[1] of Newport, who was the principal speaker at the Cambridge rally. I knew then what to expect; and while they were busy on the resolutions I wasn't less busy in the conference; and when the committee reported making reference to the "hundreds of Negro[es] coming from the South yearly begging from door to door, causing a sentiment to arise in Boston against the Negroes of our city, and placing them in a humiliating light in the eyes of the whites" I took the floor in opposition to the resolution, and I am pleased to report that the clause referring to the hundreds of beggars was eliminated entirely from the resolution. I am also pleased to say to you that I did this without disclosing my hand. My associates on the committee did not have the slightest suspicion of my stand. We organized a permanent New England Suffrage League, of which Mr. Trotter is President, and about all in it are anti-Washington men. And the majority of its officers are anti-Washington men. I accepted a position on the Executive Committee, deeming it advisable to be pretty near to the President, and the Secretary, Trotter and Rev. Johnson W. Hill[2] respectively.

You may expect a more enliv[en]ed and active opposition than you have had for some time up here with Trotter at the head, but I can promise it shall not all be one-sided while I am there. I am more convinced at each gathering that you and your cause are popular with the masses, for even with the delegates down there, largely composed of anti-Washington men, they were open to reason and they had the manhood to acknowledge the goodness that is in their opponent or his cause. At any rate I feel quite cheerful over the past and have unbounded confidence in the final outcome of our efforts.

I have taken steps to get on the executive committees of the other two associations which I spoke to you about, the Boston Historical and Literary Association, and The St. Mark's Union. This places me in a position to know what is coming before it gets to the house.

Hoping to hear from you soon, and that you are in good health, I am Very truly yours,

Clifford H. Plummer

P.S. Our friend Burrell was delighted at the out come of the Providence resolutions.

C. H. P.

TLS Con. 293 BTW Papers DLC.

1 Byron Gunner, later a minister in New York, was a long-time Trotterite and later an activist in the Niagara Movement. He was president of the Trotter faction of the National Independent Political League in 1912.

2 Johnson W. Hill, born in Virginia in 1865.

The Preface to *Twenty-four Negro Melodies*

Tuskegee Institute, Alabama, October 24, 1904

Samuel Coleridge-Taylor

It is given to but few men in so short a time to create for themselves a position of such prominence on two continents as has fallen to the lot of Samuel Coleridge-Taylor. Born in London, August 15, 1875, Mr. Coleridge-Taylor is not yet thirty. His father, an African and a native of Sierra Leone, was educated at King's College, London, and his medical practice was divided between London and Sierra Leone.

As a child of four and five Coleridge-Taylor could read music before he could read a book. His first musical instruction was on the violin. The piano he would not touch, and did not for some years. As one of the singing-boys in St. George's Church, Croydon, he received an early training in choral work. At fifteen he entered the Royal College of Music as a student of the violin. Afterwards winning a scholarship in composition he entered, in 1893, the classes of Sir Charles Villiers Stanford, with whom he studied four years or more.

Mr. Coleridge-Taylor early gave evidence of creative powers of a high order, and to-day, at the age of twenty-nine, he ranks as one of the most interesting and remarkable of British composers and conductors. Aside from his creative work, he is actively engaged as a teacher in Trinity College, London, and as conductor of the Handel Society, London, and the Rochester Choral Society. At the Gloucester Festival of 1898 Mr. Coleridge-Taylor attracted general notice by the performance of his *Ballade in A minor,* for orchestra, Op. 33, which he had been invited to conduct. His remarkably sympathetic setting in cantata form of portions of Longfellow's *Hiawatha,* Op. 30, has done much to make him known in England and America. This triple choral work, with its haunting melodic phrases, bold harmonic scheme, and vivid orchestration, was produced one part or scene at a time. The work was not planned as a whole, for the composer's original intention was to set *Hiawatha's Wedding Feast* only. This section was first performed at a concert of the Royal College of Music under the conductorship of Stanford, November 11, 1898. In response to an invitation from the committee of the North Staffordshire Musical Festival *The Death of Minnehaha,* Op. 30, No. 2, was written, and given under the composer's direction at Hanley, October 26, 1899. The overture to *The Song of Hiawatha,* for full orchestra, Op. 30, No. 3, a distinct work, was composed for and performed at the Norwich Musical Festival of 1899. The entire work, with the added third part — *Hiawatha's Departure,* Op. 30, No. 4 — was first given by the Royal Choral Society in Royal Albert Hall, London, March 22, 1900, the composer conducting.

The first performance of the entire work in America was given under the direction of Mr. Charles E. Knauss by the Orpheus Oratorio Society in Easton, Pa., May 5, 1903. The Cecilia Society, of Boston, under Mr. B. J. Lang, gave the first performance of *Hiawatha's Wedding Feast* on March 14, 1900; of *Hiawatha's Departure* on December 5, 1900; and on December 2, 1902, *The Death of Minnehaha,* together with *Hiawatha's Departure.*

In 1902 Mr. Coleridge-Taylor was invited to conduct at the Sheffield Musical Festival his orchestral and choral rhapsody *Meg Blane,* Op. 48. The fact that this work was given on the same program with a Bach cantata, Dvořák's *Stabat Mater* and Tchaikovsky's *Symphonie Pathétique* indicates the high esteem in which the composer is held.

A sacred cantata of the dimensions and style of a modern oratorio, *The Atonement*, Op. 53, was first given at the Hereford Festival, September 9, 1903, under the composer's baton, and its success was even greater at the first London performance in the Royal Albert Hall on Ash Wednesday, 1904, the composer conducting. The first performance of *The Atonement* in this country was by the Church Choral Society under Richard Henry Warren at St. Thomas's Church, New York, February 24 and 25, 1904. Worthy of special mention are the *Quintet for Clarinet and Strings*, Op. 6 (1897), which Joachim has given, and the *Sorrow Songs*, Op. 57 (1904) — a setting of six of Christina Rosetti's exquisite poems.

Besides the works already mentioned are a *Nonet for Piano, Strings and Wind*, Op. 3 (1894), *Symphony in A minor*, Op. 7 (1895), *Solemn Prelude for Orchestra*, Op. 40 (1899), between thirty and forty songs, various piano solos, anthems and part songs, and works in both large and small form for the violin with orchestra or piano.

Mr. Coleridge-Taylor has written much, has achieved much. His work, moreover, possesses not only charm and power but distinction, the individual note. The genuineness, depth and intensity of his feeling, coupled with his mastery of technique, spontaneity, and ability to think in his own way, explain the force of the appeal his compositions make. Another element in the persuasiveness of his music lies in its naturalness, the directness of its appeal, the use of simple and expressive melodic themes, a happy freedom from the artificial. These traits, employed in the freedom of modern musical speech, coupled with emotional power and supported by ample technical resource, beget an utterance quick to evoke response.

The paternity of Mr. Coleridge-Taylor and his love for what is elemental and racial found rich expression in the choral work by which he is best known, and more obviously in his *African Romances*, Op. 17, a set of seven songs; the *African Suite* for the piano, Op. 35; and *Five Choral Ballads*, for baritone solo, quartet, chorus and orchestra, Op. 54, being a setting of five of Longfellow's *Poems on Slavery*. The transcription of Negro melodies contained in this volume is, however, the most complete expression of Mr. Coleridge-Taylor's native bent and power. Using some of the native songs of Africa and the West Indies with songs that came into being in America during the slavery regime, he has in handling these melodies preserved their distinctive traits and individuality, at the same time giving them an art form fully imbued with their essential spirit.

It is especially gratifying that at this time, when interest in the plantation songs seems to be dying out with the generation that gave them birth, when the Negro song is in too many minds associated with "rag" music and the more reprehensible "coon" song, that the most cultivated musician of his race, a man of the highest aesthetic ideals, should seek to give permanence to the folk-songs of his people by giving them a new interpretation and an added dignity.

Negro music is essentially spontaneous. In Africa it sprang into life at the war dance, at funerals, and at marriage festivals. Upon this African foundation the plantation songs of the South were built. According to the testimony of African students at Tuskegee there are in the native African melodies strains that reveal the close relationship between the Negro music of America and Africa, but the imagery and sentiments to which the plantation songs give expression are the outcome of the conditions in America under which the transported children of Africa lived. Wherever companies of Negroes were working together, in the cotton fields and tobacco factories, on the levees and steamboats, on sugar plantations, and chiefly in the fervor of religious gatherings, these melodies sprang into life.

Oftentimes in slavery, as to-day in certain parts of the South, some man or woman with an exceptional voice was paid to lead the singing, the idea being to increase the amount of labor by such singing.

The Negro folk-song has for the Negro race the same value that the folk-song of any other people has for that people. It reminds the race of the "rock whence it was hewn," it fosters race pride, and in the days of slavery it furnished an outlet for the anguish of smitten hearts. The plantation song in America, although an outgrowth of oppression and bondage, contains surprisingly few references to slavery. No race has ever sung so sweetly or with such perfect charity, while looking forward to the "year of Jubilee." The songs abound in Scriptural allusions, and in many instances are unique interpretations of standard hymns.

The songs that had their origin in Virginia and the more northern of the Southern States, where the slave changed masters less often, and where he was under the personal care and guidance of his owner, are more bright and joyous in tone than are those which were sung in the Gulf States, where the yoke of slavery was more oppressive. The songs of the lower South are sadder in tone, less buoyant than are those of the upper South.

The plantation songs known as the "Spirituals" are the spontaneous outbursts of intense religious fervor, and had their origin chiefly in the camp meetings, the revivals and in other religious exercises. They breathe a child-like faith in a personal Father, and glow with the hope that the children of bondage will ultimately pass out of the wilderness of slavery into the land of freedom. In singing of a deliverance which they believed would surely come, with bodies swaying, with the enthusiasm born of a common experience and of a common hope, they lost sight for the moment of the auction-block, of the separation of mother and child, of sister and brother. There is in the plantation songs a pathos and a beauty that appeals to a wide range of tastes, and their harmony makes abiding impression upon persons of the highest culture. The music of these songs goes to the heart because it comes from the heart.

The question is often asked to what extent are these songs being sung by the colored people and to what extent are they being preserved. In the larger city churches they are being used but little; but in the smaller towns, and in the country districts, where the colored people live in greater numbers, their use is quite general, and new ones appear from time to time. Several schools and colleges of the South make an effort to preserve these songs, and at Fisk, Hampton and Tuskegee, they are sung constantly. New students coming from remote parts of the South occasionally bring in new ones. While some of the colored people do not encourage the singing of the songs because they bring up memories of the trying conditions which gave them rise, the race as a whole realizes that apart from the music of the Red Man the Negro folk-song is the only distinctively American music, and is taking pride in using and preserving it.

It is, I repeat, a cause for special gratitude that the foremost musician of his race, a man in the zenith of his powers, should seek to chronicle, and thus perpetuate, the old melodies that are so rapidly passing away.

Mr. Coleridge-Taylor is himself an inspiration to the Negro, since he himself, the child of an African father, is an embodiment of what are the possibilities of the Negro under favorable environment. In his preface to the *Cabin and Plantation Songs*, as sung by Hampton students, Mr. Thomas P. Fenner said four decades ago, "The freedmen have an unfortunate inclination to despise this music [Negro music] as a vestige of slavery; those who learned it in the old time, when it was the natural outpouring of their sorrows and longings, are dying off, and if efforts are not made for its preservation, the country will soon have lost this wonderful music of bondage. It may be that this people which has developed such a wonderful musical sense in its degradation will, in its maturity, produce a composer who would bring the music of the future out of this music of the past." May we not look to Samuel Coleridge-Taylor for a fulfillment of this prophecy?

Booker T. Washington

PDSr NN-Sc. A typed draft is in Con. 295, BTW Papers, DLC.

To Clifford H. Plummer

[Tuskegee, Ala.] October 27, 1904

Personal

My dear Mr. Plummer: I have received your letter which is full of valuable information. I am most grateful to you for it. I sent you something a few days ago which I hope you have received. You have done very valuable work which I appreciate most highly.

It seems rather strange that these men would object to Negro college presidents begging money in the North and say nothing about the dozens of white college presidents who are doing the same thing. It would seem in their eyes, all right for a white man to get money for the education of Negroes, but all wrong for a Negro to get money for the education of his own people. I wonder if you know who Byron Gunner is? He was educated on charity money from the North at Talladega College in Alabama. He was afterwards sent to teach school at New Iberia, La. After he had been in Louisiana for a while, he heard that the white people were going to mob him and he left town between suns and has never been back to Louisiana since. He is now engaged however, in telling colored people how to stand up and fight for their rights. Yours truly,

Booker T. Washington

TLpS Con. 293 BTW Papers DLC.

To the Archbishop of Canterbury[1]

[Tuskegee, Ala.] October 27, 1904

My Dear Lord Archbishop: Fulfilling the promise which I made to you when we met at the Waldorf-Astoria Hotel, I am sending you by this mail a copy of my book, "Up from Slavery," which I hope you may find time to read or at least glance through.

In our conversation, we touched briefly upon the subject of lynching. Investigation shows that only one-third of the colored people lynched in this country have been even charged with committing a crime against women.

I notice that you seem to be considerably interested in the subject of religious instruction in our public schools. While in the North and West the Bible has been taken almost wholly out of the public schools, I am glad to say that in our Southern states there is no effort to get rid of religious instruction in the public schools, and I do not think there is likely to be any for some time to come.

Please permit me to express to you again what a pleasure it was to have the privilege of meeting both you and Mrs. Davidson. The opportunity of being in your company for so long a time is one of the privileges of my life which I shall long remember. Yours very truly,

Booker T. Washington

TLpS Con. 283 BTW Papers DLC.

1 Randall Thomas Davidson (1848–1930) was Archbishop of Canterbury from 1903 to 1928.

From Emmett Jay Scott

Tuskegee, Alabama. October 27, 1904

Personal

Dear Mr. Washington: I am very much disinclined to bring to your attention the matter about which I am now writing, but I think it well to have you get it directly from me rather than from some one else.

For several weeks or more the officers of the Afro-American Realty Company have sought to interest me in their company, and on the occasion of my recent visit to New York made me a straight guarantee proposition of three thousand dollars a year to come with them, and also submitted other guarantees for the future which made the proposition seem favorable from some points of view. I told them on the spot that it was not possible for me to consider the proposition because of my interests at Tuskegee and my interest in Tuskegee and its work, and because of all your interest in me and decided helpfulness in many directions; but upon being urged to at least keep the offer open and give it consideration I brought the matter home and am today definitely writing them that it is impossible for me to at all consider it. Of course *I cheerfully appreciate the fact that my relations with you and the opportunities you have given me give me, in large part, the prominence which this company thinks it can utilize to its advantage.*

I do not bring this matter to your attention for any sinister purpose; I am well satisfied with the status of affairs at Tuskegee so far as I am at present concerned, but I thought it well to place it before you so that you would not misunderstand me should it come to you in some other way that I had such an offer made me. Yours truly,

Emmett J. Scott

TLS Con. 24 BTW Papers DLC.

An Editorial by Washington in *Outlook*[1]

29 October 1904

President Roosevelt and
the South

The Outlook happens to be in possession of information which leads it to suggest that no man, perhaps, ever went into the White House with a keener desire to be of real and permanent service to the former slave States than Mr. Roosevelt.

In the most careful manner, the President has sought information from the highest type of both white and colored people concerning the political desires and needs of both the black and the white races and the status and defects of their relations to the Federal Government. This information was sought for by the President before he became President, and even before he became Vice-President.

The Outlook happens to know that, while Mr. Roosevelt was holding the position of Governor of New York, he outlined a policy which he would attempt to pursue if he should ever be called to the Presidency. The policy which he then stated he would pursue was one which the daily press of the South, as well as the public men of the South, had long advocated. The Outlook happens to know, further, that the President has pursued and consistently followed the policy outlined before he became President, as nearly as it has been possible for any human being to do.

Up to the time that Mr. Roosevelt became President, what were the main complaints of the South, and what were its demands? Roughly stated, they were as follows:

The South had been treated since the Civil War very much as foreign territory, so far as the National Government was concerned. In a large measure, the men who possessed the confidence of the several successive Administrations, and who held the main offices and controlled the politics of the South, were not native Southern white people, and did not possess the confidence of the Southern white people any more than they possessed the whole confidence of the negro people; this foreign, or carpetbag, element parceled out the offices by means of corrupt political machines. What are the definite facts as to how President Roosevelt met these conditions?

Let us take one State, Mississippi, for instance, for it illustrates the policy that has been followed, in the main, in other Southern States.

To begin with, in Mississippi the President, while not seeking to overthrow or ignore the old political machine, went straight to the heart of conditions, and selected for his adviser E. S. Wilson, a Gold Democrat, the former secretary to L. Q. C. Lamar,[2] the Mississippi correspondent of the New Orleans "Picayune," and the brother-in-law of Governor Longino. It would at least seem that this man had the confidence and respect of the South, and of Mississippi people especially. From the day of his appointment by the President, this gentleman has been one of the President's Southern advisers. In seeking his advice upon Southern politics the President insisted upon one limitation, and only one; his adviser was to recommend none but clean men to him for appointment, giving Republicans the first consideration, but where clean Republicans could not be found, then Democrats of good and proved character. The result is that the United States District Attorney is a white Democrat, and the same is true of the Register of the United States Land Office and the United States Marshalship. These are native Southern white men who stand high in the estimation of their neighbors; and these are but examples of what has been done in dozens of other cases in Mississippi alone.

Now, as to the negro office-holder in the South: the complaint that has been made against every Republican President since the Civil War has been that many offices were filled by a horde of ignorant and characterless colored politicians. How did President Roosevelt meet this situation? He has appointed to office in the South fewer colored men than any other President, and, in doing so, has not only decreased the quantity, but improved the quality. He has not only tried to do so, but has actually done it.

To how many of our readers has it ever occurred that, notwithstanding all the discussion that has taken place regarding Mr. Roosevelt and the South, practically no criticism has been made upon the character of the men holding office under him, white and black alike. Fault has been found in a few cases because of their color, but not with their character. Not only has the class of white and colored men appointed to office in the South been of such a high character as to escape criticism, but Mr. Roosevelt has done what no other President has done, and what the South has all along claimed should be done: he has appointed colored men living in the North to important positions in that section, as, for example, William H. Lewis, appointed to the place of Assistant United States District Attorney for Massachusetts.

What the President has done in Mississippi in lifting up and purifying the public service has been done in a larger or smaller degree in every Southern State. Special examples were the throwing over of the old and corrupt gang in Louisiana; the appointment of former Governor Thomas G. Jones and Judge Roulhac, native white Southerners, to important positions in Alabama.

The main thing, however, that the public ought to know about is that in failing to be controlled by old and corrupt political organizations, in going outside of his party to select men of high character for office, the President was running a political risk which required the very highest degree of moral courage and devotion to public duty to perform. He was taking a chance, as far as his political fortunes were concerned, which no other President had ever taken. We mean this: If Mr. Hanna, or any other strong man, had announced his candidacy for the Presidency, there is little question but that Mr. Roosevelt would have lost a large proportion of the vote of Southern States in the Republican nominating Convention, because of the power of the old-time political organization. It is not going too far to say that these Southern votes would have gone far in the direction of defeating Mr. Roosevelt for the nomination, if his defeat could have been compassed; while, on the other hand, the President could have had the vote of practically every Southern Republican delegate by simply yielding to the wishes of the lower element of Southern Republican bosses. Time and time again Mr. Roosevelt was warned of the political risk he was taking, but not once did he change his policy in the slightest degree, and on more than one occasion replied to friends that he would rather be defeated for the Presidential nomination than secure it by yielding to the vicious element of the South, Republican or Democratic.

Over and over again it has been asserted, by those who have not taken the time or the pains to investigate the real facts in the matter, that President Roosevelt's Southern policy has caused an increase of lawlessness at the South, as indicated by lynchings, burnings, etc. What is the truth? Lynchings in this country reached the highest number in 1892, when Benjamin Harrison was President, the number of lynchings for that year being 236. The next highest number was in 1885, under the Presidency of Grover Cleveland, when they numbered 210. In 1893, also during the Presidency of Grover Cleveland, there were 200 lynchings. These periods represent the high-water mark of lynching. During the two years in which Mr. Roosevelt has been in the White House there have been fewer lynchings than in any year since 1885; in 1902 there were 96 lynchings, and in 1903 there were but 104. These two years represent the smallest number of lynchings since 1885.

We make the prediction that before he leaves the White House the South will learn that it has never had a warmer or more consistent friend in the Presidential chair than Theodore Roosevelt.

Outlook, 78 (Oct. 29, 1904), 511–13.

1 For proof that BTW wrote the unsigned editorial, see BTW to Roosevelt, Oct. 17, 1904, above.

2 Lucius Quintus Cincinnatus Lamar (1825–93), Confederate veteran and former congressman and senator, was associate justice of the U.S. Supreme Court from 1888 to 1893.

From William Reuben Pettiford

Birmingham, Ala., Nov. 7th. 1904

My dear Sir: If Mr. Roosevelt, on tomorrow is elected with a larger electoral vote than Mr. McKinley was, our people can claim that the "Negro Question" injected by the south has popularized his campaign instead of reducing the vote. The frequent references to yourself by J. T. Heflin, of the fifth district is becoming distasteful with a number of the best citizens, and I write to say to you to be of good courage, and go forward in the even tenor of your way, with a determination as strong as life itself; and God the father of all will see that you accomplish your purpose. I am not, nor will I be discouraged. We are praying for you that God may continue to use you in accomplishing great things. I am, sincerely yours,

W. R. Pettiford

TLS Con. 293 BTW Papers DLC.

To Whitefield McKinlay

[Tuskegee, Ala.] Nov. 8, 1904

My dear Mr. McKinlay: There is absolutely no foundation for the story about my son going into the army, in fact he is only 16 years old; he is now here at Tuskegee studying. I cannot understand how such a falsehood originated.[1]

I have just come from casting my vote for Roosevelt and Fairbanks.

While I could not just now say so publicly, more and more I feel that great good is going to come out of the changed conditions so far as the election is concerned in the South. For example, 15 years ago in this county the elections were a mere farce; the colored people voting and their votes being thrown out or in some way destroyed. How different it is now. When I went into the polling place I found two intelligent Republican watchers and an equal number of Democrats of the same character. While there will not be more than 50 Negro votes cast in this county, perhaps 40 of them being cast right here in Tuskegee, every Negro vote will be counted as cast, and it seems to me that, after all, there is great gain. When I went into town this morning to vote, I heard of a good many of my white friends who had refused to vote for Heflin on account of his remarks regarding me. When I went into the room to vote, I could not have been accorded more respect in Boston than I was in Tuskegee. Yours truly,

Booker T. Washington

TLpS Con. 555 BTW Papers DLC.

[1] The Washington *Post*, Montgomery *Advertiser*, and other papers on election day published a report that BTW Jr. had sought a position as paymaster in the U.S. Army as evidence that BTW encouraged black office-seeking. BTW on Nov. 9, 1904, gave a statement to the Associated Press categorically denying the report. (Press release, Nov. 9, 1904, Con. 293, BTW Papers, DLC.)

To Walter Francis Willcox

[Tuskegee. Ala.] Nov. 9, 1904

My dear Mr. Willcox: I have received the letter of recent date in which you ask me to state my views as to the amount of property accumulated by the Negroes of the United States. I find it difficult, if not impossible, to get data sufficiently extensive and trustworthy to base an estimate upon.

So far as I am able to discover, only a few states — North Carolina, Georgia, Virginia and Louisiana — keep the tax record in such form as to exhibit upon just what amount of property each race pays taxes. However, when I made the statement to Mr. Schurz that his estimate, $800,000,000, was too high, I was basing my belief upon the statistics from these states. In 1902 the Negroes of Virginia, leading the rest, owned property assessed at $17,580,000. Just after the War the tax collectors used to say that the Negroes took pride in placing a high valuation upon their property but, perhaps the Negroes have learned differently by this time from the example of the white people. At any rate there seems to be no doubt that the assessed value is considerably less than the real value of this property. Just how much less, I have at my disposal no means of satisfactorily determining; but, upon the most liberal estimates possible, I do not see how it could be denied that, in view of the statistics we do possess, Mr. Carl Schurz's estimate is much too high.

Taking the Virginia report of the assessed value of property owned by Negroes . . .[1] liberal assumption — we find that the Negroes of the United States (the Virginia Negroes constituting 7.5 per cent of the total black population) own property to be valued at $234,405,200. Add to this 50 per cent to account for under valuation, non-taxable property, tax dodging, etc., you can get only $352,000,000. Of course this figure is of no value except that it supports my contention that Mr. Schurz's estimate is much too high. My opinion is that the best way of getting at the matter is by taking into account the estimate of the Census report, which of course you have noted, that the total farm property of the Negro in 1900 aggregated in value $230,000,000. Of course the great mass of property accumulated by my people is farm property. It is obvious that any estimate which involves the proposition that the value of the farm property is less than one-half of the aggregate accumulation of the American Negro is incorrect on this ground, too; I told Mr. Schurz that his estimate was too high. Yours truly,

Booker T. Washington

TLpS Con. 20 BTW Papers DLC.

[1] Obliterated word or words in original.

From Robert Heberton Terrell

Washington, D.C. November 9, 1904

My dear Mr. Washington, I think that the Negroes of this country are to be especially congratulated on the election of Mr. Roosevelt. It means a great deal to us to have him achieve such a magnificent triumph over opponents who attempted to use the race issue as a cudgel to break his head. The very fact that he has been elected advances our cause immeasurably.

It will not be an easy thing to make our own people see the propriety of making every kind of a sacrifice to help our great and good President solve our delicate problem. We have got to work harder than ever to prove ourselves worthy of all that he thinks of us. We can afford to do nothing that will embarrass the efforts of Mr. Roosevelt. I hope that you will talk to our leading men along this line.

You yourself must come in for congratulations, too. For your fame was constantly linked with the President's in the campaign just passed. You were almost as much an issue as he was. I see you are paying the penalty of greatness by having yourself misrepresented and lied about. The report to the effect that your son was trying to get a commission in the Army is absurd on its face when one knows his age. I was glad to see your telegram to McKinlay which was published in the Star today. Of course your son has a right to aspire to any thing he wants, but it would be contemptible to make his ambitions an excuse for an attack on you.

To recur to the President, I know that your great common sense will greatly help him in dealing with our phase of American life.

The colored voter has stood for him manfully as he should have done, in keeping with all canons of decency. However, we must not think that we own the man. Tell our men not to crowd him. I believe that Roosevelt will accomplish wonders for us during his term.
Very sincerely yours,

R. H. Terrell

ALS Con. 25 BTW Papers DLC.

To James Sullivan Clarkson

[Tuskegee, Ala.] Nov. 10, 1904

Personal

Dear General Clarkson: I have your letter of November 7th, and I write to say that I think most, if not all, of the boys will be ready to start to the Soudan within a few weeks. Mr. Scott will keep you informed about matters.

The information which you give me about Mr. Hunt[1] is very interesting and valuable. He certainly is an extraordinary man in whom I have full faith.

Now about the election. The result of course is more magnificent than any of us could have dared anticipate. In my opinion the victory is as complete as it is because of two reasons; first, because of the personal abuse heaped upon the President, second, because of the useless raising of the race question in the South. You of course have seen something of the flurry created by Heflin's speech in the town of Tuskegee in which he attacked the President and myself in the most bitter manner. His whole object was to frighten me in a way to prevent my voting in the first place, and in the second place to prevent my testifying against him in case of a contest. So far as the first point is concerned, I am glad to say that I voted within thirty minutes after the polls were opened and I am sure my vote was counted as we had two strong intelligent white men as watchers in the election booth, a thing that has not been true within twenty years in Alabama. I shall hope to talk with you about all these matters further when I see you.

The attached editorial was taken from a Montgomery Democratic paper the day before the election. Yours very truly,

Booker T. Washington

TLpS Con. 19 BTW Papers DLC. No clipping was found with the letter.

[1] Clarkson had written BTW an account of Leigh Hunt's business career in the United States, China, and Korea. He assured BTW that Hunt was "the soul of honor" and would treat the Tuskegee graduates in his employ fairly. (Nov. 7, 1904, Con. 847, BTW Papers, DLC.)

To E. H. Thornton[1]

[Tuskegee, Ala.] November 10, 1904

Dear Sir: Enclosed I send you my check for twenty-five dollars as a small subscription towards the erection of the monument in memory of the late Gen. John B. Gordon. Just before he died he visited the Tuskegee Institute and spoke in our Chapel to our students and teachers, together with a large number of white and colored citizens, and his instructive, tender and sympathetic words will remain for a long time one of the most precious memories of this institution. I am led to make this contribution further because General Gordon represented in a most perfect degree the cultivated, brave and unselfish Southern man who was not only interested in the white race but in the elevation of my own people. He was indeed a true type of the connecting link between the best class of Southern white people and the truest type of my own race, and I believe that in the future there will be many to emulate his example. Yours truly,

Booker T. Washington

TLpS Con. 288 BTW Papers DLC.

[1] E. H. Thornton, treasurer of the Gen. John B. Gordon Monument Fund, was a banker in Atlanta, Ga.

To Joseph Oswalt Thompson

[Tuskegee, Ala.] Nov. 12, 1904

Personal

Dear Mr. Thompson: Since talking with you over the telephone I have just read your very kind letter and thank you very much for it, and I thank you especially for letting me know about the editorial in the World.

I appreciate of course your kindness and your motive in asking me to call at your office after the lecture, but I always go on the principle that it is never safe to do anything in public matters that you do not expect to become public, and I feel absolutely certain that it will be impossible for me to go to the government building without it leaking out and being heralded all over the state and perhaps the South, that my visit to Birmingham was for the purpose of parceling out offices in the state. After considering the matter, I believe you will take this view of the case. I very much prefer to see you alone in regard to any matters that I can be of service to you. You know I can see you at any time here at Tuskegee or elsewhere and that out, it seems to me to answer all purposes. If I should see one additional person there will come a call to see a second and then a third and fourth and so on without end. This suggestion is as much for your protection as for mine. You know that there are certain parties who are continually giving currency to the report that you are only a figurehead as a Referee, and if the report of my meeting you got out it would add weight to that impression. I shall hope to see you at the meeting, and it would be a genuine personal pleasure for me to call upon you at your office, especially in view of the fact that I have never been in the government building in Birmingham and seen you in new surroundings since you took your office, but even this pleasure I fear, for the reasons I have mentioned, I shall have to forego as much as I should like to do so. Yours truly,

Booker T. Washington

TLpSr Con. 25 BTW Papers DLC.

George Washington Albert Johnston to Emmett Jay Scott

Birmingham, Ala., Nov-12-'04 1.30 P.M.

Dear Mr. Scott: Your communication just received and is fully understood & appreciated by both Mr. Thompson and myself. We had already had a long conference along this line and even more.

We have planned to keep a sharp lookout on Mr. Albert Davis as well as a few others while Mr. Washington is in the city even though we do not really believe there will be any real necessity for so doing.

However, I may state to you honestly, that I will feel far better when Mr. W. is safe out of this town & Montgomery & with you all once more. Sincerely,

G. W. A. Johnston

ALS Con. 22 BTW Papers DLC.

To Robert Heberton Terrell

[Tuskegee, Ala.] November 14, 1904

My dear Judge Terrell: I thank you very much indeed for your kind letter of November 9th. It is indeed, as you say, a generous victory, and we must do our part to sustain the President. I like especially the position you take in the matter. We must do nothing to make him feel that we own the President, and I shall counsel our men as you suggest, that we properly restrain ourselves and help the President in every way we can to accomplish the great purposes he has in mind. Very truly yours,

Booker T. Washington

TLpSr Con. 25 BTW Papers DLC.

From Walter Francis Willcox

Ithaca, New York, Nov. 14, 1904

Dear Mr. Washington: Thank you for your letter of November 9th about the amount of property accumulated by negroes. I am inclined to think that the figures of the last Census make it safe to venture a very rough estimate on the subject and am pleased to find that your general conclusion derived independently and from different data is in fair agreement with mine. I am disposed at present to set it down at about 300,000,000, and probably neither less than two hundred and fifty or more than three hundred and fifty. I have submitted my argument in manuscript to Professor Du Bois of Atlanta, who is a member with me of a committee of the American Economic Association on this subject, and he thinks my figures should be raised fifty million dollars. I have submitted them also to Mr. L. G. Powers of the Census Office and he agrees with them. At present I am not disposed to agree with Professor Du Bois that they are too small, but shall carry on a discussion with him by correspondence in the hopes that we may eventually reach an agreement and so unanimously report.

With renewed thanks for your full reply I remain, Yours sincerely,

W. F. Willcox

TLS Con. 343 BTW Papers DLC.

To Oswald Garrison Villard

Tuskegee Institute, Alabama. November 16, 1904

Personal

My dear Mr. Villard: When we last met, you will remember that you requested that I make some suggestions for your speech before the colored people in the city of Boston.

So far as I can get hold of the facts, I think you will find that many of the colored people composing the literary society which you will address, have the idea, or have had it, that I was willing to surrender all the rights of the colored people and cater to all the unreasonable wishes of the Southern whites. I have had a good deal of sympathy with this class of our race in the North, because many of them have been graduated from Northern colleges and have lived the greater part, if not all, of their lives in the North and have never had the opportunity of seeing what the conditions are in the South. Some of them are really honest in their opposition to my view and policy; others are simply pretending to be honest, and would oppose any other person who stands in the same position I do. Of course it is very natural that the colored man in the North should chafe and become restless and impatient over conditions which the race has to endure. I become just as impatient as they do, and wish just as much as they that I could change conditions, but you and I both know that the mere wishing will not make a change, that we have got to go through a long process of evolution which can only be brought about by development in property, education and character.

There is another class of our people who have always thought that a colored leader was brave in proportion as he cursed the Southern white man regardless of the effect of such cursing. It takes more courage, in my opinion, for one to keep his mouth closed than to open it, especially when he is a thousand miles from the seat of danger.

Summed up briefly, I think their opposition centers around these points: first, they have misunderstood the object of industrial education; they have felt that I have insisted upon all colored people getting industrial education only; that is far from the fact. In all my writings I have emphasized the necessity for college and professionally trained men and women as well as those with industrial education. The fact is that at Tuskegee we employ more college and university graduates than is true of any other similar institution in the world. Just as in Massachusetts they have the Institute of Technology and the Simmons Industrial School, so in the South there should be the Atlanta University, the Tuskegee Institute and others. There is a place for all of these institutions to do their work. I do not believe in placing any limitation upon the mental development of the black man. I also believe that in proportion as he gets an economic foundation that it would add to the opportunity of future generations to secure the very highest training. Another objection has been that I have been willing to surrender all of the political rights of the black man, and some even charge that the Negro in the South would be in possession of his political rights but for my influence. You and I both know that before Frederick Douglass died the Negro had lost practically all political control and power in the South; that occurred when I was a mere boy attending school at Hampton, and before my name was known outside of Tuskegee the Southern states, leading off with Mississippi and South Carolina, began to pass new constitutions disfranchising the colored people. In every case, however, where a state has made an attempt to take from our people the political franchise, I have spoken out frankly and directly to the people in that state through the public press regarding the injustice of not making the same conditions for one race as for the other. On all these subjects I have stated my views fully in my book, "Up from Slavery," and more fully in "The Future of the American Negro."

On the subject of lynching this same group of people has charged me with cowardice. It is true I do not speak out every time a lynching occurs in the South, if I did my words would soon become so frequent and so common that the public press would give no attention to what I said, but when I think the proper season has come I never fail to speak out and rebuke the lynchers in every part of the country, and I have always been careful to speak directly to the Southern white people and while in the South. If necessary I could send you all of my utterances on these various subjects.

The fact is, all of us are aiming at the same thing; we may be pursuing different methods, trying to reach the same goal by different roads, and there is no necessity for quarreling. I think if you would suggest pretty strongly to these people that they could help more by friendly and sympathetic cooperation than by mere abuse that it would help them. I am always willing to take suggestions, always willing to change my policy when I am convinced that I am wrong, but heaping abuse on individuals amounts to very little in bringing about a change as a rule.

Please excuse me for inflicting so long a letter upon you, but you know my views so well that I think it unnecessary to state them further. I enclose to you, however, an extract from an address which I delivered in Athens, Georgia, a few days ago, referring to the subject of white capping and lynching.[1] I am pleased to state that the white people who were in the audience were most enthusiastic over this portion of my address. Yours very truly,

Booker T. Washington

TLS Oswald Garrison Villard Papers MH.

[1] BTW refers here to his address at the Northeast Georgia Agricultural Fair, Oct. 15, 1904, where he said that "the way for the white man to secure the most lasting and beneficial control of the Negro is not through the inciting of fear or through the method of terrorism and inhuman punishment. . . . There is almost no race in existence that can be so largely and fully controlled through kindness and justice as is true of the black race." (Typescript, BTW Papers, ATT.)

From W. A. Johnson[1]

New York November 16th, 1904

Dear Mr. Washington: I have your letter of November 14th, with the enclosure from Alexander Kuhn. I find that the German edition is published by Dietrich Reimer of Berlin. We are sending this information to Mr. Kuhn, and also suggesting that if he wants a German edition for South Africa, he might arrange with Reimer. Or if he prefers to get out a separate translation, we may secure Reimer's permission for him to do so. We think that the German edition which has already been published would answer his purpose.

The memoranda I have before me show the following applications for translations, a part of which have been completed, and others were never undertaken at all:

French.	Plon et Cie;
German.	Dietrich Reimer;
Cuban-Spanish.	D. Appleton & Company.
African.	Bishop Hartzell (Did not complete).
Indian.	Serial published in "Kankali-i-Hind" by Lilavati Singli.
Indian.	(Another native language). H. Gulliford. (Permission given to make a brief story as he requested).

Finnish.	F. K. Jauhiainen. (Not completed).
Arabian.	A. A. Kahil. (Nothing done).
Dutch.	F. L. Pierson, U.S. Minister to Holland. (Not completed).
Zulu.	James Dexter Taylor, Natal, South Africa. (Reported to be published serially soon).
Malaysian.	A copy of which you have.
Danish.	M. Johannes Knudson. (Not completed).
German.	School edition in English. (Negotiations are going on with our London representative).
Norwegian.	Aschelong & Co., Christiania. (Permission given).
Polish.	Miss Eva Landowski. (Permission given).
Spanish.	E. Marquina, Barcelona. (Permission given).
Russian.	Professor A. D. Romanoff. (Permission given).
Chinese.	Cheng Han, St. Petersburg, Russia. (Permission given).

These applications have been coming in right along and we have given permission in most cases free. From the German, French, and Cuban-Spanish, and one or two others, as you know, there is a small royalty coming in from time to time. We have written several times to the others urging them to complete the work if they wish to undertake it, and in some cases have secured definite promises. In others, where nothing seems to be doing, we stand ready to give permission to other people who apply. Respectfully yours,

W A Johnson

TLS Con. 293 BTW Papers DLC.

1 A staff member of Doubleday, Page and Co.

To Joseph Oswalt Thompson

[Tuskegee, Ala.] Nov. 17, 1904

Personal

My dear Mr. Thompson: Just on the eve of leaving for the North I want to send you a line in order that you may not misunderstand me. I speak rather frankly when I say that I very much fear that you have gotten a wrong impression. In the first place it would have been a physical impossibility for me to have seen you and your friends after the meeting in the church as there was another program which kept me until two o'clock in the morning, but aside from that I feel sure it would have been a mistake and would have done no good to either you or myself for me to have gone to the post office, although you know how very much it would have pleased me to have seen you there. I may make a mistake in having such feelings, but the only motive that actuated me in not even calling at your office was the fact that I do not like to have any one get the impression that after I have been of service in helping one secure a position of honor and responsibility that I am trying to dictate that individual's actions, and perhaps in trying to avoid that impression I have been going too far or have been too timid.

In the second place, as much as anything else I was seeking to protect you from the feeling on the part of the public that you are not standing in your own boots and are merely carrying out the wishes of some one else. You do not know how much faith I have in you, how much I respect you and how much I appreciate your bravery and disinterested unselfishness in regard to my race. It is because of my faith in you and high respect for you that I am very anxious not to do anything, and perhaps too anxious, that would embarrass you.

In this connection I ought to state that I have not found a colored man in Alabama who does not have faith in you, and in fact the whole race almost worships you.

On more than one occasion I have had to caution the President about places and times of seeing me, in fact at one time when he sent me a telegram to come to Washington to see him at once I did not go but sent Mr. Scott to explain to him that it was not best for his own interests that I should appear in Washington at that time. I think he felt a little nettled at the time, but I am sure he afterwards appreciated the situation and agreed with me in the wisdom of my course. I have just received two letters from him urging me to come to Washington as soon as possible, and I shall leave tonight or tomorrow morning, and may telegraph you from there the result of my visit.

I hope you know how very glad I am to see you at any time you come to Tuskegee, and often wish I could spend more time with you either in Birmingham or in Tuskegee. Sometime I shall hope in the near future to go to Birmingham when I am not advertised to speak and when the general public does not know about it, and spend some time in your office when I can see you and your friends. I realize thoroughly that in Alabama there are quite a number of brave, strong, unselfish white men who are standing up for right regardless of official position or future gain, and I am most anxious to come in contact with and have a heart to heart talk with that element of your friends. Yours very truly,

Booker T. Washington

TLpS Con. 25 BTW Papers DLC.

To Portia Marshall Washington

[Tuskegee, Ala.] November 17, 1904

My dear Portia: I have just received your note of the eve of my taking the train for the North. It will be impossible for me to take up such matters with you as you write about as those belong more properly to your mamma. I have turned your letter over to her and asked her to do as she thinks wise. I do not know about such matters, and, besides, I am so much occupied I could not attempt to attend to them in detail. I am sure you will hear from her in a day or two and she will do the right thing.

In haste. Your papa,

B. T. W.

TLpI Con. 17 BTW Papers DLC.

To Emmett Jay Scott

Crawford House, Boston, Mass. November 21, 1904

My Dear Mr. Scott, Our train reached Washington about 11 o'clock Saturday night. The President had a man at the depot to meet me and had arranged for me to come to the White House at once, so that does away with the necessity of my returning there tomorrow.

I found the main matters he wanted to discuss, as follows, the reduction of Southern representation, and the matter of continuing his present Southern policy, especially, as to the recognition of worthy democrats, of the Judge Jones type.

I told him I was opposed to the plan of the reduction of Southern representation as a cure to our present difficulties, and he agrees to oppose it. Later on I am to return and take up with him, other matters in detail.

We have had two very successful meetings. Very truly yours,

Booker T. Washington

TLS Con. 550 BTW Papers DLC.

To Henry A. Rucker

Crawford House, Boston, Mass. November 21, 1904

(Personal & Confidential.)

My Dear Mr. Rucker: I saw the President, a few minutes as I passed through Washington last Saturday night. I did not take up your matter in detail for very soon after I began talking, he told me his policy would be to make no changes in Officials, in the South, where they were rendering good service. I am quite sure no [one] will wean him away from his policy of treating colored people according to their merit.

Please remember me to Mrs. Rucker and the family. Very truly yours,

[Booker T. Washington]

TLc Con. 23 BTW Papers DLC.

NOVEMBER · 1904

An Article on Black Labor in the South[1]

Tuskegee, Ala., November 21, 1904

THE NEGRO AND THE LABOR PROBLEM OF THE SOUTH

Recent industrial changes bring into prominence two facts, first, that the South is likely for all time to be the cotton center of the world, and second, that the continued increase in the use of cotton goods among all nations will give to every acre of land in the South a value that it has not heretofore possessed. With these facts in mind, a natural inquiry is, what can the Negro do to help forward the interests of the South, and what can the white man do to help the Negro and himself?

I shall hope to suggest an answer to both of these questions. A few days ago I spent a day in one of the rural counties of Georgia and heard a great deal of discussion about the scarcity of efficient farm labor. After spending the day in the country, I returned to Atlanta for the night. Between 10 and 11 o'clock I made a tour through Decatur Street and several streets in that vicinity. I think I do not exaggerate when I say that I found in and near Decatur Street enough people who were not regularly employed to operate successfully fifty of the largest plantations in the state of Georgia. This single example would mean little except that it represents a condition more or less prevalent in practically all of our larger cities and all of our Southern States.

As an economic problem, we have on the one hand a surplus of idle labor in the cities, and on the other, much vacant land, unpicked cotton and a scarcity of farm labor; it is a tremendously difficult situation. The problem of changing these conditions not only confronts the South, and it is not by any means confined to my race, but for the present I desire to deal with it mainly as it affects my race and the land owner of the South, be that land owner white or black.

In order that what I may say on this subject be of any value to the white man or to my own race, I shall have to ask the privilege of perfect frankness. The many subjects affecting the interests of both races require perfect frankness on both sides. Your readers will agree with me, I think, when I say that it is possible for a Negro to know more of the feelings and motives of colored people than a white man can possibly know.

In my recent visit to Atlanta I did that which I have often done in large cities of the South wherever I have found a floating class of colored people. I made individual inquiry as to why they preferred uncertain existence in the city to a life of comparative prosperity upon a farm, either as owners, renters, or laborers. While I shall not attempt to use their exact words, I sum up the reasons they gave me in a few sentences. Just now the South is in the midst of the season when land owners are making plans for another year's crop, some of the matters that were brought out, and which I shall try to discuss a little fully and maybe with profit to land owners.[2]

In the South, as elsewhere, there are two classes: those whom labor seeks, and those who have to seek labor. The first group is comparatively small, but such a class exists; it can and ought to be increased. There are, in my opinion, two classes of faults as between white farmers and black labor: one, on the part of the white people, the other on the part of the black people. To find and state faults, however, is easy. To suggest a remedy, one that shall promote the prosperity and happiness of both races is the aim of this article.

To return to the main complaints of the colored people as they have stated them to me time and time again — These people who have talked may be right, they may be wrong, they may state facts or they may state untruths, but this I know, they represent the attitude of a large class of colored people, who give the following as chief reasons for leaving the farms: Poor dwelling houses, loss of earnings each year, because of unscrupulous employers, high priced provisions, poor schoolhouses, short school terms, poor school teachers, bad treatment generally, lynchings and whitecapping, fear of the practice of peonage, a general lack of police protection and want of encouragement. Let us assume that these conditions do exist in some sections, and with certain individual planters. As a mere matter of dollars and cents, if for no higher reason, I believe that it will pay every owner of a plantation throughout the South to see to it that the houses of the tenants are not only made comfortable, but attractive in a degree. The land owner who thinks that he can secure the best class of colored people when he provides only a broken-down, one-room cabin for them to live in, will find himself mistaken. The chances are that the planter who provides comfortable houses for his tenants will keep them much longer, and will have a more reliable service. The matter of being cheated out of his earnings at the end of the year is, of course, a complaint that is very hard to discuss, and I know is likely to involve much exaggeration, and the more ignorant the aggrieved person is, the more given is he to such complaint and exaggeration, but I must not conceal the fact that such feeling is deep and wide-spread, and I ought to make the same statement regarding the high prices charged during the year for provisions, etc., supplied.

Some of the colored people who have migrated into the cities give as their reason for leaving the country the poor school facilities in the rural communities. In practically every large city in the South the colored man is enabled by public, missionary, and private schools, to keep his child in school eight or nine months in the year. Not only is this true, but the schoolhouses are comfortable, and the teachers are efficient. In many of the rural communities, the location of the schoolhouse is far from the home of the child, the building is uncomfortable, the term lasts but four or five months, and the teacher's salary is so small that it generally invites a most inefficient class of teachers. I know one community that has had great trouble this year in getting cotton pickers and other laborers, and inquiry reveals the fact that the Negro children in that community were in school last year only four months, and the teacher received from the public fund but eleven dollars per month for his services. Under such conditions who can blame a large number of colored people for leaving the plantations of the country districts?

Purely as an economic proposition, I believe that it will not only pay the land owners of the South, either as individuals, or by united effort, to see that good schoolhouses are provided on or near their plantations, that the school is kept open six or eight months in a year, and that there is a good teacher regularly employed; where the school fund is not large enough to supply a good schoolhouse, they should extend the school term and provide a first-class, moral teacher. Further, it will pay to lead the way in seeing that reasonable facilities are otherwise provided.

This, I repeat, will lead to a demand for land and increase of efficiency in the labor force. Financially, there will soon be a great difference in the price of land when there are tenants bidding for opportunities instead of going to cities as now. Wherever it is practicable, I would urge that at least a primary course in agriculture be given in every country school. This would lead to a love of farm work and of country life. Again, many are not on the farms, as they say, because they have not been treated fairly. To illustrate: I recall that some years ago a certain white farmer asked me to secure for him a young colored man to work about the house and to work in the field. The young man was secured, a bargain was entered into to the effect that he was to be paid a certain sum monthly and his board and lodging furnished as well. At the end of the colored boy's first day on the farm he returned. I asked the reason, and he said that after working all the afternoon he was handed a buttered biscuit for his supper and no place was provided for him to sleep.

At night he was told he could find a place to sleep in the fodder loft. This white farmer, whom I know well, is not a cruel man and seeks generally to do the right thing, but in this case he simply overlooked the fact that it would have paid him better in dollars and cents to give some thought and attention to the comfort of his helper. This case is more or less typical. Had this boy been well cared for he would have so advertised the place that others would have sought work there.

The readers of your paper know too well that in a few counties of several of our Southern States there has been such a reign of lawlessness led by whitecappers and lynchers that many of the best colored people have been driven from their homes and have sought in large cities safety and police protection. In too many cases the colored people who have been molested have been those, who by their thrift and diligence, have secured homes and other property. These colored people have been oppressed in most instances not by the property-holding, intelligent white people, but by the worst and most shiftless element of whites. Have the higher class of whites escaped responsibility for letting their affairs be controlled by the worst element? The practice of peonage in a few counties of the South has also caused a fear among an element of the colored people that prevents their going into or remaining in the country districts that they may be forced to labor involuntarily and without proper remuneration. I have said that such lawless conditions exist in only a "few" counties in the South, and I used the word advisedly. In the majority of the counties in the South life and property are just as safe as anywhere in the United States, but the harm comes because of the wide-spread notoriety that a few lawless communities and counties have given the South, and this serves to spread the idea pretty generally among the colored people that if they want police protection when they are charged with crime or under suspicion they must hastily seek the confines of a city. I repeat that fear has stripped some counties of its most valuable colored labor and left the dregs of that population. In the matter of law and order, my constant appeal is that there be hearty co-operation between the best whites and the best blacks.

Nothing is clearer than that crime is rarely committed by the colored man who has education and owns property. I have not failed either to say to the colored people on more than one occasion, "We should see to it that crime in all its phases is condemned by the race and a public sentiment kept alive that will make it impossible for a criminal to be shielded or protected by any member of the race, at any time or in any place."

Few white people realize how far a little encouragement goes in helping to make better and more useful citizens of the colored people. Some months ago I recall that I listened for an hour to a white man in the South who was making a political speech. He was in a state where a revised constitution had disfranchised nineteen-twentieths of the colored voters fifteen years ago and there was not the slightest chance of any political uprising, or even opposition on the part of the colored people, yet two-thirds of this man's address was devoted to ridicule and abuse of the colored people. The sad feature of such an address lies in the fact that in many parts of the country such a speech is taken seriously. To most of those who heard it and to those who knew the man in that community it did no especial harm, for the people knew that his talk did not tally with his actions, but he had become so accustomed to making that kind of speech that he repeated it by force of habit. This man had drawn his first life's sustenance from the breast of a colored woman, had been reared by one, and at that moment he had dozens of the best colored people in that section on his plantation, any one of whom would have laid down his life for him, and the man himself would have fought to the death in defense of these colored servants of his.

Every year these same laborers were making him richer and richer by their patient, faithful labor, and he would trust them with all that he possessed. In this community the Negroes have never made an unavailing appeal to this man for aid in building churches or schoolhouses, or in supporting a school. Few white men anywhere in the world in their actual daily practice had done more to help the black man. Yet, such a speech read in the newspaper at a distance would give the impression to thousands of colored laborers that the county in which the speaker lived was for them absolutely unsafe. Such a speech was not calculated to gain a single vote, but it was calculated, in my opinion, to lose to the community a good many bales of cotton. I repeat that few understand how much good could be accomplished in the way of helping the colored people to lead law-abiding and useful lives if more white people would take occasion both in private and in public to praise their good qualities instead of reviling and ridiculing them.

In regard to the duties and obligations of my own people, I would say that unless they realize fully the opportunities that are before them in the South and seize every chance to improve their methods of labor, the time will come when Italians and other foreigners will attempt to displace them in the labor work of the South, just as the Chinese are displacing the Negro in South Africa.

One charge frequently brought against us is that we cannot be depended upon for constant and uninterrupted labor; that an excursion or other excitement will take laborers from the very places where their services are most needed. The complaint is frequently made that if paid on Saturday night the laborers will probably not return to work until all the cash received has been expended, and that on the plantation the colored tenant takes little interest in caring for the property of the landlord. These things our people should change.

I hope I may be pardoned for speaking so plainly and in so much detail and at such length, but I believe that the South is on the eve of a season of prosperity, such as it has never before experienced, and that by mutual understanding and sympathetic co-operation each of these two races of the South can help forward the interests of the other, and thus cement a friendship between them that shall be an object lesson for all the world.

Booker T. Washington

Atlanta *Constitution,* Nov. 27, 1904.

[1] BTW wrote this originally for the Atlanta *Constitution,* but its editor was so impressed by it that he arranged for its simultaneous publication in thirty southern newspapers on Nov. 27, 1904. (BTW to R. C. Ogden, Nov. 25, 1904, Con. 33, BTW Papers, DLC.) It also appeared in pamphlet form, and a copy is in Con. 956, BTW Papers, DLC.

[2] This garbled sentence appears thus also in the pamphlet version.

To Timothy Thomas Fortune

Crawford House, Boston, Mass. November 22, 1904

My Dear Mr. Fortune: I had a long talk with the President Saturday night, regarding the interest of the race: There is one point I speak of now, other matters I will leave until I see you.

The time is now here when we shall have to take a decided stand upon the question of reduction of Southern representation as a cure for our present ills. In advising the President on the proposition I took the same ground as you take, that reduction of Southern representation will not help us, and he agrees to advocate that view of the case. He will omit touching the subject in his next message.

But the main point to which I want to call your attention is the importance of our taking important measures to back up our side of the question. If you will lead off in a strong editorial about the matter, and then follow it up from week to week, I am sure there will be little trouble in getting the other Afro-American journals to assist.

The more I think of it, the more dangerous the proposition appears. Aside from the evil of legalizing a wrong done the Negro in the South, such action would establish a right to disfranchise colored people because of their color and the exercise of that right would soon extend to the Northern and border states; take for instance W. Virginia and Indiana, the Negro could be disfranchised with practically no loss of representation in Congress, because of the small number of Negro voters.

Such action would help Northern white men in securing additional power, but would not add one iota to the Negro's struggle in the South.

I hope you are well and having a good rest. Very truly yours,

[Booker T. Washington]

TLc Con. 1 BTW Papers DLC.

To Hugh Mason Browne

Crawford House, Boston, Mass. November 23, 1904

My Dear Mr. Browne: Your letter received; would it not be a good plan to print under the words, "Committee of Twelve," on your letter heads, "For the advancement of the interests of the Negro race?"

I have asked Mr. Scott to send you from Tuskegee, the list of names I think it would be well to send the "Grimke Article."

Dr. DuBois' letter[1] is very interesting and instructive as well. I very much fear you will be in danger of ass[ass]ination if you write him again. Very truly yours,

Booker T. Washington

TLS BTW Papers ATT.

[1] Du Bois had written to Browne: "Under no circumstances whatsoever is my name to be used in connection with the so-called 'Committee of Twelve,' nor do I wish any further communication concerning it." (Nov. 10, 1904, BTW Papers, ATT.)

From Emmett Jay Scott

Tuskegee Institute, Alabama. November 23, 1904

Dear Mr. Washington: I have your letter telling of your visit to President Roosevelt. I make note of the subjects mentioned as having been discussed with him. That the President should be concerned as to the precise attitude he should assume towards the South and with our problem, goes without question, considering the abuse and the great amount of discussion which have followed fast upon everything he has done in his treatment of us.

The position which you yourself should assume, is also one which no doubt has caused you much serious consideration. I am quite sure that you would not have come to your decision with reference to the recommendations you have made, without having weighed every side of the question. Nevertheless, you will not mind my admonishing you that it is rather a tremendous responsibility to shoulder alone. You may be quite sure that in the end, you are going to be held directly responsible for the position which the President has taken. The Boston newspaper for instance, last week devoted all of its editorial space to calling upon the Negro press and the Negro people, to watch you most particularly in these later days, especially when you come to advise with the President. There is an editorial on this very matter of Southern reduction, which has been up for discussion. The position taken is that the colored people of the country should hold Congress responsible as much as possible for the redemption of that plank in the platform referring to suffrage limitations in the South.

I suppose of course you take the position that we must choose the lesser evil, but the battle was especially fought out on this issue and it is hard to decide whether a specific plank in the platform should be ignored altogether, and whether the Republicans should because of their insidious maneuvering, permit them to hold their own in spite of the endorsement given by the country to the claim of the Republicans. Personally it seems to me that it would be much wiser both from your own and the President's point of view, if Congress were left to deal with this matter altogether in accordance with its specific decision as stated in the platform, which did not call as you remember, for the reduction, but only for an investigation. In this way, neither you nor the President could be held responsible for attempting to thwart the declared will of the American people, as you will be — & for a long time too.

I am only interested in this matter that you should be saved from malignant misrepresentation and from being misunderstood by hordes of the maliciously inclined, and then too, as I wrote you yesterday in a personal letter, it is very hard for me to believe anything you or the President can ever do will win the South, except along its own declared lines.

I take it that the case is now closed and cannot be reopened, but I certainly hope that you have weighed every side of the case before finally accepting this tremendous responsibility. Very truly yours,

Emmett J. Scott

TLS Con. 24 BTW Papers DLC.

To Emmett Jay Scott

Crawford House, Boston, Mass. November 28, 1904

My Dear Mr. Scott, Referring very briefly to your letter of November 25, concerning the question of Southern Representation. The more I think about it the more convinced I am right in my opinion. To save repetition, I enclose a copy of a letter sent Mr. Fortune a few days ago, on the same subject.

The fact is, the Negro plank at Chicago, was slipped into the platform without the knowledge of the President, or that of his friends on guard there.

The President, I am sure, takes the view that the platform calls for congressional action and not executive action.

I note what the Boston Guardian says of me in this respect. I wish you would get in touch with R. W. Thompson and inform him of the points involved, so that we might all work in harmony, that is, if he has not already taken a position. Very truly yours,

Booker T. Washington

TLS Con. 550 BTW Papers DLC.

From Franz Boas[1]

New York, Nov. 30, 1904

Dear Sir, A young gentlemen, Mr. J. E. Aggrey,[2] of Livingstone College, Salisbury, N.C., desires to study anthropology at Columbia

University. He is a full-blood negro, and, so far as I can learn, his standing is such that he will require at least one year of undergraduate work before he can be admitted to university study. That is to say, it will require at least five years before he could become an independent investigator in the science in which he is interested. From what I hear from my colleagues who made his acquaintance at the session of the summer school, he is a very bright man. He is, however, without means, and will require support in order to complete his studies. I do not know whether it would be possible to obtain this support here in the city, but I do not think it is unlikely. On the other hand, I very much hesitate to advise the young man to take up this work, because I fear that it would be very difficult after he has completed his studies to find a place for him. On the other hand, it might perhaps be possible for him to study for two or three years and to take his degree of master of arts, and then to obtain a position in one of the higher schools established for his race. I feel that the matter is a rather delicate one, and I do not wish to advise the young man or to assist him in beginning a study which may ultimately put him in a most unfortunate position. I should be very much indebted to you for your advice in this matter.

It is of course evident that if he developed into a good scientist, he could do excellent work particularly in Africa, which would be of the very greatest service to science. This is a consideration which makes me desirous of assisting him. On the other hand, I am very much afraid that it would be almost impossible to find a place for him even in this field. Perhaps by proper application, and if he were the right man, it might be possible to get him into Colonial service of one of the European countries that have colonies in Africa. Yours very truly,

Franz Boas

TLS Con. 550 BTW Papers DLC.

[1] Franz Boas (1858–1942), the anthropologist and ethnologist, taught at Columbia University beginning in 1896 and was curator of anthropology at the American Museum of Natural History from 1901 to 1905. He was a leader in promoting the idea that inferiority or superiority based on racial characteristics had no foundation in science. Boas was an outspoken critic of the racist theories of Nazi Germany.

[2] James Emman Kwegyr Aggrey (1875–1927) was a West African educational leader, blending Hampton-Tuskegee methods with those of higher education. A Fanti born in the Gold Coast, he completed his education in the United States with a B.A. at Livingstone College in 1902 and an M.A. there in 1912. He also earned a D.D. degree

from Hood Theological Seminary, and in 1922 an M.A. from Columbia University. In the early 1920s Aggrey was a member of the influential Phelps-Stokes Committee on Education in Africa. In his last years he was vice-principal of Achimota Prince of Wales College and School. Aggrey is perhaps best remembered for his statement of his philosophy of interracial cooperation: "You can play a tune of sorts on the white keys, and you can play a tune of sorts on the black keys, but for harmony you must use both the black and the white." (Smith, *Aggrey of Africa*, 122.)

A Memorandum for Theodore Roosevelt

[Boston, ca. November 1904][1]

Memoranda for the President

Personal

1. I have taken the liberty of saying to Mr. J. O. Thompson and Captain C. H. Scott that I am going to write you about some matters which I am sure they would not care to state themselves prior to their seeing you in a few days. I make these suggestions because of the pressing importance of each one of them being considered most carefully.

2. The party in Alabama is united to a greater extent than has been true for 20 years.

3. Those holding office have the confidence and respect of all classes, including Democrats, in a greater degree than has been true since the war.

4. Culminating with the holding of the Lily White convention in Birmingham, Alabama, in 1903, when Judge Pri[t]chard of North Carolina, was present, the Republican party was almost completely blotted out in Alabama and the Lily White party was substituted in its stead.

5. The task of re-organizing the party upon the principles as represented by you and followers has been a delicate and herculean one, and in order to get any kind of a basis for reorganization, Mr. Thompson and Mr. Scott were compelled to put those who held office in many cases as members of the State Committee, otherwise there would have been no possible manner of getting the party out of the control of the Lily Whites. The result is, the party is united

and it is the intention of Mr. Thompson and Mr. Scott to gradually get rid of so many office holders as members of the State Committee, but this should be done gradually. In Mr. Thompson's own case, he objected strenuously to being made Chairman of the State Committee, and only consented when the position was virtually forced upon him by his friends in order to save the party.

6. My attention was first called to both Mr. Thompson and Mr. Scott by reason of the fact that I saw them standing out almost unaided and alone for the rights of all the people to be members of the Republican party regardless of race, when practically every white Republican in the state was against them because they got the idea that you favored the Lily White party in this state. At the time Mr. Scott and Mr. Thompson were bearing the jeers and hoots of the Lily White element, they had no idea of any reward being given them in the direction of office, they simply stood up for principle.

7. Now that you have won such an overwhelming victory in the United States, it has become popular in Alabama as elsewhere to be a friend of the President, & any number of Lily Whites and Democrats are trying to accomplish the downfall of Mr. Scott and Mr. Thompson and give them all kinds of trouble, making their lives miserable. When it was unpopular to support you and your measures these Lily Whites kept themselves in the background or abused you. Now that victory and popularity are with you these elements want to . . .[2] Messrs Thompson & Scott. It will be difficult for me to make you understand the sacrifices and hard work which Mr. Thompson and Mr. Scott have endured for the sake of standing by you and the principles you represented. I have known a good many white men in the South, but I have never known two whose personal and official lives were cleaner and more straightforward than is true of Mr. Thompson and Mr. Scott. I do not confine my comparison to the South, they are as clean, true and straightforward as any men I know anywhere in the country.

8. I am writing thus plainly because just now I fear a crisis is being approached in this state, because of the fact that the Lily Whites and certain Democrats are willing to endorse anybody or any movement that will bring friction in the Republican party, are putting themselves very much in evidence.

9. I think you will agree with me that you have had as little

trouble in the state of Mississippi as in any state in the South or in the Union. Matters have gone well there because almost without exception you have followed the recommendations of Mr. Edgar S. Wilson and everybody knows you intend to stand by him so long as he is right. There will be no trouble in Alabama if the same policy is carried out, that is if it becomes thoroughly understood that you intend to stand by Mr. Thompson and Mr. Scott so long as they are right everything else will settle itself; otherwise, all the hard work a number of us have tried to do in order to put things in decent condition in this state will count for little. Yours Sincerely

[Booker T. Washington]

TMd BTW Papers ATT. Corrections and additions in BTW's hand.

1 Internal evidence suggests that the document was drafted after the November presidential election. BTW visited the White House on November 19 and December 21. During this time his headquarters was the Crawford House in Boston.

2 Illegible word.

To Franz Boas

Crawford House, Boston, Mass. December 9, 1904

My Dear Sir: Replying briefly to your letter, I would state it is a very difficult thing to give my impression of the young man, that would be of much value, without knowing more about him, than I do.

Judging by what you state in your letter and knowing what I do, I cannot rid myself of the feeling that the course which he is planning to take, will be of little value to him.

At the present time I know of so many cases where young colored men and women would have done well had they thoroughly prepared themselves for teachers, some kind of work in the industries, or in the applied sciences, but instead, they have made the mistake of taking a course that had no place [of] practical benefit, or in the needs of the race; the result being they ended up as hotel-waiters or Pullman car porters.

If I could see you I would be glad to talk the matter over with you. Very truly yours,

[Booker T. Washington]

TLc Con. 1 BTW Papers DLC.

To Warren Logan

Boston, Mass. December 9, 1904

Dear Mr. Logan: I find there is criticism, among some of our friends, over the matter of the students' "yells" in the Chapel. Our friends get the idea that it is "aping," too much, after the Northern colleges. Very truly yours,

B. T. W.

While Dr. Buttrick is there, have Captain Stevenson,[1] County Superintendent come up and interview him.

TLIr BTW Papers ATT.

[1] W. G. Stevenson, Macon County superintendent of education.

To Cain Washington Triplett and Others[1]

Crawford House, Boston, Mass. December 12, 1904

My Dear Triplett: I am very sorry I shall not be able to see you and the others to say good bye to you, on your departure for the Soudan, but I wish to say I shall watch your work there, with a deep interest and anxiety.

In a large degree you will have in your keeping, the reputation of the school in your hands and in your work and deportment, you must measure up to the highest standard.

One point I wish to impress upon you is this, a great many persons going to a warm climate, go to ruin from a moral standpoint. I hope you will all keep this in mind and remember that if you yield to the temptation and lower yourself in your moral character, you will do yourself, the school and the race the greatest injustice, but I feel sure you are going to stand up and be men.

I have known or known of Mr. Hunt for a long time and I want you to know he has my confidence in his judgment. I want you to take his advice, as his long experience and deep interest in matters of this kind, amply fit him to give you good advice.

I shall hope to have good and full reports of your work in the Soudan.

Wishing you and your company all the success possible, I am, Very truly yours,

[Booker T. Washington]

TLc Con. 294 BTW Papers DLC.

[1] John Powell, Poindexter Smith, Ocie Romeo Burns, and John Brown Twitty.

From Roscoe Conkling Simmons

New York, N.Y., December 13, 1904

My dear Uncle Booker: I want to call your attention to several things about the December number of "The Voice of the Negro," which are so directly flings at you, that if you cannot answer them, which no one would have you do, certainly you can refrain from contributing to its circulation, and adding dignity to its columns.

In an editorial on "What is a Good Negro," the two first paragraphs are as follows:[1]

" 'A good Negro' is one who says he does not want the ballot. He orates before his people and advises them against going into politics. He says to them 'Keep out of politics.' Go to the farms; keep quiet and let the whites handle the government." The next hits hard:

" 'A good Negro' is one who says that his race does not need the higher learning; that what they need is industrial education, pure and simple. He stands up before his people and murders the truth and the Kings English in trying to enforce upon them the evils of a College Education and the beauties of a plow."

Now, sir, this is so clearly a thrust at you, that I can hardly reconcile the announcement that you are to contribute to the columns during the coming year.

In the announcements for 1905, after naming and presenting the photographs of about half dozen unknown characters, as some of those engaged, your cut accompanied by nine lines of three letters each, appears. I have seen your name first in the Atlantic Monthly announcement. And so bent are these people on having Dr. Du Bois, who is known not beyond the clique of academic theorists that infest the country, appear as great, if not greater, than you in the eyes of its readers, that on page 629, in the announcement of the January issue of their paper, they tell us "Dr. W. E. Burghardt Du Bois and Dr. Booker T. Washington" will contribute, and further, that "each man is known and respected among both races the country over," when there are millions of people who do not know Du Bois lives, and would not know if he should die; and on the other hand, your fame rests throughout the world. The plan is to have you and Du Bois contemporaneous. I object, and every body else objects, and the world has long ago registered its objection. If you cannot see through all of this, then like Ajax you are blind because you want to be. There are magazines that pay large sums of money to have things written about you; here is a little sheet seeking to humiliate you, and has always sought to do so, and announces in the same breath, that you have not only acquiesced in the humiliation, but will actually contribute to the spreading of the gospel among its readers.

Who is Du Bois? Who knows him? Who cares anything about him, or what he writes? What does he lead?

The world has long ago placed the laurel wreath of leadership, not only of a race, but of a thought, on your brow, and as long as I can see to write, none shall disturb it. And I intend to make you see these marplotic thrusts, even if you do not care to see them. The Colored American Magazine, by far the largest and best of these two publications, has a magnificent article on your worth and work in the last edition. It espouses the cause, and agrees with the world that you have no compeer in the world's estimate. And will you write for the one, and ignore, in your writings, the other? Nay, Nay. If there is any writing to be done, it should and must come this way.

Let me see you when you are here again. Most affectionately your nephew,

Roscoe

This case is something like one of your New York friends whom you have recently placed here. He writes alright, but how he does curse you in conversation. You and your friends!

TLS Con. 3 BTW Papers DLC.

[1] *Voice of the Negro,* 1 (Dec. 1904), 618.

From Clifford H. Plummer

Boston, December 22, 1904

Dear Mr. Washington: I thought I would write and inform you that I attended, as you requested, the meeting of the Historical Association[1] on Monday evening last and heard the address of the editor of the New York Post.[2] He must have talked about an hour and a half, and "said something all the time." In all the history of this association we have never had a paper to equal it. No one there could help indorsing all that was said by him, other than a few who were there who must have felt a pang when he made reference to you several times in glowing terms, using words of this kind: "That able and noble statesman, Booker T. Washington"; "That courageous man of your race, Booker T. Washington"; and terms of this kind he brought in at intervals when he had made some most striking point. Most all of his points were striking.

As usual it is customary to have comments made after the address, but in this case a few words would have answered the purpose, and they should be of this kind: That the speaker had said it all. And that that was the sentiment was evinced by the silence of all but about three, namely Rev. Scott[3] (who can talk all day and say nothing), Clement G Morgan (the acknowledged failure, by his friends), and another friend of yours, Monroe Trotter. As usual, what they had to say was not germane to the matter at all. They made no reference to you in what they had to say. In fact they made no reference to what the speaker said; and I have doubts if they know what they said themselves, for the Lord knows I can't recall it now.

I am glad you suggested to me to attend the meeting, for otherwise I would not have been present, for by his words I have been greatly inspired, and for the future shall read after him. I wish you and your family a Merry Christmas and a Happy and Prosperous New Year. Yours,

Clifford H. Plummer

TLS Con. 293 BTW Papers DLC.

1 Boston Literary and Historical Association.
2 Oswald Garrison Villard.
3 William H. Scott.

Emmett Jay Scott to Wilford H. Smith

[Tuskegee, Ala.] Dec. 22, 1904

Personal

Dear Mr. Smith: This letter I am writing to you directly and not to Payton.

You will remember my speaking to you with reference to the advertisement of the company running in the Voice of the Negro. It is pure presumption for me to make the suggestion I do, but if the results are not altogether flattering I should be happy if you could see your way clear to use your influence in the direction I indicated. In the October number of the magazine a very direct clash of the Business League appeared, and it was followed up in the December number with another ("a Good Negro" etc) which I am sure is meant to refer to no one but Dr. Washington.

Please do not dictate a reply to this letter, and please be good enough to respect my confidence to the extent of not placing this letter on file but destroying it. Let me know what you think of it however.[1] Yours very truly,

Emmett J. Scott

TLpS Con. 24 BTW Papers DLC.

1 Smith replied that he would arrange for the Afro-American Realty Co. to cancel its advertising contract with the *Voice of the Negro*. (Dec. 26, 1904, Con. 24, BTW Papers, DLC.) Scott, however, later sent Smith a draft of a letter canceling the advertising on the grounds of an alleged opposition not to BTW but to the NNBL. (Dec. 31, 1904, Con. 25, BTW Papers, DLC.)

To Charles William Anderson

[Tuskegee, Ala.] December 23, 1904

Personal

My dear Mr. Anderson: I was with the President for an hour and a half on last Wednesday night, and we took up matters pretty thoroughly, including your own case. When I brought up the matter in reference to yourself I informed him that Mr. Sharkey's term of office would not expire for two years, and he said that he had already found that out and was looking for another place and at once suggested that he hoped to give you the place of Deputy Appraiser at a salary of $3500. I told him at once that you are now receiving more than that salary and I felt sure that you would not take that place. He seemed surprised to know that such a position would be no promotion to you and that you would hardly consider it. This is where our friend the General has evidently tried to get in his work, but I soon convinced him that it would be folly to consider you for any such place and that it would be no proper recognition nor would it answer the purpose to any great amount in reference to its influence on the South. I then asked him if there were not other positions in New York which he could give you, and he then took up at once with a great deal of interest the matter of making you U.S. Marshal or Collector of Internal Revenue. The place which he now is evidently leaning toward is the U.S. Marshalship. He thinks he could in some way make a place for you by failure to appoint and thus making a vacancy in that position. *Unless his mind changes* he proposes, as he said, to give you one of those two offices. Now I want to get your own opinion in regard to both of these offices. First, you must be perfectly frank and fair with the President. He told me that he had a little fear that some of the people in the Marshal's office might resent your appointment and resign and make trouble; do you think that would be likely to happen? Which office do you prefer to have, and how do the offices rank as to salary and general importance? I reminded him that he would have a precedent in making you U.S. Marshal, owing to the fact that Frederick Douglass held the same position in the District of Columbia. Of course it is possible that some of the newspapers and small fry politicians might make a great outcry over the fact that a Negro was put in a place where he would have to arrest white people. About all these matters you know more than I do. You also know about the importance and value of the Collectorship of Internal Revenue. He is thoroughly committed to you, and our only danger at present is to keep the matter quiet and to break the influence of such men as Clarkson who I am sure, want to give you an inferior position. I told him that I thought it very important to settle this matter before making his Southern trip, and he agreed with me on that point.

If you have not said anything to Gov. Pinchback regarding my last conversation with you bearing upon him I wish you would not do so until I see you again. Yours truly,

Booker T. Washington

TLpS Con. 18 BTW Papers DLC.

To James Calvin Hemphill[1]

[Tuskegee, Ala.] December 23, 1904

Personal

Dear Sir: Replying further to your telegram sent me in Boston, I enclose to you in this envelope a marked copy of the New York Age containing an editorial on the South and the Platt Bill[2] written by T. Thomas Fortune, who, without doubt, is the most influential Negro editor. You will find, I think, that with few exceptions the colored press will take the view as outlined by Mr. Fortune.

Perhaps I ought to add that Mr. Fortune had a long interview with me before taking this position.

You will note another marked article on the same subject signed "Citizen."[3] Yours truly,

Booker T. Washington

TLpS Con. 289 BTW Papers DLC.

[1] James Calvin Hemphill (1850–1927) was editor-in-chief of the Charleston *News and Courier* (1888–1910), editor of the Richmond *Times-Dispatch* (1910–11), and editor of the Charlotte *Observer* (1911); and later he was on the editorial staffs of the New York *Times* and the Philadelphia *Public Ledger*. In 1909 he was a vice-president of the Associated Press.

[2] Senator Thomas Collier Platt of New York introduced a bill (S. 5747) to reduce representation in Congress of eleven southern states under provisions of Section 2 of the Fourteenth Amendment.

[3] A carbon of this letter to the New York *Age*, perhaps written by BTW though addressed from New York, is in Con. 23, BTW Papers, DLC. It included the arguments against reduction of representation that BTW made in his letter to J. S. Durham, Dec. 24, 1904, below.

To John Stephens Durham

[Tuskegee, Ala.] December 24, 1904

Personal

My dear Mr. Durham: Your very good letter comes to us just on the eve of our Christmas holidays, and I am taking part of my evening before Christmas to write you. I am very glad to hear that Mrs. Durham and the baby are in such good condition. Only this morning Mrs. Washington showed me a present which I believe is now on the way to your boy; I am sorry that it is so much delayed, but I have been away from home and it seems that she was uncertain about your address.

Matters move on about as usual at the school. We are still making progress in the effectiveness of the work and in our material growth I think.

I have seen the President twice since the election. Last Wednesday I spent an hour and a half with him. He is principally occupied now in the preparation of an address which he is going to deliver on Lincoln's Birthday in New York. He went over the address with me rather carefully and is to send me a revised copy of it for inspection within the next few days. He is going to discuss the Southern question from the Negro's point of view and from the white man's point of view. The only danger point in the address, and I have warned him about it rather frankly and am going to do so again in a letter tonight, is his treatment of the subject of "social equality." By social equality the Southern white man understands one thing and the Northern white man quite another thing, besides, where the lines are drawn in the South in the matter of public conveyances the Negro always gets the small end. I suggested to him that I hoped he would let the subject alone, but, as you know, he has such a horror of dodging any question that I very much fear he is going to pitch into it. Aside from what he will say on that subject, I feel satisfied with his address. He is going to take the position against the Platt bill. I do not know whether you have studied it, but the Platt bill is a dangerous measure. In so many words it says to the Southern states, if you will give up so many of your representatives you can disfranchise your Negroes. It goes into the state of Texas where the subject of disfranchisement has never been raised, and says if you will give up one of your 18 representatives you can have the privilege of disfranchising all the colored people.

The President spoke most strongly of you and your work without any suggestion from me. I hope you will not fail to see him when you are in this country again, as he thinks most highly of you.

Fortune is far from well, but he is doing his work after a manner. He writes me that the Age is having hard sledding financially again.

Mr. Scott and Mrs. Washington desire to be kindly remembered to you, Mrs. Durham and the boy. Yours very truly,

[Booker T. Washington]

TLp Con. 20 BTW Papers DLC.

To Theodore Roosevelt

[Tuskegee, Ala.] December 26, 1904

Personal

My dear Mr. President: So anxious am I about your Lincoln Birthday speech that I am writing you again, and may write you several times on the subject before the address is delivered.

I hope you will bear in mind in the preparation of this address

First, that the whole country has endorsed your principles and acts in a way that no other President has ever been endorsed, and that nothing will creep into the address which will give those who have stood by you so loyally the least impression that you are not standing by the principles upon which you were re-elected so overwhelmingly. In stating your position on the Platt bill for reduction of representation, I wonder if it would not be wise in some way to recognize the fact that the national platform adopted at Chicago called for an investigation of conditions. This, of course, does not commit the party to reduction. You stated very clearly in your letter of acceptance that you approved of the whole platform. The average man has the idea that the platform called for reduction, which it did not. This is merely a suggestion. Second, the discussion of the question of "Social Equality" is a very delicate matter and one out of which all kinds of harm may grow unless it is handled very carefully. The Southern white man understands one thing about social equality and the Northern and Western white man quite another thing. The Southern white man is constantly confusing civil privileges with social intercourse. The more I have thought over it since I saw you . . .[1] cussing that subject rather than to hear from Bishop Strange.[2] I happen now to recall that I am quite sure this is the same address which I heard Bishop Strange deliver in St. Thomas's Church, New York, about two months ago, and the effect which it made upon the audience, I mean the part relating to social equality and the separation of the races, was not satisfactory to any element in the congregation and I heard it rather severely criticised by many afterwards. On the question of Negro domination and social equality I send you an extract from an address which I delivered in Montgomery, Alabama, a short while ago.

So far as I can discern, the Negro in no part of the country feels it necessary to have purely social intercourse with the white man, nor does he hanker after it, but the difficulty in discussing the question grows out of the fact that in the South many of the white people regard the matter of riding in the same railroad coach or on the same seat in a street car or in the same waiting room at a depot "social equality." The Negro does not object so much to the separation of the races in these regards in itself, but he knows by experience that in nine cases out of ten where the Negroes are so separated the colored man gets the bad end of the bargain, that is to say in the vast majority of the cases in the South the colored man pays the same fare as the white man on the railroad trains but gets an accommodation that is far from equal. This is the ground of opposition.

It will be very hard for you to use the quotation from Bishop Strange's address without making the Northern white people feel that they must begin drawing the same lines that are drawn in the South.

I wonder if what you have to say against the amalgamation of the races would not go far towards answering the point which you have in mind:

These are mere suggestions. The Address so far as it is completed is strong and is going to produce a great impression as a whole as I said to you when you read it to me. Yours very truly,

Booker T. Washington

P.S. I wonder if you could not properly, in your Lincoln Birthday address, congratulate the country and the South upon the fact that now for two months there has not been a single lynching in any part of the country. This, I think you will find has not been true for any two months since the year 1885. This will be all the more powerful since so many have tried to produce the impression that your administration had resulted in creating more lynchings in the South than had ever occurred before. If you decide to take this matter up, it might be safe for you to get the latest and most direct information from the Chicago Tribune which is an authority on the subject.

If you take up the subject of lynching, I think it well for you to bear in mind that most of the daily newspapers, especially the Atlanta Constitution, Montgomery Advertiser as well as the grand juries and ministers, deserve great credit for taking the lead in this movement in the South to blot out lynching. Not the least part of the effective work has been the fact that the intelligent classes of colored and white people have both cooperated actively and heartily together in forming public sentiment.

TLpS BTW Papers ATT.

[1] Illegible line.

[2] Robert Strange (1857–1914), Episcopal bishop of North Carolina, a moderate on racial issues.

To Judson Whitlocke Lyons

Tuskegee Institute, Alabama. December 26, 1904

Personal and Confidential

My dear Sir: Replying to your letter of December 22d concerning the possible policy of the President toward the South and the race,[1] permit me to say that I have seen the President twice since his re-election, being with him for an hour and a half last Wednesday night. In each of these visits the time has been occupied mainly in a discussion of the general policy rather than matters relating to individuals. On each occasion he said to me frankly and strongly that he did not mean to change his attitude toward the race. Of course [after] his making such a statement it is a little difficult to go into details with him, that would seem to doubt his ability to maintain his former high standard. I think, however, since your letter states the fear of many colored people so clearly and emphatically, I will leave off your name and address and send the letter to him telling him that it states what many of the colored people feel and fear. I told him, however, the same thing very strongly last Wednesday night, that is, that many had the fear that he would be captured by the South. In reply to that assertion he said that the fact that he sent in Crum's name immediately after the assembling of Congress ought to convince the colored people that he seems to stand as he has always stood. He is going to make an important utterance on the subject in his address in New York City on Lincoln's Birthday, and I am very anxious that he say the proper thing and refrain from saying anything that will be harmful.

Regarding colored men in office, I think his general policy is going to be to put more colored men in office in the Northern states and fewer in the South. That does not mean, as I understand him, that he is going to remove colored men who are now giving satisfaction in the South, but his new appointments will be largely confined to the Northern states where the Negro vote is more potent in national elections.

Regarding the activity and hopes of the Lily Whites and others who masquerade under that banner, we have several illustrations of it right here in Alabama. While that element is sleeping or seemingly dead, it pops up its head whenever there is the least hope of recognition, but in anything I may say to him or write him I shall certainly keep in mind the views which you have so clearly expressed. My own opinion is that he is going to make no change in his attitude whatever toward the race.

I do not know what your own individual opinion is regarding the Platt bill recently introduced in Congress, but I have no hesitation in saying to you that I am opposed to it. It will accomplish no good for the black man in the South. It virtually says to the Southern states that if they will give up one or two of their representatives in congress that they can have the privilege of disfranchising all the colored people; besides, the passage of such a bill will be legal recognition and endorsement of the right of the Southern states to draw the color line at the ballot box, a matter which the Southern states themselves have never dared to come out and admit in their new constitutions, while of course they have drawn the line in the administration of the law. Take a state like Texas where the Negro vote has never been seriously questioned, the Platt bill virtually says that if that state will give up one of its 18 representatives the colored man can be disfranchised, and if such a practice will get root in the South very soon it would spread to the border states like West Virginia and Indiana where the states could give up one or two representatives with practically no loss to the white man. Largely for the reasons mentioned, I think you will find that the President will oppose the Platt bill. Some relief is necessary, but I am quite sure that this is not the measure.

Wishing you the compliments of the season, I am, Yours very truly,

Booker T. Washington

TLS Con. 1 BTW Papers DHU. A press copy is in Con. 3, BTW Papers, DLC.

[1] Lyons had written urging BTW to use his influence with the President to persuade him to concede nothing to the lily whites. He estimated that four-fifths of the votes for Roosevelt in the cotton states were cast by blacks. (Con. 25, BTW Papers, DLC.)

To Theodore Roosevelt

Tuskegee, Alabama. December 27, 1904

Personal

My Dear Mr. President: I write you on two points. First, it may interest you to know that, with probably three exceptions, every Negro paper in the United States has spoken out against the Platt bill, that is against reduction of Southern representation, as proposed by the terms of that bill.

Second, would it not be possible to send Mr. Tebbetts[1] to some foreign country as a Consul, or something of that kind, and thus provide the way for settling the muddle in this state? He is a young man without family, and could easily leave Mobile I understand.

Enclosed I send you a clipping from the Boston Transcript written by Hon. T. G. Bush[2] of Alabama, perhaps one of the strongest white men in the state, in which he gives his opinion concerning the kind of appointments you have made in Alabama. More and more I am sure this kind of thing is going to come to the surface. Yours very truly,

Booker T. Washington

TLS Theodore Roosevelt Papers DLC.

[1] William Frye Tebbetts, born in New York City in 1872, settled in Alabama after service in the Spanish-American War. In December 1900 President McKinley appointed him collector of customs of the port of Mobile. Tebbetts was prominent among Alabama Republicans, organizing the Mobile Republican Club and later serving on a Mobile rivers and harbors committee.

[2] Thomas Greene Bush (1847–1909), an Alabama merchant, manufacturer, and railroad magnate. He was the first president of the Mobile Chamber of Commerce (1884) and founder and lifelong president of the Mobile & Birmingham Railroad. He had interests in other railroads and in several coal and iron companies. In 1907 President Roosevelt appointed him as a representative of the South to the "Foundation for the Promotion of Industrial Peace."

To John Wesley Edward Bowen

[Tuskegee, Ala.] Dec. 27th, 1904

PERSONAL AND CONFIDENTIAL

My dear Dr. Bowen: When I agreed sometime ago to write an article for your magazine for publication during the year, I had no idea of any change of your attitude towards me and the work of this Institution at that time. So far as my own experience and observation are concerned, you and I have thoroughly understood each other, and I think you have appreciated my position. I certainly have both appreciated and respected yours, but the general tone of the magazine for which you are responsible, as senior editor, lately is so surprising in its attitude toward me that I am really at a loss as to how to proceed.

In order that you may get some idea of what I have in mind, I send you copy of a letter just received from a Northern friend.[1] Many others have written me almost to the same identical effect. I do not wish to give this letter anything like a personal tone, but I believe that it is well for us to be entirely frank with each other. The magazine undoubtedly has sought recently, to cast unwarranted slurs at me and the organizations with which I may be affiliated. I refer now of course, to the editorial of some time ago, on the Business League. If one is disposed to cavil of course the query can well be addressed, how do you know that the insinuations and slurs are meant for you? My friends entire have recognized in the references referred to, that they were meant for me, and I myself, am perfectly frank to say that I have been inclined to believe that the paragraphs referred to by my friend were meant for no other than me.

I do not believe that a magazine that makes pretentions to being a high class one, would permit writing like this to appear in its columns, and I believe that your readers will be inclined with me to agree to the same opinion.

I do not have to apologize for myself, for the position I have maintained with reference to your writings. I have only time now to ask you the following:

Do you know a single Negro in the history of the whole South, who has for two years, borne the curses of the entire Southern white people for standing up for principle and asserting his rights as a citizen in accepting the hospitality when offered, of a gentleman with whom he had a right to dine? I would ask one other question: Do you know of any other colored man who has stood up for the political rights of the Negro amid the abuse and curses of the Southern white people to the extent that I have during the past two years? My check book will show that I have spent at least four thousand dollars in cash, out of my own pocket, during this same period, in advancing the rights of the black man. If necessary, I could give you the details as to the expenditure of this money. Very truly yours,

[Booker T. Washington]

TLp Con. 26 BTW Papers DLC.

1 Probably excerpts from the letter of Roscoe Conkling Simmons, Dec. 13, 1904, above.

From James H. Hayes

Richmond Va., Dec. 27th, 1904

Dear Mr. Washington: As I am about to press another case through the courts, with the hope of obtaining a decision upon the question of Negro Disfranchisement, and feeling the need of good counsel and advice, I send you the following lines.

About three weeks ago, upon invitation from the Committee of the Republican Club of New York, six in number, headed by former U.S. Senator, Warner Miller, together with Mr. Cummings of Baltimore, we spent more than an hour at the White House, discussing the question with the President. I feel certain that some action will be taken in the new Congress, but we, as a people, certainly do not want the question settled under the 14th Amendment by the cutting down of Southern Representation. I think this the most dangerous proposition relative to Negro citizenship that could be enforced.

But as something is going to be done, ought not the Negro to take the initiative, as far as he can, in shaping the way in which that something is done?

Fate has been against me seemingly, since election day, and as much as I have desired, we have not crossed each others paths. A suggestion has been thrown out of a conference at Washington during the week of March the 4th – not a large nor a public conference, but a selected and private one.

We think that some active lobby work ought to be done, and that conferences with such Congressmen, as Messrs. Morrell,[1] Crumpacker and Keifer[2] ought to be had and an attempt made to turn the tide of congressional legislation from the 14th to the 15th Amendment.

Knowing full well your position as to publicity, permit me to say that I am not writing for publicity of any kind, but simply to see if you will not in this (to my mind) critical time, lend us your wisdom, experience, and personal influence to set the current of legislation in the right channel. I am not even writing this letter for the purpose of getting a reply so that I can quote you even in private, but to enlist your powerful aid.

I hope to be in New York about the middle of January, and as I have not the slightest idea as to your whereabouts, I send this to Tuskegee.

With the hope that your Xmas has been pleasant and that God will spare you to us, many and many New Years yet to come, I am, Very Respectfully,

Jas. H. Hayes

TLS Con. 3 BTW Papers DLC. Written on stationery of the National Negro Suffrage League.

[1] Edward de Veaux Morrell (1863–1917) was a Republican congressman from Pennsylvania from 1900 to 1907. He was a member of the Philadelphia Board of Education from 1912 to 1916.

[2] Joseph Warren Keifer (1836–1932), Republican congressman from Ohio from 1905 to 1911.

To James H. Hayes

[Tuskegee, Ala.] December 31, 1904

Personal

Dear Mr. Hayes: Replying briefly to your kind letter of recent date I would say that I am planning to be in New York and vicinity during the greater part of March and April, and I shall be very glad to see you and talk these matters over in a more extended manner.

While I have not as yet said so publicly, I do not mind letting you know that I do not favor the Platt bill. It is a very dangerous measure in my opinion so far as the rights of the Negro are concerned. It virtually says to the Southern states that if you will give up one or two of your representatives we will give you a free hand to disfranchise all Negroes regardless of their qualifications. Further, it goes into a state like Texas where the question of the Negro's voting providing he pays his poll tax, has never been seriously questioned and says to that state if you will give up one of your 18 representatives you can disfranchise all the colored people. In a word, for the first time in our national legislatures it proposes to enact the color line into law. If such a practice becomes common in the South it will be very easy to extend it to states like Indiana and West Virginia where they can disfranchise all the colored people by losing almost no representation in the lower house of Congress. The bill is almost vicious in my opinion. I do not believe that anything could be gained by a conference in Washington. The entire atmosphere of Washington is of such a nature that nothing, in my opinion, could be accomplished except the conference were confined to a half-dozen. New York, Philadelphia or some other city I think would be a much better place.

My own feeling on the subject of the enforcement of the constitution is that we ought to insist upon Congress taking up each individual case and each individual state and wherever the constitution has been violated by a member being sent to that body through fraud the individual or state should be made to suffer the consequences. If that were done consistently we would have a different state of affairs.

One other point ought to be kept constantly before our people, and you are in a good position to do this. If you will study the constitutions in the South carefully you will find that almost as many colored people disfranchise themselves as the white people disfranchise, that is by not paying their poll taxes or by not qualifying themselves to vote under the old constitutions or under the new constitutions. I think you will find in states like Tennessee and Texas where there is nothing but the poll tax qualifications that at least half of the colored people could not vote today because they have not paid their poll taxes. Even right here in this county where we have succeeded in getting an unusually large number of colored people upon the permanent voting list, it is almost impossible to get any large proportion of them to pay their poll taxes. I believe that more of our effort and energy ought to be turned in the direction of arousing our own people to perform their duty in regard to the suffrage and in regard to representation upon juries, but, as I have said, I shall talk matters over further with you when I see you.

Yours truly,

Booker T. Washington

TLpS Con. 3 BTW Papers DLC.

To Theodore Roosevelt

Tuskegee, Alabama. December 31, 1904

Personal

My dear Mr. President: Herein I return the copy of the address which you sent me. I take for granted that you have purposely omitted any reference to the reduction of Southern representation. You will recall that in the address which you read to me you covered that subject. I have gone carefully over this address several times and have taken the liberty also of letting one or two intelligent colored people whose views are more radical than mine read it, and I do not see anything in it which I would have changed. It seems to me it covers the case fully. It is much stronger in many ways than the address which you read to me. I am sure that it will satisfy and help the colored people and the Northern white people and the sensible Southern white people. The only element that will be disposed to object will be the professional politicians in the South who for thirty years have used the Negro question and the cry of "social equality" to frighten and deceive the ignorant white people and keep themselves in office. This class of Southern white people of course do not want to be converted nor satisfied; their stock in trade would be gone from the moment the Negro question disappears.

I thank you sincerely for letting me see this address, and I hope that you will use it on Lincoln's Birthday as I think it is a fitting word to say on that occasion. Yours truly,

Booker T. Washington

TLS Theodore Roosevelt Papers DLC.

From Henry Hugh Proctor

Atlanta, Georgia, Jan. 2, 1905

My dear Mr. Washington, Mr. H. A. Rucker, Prof. W. H. Crogman and myself went over the address[1] carefully to-night. We regard the matter taken up an exceedingly delicate one for him. On the whole we think it a strong statement. We unanimously agreed on the following suggestions:

1. On the top of page "E," we would insert the words "moral" and "intellectual" after the word "social," making the sentence to read: "But the prime requisite is social, moral, intellectual and industrial uplifting." We think that would make a completer statement and avoid ambiguity raised by the word social in view of its double meaning.

2. In the sentence following the one just referred to on the same page we would omit these words: "Arrogance and insolence, laziness and shiftlessness these and above all vice of every kind." We would substitute the following so that the whole sentence would read: "Internal vice is capable of more harm to the black race than all acts of oppression of white men put together." To make the

statement he does while true would likely be construed as his giving assent to the possession of these traits as a whole by the black race. The one we suggest would be an abstract statement which could not be construed.

3. The other suggestion is that in the fourth line from the bottom on the same page where the question of social equality is referred to that instead of making it a matter for the locality to settle make it a matter for the individual to settle. That is the position he took and the country has sustained him in it. This statement would be weaker than his action. Dr. Bradley[2] of this city has stated in a public address and printed in the Constitution with approval that social equality is an individual matter. We believe that he can afford to say that.

H. H. P.

TLIr Copy Con. 305 BTW Papers DLC.

1 Theodore Roosevelt's Lincoln Day address in New York City.

2 Henry Stiles Bradley, born in Jackson County, Ga., in 1869, was a biology professor and vice-president of Emory College from 1890 to 1901. A Southern Methodist minister, he was pastor of Trinity Church in Atlanta from 1901 to 1905, of St. John's Church in St. Louis from 1905 to 1909, and of Piedmont Congregational Church in Worcester, Mass., after 1909.

To Ruth Standish Bowles Baldwin

Tuskegee, Alabama. Jan. 3, 1905

Our hearts are bou[n]d in inexpressible sorrow and sympathy with you and all the family. We have all been made better and we believe more useful, because of have [having] been permitted to touch such a strong and pure life. The inspiration of his faith and example will always remain with us and make us all work harder to complete the work which was so near his heart.

I leave for New York tonight.

Booker T. Washington

ALdS Con. 873 BTW Papers DLC.

A Press Release by Emmett Jay Scott

Tuskegee, Ala. Jan. 3, 1905

The death of Mr. William H. Baldwin, Jr., President of the Long Island Railroad, at his home Locust Valley, New York, early this morning brought acute sorrow to the Tuskegee Normal and Industrial Institute for Negroes located here. Mr. Baldwin for many years has been a trustee of the school and one of Booker T. Washington's staunchest friends and supporters in carrying on this work, in addition to holding trusteeship in the General and Southern Education Boards. Principal Washington left Tuskegee tonight for New York to be present at the funeral later in the week. Referring to Mr. Baldwin's death he said: "This news brings inexpressible sorrow to me personally, and to the officers, teachers and students of the Tuskegee Institute. Mr. Baldwin was interested in the whole cause of Southern education and did all that he could to advance the best interests of every child in the South who needs educational advantages. The chief legacy of the Tuskegee Institute is in having been permitted to touch so pure and strong a life. The inspiration of his faith and example will always remain with us and make us work harder and harder to complete the work that was so near his heart."

Emmett J. Scott

TLpSr Con. 305 BTW Papers DLC. A fragment of a draft in Scott's hand is in Con. 293, BTW Papers, DLC.

From Charles William Eliot

Cambridge, [Mass.] January 5, 1905

Dear Mr. Washington: There is a pleasant club in Boston called the Tavern Club, composed of professional men, authors, musicians, artists, etc., who like to give private dinners at their small club-house to public men who are visiting Boston, and particularly to writers, speakers, teachers, and artists. These dinners are entirely private, although from a hundred to a hundred and fifty persons sit down at the tables. There is some speaking after dinner, and often music or a play. Now, the Tavern Club would like to give you a dinner some evening in February or March when you are to be in this part of the country. Could you accept such an invitation? Major Henry L. Higginson is President of the Club. The good effects on Tuskegee would be only indirect; for the Club is not a place for raising money directly. So far this year they have entertained Professor Barrett Wendell and Mr. James Bryce. The Club is non-political, and its membership is rather younger than that of most clubs. Sincerely yours,

Charles W. Eliot

TLS Con. 301 BTW Papers DLC.

To Bradley Gilman

Manhattan Hotel, New York, January 9, 1905

My dear Mr. Gilman: I thank you for your kind letter which I have just had time to read. Both Mr. Villard and Dr. Courtney told me about your sensible and helpful address, and I thank you for what you said.

I have it on pretty good authority, that the persons having in charge the Literary Society, have forbidden Mr. Trotter to use my name and that may account for his course on the evening you were there.

It is very difficult to tell just how to deal with him. Among the rank and file of our people, I am sure he has no influence, especially in Boston, but he has among a certain element.

Just before I left Boston, on Sunday evening with almost no previous notice, I went into a colored church, in Cambridge to speak, after my meeting in a white church and notwithstanding it was the Sabbath day, I have seldom received such an ovation and hearty congratulations as from the members of that church. This is my experience throughout the country.

I think you can help the cause by strengthening Mr. Alexander's paper any way you can. I hope you will have a conference with him.

I do not feel that Trotter's paper can live much longer, unless it changes its policy, by having no regard for truth in its statements. A friend told me that in one of its recent issues, it made the statement that I was not a registered voter; the fact of the matter is, I am a registered voter and cast my vote for Roosevelt within an hour after the polls opened and I have always voted in the state.

I shall hope to see you while in Boston and talk matters over with you. Very truly yours,

[Booker T. Washington]

TLc Con. 302 BTW Papers DLC.

Roscoe Conkling Simmons to Emmett Jay Scott

New York Jan. 12, 1904 [1905]

My dear Friend: I want to tell you what a magnificent audience, both in numbers and character, greeted Dr. Washington yesterday afternoon at the Church of the Messiah, where a memorial service for the late Mr. Baldwin was held. The Church was really packed, and standing room at four could not be had. Perhaps as the New York Sun said, so many celebrated people had never gathered at one time on such an occasion, in New York. I think the most impressive thing about the whole gathering, were the colored men and women who were present. There were at least 150 representative men and women of the race present, who came to show their appreciation for the labours of Mr. Baldwin in their behalf, and to hear Dr. Washington pronounce their eulogy.

The speakers were Felix Adler, Dr. Washington[,] Minot J. Savage[1] and Dr. Thomas Colyer.[2] Mr. Adler and Mr. Washington made the principal addresses. I have never heard Mr. Washington so eloquent, so soul-inspired, so simple. The audience gave him almost breathless silence.

I might mention that Mr. Carnegie sat in what we call "The Amen Corner." H. H. Rogers,[3] St. Clair McKelway, most of New York's Railway Presidents, Seth Low, Rob't C. Ogden, Lyman Abbott, Walter Page — in fact New York's best men and women crowded the church, in order to show how highly they appreciated Mr. Baldwin's life, and how deeply they mourn his loss.

I hope you are well. Yours truly

Roscoe C. Simmons

ALS Con. 30 BTW Papers DLC.

[1] Minot Judson Savage (1841–1918), a Unitarian clergyman, was a pastor of the Church of the Messiah in New York City from 1896 to 1906.

[2] Robert Collyer (1823–1912), a Unitarian clergyman and pastor at the Church of the Messiah.

[3] Henry Huddleston Rogers (1840–1909) was an early oil refiner whose company was incorporated by John D. Rockefeller into the Standard Oil Company in 1874. Rogers was a technical expert in the oil industry, designing the machinery for separating naphtha from crude oil. He was also an organizational genius, and he used his wealth from Standard Oil to invest in natural gas, traction, copper, railroad, and insurance companies. While a ruthless businessman in the "robber baron" tradition, Rogers in private life was an imaginative philanthropist, paying for the education of Helen Keller and saving Mark Twain from financial ruin. BTW knew him in his more benign role, and after Rogers's death wrote that whenever he visited Rogers, the philanthropist would open his desk drawer and hand BTW a large sum in cash. At the end of his life Rogers was constructing the Virginian Railroad into the West Virginia coal regions, and when the railroad was completed BTW made a speaking tour of the towns along the route. See An Article in the New York *Evening Post*, May 29, 1909, below, vol. 10.

From George Foster Peabody

New York City. Jan. 16th, 1905

Dear Mr. Washington: I hope my telegrams did not disturb you. Some things I heard gave me the impression that Mr. Carnegie might be amenable to some influence from you just now but later I heard that he intimated to Mr. Villard that he did not now care to consider Tuskegee further which was in line with my own idea as to what Mr. Carnegie's present thought would be. Therefore I now think that it would be harmful to approach Mr. Carnegie just yet although I do think that ultimately, perhaps later in the year, a strong presentation might be made to Mr. Carnegie to see if he could not consider adding $1,400,000. bonds to the $600,000. which he has already given, making his total gift $2,000,000. which would really relieve you. However, as I say, this is a matter for the future.

I trust that you are having satisfactory results from your trip and hope that the strenuous life of your travel is not too fatiguing.

I am sorry myself to be in such need of rest that it seems wise, on all accounts that I go to my place at Lake George until Thanksgiving Day. I go up Wednesday to come down only once in a while for something special. Very truly yours,

George Foster Peabody

TLS Con. 30 BTW Papers DLC.

Emmett Jay Scott to James Weldon Johnson[1]

[Tuskegee, Ala.] January 18, 1905

My dear Friend: At some time in the near future, date not yet announced, President Roosevelt is planning to visit Tuskegee, and we want to sing for him when he does come, your song, "You're all Right Teddy." We ought to have sixty-five copies of the song.[2] Please let me know for how much you will let us have this number.

Thanking you in advance, and with cordial regards to your brother[3] and Mr. Cole,[4] I am, Very truly yours,

Emmett J Scott

TLpS Con. 303 BTW Papers DLC.

1 James Weldon Johnson (1871–1938) was a member of the Talented Tenth who joined BTW's camp, and after the Tuskegean's death became a staff member of the NAACP. Born into the middle class in Jacksonville, Fla., he graduated from Atlanta University in 1894 and returned as principal of Jacksonville's black high school. In the same period he edited a short-lived newspaper and passed the Florida bar examination in 1898. Johnson also became a successful songwriter. For Lincoln's birthday in 1900 he composed "Lift Every Voice and Sing," later known as "The Negro National Anthem."

In 1902 Johnson moved to New York as the partner of his brother Rosamond and Bob Cole in the production of musical shows. He was also active in politics as the protégé of Charles W. Anderson. He was treasurer of the New York Colored Republican Club in the election year 1904, and its president in 1905. Under BTW's influence, he joined the NNBL but refused Du Bois's invitation to join the Niagara Movement.

As a reward for Johnson's loyalty to the party and to the Tuskegee Machine, BTW and Anderson pressed the State Department to give him an appointment. He became U.S. consul at Puerto Cabello, Venezuela (1906–8), and Corinto, Nicaragua (1909–12), but was frustrated in his efforts to secure an appointment in Europe. (Levy, *James Weldon Johnson*, 102–19.)

While a consul Johnson wrote the anonymous novel, *The Autobiography of an Ex-Colored Man* (1912). When Woodrow Wilson became president, Johnson resigned his consular post, wrote editorials for the New York *Age* for a year, joined the NAACP in 1915, and became its field agent in 1916. From 1920 to 1930 he was the executive secretary of the NAACP and the leader of its lobbying effort for the Dyer anti-lynching bill. Outstanding among Johnson's many works were *God's Trombones* (1927), *Black Manhattan* (1930), and *Along This Way* (1933).

[2] Johnson sent seventy-five copies and offered to make a manuscript copy, autographed, to be presented to Roosevelt at the time of his visit. (Johnson to Scott, Jan. 25, 1905, Con. 303, BTW Papers, DLC.) Roosevelt expressed his enthusiastic approval of the song through Scott. (Levy, *James Weldon Johnson*, 102.)

[3] John Rosamond Johnson (1873–1954) was a popular vaudevillian and a member of the songwriting team of Bob Cole and the Johnson brothers.

[4] Robert "Bob" Cole (d. 1911) contributed toward the transformation of the stereotypical, Negro-dialect "coon songs" into more genteel, ragtime songs.

To Hugh Mason Browne

Tuskegee Institute, Alabama. January 23, 1905

Personal

My dear Mr. Browne: I take for granted that the enclosed letter is a copy of one sent to all the members of the Committee including Mr. Grimke and Prof. Du Bois; I am very anxious that they see that their resignations are not affecting our work.

Now as to future work, I am wondering if we could not get up some little newspaper squibs bearing upon the decrease in lynching during the last three or four months. This would tend, I think, to encourage the white and colored people. If I have the facts correctly in my mind, I think you will find that there was no lynching in November, only two in December, and so far none have occurred in January. These figures will have to be verified, however, by direct information from the Chicago Tribune.

I have been much on the train lately and have not been able to keep in touch with you, but I shall hope to do so hereafter. I am to be in Philadelphia during the first week in February and perhaps we can have a conference. Yours truly,

Booker T. Washington

TLS BTW Papers ATT.

To Ruth Standish Bowles Baldwin

[Tuskegee, Ala.] January 24, 1905

My dear Mrs. Baldwin: I have received both of your kind letters, that is the letter of January 15th., and the one of January 19th.

We were very sorry about the bad picture which appeared in one issue of the Student. Mr. Scott had no cut, and so sent to the Atlanta Journal, Mr. Atkinson's paper, supposing they would have a good one and used the one which the Journal people sent.

I have asked Mr. Scott to make a collection of what the colored papers throughout the country have said regarding Mr. Baldwin and shall send it to you. I think you will be surprised, as well as pleased, at the many beautiful references which the colored press has made.

I was very glad to note on the day of the Memorial exercises, that there were so many of the best colored people of New York present.

Mrs. Washington and I are very grateful for the check which you send, and we can think of no better way of using it than in securing as many large photographs of Mr. Baldwin as we can, and placing them in our various public buildings on the grounds. We are very anxious to have our students constantly reminded of his beautiful and helpful face. The small picture which we have in our home, is the one which we like best, and we are going to make an effort to get it enlarged and get as many copies as possible.

We are all delighted with the possibility of your coming here in February, and I hope by all means that you will bring Billy with you. I am very anxious to have our students and teachers see and know him. I have a strong feeling that in a remarkable degree, he is going to take his father's place.

You perhaps know that our Conference takes place on the 22d and 23d of February.

I am planning to be in New York on the 29th 30th and 31st, and shall hope to see you while I am there.

You do not know what a great pleasure it is to have your letters. Very truly yours,

Booker T. Washington

TLpS Con. 27 BTW Papers DLC.

To William Eleroy Curtis[1]

Tuskegee Institute, Alabama. Jan. 24, 1905

Personal

My dear Mr. Curtis: I have received you kind letter of January 21st[2] and I thank you very much for the suggestion which you make. I am especially pleased to know that you are thinking of making a trip in this direction during the spring; we shall be very glad to give you a hearty welcome, and I hope nothing will prevent your coming.

I wonder if you know about the Negro Conference which takes place on the 22d and 23d of February? Enclosed I send you a little slip relating to it. Perhaps you might like to be present on that occasion.

Now in regard to the suggestion of your publishing something concerning my dining with the President. I would state that at present I cannot see my way clear to consent to give out anything in reference to the dinner. I question whether I should do it while Mr. Roosevelt is in the White House. I agree with you for the sake of history that the correct story ought to be told at some time. I might state for your own private information that I have never seen the story published as yet correctly; I wondered how it was possible for so many falsehoods to be concocted concerning one single, to me, unimportant incident. I should be glad, however, to talk the whole matter over with you when I see you.

Mrs. Bruce is now in Mississippi, but I shall let her know what you say when she returns to Tuskegee. Yours truly,

Booker T. Washington

TLS NN-Sc. A press copy is in Con. 299, BTW Papers, DLC.

1 William Eleroy Curtis (1850–1911) had been Washington correspondent of the Chicago *Record-Herald* since 1887. From 1889 to 1893 he was also the first director of the Bureau of American Republics, later called the Pan-American Union. A globe-trotter, he wrote a number of travel books.

2 Curtis had written BTW that as the President was soon to visit the South, "it would be a good thing to publish a correct version of your famous luncheon with him, and explain how you happened to be there that day." If BTW would consent, Curtis said, he would ask Roosevelt also for permission. (Jan. 21, 1905, Con. 299, BTW Papers, DLC.)

Emmett Jay Scott to Wilford H. Smith

[Tuskegee, Ala.] January 25, 1905

My dear Mr. Smith: It is very kind of you to transmit copies of the correspondence with The Voice of the Negro people, and I am glad that the matter has been thrashed out as it has been. It rather shows to them that "The Wizard" has friends who resent the untoward position of that publication.

Please thank Mr. Payton most heartily, for his firmness in this matter. I am sorry to learn that he has been ill. No direct word to that effect has come.

I have brought this whole matter to the Doctor's attention, and he is most grateful to you, and Mr. Payton, for what you have done.

Shall I hear from Mr. Chisum, I shall do all that I can to push any matter along which has your endorsement. Very truly yours,

Emmett

TLpS Con. 307 BTW Papers DLC.

From Bradley Gilman

Boston Mass Jan 25/1905

My dear Mr Washington, I had a long talk last week with Mr Alexander editor of the "Colored Citizen," of this city. He presented the work of his paper mainly. He also went over the situation here in Boston and New England, so far as it is being affected by the "Guardian."

Later, after a talk with Rev. Edward Cummings,[1] of the South Congl. Church, it was agreed by us two that I should write you this letter to ask advice.

I think that you believe that the best and only wise way in which the Guardian's evil work can be met is by making the "Colored Citizen" as good a competing paper as possible.

To do this, money is needed. Now what do you think of the plan of Cummings and myself taking from you a list of a dozen or more generous white men of Boston, and trying to get them interested in backing the "Citizen"?

Incidentally I ask if you feel full confidence in Mr Alexander. He certainly seemed to me intelligent, well educated, discreet, and kindly disposed; but one would wish to be very sure about him and his methods, before enlisting money in his enterprise.

If you favor the plan, will you send a dozen names of men or women, favorably disposed to negro education etc.

If you are to be here before long I would be glad to have you dine with my family, here at above address. Telephone in our suite of rooms.

I suggested to Mr Dole, president of the Twentieth Century Club, that we have Prof. Dubois speak before that club, when he is in Boston. Some of us would like to ask him some questions.

I have heard it asserted strongly that Atlanta University gives money to the "Guardian," thinking that by aiding it to cripple *your* work, more attention and aid will be given *it*. Do you suppose that can be true? Very truly yours

Bradley Gilman

ALS Con. 302 BTW Papers DLC. No enclosures were found with the letter.

[1] Edward Cummings (1861–1926) was minister of the South Congregational Church in Boston from 1900 to 1925. Earlier Cummings had taught sociology at Harvard (1891–1900), and had William Monroe Trotter as a student in 1895.

From Charles Alexander

[Boston, Mass.] January 26, 1905

My dear Dr. Washington: Trotter has sued me on account of the enclosed article. You will remember when and how it was sent to the paper. If you are to be in Boston soon I must see you and talk over this matter. I hope that the enclosed editorial of mine in this week's paper will please you. Sincerely yours,

Charles Alexander

TLS Con. 27 BTW Papers DLC. No enclosures were found with the letter.

To Grace Lathrop Dunham Luling[1]

[Tuskegee, Ala.] January 28, 1905

My dear Madam: I have your letter of some days ago with enclosure of letter from Mr. Sedgwick,[2] and certain inquiries addressed by you to me with the suggestion that you would like comment upon each of them from me.

Mr. J. N. Calloway, a member of our faculty, spent three years or more in Africa as the head of a party which went out from Tuskegee to introduce cotton raising in the German possession of Togo. After consultation with Mr. Calloway I desire to submit the following answers to the inquiries sent by you:

Mr. Calloway observes that from his experience in Africa, he can see no very great difference between the native problem there and the Negro problem in America, and that the answers to the six questions herewith submitted are based upon the recognition of that fact:

(1) Since the blacks are to live under the English Government, they should be taught to love and revere that government better than any other institution. To teach them this, they should receive their education and training for citizenship from or through the government. It is not always true that the Missions teach respect for the rulers in power.

(2) There is no universal language among the tribes of Africa, and therefore they could have no books that would be of general use to the several tribes in the colonies. They should be given a language that will open up to them a knowledge of the world they live in and of western civilization. No other language will do this so well as the English language. Aside from this, all the laws and business of the colony are to be in English form and by English methods.

(3) The State should not only give a common school education but an industrial training that will fit them to go out into this rich country and be skilled laborers in agriculture, mining and the trades.

(4) As far as native men become educated and refined they should be shown, in a social way, a proper recognition of their worth and in civil standing be the equal of Europeans. To undertake to settle

this problem in any other way means, eventually, more or less civil discord.

(5) The tribal system of government should gradually be replaced by an allegiance directly to the government of the land. Some native blacks have already gone to the United States for an education and when they return to their homes in Africa they will not be satisfied to give their allegiance to the old time superstitious chiefs.

(6) Experience shows that the black, as other men, work better and more profitably when induced to this labor by reward and it is voluntarily performed. If proper inducements are offered these people they will labor more and more as their wants are increased by education.

Thanking you for affording me the opportunity to be of service in this matter, I am, Yours very truly,

Booker T. Washington

TLpSr Con. 303 BTW Papers DLC.

1 Grace Lathrop Dunham Luling (b. 1876), a New York socialite married to the Englishman Theodore William Luling, was among those who heard BTW when he spoke in Stockbridge, Mass., during the summer of 1904.

2 Alexander Sedgwick. The letter was actually from Edmund Beale Sargant (1855–1938), director of education for the Transvaal and the Orange River Colony after the Boer War. He had written to Grace Lathrop Luling in November 1904, asking advice about the best course of development for "native" schools, and Mrs. Luling had sent the inquiry to BTW.

From Warren Stone Reese, Jr.[1]

Montgomery, Feb. 1, 1905

Dear Sir: I am forwarding to you by this day's mail the argument of the Attorney General of the United States in the now famous peonage case, this case is similar to those we have pending in this district, and the result of the decision in the Clyatt case[2] settles the question whether we will be able to proceed further in this district in the prosecution of those parties who have already been indicted for a similar offense, and those we intend to indict at this term of Court. I know that the Attorney General is taking a very great interest in these peonage cases. In fact it is my information that he has stated that he considered the Clyatt case the most important matter now before the Supreme Court of the United States – I thought that the reading of these briefs would throw much light upon this subject that a layman ordinarily would not be in possession of.

I am about to embark upon the prosecution for the lynching of a colored man (by name of Edmund Bell) at Sardis, Ala. on the 6th of August, 1904. This place Sardis is only a few miles from Selma the home of Senators Pettus[3] and Morgan. Two terms of the State Grand Jury have been held at Selma one closing Saturday last, and neither of them found any indictments against the parties who lynched Bell. The facts are about like this: Bell was charged with the murder of a colored woman, and three constables, Stanfield, Cherry and Ransom started from Sardis to convey him to the Selma jail. These three constables claim that as they were passing through a clump of woods, they were overpowered by a mob of negroes who took Bell from them and lynched him in their presence. It has since been shown, I think, conclusively that it was a scheme between the white constables and the colored mob that this should be done as it was done. The strength of this case is that no charge can be made that it was a scheme or that it was done because the parties accused were negroes, for if any are guilty the whites and the negroes are both guilty. I know that a great hue and cry will be raised in the State in reference to this matter, claiming that it is an interference with State's rights etc., and that when the matter of my reappointment comes up January next that there will be made a violent attack on it, but I consider that it is my duty to move in this matter because in my humble opinion it is right. The State Grand Jury has had the right twice to indict and refused to take advantage of it, and therefore, it is the duty of the other co-ordinate branch of this great Government to take some action under the authority given to it under the fourteenth amendment. I know that attacks personal and political will commence to be made upon me as soon as this matter is known, and I must of necessity look to those who feel friendly to the fight that I have made to protect me, because in a short while with the methods that are going on in this State the regular organization will be disbanded and every man will have to strike out for himself. I say this because it is as clear to me as the noon day sun that there is a plan on foot among the Democrats to get the President to replace Republican office holders by Democrats, and in no district is this more apparent than the Middle District of Alabama. At the present writing there is one Colonel Mosby[4] (of Confederate fame) who is here and by his actions, if not his words has claimed that he is sent here by the administration to get the standing of acceptable Democrats to replace Republicans in case Republicans are not *fit*. That means that all sorts and kinds of accusations are to be made upon Republican office holders to make them withdraw.

It is my intention to be in Washington on Monday next. I would appreciate it very much if you would write a personal letter to the President on receipt of this in my behalf, letting him know of the good fight I have made in these peonage cases. I would prefer that the President should not know that I have made such a request, as of necessity that would weaken it. I would be glad if you would reply to this letter and address the reply to the Hotel Hamilton, Washington, D.C. Yours truly,

W. S. Reese

TLS Con. 4 BTW Papers DLC.

1 Warren Stone Reese, Jr. (1866–1953), was a U.S. district attorney in Alabama from 1897 to 1905 and from 1909 to 1913. He led the exposé and prosecution of peonage practices in Coosa and Tallapoosa counties in the summer of 1903 and also publicized the extent of peonage in other parts of the state. For a further discussion of Reese's role in the Alabama peonage cases, see Daniel, *Shadow of Slavery*.

2 Samuel M. Clyatt, owner of a turpentine plantation in Georgia, was the defendant in the first test case of the federal peonage statute of 1867 in Clyatt *v.* United States 197 U.S. 207. In February 1901 Clyatt traveled to Florida to retrieve several black laborers who had formerly worked for him and who, he claimed, had run away while owing him money. He forced two men at gunpoint to return with him to Georgia. To federal prosecutors this act of compelling persons to work because of debt violated the peonage statute. In 1904 the U.S. Supreme Court overturned a lower court conviction of Clyatt on grounds that the Justice Department had failed to prove that a condition of peonage existed before Clyatt forced the men back to Georgia. The Supreme Court did, however, uphold the constitutionality of the 1867 peonage statute, which paved the way for other peonage cases. (Daniel, *Shadow of Slavery*, 4–18.)

3 Edmund Winston Pettus (1821–1907), U.S. senator from Alabama (1897–1907), a Democrat and Confederate brigadier general.

4 John Singleton Mosby (1833–1916), a Confederate military hero, returned to his law practice in Virginia after the Civil War and joined the Republican party in the Grant era. He held several appointive federal offices, including that of attorney in the Department of Justice from 1904 to 1910.

Julius Robert Cox to Emmett Jay Scott

New York, February 1, 1905

Personal.

Dear Mr. Scott, Mr. Washington has gone to Maine, leaving me here to look after a few matters in N.Y. He returns here Friday, leaving immediately for Philadelphia.

What I wanted to write you about is this, I do not think my views are in accord with Mr. Washington's therefore its personal.

Last Saturday we were in Washington, among those present at the depot to see Mr. Washington away, were Messrs Dancy, Lyons, Terrell, McKinlay, (Chas. Anderson was there, but not in their crowd) after it was discovered that we could not leave as we intended, a dinner was proposed; that Washington crowd fairly fell over each other making the arrangements: to make a long story short, when the time came to settle, it would have amused you to see each one equally as active in maneuvering, "to get out from under." I was most thoroughly disgusted with the whole "push." I do not include McKinlay in that crowd.

Of course you know what a thorough-bred Anderson is, also Wetmore,[1] they wanted to settle the bill between them, but the Governor, good hearted as he is, would not listen to such an arrangement and settled the whole thing himself.

Now of course there are "methods" and there are "methods," but putting aside all the finer reasons of politics, and obligations that these men, if they are men, have placed themselves under to the Dr. I think Mr. Washington is too big, for that, hungry set of office-hunting, blood suckers, to pander to their, or for their influence. Then the feelings of the desire to act as hosts should have played some part, and perhaps it would had we been among men.

I think Wetmore was about as sore as I was, while neither of [them] said anything, excepting to each other.

There they were, all day Saturday, hunting Mr. Washington like they were half-crazy to "see him just a minute" only to return their splendid appreciation of him, by allowing him, (a man whose feet they should not allow to touch the ground, while among them), to feed them.

In the gutter-language, they are a set of "peaches" and personally, I don't care whether I ever see them again.

I guess you are thinking I have lots to learn in the game of politics, but while that may be true, I hope I shall never get so deeply lost in its meshes as to lose all sense of chivalry or just plain, common every-day decency.

I trust every thing in Tuskegee is humming along. Very truly yours,

Julius R Cox

TLS Con. 556 BTW Papers DLC.

[1] J. Douglas Wetmore, born in 1870, was a lawyer in Jacksonville, Fla., from 1898 to around 1908. In 1905 he served on the Jacksonville City Council. He frequently praised Jacksonville as fairer to blacks than most southern cities, but after 1904 he sought an opportunity to leave it. After supporting Theodore Roosevelt and the Republican ticket, he tried unsuccessfully to secure appointment as consul in Santo Domingo. He kept BTW informed of affairs in Florida and was a member of the NNBL, but he also sought support from W. E. B. Du Bois and other critics of Washington. During 1906 he prepared two test cases of the Jim Crow car laws in Jacksonville and Pensacola. At about this time he turned against Roosevelt's political leadership, and he was one of the speakers at a Brownsville protest meeting in Washington in 1907. Moving to New York City in 1908, Wetmore sought opportunistically to retain the favor of BTW while associating also with his enemies and, according to reports, passing for white in his social life. Washington and his New York lieutenant, Charles W. Anderson, seized every opportunity to block Wetmore's efforts to secure political appointments.

From Charles Alexander

Boston, Mass., February 6th, 1905

My Dear Doctor Washington: I have hesitated for sometime to write you this letter for many reasons. I did not like the idea of calling to your attention matters that would have a tendency to make you feel uncomfortable, and for this reason I have delayed writing about a very important matter which I have discovered here in Boston. I think you ought to know that a certain element of Bostonians, the so-called four hundred, have organized very strongly to kill the influence of the Boston Colored Citizen. They have circulated all sorts of reports concerning the paper and have made it impossible in many instances for us to secure news items that would be of real value to the paper. More over, the suit which Trotter brought against me concerns the enclosed article.[1] I do not know that you remember how this article came to my office, but if you will ask Mr. Scott he will inform you that it was sent by him from New York, and that I altered it so that there would be no personal reference in it. I did not use either the name of Trotter or the name of his paper, and my lawyer informs me that there is no chance of his winning except by a preponderance of evidence and by a preponderance of witnesses. Now, I have absolutely no witnesses in this particular case and it is giving me great concern to know how I am going to secure evidence to show that everything stated in the article is absolutely true. Of course, I realize that I must go to New York and see General Clarkson personally in order to verify the statement concerning the interview, and there ought to be a few others who know about the matter who would be willing to testify in the case. I hope you will see the necessity of helping in this matter. We cannot win out unless we have funds with which to win out. I am doing a very good business at this time but the money which I earn in my printing business is consumed in the paper. The paper is paying now about 25% of its actual cost. It is increasing steadily in circulation and in efficiency as a news medium, but the advertising patronage has not increased and is not likely to increase except I can find someone who will work steadily on that particular department, and no one is willing to do that unless I offer good pay at the very start. I need immediately about two hundred and fifty dollars ($250) to fight this fellow to a finish. I am sure that if I can tell my lawyer that I have funds at my command to meet the demands of the court, that there will be no trouble of swamping him. I have not purchased the cylinder press which I proposed for the reason that I could not do so owing to the obligations which must be promptly met in order to save my honor and name among people who are known to and by this fellow Trotter.

You probably know that they are getting up a great banquet here in honor of Professor Du Bois of Atlanta. I thought at first that I would accept their invitation and subscribe two dollars and attend the thing in order to see just what would be said, but upon second thought I decided not to go and have held up the letter which I wrote this morning. I do not think that I can advance our interest by subscribing even five cents to the other fellow's scheme. Professor Du Bois wrote me a very ugly letter recently which showed a spirit not at all becoming a man of his great experience and large scholarship. Again, I very much fear that if I attended the affair I would come in contact with Trotter and he would say something to insult me, and if he insulted me, I am very sure that I could not refrain from striking back as is my nature, and in thus I would bring disgrace upon myself and upon those who might be associated with me. I do not want to be the cause of any commotion or sensation in Boston and will not be unless circumstances arise over which I can have absolutely no control.

In the last issue of the Guardian Rev. Mr. Callis[2] seems to have jumped over the fence suddenly. He borrowed from my office a cut of his church and another cut and had the same run in the paper, and the only excuse he offered to his congregation for so doing was that we ought to forget and forgive our enemies according to the good christian view point. I sent a man to see him personally about the matter and the excuse he offered him was that there was a certain element in his church which had refrained from giving the church such support as it required of them. I very much fear that he has taken a step in the wrong direction. A step once taken in the wrong direction usually leads further from the goal. It is my belief that he is somewhat disappointed because I was not able to secure your services for a lecture at his church during the summer. To me personally he is very cordial and has been sending considerable work to the office, but Trotter's gang is so well organized and he has so many good looking young women working in the interest of his paper that I very much fear that a man of gifts and proclivities cannot resist the wiles of a pretty woman's smiles. I do not know that you quite understand this sort of language but if you were here I could talk with you freely and you would quite understand, something like what I have hinted at is the trouble. I have had many complimentary letters lately from some very distinguished white men in this community concerning my recent editorial regarding your visit to the West. Not a few have said that it is one of the best estimates of a great man that they had ever read. I received a beautiful letter from Elbert Hubbard, the editor of the Philistine in which he also commends the Citizen and agrees that my estimate of you is about as accurate as anything he had read.

I hope that you will give this letter your personal attention and will let me hear from you promptly. If you are in New York soon let me know. I must see you and talk it all over. I very much fear that vigorous protests are not being made here in Boston against the workings of Trotter and his element which means harm for us. I could explain more if I could see you, but long letters are not read and rarely digested. Sincerely yours,

Charles Alexander

Send what money you can to help in this matter. I am working hard to hold up the dignity and honor of the *cause.*

TLS Con. 27 BTW Papers DLC.

[1] Enclosed was a clipping of a newspaper article headlined "Doing the Circus Act," a "Special Correspondence" from New York on Sept. 26, 1904. It reported that the editor of "the Colored Democratic newspaper published in Boston" came to New York and "sought an interview with General James S. Clarkson at the Custom House and for two hours and more pleaded for the General's influence and power to secure a seat on the Roosevelt bandwagon, pledging good behavior in the future and renunciation of past strictures on the President and the Republican party." The article denounced such "political buccaneering" and remarked of Trotter, though without naming him: "The brave, roaring, make-believe lion cringingly begs for political cash!!"

[2] Henry J. Callis was pastor of the Columbus Avenue A.M.E. Zion Church in Boston in 1905.

Charles Alexander to Emmett Jay Scott

Boston, Mass., February 6th, 1905

My Dear Scotty: Trotter has sued me on the enclosed article. I will want you to help me in every way possible. If this fellow wins out in his case, he will of course kill the influence of the Boston Colored Citizen, but if he loses, the Boston Colored Citizen will be more firmly rooted in the confidence of the people and will really have a boom that will be worth while. I hope you will advise at once the best steps to take. I depend largely upon your judgment; you are such a careful little fellow and have had such great experience with men and matters that I believe that it is almost impossible for you to err in such matters. Sincerely yours,

Charles Alexander

TLS Con. 27 BTW Papers DLC.

To Bradley Gilman

Philadelphia, Pa. February 8, 1905

My dear Mr. Gilman: I have just received yours of January 25th in reply permit me to say I thank you for the interest which you manifest. I shall write you more fully from Tuskegee.

The Tavern Club, in Boston, is to tender me a dinner some time next month, and I think just now, it is best to let matters stand until I can see you in Boston.

I do not believe the Atlanta University, as an organization, or any other school contributes money to the support of the Guardian. Individuals doubtless help it, but I hardly think there is a school in the South that would embark in such work.

I shall write you more fully from Tuskegee. Very truly yours,

[Booker T. Washington]

TLc Con. 302 BTW Papers DLC.

To Samuel Laing Williams

[Tuskegee, Ala.] Feb. 15, 1905

Personal

My dear Mr. Williams: I meant to have written you some days ago to the effect that I saw the President about three weeks ago, and at the time he told me it was very likely that Prof. Greener would be recalled from Vladivostok because of incompetency and several other troubles. I urged the President to appoint you to the place. He said he thought it best not to send you so far North into such a cold country but he would be willing to give you a consul-ship in a warmer country, if you wanted it when Prof. Greener was recalled. I wish you would keep this in mind. Of course you will not say anything about the probable recall of Greener. Yours truly,

Booker T. Washington

TLpS Con. 31 BTW Papers DLC.

Emmett Jay Scott to Roscoe Conkling Simmons

[Tuskegee, Ala.] February 17, 1905

Personal

Dear Mr. Simmons: I wish you would forward in a plain envelope to the editor of the Boston Guardian, the enclosed editorial sheet of the Scranton (Pennsylvania) Defender. Address it directly to the editor at his address, 3 Tremont St., Boston. Very truly yours,

E. J. Scott

TLpS Con. 30 BTW Papers DLC.

To the Editor of the New York *Times*

New York, N.Y. February 20, 1905

Dear Sir: Writing as a colored man, I beg to say that the enclosed clipping from the Buffalo Commercial, strikes me as rather a deserved rebuke of your newspaper, so valued in many other respects:[1]

The whole New York press has recently overworked the term "Negress," in referring to any colored woman with whose doings it has had to do. Surely you would not expect, using the term of the Buffalo Commercial, to have the women of your race[2] referred to as Jewesses whenever it became necessary to in any way refer to them. Very truly yours,

[Booker T. Washington]

TLp Con. 305 BTW Papers DLC.

[1] No enclosure with press copy.

[2] Adolph Simon Ochs (1858–1935) was publisher of the New York *Times* from 1896 until his death. BTW evidently assumed that he was writing to Ochs. The editor-in-chief was Charles Ransom Miller (1849–1922), of English origin and an Episcopalian.

Emmett Jay Scott to Charles William Anderson

[Tuskegee, Ala.] February 20, 1905

PERSONAL

Dear Friend: You were sent a wire today advising you to be in Washington during the inauguration so as to keep your eyes on the enemy.

The particular point is that Du Bois, Kelly Miller, Trotter, Grimke, and some of that crowd are to have special meetings during the inauguration, and are planning among other things, to call upon the President.

Hershaw is arranging to resuscitate the Pen and Pencil Club for a banquet during inaugural week, and of course will be very anxious to feature your little Atlanta friend[1] as a big attraction. The Wizard believes that it would be well for you to be on hand and if possible, as you easily can, secure an invitation to the Pen and Pencil Club banquet so as to meet the enemy on any ground that may be offered.

I have no word yet that I am to be there with you, as I should like to be. Perhaps however, the Doctor may decide in the end to have me go, but on this point I have no word yet.

With sincere good wishes and a hope to hear from you soon, Very truly yours,

Emmett J. Scott

TLpS Con. 27 BTW Papers DLC.

[1] W. E. B. Du Bois.

To Whitefield McKinlay

[Tuskegee, Ala.] February 21, 1905

My dear Mr. McKinlay: I have received your letter with enclosures. I think it very important that you be present at the meeting at Kelly Miller's house also at the meeting of the Pen and Pencil Club. You will have to keep your eyes wide open during the inauguration week. Yours truly,

Booker T. Washington

TLpS Con. 4 BTW Papers DLC.

Charles Alexander to Emmett Jay Scott

Boston, Mass February 21st, 1905

My Dear Mr. Scott: It appears through the many revelations made in the Court Room today by William Monroe Trotter that he has been looking forward to a time when he could get me into court. He has carefully filed every copy of the Boston Colored Citizen making any reference whatever to himself or his paper, and as an evidence of this his lawyer[1] today produced a great number of copies of the Citizen marked in various places where references were made to a Democratic newspaper or to "A leader of his Race," and like references, all of which were, of course, regarded by him as referring to himself and his paper. He crowded the Court Room with witnesses and friends whereas I had not a single witness and had not invited a single person to be present. Unfortunately, both his case and mine were on docket to be tried together, so that while I was on the stand the questions referring to my case were quickly disposed of and a hundred or more questions asked in regard to articles appearing in my paper at various times as supporting his case against me. I had been advised by my lawyer that if I would assume the responsibility for the publication of the article that it would not be necessary for me to disclose the author or to furnish the name of the writer of such an article, and I believe that my lawyer advised me in good faith, but when we got into court Trotter's lawyer asked the question who is the author of this article, referring to the article in the Boston Colored Citizen headed "Doing the Circus Act," and I declined to answer the question and stated that I myself was in part the author of the article and assumed the entire responsibility for its publication. He then appealed to the Judge and the Judge ruled that the question which he put was perfectly in order and the Court ordered that I answer, and, of course, I had to state who the writer of the article was and how it came into my possession. This was unfortunate because I did not care to have anyone mentioned or mixed up in my personal affairs and it is with sincere regrets that I have to tell you about it. In regard to Reverend Mr. Johnson's testimony, he threw Trotter in the shade. His testimony was the strongest sort of evidence; that Mr. Alexander showed the proper spirit at the Prayer Meeting mentioned in the article sued upon and that in every way Mr. Alexander had his most profound regard and confidence, and the Court permitted him to make further explanation, that there was nothing in his address, or reference to myself at the Prayer Meeting that could by any possible stretching or exaggeration be construed to mean anything like [what] was published in the Guardian, and he further said that he regarded it as a vicious attack. You may imagine how Trotter, and his lawyers, and his witnesses felt when their witness testified so strongly against them.

My lawyer thinks that it is barely possible that both of us will win, that is Trotter will win his case against me and I will win my case against him which will be no victory at all for either of us. I cannot see myself how I can lose my case, and I am fair enough to conceive that Trotter has a pretty fair case since I did testify and acknowledge that the articles referred to were directed at him and at his paper, there being no other Negro newspaper published in Boston with the peculiar proclivities of the Guardian. I am inclined to believe that Trotter will be more careful in the future as to what he publishes concerning people in and about Boston, but he is so strongly organized and his paper is so subsidized by those who are interested in fighting the Doctor and those who believe as the Doctor believes that he will not cease his abuse of people out of his immediate reach. If, however, we can fix it so as to discontinue his harsh abuse and criticism of those immediately around him, we will have accomplished something for the good of the cause.

The case is carried over until Thursday morning at 9:30 at which time I sincerely hope the whole business will be concluded and, of course, I will immediately let you know the outcome. I have never before been into a Court Room either as a witness or the principal in any case and you can imagine my nervous state when I was asked to take the platform. I never will, if I can possibly avoid it, go into Court again. I rather think I will let the fellow besmear me with mud and skunk water, as Fortune calls it, to his fill, but I will not do anything in the future to hinder him. I do not like it, I cannot stand it. I will be very glad to see the villain punished but I do not believe that I have the courage to do the punishing. If I could see you personally, of course, we could go over the matter and perhaps you would get a more definite idea of the situation.

Let me hear from you very soon. Sincerely yours,

Charles Alexander

TLS Con. 27 BTW Papers DLC.

1 Edgar P. Benjamin, a black man born in South Carolina in 1871, was W. M. Trotter's attorney. He was a graduate of the Boston University Law School.

From Whitefield McKinlay

Washington, D.C., Feby 22/05

Dr Mr Washington Yr telegram at hand. Kelly Miller called at my office today & remained some time & during the conversation I got the following names without [his] suspecting my object. He said that Bishop Grant will probably attend the Conference at his home tho he did not sign the memorial which has been sent to the Presdt. Neither Pinchback, Lyons, Dancy nor Terrell have been invited to the Conference, but I shall do all in my power to have Pinchback there to aid me in suppressing those ambitious only for notoriety.

J W E Bowen; W E B Dubois; Bishop A Walters; D. A. Straker; Rev Proctor, Atlanta; S. L. Corrothers; Kelly Miller; Archie Grimke; M. Trotter; Dr Boyd,[1] Nashville, Tenn; Rev Bird, N.C.;

Rev. H. T. Johnson Phila, Pa; W. Ashby Hawkins, Balt, Md; Jno. A. Hagan, New Haven, Conn & myself.

Enclosed I send you some clippings which are interesting. Very truly

W McKinlay

ALS Con. 4 BTW Papers DLC.

[1] Richard Henry Boyd was the founder and for decades the head of the National Baptist Publishing House in Nashville. Though nominally under the control of the National Baptist Convention, the publishing house was so dominated by Boyd and his friends that another faction of black Baptists established another publishing house. Boyd was a staunch supporter of BTW and of black business enterprise, and was a vice-president of the National Negro Business League. He was president of the One-Cent Savings Bank and Trust Co., of which his good friend J. C. Napier was cashier. He took a leading part in the Nashville streetcar boycott in 1905. Boyd died in 1922. (Lamon, *Black Tennesseans*, 5–6, 18, 26–27, 193.)

From John B. Nail

New York 2-22-1905

Dear Doctor: As your personal friend and loyal supporter, I think it my duty to inform you of the meeting last night and to explain, as far as I am able, just what took place. In the first place there was *no* attack on the President: Secondly, there was no *intended* attack on you. Dr Morris, in his address, was comparing two men — you and Mr Hayes. He said that it was *impossible* for you to beg with one hand and fight with the other. He said that your policy of conciliation was *not* as effective as the policy of Mr Hayes's *agitation* — that both of you sought the betterment of the Negro race but by different methods and that so far as the *right of franchise* was concerned he *thought* that Hayes struck the keynote. The whole purport of the addresses was distorted and you can readily see the reason when you recall the fact that the South is fighting for its *full* representation and that the Associated Press is filled with southern sympathizers who are willing to adopt any means to cause strife among the colored people.

There was no fainting of women — *no appearance of disorder* and only words of praise for you and Mr. Roosevelt. I was Chairman of the Finance Committee and was there from the beginning until the close of the meeting and sat within five feet of the speakers. Mr Hayes has *never*, by voice or pen, assailed you, but on the contrary has spoken of you in the highest terms and the only thing upon which anyone could base exceptions was Dr Morris's address and I assure you that he meant no assault upon your noble work.

As for politics, I think it is too dirty a business for a clean man like you and one engaged in the noble work of education, to venture into. Hayes, being a game and fearless agitator and no great cause to endanger, is just fitted for the work. I think that his calling in that line is just as legitimate as yours is in education and I hope that you two strong men may work in harmony toward the betterment of our race.

With highest regards for you & your family, I am your humble servant,

John B. Nail

ALS Con. 305 BTW Papers DLC.

From Charles Alexander

Boston, Mass. February 23, 1905

Victory. Won my case. No damages paid as yet. He had twenty witnesses, I had nine [none].[1]

Charles Alexander

TWSr Con. 27 BTW Papers DLC.

[1] See Alexander to Scott, Feb. 21, 1905, above.

To Timothy Thomas Fortune

[Tuskegee, Ala.] February 24, 1905

My dear Mr. Fortune: I have received both of your communications. I think it would be wise for you to sleep a few nights over your relations with Mr. Moore before taking action. You have no warmer or better friend anywhere in the country than he is. He is one that you can always depend upon. In regard to his business, I know absolutely nothing about it. I did not know that he had a printing office until after he had been operating it for some time. I have no business relations with him whatever.

Your letter regarding the President's speech leads me to make a statement that I meant to make some days ago and that was that I wanted to have you go over with me the advance copy of the President's speech when I was last in New York, but in some way I had mislaid it and did not have it with me at the time when I saw you. The President was kind enough to consult me on the subject, and I went over the address several times, and it is a great pleasure to know that you and others are greatly pleased with it. I do not mind saying to you in confidence that if the speech had been delivered as it was first prepared it would not have given any great satisfaction to our people. I will tell you more about it when I see you.

Are you going to be in Washington during Inauguration week? I cannot stand the Washington crowd and like to keep as far away from them as possible. I am planning to be in New York by March 5th and shall hope to see you.

We were very sorry that you could not come to the Conference, but considering everything I think you were pursuing the wisest course. The main thing is to get your paper upon a paying basis, and I know by experience one has to stick very closely by such efforts to make them succeed. Yours very truly,

Booker T. Washington

TLpS Con. 1 BTW Papers DLC.

From Anna Thomas Jeanes[1]

Germantown [Pa.] 2/25—1905

Booker T. Washington Principal Tuskegee Institute Is not aid for "Rural Schools" more desirable and important than the Tuskegee dining room, (to cost $54,000)? that might benefit the few while the influence of Rural Schools might benefit the *many*. Hollis Burke Frissell, Principal of Hampton Institute, called on me recently (I had not previously known him). He approved of Rural Schools and a Fund[2] to assist them, so I gave him my check for Ten Thousand dollars, he has written to me saying, "I am sending your check to Mr. Geo. Foster Peabody the treasurer of our Endowment Fund asking him to invest it as a special fund the interest of which is to be applied to the assistance of Rural Schools — and farther he says, "Perhaps as you suggested it may be the beginning of a larger fund that will accomplish much good for the Country people of the Negro race in the South." I copy this for you, although I do not know what may be the result, but if you "*see your way clear*" to invest Ten Thousand dollars for the assistance of Rural Schools, I am willing to send you a check for that purpose — but not for the dining room. Sincerely

Anna T. Jeanes

ALS Con. 29 BTW Papers DLC.

1 Anna Thomas Jeanes (1822–1907), the youngest of ten in a Philadelphia Hicksite Quaker family, came into possession of the considerable fortune she was to devote to philanthropy by virtue of outliving her brothers and sisters; she made her first charitable donations in 1894, at the age of seventy-two. Anna's father, Isaiah, was a shipping merchant. Her brothers went into the dry-goods business and invested in Schuylkill County coal properties. Anna T. Jeanes had only a secondary-school education, but her intellectual interests ranged from the fine arts to the natural sciences. Although an active member of the Society of Friends, she also studied other religions, especially Buddhism, and wrote two books on religious subjects.

Her first gifts went to Quaker projects—education, improvements in meeting houses, relief work, and homes for the elderly. Her donations to Negro causes may have been influenced by her sister Mary's activities. Anna's mother died when she was four, and Mary took her mother's place in rearing Anna. In 1855 Mary started a Home for Destitute Colored Children. Anna's will benefited this orphanage as well as a Home for Aged and Infirm Colored Persons and a Friends' school for freedmen.

Having learned of her earlier modest gift to the Fort Valley (Ga.) Institute, George Foster Peabody advised Hollis Burke Frissell of Anna Jeanes's potential as a donor, and Frissell in turn told BTW. She steadfastly refused their joint requests for aid to Hampton and Tuskegee, but appointed them trustees of the Negro Rural School (Jeanes) Fund.

2 This donation was the beginning of the more formalized Anna T. Jeanes Foundation (Negro Rural School Fund, Inc.), which came into existence in 1907 through Anna Jeanes's million-dollar bequest. In the early years Jeanes supervising teachers traveled from school to school within their counties, applying the Hampton-Tuskegee principles of rural-school improvement. Virginia Randolph, a Hampton graduate and the first Jeanes teacher, was the chief figure in implementing this approach. As Jeanes teachers grew more numerous they often served as the de facto superintendents for

Negro schools, reporting on conditions to the white county superintendents. By calling attention to the inadequacies of most rural schoolhouses, Jeanes teachers helped begin the campaign for modern buildings which the Rosenwald Fund later took up systematically. Many African countries, including Kenya, Angola, and South Africa, experimented with the Jeanes teacher plan. When James Hardy Dillard became the general agent of the Slater as well as of the Jeanes Fund in December 1910, the latter joined the interlocking directorate of the Rockefeller philanthropies. Under Dillard's leadership county agricultural and industrial training schools, where graduates of Negro elementary schools could train to become teachers, evolved into bona fide high schools for blacks. Jeanes teachers were most numerous in Virginia, but many also worked in Missouri, North Carolina, and Alabama.

From Robert Ezra Park[1]

Tuskegee Institute, Alabama. Feb 25, 1905

My dear Mr Washington — Our agreement, as I understand it, is this: I give my services to your school and in return the school guarantees me $1800 a year, or $150 a month as long as those services continue, with traveling expenses, (railway fare and sleeping car, but not hotel). During the time I am in its employ all that I earn by writing or any other means whatever, whether more or less than $1,800 per year, unless by special agreement, shall be either turned over to the funds of the school or charged against the $150 per month guaranteed me in this agreement. I am very truly

Robert E. Park

ALS Con. 30 BTW Papers DLC.

1 Robert Ezra Park (1864–1944) was BTW's ghostwriter from 1905 to 1914. A white journalist and sociologist, he was educated at the University of Michigan (Ph.B., 1887), Harvard (M.A., 1899), and the University of Heidelberg (Ph.D., 1904). After more than a decade of newspaper work and years of travel and study, Park was employed by the Congo Reform Committee in Boston when he first made BTW's acquaintance in 1904. He wrote not only several of BTW's books but also articles, speeches, and even some letters dealing with matters beyond BTW's knowledge. Park spent part of every year at Tuskegee, but most of the time his headquarters were at Wollaston, Mass., a suburb of Boston. He traveled with BTW in Europe to aid in the investigation of the poor that led to BTW's book *The Man Farthest Down* (1912). He also wrote large parts of *The Story of the Negro* (1909) and *My Larger Education* (1911) under BTW's name.

At the International Conference on the Negro at Tuskegee in 1912, Park's address so impressed Professor W. I. Thomas of the University of Chicago sociology department that he offered Park a lectureship in 1914. Park was connected with the University of Chicago for the remainder of his career, becoming a professor in 1923 and an eminent pioneer student of race and urban sociology, author of many scholarly books and articles, and graduate director of what became known as "the Chicago school" of sociology. (For biographical information and an account of Park's sociology, see Matthews, *Quest for an American Sociology*.)

From Whitefield McKinlay

Washington, D.C., Feby 25/05

Dr Mr Washington I telegraphed you last night that Crum's letter was a complete success especially as he carried his audience by storm. When yr name was mentioned, the applause that greeted it showed that this community has not forgotten your lecture & if there were any of the anti's there it would serve to further emphasize the hold you have on the affection of these people.

Crum paid you & your work a deserved tribute.

We called on the Presdt the Sec of Treasy[1] & Mr Leupp yesterday.

The Presdt was immensely pleased to see him. I took advantage of the visit to thank & praise the recent Lincoln speech.

I also called with Crum on Editor's Bone of Post & Noyes of Star, so that they could see for themselves the man who has been so misrepresented.

Crums deportment has been excellent and I have had some heart to heart talks about several matters of interest to him. I told Kelly Miller to day that I shall insist upon the Gov. being invited to the Conference — to this he agreed.

It was not my intention to go to the Pen & Pencil, but I concluded today to subscribe. As a rule I take no interest in such affairs.

Enclosed please find Stars acct of C.'s lecture. Also editorials from Post on you. Mr. Leupp told me that Weightman has quit the Post for the Chicago Tribune. Very truly

W McKinlay

Several errors in Star's article.

ALS Con. 4 BTW Papers DLC.

[1] Leslie Mortier Shaw.

Frederick Randolph Moore to Emmett Jay Scott

New York, N.Y., 2/25 1905

My dear Emmett: I always thought that *your* friend Alexander was a *damphool.* I did not however believe him as big as he has shown himself to be in his recent testimony — wherein he mentions you as the responsible user of "Toad." Woul[d]n't it *jar* you, or, didn't it *jar* you. You will pardon the slang. Why didn't he stand up like a man and, face the music. Yours sincerely,

Moore

Will write you as [to] Business League and other matters lately.

F.

ALS Con. 29 BTW Papers DLC.

To Whitefield McKinlay

[Tuskegee, Ala.] February 27, 1905

Dear Mr. McKinlay: I do not intend in any way, to take part in the inaugural parade, but I thought perhaps I could secure for myself and one of our teachers, admission to the reviewing stand, or to the stand from which the President will deliver his inaugural address. Very truly yours,

Booker T. Washington

TLpS Con. 4 BTW Papers DLC.

To Jesse C. Duke

[Tuskegee, Ala.] February 28, 1905

My dear Mr. Duke: I am in receipt of your letter of February 23d. I had not forgotten about your boy, but I have been unable to find any place where we could put him. I should dislike very much to see so bright a young man enter the government service. Under no consideration would I have a son of mine accept a federal position; it simply means in the long run that all the ambition is taken out of a boy and he becomes a mere machine.

Am I right in thinking that your son is a civil engineer? Someone told me that he graduated at Harvard from that department; if so, please let me know, and there is a bare possibility I might find something for him. Yours very truly,

Booker T. Washington

TLpS Con. 300 BTW Papers DLC.

Emmett Jay Scott to Frederick Randolph Moore

[Tuskegee, Ala., ca. February 1905]

PERSONAL

Dear Mr. Moore: Dr. Washington has suggested that I write you rather freely as I am sure you would like to have me do, in regard to the February number of the Colored American Magazine. He does not feel that the treatment of the Du Bois matter, page 67, is dignified,[1] and in fact thinks there is altogether too much of Tuskegee in this number, giving vindication to the impression that a great many enemies of the magazine have endeavored to foist on the general public.

Tuskegee appreciates most sincerely all that you and your magazine have done toward helping our work, but we would not for one minute have the magazine interfered with by any too general impression that it is a Tuskegee publication. As a whole, I think the magazine for this month is rather satisfactory, and I congratulate you upon the . . . in evidence.

Emmett J. Scott

TLpS Con. 268 BTW Papers DLC. Last line too dim to be read in its entirety.

1 The *Colored American Magazine* (Feb. 1905), 67, called for Du Bois to be more specific in his charge, made in the January issue of *Voice of the Negro*, that $3,000 had been used to bribe black newspapers and silence criticism of BTW. The magazine

called for Du Bois to name his sources, and the recipients of the bribes or readers would have to conclude that he "has sunk to blackguardism; and that his right eye is an evil one, and his tongue is greased with slanderous oil." For Du Bois's full indictment of BTW's involvement with the black press see Du Bois to Oswald Garrison Villard, Mar. 24, 1905, below.

To Anna Thomas Jeanes

[Tuskegee, Ala.] March 1, 1905

My dear Miss Jeanes: I have just received your kind letter of February 25th. I write to say that I could use to the very greatest advantage $10,000 in the way that you suggest. There are few greater needs than that, especially if the money is used in a way to stimulate self-help, and that would be the manner in which I should like to use it.

I want to thank you for giving me the opportunity to serve you in this way.

I shall try to get some others to help in the matter of the dining room. Yours very truly,

Booker T. Washington

TLpS Con. 29 BTW Papers DLC.

To Timothy Thomas Fortune

[Tuskegee, Ala.] March 1, 1905

My dear Mr. Fortune: I have your letter of February 24th regarding the Hayes meeting. I think the whole difficulty grew out of the fact that most of our pretended leaders are filled with jealousy to such an extent that it is impossible for them to pursue any constructive policy; their whole stock in trade consists in trying to tear down or minimize the work of somebody else. They seem to think that they will build themselves up in proportion as they can curse one of their fellows. Charley Morris I think is mentally unbalanced.

You have not said anything about going to the inauguration. I take for granted that you are not going to be there. Neither am I. I cannot bear such crowds, and especially the Washington crowd. Mr. Scott, however, is likely to be there.

I presume you know about the meeting referred to in the enclosed communication. You and I both, it seems, have been given the black eye.

It seems that the President is going to do something for Charley Anderson sometime during the spring.

I am anxious to see you. Yours very truly,

Booker T. Washington

TLpS Con. 1 BTW Papers DLC.

From Emmett Jay Scott

Washington D.C. March 6/05

My Dear Mr. Washington: I have tried to keep my eyes & my ears open since I have been here. There is really not much to report.

I attended the meeting of the Pen & Pencil Club Saturday night. Anderson, Kealing, Wetmore, McKinlay and a host of *your decided* friends were there. It was not a formal banquet. The men sat in the middle of the hall & on a screen certain caricatures were thrown. These were designed to show "signs of the Times" as they said. These were all very funny & without bitterness. The program was arranged by Pelham,[1] Slaughter[2] & A. S. Gray.[3] When your picture was shown the whole company came to its feet with more & continued applause than fell to anything during the whole evening. My own picture was shown in connection with my work at Tuskegee & with you, with comment of a nature not unflattering.

An imaginary conversation over the telephone was the only thing you might have objected to, but it was designed to be funny & not malicious. The White House was supposed to be calling up to ask if you were present. The reply was sent as follows without mentioning your name: "No he is not here, but Emmett Scott his secretary is with a military attache (Maj. Ramsey) – & that the Tuskegee folks do not wish positions. They are content to stand behind the throne & make them &c." It caused much laughter & was the cause of some merriment. Hershaw was not present & nothing occur[r]ed to cause any real annoyance.

I went with Anderson to White House this morning. Loeb said it was absolutely impossible to get a chance to talk over anything — tho' he spoke to Anderson about the situation & said it is absolutely alright without change of purpose. We c'd not get the Register matter before either of them. The crowds were simply awful & nobody c'd see him for anything but a handclasp. We did get in line however & he held us to say what the plan is just as it appears in newspapers, & that he will have it ready by June 1 for announcing the appointment, that being date of close of Roberts[4] commission as Treasurer of U.S. Loeb *however* agrees with Anderson that it ought to go in right away — so that it may be confirmed before Senate adjourns. Loeb made note & said he w'd bring it before President *at once*. If not done it will give Odell[5] who is said to be unfavorable a chance to organize opposition. Odell is now in Europe but will return in six weeks — besides most of the whole sale liquor dealers buy their goods from Kentucky distillers & other Southern dealers, & Odell might organize them *against* the plan, & have them work on Southern senators. If appointed now he can take hold June 1 — if held up cannot take charge till confirmed & Senate will not be in session till next December in regular session. It w'd be unfair to hold him in air he thinks under these conditions. Anderson will be here till Thursday. He goes South then.

The Conference crowd has nobody so far in attendance. McKinlay, Grant & Wetmore will camp with them. I went over the whole call & Loeb says he will take care of them. Anderson asked him directly to say that they are asking just what you have been recommending & he says he'll take care of them in a way they will not forget. I think however they will not get to see the President however except for a very few minutes. For 4 days this rush is to be on at least — with cabinet day on Tuesday & Friday. I think they will pull out if they can't get in on Tuesday or Wednesday & they won't on either of those days. We told him (Loeb) who each man is — of Trotter's democratic pa[per] his antagonism of President & in a way that have them "fixed."

Yesterday I went to Grimke's church. He spoke on citizenship & *of course* rapped at you about four times, misrepresenting your views on suffrage — the Separate Car laws — &c &c. He did *not* call your name a single time however in his usual cowardly way.

I shall go South Tuesday night. Phil Waters has the paper signed by both Senators[6] & his representative.[7] What am I to do with it.

Everything from the viewpoint of all of *us* is most satisfactory. Of the Conference I'll wire you on Tuesday. Yours sincerely

Emmett J. Scott

ALS Con. 24 BTW Papers DLC.

[1] Robert A. Pelham, who received an LL.B. from Howard University in 1904 and was employed by the U.S. census office.

[2] Henry Proctor Slaughter (1871–1958), a graduate of Howard University (1900), was employed by the U.S. Government Printing Office from 1896 to 1910. Beginning in 1910 he was editor of the *Odd Fellows Journal* and a director of the Odd Fellows Hall Association in Washington, D.C. He was a director of a bank in Staunton, Va., and served a term as president of the Pen and Pencil Club. A bibliophile, Slaughter donated over 10,000 volumes to the library of Howard University.

[3] Arthur Smith Gray (1869–1917), a Howard University graduate (1893), was a stenographer and private secretary to the chief of the Bureau of Statistics from 1898 to 1905 and later a statistician for the Bureau of Foreign and Domestic Commerce. He was also a partner with his wife in the ownership of the Fountain Pharmacy in Washington, D.C. Gray was a member of the NAACP.

[4] Ellis Henry Roberts.

[5] Benjamin Barker Odell (1854–1926), Republican governor of New York (1901–5) and chairman of the state Republican committee during and after his governorship, defied the boss rule of Thomas C. Platt but confined his reforms to economies in the operation of the state government.

[6] Stephen Benton Elkins and Nathan Bay Scott.

[7] Joseph Holt Gaines.

To Charles William Anderson

Hotel Manhattan, New York, March 7, 1905

(Personal & Confidential.)

Dear Mr. Anderson: I have received all your communications[1] and wired the President early this morning in the way you suggested.

I do not believe your fears are well grounded. I know something of the public sentiment in New York, and judging from what the New York papers and individuals say, they take it for granted that your appointment is settled. A big row would be kicked up if any backward step would be taken now or later.

There are three points however that you will have to settle with the colored brother, they are waiting for you on every corner, the first one is, the papers say you have fifty positions to dispose of; second, you are the best dressed colored man in the city; third, you own more property than any other colored man in the city, these are the points you will have to square yourself with the colored brother. Very truly yours,

[Booker T. Washington]

TLc Con. 27 BTW Papers DLC.

1 Anderson had written BTW the preceding day urging him to ask the President to appoint Anderson at once rather than wait until June, as the President had intended. (Con. 27, BTW Papers, DLC.)

To Anna Thomas Jeanes

Hotel Manhattan, New York March 9, 1905

Dear Friend: I would have written earlier, but was waiting to have a conference with Dr. Frissell, I learn however that he is sick. I have talked with Mr. George Foster Peabody about the way of taking care of the ten thousand dollars you have placed in our hands for the benefit of the rural colored schools, and we are going to attend to the investment this week.

We are all most grateful to you for the timely and practical help. I want to report to you from time to time of the results of the investment. I shall be passing through Philadelphia some time soon and would like to talk with you a little further before you finally decide on the larger amount for a school.

If none of the existing Boards or organizations would serve your purpose I have been wondering just a little if a small special board might not be wise. As I said however, I should like to talk with you about this matter and some of the various methods concerning the investment of the money. Very truly yours,

[Booker T. Washington]

TLc Con. 716 BTW Papers DLC.

To George Foster Peabody

New York, March 9, 1905

My dear Mr. Peabody A lady in Philadelphia has placed in our hands ten thousand dollars with the request that the interest be used in helping small rural Negro schools in the South. I am writing especially to ask permission of the Endowment Fund Committee to invest this fund at Tuskegee under the supervision of Mr. Logan our Treasurer, Mr. R. R. Taylor our Architect, Mr. Hare one of our local Trustees, or some other persons who will answer as well. I ask this for the reason that I do not think this money constitutes a part of our legitimate endowment fund and mainly for the reason I am sure this amount could be loaned out in small amounts to the colored people in the vicinity of Tuskegee, well secured, for the purpose of aiding them in building small homes.

In that way I think 6% could be realized on the money. The principal would be serving a double purpose in aiding worthy people to build homes and aiding the rural schools.

I should urge that only a small per cent of the value of the property be loaned in every case. Very truly yours,

[Booker T. Washington]

TLc Con. 29 BTW Papers DLC.

To Emmett Jay Scott

New York, N.Y. March 11, 1905

Dear Mr. Scott: Enclosed I send you an editorial,[1] kindly pass it on to Davis[2] of the Independent.

I have urged Mr. Fortune to stop giving attention to Du Bois and The Voice, and I think this ought to be observed in all the rest of the Afro-American papers excepting the local papers in Atlanta.

By paying attention to them only advertises them all the more. Very truly yours,

B. T. W.

TLI Con. 557 BTW Papers DLC.

1 See A Draft of an Editorial, Mar. 11, 1905, below.

2 Benjamin Jefferson Davis, Sr. (1870–1945), was a journalist and leading black fraternal and political figure in the South. In 1903 he founded and edited the Atlanta *Independent* and was for many years a delegate-at-large from Georgia to Republican national conventions. He was secretary of the Republican state organization in Georgia for ten years. Davis held high positions with the Odd Fellows, YMCA, and the Atlanta Community Chest. His son, Benjamin Davis, Jr. (1903–64), was a high-ranking member of the American Communist Party and was a member of the New York City Council from 1943 to 1949.

A Draft of an Editorial[1]

[New York City, Mar. 11, 1905]

A Base Slander of the Afro-American Press

In a recent issue of a magazine, published in Atlanta, Ga., one of the Professors of the Atlanta University makes the statement that $3000 of "Hush Money" had been used to subsidize the Afro-American Press in five of the leading cities.[2]

This is a statement which calls for proof, explanation or retraction. No institution, for the uplifting of the Afro-American has stood out more strongly for forty years, than the Afro-American Press. Many of the Editors and publishers have almost pauperized themselves in standing for the rights of the race. The Afro-American press has held their columns open in defence of the Negro and has advocated his advancement and education in Industrial schools, Colleges and Universities.

From the inception to the present, the Afro-American press has stood loyally by the Atlanta University in all its struggles and its triumphs. At the present time, when there is existing a spirit of peace, harmony and unity, among our people all over the United States, such as has never existed before, for a Professor in the Atlanta University to make the bold bare statement that a large proportion of the Afro-American press has been bribed, is an insult to the race and to our Negro press, unless such a statement can be proven. We want the Professor to name the five leading cities and name the five newspapers. If he cannot do this, or does not, the race will decide to [that?] in making this statement, the Professor had no other idea than to stir up strife, or to slander the Afro-American press.

As the matter now stands, every Negro paper and every city, according to the Professor, is now under suspicion. We know individuals and organizations that have and are spending money in order to enable a Negro paper to speak out in defence of the race, but we repeat we want the names of the papers who have received $3000 to prevent them speaking out their sentiments.

TMdc Con. 305 BTW Papers DLC.

1 Presumably this is the editorial referred to above in BTW to Scott of the same date. Newspaper material was often separated from covering letters at Tuskegee Institute and filed under *N*, as in this case. While it is not certain that the same typewriter produced the letter and the editorial, the typeface is the same. The fact that the term "Afro-American" appears in the letter and the editorial, when BTW did not customarily use that expression, also suggests that the two items were drafted together.

2 W. E. B. Du Bois, "Debit and Credit," *Voice of the Negro*, 2 (Jan. 1905), 677, in a New Year summary of the black gains and losses of the year 1904, listed in the debit column: "To $3000 of 'hush money' used to subsidize the Negro press in five leading cities." Though Du Bois did not mention BTW or Tuskegee, the source of the money was probably obvious to most of his readers.

From Ralph Waldo Tyler

Columbus, Ohio. March 11, 1905

My Dear Mr. Washington: I am enclosing you herewith marked editorial[1] which I wrote concerning the visit of the colored bishops to the President. That request they made, I am satisfied, was a veiled effort to discredit your work. These bishops, as you well know, have always opposed you. Arnett, who was the Poo Baw of the McKinley administration, who dictated all appointments, with an eye singled to his own financial success, is trying to get in out of the wet where President Roosevelt has permitted him to remain.

The whole scheme was one to detract from your work and prestige, and I thought it wise to take a shot at them. Very truly yours,

Ralph W Tyler

Am sending a marked copy to the president.

TLS Con. 308 BTW Papers DLC.

[1] The enclosure, presumably from the *Ohio State Journal*, opposed a congressional investigation of the race problem and endorsed BTW's emphasis on economic opportunity.

To Austin N. Jenkins

[New York City] March 12, 1905

(Personal and confidential.)

My dear Mr. Jenkins: I have scarcely ever been placed in such an awkward position as I am at present. As a member of your publishing family, with your firm praising and selling my books on the one hand and your magazine doing all it can to destroy the effect of my books on the other hand.

I have never heard of such a condition before in connection with any book publishing firm.

Since seeing the last issue of your magazine I confess that but for our agreement, which we reached at Tuskegee, and your promise, I would not endure it any longer. My first impulse was to write Bowen a strong letter, regarding his hypocrisy, but on further consideration I have decided to be patient and leave the whole matter in your hands, for the present, believing you will find a wise way to remedy present conditions.

You will note two editorials, one in the first part of the magazine, the other in the latter part, both wholly directed towards me.

I think the idea of having Mr. Hertel writing you the kind of letter you suggested to Mr. Scott a good plan.

I have a plan for the distribution of my large pictures, without cost to you in connection with the sale of The Negro in Business, which I want to talk with you about some time soon.

I shall be glad to hear from you. All your correspondence will be treated confidentially and I wish mine treated the same. Very truly yours,

[Booker T. Washington]

TLc Con. 29 BTW Papers DLC.

To Margaret James Murray Washington

[New York City] Mar 13 [190]5

You can write President Merrill that saw Mr Carnegie today regarding library for Fisk and he decided to give it but ask Merrill not to make matter public until he hears from Carnegie directly. He was especially glad to give it as you were educated there.

B. T. W.

HWIr Con. 563 BTW Papers DLC.

To James Griswold Merrill

Hotel Manhattan, New York, March 14, 1905

My dear President Merrill: I am very sorry indeed, that I have been so very tardy in regard to attending to the matter concerning the Library for Fisk University, but as you know, I have had the Conference and others matters engaging my attention to such a degree, that I have not had the opportunity of speaking with Mr. Carnegie until yesterday, when I went over the matter with him and his Secretary.[1]

Mr. Carnegie will give the building, and one of the reasons, that made him especially pleased to do so is the fact that Mrs. Washington was educated there.

I am quite anxious however, that you not make this public until you have heard directly from Mr. Carnegie, which will be within a few days.[2] Very truly yours,

[Booker T. Washington]

TLc Carter G. Woodson Collection DLC. Another carbon is in Con. 304, BTW Papers, DLC.

1 James Bertram (1872–1934) of Edinburgh, Scotland, came to the United States in 1898 as an associate of Andrew Carnegie in his educational and library interests. In 1911 he became secretary and life trustee of the Carnegie Corporation.

2 BTW sent this copy to Whitefield McKinlay, Mar. 14, 1905, suggesting, "If proper occasion offers, you might show it to some of my Washington critics." (Con. 4, Carter G. Woodson Collection, DLC.)

From John Campbell Dancy

Washington, D.C. March 14th, 1905

My dear Dr. Washington: I write simply to thank you for your success in securing for Livingstone College the Library building from Mr. Carnegie. Had they listened to me they would have appealed to you long ago. But since they did not I thank you even now for the masterly stroke you have made in our behalf. You have put the entire Zion Church under renewed obligations to you. I suppose you saw Bishop Hood's[1] defense of you in the last issue of the *Star of Zion*. The Church is your friend, and you may depend upon it. We will make the best possible use of this recent effort of yours in our behalf.

When you pass this way again I would suggest that you say to the P. that he give out a definite statement as to this place in order to stop the constant pleas of candidates who would like to have it. Yours very sincerely

Jno. C. Dancy

ALS Con. 1 BTW Papers DLC.

1 James Walker Hood, born in Pennsylvania in 1831, founded more than 600 A.M.E. Zion churches in the Carolinas and Virginia during the Civil War and Reconstruction. He was elected bishop in 1872, with headquarters in Raleigh, N.C.

To John A. Hertel

[New York City] March 15, 1905

Personal and Confidential.

My dear Mr. Hertel: I am in receipt of your letter and in reply would say I am very sorry the book falls so far short in words, it seems that I overlooked the fact that you desired the number mentioned. It will be an easy matter however to remedy this fault as there are quite a number of worthy persons left out that can be added. I have in preparation, several chapters which will reach you very soon. I shall press the work forward as rapidly as I can as I realize the awkward position in which you are placed.

Now in regard to the other matter about which Mr. Jenkins wrote you; I have never done business with any firm that has treated me better than you, with one exception, and that is, in the matter concerning the Magazine.

Please understand that it is not a matter between your firm and Mr. Scott, but between your firm and myself, and I am sure at a glance you will see it is unwise to try to serve you, with your magazine trying to damn me on the one hand and you trying to praise my books on the other. Every thing you say in praise of my works is slandered by your editors.

I am sure you will appreciate, as Mr Jenkins, that there should be cordiality and cooperation. I would not work for Doubleday Page & Co. if they tried to damn me in their magazine. I am deeply interested in your magazine and will do all I can to help it if it pursues the policy of upbuilding the race instead of tearing it down.

I am quite sure however that you and Mr. Jenkins understand the situation and I shall leave the matter to you for solution believing you will solve it in the wisest way. Very truly yours,

[Booker T. Washington]

TLc Con. 29 BTW Papers DLC.

From Emmett Jay Scott

Tuskegee Institute, Alabama. March 17, 1905

Dear Mr. Washington: I just learned that on yesterday, Thursday, March 16th, Dr. Massey specifically notified the girls of his school that any of them caught reading von Grabill's book[1] would be suspended from the school. He also said that it was true of any institution that there would be lapses from time to time, but that this book had exaggerated everything and reflected no credit either upon the writer nor upon those who were selling the book. I thought you might like to know this. Yours truly,

E J Scott

TLS Con. 556 BTW Papers DLC.

1 S. Becker von Grabill (1871?–1950), a German immigrant, was a concert pianist who settled in Tuskegee for about three years beginning in 1903 and taught music at the Alabama Conference Female College. In 1905, under the pseudonym of Ruperth Fehnstoke, he wrote *Letters from Tuskegee, Being the Confessions of a Yankee*, a scurrilous anti-black booklet of 43 pages on Tuskegee Institute's faculty and students. Von Grabill condemned the work of BTW and Tuskegee Institute and proclaimed that the Negro race was degenerating into a hopeless state of immorality and ignorance. He accused BTW of covering up many seductions, sexual affairs, illegitimate births, and abortions at Tuskegee Institute among both faculty and students. He also charged that contrary to BTW's claims, the school buildings were built by professional builders rather than student labor. He claimed that BTW's ultimate goal was social equality and racial amalgamation, and that Tuskegee Institute was a conspiracy to that end. The reason Von Grabill wrote such a book is unclear, but BTW and Emmett J. Scott attributed it to the fact that Von Grabill was turned down in 1903 when he offered to give piano recitals at Tuskegee Institute and to act as an agent in the purchase of pianos. (Von Grabill to BTW, Mar. 12, Nov. 8, 1903, Con. 259, BTW Papers, DLC; see also Scott to R. R. Moton, Mar. 22, and BTW to James M. Henderson, May 16, 1905, below.) The book caused some stir locally and among a few of BTW's northern supporters, but BTW refused to make public comment about it and claimed that he never bothered to read it. BTW did, however, have Emmett J. Scott prepare a summary of the main accusations. (See Emmett Jay Scott's Summary of *Confessions of a Yankee*, ca. Apr. 20, 1905, below.)

Emmett Jay Scott to Timothy Thomas Fortune

[Tuskegee, Ala.] March 18, 1905

Dear Mr. Fortune: I wrote you yesterday with reference to the New York trip. That is still in the air until I can hear from Ye Wizard. I do not wish to make the trip to New York unless I can really have time to get through with the work. I am most anxious to complete it but have done no great amount so far. How much real help can you be to me in the writing of that biography?

With reference to the whisper which comes to you from Washington I can say to you frankly that there is absolutely nothing in it. The Wizard would not stand for any political job for me for several reasons, and then, too, I am not hiking so strenuously as I might have been at some time in my life for recognition. The only place I would have is the one mentioned by you, and that ambition is based upon a heritage such as it would be for my children. You may be very sure that if any such good luck was about to befall me I should write you. I am doing pretty well at Tuskegee all things considered, and shall try to carve out a career here. I hope I may be limitedly successful. Yours very truly,

Emmett J. Scott

TLpS Con. 29 BTW Papers DLC.

To John Campbell Dancy

Hotel Manhattan, New York, March 20, 1905

Personal.

My dear Mr. Dancy: It has been a great pleasure to know that I have been of any service to the great Zion Church. Mr. Carnegie was all the more willing to give when I told him the Tuskegee Institute had its birth in one of the Zion churches, at Tuskegee.

I do not believe you need worry in regard to your place, as I believe the President has fully made up his mind to keep you there, and the more candidates there are the better for you.

I hope to see you as I pass through there. Very truly yours,

[Booker T. Washington]

TLc Con. 1 BTW Papers DLC.

To Robert Charles Bedford

Hotel Manhattan, New York, March 21, 1905

Dear Mr. Bedford: I am very glad to receive your letter regarding your trip to Birmingham, I shall read your full report as soon as I reach Tuskegee.

I am writing Mr. Thompson today, thanking him for the kindness shown you.

As soon as you reach Tuskegee, which I hope will not be very long, I have an important matter to take up with you in reference to some land on Hilton Head Island, S.C. owned by Mr. William P. Clyde.[1] Mr. Clyde practically owns the island consisting of about 10,000 acres of land and he is thinking of trying to make an ideal settlement, as an illustration of what Tuskegee graduates can teach the people to accomplish. He is thinking of financing the scheme, in case we care to undertake it.

I should think there are about 1,000 colored people, and about a dozen whites on the place.

It is one of the places where the finest sea-island cotton has grown, but matters have very much retrograded there now. I wonder if you could go there and look the whole thing over. Very truly yours,

[Booker T. Washington]

TLc Con. 28 BTW Papers DLC.

1 William Pancoast Clyde (1839–1923) founded and directed the Clyde Steamship Co. An avid sportsman, Clyde eventually purchased about 9,000 acres of Hilton Head Island for use as a personal hunting retreat. For a decade BTW and officials of Hampton Institute, particularly W. T. B. Williams, counseled a Tuskegee graduate at the school on Hilton Head. BTW also encouraged a scheme whereby farmers on the island bought the land they worked on long terms at low interest. Economic crises, human failings, and natural disasters, however, prevented the plan from prospering.

Charles Alexander to Emmett Jay Scott

Boston, Massachusetts March 21st, 1905

My Dear Scotty: I have just received a letter from my lawyer stating that in the case of Alexander vs. Trotter the Judge fines in my favor in the sum of $500 and in the case of Trotter vs. Alexander fines in Trotter's favor $100. I regard this as a decided victory as Trotter put forth every effort to advertise and emphasize the importance of his fight. My lawyer advises me to appeal to a higher court where we might secure even a larger damage. What do you think about it, advise me? Sincerely yours,

Charles Alexander

TLS Con. 27 BTW Papers DLC.

Emmett Jay Scott to Robert Russa Moton

[Tuskegee, Ala.] March 22, 1905

PERSONAL

Dear Major Moton: I write at once in acknowledgment of your letter of March 20th to say that there is living in the town of Tuskegee, no such individual as you mention.

Of course you know that there must have come into your possession a hideous book, recently prepared, with this fictitious name as the author. It is an abominable libel upon the school, and upon the teachers here, but it is a kind of craven courage which hides behind anonymity, and so of course, has not greatly disturbed us.

The real author of the book is a German who came here about three years ago to teach in the white college. He was unable to hold us up for one or two musical concerts at from One Hundred to One Hundred Fifty Dollars an evening, and was further unable to persuade us to empower him to order our pianos so that he might get a commission on them.

Possessing some latent prejudice, he must have had his fury

aroused because of the failures mentioned and has proceeded to libel us in this book.

You have not asked for this information and I am only sending it to you confidentially. We have positively refused to discuss with anybody, the book, its purpose, the animus of the writer, or anything that would let him feel that we attach any significance to his publication.

You will treat what I say in confidence then. Very truly yours

Emmett J. Scott

TLpS Con. 30 BTW Papers DLC.

To Emmett Jay Scott

New York, March 23, 1905

Dear Mr. Scott: The very best way to treat Wetmore, I think, is to let him alone for a while. I think he has overestimated himself. He has written Mr. Anderson a very saucy letter, without cause. Too much attention has spoiled him, so the best thing to do now, is to let him alone.

I did something for him I have never done for another colored man, living, I left my work and called upon him, at his hotel, when he was here sick.

He evidently has too high an opinion of himself. He is also lacking in good breeding and common sense; if he had the least common decency he would not write around his private business, such as he has in the case with Mr. Smith.

One of his troubles seems to be that while he did not want to beg for a position, he also wanted to take the dignified stand and have the position seek him.

I wrote Mr. Williams that the President wanted the endorsement of his two Senators. I find that practically all these people are unable to help themselves, but want some one to pick them up, then carry them. Very truly yours,

B. T. W.

TLI Con. 24 BTW Papers DLC.

To Phil Waters

New York, March 24, 1905

Personal & Confidential.

My dear Mr. Waters: I had a long talk with the President last night and he tells me that he does not want to make any changes, or new appointments of colored people for some time; he has the feeling that he has done enough already in this line for the present, and to make any more now would hurt the race, as it only opens the question for discussion.

In making changes he is pursuing the same policy he has in regarding white people. Very truly yours,

[Booker T. Washington]

TLc Con. 5 BTW Papers DLC.

William Edward Burghardt Du Bois to Oswald Garrison Villard

Atlanta, Ga., March 24, 1905

(confidential.)

My dear Mr. Villard: In reply to your letter of the 13th inst, I am going to burden you with considerable matter. I do this reluctantly because it seems like imposing on a busy man. At the same time I want to say frankly that I have been sorry to feel in your two letters a note of impatience and disbelief which seems to me unfortunate and calling for a clear, even, if long, statement.

In the *Voice of the Negro* for January, I made the charge that $3000 of hush money had been used to subsidize the Negro press in five leading cities. The bases upon which that charge was made were in part as follows:

The offer of $3000 to the editor of the Chicago *Conservator* on 2 separate occasions to change its editorial policy, and the final ousting of the editor by the board of management, and the installing of an editor with the required policy; with the understanding that financial benefit would result. (Exhibit A.) The statement of the former editor of the Washington *Record* that he was given to understand that the *Record* received $40 a month from the outside to maintain its policy. (Exhibit B.)

The statement of one of the assistant editors of the Washington *Colored American* that it was worth to them $500 a year to maintain its policy. (Exhibit C.) There is similar testimony in regard to papers in other cities particularly the *Freeman* of Indianapolis, the *Age* of New York and the *Citizen* of Boston. All these papers follow the same editorial policy, print the same syndicated news, praise the same persons and attack the same persons. Besides the more definite testimony there is a mass (Exhibit D) of corrob[or]ative circumstantial evidence, and all this leads me to estimate that $3000 is certainly the lowest possible estimate of the sums given these 6 papers in the year 1904; I firmly believe that the real sum expended was nearer $5000 and perhaps more than that.

The object of this distribution of money and other favors was, I believe, to stop the attacks being made on the policy of Mr. B. T. Washington. The reason for this belief is as follows:

1. The fact that these papers praise all that Mr. Washington does with suspicious unanimity.

2. The existence of a literary bureau at Tuskegee under Mr. Washington's private secretary, Emmett Scott. (cf. Exhibit B and F. No. 2.)

3. The sending out of syndicated matter from the bureau to appear simultaneously in the above mentioned papers and several others. This appears often in the form of editorials. (Exhibit E.)

4. The change of policy toward Mr. Washington of such papers as the *Age*, which formerly bitterly opposed his policy.

4.[1] The creation of new papers and buying up of old papers by Mr. Washington's friends or former employes. (Exhibit F.)

5. The rewarding of favorable newspapers by Mr. Washington. (Exhibit G.)

6. The abuse and warning of enemies through the syndicated papers, sending out of cartoons, etc. (Exhibit H.)

7. The use of political patronage to reward and punish.

Finally I was not the first to make this charge. It was common property among colored people, spoken and laughed about and repeatedly charged in the newspapers. (Exhibit J.)

What now ought to be the attitude of thinking Negroes toward this situation, assuming the facts alleged to be substantially true? Two things seem certain:

1. There was some time ago a strong opposition to Mr. Washington's policy developed among Negroes. In many cases this opposition became violent and abusive and in one case even riotous.

2. Since that time by the methods above described and also as the result of conference and statements by Mr. Washington, this opposition has been partially stopped.

Now personally I strongly oppose Mr. Washington's positions: those positions have been considerably modified for the better since the time of my first public dissent from them; but they are still in my mind dangerous and unsatisfactory in many particulars.

At the same time I have been very sorry to see the extremes to which criticism has gone. I anticipated this mud-slinging in my book and deprecated it, although I knew it would come. My rule of criticism has been, (a) to impute no bad motives (b) to make no purely personal attack. This has I think been adhered to in every single public utterance of mine on the subject hitherto. And when others have not adhered to it I have not hesitated to criticise them.

Moreover most of the criticism of Mr. Washington by Negro papers has not been violent. The *Conservator* was insistent but courteous; the *Record* under Cromwell was always moderate and saw things both to praise and condemn; The *Freeman* and *American* were open to the highest bidder on either side; the *Guardian* was at times violent although more moderate now than formerly, and has gained in standing as it has become less bitter. All this was a good sign. The air was clearing itself, the demand of the people known, and a healthy democratic out-come of the controversy seemed possible. It seemed at one time indeed possible that even the *Guardian* would see the situation in a better light. Then gradually a change came in. Criticism suddenly stopped in many quarters and fulsome adulation succeeded. Violent attacks on all opposers were printed in a certain set of papers. National organizations of Negroes were "captured" by indefensible methods. (Exhibit K.)

It thus became clearer and clearer to me and to others that the methods of Mr. Washington and his friends to stop violent attack had become a policy for wholesale hushing of all criticism and the crushing out of men who dared to criticise in any way. I felt it time to speak at least a word of warning.

I could not however make this warning as definite as I would have liked for three reasons.

1st. I did not want to drag Atlanta University into the controversy since the proceeding was altogether of my own initiative.

2nd. I did not want to ask those who privately gave me information to do so publicly. They are poor men and if, for instance, Mr. Cromwell, a teacher in the Washington Colored schools, were to testify as to the facts in public he might lose his position.

3rd. I uttered the warning to a Negro audience and it was addressed particularly to them; so far as possible I want to keep the internal struggles of the race in its own ranks. Our dirty linen ought not be exhibited too much in public.

For this latter reason many of my friends do not agree with me in the policy of speaking out. Kelly Miller, A. H. Grimke and others have repeatedly expressed to me that they are perfectly satisfied that Mr. Washington is furnishing money to Negro newspapers in return for their [the newspapers'][2] support.But they say: What are you going to do about it? He has the support of the nation, he has the political patronage of the administration, he has apparently unlimited cash, he has the ear of the white press and he is following exactly the methods of that press; and moreover his attitude on the race question is changing for the better. These are powerful arguments, but they do not satisfy me. I am however constrained by such representations to take up the matter cautiously and to see what warnings and aroused conscience in the race will do toward stopping this shameful condition of affairs.

On the other hand when I am convinced that the time has come, that bribery is still going on and gag law manifest, and political bossism saddled on a people advised to let politics alone, I will speak again in no uncertain words and I will prove every statement I make.

I regret to say that honest endeavors on my part in the past to understand and cooperate with Mr. Washington have not been successful. 'I recognize as clearly as anyone the necessity of race unity against a common enemy – but it must be unity against the enemy and not veiled surrender to them.' My attitude is not actuated by my sympathy with Mr. Trotter, editor of the Guardian. There was once a rumor that I was acting jointly with him. My reply to that was made in a letter to George F. Peabody, which I venture to enclose as Exhibit L. I went into conference last winter with Mr. Washington and his friends. Mr. Washington selected the personnel of the conference and it did not altogether please me but I attended and urged such of my friends as were invited to come also. In that conference I did not beat around the bush but told Mr. Washington plainly and frankly the causes of our differences of opinion with him.

Mr. Washington replied in a very satisfactory speech and his friends asked me to draw up a plan of a central committee of 12. This I did. The resulting committee which I helped select was good save in two cases where I was overruled by Mr. Washington and his friend. I was taken ill during the summer and the meeting of the committee was postponed; finally the committee was organized at a meeting to which I was not invited, and of which I knew nothing till 2 weeks afterward. Whether this was by accident or design I do not know. At any rate the committee was so organized as to put the whole power virtually in the hands of an executive committee and the appointment of that committee was left to Mr. Washington. Upon hearing this some two weeks after, I resigned my membership. I could not conscientiously deliver my freedom of thought and action into the hands of Mr. Washington and his special abettors like Fortune.

I am still uncertain as to how Mr. Washington himself ought to be judged in the bribery matter. I especially condemn the bribetakers and despise men like Fortune, Cooper, Alexander, Manly and Knox who are selling their papers. If they agree with Mr. Washington and he wishes to help them, the contributions ought to be open and above board; and if the contrary is the case and it is, to my unwavering belief, in 3 or 4 of the above instances, these men are scamps. Mr. Washington probably would defend himself by saying that he is unifying the Negro press, that his contributions are investments not bribes, and that the Tuskegee press bureau is a sort of Associated Negro Press. The reply to this is that the transactions do not appear to be thus honorable, that the character of the matter sent out is fulsome in praise of every deed of Mr. Washington's and abusive toward every critic, and that the men who are conducting the enterprises are not the better type of Negroes but in many cases the worst, as in the case of Fortune, Cooper, Knox and Thompson. (Exhibit M.)

In the trying situation in which we Negroes find ourselves today we especially need the aid and countenance of men like you. This may look to outsiders as a petty squabble of thoughtless self-seekers. It is in fact the life and death struggle of nine million men. It is easy of course to dismiss my contentions as the result of petty jealousy or short-sighted criticism — but the ease of the charge does not prove its truth. I know something of the Negro race and its condition and dangers, and while I am sure, and am glad to say, that Mr. Washington has done and is doing much to help the Negro, I just as firmly believe that he represents today in much of his work and policy the greatest of the hindering forces in the line of our true development and uplift. I beg to remain Very respectfully yours,

W. E. B. Du Bois

Exhibits A, B, C, D, E, F, G, H, J, K, L, M.

Please return.

Nota Bene. No attempt is made in the following exhibits to present all the evidence obtainable — I am simply giving typical examples of the sort of proof upon which I rely.

W. E. B. D.

Exhibit A (1).

(Copy of a part of a letter addressed to ——— from the editor of the Chicago Conservator.)

Chicago, Feb. 19, 1904.

. . . .

"Less than six weeks ago, I could have gotten Three Thousand Dollars for the use of the *Conservator* as a special booster of the Idol with a strong stipulated annuity — but we don't need it."

. . . .

Truly yours,
(Signed) D. R. Wilkins

The above letter was sent by the editor of the Conservator to a friend of mine. To corroborate the statement I asked my friend

Dr. C. E. Bentley, a prominent dentist of Chicago* to look into the matter; his answer follows:

Exhibit A (2).

Copy of a part of a letter to W. E. B. D. from Dr. Bentley.

Chicago, March 18, 05.

. . . He was approached by a gentleman and his wife of this city who are upon intimate terms with B. T. W. They also have the respect of the community. They submitted the proposition: if he — Wilkins — would use the columns of the Conservator in support of the work done at Tuskegee and cease to criticise Washington as a leader, that the sum of $3000 per year would be paid quarterly to him in advance. He took the matter under advisement, he says; that receiving no answer they came a second time and repeated the proposition adding that if he did not agree in all Mr. Washington said he need not stultify himself; but to give unqualified support to his work at Tuskegee, and that they would trust to time for his conversion upon all things else as represented by Mr. Washington.

Later on Mr. W. came to Chicago to lecture at Quinn Chapel. After he had gone Mr. Allison Sweeney — late editor of the *Conservator* — approached Wilkins and said there was $3000 per year, in advance for him — Wilkins — if he would change the policy of the paper as regards B. T. W. Wilkins says you are at liberty to use this data as you see fit. He would not divulge the names of the man and wife — altho that would not be hard guessing — but had no hesitancy in calling Sweeney's name. He also says that Sweeney became editor largely upon the representation made by him to the stockholders — that certain substantial contributions could be had from B. T. W. if he were made editor.

The *Conservator*, as you may know has gone under through the mismanagement of Sweeney — and the Charter, good will and mailing list are now matters of litigation between its owners and Wilkins. He has no doubt of finally securing the paper. Some of us are helping him in the fight. . . .

Hastily yours,
(Signed) C. E. Bentley.

* Elected head of the dental clinics at the St. Louis fair.

Exhibit A (3).

The "gentleman and wife" mentioned are Mr. & Mrs. S. Laing Williams.[3] He is secretary of Mr. Washington's Business League and she is a newspaper writer who usually reports the league meetings for the newspapers. Mr. Williams must have had ample ground for his promise as he is a careful truthful man.

Sweeney was formerly connected with the *Freeman* of Indianapolis one of the accused papers.

Exhibit B.

Washington, D.C. March 18, 1905.

. . . .

While I was with the *Record* I got definite information that there was a literary bureau at Tuskegee. In the month of September 1903, Mr. Frank Manly one of the owners of that paper, almost immediately after the adjournment of the Business Men's Convention held at Richmond, left this city to take a place at Tuskegee. Shortly after this items respecting Tuskegee and Mr. Washington appeared quite regularly. It was rare that this copy passed through my hands. . . .

When your (?) famous N.Y. conference was held I picked up the salient points of the gathering and gave it out. So accurate was the account that The Wizard was evidently baffled. But Frank Manly suddenly came here from Tuskegee and had published an account diametrically opposite in spirit to the story of Morris' celebrated talk on "Shams" that I had published, as the contribution of a "Staff correspondent." I was consulted about its publication and the understanding was that it should appear only as that of an "occasional" correspondent and not on the editorial page. When this understanding between me and Mr. G. was violated, my self-respect forced me to resign. It was the general belief that F. M. came here all the way from Tuskegee to bring things to a head and provoke a disagreement. I learned from a brother of his that a certain sum — say $40 a month — was received *regularly* here by the business manager to help float the paper. It will naturally suggest itself to you that Mr. F. M. could not afford to send that amount out of his own pocket regularly to help the paper.

. . . .

Very truly yours,
(Signed) J. W. Cromwell.

From the Washington *Bee*, March 11, 1905.

"It is true that Editor Cooper supported Mr. Washington when other papers were opposed to him. Whether he was paid for it, the Bee only knows what Mr. Cooper has said from time to time."

Exhibit C.

Mr. W. H. Ferris, a colored Yale graduate, and at present an American Missionary Association pastor, was in the office of the Washington Colored American discussing the race question; he heard J. Will Cole, an assistant editor say: "Industrialism is worth $500 a year to us."

[Told by Mr. Ferris to a friend of mine whose word can be depended upon][4]

Exhibit D.

Some of this proof is as follows:

1. The well known fact that the New York *Age* was in financial difficulties until its editor's intimate association with Mr. Washington began. The policy of the *Age* has in recent years been quite different than earlier.

2. The venality of the *Freeman* is proverbial. Its columns are for sale and have been offered to me indirectly, but plainly.

3. Mr. Charles Alexander, editor of the *Citizen* of Boston was quite without capital according to his statement to me in 1902, and is running his paper at a loss according to his sworn testimony in court.

4. The printers of the Boston *Citizen* speak of it as B. T. Washington's paper.

5. The purchase of the *Colored American magazine* by representatives of Mr. Washington and its removal from Boston to New York. The present editor[5] is a relative of Mrs. Washington and the business manager is Mr. Washington's assistant private secretary, Mr. Stokes.[6] Mr. Stokes also acts as business manager of the *Age*. The

former business manager of the Age[7] was appointed to a consulship in South America on recommendation of Mr. Washington.

Exhibit E.

The following "editorial" appeared in three or four papers of the "group."[8]

Indianapolis Freeman, Feb. 6, 1904.

Booker T. Washington's recent interview of two hours at the White House has attracted much attention. It is most satisfactory that the president and Mr. Washington continue their cordial relations. The president is entitled to every credit for his dependence upon this representative of the race in matters affecting our best interests.

Copy of part of an open letter to Mr. Washington published in the Jersey City *Appeal*, June 27, 1903:

An Open Letter.

Jersey City, N.J. June 27, '03.

Professor Booker T. Washington, Tuskegee, Ala.

My dear Mr. Washington: I have your letter of the 20th inst., with type-written paragraphs for the *Appeal*, which I marked "Refused" on the envelope and returned the same to you; I see your smooth way in subsidizing the Colored papers to boom yourself, by sending out editorials prepared at Tuskegee. . . .

I am yours for God and my race, fraternally

Joseph Summers.

Exhibit F.

1. After the Boston "riot" against Mr. Washington, the Boston *Citizen* was started by P. J. Smith a former collecting agent employed in the North by Tuskegee. He was succeeded in management by J. Will Cole, assistant editor of the *Colored American* of Washington D.C. Later Charles Alexander, formerly head of the printing department of Tuskegee took charge. None of these men had ever before given evidence of having any capital themselves.

2. In that paper, notes like the following have appeared. "If Washington would notice this toad he would be satisfied, and, as a friend of that good man, I would suggest you mentioning to Washington that if he will invite this creature to dinner, or show

him any courtesy whatever, he will cease his continued meanness, and sell himself for 'recognition.' "

. . . .

This led to a libel suit and a cross suit.

Under cross examination of Mr. Alexander by Attorney Benjamin the following was brought out, in regard to the above article.

Question. To whom did you refer in your article?

Answer. The editor of the *Guardian.*

Q. By whom was it written?

A. I assume the responsibility of its authorship.

Q. By whom was it written?

A. I assume the responsibility of it. I could not tell who wrote it. In fact I wrote some of it.

Q. How did you get it?

A. Through the mail.

Q. Do you know who sent it?

A. Yes.

Q. Who sent it?

A. Mr. Emmett J. Scott.

Q. Where does he reside?

A. In Tuskegee, Alabama.

3. Mr. Wilford Smith who has formerly acted as Mr. Washington's lawyer in various cases and has spent considerable time at Tuskegee, came from New York, and offered the publishers of the Boston *Guardian* $500 for the outstanding notes of that paper which represented their full value. He stated to the firm: "We have plenty of money behind us as you, of course, know."

Exhibit G.

(Copy.)

South Weymouth, Mass.

Mr. J. E. Dickerson, care The Norfolk News, Norfolk, Va.

Dear Mr. Dickerson — I am in receipt of your kind letter of July 9[9] and greatly regret my delay in answering it. I have been away from my mail a great deal lately and could not reach your letter sooner.

I am very grateful to you for the policy your paper has pursued and is pursuing. I have asked my publishers to send you an advertisement for my book "Up from Slavery" and I think they will do so. In addition, I shall place in the News an advertisement for my Agricultural Department at Tuskegee Institute. I shall be glad to hear from you from time to time and to see copies of your paper.

I hope you will see your way clear to attend the meeting of the National Negro Business League at Nashville, Tenn., during August 19, 20 and 21. It is an excellent organization and you would meet many fine men. We could thus become better acquainted.

Very truly yours,
Booker T. Washington

The above letter was printed in the news and kept standing for several issues. The *News* has severely attacked all newspapers criticising Mr. Washington.

Exhibit H.

Mr. L. M. Hershaw of Washington, D.C. a clerk in one of the departments publicly criticised Mr. Washington in a speech. There upon the following editorial note appeared in 3 or 4 of the group papers:

"It seems rather strange that Mr. L. M. Hershaw, a department clerk employed here, should be interested in contributing constantly to anti-Roosevelt Negro newspapers. It is a well known fact that Mr. Hershaw is the Washington correspondent for an anti-Roosevelt Colored paper published in Boston, and he now has the Washington *Bee* very largely on his shoulders. We repeat, it is strange that a man holding a position under President Roosevelt should contribute both editorially and otherwise so constantly to papers that are doing everything they can against the very administration under which Mr. Hershaw is holding his office."

To these, Mr. Hershaw replied in an open letter:

. . . I am now and always have been a Republican without variableness or shadow of turning. I have voted the Republican ticket, contributed cheerfully, willingly and without solicitation to Republican campaign funds and made speeches for that party, always paying my own expenses.

There are questions, however, in no way connected with the policy of the Republican party and the administration of the government, about which I have honest, fixed and conscientious convictions, and on those questions I have expressed my convictions orally and in writing, publicly and privately, and I have neither apology nor explanation to offer for having done so. As to such questions, I carry my sovereignty beneath my hat, and shall continue to do so while liberty endures and speech is free.

L. M. Hershaw

February 15, 1904.

Exhibit H-1½.

When the *Voice of the Negro* was started in Atlanta, Mr. Washington paid the business manager's fare to Tuskegee and asked to have his private secretary put on the staff as assistant editor to look after his (Mr. Washington's) "interests." This was done and Mr. Scott began to send editorials praising Mr. Washington and ridiculing opposition. He sent one poem "to the bronzen lion-faced" leader. That Mr. Barber, the managing editor refused to print. Thereupon Mr. Washington and Mr. Scott went to Mr. Hertel, head of the firm which finances the magazine, who has offices in Chicago and criticised the editors in various particulars. After some controversy Mr. Barber asked Scott to resign, and again Mr. Washington wrote the firm and complained that the policy of the magazine was against him. The publishers however refused to take any action against Mr. Barber.

(Above facts given me personally by Mr. J. Max Barber, managing editor of the Voice of the Negro. Documentary evidence of the same was shown at the time.)

In a recent meeting in New York, Mr. Washington was criticised, and Mr. Hayes in honor of whom the meeting was held did not resent the criticism but seemed to approve it. Thereupon the New York *Age* attacked him violently in a bitter editorial. This the *Home News* of Alexandria, Virginia, resents:

Exhibit H (2).

(From the Home News, Alexandria, Va. March 18, 1905.)

"Are we to understand that every Negro is to be stoned to death who dares, in any company or any cause, to raise his head in public without wearing the insignia of the house of Tuskegee? Shall we, even when we seek to serve the cause of true freedom at the altar of human liberty, be obliged to dress in the livery of the Washington cult?

"The signs multiply that such is the condition that confronts us. To quote Joseph Chamberlain, there seems to be 'a treaty, a compact, or an understanding if you please,' to that effect. If not, why then this bitter boycott against every man and every movement which bears not the Tuskegee label?

"These questions press for answers."

In the Boston *Traveller* of July 16, 1901 appeared a cartoon "Washington crossing the Delaware" and impeded by Negro hate, envy, jealousy, etc. One of Mr. Washington's secretaries came up from South Weymouth, Mr. Washington's summer home and paid an engraver $10 a piece for a number of these plates which subsequently appeared simultaneously in 6 or 7 Negro papers.

The above was told me by one who saw the plates being made and asked the cost. I rely implicitly on his testimony.

Exhibit J.

These charges have been made by several papers and very generally in private conversation for 2 or 3 years back. Recent instances are:

The Boston Guardian, July 30, 1904.

"We submit that in the evidence we have brought forth that there is a strong odor of corruption. Is it not corrupt for a man who is begging money for a philanthropic institution to be offering money for the notes of a Colored paper that is supposed to be in trouble? Can such a man legitimately secure the chief space in ten or a dozen weekly papers to boom himself? Can he legitimately hire a man to write for him in several papers each week? Is not corruption apparent when a newspaper arises from nobody knows what source, but espoused by men notoriously without money, who have been the employees or agents of a Negro educator, supposed to be, and which paper on some occasions has ten out of thirteen editorials in praise of said educator and whose columns are ever open for any attack on a paper that opposes him? Is a man corrupt who recommends corrupt men for political appointment, and who depends upon men of bad reputation to do his work for him?"

From the Washington *Bee,* March 11, 1905.

. . . We supported him* loyally from the day he was nominated at Chicago, and we are willing to have the matter which appeared in our columns for the period covering the Presidential canvass compared with the matter which appeared in the columns of the known subsidized organs, and leave it to any just person to judge if our support was not as thorough and whole hearted as the support of the subsidized organs.

It is discouraging to say the least, to see those charged with the formation of the minds and characters of those who are to greatly influence the race resorting to the methods which have made Tweedism, Crokerism and Tammanyism synonyms for corruption and graft.

Exhibit K.

The Afro-American Council when it met in St. Paul in 1902 was 6 or 7 years old and in shape to do good honorable work. Its president was Bishop A. Walters of the Zion Church. His logical successor was Bishop Scott, a man of sterling honesty, recently sent by the white M. E. Church as bishop to Africa. Mr. Washington and his private secretary appeared on the scene and to my astonishment announced his preference for T. T. Fortune as president. I pled with him because I knew the selection would kill the organization among decent Negroes. Mr. Washington was non-committal; Then by a scheme engineered by Mr. Washington's private secretary and Bill Pledger the chairman, the election was sprung on the body at the noon hour when a majority of the members were at dinner, and the proceeding was veiled under the guise of "accepting the report of the nominating committee." This the chairman ruled was equal to an election and installed Mr. Fortune over the protest of the majority of the body.

In 1903 the council met at Louisville. I refused to attend and went to Tuskegee to lecture to the summer school. Only last week a prominent lawyer in St. Paul, F. L. McGhee, explained the outcome there to me. He said "We had them easily beaten and would have elected Bishop Scott president, when a lot of new voters qualified by paying their fees of $5 and beat us by re-electing Fortune.

* (i.e., Roosevelt; above is in answer to an attack by the group papers.)

It must have cost Washington over $300 to carry the organization!" Fortune however was unable to do anything with the council and soon resigned the presidency. The organization is now practically dead.

Exhibit L.
Copy.

December 28, 1903.

Mr. George Foster Peabody,

My dear Mr. Peabody: Some time ago Mr. Ware,[10] our Chaplain spoke to me of a letter received from you in which you spoke of certain rumors as to my connection with the disturbances over Mr. Washington in Boston last summer. Later Dr. Bumstead wrote me of a similar letter not mentioning from whom he had received it, but I took it that it was probably from you.

I want therefore to write you frankly of my position in this matter that there may be no misapprehension, and I want you to feel at liberty, to use the letter as you may wish.

Mrs. Trotter, the wife of the editor of the Guardian is an old friend of mine of school days. Mr. Trotter I have not known as long or so well but met him in college. I had then and afterward disagreed with him rather sharply over many quetsions of policy and particularly over Mr. Washington but nevertheless both then and now I saw in him a clean-hearted utterly unselfish man whom I admired despite his dogged and unreasoning prejudices. Last summer while Mrs. Du Bois and I were looking for a boarding place, Mrs. Trotter offered to share her home with us and we gladly accepted. I went first to Tuskegee and then made a trip on a coast steamer. I did not arrive in Boston until after the Zion Church disturbance. Before seeing the account in the morning papers I had had no inkling or suspicion in any way of the matter. I did not know Mr. Washington was in Boston or intended to go there as I had just left him in Tuskegee. I had had no conference with Mr. Trotter for 6 months save in regard to the boarding place. When I arrived in Boston and heard of the meeting, I told Mr. Trotter and Mr. Forbes in plain terms my decided disapproval of the unfortunate occurrence and my conviction that it would do harm. Altho I was unable at that time to defend Mr. Washington's position as I once had, I nevertheless took occasion to address a meeting of men at Mr. Trotter's house and remarked of the vast difference between criticising Mr. Washington's policy and attacking him personally.

Nevertheless, brought into close contact with Mr. Trotter for the first time, my admiration for his unselfishness, pureness of heart and indomitable energy even when misguided, grew. And, too, I saw how local jealousies were working to make mountains out of mole-hills. So far as I could learn, had it not been for Mr. Lewis, the chairman of the Washington meeting, there would have been no riot — the disturbance could have [been] easily and quickly quelled and the dignity of the occasion saved. This same Mr. Lewis a few years ago was a rabid Anti-Washington man and wanted to "burn down Tuskegee." I labored with him and Trotter and Forbes in past years and was instrumental in getting Mr. Washington and Mr. Lewis together at a small luncheon so that they might understand each other. They evidently came to understand each other so well that Mr. Lewis got a political appointment and turning around proceeded to abuse his former comrades — a conversion in which I had as little faith as I had in his former radical stand.

There were a great many other things not generally known that made me pity and admire Mr. Trotter as well as condemn his lack of judgment and there were also things that made me have less and less faith in Mr. Washington. Nevertheless, I steadfastly condemned Mr. Trotter's action from that day to this — a fact which he will frankly testify to. When the matter was pushed to the extent of actual imprisonment I felt this was too much in view of all the facts and still feel so and I wrote an open letter to the "Guardian" expressing my disagreement on many points with him but my admiration for his honesty of purpose.

While then I had absolutely no knowledge of the Washington meeting before hand and no part active or passive in the disturbance and while I did then and do now condemn the disturbance, I nevertheless admire Mr. Trotter as a man and agree with him in his main contentions. When I think him in the right I shall help him, when his methods or opinions go beyond law and right I shall condemn them.

As between him and Mr. Washington, I unhesitatingly believe Mr. Trotter to be far nearer the right in his contentions and I only pray for such restraint and judgment on Mr. Trotter's part as will save to our cause his sincerity and unpurchasable soul, in these days when every energy is being used to put black men back into slavery and when Mr. Washington is leading the way backward.

I am sorry that I was not at the University when you called to welcome your party.

Very sincerely,
(Signed.) W. E. B. Du Bois.

Exhibit M.

Fortune is a man of ability and once bade fair to be a force, but he has degenerated fearfully and is now generally regarded as a drunkard, of loose private life, and unscrupulous and abusive in public life.

Cooper is notoriously dishonest, e.g.: Copy of part of letter from A. J. McN. to W. E. B. D.

February 1, 1905.

"My dear Sir: I have learned to my sad misfortune that Mr. E. E. Cooper is neither a reliable truthful nor honest man. . . ."

A. J. McNorton,
(Editor Colored Catholic Herald, Washington, D.C.)

Knox will do anything for money; witness his recent candidacy for Congress in Indiana where he appears to have been the paid puppet of Tom Taggart.

Thompson, who is joint editor of Bureau news with Emmett Scott (or at least signs much of the circular matter) left Washington D.C. under a cloud and was through Mr. Washington's influence given a political position in Indiana.

TLS Oswald Garrison Villard Papers MH. Occasional corrections or comments in Du Bois's hand.

1 Error in numbering in original.

2 Brackets in original.

3 Samuel Laing Williams and Fannie Barrier Williams.

4 Bracketed phrase in Du Bois's hand.

5 Roscoe Conkling Simmons.

6 Richard Le Roy Stokes, a stenographer in the principal's office at Tuskegee in 1903–4.

7 Jerome Bowers Peterson.

8 Du Bois submitted copies of editorials from the *Odd Fellows' Journal,* Feb. 6, 1904, and the Jacksonville *Florida Sentinel,* Feb. 6, 1904, identical with the editorial of the Indianapolis *Freeman.*

9 Dickerson wrote to BTW on July 9, 1903, asking for "your encouragement, indorsement and support to the work I am doing in this vicinity." "I have always been an enthusiast over your great work at Tuskegee," he wrote, and mentioned "the many indorsements of your work that have appeared from time to time in the News." He said he "would be grateful to receive any amount you can spare me." (Con. 256, BTW Papers, DLC.)

10 Edward Twichell Ware (1874–1927) was connected with Atlanta University for most of his life. He was born there during the presidency of his father, Edmund Asa Ware, founder of the school. After graduation from Yale and Union Theological Seminary, he was chaplain of the university from 1901 to 1907 and president from 1907 until 1922.

To Emmett Jay Scott

New York, March 25, 1905

Dear Mr. Scott: I had a very long talk with the President Thursday night. It is his general wish not to make any prominent appointments or changes, in the cases of colored people, for the present. Later on I think he will remove Lyons. He may give Ferguson a small Consularship.

~~Tell Mr. Thompson, by telephone, that the President was disturbed, because he found out that some of the endorsers of Tibbets did so thinking Mr. Thompson favored the appointment, that seemed to smack too much of machine methods.~~ Tell him also, that he is very desirous that all the appointments be of the highest type of efficiency, and that in once in a while it gives him the opportunity, as he calls it, "A spectacular appointment."

I went from the President, at his suggestion, to see Mr. Cortelyou, and I found him, much to my surprise, a completely changed man. He talked with me fully and freely on all matters discussed, and did not want me to leave his house. He has a very high opinion of Messrs Scott[1] and Thompson and will send for one or both of them to come and see him, very soon.

There is no doubt in my mind but that he is a candidate for the Presidency, and he may be the coming man. Very truly yours,

Booker T. Washington

TLS Con. 24 BTW Papers DLC.

1 Charles Herrington Scott.

From Anna Thomas Jeanes

Germantown [Pa.] 3/25–1905

Mr. Booker T. Washington Do you approve of the enclosed copy of my letter and check to Mr. George Foster Peabody, Treasurer of the General Education Board – I think it is all that is required, and the Bank will recognize my usual practice of identifying a check with its purpose. Respectfully

Anna T. Jeanes

Copy
Mr. George Foster Peabody,
Treasurer of General Education Board

I defer[r]ed answering your letter until I had seen Mr Frissell and Mr Washington – they now leave it to me to inform you of my gift of Two hundred Thousand dollars ($200,000.) as a Special Fund for the Assistance of Rural Colored Schools in the South, and also to request that for a limited time, their own Institutes may make use of the Interest accruing therefrom. Respectfully

Anna T. Jeanes

ALS Con. 29 BTW Papers DLC. Copy of Peabody letter in Anna Jeanes's hand.

Edward Elder Cooper to Emmett Jay Scott

Washington, D.C. Mar 25 1905

Dear Mr Scott – I am so amused over an incident which took place yesterday that I thought I would write you about it. For weeks the emis[s]aries of the Boston Guardian have been trying to have a confab with me and thinking that they wanted me to take up work on that paper I ignored them. Yesterday I was asked "in confidence" of course if I had the correspondence between Mr W– and you and myself. Without answering I indignantly asked why. Well, no harm was meant but they just wanted to look it over. My reply was – "not on your life" with epithets that would not look well in print. They are mistaken in their man. How are you anyway? I am still hunting for work and hope to find some ere long. If you know of anything do not fail to tell me. I hope to be on my feet again and when I am I shall remain on them. The Wizzard continues to do great work and like old wine he seems to improve with age. With best wishes I am sincerely

E E Cooper

ALS Con. 28 BTW Papers DLC.

To Abram L. Grant

Hotel Manhattan, New York, March 26, 1905

Personal & Confidential.

My dear Bishop: I saw the President at some length Thursday night, and we went over the matter, you are especially interested in. I told the President, as I told you I would, what I had in mind concerning the candidate[1] and friends. That part is now over.

The President is still undecided, but says if he does make a change, he will put in your friend.

My belief is that as soon as he returns from his Southwestern trip, that if you and some of his forceful friends from Kansas, perhaps one of the Senators, appear and talk the matter over with him, he will make the change. I think it would be a good idea to bring letters from several important persons to bear also.

He wants to please you in the matter, and he said quite frankly that since the other man[2] had been there eight years, he felt under no obligations to him: so I think the main thing needed now is a little bit of judicious pushing, guided by yourself. Very truly yours,

[Booker T. Washington]

TLc Con. 3 BTW Papers DLC.

1 William Tecumseh Vernon (1871–1944) was chosen in 1906 at the suggestion of Bishop Abram Grant to fill the post of register of the treasury, then the highest ap-

pointive office open to blacks. Educated at Lincoln Institute (Mo.) and Wilberforce, Vernon was converted to the A.M.E. Church in 1896 and became president of the denomination's Western University, Quindaro, Kan., in the same year. When S. Laing Williams, BTW's candidate for register, proved unacceptable to the Illinois congressmen, BTW accepted Vernon, perhaps because Vernon's educational philosophy was similar to his own. BTW's lieutenant Ralph W. Tyler gathered evidence that Vernon during the 1908 campaign pocketed expense money from two separate sources for the same Republican party errand. After his removal as register in 1910 he became president of another A.M.E. school, Campbell College in Mississippi (1912–15). Mockingly dubbed "the eloquent one" by Tyler, Vernon did have genuine oratorical gifts, and he was a popular pastor of Avery Chapel in Memphis from 1916 to 1920 and a bishop after 1920. He was suspended as bishop from 1932 to 1936 in a dispute over a shortage in his accounts. Soon after his restoration he retired to Quindaro.

2 Judson Whitlocke Lyons.

To Anna Thomas Jeanes

[New York City] Mar. 28, [190]5

Letter and contents received. Will see Dr Frissell today. Am sure he will agree with me in saying you have put the whole matter in the very best form. Your words are wiser than ours. Will Write.

Booker T. Washington

HWcSr Con. 716 BTW Papers DLC.

Emmett Jay Scott to Edward Elder Cooper

[Tuskegee, Ala.] March 28, 1905

Dear Mr. Cooper: I have your letter of March 25th, and make especial note of what you say with reference to the emissaries of the Boston Skunk, as Mr. Fortune inelegantly terms this newspaper. You have acted of course in this matter just as I knew you would. Sometime ago I saw in the Washington Bee a statement to the effect that you were planning to turn over all this correspondence to the enemy, ignoring of course, the fact that there is absolutely nothing in the correspondence that could not see the light of day and intimating at the same time that you were the type of man who could be used in such manner. I am very glad that you have indignantly replied to this suggested aspersion.

I trust that employment of a kind commensurate with your ability will soon be found and that, to use your phrase, you will soon be on your feet again. Yours very truly,

Emmett J. Scott

TLpS Con. 28 BTW Papers DLC.

From Emmett Jay Scott

Tuskegee Institute, Alabama. March 28, 1905

Dear Mr. Washington: I sent you several days ago a statement which I noticed in one of the Washington papers, The Bee I think, to the effect that Cooper intended turning over all the correspondence he had received from you and me. Cooper writes me today, however, of what he calls an amusing incident, namely, that for several weeks emissaries of the Guardian have been seeking to court him and that last week he was confidentially approached and asked if he had all of the correspondence in his possession written by you and me to him. Indignantly he says he asked why, and that he was told that no harm was meant, etc., which shows the depths to which this malignant crowd is willing to go. Cooper claims that he is not their kind of man and that he resents the opinion entertained that he would turn over to them our correspondence. Of course I have written Cooper that I appreciate this, but that even if he had turned the correspondence over to them there is nothing in the correspondence which we would seek to hide. Yours truly,

Emmett J. Scott

TLS Con. 556 BTW Papers DLC.

From William Eleroy Curtis

Washington, D.C. March 31. 1905

Dear President Washington: I have returned from my southern trip with renewed interest in Tuskegee. For fear you may not have received copies of my letters I enclose them herewith, and I have more material which I intend to use later. I did not wish to say too much upon the same subject at once, so limited myself to two letters, (which I send you) with an occasional reference when other subjects are under discussion. I congratulate you upon the great success and usefulness of your work; and it was gratifying to find such general approval of you and your methods from white people of all classes.

The only criticism I heard was based upon your intimate relations with Mr. Thompson; who, many people think, is using you to promote his own purposes, and some of your friends fear that he may involve you in embarrassments that will injure your usefulness. I saw no politicians in Alabama, but I saw a great many business men from whom I received information that convinced me that Thompson is trying to build up a political machine like that of Platt in New York and Quay in Pennsylvania. I have had a long talk with the President since my return and he has the same conviction. He told me he had promised you to retain Thompson until his (the President's) return from his vacation.

I have no doubt you have good reasons for supporting your protege so earnestly, but at the same time the President agrees with me and I am sure that many of your most sincere friends, who are familiar with the facts, are of the same opinion: that you are running dangerous risks in your relations with politicians. You cannot afford to guarantee the good faith of professional politicians. I took occasion to print something about Mr. Thompson in connection with Republican appointments which has given him great offence, and I intended to follow it up with other letters, showing his unfitness to be trusted with the responsibilities that have been placed upon him. But the President fears that my criticisms of Thompson may reflect upon you, because he is known to be your protege. I have therefore promised that I will not print anything more about him until the President returns from his vacation. But in the meantime I propose to investigate the character of his recommendations for appointment and satisfy myself whether he is honest or not. He has published a very intemperate attack upon me personally and threatens a libel suit, which shows bad judgement.

On your way from New York to Tuskegee I wish you would make it convenient to stop over here and let me talk with you, because there are several things in connection with the institution that I should like to ask you about.

With kind regards and great respect, I am, Your obedient servant,

William E. Curtis

TLS Con. 299 BTW Papers DLC.

To Alfred Holt Stone

[Tuskegee, Ala.] April 6, 1905

Personal

My dear Sir: Your letter of April 5th has just been received. By this mail I am sending you a copy of the "Successful Training of the Negro." I am sorry that you did not receive the last copy.

Some days ago I received a copy of the paper read by you recently in Philadelphia, and have read it with interest. In the latter part of this paper you speak of the fact that I make no reference in my recent article to the shortcomings of the colored people. I think you are mistaken; if you will read the marked portion of the whole letter which I send you, you will agree with me, I think, that I did not omit reference to the matter. I did not dwell upon the colored people's shortcomings in the letter, however, as much as I would do in an address to the colored people for the reason that I was speaking mainly to the white people concerning what I considered to be their duties. In my addresses to my own race I never fail to dwell upon the very points that are brought out in your paper.

I wish very much that you might see an experiment that is being conducted within about five miles of this institution. I was talking with the man who has charge of it this morning, and he tells me that he has this year 65 or 67 families on the plantation. I asked him how many moved away this year, and he said one, and I asked him how many last year and he said two at his request, and the year before only one left. This man has the greatest faith in the capacity and the character of the colored people upon his plantation, and because the people know that he has faith in them and trusts them, they stand by him.

I am very sorry that we have never been able to meet each other, and hope at some time that we can. Yours very truly,

Booker T. Washington

P.S. One other point I omitted to mention. I think that one of the fundamental diffculties in regard to the trouble in the South is in this direction: Within the last twenty years the industrial operations of the South have increased three or four fold perhaps. While this tremendous increase has been taking place, the South, unlike the rest of the country, has been depending upon the native population unaugmented by emigration to take care of the increased industrial operations. If New England or any other section of the United States had to depend upon natural increase of population to keep pace with the tremendous growth in industrial operations with other sections of the country, it would be in the same position that the South is.

The scarcity of labor, brought about largely in the way that I have mentioned, makes the laborers, in my opinion, feel an independence that results very often in their not sticking to a job in the way they would if they felt that if they gave up their present job they would have to seek many months before finding another.

B. T. W.

TLpS Con. 307 BTW Papers DLC.

To George Foster Peabody

[Tuskegee, Ala.] April 6, 1905

My dear Mr. Peabody: I have received all of your communications, and am very glad to know that you are so well pleased with the suggestion of putting Mr. Low upon our Board. After receiving your telegram I called to see him and asked him if he would be willing to consider the matter, and I found that he seemed to be most glad of the opportunity of going upon our Board should he be elected.

I wrote Mr. Hanna on the same subject but have not heard from him as yet.

The death of Mr. Purves[1] is a very severe blow to all of us. I cannot understand how Mr. Ogden holds up under all the afflictions that seem to come upon him. He teaches us all a great lesson.

I do hope that Mr. Murphy's present illness will not prove fatal. Yours very truly,

Booker T. Washington

TLpS Con. 30 BTW Papers DLC.

[1] Alexander Purves (1866–1905) was Robert C. Ogden's son-in-law. A banker with the Fielding Trust Co. in Philadelphia, he resigned this position to become treasurer of Hampton Institute in 1899. From that time until his death of typhoid fever in 1905 he was also administrative head of the Southern Improvement Co., which bought tracts of land near Hampton and Tuskegee and sold them on long terms at low interest to local black farmers, while also furnishing tools on credit and some rudimentary agricultural instruction.

To Josephine Turpin Washington[1]

[Tuskegee, Ala.] April 8, 1905

Personal and Confidential

My dear Mrs. Washington: I do not want you to think that I failed to act in good faith with you regarding the library. After considering the matter carefully and receiving a letter from your husband, it seemed that the proper way would be to do that which would secure a library to the race regardless of individuals. Perhaps Mr. Paterson has already explained to you that when we saw Mr. Carnegie, I endorsed Mr. Paterson's request that he give $10,000 for the school library on consideration that the trustees supply $1,000 annually towards current expenses, and that Mr. Carnegie give $5000 additional provided the city of Montgomery would give $500 annually towards its current expenses, all this with the understanding that your organization was to be permitted to share in the use of the library. Mr. Paterson perhaps has already explained all this to you.

It seemed to me it would not have been wise to let the opportunity to get a library slip by on account of a difference of ideas as to the use of it. The main thing, it seems to me, was to secure the building for the race, and to this I think you will agree with me that perhaps the wise thing has been done. Yours very truly,

Booker T. Washington

TLpS Con. 882 BTW Papers DLC.

[1] Josephine Turpin Washington, the wife of Samuel Somerville Hawkins Washington, taught mathematics at Tuskegee from 1894 to 1896 while her husband was the school physician. They later resided in Montgomery, Ala.

Francis Jackson Garrison to Oswald Garrison Villard

The Cedars, [Lexington, Mass.] April 9, 1905

Dear Oswald: I return the Du Bois letter & documents herewith, after showing them to Uncle William, who sympathizes with my view of the matter as expressed in my hasty letter of Friday to you. I do not know that I have much to add to what I then wrote. It will take a great deal more than what Du Bois has written or presented to shake my faith in Washington's purity of purpose & absolute freedom from selfishness & personal ambition. In spite of all the praise & honors & laudation that he is constantly receiving, I do not believe that he has any thought or purpose but the uplifting of his race, & I am sure that whatever he does is with that single object in view. Nor have I ever seen the slightest trace of personal jealousy, bitterness or resentment in him towards those who have been so despiteful towards him. His spirit & temper have been wonderfully calm & patient & enduring. Certainly the same cannot be said of Trotter & his sympathizers, & I cannot take any such stock in him as Du Bois does. I believe there is a vast deal of petty jealousy & spite in all this criticism of Washington, & I have never liked the bitterness betrayed by my friends the Wilsons,[1] (Mrs. W. especially) & by Mrs. Bumstead, when B.T.W. was mentioned. Their spirit seemed to me far, far below his, & their "atmosphere" was as unpleasant as his was inspiring. Trotter's behavior & speech at the mob meeting were that of a blackguard, & his purpose to wreck the meeting was deliberate.

Now as to the charges of subsidizing the negro press, the evidence offered by Du Bois is circumstantial & plausible, & I do not doubt that B.T.W. is doing all he can to influence the colored papers & secure unity rather than contention & discord, & this not because he cares for the attacks on himself, but because he knows that some of his assailants would gladly see Tuskegee wrecked if necessary to discredit & pull him down. He does show bad taste, or careless supervision of Scott, in allowing the latter to send fulsome praise of himself as syndicate matter. Theresa[2] suggests that he may draw on his personal income ($7500) from the Carnegie gift for this press business.

As for the men he influences, those mentioned by Du Bois are for the most part poor sticks, & like the mass of white politicians ready to sell their principles for an office or an income. I dare say Lewis would, though I have never heard before that B.T.W. had anything to do with his appointment, which was Roosevelt's reply to the taunt that he made colored appointments at the South only, & R. of course knew Lewis through his Harvard athletic career, which was sufficient without any prompting from W.

I must close abruptly for the mail, but shall be glad to respond to any points which you may wish to ask specifically about. In haste, affecty

Uncle Frank

I see B.T.W. quotes you in the April *Southern Workman* (p. 200) without naming you.[3]

ALS Oswald Garrison Villard Papers MH.

[1] Butler Roland Wilson.

[2] Theresa Holmes Garrison, second wife of Francis J. Garrison.

[3] In a brief note the *Southern Workman* quoted, from BTW's recent address at Augusta, Ga., his views on the "servant problem." BTW remarked: "The grandson of William Lloyd Garrison said to me a short time ago in New York that in his opinion, and he said this after having traveled through the South, few forces would go farther in the solution of the race problem than the placing in every white home in the South an intelligent and conscientious servant. This element of training we have too long avoided in our system of education, and, understand . . . I do not insist upon this kind of training being confined to the Negro race." (*Southern Workman*, 34 [Apr. 1905], 200–201.)

To John Stephens Durham

[Tuskegee, Ala.] April 10, 1905

Personal

My dear Mr. Durham: I received your letter while in New York. I have not written you lately because I have been under the impression that you owed me a letter. When I saw Mr. Fortune some days ago, he told me that he felt sure that you had written me last; however, that is a minor matter.

Matters seem to be going reasonably well at present. The President is now traveling in Texas and is receiving a royal welcome. I had a great fear that he would go into Texas and say something that would overturn the impression that his Lincoln Birthday speech made regarding the Negro. So great was my fear in this respect that I took occasion to see him before he started to Texas and he promised me that he would not say anything regarding the Negro while in the South, and so far he has kept his promise.

I do not mind saying to you confidentially, that I went over his Lincoln Birthday speech with him three times, and I am quite sure I helped him get it into shape so it would not hurt our cause. The first draft gave our cause away completely without the President, of course, knowing it. As soon as I called his attention to it, however, he was quick to see the point and most willing to make all the corrections I indicated. In fact, I do not think throughout the whole speech there was a single change which I asked him to make that he did not readily consent to.

I had hoped that in the reorganization of commissions in San Domingo there would be some hope for you to be of service and I have been on the lookout for that, but the fact that the President is out of Washington has made it rather awkward for me to keep in close touch with matters. I very much fear that many months will not pass before San Domingan affairs will be in the hands of some other government, and I suppose Haiti will follow soon.

I have been spending some weeks in New York City and vicinity, and I find that Fortune is down at hard work and is keeping himself very straight. He has the Haitian Ministership bee in his bonnet pretty stiff just now.

The policy of the President at present is to make no important changes where colored people are holding office. He does not want to stir the question up too much. He feels that the appointment of Anderson ought to be enough for a while.

It will interest you to know that many of the Republican leaders in New York whom Anderson most faithfully served for many years, made a most desperate attempt to stab him in the back; in fact, the truth is Anderson would not have been confirmed had not the President laid aside everything else and took hold of matters and forced his confirmation through the Senate. This I have not told even Anderson.

I am sorry to tell you that our friend Greener has gone wrong in Vladivostock. I have it from headquarters that he was head over heels in debt. He has gotten the drink habit, and would not answer the Department's letters.

Will you be kind enough to remember us all to Mrs. Durham. When are you coming North?

We are hoping to secure a summer residence on or near Long Island, and in that case we shall be able perhaps to see more of each other during the summer in case you come North in the future.

The death of Mr. Baldwin is a great calamity to all of us. Mrs. Baldwin comes here next week for a few days' visit. The fund in his memory has now reached the figure of about $130,000, and I am sure Mr. Schiff[1] would appreciate anything you might contribute toward it. Yours in great haste,

Booker T. Washington

TLpS Con. 20 BTW Papers DLC.

[1] Jacob Henry Schiff (1847–1920) was for many years a major contributor to Tuskegee, and for about a decade he permitted BTW to select each year about ten small black industrial schools, most of them outgrowths of Tuskegee and conducted by Tuskegee graduates, to which he gave varying amounts from $50 to $300. Though he never served as a trustee of Tuskegee, Schiff kept in touch with the school through BTW's frequent visits to his office, and his partner, Paul M. Warburg, was a trustee.

To William Eleroy Curtis

Tuskegee Institute, Alabama. April 11, 1905

My dear Mr. Curtis: The enclosed are the principal men in different parts of the country who hold Presidential offices. I have not been able to hear of but one of these during President Roosevelt's term of office who has gone wrong.

Two colored officials have been recalled from foreign countries during Mr. Roosevelt's administration, but not for defalcation but by reason of the fact that they did not seem to fill their places well. One of these, Mr. Richard T. Greener, was appointed by Mr. McKinley, and the other, Dr. Crossland, was appointed by President Roosevelt. Yours very truly,

Booker T. Washington

TLS NN-Sc. The enclosure was a list of nineteen black presidential appointees.

To Wallace Buttrick

[Tuskegee, Ala.] April 11, 1905

My dear Dr. Buttrick: Answering briefly your letter of recent date asking for a brief statement covering the conversations I had with Miss Jeanes concerning the fund which she has given to the General Education Board, I would say that I first met Miss Jeanes some eight or ten years ago and have kept in touch with her ever since. Some months ago I applied to her for a donation to help build a new dining room; she refused to give in that direction, but stated that Dr. Frissell had just seen her and had spoken to her concerning the good that a small sum of money might accomplish in assisting and encouraging the Hampton graduates who work in the small rural schools of the South. She said that Dr. Frissell told her it would be a Godsend in many cases if Hampton had a sum that it could use in encouraging worthy graduates to go back to their homes where they receive small salaries from the public fund and build up a good and creditable local rural school. The fact that Dr. Frissell told her that he himself received his first education in such a school seemed to impress her very much. She became so much interested in that phase of what Dr. Frissell told her, and recalling, as she told me, what she had read in the same direction in our little paper, the Southern Letter, concerning the struggles of our own graduates, that she decided to give $10,000 to the Hampton Institute, the interest of which was to be used in the direction that I have mentioned, and the same amount to the Tuskegee Institute.

After receiving the letter containing this offer, as I was passing through Philadelphia, I called to see Miss Jeanes, and I found that the subject of doing something to aid the small rural schools for colored people was very much in her mind. We talked for an hour or more on the subject, and at that time I think she stated she had already written to Dr. Frissell concerning her intention or wish to do still more in the same direction, at any rate, she told me when I saw her that if the project met the approval of Dr. Frissell and myself that she would be glad to give $200,000, the interest of which might be used for helping Negro rural schools.

Still later, Dr. Frissell and I both called in person to see her and talked with her for an hour or more, and encouraged her in the direction of giving her money for the purpose named. We discussed the subject of just the form that her letter of gift would take, and several drafts were made, and finally the one which has gone to Mr. Peabody was settled upon as being satisfactory.

So far as I could glean from her conversation, she had two objects in view so far as the Hampton Institute and the Tuskegee Institute were concerned. She did not care to give the money directly to these two institutions for the reason that it would seem to the public that these two schools were receiving money for their immediate work which, in fact, they were not receiving.

In the second place, she stated, and repeated it, I believe, in the letter of gift, that she wished the interest on this fund to be directed by the Principals of the Hampton Institute and the Tuskegee Institute for a limited period for the reason that until the fund was enlarged she did not think it wise to attempt to spread out the interest over too large a field. She expressed the hope that the fund would be added to from time to time, and that when it grew to a considerable size that the limitations so far as Hampton and Tuskegee were concerned, might disappear. She seemed very much averse to putting her wishes in definite form as to terms, dates, etc; these matters of detail she preferred to leave to the discretion and wisdom of the Trustees of the General Education Board. Yours very truly,

[Booker T. Washington]

TLp Con. 28 BTW Papers DLC.

To William Eleroy Curtis

[Tuskegee, Ala.] April 13, 1905

Personal and Confidential

My dear Mr. Curtis: I very much fear that you have been imposed upon by the persons who gave you the information brought out in the enclosed paragraph from one of your letters. I think you will find that a close personal examination will reveal the fact that in the Black Belt counties of Alabama that not a dozen white people altogether were required to pass any kind of an examination before registering. While in many cases colored people were required to pass the most severe examination, in fact I believe the registers would tell you frankly that the color of a man's skin decided the question largely as to whether he was allowed to vote.

It is true, however, and I want to say it to the credit of the white people of Alabama, that the 3600 colored people who are registered represent the very highest type of the colored people in the state, and I believe that in this 3600 we have a basis for a voting citizenship that shall mean much more in the future than the thousands of ignorant voters whose ballots were thrown aside.

I also believe, now that the temporary provisions for voting have disappeared, that in the future the law is going to be applied to both races with nearly equal strictness.

Now that I have found this little fault, I want to thank you again most earnestly for the kind, most helpful and generous things which you have said about our work. We are constantly hearing of the good that your words are doing.

[Booker T. Washington]

TLpf Con. 32 BTW Papers DLC.

To William Eleroy Curtis

[Tuskegee, Ala.] April 13, 1905

My dear Mr. Curtis: This is another one of my installments. I find that all of the ex-slave states give a certain amount of money for the support of some special institution, except Tennessee. In Tennessee the money that comes from the U.S. Land Script Fund is apportioned out among several existing colored institutions. I say that a colored school is supported, meaning that in most cases the larger proportion of the support simply passes through the state treasury from the United States Treasurer, the colored schools receiving their pro rata share of the various funds devoted to the Mechanical and Agricultural Colleges. These state institutions I would say, have on an average an attendance of 200 students.

It will be very difficult for me to answer your questions as to how much state money and how much Northern money goes into the education of the colored people in the higher institutions. I think it is fair to say, however, that 9/10 of the money for the support of the higher education of the Negro or their industrial education comes from the North. It may interest you, however, to know that there are several cases of colleges and industrial schools that are wholly supported by Southern white people; the most notable case is that of the Paine College of Augusta, Ga., supported almost wholly by the Southern white Methodist Church. There is a theological seminary at Tuscaloosa, Ala., supported wholly by the Southern Presbyterian Church. There are several other cases that I cannot now recall.

Our greatest need at Tuskegee just now is the increase of our Endowment Fund from its present figure, $1,040,000 to at least three million dollars so that we shall not have to depend upon miscellaneous begging for so large a proportion of our current expenses.

Next to the matter of an increased Endowment Fund, we could expend at least $100,000 in putting up much needed dormitories for both boys and girls.

If we had the funds, we could enlarge and improve our work in the direction of training more students in the various branches of agriculture, and when I say training more students that includes more thorough teaching in the way of additional appliances and instructors. Agriculture, in my opinion, is the one great industry in which the Negro is most likely to succeed and which is the base for him to lay the foundation for his future career.

If I can furnish further information at any time, please do not hesitate to call upon me. Yours very truly,

Booker T. Washington

TLpS Con. 2 BTW Papers DLC.

From Neal L. Anderson

Montgomery, Ala. April 14th 1905

My dear Prof. Washington: Prof. Paterson has spoken to me of your letter to him of recent date concerning the interview in the Advertiser of April 1st giving an account of the gift by Mr. Carnegie of $10,000 for a Library for the State Normal School of Montgomery, in which there is no reference made to your relation to Prof. Paterson's visit to New York City.

I think it due Prof. Paterson to state that when he returned to Montgomery he spoke most appreciatively of the assistance you rendered him, and made special mention of this in his first report to our Executive Committee held this afternoon.

It was my earnest desire that there should be no newspaper notice of this gift until the money was actually in hand, and the interview was given the Press only because of the fact that through other parties the matter had become general rumor on the streets, and it was thought best to have a brief authoritative statement made instead of having the papers publish what had been told the reporters on the streets.

When this interview was given it was not known by any one in Montgomery that you were even in New York at the same time with Prof. Paterson. Knowing Mr. Murphy's kindly interest in the matter it was supposed that he had continued to be of great assistance to Prof. Paterson.

As it is the policy of the Board to keep the School out of the papers as much as possible no further reference has been made in the local Press to this gift. Very truly yours,

Neal L Anderson

TLS Con. 297 BTW Papers DLC.

To Charles Betts Galloway

[Tuskegee, Ala.] April 15, 1905

Personal

My dear Sir: I have received your note concerning aid from Mr. Carnegie for Millsaps College. I shall be most happy to serve you in any manner I can in securing this aid, but before moving in the matter I think it well to put one or two facts before you.

Mr. Carnegie was kind enough to go over his plans pretty fully with me some days ago for future giving, and he is intending to devote considerable money to the aiding of such colleges as you mention, but his present plan is to stick to the policy of requiring the college to raise from friends as much money as he gives, in that case, your college would have to raise $25,000. If you [think] this could be done, I have no doubt but what Mr. Carnegie would make the conditional gift at once. If, on the other hand, you feel that the additional gift could not be raised, I should not mind making an attempt when I see Mr. Carnegie to get him to waive this condition in your case, but with what success I do not know. If the latter plan were tried, it would be best to wait until the fall as he is preparing now to sail for Europe in a few days. If it could be arranged when he returns in the fall for you to make a personal call upon him, I think that would accomplish a great deal more than much writing. Of course he sees very few people, but I think the way could be opened for you to see him. In several cases by judicious methods I have been able to get him to make exceptions to his rule, but the most direct and surest way in securing aid would be to let him follow his usual plan, and I repeat, in that case I should not mind writing him at once.

Now as to the book which you have received. I have heard of the book but have never seen or read it and do not expect to. I knew several months ago that it was being prepared, and I am glad to say that it was not written by a Northern white man or by a Southern white man, but by a German who has been in this country only a short while, and the best evidence I can get seems to indicate that he wrote it for the purpose of creating a sensation and making money out of it. I consider that the results of the circulation of this book bring the highest testimony as to the esteem in which our work is held in the South. Care has been taken to send the book to practically every newspaper of importance in the country, North and South, and this was done two or three months ago. So far, only three papers in the United States have even mentioned the book, and it has fallen completely flat. Only one paper in the South has referred to it, and not a single one in Alabama.

Of course it would be idle for me to deny the assertions mentioned in the book, because any man who would permit such a condition of things to obtain would have no hesitation in making a denial. My policy is to let our work speak for itself.

Whenever I can serve you in any manner, please do not hesitate to let me know. Yours truly,

Booker T. Washington

To try to express myself still more plainly, I think if Mr. Carnegie is applied to and pressed for an answer now, he will lay down the usual conditions; that, of course, would shut off, perhaps, future negotiations with him.

TLpS Con. 302 BTW Papers DLC.

Oswald Garrison Villard to William Edward Burghardt Du Bois

[New York City] April 18th, 1905

Dear Dr. Du Bois, I found your long letter with its enclosures on my return from the South. I must say frankly that it will take a great deal more than the evidence you have presented to shake my faith in Mr. Washington's purity of purpose, and absolute freedom from selfishness and personal ambition. At the same time, the evidence would seem to show that the literary bureau at Tuskegee under Mr. Scott has been extremely injudicious. It also looks as if money aid had been given; but you have failed to substantiate your positive statement in the Voice of the Negro that three thousand dollars was the sum used, since you say the testimony "leads me to estimate." Several of your counts I do not think you substantiate at all, notably the use of political patronage. So far as your witnesses are concerned, I am unable to judge of their reliability. Your "Exhibit C.," for instance, contains the statement of an assistant editor heard by Mr. Ferris, and repeated by Mr. Ferris to a friend who in turn repeated it to you. This sort of thing would have no weight in court. I cite this merely as an instance.

I shall certainly speak to Mr. Washington about Scott's ac[tivities][1] and I think it would be a very good thing if you would let me submit the whole correspondence the next time he comes to New York. I want particularly to take him to task for your connection with the council, and ask him whether the apparent slight to you was not really due to accident. I think you made a great mistake in resigning from it.

I hold no brief for Mr. Washington. As my writings show, I am a sincere believer in the higher education of the negro, and I am doing what I can to help Atlanta and similar institutions. I may also lay claim to being a devoted friend to the race, to whose interests I am giving a very large share of my time. You will perhaps permit me therefore to say frankly that I greatly regret your position and your attitude towards Mr. Washington. I do not think that there are any essential differences between your positions. I do believe that for the masses of the negro race industrialism is the all-important question of the hour. It goes without saying that to have proper industrial schools we must have such institutions as Atlanta and Fisk to furnish proper instructors.

As for Trotter, he was under me at Harvard, and his father was a sergeant in my uncle's company in the 55th Massachusetts. I consider young Trotter a very dangerous, almost irresponsible, young man, whose conduct at the Boston riot should make it impossible for anyone to consider seriously his opinions upon any subject relating to his race.

In the hope that you will grant me the permission I desire, Yours very truly,

[Oswald Garrison Villard]

TLc Oswald Garrison Villard Papers MH.

[1] Manuscript torn.

To Emmett Jay Scott

Tuskegee, Alabama. April 19, 1905

Mr. Scott: I want to refute indirectly each one of the principal charges made against the school by Von Grabill, and I wish you would have a short typewritten analysis of the book made covering the principal points so that I may deal with them.

Also let me have at the earliest opportunity a memorandum of any special matters that ought to be dealt with in my report.

B. T. W.

TLI Con. 557 BTW Papers DLC.

From John A. Hertel

Chicago 4/19/05

Dear Mr. Washington: I received a copy of the letter that you wrote to Dr. Bowen some days ago. I was very glad to see the excellent article in the April number of "The Voice" regarding your work at Tuskegee.[1] I also wrote our editors that I much appreciated it and that it is just what your institution and your work deserves. I feel sure, Mr. Washington, everything will come around all right in time. Both Mr. Jenkins and myself have had this matter up. Of course, we must work along pleasantly and judiciously.

I wish, however, to state confidentially that I am assured by both our editors they are not going out of the way in any manner to criticise you or your work. On the other hand, you are to a very great extent a public man and, as is the custom with magazines a man *who does things* not only receives commendation but also comes in for some criticism.

I hope that you are making good progress with our new book, "The Negro in Business." Yours very truly,

J. A. Hertel

TLS Con. 29 BTW Papers DLC.

[1] J. W. E. Bowen, "Doing Things at Tuskegee Institute," *Voice of the Negro*, 2 (Apr. 1905), 249–53, an uncritical puff obviously intended to mollify BTW.

Emmett Jay Scott's Summary of *Confessions of a Yankee*

[Tuskegee, Ala., ca. Apr. 20, 1905]

Von Grabil's Book

1. He speaks of the existing evils and immoral results of Negro education.
2. In his third chapter he treats of the influence of education upon the race as affecting Morals, Religion, Social Equality, Industry, Criminality and Fidelity. He takes direct issue with the statement (Page 249 – Up From Slavery)[1] to the effect that it is base libel to say that 90% of Negro women are not virtuous etc. He says that he will not treat of the worst elements of the race, but of the very best – those at Tuskegee. Speaks of immorality existing between male & female students & between male teachers & girl students. Says that a large number of former girl students are in questionable resorts &c. Specifically he speaks of the Dallas (Texas) girl, of Mrs. Hamilton's case & an imagined case of some female teacher who deserted a child at a railroad station. Says these things have been suppressed.
3. In speaking of influence of school on the town – & the fact that we have a "Theological Department," he gives a lot of questions

(Biblical in character) with silly answers from farmers in town during Christmas week.

4. Says there would be no Race problem but for northern philanthropists. Says Negro is alright when not spoiled & says *Social Equality* is taught & practiced at the school & by you when away from school. Says that some one from town was asked in one of the offices to take off his hat.

5. Says during building time 400 to 500 "foreign" Negroes are imported & paid. That students hate to work & that had a rebellion here once when tried to enforce a regulation for more labor. Says that these imported Negroes are given diplomas when they finish a building. Says that Montgomery woman who wrote for a cook was told that we were not educating cooks & housemaids, but preparing them for higher walks in life. Tells an imaginary story of some girl who was engaged as a seamstress you [who?] c'd not sew & who confessed that the Industrial Diploma was thrown in because she had finished with High Honors in *Vocal Culture* & *Modeling Art*. Speaks of second hand clothing being allowed to rot & mould. Says Tuskegee students crowd criminal docket — that there were two (2) terms before Tuskegee came & that there are now 6 terms held. Says crime has increased 90% & that white sheriffs & posses have had to quell riots on school grounds.

AM Con. 556 BTW Papers DLC.

[1] See above, 1:347.

William Edward Burghardt Du Bois to Oswald Garrison Villard

Atlanta, Ga., April 20, 1905

Confidential

My dear Sir: Good faith to my correspondents will not allow the proposed use of the matter sent you.

I trust you will not misinterpret my position: your attitude toward the Negro has been commendable; I am not seeking to change your opinions, I am merely showing you, at your own request, the reasons why my faith in Mr. Washington has been shaken.

It happens that in the same mail with your letter are two other letters. One is from a man who has edited a Negro newspaper 22 years; he says:

"But for the assistance Booker T. Washington has and is rendering the Cleveland O. *Journal* it would have been dead many weeks ago. The same is true of the Boston *Colored Citizen.* That he has subsidized the New York *Age* and Indianapolis *Freeman,* and owns the *Colored American Magazine* as well as assisting other alleged race papers, you are doubtless aware."

Another is from one of the most intelligent young Negro physicians in New England, who serves some of the best white families:

"He told me a story which firmly convinces me that Mr. Washington heads an organization in every large city whose purpose it is to ruin any man who openly criticises his methods in any particular. And I am now of the opinion that it is time that the decent element of the race take a stand for the things which are necessary for our further progress."

Such actions are not "injudicious," Mr. Villard, they are now *wrong.* I do not believe you can make Mr. Scott, the scape goat for them — it is scarcely conceivable that he has acted without Mr. Washington's full knowledge and consent.

As I have intimated, I am not submitting to you all the evidence obtainable, nor am I submitting it to a court of law. I am merely showing you the sort of testimony that has moved me to speak and act, and naturally its weight with me depends on the character of the witnesses whom I know and you do not.

Contrary to your opinion there was to my mind no alternative left me but to resign from Mr. Washington's committee: I thoroughly believed that by means of downright bribery and intimidation he was influencing men to do his will and had obtained a majority of such men on his committee; that he was seeking not the welfare of the Negro race but personal power; under such circumstances with the additional slight of not being invited to the most important meeting of the Committee, could I continue to co-operate with him?

You have attacked Mr. Roosevelt harshly. Does that mean that he is a rascal? No, but it does mean that you think he loans himself to indefensible deeds and measures, and that the general tendency of his policies is dangerous; if you believe this you have a right to proclaim it and act accordingly, and people must respect your intentions even if they doubt your judgment. So in this case: I am convinced of Mr. Washington's wrong course. You are not. Very well, I only ask for my convictions the same charity that you ask for yours. Respectfully yours,

W. E. B. Du Bois

TLS Oswald Garrison Villard Papers MH.

From Elkan Naumburg

New York, April 21, 1905

Dear Mr. Washington: Some years ago I visited some Southern cotton mills with my friend, Mr. Seth M. Milliken,[1] who has been the Northern pioneer in assisting the South build cotton mills. Though somewhat out of my line, I looked towards the future in that direction with great confidence, and invested in several of these enterprises.

Upon my first visit to Spartanburg, I mentioned to Capt. Montgomery,[2] who is one of the ablest manufacturers, that "it is simply a question of time when your white labor will give out, and you will have to obtain colored labor." Capt. Montgomery, a regular Southern gentleman, who had served in the Confederate Army, and a fair-minded, broad-gauged man, said "It is impossible." Well, what did happen about four years ago, which was about four or five years after the first conversation? Captain Montgomery with Mr. Milliken bought a cotton mill in Charleston, S.C. and employed colored labor. I was very enthusiastic about it, and paid a big price for some of the stock, which I am sorry to say is almost worthless today.

If you remember, I wrote you about this matter at the time when the fiasco occurred, and you were kind enough to call at my office, but unfortunately I was out. You wrote me a letter then that the fault was with the city of Charleston and not with the colored help, since the inducement to "loaf" was greater in the city than it was in the country, and at that time you enclosed a clipping about a silk mill in the South which was worked by colored labor, and apparently successful at that time; but since then I have heard that that mill also failed. Am I correct?

So much for the prelude. What I want to say to you now is this: I have just returned from a tour of observation through some of the cotton mills in South & North Carolina, and the whole cry now is the scarcity of labor. I received a letter this morning from Georgia in which the President speaks in a very optimistic way about the Southern cotton mills, but he ends up thus: "The only draw-back is the scarcity of help."

I do not need to tell you the reasons my friends give for not being able to employ colored labor — that if they are paid off on Saturday night, they do not make their appearance on Monday morning — not until their money is spent &c. And then again in some other sections when the strawberry season or other seasons begin where they can get a little better pay in out-door work, they do not report at the mill &c.

Now, I am very anxious that my prediction as to colored labor in that direction should become true. How can it be done, Mr. Washington? Of course I can see at a glance that if the majority or only a portion of the colored mill men were of the kind that you have at your institute things would be settled. Why couldn't some of your students start out in that direction, and with their influence and training get a large proportion of the colored population in any one neighborhood to follow them and to mind them? Have you any suggestions you can make that would prove profitable to the merchant and to the banker to begin cotton mills in the South with colored labor? Think the matter over, talk it over with some of your students, and see what can be done in that direction, and if I can lend an assisting hand, you will find me ready to help you, and thus obviate the scarcity of labor and make a pecuniary success to the stockholder and at the same time help the colored race. Very truly yours,

E Naumburg

TLpS Con. 879 BTW Papers DLC.

1 Seth Mellen Milliken (1836–1920) founded with William Deering in 1866 the

New York investment banking firm of Deering, Milliken & Co., with special interest in northeastern and southern manufacturing.

2 John H. Montgomery (1833–1902), a former Confederate captain, turned to manufacturing after the Civil War. From 1874 to 1884 he manufactured fertilizer, but beginning in 1881 he became involved in a number of cotton-manufacturing companies in Spartanburg and elsewhere in the Piedmont of South Carolina. From 1899 to 1901 he owned and operated the Charleston Cotton Mill. The mill had been unprofitable for some years and continued to be so when in 1897 the previous owner changed to black labor. The failure of the mill was attributed to the use of black labor, by proponents of an all-white mill-labor force. Opponents of this employment segregation, on the other hand, argued that there were many other factors in its failure, including the low-country location of the mill.

From Emmett Jay Scott

Tuskegee Institute, Alabama. April 21, 1905

Dear Mr. Washington: As I tried to indicate to you a day or two ago, a large number of my friends have written from Texas to the effect that Ferguson[1] is the only man whom Lyon,[2] the State National Committeeman, is disposed to assist in any way, and in assisting him he is only disposed to send him out of the country on a diplomatic mission. Ferguson and all of his friends say that the only thing that has kept him out of a Presidential appointment has been the Tuskegee influence; this he has acknowledged on numerous occasions. I believe that it is the old game of the white bosses to claim to Ferguson that he cannot be appointed in the state because this influence is against him, and then since he refuses to take a diplomatic position leave the Negroes high and dry without any appointment. Mr. Smith[3] seems not to make any headway with the machine, and so I am disposed to ask if it will at all be possible for you to in any way help the Negroes of the state to getting a Presidential appointment in view of the present aspect of things. I very much dislike to see them relegated to the rear, and even if I have no love for Ferguson I should like to see him rammed down the throats of the Lily white bosses since I appreciate so well what their real position is. I should like to have a moment to go over the matter with you before leaving if you are disposed to consider the matter. I hand you herewith a clipping from the Victoria

Guide,[4] of which Mr. Baughman,[5] whom you met, is the editor. Yours truly,

Emmett J. Scott

TLS Con. 30 BTW Papers DLC.

1 Charles M. Ferguson.

2 Cecil Lyons, a former Rough Rider, was the leader of the lily-white faction in Texas.

3 Robert Lloyd Smith.

4 The undated clipping endorsed Charles M. Ferguson for another federal position after he had been offered and had refused a consulship.

5 Theodore Baughman published the *Texas Guide*, a black newspaper in Victoria, Tex., from 1895 to 1910. Later he was editor of two newspapers in Tulsa, Okla., the *Oklahoma Sun* (1922–24) and the *Oklahoma Eagle* (1924–37).

Emmett Jay Scott to the Principal's Office Staff

Tuskegee: 4/22/05

The Principal has complained very earnestly that the affairs of the Office are not as carefully screened from the office boys (& such others as come into the office) as they should be.

It is his wish & I communicate it for your earnest attention that (1) Office boys be allowed to have nothing to do with any of the correspondence that comes into the office. (2) that everything be removed from the desk when you are not present yourself & that this be kept as much in mind *at twelve o'clock,* as *at 5 o'clock.* I shall ask – as I have indicated your co-operation – active & sympathetic – to the end that these things may be done. He feels in the matter strongly because he has been here at noon early morning & even evening & found matters out that he insists should not be allowed to remain out for general inspection.

Thanking you for past help & asking a continuance in this matter – I am, Yours very truly,

Emmett J. Scott

Please o.k. your name when noted.[1]

ALS Con. 556 BTW Papers DLC.

1 Sent to and initialed by J. Frank Armstrong, Nathan Hunt, Sue B. Thomas, Penelope B. Lloyd, Julius R. Cox, and Clinton J. Calloway.

From J. W. Adams

Muskogee, I.T. May 1st. 1905

My dear Mr. Washington: You will find enclosed my resignation as member of the Board of Trustees.

It is with the deepest regret that it was not possible for me to remain at Montgomery to continue to render my little service to the Institution in that field, but even though a change of residence has occurred there is no change in my feelings toward the Institution. I will always bear a Tuskegee banner and spread the Tuskegee spirit, as, to my mind, it is the right spirit to instill into the hearts and minds of this and future generations of our people.

I pray that you may ever live long to continue to press forward the great and good work in which you are engaged.

As to my successor, I would recommend Mr. N. H. Alexander[1] or Mr. V. H. Tulane. Both are strong and honorable gentlemen but I am of the opinion that Mr. Tulane will be in a position to render more service to the Institution, and again, Mr. Tulane is a practical business man and one who has the respect and confidence of the masses. Mr. Tulane has ever impressed me as one who would never tire doing what he could for the School.

I am convinced that there is no section of the Country where the Tuskegee spirit is more needed than in the Territory, as our people here own nearly all of the farm lands in the Creek Nation, but not having had the advantage of industrial training, they know not the value of their lands and are disposing of them as fast as the people from the States can come in and purchase. There are Colored farmers in this section who own as much as 3000 acres of land, as good as any land in the Country. With the Tuskegee spirit, this could be made the greatest section of the Country for the Colored man.

There is no section of the Country that shows the Negro in business more than the Territory. Some of the Towns have as many as 25 Negro business enterprises. Muskogee, the Metropolis of the Indian Territory, had the Negro in the following businesses, two Banks, two Millinery establishments, about twenty first class retail Grocery stores, one Wholesale Grocery, one Clothing and Gents Furnishing store, two Dry Goods Stores, one Steam Laundry, several Dress Making Establishments, one Drug Store, six good Hotels, several Cafes and Barber Shops. In the past twelve months quite a number of brick buildings have been erected by Colored men. Recently, Dr. Brown of Miss. came here and purchased two vacant business lots at a cost of $17,800 on which Mr. Carter also of Miss. purchased a business lot on which to erect a brick bldg. He will erect, this Summer, two three story brick buildings. As to Professional men, I don't think there is any place in the Country where we are better represented. We have nine Doctors and twelve Lawyers, some of whom are the most influential at the Bar. We also have three Weekly papers and one Daily Paper all of which have a nice circulation.

I assure you that you may continue to confide in me, and that I stand ever ready to render any service possible, to you or the Institution.

With best wishes that the good Lord may continue to shower upon you and the Institution, His blessings, I am, Yours truly,

J. W. Adams

TLS Con. 31 BTW Papers DLC.

[1] Nathan H. Alexander (1854–1915) was receiver of public moneys of the U.S. Land Office in Montgomery, Ala.

From Charles Alexander

Boston, Massachusetts May 6th, 1905

My Dear Doctor Washington: I am delighted to learn that you are to speak at Wilberforce University June 12th. I sincerely hope that the impression made on this occasion, will counteract the effect of some of the anti-Booker Washington sentiment prevailing in that little community. You will find the president[1] a two-faced sort of a fellow. He is always plausible, gifted with a wonderful flow of language and quite scientific in some of his discussions. He will tell you one thing when he means another, and will say something that will not be remembered, when he meets a person, concerning whose attitude he is not certain, but if he knows him to be opposed to

Booker T. Washington, why, he will give you many reasons why he is also opposed to him; but if you declare yourself friendly to Booker T. Washington and in sympathy with his movements and his philosophy, he will also claim that he has many reasons why he admires that gentleman. Beware of what is said to him in confidence. Of course Professor Scarborough needs no introduction, you are well acquainted with him. He is also very plausible and can tell many beautiful stories about his own successes, but I dare say you know enough about him to realize that he isn't worthy of any confidential sentiment. I am throwing these out as a suggestion to you. You are a wise man and there is hardly any necessity for my trying to post you. Mr. Anderson of Wilberforce who runs the grocery store there and who earns nearly $14,000 a year off of that community, will tell you that he admires you and your work, what he doesn't believe himself, so addicted to the habit of falsifying is he. Sincerely yours,

Charles Alexander

TLS Con. 27 BTW Papers DLC.

[1] Joshua H. Jones was president of Wilberforce University from 1900 to 1908.

From Francis Jackson Garrison

Boston, May 8, 1905

My dear Friend: I am enclosing with this a copy of a letter I have written to Charles Alexander, apropos of his appeal for my subscription to his new monthly.[1] It expresses, possibly with too great frankness, my feeling with regard to his late paper and to other race journals which are guilty of similar offenses against taste, sobriety, and self-respect, and I am not grieved to see it go under. Such papers do not deserve "boosting," in my opinion. I fear we must wait some years yet for a worthy representative race paper, edited with ability and dignity by men of character, soberness of speech and breadth of mind. College training does not always give the latter, as we know, but the more colored graduates Harvard, Yale and other strong colleges and universities send forth, the sooner we shall have the conductors and the readers for such a paper. I am glad that you have secured Leslie Hill for Tuskegee, and hope that you are finding him a worthy second to Bruce. Both those young men seem to me to be actuated by the true spirit.

I wish I could have a good talk with you. I do not see the "Guardian" often, but occasionally some one — possibly Trotter — sends me a marked copy with some malicious fling at you, and I have had other evidence lately of the covert efforts made to discredit you by those in sympathy with that sheet. It is asserted that you have subsidized and bolstered up several papers, including the Citizen, have supplied them (through Mr. Scott) with syndicate matter in laudation of yourself and Tuskegee, and that you are constantly endeavoring by fair means or foul to stifle and crush out all opposition to you and your policy, whether in the press, in conventions, or elsewhere, and all for your own personal advancement and glorification! This last charge is so preposterous to all who know you that it makes clear the animus of your assailants. As to whether you desire to avert an open rupture and alignment into opposing forces of the colored people of the North, and your fear as to its disastrous effect upon the whole educational work, has led you to take any of the measures asserted, I prefer to have your word rather than the innuendoes, inferences, and circumstantial evidence of your assailants. I know you appreciate the value and importance of keeping Tuskegee and its work before the country through the press, and that you have long done this through such agents as Mr. Thrasher; and I think it not impossible that you have deemed it legitimate to try and keep the colored press on sound lines for the reasons above mentioned, but certainly such papers as Alexander's confer no credit, and the support of any editor who is moved by purely mercenary considerations is not to be solicited or desired. If Trotter and his sympathizers are bound to assail you, they will do it in spite of all efforts to avert it, but personally I should not be troubled as to the result, which can only be a recoil on themselves. They want, no doubt, to alienate your white as well as colored friends and supporters, and hence are bruiting such statements as I have mentioned. Thus far I have taken no notice of them, though I have been tempted once or twice to free my mind vigorously, when a marked "Guardian" came to me, but they have not ventured to approach me in any other manner. I wish when you have a chance (if you are not coming to Boston soon) you would write me freely about this whole matter. If I blow a blast, I want to feel fortified at all points. Yours very truly,

Francis J. Garrison

P.S. By the way, I have just noticed, since writing to Alexander, that the "Guardian" refuses to accept those abominable advertisements. That is certainly to its credit.

TLS Con. 302 BTW Papers DLC.

[1] Garrison's letter to Charles Alexander, May 8, 1905, enclosed, expressed his disapproval that the Boston *Colored Citizen* in its news columns "lauds so indiscriminately and effusively everything done by any colored man or woman, with absurd exaggeration of adjective and display type." He added: "Even more painful to me . . . are the advertisements of fraudulent concoctions or recipes for bleaching the skin and straightening 'kinky' hair, and I am at a loss to understand how any self-respecting colored editor or publisher can admit such swindling schemes to his paper or tolerate them for a moment." He contrasted the earnest and straightforward tone of Tuskegee's *Southern Letter* with the reports of unimportant meetings and trivial society notes in the black weeklies.

To Oswald Garrison Villard

Hotel Manhattan, New York, May 10, 1905

Personal.

My dear Mr. Villard: Enclosed I send you an account of a trial of [a] young white man, for the killing of a Negro. The action of the jury and the words of the Judge are most encouraging. This was taken from the Birmingham Age-Herald.[1]

I leave for Tuskegee today. Very truly yours,

Booker T. Washington

TLc Con. 31 BTW Papers DLC.

[1] The jury in a Jasper, Ala., circuit court found a white businessman guilty of first-degree manslaughter in the shooting of a black man, and he was sentenced to eighteen months imprisonment. Judge A. H. Alston commended the jury, saying: ". . . I am glad to know that a Walker county jury has set the example of administering justice regardless of the conditions of the parties interested," and that "you have said that the majesty of the law will be upheld and justice done the black man as well as the white." (Birmingham *Age-Herald*, May 1, 1905, 2.)

To Roscoe Conkling Simmons

[Tuskegee, Ala.] May 13, 1905

Dear Mr. Simmons: I very much hope that there will be nothing whatever in the June issue of the Colored American Magazine about the school or myself. I think it was a little unfortunate that there were two articles from members of the school in the April number and still another in the May number.

Please ask Mr. Moore to leave out the Phelps Hall advertisement for June and July. Explain to him fully that I am doing this purely as a matter of caution. I do not want the public to feel that the Colored American Magazine is our organ. Later on I will put it in again. You may recall that there are three advertisements in the magazine that bear directly or indirectly on our work. Yours truly,

B. T. W.

TLpI Con. 30 BTW Papers DLC.

To Timothy Thomas Fortune

[Tuskegee, Ala.] May 13, 1905

Hope you can send completed manuscript Negro in Business early next week. Publishers pushing me hard.

Booker T. Washington

TWpSr Con. 29 BTW Papers DLC.

To Charles Alexander

[Tuskegee, Ala.] May 13, 1905

My dear Mr. Alexander: I note in one of your notices that you are going to republish my Coleridge Taylor article in your forthcoming magazine. I am very anxious that there be no other reference to me or to the school in that number of the magazine.

I hope you are having great success. Yours truly

Booker T. Washington

TLpS Con. 27 BTW Papers DLC.

To Oswald Garrison Villard

Tuskegee Institute, Alabama. May 13, 1905

My dear Mr. Villard: I am returning by this mail the International Quarterly which contains the article on The White Man's Burden at Home.[1] I think it a very fine article and wish very much that it might have a wide reading in the South. I hesitate a little about having our committee take it up and publish it in full for this reason, there is much in the article that might be twisted in the South into advocacy of social intermingling of the races, and I am wondering if that charge was made against the committee at this time before our work is thoroughly understood if it would not hurt rather than help the cause. I would like to have your judgment on this point. It might be, however, that the article might be republished with the paragraphs referred to taken out. Of course this is all on the supposition that the publishers of the magazine would allow us to republish Mr. Olivier's article. Yours very truly,

Booker T. Washington

TLS Oswald Garrison Villard Papers MH. A press copy is in Con. 31, BTW Papers, DLC.

1 "The White Man's Burden at Home," *International Quarterly*, 11 (April 1905), 6–23. The author, Sydney Haldane Olivier (1859–1943), a leading Fabian Socialist, was an officer in the British Colonial Office from 1890 to 1913, including several terms as governor of Jamaica. In 1924 he was secretary of state for India. He was the author of several books on Africa, Jamaica, and the exploitation of cheap labor in the colonies. In "The White Man's Burden at Home" he argued that whites and blacks could live together in harmony, but only if theories of racial inequality were discarded and forgotten. He maintained that the seeming superiority of intellect of whites was the result of environment and history and that blacks could achieve the same levels if properly encouraged by whites. He considered Reconstruction reforms too hasty and

insufficiently paternalistic. On race mixture, Olivier had views influenced by Jamaican experience. He approved sexual congress between white men and black women but not between black men and white women, on the grounds of "bad natural economy," for whites were so far advanced that "their maternity must be economized to the utmost."

To James M. Henderson[1]

[Tuskegee, Ala.] May 16, 1905

Personal and Confidential

My dear Dr. Henderson: I thank you for your letter of May 15th regarding the book. I would say that this book has been out, as I understand it, about four months. I have heard of it but I have never seen it. I knew before it came out that it was being prepared. I am glad to say that the book was not written by a Northern white man or a Southern white man but rather a renegade foreigner who happened to drift into the town of Tuskegee. He became offended at the school because we refused to pay him $150 to give a musical concert to the students, and also because we refused to buy musical instruments from him. Coupled with this feeling of revenge, I think he wished to create a sensation by which he would receive quite an income from the sale of these books. I am glad to say, however, that the whole thing has fallen completely flat, except in two cases not a single Southern paper has noticed the book, although it has been sent to every Southern paper and many in the North. Dr. John Massey, the president of the white female college in the town of Tuskegee, has just written a strong denial of the statements in this book and connected with this a most hearty endorsement of the school, and only five minutes ago I telephoned to the editor[2] of the local white paper urging him not to publish these endorsements because I thought it best not to notice the book in any way whatever. The whole performance I am sure has done a great deal more good than harm. Yours very truly,

Booker T. Washington

TLpS Con. 302 BTW Papers DLC.

[1] James M. Henderson (1859–1928), an A.M.E. minister, lawyer, and college president, was a graduate of Oberlin (1881). From 1896 to 1904 he was president of Morris

Brown College in Atlanta, Ga. He then moved to Selma, Ala., where he was president of Payne Institute until 1909. After retiring from Payne he returned to the ministry and a law practice in Detroit.

2 Charles Woodroph Hare.

To Elkan Naumburg

[Tuskegee, Ala.] May 17, 1905

Dear Mr. Naumburg: I have delayed answering your letter of April 21st for the reason that soon after it was received I started for New York and planned fully to call and see you and answer the letter in person, but I was prevented from calling.

To answer your letter in brief, I believe that one of the best things that can be done would be for you or some one interested in putting the Negro in the cotton mill to visit Fayetteville, N.C., and inspect the operations of a silk factory that has been under the control of colored people for a number of years and I understand is quite successful. I believe thoroughly in the view that if you would take the colored people off into the country and build houses for them in the same way that is being done for the white cotton mill operatives in North Carolina and elsewhere that the venture would be a success. The operatives in the silk mill in Fayetteville are under the control of a colored man.

If I can serve you further please be kind enough to let me know. Yours very truly,

Booker T. Washington

TLpS Con. 879 BTW Papers DLC.

To Francis Jackson Garrison

Tuskegee Institute, Alabama. May 17, 1905

Personal

My dear Mr. Garrison: I hope you will forgive me for the delay in answering your letter with a copy of one enclosed to Mr. Alexander. The last few days have been very busy ones with me, occupied mainly in catching up with work that I found on my return from New York.

I thank you for sending me the copy of the letter which you have written Mr. Alexander, and also for what you say in the letter directed to me.

In regard to Mr. Alexander's paper I would state that I have not read a copy of it for the last two or three months and am not in a position to know just what it has contained, although I know its general policy.

I wish you might have a talk at some time with Rev. Bradley Gilman who is now residing in Boston, and he can tell you on one or two occasions he has felt so deeply the attacks of the Guardian upon me and the necessity for something being done to offset this influence that he has appealed to me to give an endorsement to him or somebody else that would result in his getting money from people in Boston to strengthen Alexander's paper. On each occasion such suggestions have been made to me by Mr. Alexander, Mr. Gilman or anybody else, I have refused to give my consent or to act in the matter. I have always taken the position that my friends can do me no greater injury than to be constantly defending me. On the other hand, I have told my friends that when the Tuskegee school does anything that is worth the notice of the public they can help the work and help me by making that known to the world, but the mere policy of defense I have discouraged.

I suppose I have spoken to Mr. Alexander not less than half a dozen times against the constant use of my name in his paper. The same experience I have had with many other colored editors.

Enclosed I send you a few extracts from letters that I have written Mr. Alexander on this subject, also some extracts from letters which I have written to the editor of the Colored American Magazine published in New York.

I consider Mr. Alexander a thoroughly good and earnest man, but like most of us his judgment is often bad.

It is difficult for me to deal with a man who is so utterly wanting in truth or honor as Trotter. He has no hesitation whatever in giving assertion to the most baseless and unreasonable falsehoods. For example, he has constantly asserted that I owned the Colored American Magazine. The fact is, I do not own a dollar's worth of interest in a single Negro publication in this country. At one time

I did own fifty dollars worth of stock which I purchased simply for the purpose of helping the magazine out when it was in Boston, but as soon as I saw the assertion made that I was trying to control publications with money I gave the stock away.

Leaving aside for a minute the moral question of the action, it would be the most suicidal policy that I could pursue as a public man to attempt to control the public press with money, even if I had it to spend in that way. In the first place, any editor who would accept money one week to control his editorial utterances would want money the following week, and so on to the end.

In the second place, the minute it was known that one paper was receiving pay, each one of the 200 other colored papers published in the United States would want pay and if they did not receive it of course would jump on me with both feet. If a man wanted to kill himself with the colored press he could pursue no better policy than of trying to control their utterances through pay. The fact is, Mr. Trotter and his few followers are trying the old game of trying to get something for nothing; they want public approval and confidence without paying the price to secure it. For nearly twenty-five years I have been spending my time and strength night and day, winter and summer, in coming into contact with the colored people of every section of the United States. The result is that I know in a personal and friendly way practically all the colored editors and leaders of the country, and it is because of this personal touch and because I have given them my confidence and let them understand fully my policy and objects that they support me. The only embarrassment I have, as I stated a few minutes ago, is to keep them from lauding me too much.

What I said to you regarding my relations to the colored press can be repeated in regard to my relation to the various colored organizations throughout the country. For nearly twenty-five years I have been attending these conventions and giving them my message in the best manner I could. The result is that I know the best leaders of thought and action and they are in close touch and sympathy with me. Mr. Trotter cannot understand why he cannot get the same kind of confidence and influence over the colored people in a few months when his greatest claim to notoriety is an attempt to break up a Negro meeting. There is practically never a national organization which assembles anywhere in the country composed of our people that I do not receive an invitation to deliver an address. For example, only this week I have refused to deliver an address before the National Negro Medical Association which assembles in Richmond next summer; before the National Negro Educational Association which assembles in Atlanta; before the National Negro Southern Convention which assembles in Montgomery. This is an example of what takes place every week. Another example: I have just received an invitation to be present and deliver an address before the Afro-American Council which meets in Detroit in August. I have refused this invitation as I have done three or four times in the past on the ground that I have told the president[1] frankly that it is a political organization and that I did not want my presence at such a meeting to seem to modify or control the action of the meeting. I realize fully that such organizations can do a work which I cannot do and such organizations ought to be left free to do their work unimpaired by my presence or seeming influence. I do perhaps, attend about a third of the meetings of the organization, but for the reason mentioned I attend comparatively few of them.

Of course I am human and I believe thoroughly in the policy which I am trying to advocate, and it would certainly be wrong for me not to use every legitimate means to keep the race in harmony as far as possible with the policies in which I believe, but I have tried to do this in a manly, open manner and pursuing methods that all of my friends would approve. There is one department of our school, Phelps Hall Bible Training School, especially that is pretty generally advertised in the Negro press. This is done because the person who started this work has given us money for this special purpose, but in every case where we have put the advertisement we have said frankly to the editors that we did not want the fact that we were placing an advertisement in their columns in any way to influence their editorial policy.

Of course, with a man of Trotter's make-up it is impossible for him to understand how one may differ with me on certain vital points and still at the same time be friendly and decent toward me. There are several colored papers that differ from me in several respects, and many individuals who differ from me very vitally but all of whom at the same time are friendly and respectful. For example, Mr. Charles W. Chesnutt, the colored writer, and I differ radically on many, if not most, of the points that are before our race, still he and I have been on the most friendly and personal terms; whenever I go to Cleveland I am his guest, and he comes to Tuskegee to see me. His daughter for a number of years was one of our teachers, and I could mention a number of other such cases, but Trotter cannot understand how one can differ from me without continually heaping personal abuse upon me.

I am glad to say to you that Leslie Hill is here and is giving complete satisfaction; in fact, he and Mr. Bruce are two of the finest examples of what college education can do for our people that I know of. How much I wish that all of the young colored men around Boston could see something of the spirit and usefulness of these two men. They are entirely forgetful of self in their devotion to the cause that we all love.

In my haste I am sure that I am answering your letter very unsatisfactorily. I shall keep the whole matter in mind and when I am in Boston again I shall call to see you.

It is perhaps true that Mr. Scott in his attempt to keep the work of the school before the public, which I consider legitimate educational work, has sent too much matter to the colored papers in laudation of myself, and I shall see that he is more careful in the future.

I hope that you will write me fully at any time when you feel that there is anything that ought to be called to my attention. My only object is to do the best thing for the race and for all concerned. Yours very truly,

Booker T. Washington

We have another young man here from Harvard University by the name of David Houston,[2] who is just as fine in spirit and action as Mr. Bruce and Mr. Hill. He is a native of Cambridge.

TLS Francis J. Garrison Papers NN-Sc. Copies are in the Oswald Garrison Villard Papers, MH, and Con. 302, BTW Papers, DLC.

[1] William H. Steward.

[2] Gordon David Houston (1880–1940), a 1904 Harvard graduate, taught English at Tuskegee Institute from 1904 to 1907. When Houston left Tuskegee before the expiration of his contract to teach in the Baltimore city schools, BTW used letters critical of Tuskegee that were stolen from Houston's pastor's desk to embarrass him and force an apology. (Harlan, "Secret Life of BTW," 409.) From 1912 to 1919 Houston was director of the English department at Howard University.

An Article in *The Independent*

[May 18, 1905]

A Man about Whom the World Should Know

A great deal has been said about colored people who are trying to help their own race; much has been stated about the Northern white people who have given service and money in the elevation of my race in the South, but one hears very little of a small class of Southern white men who are quietly and privately working to help forward the interests of the colored people and therefore the interests of both races. It is for this reason that I am calling the attention of my readers to Mr. R. O. Simpson, of Furman, Wilcox County, Alabama, a man about whom the world ought to know more.

Mr. Simpson was born at Belleville, Conecuh County, Alabama, December 1st, 1842, which means that he is now 63 years old. During his youth he received some education in an academy near his home, but, like many young Southern men of his time, Mr. Simpson left school at an early age to enter the Confederate Army. He joined the Second Alabama Cavalry, in which he served through the war. Returning penniless to his home at the close of the war, Mr. Simpson took charge of a plantation belonging to Mr. Dabney Palmer, his uncle. He has prospered as a business man and now owns several thousand acres of the most valuable land in Alabama.

Wilcox County, to which Mr. Simpson came in 1861, is in the center of the "Black Belt" of the South, where the colored people outnumber the white people about four to one. There are in the immediate neighborhood of Mr. Simpson's house hundreds of colored people, many of whom were formerly owned by Mr. Simpson's family, and he, himself, also owned slaves inherited from his father. About twenty years ago the idea began to grow upon Mr. Simpson that he ought to use a portion of his wealth and time in helping to make more useful citizens of the colored people. How to begin, however, was a great puzzle to him. The way did not seem to open until a young colored man by the name of William J. Edwards, whose father lived on Mr. Simpson's plantation, began to work his way through a nearby Normal School. Mr. Simpson had loaned him several small sums of money, but with the lending the loan was forgotten. Some months afterward, much to the surprise of Mr. Simpson, young Edwards voluntarily appeared one day and repaid the loan. The act of this educated young negro impressed Mr. Simpson deeply. He began to reason that if education would help one negro to the point where he would act in this manner, it would help others, and he began to talk with Edwards about starting a school upon his plantation. After some search a vacant and abandoned log cabin was found and a little school was opened with twenty-five pupils. The results of the work of this school founded in 1898 have been marvelous. The Snow Hill Institute has now 308 students, 55 of whom are boarders, and the students this year have come from five States. There are 22 teachers and helpers. The school owns 100 acres of land and two rather large, substantial buildings, a third one having been recently destroyed by fire. In addition to these two large buildings there are many smaller ones. The whole property is valued at $35,000.

Mr. Simpson's part in this wonderful growth has been to me one of the most beautiful and inspiring object lessons that I have known in my experience in Southern education. Mr. Simpson is a doer and not a talker. I have never heard him make speeches over ten minutes in length. No man could watch over a member of his own family with more solicitude and tender care than does Mr. Simpson guard this school, and between him and Edwards there is complete faith.

Mr. Simpson had given 100 acres of land to the school, and many times when the treasury has been completely empty, when there has been no money to buy food or pay the teachers, even before an appeal could be made to him, he has from his private funds supplied the needs. Aside from what Mr. Simpson has done in the matter of gifts of land and funds for the erection of buildings, he contributes generously each year to the current expenses of the institution. From the first he has been President of the Board of Trustees. His son was Treasurer and is now Auditor, and his whole family is as deeply interested as Mr. Simpson is himself. The influence of Mr. Simpson has spread even further — many white people in that section of Alabama who formerly had little faith in negro education now contribute toward the support of this school.

One white man, Mr. C. W. Hooper, of Selma, Ala., made a few

weeks ago an unsolicited contribution of one hundred dollars.

The importance of the education of the colored children has impressed itself so deeply upon Mr. Simpson that he recently helped to found another school in another portion of the county. My readers may get some further idea of his deep interest when I say that both these schools are connected with Mr. Simpson's home by telephone. Within a few months he has placed his business in the hands of his sons in order that he might be able to devote his entire time to helping the people who need help. Mr. Simpson has not only interested himself in the material and educational improvement of the colored people, but has been equally outspoken and strong in his stand in favor of the colored man receiving justice in the courts and in favor of his being permitted to vote wherever he satisfies the demands of the State constitution.

Mr. Simpson's help and interest are not confined to the colored people. The white schools and churches share his interest and generosity, but, since the colored population is more numerous and more needy, he is especially interested in helping them.

Not many days pass that do not find this benefactor on the school grounds in consultation with Mr. Edwards. His days are now largely spent in going among the people, encouraging them to buy land and homes, to be frugal, to educate their children and to live Christian lives.

Mr. Simpson is, as I have said, a modest and unassuming man of few words, but having made up his mind that a certain course is right, and having clearly perceived his duty, he has pursued it steadfastly in spite of opposition or adverse criticism.

Independent, 58 (May 18, 1905), 1115–16. Copy in Con. 968, BTW Papers, DLC.

To Portia Marshall Washington

[Tuskegee, Ala.] May 20, 1905

My dear Portia: I think your idea of boarding in a German family is a good one, and much better than the boarding school idea. I wish you would talk the matter over thoroughly with your German teacher, and remind me to do the same thing when I see you on the 14th of June, so as to have everything thoroughly understood before you sail. Your papa,

B. T. W.

TLpI Con. 17 BTW Papers DLC.

To Francis Jackson Garrison

Tuskegee Institute, Alabama. May 20, 1905

Personal

My dear Mr. Garrison: I fear just a little that there was a paragraph in my letter which might prove misleading. I do not want you to get the impression that we do not make an attempt to send out from this institution matters of news which we think will be of value in advancing the interests of the school and of the race. That we have always done in what we hope was a judicious and commendable manner, and as I attempted to say, it may be that in doing this we have sent out matter that seems to others to be much of laudation of individuals connected with the school, but what was done we have considered legitimate advertising.

When I wrote you Mr. Scott was absent, and since his return from Texas I have taken up in detail the subject with him to find out just what has been his policy, and he tells me that he has tried to avoid sending out anything except that which contains an element of news that would advance the interests I have referred to. Aside from this, Mr. Scott has considered the whole matter in a broader light. For example, an invitation has just come to me from the King of Belgium to attend a congress of some kind in Brussels during the coming summer. Mr. Scott feels that the sending out of such an item of news helps the whole race in that it would show the narrow white people that their prejudices are not shared by other parts of the world, and at the same time such news would encourage the colored people.

I speak to you thus frankly in order that you may get wholly our point of view. Yours very truly,

Booker T. Washington

I suppose that Mr. Scott sends out a good deal of this matter in performing his duty as agent of the Associated Press in this section. So far as I know, he is the only colored agent in the United States.

B. T. W.

TLS Francis J. Garrison Papers NN-Sc. Copies are in the Oswald Garrison Villard Papers, MH, and Con. 882, BTW Papers, DLC.

To Cain Washington Triplett, John Perry Powell, Poindexter Smith, Ocie Romeo Burns, and John Brown Twitty[1]

[Tuskegee, Ala.] May 23, 1905

My dear Friends: I am writing this letter to all of you to let you know that during our Commencement season we are thinking of you, and to let you know how very much we are looking forward to your efforts in that far away land. Mr. Hunt has the most gratifying opinion of your abilities and has written me as per the enclosed issue of the Tuskegee Student shows. Mr. Scott thought it well to publish this statement in the Student so that our graduates and friends might know just how you are regarded by Mr. Hunt. I wish to impress upon you the fact that it is incumbent upon you for the sake of the institution as well as for yourselves, that you put forth every effort to make the experiment a success, if it fails it not only carries you down, but us as well, and I wish you to justify the high faith which Mr. Hunt has. I am very glad to have had the chance to talk with him several times in New York recently and to learn that he feels as warmly toward you as he does.

We shall send you copies of The Student containing our Commencement exercises so that you may keep in touch somewhat with the exercises going on during your absence. Yours very truly,

Booker T. Washington

TLpS Con. 308 BTW Papers DLC. Addressed to Zeidab, Sudan.

[1] John Brown Twitty of Lenexa, Kan., was a member of the Tuskegee Institute senior class in 1904–5.

From Benjamin Franklin Trueblood

Boston, Mass. May 23, 1905

My dear Dr. Washington: At our Annual Meeting held on the 18th instant you were, by unanimous vote, chosen a Vice President of the American Peace Society.

We all appreciate the great services which you are rendering to the cause of international peace and very much hope that it will be agreeable to you to serve as a Vice President of the Society.

The position involves no necessary duties.

We shall feel greatly honored to have you associated with us in this capacity.[1] Yours very sincerely,

Benjamin F. Trueblood

TLS Con. 308 BTW Papers DLC.

[1] BTW accepted the office and offered to do what he could to promote the aims of the society. BTW to Trueblood, May 30, 1905, Con. 308, BTW Papers, DLC.

From Francis Jackson Garrison

Boston May 23, 1905

My dear Friend: I received yesterday your very full letter of the 17th inst., for which I am heartily obliged to you. I am sorry to have taken even so much of your time as was involved in dictating it. What you say as to the certainty that, if one paper were subsidized, every other would want to be, and would be demanding its price, is perfectly true. (It is a sorry reflection on the character of the men who are running these papers that they are ready to sell themselves to anyone who has a long enough purse to buy! It is no less true, however, of the daily press in our large cities. Only a few days ago I learned of the ease with which a large brewing house, convicted and fined for the adulteration of its beer, purchased the silence of the entire daily press of Boston, with a single exception, by giving them a half-page advertisement for ten insertions, and not one of those papers informed its readers of the penalty which the courts had visited upon the adulterating firm, even as an item of news.) I am very glad to have your letter, and am much gratified by what you tell me about Leslie Hill and young Houston, of the latter of whom I had not heard before. By the way, I have just received a copy of the New York Age, sent in fulfillment of Alexander's unexpired subscriptions, and am surprised to find it so well printed and put together a sheet. I have not been familiar with it. I knew that the editor was a man of ability, but have rather regarded him as somewhat a "soldier of fortune" and open to "influence."

I presume that you and your family will spend the summer at Weymouth as usual. I am expecting to go abroad for the months of July and August, and shall spend the time chiefly in Switzerland and have much less time in England than I could wish – probably not over a week, which will be scant time to see all the people there I should like to.

With kind regards to Mrs. Washington and Miss Clark, I am Faithfully yours,

Francis J. Garrison

TLS Con. 302 BTW Papers DLC.

John Massey to the Board of Trustees of Tuskegee Normal and Industrial Institute

Tuskegee, Ala., May 23, 1905

While I concur in the sentiment of all the better class of Southern people, I wish to express my unqualified dissent from the conclusions drawn in "The Confessions of a Yankee," (1) that Social equality and mixing of the races are taught and encouraged in your school; and (2) that immorality is fostered under your management.

As a citizen of Tuskegee I have been an observer of the work of your School since its beginning. I have had in my employ some of its students for a number of years. I have not seen any thing in their conduct that caused me to think that they wished to push themselves into the association of the white people.

While such men as George W. Campbell and Wm H. Baldwin, R. O. Simpson and George Foster Peabody have been in your board and supervised your affairs, I cannot give credit to the conclusion of the writer that immorality is fostered in the institution, but, on the contrary, I believe that your management has endeavored to do the best possible, under the circumstances, for the moral development of the negroes. Instead of looking only for defects, and setting them in the strongest light, I prefer to be in the company of those whose aim is to lift human beings up rather [than] to pull them down. Yours respectfully,

John Massey

ALS Con. 255 BTW Papers DLC.

To John Massey

[Tuskegee, Ala.] May 29, 1905

My dear Sir: Owing to our closing exercises it has been impossible for me to find time before now to write for the purpose of thanking you for the letter which you have addressed to our Board of Trustees. You do not know how very deeply I appreciate it. If this letter had come from a non-resident of Tuskegee or from some one who had not been in almost daily contact with our work for twenty-four years, I should not have appreciated it half so much.

I have not seen the publication to which your letter refers and probably shall not see it, but I have heard of it several times. I have never made any reply to the falsehoods stated therein, and have prevented as far as I could others from doing so for the reason that I always try to proceed on the policy that a work in the long run will speak for itself; if it is good and wise it will last; if it is bad and unwise it will pass away. Perhaps it was largely through my own request that Mr. Hare did not publish the letter in his paper; I felt that your letter could be used to better advantage in the way that he has already explained, and the stirring up of the matter in the community would accomplish no good purpose. The publication, however, has given me the opportunity of finding out how deeply the majority of the white people in Tuskegee are interested in this school. From any number of sources without suggestion or application on my part, persons have told me that they were willing to put themselves on record as endorsing our work in the most hearty matter.

As you and other prominent citizens of Tuskegee well know, it is impossible to conduct an institution of any character or of any size without weaknesses appearing and without mistakes. We have made mistakes, and there have been occurrences from time to time of which we have been ashamed, but one policy I have always pursued and that is I have always gotten rid of any individual, whether student or teacher, who brought disgrace on the school. The wonder is that there have not been more instances of wrong doing than there have been. I think that no greater tribute could be paid to our twenty-four years of work than the fact no more mistakes and cases of wrong doing could have been brought to light than I understand this publication attempts to divulge. I shall not, of course, take your valuable time in denying many of the silly and unreasonable statements made. I consider that it would be almost an insult to an intelligent and high-minded man to ask him to discuss with me the sickening and filthy details that are covered. My main and only object is to thank you most heartily for what you have done. Yours very truly,

[Booker T. Washington]

TLc Con. 878 BTW Papers DLC.

To Francis Jackson Garrison

Tuskegee Institute, Alabama. May 29, 1905

My dear Mr. Garrison: I am writing for a Philadelphia firm a life of Frederick Douglass; it will be completed within a few weeks. One portion of it I am very anxious to submit to you in proof form before it is finally published. The portion in mind refers to two differences that came up between your father and Mr. Douglass; one was on the wisdom of his starting a newspaper, and the other regarding the methods to be pursued relating, as I understand it, to the use of politics in the abolishment of slavery. Yours very truly,

Booker T. Washington

TLS Francis J. Garrison Papers NN-Sc.

To James E. Bertram

[Tuskegee, Ala.] May 29, 1905

Personal

My dear Mr. Bertram: If you have not concluded matters in relation to the library for Professor Paterson's school at Montgomery, Alabama, I think it would be well for me to see you before you take final action. There are some developments which I should explain to you.

This information I hope you will treat as private. Yours very truly,

Booker T. Washington

TLpS Con. 298 BTW Papers DLC.

To Ellis Paxson Oberholtzer[1]

[Tuskegee, Ala.] May 30, 1905

My dear Sir: I wish to ask that Negro be spelled with a capital letter throughout the book, Frederick Douglass.

This request has been heeded by all of my publishers, and I shall be very glad if you will also see that it is observed by the printers. Very truly yours,

Booker T. Washington

TLpS Con. 27 BTW Papers DLC.

1 Ellis Paxson Oberholtzer (1868–1936), an American historian, was editor of American Crisis Biographies, in which series BTW's biography of Frederick Douglass appeared in 1907.

J. Frank Armstrong[1] to Timothy Thomas Fortune

[Tuskegee, Ala.] May 31, 1905

Dear Sir: I have been asked to hand you $50, and send you my personal check herein for the amount. You will understand why this money is sent. Yours truly,

J. Frank Armstrong

TLpS Con. 29 BTW Papers DLC.

1 J. Frank Armstrong was from 1903 to 1908 Emmett Scott's chief assistant in the principal's office at Tuskegee. He secured a medical education and in 1913 began practice in Chicago. (Scott to Armstrong, Mar. 5, 1913, Con. 470, BTW Papers, DLC.)

An Article in *Vim* by Edgar Charles Beall[1]

[May 1905]

BOOKER WASHINGTON, A.M., LL.D.
A PHRENOGRAPH FROM A PERSONAL EXAMINATION

The most conspicuous figure among the intellectual leaders of the colored race in this country, and perhaps in the entire world to-day, is Dr. Booker T. Washington. His prominence in this position is not due alone to the fact that the leadership is unique. It often happens that a man appears great because of some sort of isolation, yet who would instantly seem commonplace if a number of rivals were to appear. Dr. Washington has a pronounced individuality and many talents that would bring him to the front in any community and at any time. His position as an educator is particularly significant of the present tendency of the colored people to take higher ground, not only in the political and social world, but as regards the industrial and intellectual life.

To students of phrenophysics, Dr. Washington presents many interesting features. He is five feet, six inches in height, weighs 176 lbs., and is a remarkable example of health, strength and bodily endurance. He has an especially fine development of the chest. His breathing capacity is enormous, and has much to do with his general vigor of body and mind, as well as courage, hope, personal magnetism and general executive force. Another very interesting sign of breathing power is in the width of his nostrils.

His head measures 22 inches, which indicates the full size, although this figure does not fully denote the power of the man, for the reason that some of his best developments are in the crown of the head far above the line of the basilar circumference. Besides, some of his deficiencies are in the direction of ornate qualities which would not add materially to his power.

The back head is large, showing a full equipment of all the social attachments and affections, including love for wife, family, friends and home. In the region of the ears the width is considerable at the seat of courage. Secretiveness is also well-developed. Caution, which is near the top of the head, is not so large.

Coming forward from the ear, it will be noticed in the accompanying photograph that the lower temporal region is quite narrow. This reveals a lack of the hoarding instinct or sense of property; also want of ingenuity and construction. Southerners, both white and black, usually have narrow heads, and are generally averse to mercantile and mechanical pursuits. This is true, in fact, of all tropical races, and is more and more noticeable as we approach the equator, so that Dr. Washington is not at all exceptional in these respects. However, in the matter of music he is an exception among colored men, and it is the lack of music, imagination and ideality which accounts for the general narrowness of his forehead in the upper temples.

This peculiarity detracts from the impressiveness of the forehead, but it must not be understood to be a detriment to the intellect. In fact, it is often the case that comparatively narrow and compressed foreheads are more intellectual than the very opposite type. This is because the narrow forehead is likely to be exclusively devoted to intellectual work. Such a man wastes no time on poetry or art. He is not diverted by amusements.

Again, the brain in the narrow forehead is likely to be more closely woven than in the broad type. The convolutions are often deeper, and, altogether, the judgment will be keener, stronger and more accurate. There is the same difference as regards efficiency between this type of forehead and the very expanded, balloon-like head, that there is between the axe and the maul.

It must also be remembered that a forehead may appear low and insignificant on account of deficient qualities in the frontal top head, some of which, like suavity, for instance, or imitation, do not add to the logical power. This explanation will answer the question so often asked as to why people with small foreheads are so often more talented than those with large.

Another peculiarity in which Dr. Washington is an exception among colored men, though much like most white men in the South, is that he has unusual self-reliance, dignity, self-poise, self-confidence, or the sense of personal value and power. This faculty is so uncommon in our northern States that most of our people fail to understand it. It is the dominant trait in the English character, but is very deficient in the French, Irish, Negroes and Americans generally. As a people we lack dignity, although we have great ambition or love of approbation.

Dr. Washington is thus more proud than vain; more independent than sensitive to the opinions of others; more disposed to stand his ground in the defense of a great principle than to turn aside to consult "Mrs. Grundy," and more inclined to trust to his own judgment and ability than to lean upon others. This quality of self-esteem gives elevation to the central part of the rear of the crown, and the development is indicated by the distance from the ear. A facial sign of this characteristic is in the length of the upper lip.

Approbativeness, which is situated just outwardly from self-esteem, on the corners, as it were, is also well developed, but not so strong as the twin faculty of self-esteem, or pride. Just forward of self-esteem, on a line with the ear, the head rises to a considerable height, which denotes great firmness. These two faculties work well together. One gives the desire for leadership, the other imparts the determination and persistence so often needed in carrying out the duties of a leader.

Such men are never satisfied in subordinate positions, unless clothed with authority to control other persons still below them. Here we have the key to much of Dr. Washington's executive power, and his ability to influence the affairs of the colored people in the South. He can make other people believe in him, largely because he believes in himself. He does not wobble or waver either in his opinions, his purposes, or his methods of work. No matter what he starts out to do, everybody who knows him feels sure that it will be accomplished. He is never flurried; is never embarrassed; never has stage-fright; is never "led off" by evil companions; never breaks his resolutions, and may be counted on to stand fast under opposition of every kind.

Conscientiousness and reverence are well developed, but there is no excess of any of the sentiments that produce extravagant belief, hope or imagination.

The intellect is well balanced as regards both the perceptive and reflective groups, but with a predominance of the former. This is shown in the greater fullness of the lower forehead as compared with the upper. The width between the eyes is the sign of exceptional memory for form. He will never forget faces, but owing to the depression above the outer part of the eyebrow he will have considerable difficulty with names. He has good memory of events and of details in a general way, but is not remarkable for order.

Language is excellent. His memory of words as revealed in the prominence of the eyeball is far above the ordinary. He should have talent for the study of languages. He would learn both the spirit and the vocabulary of a language very quickly. Though not skillful as a grammarian in all respects, he would soon acquire a foreign tongue if he heard it spoken; and by means of his great perception of form he would easily master the most complex printed characters.

The upper forehead displays fair capacities for abstract reasoning, but he is not fond of metaphysics. He is nothing if not matter-of-fact. He can plan, philosophize, and co-ordinate ideas, calculate consequences, and grasp the why and wherefore of things, whenever it is necessary to do so in the discharge of his duties, but he is not given to much speculation or dreaming in any form. This is not the head of a great thinker, but rather of a practical doer.

The development in the centre of the upper forehead is the mark of ability to read character. This faculty confers the ability to understand people's motives. It prompts to the observation of all kinds of phrenophysical signs. It enables him to know what people "mean." He is not disposed to credit his enemies with being loyal, or to suspect treason on the part of his friends. He has a good deal of *savoir faire,* and can generally manage to have his own way.

His principal talents may be summed up in the one word, intelligence. He has a great deal of good, hard, common sense, which is due in part to his health of body and mind, but particularly to the subordination of all non-essential, frivolous or diverting qualities, and concentration upon the serious business of life. His character is solid and substantial, and his ability consists more in being able to say and do the right thing at the right time than in any spectacular display. His thoughts and methods are straightforward and direct. He instinctively follows the principle of the simple life. He wastes neither time nor strength. Every move he makes is sure to count, and he succeeds as much because he knows what to leave undone as because he knows what to do.

He is a born public speaker, and his oratory is due primarily to the fact that he has something to say. He is thus more effective than if he talked for the mere pleasure of expression. Some of his best addresses will doubtless prove to be among those for which he consciously prepares the least.

He has a strong sense of humor, and his mirthfulness is particularly revealed in the upward curve at the outer corners of the mouth.

With such narrow temples he would never excel as an inventor, manufacturer or merchant. His social qualities, sense of human nature and language fit him eminently for some literary pursuit. He would have neither heart nor skill for any of the technical sciences that would confine him in a laboratory with no companions except mute instruments of glass or metal. Such a man must be out among the folks. In law, journalism or politics he would do well, but he would naturally succeed best in some form of higher educational work.

Vim, 5 (May 1905), 141–44.

1 Born in 1853, Edgar Charles Beall was the author of *The Brain and the Bible; or The Conflict between Mental Science and the Bible* (1882) and *The Life Sexual: A Study of the Philosophy, Physiology, Science, Art, and Hygiene of Love* (1905).

To William Loeb, Jr.

[Tuskegee, Ala.] June 5, 1905

Personal

My dear Mr. Loeb: Enclosed I return the letter and circular regarding the proposed Frederick Douglass Memorial Exposition.[1]

I would state it is evident that John G. Jones, of Chicago, is the moving spirit in this affair. Jones does not command the serious attention of any one who knows him, in fact he is what is known as a pretty good "fakir." If the President were to write him any kind of letter he would use it in a way to make money out of various individuals throughout the country. I am quite sure he does not mean to have any exposition, and of course the idea of getting up such an exposition within so short a time is absurd. Some of the names attached to this circular are good ones, but they have evidently given the use of their names to please Jones. Yours very truly,

Booker T. Washington

TLpS Con. 261 BTW Papers DLC.

1 Loeb had written BTW that the President had "very grave doubts about the advisability of the movement," and asked for BTW's opinion. (June 3, 1905, Con. 16, BTW Papers, DLC.)

To Mrs. N. D. Colton

[Tuskegee, Ala.] June 5, 1905

Private

Dear Madam: I am in receipt of your design of a "Negro Flag" together with your letter.[1] I have received a number of letters on this subject, and several different designs have been submitted to me for my opinion, but I am yet unable to understand why the Negro should have any other flag than the Stars and Stripes. In speaking of the Germans, Irish, and other nationalities carrying their colors together with the Stars and Stripes, I think we are apt to forget the fact that the Afro-Americans in this country are Americans, not having emigrated to the country, but that those here now were born here practically without exception, and know no other country than America; the Negro here is no foreigner, but is truly an American having been identified in a most essential and important manner with the whole country's progress and development. He is an integral part of the country; its interests are his, and his are America's. They cannot be separated.

When we consider these facts, it becomes clear, it seems to me, that the Negro needs no special insignia; that America is his country, and that, as a consequence, Old Glory is his flag.

Let me thank you, however, for your letter and the design, as I have been much interested in noting both, and appreciate your thought of me in this connection. Yours truly,

Booker T. Washington

P.S. — By this mail I am returning the design.

TLpS Con. 299 BTW Papers DLC.

[1] Mrs. N. D. Colton to BTW, May 16, 1905, Con. 299, BTW Papers, DLC. Mrs. Colton's design for a Negro flag was a portrait of Abraham Lincoln surrounded by thirty-six stars. She was a white resident of Pasadena, Calif.

To Samuel Laing Williams

[Tuskegee, Ala.] June 10, 1905

My dear Mr. Williams: I have offered to submit in proof form to Mr. Francis J. Garrison, son of William Lloyd Garrison, those references which bear upon the relations of Mr. Douglass and Mr.

William Lloyd Garrison. It is especially necessary, under the circumstances, that we be careful in the treatment of that subject.

Mr. Garrison has sent me a little pamphlet, which is of great value to him, and I must ask you to take [as] good care of it as possible so that we may return it to him.

You have I infer, retained copies of the chapter and for that reason I am not returning the original to you.

If you have any suggestions in regard to the revision of this chapter I should be glad to hear from you. Very truly yours,

Booker T. Washington

TLpS Con. 31 BTW Papers DLC.

To Valentine Everit Macy

[Tuskegee, Ala.] June 10, 1905

My dear Mr. Macy: I have just received your letter of June 8th referring to the scholarships at Teachers College in which you express your wish to change the method in which the individual who received the benefit of your scholarship at the Teachers College has been selected.

In reference to this I want to say that we are most grateful for the help which you have given us in this respect in the past. All of the students helped by you are rendering excellent service, and we feel deeply indebted to you.

I think perhaps that the main, if not the only, advantage that the former method of selecting these candidates possessed was that it insured the sending to the Teachers College two or three promising colored men or women each year, and I hope the new arrangement does not mean that the colored students will not have as good a chance in the future as they have had in the past to enter the college. I appreciate thoroughly, as I think you already know, the advantage of educating as many Southern white men and women in the North as possible because the more thoroughly they are educated the more are the colored people helped; at the same time, I think for a few colored men and women to have such advantages as the Teachers College offers is also a good thing.

You have been wholly misinformed concerning any sum of money being given to the General Education Board for the use of Tuskegee students, that is in the way of helping them in the way that you have been helping at the Teachers College. A lady has given $100,000 to the General Education Board to both Hampton and Tuskegee with the distinct proviso, however, that the income must be used in helping small rural colored schools in various parts of the South; we could not spend a single cent of it in helping to pay our teachers nor in sending any student to the Teachers College or elsewhere.

You will be very glad to know that ex-Mayor Low has become one of our Trustees.

I hope very much that I shall have the privilege of seeing you and Mrs. Macy during the summer. Yours truly,

Booker T. Washington

TLpS Con. 878 BTW Papers DLC.

To Harris A. Wheeler[1]

[Tuskegee, Ala.] June 10, 1905

Personal

Dear Sir: I am writing to know whether or not it will be possible or practicable for me to have a short conference with you sometime this summer, perhaps in June, in Detroit or Chicago. While my plans are not quite matured in detail, I now feel reasonably sure that I shall be passing through one or both [of] these cities during the summer.

The subject about which I wish to talk with you is the entering of one of my sons into your academy next fall, but before reaching any decision I should like to have a personal interview. In the meantime, I am sure that you will see that nothing concerning this correspondence reaches the public press.

An answer to this letter sent to the Manhattan Hotel, New York City, will reach me. Yours truly,

Booker T. Washington

TLpS Con. 1 BTW Papers DLC.

[1] Gen. Harris A. Wheeler was president and superintendent of Michigan Military Academy at Orchard Lake, Mich. He arranged to meet BTW at his Chicago office in late June. (Wheeler to BTW, June 23, 1905, Con. 882, BTW Papers, DLC.)

Portia Marshall Washington's Report Card

Bradford Academy, Bradford, Mass. June 14, 1905

Report of Miss Portia Washington
for the term ending June 14, 1905.

Composition. B
English Literature IV. B+
Economics. B+
Evolution of Christianity A
Bible. B+
Music. A−
Gymnasium Work. C−
Care of Room. A
Deportment. A
Punctuality. A

Laura A. Knott
Principal

A = excellent. B = good. C = fair. D = poor, but passable.
E = not passable.

PD Con. 17 BTW Papers DLC. Condensed from a longer list of subjects for which no grades are listed.

A Commencement Address in Washington, D.C.[1]

Washington, D.C. June 16th, 1905

Mr. Commissioners, Gentlemen and Ladies of the Board of Education, Principals, Teachers, Members of the Graduating Classes:

It is a pleasure and a privilege for me to be permitted to stand before you for a few minutes this evening. When your invitation came to me in the midst of the many duties and responsibilities which press so heavily upon me at this season of the year, I hesitated long as to whether or not I could, and ought accept the invitation which was so generously extended to me. And then when I thought that, perhaps, I might be able to speak a word that might be of some comfort — that might, perchance, be of some profit to some struggling and ambitious soul, I said that my duty leads me to accept this invitation, and so I am here.

The influence of a man of our race who resides in the District of Columbia is far from local — it is national; in the words and in the thoughts of another — "It is almost continental, almost IMPERIAL!" No other group of ninety thousand members of our race, and I weigh my words when I make this assertion, no other group of ninety thousand members of our race to be found in this or in any other country, is so high in the general average of intelligence as is true of the ninety thousand of our people to be found in the District of Columbia. There is no other group of ninety thousand members of our race where so much money is being expended as a whole and per capita, so far as school population is concerned, as is true in the District of Columbia. In order that I may enforce this thought, that I may emphasize this truth, if I may, let me give you one or two definite facts. In 1901, according to your reports, there was expended for the education of the twenty thousand children of our race in the District of Columbia, about $275,000, or to put it in a different form, a per capita expenditure to school population of $13. During that same year, in one of our Southern commonwealths there was expended for the education of 287,000 children of our race $60,000 less than you spend for the education of these 20,000 children in the District of Columbia. Here there was an expenditure of $13 per capita, THERE — there was an expenditure of less than $1 per capita. I mention these facts, my friends, in your presence, not with the idea of indicating that there should be spent less here — rather more than less, for there IS NO COMMODITY THAT, IN THE LAST ANALYSIS, IS SO WORTHLESS AS CHEAP EDUCATION. I would rather encourage the expenditure of more dollars per capita in the District of Columbia than fewer dollars, and I would likewise encourage more dollars in the South rather than fewer dollars. I give you these facts in order to impress upon you, as teachers, as parents and as students, the immense responsibility that is resting upon all of you.

The question that presents itself to the thinking mind is — "Are you justified — can you justify in actual, indisputable results, the difference between $13 per capita and 73 cents per capita as is true in one of our Southern States?" *In order that you may justify that difference it is important that, as parents, important that as teachers, important that as as students you sink all personal differences, all localisms, all mere temporal considerations and let your influence for good go out to the people of the United States.* Because you do not teach alone in the District of Columbia, *twenty thousand* children, but in a very large degree you are the teachers of the THREE MILLIONS of children of our race scattered throughout this nation. That brings to you (I repeat) as teachers, parents and pupils, a tremendous responsibility. We are looking to you more and more each year for example, for guidance, for inspiration in our educational methods throughout this country. Failure here is not local but national, and success here is not local but national, reaching the people in every part of this country. You have an opportunity here as few people have ever had — an opportunity to actually put into visible form the teaching of the "Teacher of teachers" when he said: "Go ye into all the world and teach the peoples and the nations the commandments which I have impressed upon you."

And, my friends, I am glad that for a number of years I have had by my side a young man who went through your public schools, who graduated at your High School (Old M Street) and later graduated at one of our great universities, who has manifested in his daily life the fact — the great truth that THE MONEY SPENT IN THE EDUCATION OF OUR PEOPLE HERE HAS NOT BEEN SQUANDERED. And just in proportion as your public school system can produce and continue to turn out and can multiply by the score and by the thousand, men of the character and type of ROSCOE CONKLING BRUCE

— in the same degree you will justify the Nation and the District of Columbia in expending every dollar that is now expended here in the education of your sons and your daughters. But in order that the men of the type of Bruce (and others whom I could name) may be multiplied, you must remember that the men and women who go out from your public schools must be "doers of the Word" and not mere "talkers of the Word."

You have here an equipment for giving to our people, training in every form of education that is necessary for any race to have. You have facilities in the District of Columbia for the most complete education — from the kindergarten up through the University, and, my friends, I believe thoroughly in every form of education which your equipment has provided for. I believe thoroughly in the work of your Normal School. I believe thoroughly in the work of your High School. I believe thoroughly in the work of your Manual Training School, and I believe thoroughly in the work of the University which is situated in the District of Columbia. I believe in them all. If I did not believe in them all I should not be surrounded, as I am day by day, by graduates, by the score, of manual training schools, colleges and universities. OUR RACE NEEDS ALL THE FORMS OF EDUCATION THAT ANY RACE HAS NEEDED AND DOES NEED. You will find as you go out into the great world, that there is a use, varying in proportion, for all kinds of education given in the District of Columbia. We should bear in mind, however, that all education, whether obtained through the medium of the song; whether through the medium of the hammer; whether through the medium of Caesar; whether through the medium of the Bible; whether through the medium of the laboratory — any form of education — means not the *end*, but a MEANS TOWARD REACHING THE END in education. What is the end — what is the end at which all education should aim? Whether of hand or head or heart, whether that obtained in the industrial school, or the high school, the manual training school, or the college or the university — the great END should be the MAKING OF STRONG CHRISTIAN CHARACTER. Without that, all education is meaningless — without that all education is, in a degree, valueless! I believe that if we would make the best of education — if we would use it as a tool in the perfection, in the advancement of human character in the direction to which I am referring, regard must be had as to the emphasis which we must place upon these various kinds of education; emphasis in proportion to the USE — the opportunity that there is for the use of these various kinds of education. I believe in any kind of education which will reach and be the most effective in regard to the lifting up of a race of people, and in determining that education you have *got* to keep in mind the age — the chronological needs of the race for whom that education is designed. In this regard I think it was the philosopher Emerson who said: "One generation clears the forest, the next builds the palaces." I repeat for emphasis: "One generation clears the forest, the next builds the palaces." Now it is true of all races — our race not excepted, *that very often the temptation has come to that race to build the palaces without clearing the forests, and wherever and whenever that mistake is made, we have got to begin over and clear the forest and then have the palaces follow.* Now that is a hard and stubborn truth in human nature which you and I cannot and should not disregard in our educational methods. No matter how much courage it takes to apply that truth, it should be applied wherever and whenever it is necessary. I have never advocated (and I do not now advocate) a single application of education to my race that I would not advocate in reference to any other race, whether it were black, white, brown or blue! (Dr. Washington remarking, however, "DON'T CHEER TOO SOON" and finishing the sentence by saying) THAT WAS IN THE SAME RELATIVE STAGE OF CIVILIZATION. There are certain hard, fundamental, material needs which in the early history of any race are of imperative importance and rightfully command the attention of the members of a young race only forty years old and who are just "clearing the forests"; and you, perhaps say when I make that remark, that the Negro race has been "clearing the forests" for the last 250 years. Doubtless some of you would say that the Negro has been working for the last 250 years. No, my friends, the Negro has been doing something else. He has been "*worked*" during the past 250 years and now, my friends, what he wants to do is to *learn how to work.* THERE IS A VAST DIFFERENCE BETWEEN "WORKING" and "BEING WORKED." That is what our schools are teaching our race; a great work, among others, that is being done in your public school system, in all its ramifications, is to teach us the difference between "BEING WORKED" and "WORKING."

A young race (and, my friends, it is no disgrace to belong to a young race) — a young race *has its future before it,* while an "old" race has left its future behind. And I like the distinction of belonging to a young race. A young race has, very largely, got to concern itself with the getting of the soil, providing food, providing houses. For example, Liberia is a young nation; it is without roads; it is without farms sufficient to supply its needs; it is without sufficient bridges, and railroads and telephones, telegraphic appliances and other public conveniences, and, my friends, I believe that under such circumstances it is a part of the function of education to pay attention to the crying needs of a Republic that is in that condition. In other words, while I believe that in Liberia we need lawyers, doctors, ministers and teachers — yet at the same time we need mechanical engineers who can construct bridges, install public utilities, and project railroads. We need, there, civil engineers who can lay out and construct public roads; that is what the white race has done, and what every other race under the sun has done that has gone forward, and the black race can be [do?], and must not be an exception to the rule. If our young race is without houses, I believe that out from the black people there should grow black architects to build those houses and black farmers to intelligently till and cultivate the soil; if our young race is without roads, there should grow up from among us black civil engineers to lay out and construct those roads, and if our neighborhoods and houses are without proper lighting appliances, there should grow up among us black electricians to light our streets and our homes, and I believe that teachers and ministers and lawyers and doctors should go forth just as fast as there is need for them and demand for them and as fast only as the young race is able to support them.

I believe that in education we have got to consider certain geographical and climatic conditions. For example, if the masses of the people for whom you are educating, are so situated as to climatic and geographical conditions that they live an out-of-door life, an agricultural life, if the education is good and destined to be effectual it will take account of that condition. In the South we live an out-of-door life in a large degree; in New England the life is an in-door life in a very large degree. In the South the masses of our people are engaged in the production of cotton; that leads to cotton manufacturing, and in every state of the South, with one or two exceptions, you will find that there is a large and thoroughly equipped technical institution to teach white boys who are going out to become masters and leaders in the industry of cotton manufacturing. AND I BELIEVE THAT THE NEGRO BOY SHOULD HAVE THE SAME KIND OF A CHANCE. And if you don't give him the same kind of a chance, he is going to become a "hewer of wood and a drawer of water" while on the other hand, the white man will be his "boss" and "the proprietor." In Massachusetts certain conditions have made the manufacture of shoes — the working in leather, a paying investment, and the result is that the educational system in Massachusetts has concerned itself with that condition and within the last three years, there has been opened in Lowell, in Brockton and in other great shoe-manufacturing centers, large and well-equipped institutions to teach young men how to become masters and producers in the manufacture of shoes. Certain climatic conditions have made Sweden one of the most remarkable countries for the dairy industry, and the result is that from the public school up to the university, the industry of dairying finds a place in the educational system of the Kingdom of Sweden, with the further result that there is today sent out more fine dairy products from the country of Sweden, in proportion to population, than is true of any other kingdom or country in the world.

A Missionary who was going into Mexico some years ago asked me what advice I would give him in regard to getting along with the people among whom he was going to cast his lot — how to get the confidence of the people among whom he was going to labor. I said to him: "Will you tell me what industry the people in that section depend upon for their living?" He said: "Sheep grazers." I said: "First of all, show them by your American intelligence and improved scientific methods how they can raise better and more sheep than they are now raising in their section, and you will get their confidence and their co-operation, and after that you will not have much trouble in getting them to read the Bible, to attend your church and to believe in the Gospel which you are commissioned to preach to them."

Further, I believe that in any proper system of education, whether for black people or for any other race of people, you have got to take into consideration the *racial needs*, the *racial opportunities*, and the *racial characteristics* that surround the people for whom that education is given. Now I know that some of you will argue that that is a wrong point of view, that there is no difference between a white child and a black child, and therefore you should not bring that in as an element in education. I take you at your word. Twelve of these bright, interesting young men graduate from your school tonight; they see in tomorrow morning's newspaper an advertisement asking for twelve positions to be filled in business houses. Twelve other young men graduate tonight at another school and of another race; they see the same advertisement in the morning's newspaper; these young men — twelve black and twelve white — all start out in the morning to fill those twelve positions; tomorrow night at six o'clock how many of those black boys will have found employment, and tell me, if you please, how many of those white boys will most likely have been employed? You have got to consider the question practically; you have got to consider this question frankly. If, for example, custom, race prejudice, or any other consideration has, for 250 years, taught a race that laboring with the hand was a disgrace — was degrading — was fit only for certain races, whether the Filipino, the Mexican, the American Indian, the American Negro or any other race, then I believe that it is a part of the function of education to teach that race how to lift itself up out of the drudgery into that atmosphere where the children of that race will feel that all forms of labor are honorable and all forms of idleness — a disgrace!

We have got to consider further in any educational system how a majority of the people for whom that education is given, earn their daily bread — not the exceptional man — the EXCEPTIONAL usually takes care of himself, whether he be black or white; I don't concern myself so much about him; I concern myself about the masses — those who are unable to look out for themselves as yet. Any proper educational policy has got to consider the employment of the masses of the people for whom that education is given. I speak to you, not as educating solely the twenty thousand children of the District of Columbia, but I speak to you as planted at the head of the educational system of the United States so far as our race is concerned; I repeat that you are teaching by precept and example three million members of our race and in doing that, you have got to consider the occupations of our race. They divide themselves largely into three groups: (1) Agricultural; (2) Mechanical; (3) Domestic. Now, I don't advocate for the black man more than I would advocate for the white man, that a majority of the members of our race should remain in one of these three groups, but I do say that inasmuch as the majority of our people are now interested in one of these three groups, we should help this majority to perform that service well, whether it is in service for themselves or for others. We are looking to education to benefit the race just in proportion that we teach the race to put brains and skill and dignity into all these three great groups of service; and just as fast as that is accomplished, and just in proportion as that sure foundation is laid, in that proportion will there step out of the three great groups, ministers and lawyers and doctors and other professional men and women from colleges and universities to be supported by the members of our race.

We have got to consider the local and, perhaps, the pressing need of the people whom we are educating. Just here I apply my remarks more especially to those who are receiving their diplomas from these three institutions tonight. In the District of Columbia it is not only true of our race, but in equal degree true of all races, you live in an atmosphere where one is perhaps likely to yield to the temptation of becoming dependent for his living upon the activities or upon the thoughts of somebody else. In all capitals you will find (in the capitals of Europe and almost every nation) that where a group of people reside at the center of government they have got to be careful not to yield to the temptation of becoming dependent on the government for their support. I want to see our educated young men and our educated young women grow to the point where they shall not *look to the government for support,* but get to the point, as soon as possible, where they will "*support the government.*" I repeat, I want to see you exercise that independence that will make you strive to get to the point where you will not be dependent upon the government for support, but through your education you will support the government, and make the government depend upon you for something. *And, my friends, the great men and women who control this government are the men and the women who pay its taxes.* I mean by that — that I want to see you get to the point where, in a large degree, you will become PRODUCERS and not mere CONSUMERS. *Any man, ignorant or educated, who consumes more than he produces, is a pauper!* I repeat: "Any man, ignorant or educated, who consumes more than he produces is a pauper," whether he earns his living by the body, by the mind or through the exercises of his heart. I don't want to see our educated men and women become machines; we can leave that to the ignorant. I want to see our educated men and women step out boldly and become pioneers in many of the walks of life, industrial, educational, spiritual and otherwise. My friends, DON'T SEEK TO BECOME A CLERK, BUT SEEK TO BECOME THE EMPLOYER OF A CLERK! To be the EMPLOYER OF CLERKS is greater than to be a CLERK! Now you ask me: "How are you going to manage that — what condition is going to bring it about?" Go out here about twenty-five miles from the city of Washington, where ground is cheap, and start a flower garden or something of the kind; bring your flowers into the market and sell them; after a while you can afford to rent a little space on the market square; this will increase your business and you can afterward enlarge your room; by hard, intelligent study and work you can build up a big trade so that you can take your sister into the business as a clerk and your brother as a partner; and after a while you can see the humble little effort developing into a great flower shop; you can employ more clerks, and a typewriter and a bookkeeper and an overseer, and you are the "boss of the whole establishment!" And I don't care who is in power — the Democrats or the Republicans, you are independent and you are safe — because you have created a position for yourself.

Now don't get the idea that you will succeed by mere abstract thinking — however clear and however strong your thinking may be. My friends, WE HAVE GOT TO WEAVE IDEAS INTO ACTIVITIES! Why there are enough ideas floating about to float a ship. Why, my friends, the whole world a few days ago was doing a good deal of abstract thinking — thinking of the great war in the Orient — thinking that it should stop — and thinking what the diplomats of the world could do to bring about peace, but while these people were thinking out their abstract ideas, there was a great, good man in the White House WHO WAS DOING and very soon we heard of the definite steps which have been taken to bring about peace between the two conflicting nations.

Suppose I put into a boat two bushel baskets of gold dollars; suppose I put you into the boat by the side of those gold dollars, and then shove or draw that boat two miles out from the shore of Chesapeake Bay and leave you there by the side of those two bushel baskets of gold dollars; where will you be at the end of thirty days?

Gold dollars are sometimes valuable, but *gold dollars that do not touch the world's commerce are valueless.* IDEAS ARE VALUABLE, but IDEAS THAT DO NOT BRING THEMSELVES INTO THE ACTIVITIES OF THE WORLD ARE VALUELESS. And as you go out into the world and attempt to apply the principles which I try to emphasize, my friends, you will find abundant use of the exercise of courage; especially just now as they surround and apply to the members of our race in various parts of this country. And I say "courage" — not so much that kind of courage which manifests itself in loud boasting — in blatant talking, but that kind of courage which will enable you to keep silent when you are sorely tempted to speak (*and, my friends, it often requires more courage to be silent than it does to speak*). That beautiful flower in that vase has not spoken a word to-night; it will never speak a word, but, nevertheless, through its beauty and magnificent silence it is lifting up, and making more Christlike every human being in this room. It is not necessary for us to talk or even act in order to exert an influence. We have got to live a life of beauty, of truth, of usefulness, of honor! And remember, friends, in exercising this courage, that no human being in this country can degrade you. People may make it inconvenient for you; they may place obstacles in your path; they may try to insult you; but, my friends, no man or set of men can degrade you! *You, yourselves, are the only individuals who can inflict that punishment.*

And I am most anxious that as our educated young men and women go out to begin their life-work, that they shall not overlook the sacrifices, the interest, the love and the prayers of the mothers and fathers who have supported them — of the mothers and fathers who have stood by them. *Doubtless in many cases these mothers and fathers have sacrificed in shop, in field, in laundry room, before the cooking stove, over the ironing table, in departmental work, in professional life for your benefit — they have given themselves, as best they could, in order that you might get to the point where you could get your diplomas, and on the morrow, when you go home with your diploma in your hand — remember those sacrifices — their love and their interest.* Be not ashamed to begin life just where your fathers and mothers are — I DON'T SAY REMAIN THERE. Rise up to a better sphere — a larger sphere of usefulness if you can; if your father is a mechanic, help him; if your mother is a laundress, help her; don't be ashamed to spend your education upon them — don't be ashamed to begin life just where they are! And put so much brains, so much science, so much literature, so much language, so much skill into their occupations that you will help them and help yourself to rise up higher and higher to enlarged and more important usefulness.

Just before he died, I was in the office of the late Collis P. Huntington. He told me a story that I shall never forget. He said: "Some fifteen years ago an acquaintance of mine came into my office and requested a loan of five dollars. I said to him, 'I am your friend; I honor you; I trust you, and I don't mind lending you five dollars, but, my friend, I can perform a better office for you. Will you make me the promise that the very first thing which your eyes fall upon — the very first work which you see to be done as soon as you leave the elevator and go out into the street — will you put your hands to that work and do it — will you begin service in that connection?' The man promised he would. Upon leaving the elevator, and turning down Broad Street he found a man unloading coal; he immediately asked the man for the job of putting in the coal and afterward worked in the service of that Coal Company for a week, for a month, was later promoted and stayed with the firm for over fifteen years, and now he is one of the largest wholesale coal dealers in the city of New York!" *Begin life*, my friends, *just where you are*, but DON'T STAY THERE; work up to the highest position which your opportunities and your faculties can command.

Don't get the idea that some of our young men and women are fond of imbibing — that is, when you get an education, don't be ashamed to attend Sunday School and church. You know it gets to be fashionable among a certain class of our "educated" people that as soon as they graduate from High School and college, *that they can find no minister intelligent enough to preach to them.* And no church that is FASTIDIOUS enough to hold their bodies. Show your education by going away out here on the edge of the District of Columbia and find the humblest, the most desolate, the most forsaken place of worship and give that minister — that church your undivided service. Lift them up to a higher plane and live a life of Christian usefulness.

You will find that your education is going to increase your wants many fold. Some of your wants are going to be multiplied ten-fold by to-morrow morning, and, my friends, unless you can get an income that is in keeping with those multiplied wants, you will find yourself in trouble inside of the next twelve months.

Now be sure that you manifest your education by cutting off or denying yourselves some of these wants. When the springtime comes, if your father and mother have had a hard winter, go to your mother and father and say: "I was ignorant a few years ago; I am educated now; I don't want you to spend your last dollar in order to buy me a fine, new spring hat when you are not able; I will just take out my old hat, and rebuild it, and place a new ribbon on it, redress it and make the old hat answer for a few springs to come. That, my friends, is the best kind of education. I don't speak idly — I don't speak abstractly in this regard. More money has come from New England for the education of our people during the last forty years than from any other source. The very class of people who have poured out their love and their sympathy and their treasures for the benefit of our people in the South are the very people who retrim old hats, rebuild old gowns, deny themselves of many luxuries and wear the same apparel summer after summer, and winter after winter in order that they may eke out a few dollars to give to the education of our people. The education of our young people should have the same results.

And, my friends, don't be ashamed to be just what you are. Now the man who has the hardest time in this world, in my opinion, is the individual who is poor and trying to be rich, is the individual who has a $50 income and who is living at a $100 rate per month. Now don't make that mistake. If you have a $50 income, live at a $25 rate and you will find yourself making progress in your life. Life, to the educated man or woman, should not be a life of "spending," but a life of "giving" — should not be a life of "hoarding," but a life of "scattering."

My friends, I like to encourage our young educated men and women to have faith in their own race and in their own racial possibility, and when I say that I don't mean that we should not love and have faith in all other races, but I LIKE TO SEE A RACE HAVE FAITH IN ITSELF. Quite as much in itself as it has in any other race. Did you ever see a Hollander ashamed of being a Hollander, or a German ashamed of being a German, or a Chinaman ashamed of being a Chinese, or a Japanese ashamed of being a Japanese? And now, my friends, don't you know that they are even saying the Japanese is a white race. Yes, it is now a white race — a white race. Why I met a man on the train not long ago — only a few weeks ago, and he said: "Why, Washington, don't you know that I have been studying into the origin of those Japanese people, and don't you know that we have been deceived about them; why they have had a civilization for a thousand years and I tell you, Washington, THEY ARE A WHITE RACE — THEY ARE NOT A YELLOW RACE. The Japanese, as we all know, have solved their problem — I don't care what you call them.

I believe, too, my friends, in looking on the bright and sunny side of life. I believe in a man having faith in the future of himself, faith in the future of his race and faith in the future of the country to which he belongs. You know there are some *leaders* of our race who are always gloomy, dark, sullen and disappointed. Why there are some preachers, who are fit for nothing but to PREACH FUNERAL SERMONS. You meet them in the street and say: "Good morning, it is a bright, beautiful, sunny day," and they will reply: "Yes, but it is going to rain to-morrow." Now, my young friends, such as you who come out from the High School, the Normal and the Manual Training School, cannot afford to look upon the dark and gloomy side of life. You must be cheerful and hopeful in order that you may inspire the masses of our people to nobler, higher effort. I like the spirit — the determination of that colored soldier who lay dying upon the battlefield during the late war. After the doctor came and saw his wounds, he told the dying comrade that he had but a few minutes to live, and asked him if there was some message or some token he would like to send to any of his loved ones at home; the helpless soldier looked Surgeon Jones straight in the eye with not the slightest fear of death upon his countenance; and when the Chaplain later came in a few minutes and told him that he must soon pass into another world, and asked him if he had some last word to send to mother, or wife, or loved ones at home, he turned to the Chaplain and said, as he lay there trembling on the grass: "Chaplain, place your hand in my vest pocket; take out that little memorandum book, open it please, and get out that bill." The Chaplain quietly obeyed, and then the soldier said: "Hold that bill up before my eyes so I can see it. Now," said he, "Chaplain, I'll bet you that five-dollar bill I'm going to get well." And, my friends, I WILL BET THE PEOPLE OF THIS NATION FIVE DOLLARS THAT THE NEGRO

RACE WILL GET WELL! Because out from these three schools I see the bright faces and the earnest hearts of these graduates who are going out into every corner of these United States and who shall help make the race "well" — well in body — well in mind — well in heart.

And Jesus said unto His disciples: "If ye have faith as a grain of mustard seed, ye can say to yon mountain, 'Be thou removed and planted by the sea and it shall be done.' " When I read those words I doubted even the words of the Master. I could not understand how a man's faith could accomplish such magnificent and far-reaching results. Soon after that I was in New York City and had occasion to cross the Brooklyn bridge; I saw that great bridge spanning the water between Brooklyn and New York City, and I thought of the passage in the Bible about the little grain of mustard seed, and I analyzed the mountain and found that it was composed of soil and timber, of iron and stone; then I analyzed the bridge and found that the bridge was composed of soil and wood and stone and iron, and I said, "Now, I understand it — I know what the Master meant." Man, by following God's laws — Man, by following Nature's laws, by applying brains and brawn, and chemistry and physics to the forces of nature and the laws of gravitation; by having faith in the laws that govern chemical affinity; faith in the laws that govern cohesion — has not only moved the mountain and brought it to the edge of the sea, but has poised it here between heaven and earth as an everlasting lesson as to what man's faith can accomplish when following the eternal laws of the Master.

And so, my friends, in closing, I say to the teachers in your Normal Schools, your High Schools, and your Manual Training Schools, and to you all — your faith in your race — your faith in your people will remove mountains in the material world — mountains in the educational world, mountains in the racial world — mountains in the spiritual world, and in all these directions, mountains, through your efforts, will be removed, until the race works itself into the citizenship of the KINGDOM OF GOD.

PD BTW Papers ATT.

[1] The first joint commencement of Normal School No. 2, the Armstrong Manual Training School, and the M Street High School held in Convention Hall.

To Elbert B. Williams[1]

[Tuskegee, Ala.] June 24, 1905

Personal and Private

Dear Mr. Williams: We have been making a request of the Secretary of War for the detail of a band master from the Army, to come to Tuskegee and take charge of our band.

The Secretary of War has very kindly consented, I beg to say for your private information, to detail you on furlough for the position. I very much hope that you will feel disposed to take up this new service at Tuskegee. Mr. Townsend[2] was with us only for the year.

As I understand it, under this regulation, your salary will be paid by the army, and you will in every way be to the army just what you are now, simply that your service will be at Tuskegee.

President Roosevelt will be here in October, and we are very anxious to have a good band when he comes, and so for that reason, I have asked the Honorable Secretary of War to detail you at once, if you decide to accept this service. Very truly yours,

Booker T. Washington

TLpSr Con. 882 BTW Papers DLC.

[1] Elbert B. Williams, born in Brooklyn, N.Y., in 1862, served for some thirty years after 1895 in the U.S. Army, principally as a bandsman in the 10th Cavalry and the 24th and 25th infantry regiments. He was furloughed from August 1905 until June 1907 to serve as bandmaster of Tuskegee Institute. He also played the trumpet and clarinet.

[2] William H. Townsend.

From Clinton Joseph Calloway

Tuskegee Institute, Alabama. July 3d, 1905

Dr. B. T. Washington: I succeeded in getting an opportunity to speak to two audiences as well as do some personal canvassing on the whiskey, home improvement, and school building questions since my last report. The first meeting was held at about eight miles from Tuskegee near a bridge in the woods and was on the style of the old fashion picnic. The number there was not so large but the people seemed very attentive and promised to help do something to better the community in which they lived along the lines mentioned. The second meeting was held yesterday at Baptist Cluster church i.e. I was given as much time as I wanted to speak during the church service. The people in this community are trying to build a school house and have a good school but they had grown somewhat cold on the subject during the past few months. It seemed from their promises that they mean to begin afresh and complete the school house already begun. I also got quite a number to promise to help in getting every Negro in Macon county to quit buying whiskey and put that money in land and home improvement, schools and churches. Slowly but surely the Negro in Macon county is getting his eyes open and I am quite sure that he is making progress in at least the same proportion. Yours very truly,

Clinton J Calloway
Conference Agent

TLS Con. 556 BTW Papers DLC.

To the Editor of the Columbia [S.C.] *State*

[Tuskegee, Ala.] July 8, 1905

Personal and Confidential
Dear Sir: I have just had time to read the enclosed editorial from your paper, and the following statement I am making for your personal information and use because I do not think that you will willingly do any one an injustice.

I would state that I am quite sure that no one can put his hands upon a single statement made over my signature, or in any interview, or in any public address wherein I have claimed that the Negro was superior to any other race. The fact is, I have always discouraged our people from making boasts of any character.

I presume the editorial is based upon a speech which I made before the National Educational Association in St. Louis just about a year ago. That was the first time that I have ever made any comparison as to educational progress. I have used the same sentence in several other speeches on various occasions since that time, but evidently the St. Louis speech furnished the basis for the discussion. If you care to trouble yourself to get the official report of that convention, it can be gotten by addressing Mr. Erwin Shepard, the Secretary of the National Educational Association, Winona, Minn., you will find that you have been misinformed concerning the spirit and tone of my address. I made no boast; what I did say was simply to quote the public statistics showing the proportion of illiteracy in Italy, Spain, Russia, and South America, and then called attention to the amount of illiteracy existing among our people in the South. I did so because I felt, and in fact said, that it should be a subject of congratulation both to the North and South that after only forty years that the Negro had gotten rid of so much of his illiteracy. I am perfectly aware of the fact that one man can possess a certain degree of education without being the superior of the other; that would be no more safe proposition than to say that one man is superior because he owns $100 worth of property and the other only $25 worth. I simply stated facts. Yours truly,

Booker T. Washington

TLpS Con. 879 BTW Papers DLC.

To Margaret James Murray Washington

[Tuskegee, Ala.] July 8, 1905

Mrs. Washington: I hope you are bearing in mind that the whole matter of teaching cooking, table serving and general housekeeping is to be overhauled and improved by the beginning of next school term. Instead of dabbling with the study as we are now doing, we are going into it with real earnestness and have the students have at least three lessons a week, I mean all the girls.

Miss Lane says that practically every girl now on the place who knows how to cook learned before she came here. Yours truly,

[Booker T. Washington]

TLp Con. 563 BTW Papers DLC.

To Margaret James Murray Washington

[Tuskegee, Ala.] July 8, 1905

Write Mrs. Talbert[1] to keep you closely informed about proceedings and names of people connected with the Buffalo meeting next week.

Booker T. Washington

TWpSr Con. 563 BTW Papers DLC. Addressed to South Weymouth, Mass.

1 Mary Burnett Talbert (1865–1923) of Buffalo, N.Y., was a prominent black clubwoman. Born in Oberlin, Ohio, she graduated from Oberlin College in 1887. A high school teacher and a lecturer on racial subjects, she was president of the Empire State Federation of Women's Clubs, chairman of the executive board of the National Association of Colored Women, and a member of the Phillis Wheatley Club of Buffalo.

To Charles William Anderson

[Tuskegee, Ala.] July 8, 1905

Tell Crosby[1] look after Buffalo meeting sharply. It is to be held next week. Inside data can be gotten from Talbert.[2] Keep me closely informed my expense. Think they are making effort to rope Crosby in.

B. T. W.

TWpIr Con. 27 BTW Papers DLC.

1 Possibly a pseudonym for Melvin J. Chisum or Clifford H. Plummer, both spies for BTW. The name Crosby also occurred in 1911 when Anderson and Wilford H. Smith assisted BTW's efforts to gather information after the Ulrich affair.

2 William Henry Talbert (1866–1918?) was a Buffalo realtor and a clerk in the city treasurer's office. In 1911 he became president of the Buffalo Colored Republican League.

To Julius Robert Cox

Tuskegee Ala July 10 1905

See Plummer at once give him fifty dollars tell him go to Buffalo to night or tomorrow morning ostensibly to attend Elks convention but to report fully what goes on at meeting to be held there Wednesday and Thursday. Get into meeting if possible but be sure name of all who attend and what they do answer when you have completed this matter.

B. T. W.

HWIr Con. 556 BTW Papers DLC. Addressed to South Weymouth, Mass.

To Julius Robert Cox

Tuskegee Ala July 10 1905

If you need money for Buffalo matter draw on Mr Logan for fifty dollars.

Booker T. Washington

HWSr Con. 556 BTW Papers DLC. Addressed to South Weymouth, Mass.

To Oswald Garrison Villard

Tuskegee Institute, Alabama. July 10, 1905

Personal

My dear Mr. Villard: Enclosed I send you a letter[1] which you might like to see. It is most encouraging from every point of view.

Do you think it would be possible and practicable for you to send a man into the South who would find out the real facts bearing upon the distribution of the public school money as between the races. You will note in the enclosed letter this man says in his district $15 per capita is allowed every white child and 35 cents per capita for every Negro child. If this is true and this condition exists in any large proportion in our counties, you can easily see what the results would be.

Enclosed I also send you a marked copy of the Atlanta Constitution containing one of the bravest and most encouraging sermons that I have ever read. Mr. Bradley is a Southern white man. Thus, you see, that in the midst of seeming darkness there are many rays of sunshine. Of course the letter from Mr. Little is wholly private. Yours very truly,

Booker T. Washington

TLS Oswald Garrison Villard Papers MH. A press copy is in Con. 31, BTW Papers, DLC.

[1] I. T. Little, a white man of Ackerville, Ala., wrote on July 2, 1905, to BTW, who forwarded the letter to Villard. (Oswald Garrison Villard Papers, MH.)

To John Henry Washington

[Tuskegee, Ala.] July 10, 1905

Mr. J. H. Washington: I think it will be well for you to reduce the amount now being paid to John[1] and Charley[2] for their work. I find it is above the price of work being paid other students. In the case of Charley, it requires effort to keep him in the office, and I think the same is true of John. I think it will really help the boys to let them begin low and work up to a good salary in proportion as they prove themselves worthy. For example, the girl in Mr. Palmer's office does the same kind of work and as good work as Charley, and besides she gives no trouble about being kept at work, but Charley gets about twice as much as the girl receives.

[Booker T. Washington]

TLp Con. 558 BTW Papers DLC.

[1] John Henry Washington, Jr. (b. 1886), eldest son of John H. Washington, graduated from Tuskegee Institute in 1909.

[2] Charles Dean Washington (b. 1888), son of John H. Washington, graduated from Tuskegee Institute in 1906.

Samuel Laing Williams to Emmett Jay Scott

Chicago, July 10–1905

My Dear Mr Scott: I have from time to time postponed my good intention to answer your last letter and also gratefully to acknowledge receipt of your book "Tuskegee and its People." I sincerely thank you for the book and congratulate you in getting out a volume of such absorbing interest and attractiveness. "Tuskegee and its People" is unique in its way and you may well feel proud of your work.

Mrs. Williams was so much pleased with it that she has written a review of the Book for the New York Age.

I send you by even mail a copy of the Herald with an interesting article by Curtis on the Negro in Oklahoma and Indian Territory, confirming what I said to you in a former letter. When Dr Washington was in the city a few days ago I gave him a copy but he mislaid it and asked me to send him one, so when you get through with it you may pass it along to him.

I got a telegram from Dr. Washington yesterday asking for some data concerning the Buffalo Conference to be held Wednesday and Thursday of this week. I did my best to get hold of some facts about the matter, but those who have knowledge are very secretive. What I said in my reply telegram represents the extent of my knowledge. Invitations were sent to the following Chicago people, Morris, Bentley, Wilson Wesley[,] E. H. Wright,[1] Oscar De Priest[2] Dr Wesley Col Marshall and James S Madden.[3] Of these Madden and Bentley have gone, and I understand Wilkins is going. I have not heard for certain of any others going. Magee[4] of St. Paul, Woodson[5] of Iowa, and Smith[6] of Kansas City – all lawyers have passed through the City on their way to Buffalo.

As an evidence of the meanness of some of these people, Smith of Kansas City Kans. said to a friend of mine that Mr Washington's visit to Kansas recently was responsible for a law recently enacted providing Separate High Schools for Colored Students! Smith admits that Mr Washington said nothing in his addresses in that State to justify such action, but such was the "impression" of Mr Washington's presence that the law providing for separation followed as a matter of course!

It occurred to me that it might be a good thing for you to write to Mr Ira Guy[7] of Topeka, Secretary of the Topeka Negro Business League and get from him the facts in the case. Guy is a strong friend of Mr Washing[ton] and I know if there is any gossip or general impression that in the least justifies Smith's extravagant assertion he would know it.

Referring to League matters there is prospect for a large delegation from the West. I am just in receipt of a letter from Topeka asking me to arrange for the Kans and Ills delegates to cooperate.

Hope you are succeeding in getting up an attractive program, as the Eastern people are quite critical.

Referring to my personal matter, I promised Dr Washington to find out and let him know the exact date of expiration of L's[8] term. I have not as yet got the reply that I am looking for. Bruce died in the Spring of 1898, and L was an early successor. If that be the case he has a year yet.

I expect to know in a few days the exact date and will advise Mr Washington. Referring, again, to your new book I think it would be a gracious thing to send a complimentary Copy to Mrs Celia Parker Wooley[9] head of the "Frederick Douglass Center." She is now at Coldwater, Mich. She is a great admirer of the Dr notwithstanding the effort [of] the Old Equal Opportunity etc to get her to endorse their foolishness.

Hope Mrs Scott and children are enjoying themselves "down East."

Remember me kindly to Wheeler et. al. Sincerely yours,

S. Laing Williams

ALS Con. 31 BTW Papers DLC.

1 Edward H. Wright (1864–1930), a black lawyer and Republican politician, was a graduate of the College of the City of New York. Moving to Chicago, he was a commissioner of Cook County from 1896 to 1900. In 1900 he founded the Appomattox Club for Negro Republican politicians, one of the sources of his influence on the South Side. In 1915 Mayor W. H. Thompson appointed him assistant corporation counsel. He held other local and state offices in the 1920s and was active in the Republican party. In 1927 he lost favor by opposing Thompson's successful bid for re-election as mayor. (Spear, *Black Chicago*, 78.)

2 Oscar De Priest (1871–1951), Chicago's leading black politician for decades, was born in Alabama and reared in Salina, Kan. Leaving home at seventeen, he went to Chicago as a painter, decorator, and real estate dealer. An active Republican, he was county commissioner from 1904 to 1908 and in 1915 became Chicago's first black alderman. Though indicted for conspiracy to permit prostitution, gambling, and the bribery of policemen, De Priest was successfully defended by Edward H. Morris and

Clarence Darrow. He organized his own faction, the People's Movement, stressing black solidarity. When W. H. Thompson resumed control of the Republican machine in Chicago, De Priest also prospered politically. In 1928 he was elected to Congress as the first black member since 1901. In 1934 he lost his seat to a black Democrat and retired to run his real estate business. He served as an alderman again from 1943 to 1947.

3 James S. Madden, a Chicago black bookkeeper, was one of the founders of the Niagara Movement, attending its first meeting in 1905 and aiding Charles E. Bentley to establish a branch in Chicago. He was a trustee of Provident Hospital in Chicago and helped form the Equal Opportunity League to protest school segregation in Chicago.

4 Fredrick L. McGhee.

5 George H. Woodson, an attorney of Des Moines, Iowa.

6 Brown Sylvester Smith (b. 1863) was a graduate of the University of Michigan Law School. He practiced law in Kansas City, Kan., was active in the Republican party, and served on the city council from 1892 to 1896.

7 Ira O. Guy owned a grocery store in Topeka, Kan., and was active in the NNBL.

8 Judson Whitlocke Lyons.

9 Celia Parker Woolley (1848–1918), a white novelist and Unitarian minister, founded in 1905 the Frederick Douglass Center, the first black settlement house in Chicago.

From Clifford H. Plummer

Buffalo N.Y. 7/12 1905

Arrived this morning. It is raining. Off to Ass'd Press. Then will get a line on what is doing.

If necessary address telegram to this office.

C. S. [H.] P.

HWIr Con. 305 BTW Papers DLC.

From Clifford H. Plummer

Buffalo N.Y. 7–13 190[5]

Few of them here nothing serious so far. Will try to stop their declaration of principals from appearing.

C. H. Plummer

HWSr Con. 305 BTW Papers DLC.

From Charles William Anderson

New York, N.Y., July 14, 1905

Personal.

My dear Doctor: Enclosed you will find clippings from the Buffalo papers relative to the Du Bois conference, together with a letter from Crosby. As you will note, they failed to interest Crosby in the movement, and as you will also notice, Crosby in his note to me, makes the point that the true measure of their influence and their honesty of purpose is revealed in the fact that they had to seek a meeting place outside of the United States. The meeting seems to have been held at the Fort Erie Beach Hotel, Fort Erie, Canada. Concerning the list of names printed in the enclosed clipping, you are doubtless aware that not one tenth of them were present. I know the men too well to believe that they would spend one dollar to support the holiest cause ever devised by the wit of man. The printed list of names was undoubtedly prepared by Professor Du Bois or some other enterprising citizen, and handed to the newspaper. I think perhaps you ought to make an effort to have that man Hershaw removed. Can that not be done in some way? Can you in any way find out just how many of these men really attended the conference? Of course the movement will never be dangerous, because there is not a man in it who would be willing to finance it over, or contribute anything towards that end. They are a lot of "unmoneyed" patriots, and you know better than almost any other man living, how much an unmoneyed patriot can accomplish.

Hoping to hear from you soon, I remain Yours truly,

Charles W. Anderson

TLS Con. 27 BTW Papers DLC. Addressed to South Weymouth, Mass. Enclosures no longer attached.

From Emmett Jay Scott

Tuskegee Institute, Alabama. July 14, 1905

Dear Mr. Washington: While here I meant to discuss with you the matter of your stopping place in New York during the Business League.

Perhaps you did not take any especial account of some of the criticism made at Indianapolis last year with reference to stopping at a white hotel with colored hotels available, etc., etc. You will recall the general comments! Of course I know you will hardly want to stop during the present League meeting at the Manhattan Hotel with the liability of so many of the delegates calling there to see you, and if you should stop at the Stevens House I feel quite sure that this same kind of comment would ensue, especially with a number of colored hotels available. Under the circumstances, then, I feel you will not object to my directing your attention to this matter. I am sorry that I failed to go over this matter with you while you were here. Yours truly,

Emmett J. Scott

TLS Con. 557 BTW Papers DLC.

To Charles William Anderson

[South Weymouth, Mass.] July 15, 1905

Get Crosby to send you twelve copies Buffalo paper containing names.

B. T. W.

TWpIr Con. 27 BTW Papers DLC.

From Clifford H. Plummer

Boston, Mass., July 16, 1905

My dear Dr. Washington: I arrived home this morning and called you up first thing; but Mrs. Washington informed me that you left home last evening. Dr. Courtney gave me your address. He also showed me the article in the Transcript;[1] he was not aware that I was anywhere near the scene. And therefore he could not imagine my thoughts in the matter. I have not had such a feeling of indignation for a long time as I had when I saw it. Knowing as I did that the report was not true; in fact there really was no conference in Buffalo where delegates were in attendance. The names of the delegates might have been communicated to a certain gentleman and they were carried to Buffalo; but the gentlemen themselves were not there. I was located near 521 Michigan Avenue from Wednesday morning until Friday and I can state positively that none of the men named in the report were present except Du Bois. Notwithstanding the fact that the conference amounted to nothing, the local editors informed me that some colored man did bring in a report such as appeared in the Boston papers; but no reporter was assigned to the seat of the conference. Sincerely yours,

C. H. Plummer

TLS Con. 305 BTW Papers DLC.

[1] BTW's agents were able to prevent the Associated Press and most daily newspapers from reporting the meeting, but W. M. Trotter on his return to Boston gave a detailed account, which appeared as a news item in the Boston *Transcript*, July 15, 1905, 14.

To Emmett Jay Scott

New York 7–17 190[5]

Telegraph Thompson and other newspaper men that you can absolutely trust to ignore Niag[a]ra movement Fortune, Anderson and I think this best white papers in the north leave [have] practically ignored it all together.

B. T. W.

HWIr Con. 31 BTW Papers DLC.

From Emmett Jay Scott

Tuskegee Institute, Alabama. July 18, 1905

Dear Mr. Washington: I send you herewith a copy of Du Bois' suggestions for the Committee of Twelve.[1] Perhaps you will want to go over them with some of the friends. They seem to indicate, I should say, some of the plans he will try to follow in the work of his Niagara Movement committee. Yours truly,

Emmett J. Scott

TLS Con. 557 BTW Papers DLC.

[1] Du Bois sent "Suggestions as to the Committee of Safety," Feb. 20, 1904. (Con. 164, BTW Papers, DLC.) He proposed not only a committee of twelve but also a committee of 120 to meet annually, and "Committees of Correspondence" in each state.

From Emmett Jay Scott

Tuskegee Institute, Alabama. July 18, 1905

Dear Mr. Washington: I have taken measures, in accordance with your telegram, to have Thompson ignore the Niagara Movement. He will be willing to abide by your suggestion. I have asked him on his own initiative to influence other of our friends similarly.

The Boston Transcript of Saturday, July 15th, has an extended telegram from Buffalo bearing upon this movement. You must have seen it. Their purpose most likely will be to secure issues of the Transcript or Buffalo papers if any of them carried the report, and send marked copies to all of our newspapers.

I am very glad that you have been in conference with Mr. Fortune and Mr. Anderson.

I fear nothing from it beyond the ordinary ripple which a new movement of any character usually creates. Yours truly,

Emmett J Scott

I hope you sent, or will send, Mr. Laird[1] of Montgomery Journal last Saturday's Transcript Editorial.

TLS Con. 557 BTW Papers DLC. Postscript in Scott's hand.

[1] Hervey W. Laird was editor of the Montgomery *Times* and the Montgomery correspondent of the Birmingham *Age-Herald*.

Emmett Jay Scott to Richard W. Thompson

[Tuskegee, Ala.] July 18, 1905

Personal

Dear Thompson: I have just wired you today to the effect that a conference of our friends thinks it wisest to in every way ignore absolutely the Niagara Movement. I am sure you can trust their judgment in this matter. The best of the white newspapers in the North have absolutely ignored it and have taken no account of its meetings or its protestations. I think, then, as I have intimated, if we shall consistently refuse to take the slightest notice of them that the whole thing will die a-borning.

With kindest regards ever, I am, Yours truly,

Emmett J. Scott

P.S. Of course anything you may do in the direction of influencing others to ignore them, as I have intimated, will be a good thing. By all means try to influence the Freeman people and the Charleston Advocate accordingly.

TLpS Con. 31 BTW Papers DLC.

From Emmett Jay Scott

Tuskegee Institute, Alabama. July 24, 1905

Dear Mr. Washington: I am sending you with papers today a number with the item sent out from here bearing upon the coming meeting of the Business League. They represent a wide strip of territory and show that we have been able to reach the papers pretty well. We sent it out to the complete list of all that we have, and I feel reasonably sure that the notice will appear in 90 per cent of them any way. They are running the notice with extended head lines and in other ways are stirring up interest in the meeting.

I also include a number of papers that have references to the Niagara movement. I do not believe that aside from the Atlanta Age, and it straddles, that any papers that have been heretofore favorable will be deflected from support of the great principles for which you have been laboring. I shall be very greatly surprised if it does not turn out in the end that the whole effort of these brethren is to secure a little notoriety. Yours truly,

Emmett J. Scott

TLS Con. 557 BTW Papers DLC.

To Emmett Jay Scott

South Weymouth, Mass., July 27, 1905

Dear Mr. Scott: On your way North I wish that you would stop and have a conference with the Atlanta Age man, I forget his name, and show him the true inwardness of Du Bois. Perhaps it would be better to have him come to Tuskegee, at our expense, for a conference, without you letting him know the exact reason. I am very anxious that we lose not one of our friends on the account of this new movement.

Enclosed find the letter returned from Mr. Williston, tell him to go ahead at the figures named.

I think it would be a good plan to arrange for the expenses of R. W. Thompson to N.Y. for the League. Very truly yours,

Booker T. Washington

TLS Con. 30 BTW Papers DLC.

Emmett Jay Scott to W. Allison Sweeney

[Tuskegee, Ala.] July 27, 1905

Personal

Dear Mr. Sweeney: I have your kind letter of July 25th asking "a thought" as to the Niagara Movement. I have only to say that a number of my newspaper friends have written me that it is not their purpose to take the slightest notice of the organization since Du Bois was, as is well known, a member of another committee at work along the same lines, but because he could not be, as he wanted, the central figure in the movement and at the expense of others, he has gone out to duplicate that movement.

With sincere regards, I am, Yours truly,

[Emmett J. Scott]

TL Copy Con. 307 BTW Papers DLC.

An Article in the *North American Review*

[July 1905]

THE RELIGIOUS LIFE OF THE NEGRO

In everything that I have been able to read about the religious life of the Negro, it has seemed to me that writers have been too much disposed to treat of it as something fixed and unchanging. They have not sufficiently emphasized the fact that the Negro people, in respect to their religious life, have been, almost since they landed in America, in a process of change and growth.

The Negro came to America with the pagan idea of his African ancestors; he acquired under slavery a number of Christian ideas, and at the present time he is slowly learning what those ideas mean in practical life. He is learning, not merely what Christians believe, but what they must do to be Christians.

The religious ideas which the Negroes brought with them to America from Africa were the fragments of a system of thought and custom, which, in its general features, is common to most barbarous people. What we call "fetichism" is, I suppose, merely a childish way of looking at and explaining the world, which did not, in the case of the people of West Africa, preclude a belief in the one true God, although He was regarded by them as far away and not interested in the little affairs of men.

But the peculiarity of their primitive religion, as I have learned from a very interesting book written by one who has been many years a missionary in Africa, consists in this, that it sought for its adherents a purely "physical salvation."

In the religion of the native African there was, generally speaking, no place of future reward or punishment, no heaven and no hell, as we are accustomed to conceive them. For this reason, the Negro had little sense of sin. He was not tortured by doubts and fears, which are so common and, we sometimes feel, so necessary a part of the religious experiences of Christians. The evils he knew were present and physical.

During the period of servitude in the New World, the Negro race did not wholly forget the traditions and habits of thought that it brought from Africa. But it added to its ancestral stock certain new ideas.

Slavery, with all its disadvantages, gave the Negro race, by way of recompense, one great consolation, namely, the Christian religion and the hope and belief in a future life. The slave, to whom on this side of the grave the door of hope seemed closed, learned from Christianity to lift his face from earth to heaven, and that made his burden lighter. In the end, the hope and aspiration of the race in slavery fixed themselves on the vision of the resurrection, with its "long white robes and golden slippers."

This hope and this aspiration, which are the theme of so many of the old Negro hymns, found expression in the one institution that slavery permitted to the Negro people – the Negro Church. It was natural and inevitable that the Negro Church, coming into existence as it did under slavery, should permit the religious life of the Negro to express itself in ways almost wholly detached from morality. There was little in slavery to encourage the sense of personal responsibility.

The attitude of some Negro communities in this respect is very clearly illustrated in the story of the slave who was a "professor" of religion, in the current phrase of the time, but made his master so much trouble by his persistence in certain immoral practices that it was finally necessary to call in a clergyman to try to reform him. The clergyman made the attempt, and sought to bring the terrors of the law to bear upon the slave's conscience.

"Look yeah, Massa," said the culprit, "don't de Scripture say, Dem who b'lieves an' is baptize' shall be saved?"

"Certainly," was the reply, and the clergyman went on to explain the passage to him, but the slave interrupted him again.

"Jus' you tell me now, Massa, don't de good book say dese words: 'Dem as b'lieve and is baptize' shall be saved?' "

"Yes, but —"

"Dat's all I want to know, sar. Now, wat's de use of talkin' to me. You ain't ago'n to make me believe wat de blessed Lord say ain't so, not if you tries forever."

This illustrates one of the difficulties that we have to contend with to-day. In our Tuskegee Negro Conference, we have constantly to insist that the people draw moral distinctions within the limits of their own communities, that they get rid of immoral ministers and school-teachers, and refuse to associate with people whom they know to be guilty of immoral practices.

It has been said that the trouble with the Negro Church is that it is too emotional. It seems to me that what the Negro Church needs is a more definite connection with the social and moral life of the Negro people. Could this connection be effected in a large degree, it would give to the movement for the upbuilding of the race the force and inspiration of a religious motive. It would give to the Negro religion more of that missionary spirit, the spirit of service, that it needs to purge it of some of the worst elements that still cling to it.

The struggle to attain a higher level of living, to get land, to build a home, to give their children an education, just because it demands more earnestness and steadfastness of purpose, gives a steadiness and a moral significance to the religious life, which is the thing the Negro people need at present.

A large element of the Negro Church must be called from its apocalyptic vision back to the earth; the members of the Negro race must be taught that mere religious emotion that is guided by no definite idea and is devoted to no purpose is vain.

It is encouraging to notice that the leaders of the different denominations of the Negro Church are beginning to recognize the force of the criticism made against it, and that, under their leadership, conditions are changing. In one of these denominations, the A. M. E. Zion Church alone, $2,000,000 was raised, from 1900 to 1904, for the general educational, moral and material improvement of the race. Of this sum, $1,000,000 was contributed for educational purposes alone. The A. M. E. Church and the Baptists did proportionally as well.

The mere fact that this amount of money has been raised for general educational purposes, in addition to the sum expended in each local community for teachers, for building schoolhouses and supplementing the State appropriations for schools, shows that the colored people have spent less money in saloons and dispensaries; that less has been squandered on toys and gimcracks that are of no use. It shows that there has been more saving, more thought for the future, more appreciation of the real value of life.

In this connection, it is well to have in mind that the industrial schools have performed a great and useful service, in so far as they have impressed upon the young men who go out from these schools as preachers the importance of learning a trade, something of agriculture, so that they can give the members of their congregations an example of industrial thrift.

At Tuskegee Institute, we insist upon the importance of service. Every student in this department is expected to do, in connection with his other work either as a teacher or preacher, some part of the social and religious work that is carried on under the direction of the Bible Training School in the surrounding country. We are seeking to imbue these young men who are going forth as leaders of their people with the feeling that the great task of uplifting the race, though it may be for others merely a work of humanity, for them, and every other member of the Negro race, is a work of religion.

In this great modern world, where every individual has so many interests and life is so complicated, there is a tendency to let religion and life drift apart. I meet men every day who, honest and upright though they be, have lost in their daily lives this connection with religion, and are striving vainly to regain it. There is no one great dominating motive in their lives which enters into every task and gives it significance and zest.

It is one of the compensations which hardships bring, that the race problem is a thing so real and so present to the Negro people that it enters, as a motive, into everything they do. It is this that makes it possible for them to realize that the acts of every individual have an importance far beyond the measure in which they make or mar his or her personal fortunes.

So soon as a man, white or black, really learns to comprehend that fact, he will cease to whine and complain, and he will be content to do his best, humble though it be, to improve his own condition, and to help his less fortunate fellows.

Slowly but surely, and in ever larger numbers, the members of my race are learning that lesson; they are realizing that God has assigned to their race a man's part in the task of civilization; they are learning to understand their duty, and to face uncomplainingly and with confidence the destiny that awaits them.

Booker T. Washington

North American Review, 181 (July 1905), 20–23.

To Emmett Jay Scott

[South Weymouth, Mass.] August 7, 1905

Dear Mr. Scott: I am quite sure it will interest you to know that Kelly Miller and Grimke have broken off completely from Du Bois and his crowd.

It seems that Du Bois has insulted both of them. Grimke had a long talk with me and went over many of the details covering the devilment of the whole gang. He seems more than anxious now to line up with us.

Kelly Miller feels the insult very keenly and resents it in very strong language, but he is mushy and cannot be depended upon for a straight out fight. Very truly yours,

Booker T. Washington

TLS Con. 24 BTW Papers DLC.

To Emmett Jay Scott

South Weymouth, Mass., August 7, 1905

Dear Mr. Scott: I am returning Cable's letter to you the one written to Thompson.

Mr. Cable's views are all right when dealing with gentlemen, but not scoundrels, whose purposes are wholly known.

Some of our friends of the colored press have taken for granted that those connected with the Niagara Movement are honest and from that point of view have discussed the declarations, which makes it a rather puzzling condition to deal with, but in the end, I am sure they will find out their ultimate purpose. Very truly yours,

Booker T. Washington

TLS Con. 24 BTW Papers DLC

To Emmett Jay Scott

[South Weymouth, Mass.] August 7, 1905

Dear Mr. Scott: I am of the opinion it would be well to stop in Washington, on your way North, and see Terrell and Dancy; let them understand that I do not feel exactly comfortable over the fact that the three papers, in or near Washington, are continually knocking me and there is nothing to indicate an action on the part of my friends, or supposed friends.

You can use your own judgement in this matter. Very truly yours,

B. T. W.

TLI Con. 24 BTW Papers DLC.

To John A. Hertel

South Weymouth, Mass., August 7, 1905

Personal & Confidential.

My dear Mr. Hertel: The enclosed clipping from a Buffalo paper, where the meeting was held, will give you the true aim of the persons in it. I have found out definitely that not over 12 or 15 persons were in the meeting, and as I said to you, you will find that they will attempt to use your magazine as a propaganda, and if permitted, you will find that Barbour[1] will show his hand more fully in the September number. Very truly yours,

[Booker T. Washington]

TLc Con. 29 BTW Papers DLC.

1 Jesse Max Barber.

From Emmett Jay Scott

Tuskegee Institute, Alabama. August 7, 1905

Dear Mr. Washington: A letter received from Thompson assures me of his willingness to work with us in good spirit and heartily in connection with the coming meeting of the League. I think that he and Mr. Simmons will help us out very materially. Mr. Attwell[1] is planning to be there, and I can utilize both him and Mr. Cox should it become necessary and your approval is given.

Thompson tells me in his letter that the Bishop[2] writes him that the new Council matter is to kill off the Niagara movement and that he, the Bishop, is with you now till death. The Bishop is quite mercurial in temperament, but I feel sure he will be disposed to stick since he was crowded out of recognition by the other fellows. Yours truly,

Emmett J. Scott

TLS Con. 557 BTW Papers DLC.

1 Ernest Ten Eyck Attwell, after serving for two years as chief clerk and stenographer in the business office of Tuskegee Institute, had recently become assistant to the principal's private secretary. From 1907 until after BTW's death he was the institute's business agent and a member of the executive council. BTW trusted Attwell's discretion and sent him occasionally on confidential missions unconnected with Tuskegee Institute.

2 Alexander Walters.

From John A. Hertel

Chicago 8/9/05

Dear Mr. Washington: Yours of the 7th inst. is just at hand. I wish to thank you for the clipping that you have sent and also for your letter.

As stated to you verbally several days ago, I shall keep an eye on the magazine, and you can count on me to always stand for fair play. I am aiming, and in fact, working very hard to make ours a magazine not only in name but in reality, a journal that will stand for the progress of the race and that will commend the good among all classes.

I must, however, handle our young editor very carefully and very diplomatically. I cannot place the magazine under censorship, but I will be on the alert and endeavor to put in the proper word at the proper time. Everything will come out all O.K. if you are patient and keep me informed.

I might add that we have a pretty extensive enterprise in the way of a publishing house and I am worked superlatively hard. Our business in the South has also developed wonderfully the last year or two and the Voice so far as I have been able to learn, has enjoyed a very healthy growth. To be sure, it is still in its infancy, but it shows very vigorous signs of life and with proper nourishment I am confident it is going to become a giant in the course of two or three years.

Again thanking you for the confidence you have placed in me and assuring you I am always glad to hear from you, I remain, Yours very truly,

J. A. Hertel

TLS Con. 29 BTW Papers DLC.

From Fannie Barrier Williams

[Chicago] Thursday 8/10/05

My dear Friend: Your telegram requesting some statistics as to recent lynchings received. I take pleasure in forwarding to you the following facts & figures.

There have been in the U.S. from January first to August first, 38 lynchings while in the same length of time in 1904 the number was 57 showing a decrease of 19 for this year or 1905. These figures, of course, include the statement given in response to a previous request.

From the first of June to the first of August 1905 there have been 22 lynchings, all occur[r]ing in the South. Of these cases 14 were for murder, and 7 for criminal assault, and one for larceny. Of this number also 21 were colored and 1 white, occurring in different states as follows: La. 1, Tenn. 1, Miss. 5 Ga. 8, Fla. 1 Ark. 1 Ky 1 and Texas 4.

Again thanking you for the privilege of serving you, I am Cordially, but hastily yours

Mrs. Fannie B. Williams

ALS Con. 308 BTW Papers DLC.

An Editorial in the Montgomery *Advertiser*

Montgomery, Ala., Aug. 16, 1905

BOOKER WASHINGTON'S SARATOGA PERFORMANCE

Since the fateful day when Booker T. Washington sat down to the dinner table in the White House with President Roosevelt, he has done many things to hurt the cause, of which he is regarded as the foremost man. The people of the South have voluntarily taxed themselves many millions of dollars for the education of the negroes. There has been no discrimination except — in the matter of taxpaying — nine dollars and fifty cents coming from the white people for every fifty cents paid by the negroes for education of negroes. There can be no just complaint, therefore, by Northern, Western, or any other people on this score against Southern white people. That Washington's persistent way of turning up at big affairs in the North, and occupying prominent places at banquet tables, where white men and women abound has caused some trouble in the South is not to be disputed. The Roosevelt affair was talked of among negroes in every part of the South as evidence of what was coming for all of them. This was so widespread as to become a topic of conversation in the humblest and most isolated negro cabins.

The true friends of Washington and of the real advancement of the negro race, which it was hoped might be accomplished through policies he advocated and proposed to carry out, have been sorely grieved by his continual exhibition of desire for social equality, knowing that what he did would make a deep impression upon the more ignorant negroes of this country. What excuse, in view of conditions, North and South, can he offer for the exhibition of himself as escort to the dinner table at Saratoga's leading hotel, of the daughter[1] of late Postmaster General John Wanamaker.[2] Leaving out of question the lack of delicacy and self-respect manifested by Wanamaker and his family, blame must rest upon Washington because he knows how deep and impossible is the gulf between whites and blacks in the South, when the social situation is involved.[3] He deliberately flaunts all this in the face of the Southern people among whom he is living and among whom his work has to be carried on. He could have given no harder blow to his institution than he gave when he marched into that Saratoga dining room with a white woman and her father.

Montgomery *Advertiser*, Aug. 16, 1905, 4.

[1] Mary Brown Wanamaker (Mrs. Barclay H.) Warburton, wife of the publisher of the Philadelphia *Evening Telegraph*.

[2] John Wanamaker (1838–1922) was a self-made millionaire department-store owner. He was also involved in many other investments and philanthropies in Philadelphia. An anti-machine Republican, he was Postmaster General in the cabinet of Benjamin Harrison. He was active, from 1858 until his death, in the Young Men's Christian Association, and contributed to college and YMCA buildings in the United States and several foreign countries. His connection with BTW perhaps came through his New York partner, Robert C. Ogden, who was chairman of the Tuskegee trustees

and a longtime supporter of BTW. A few days after the Saratoga incident, Wanamaker addressed the National Negro Business League meeting in New York. He expressed the viewpoint of many conservative Republicans in remarking of the Negro after Reconstruction: "You are like the man who was kicked by a mule. You're not quite so handsome, but you've learned a great deal." (New York *Times*, Aug. 19, 1905, 12.)

3 This incident on Aug. 14, 1905, occasioned a brief outburst of southern newspaper criticism of BTW, but it was neither as intense nor as lasting a furor as that which followed the dinner at the White House four years earlier. "BOOKER WASHINGTON'S ARM AIDED WANAMAKER'S GIRL AS SHE WALKED TO DINNER" was the front-page headline in the normally pro-BTW Atlanta *Constitution*, Aug. 15, 1905. The Birmingham *Age-Herald*, Aug. 17, 1905, 4, published a review of southern press comments, all unfavorable. William H. Councill, Washington's old rival, seized the opportunity to criticize Washington for his "mistake," which he was sure "could not and would not be permitted." Councill slyly suggested in an open letter to the governor of Alabama that he himself was more conservative than Washington. (Montgomery *Advertiser*, Sept. 1, 1905, 5.) A Montgomery white friend wrote Scott that a man from Elmore, Ala., had threatened to kill BTW with a shotgun and boasted that no court would convict him. (Benjamin W. Walker to Scott, Aug. 27, 1905, Con. 32, BTW Papers, DLC.) Scott urged BTW to stay out of the South until the furor died down.

To the Editor of the Montgomery *Advertiser*

New York, Aug. 20 [1905]

I have just seen for the first time the misleading and false reports in Southern newspapers referring to my escorting female members of Mr. Wanamaker's family into the dining room of a Saratoga hotel.[1]

I have not referred to these reports before, because they have just come to my notice. I did not escort any female member of Mr. Wanamaker's family to, or out of the dining room. I did dine with Mr. Wanamaker and members of his family at a hotel, at his request, for the purpose of talking on a matter of business, but at the time was a guest myself at a colored hotel in Saratoga.

During the last fifteen years, I have been at the hotel where Mr. Wanamaker was on three different occasions, when I was to speak at public meetings, as I was this time and no comment was made of it.

When in the South I conform like all colored people to the customs of the South, but when in the North, I have found it necessary, during the last twenty years, as stated fully in my book, "Up from Slavery," to come into contact with white people in the furtherance of my work in ways I do not in the South.

Booker Washington

Montgomery *Advertiser,* Aug. 21, 1905, 1. The newspaper ran the letter with bold headlines: "STATEMENT OF WASHINGTON / NEGRO MAKES PARTIAL DENIAL / DINED WITH WANAMAKER / SAYS HE DID NOT ESCORT THE DAUGHTER TO TABLE / TUSKEGEE TEACHER ADMITS SITTING DOWN TO DINNER WITH PHILADELPHIAN AND HIS FAMILY AND STATES IT AS HIS CUSTOM."

[1] In addition to the editorial of Aug. 16 above, the Montgomery *Advertiser* ran another editorial on Aug. 18 which criticized BTW further. Quoting from BTW's speech before the NNBL in New York, the newspaper accused him of being a "false pretender" for saying "we should see that no fire of racial hostility is lighted," and then escorting a white woman to dinner a few hours later. "The best and truest friends of Washington will have to drop him," the editorial stated. (Montgomery *Advertiser,* Aug. 18, 1905, 4.)

To Charles Woodroph Hare

Chicago, Ill., August 22, 1905

Dear Sir: I presume that you received the telegram which I sent you yesterday from New York. The clippings which you sent contain the first information I had seen concerning the Saratoga matter. It now seems that the report was first published in an afternoon sensational sheet. I judge then that some one took it from this paper and sent it South.

It seems I am at the mercy of a sensational press. For fifteen years I have been spending a large portion of my Summers in going to Summer resorts and hotels in the North and West for the purpose of making addresses and seeing individuals in order to get money. I went to Saratoga in the same way and on the same mission as I have always done. I have been going to the people who wanted to talk with me about the work, and in the same manner, I met Mr.

Wanamaker and so far as I know, little has been said about it. The report telegraphed South did not appear in a single New York paper, excepting the one mentioned, so far as I can learn.

I have tried to be more than careful and I did not change my method of work or mode of life in recent years. I have not taken a single day of vacation this Summer, all of my time, strength and energy being devoted to work.

For fifteen years I have visited such resorts as Poland Springs, Me., Lake Mohonk, N.Y. and Bar Harbor, Me. to meet the people who go there, and the proprietors have gladly given me accommodation for the purpose of reaching their guests. On two or three occasions, when I have been in Saratoga, to speak or see individuals, I have stopped at the same place where Mr. Wanamaker was and no comment was made. On this occasion however, finding that there was a good colored boarding house, I went to it, a thing I always prefer doing when possible, but on this occasion I had especially in mind, avoiding all appearances to occasion remarks.

So far as Mrs. Wanamaker[1] is concerned, I have never met her in my life. She is at present in Europe. Mr. Wanamaker told me his daughter was especially anxious to hear about our work. She was present and no other lady. I went into the dining-room with Mr. Wanamaker and came out with him. Besides, over a month ago, Mr. Wanamaker wanted to speak with me at length about some special plans he had in mind and wanted me to come to his hotel.

But the main point is if I am to do my work in the same manner as I have in the past, I cannot see how I can escape these sensational and false reports. The same kind of a report would have found lodgement in the South, except for the fact that the white men from Birmingham, who composed the committee to invite the President to come to Birmingham, had the opportunity of denying the false report themselves. That example illustrates what I am called on to bear.

I thank you very much for sending the clippings and writing me. Very truly yours,

[Booker T. Washington]

TLc Con. 29 BTW Papers DLC.

[1] Mary Brown Wanamaker (1839–1920), who married John Wanamaker in 1869.

From Roscoe Conkling Bruce

Tuskegee Institute 26 August 1905

My dear Mr. Washington, I write to ask you if you would countenance my accepting the principalship of the Armstrong Manual Training School, in case it were proffered me. For three years I have sought to serve you and Tuskegee to the very best of my ability, and I realize clearly and willingly the profound obligations your courtesy and generosity have placed upon my shoulders. How the other position, wholly unsolicited, was suggested to me by a member (I think, the President) of the Board of Education and what is my personal attitude in the matter, the enclosed copy of a letter I am now sending to Mr. J. Holdsworth Gordon,[1] explains in full.

My reasons for considering the change are:

1. The happiness of my family — Tuskegee is isolated and travel is costly.
2. My health cannot long sustain the amount of indoor work and the hours entailed by my present position. The other position incurs only nine months' work, and night work is optional.
3. With better facilities for study, I should have every day and night much more leisure for recreation, for my own intellectual development, and for serious literary production.
4. I could make and save more money.
5. The city Negro population offers practically a new field for applying that philosophy of education which I have learned at Tuskegee; and, therefore, a highly significant and useful career.

In case of your approval and my appointment, this plan would involve my completing the charts, diagrams, etc. for the Exhibit; and my remaining here at Tuskegee until you had time to secure my successor.

I place the situation frankly and freely before you, requesting your consent and approval. Wherever my field of effort, I shall always regard faithful service to you and to Tuskegee as a proud privilege. You have always treated me with a consideration that is almost fatherly. Sincerely yours

Roscoe C. Bruce

TLS Con. 565 BTW Papers DLC.

[1] J. Holdsworth Gordon (1847–1924), a Washington attorney for more than fifty

years, was a member of the District of Columbia Board of Education throughout Roosevelt's presidency. He was vice-president from 1903 to 1905 and president for the school year 1905–6.

To Benjamin Jefferson Davis

[New York City] August 29, 1905

Personal.

My dear Mr. Davis: Yours of August 20th has been received and I note that it was written before my statement was given to the Atlanta Constitution and other Southern papers.

Of course you are aware that I would not permit myself to be drawn into a display of folly. There was absolutely nothing unusual in my conduct at Saratoga. The whole thing, so far as I have been able to learn, the sensational part, was started in an afternoon "yellow journal" in New York City. The fact that the New York papers did not notice it ought to be proof enough that there was nothing unusual connected with the incident.

I try to be as careful as possible in such matters but it is impossible to act, in the North, as the Southern people demand.

Some time soon, I want to talk with you at length regarding the meeting of the Business League in Atlanta next year. Very truly yours,

[Booker T. Washington]

TLc Con. 28 BTW Papers DLC.

To Seth Low

[New York City?] Aug 31 [190]5

If not too late am inclined to ask you to let sentence remain about my walking in and out of dining room alone with Mr. Wanamaker.

Also to make it plain I have been going to watering places and summer hotels for fifteen years in the interest of my work, and not for pleasure.

Booker T. Washington

HWcSr Con. 878 BTW Papers DLC.

Seth Low to the Editor of the Atlanta *Constitution*

North East Harbor, Maine, August 31st, 1905

Dear Sir; I have noticed with surprise the recent outbreak of criticism of Booker Washington in the South, because of a supposed happening at Saratoga. Mr. Washington did walk into the hotel dining-room with Mr. Wanamaker, and he walked out with him after luncheon; he did not serve as escort to any of Mr. Washington's [Wanamaker's] party. The criticism based upon this incident seems to me to make no allowance for the differences of condition existing at the North. The South very properly asks the North to be considerate of its views upon this subject, and it is only fair in return that the South should give some heed to the point of view of the North. Very likely neither is wholly right nor wholly wrong.

I apprehend that the fundamental difference between the two sections is very slight. Race purity is as strong an instinct at the North as it is at the South; but, there being at the North so much larger a proportion of whites to blacks, this is maintained in the North by much less drastic measures than are believed by Southerners to be necessary in the South. It is inevitable, in a community that feels itself safe enough to discriminate between an individual and his race, that such discriminations will be made; and individuals at the North are likely at any time to give invitations to Booker Washington and exceptional colored men like him that would be unthinkable in the South. This does not mean that the North differs from the South as to race purity, nor that it criticises the South for its attitude. It only means that in the North, for various reasons, a greater freedom is possible, without injury.

The South does itself injustice when it gives to such happenings an exaggerated significance.

Booker Washington's attitude to this matter seems to me to have been as wise as it is upon so many other questions. For fifteen years he has been going to summer resorts in the North, never for pleasure but always in the interest of his work. Although often invited to functions of every kind, he has accepted no invitations but those that bear directly upon his work. It was by Mr. Wanamaker's invitation, and for the purpose of talking about Tuskegee and other work affecting colored people, that Booker Washington lunched with Mr. Wanamaker at Saratoga. To found upon an incident like this a serious criticism of a man who is trying to serve the South in serving his own race, seems to your fellow-countrymen in the North neither generous nor wise. Not wise, because it advertises the fact, if it be objectionable; and not generous, because it attributes ignoble motives to a man whose life of generous service ought to exempt him from such misunderstandings.

I realize fully, Mr. Editor, how impossible it is for one living out of the South to enter completely into the South's feelings upon this subject, try as he will; but at least I may claim sincerely to desire to do so. My hope is that, as the years go on, we may all be able to do more justice to the point of view of the other. Yours respectfully,

[Seth Low]

TL Copy Con. 878 BTW Papers DLC. Redated Sept. 12, 1905, the letter appeared in the Atlanta *Constitution*, Sept. 18, 1905, 4.

Seth Low to Clark Howell

North East Harbor, Maine, September 1st, 1905

Confidential.

My dear Mr. Howell: I venture to send you the enclosed letter for publication in the "Constitution," in the hope that it may do some good; for it seems to me that some effort ought to be made to interpret the North to the South in this matter, in the interest of the South itself. The attitude of the South, as expressed in criticism such as I have made reference to, seems to many and probably to most men at the North simply hysterical; and I cannot help thinking that the root of it is to be found in the South's failure to understand that the North is as firmly set upon race purity as our good friends of the South. There is no evidence anywhere that race purity in the North is endangered by the courtesies shown to exceptional colored men; and if the South will only take this for granted it will do much to bring the two sections into closer sympathy with each other. I suppose the point of view of the South is that such an incident, when made known to the negroes at the South, will fill the race with social ambitions which otherwise it would not have. It certainly does not have this effect in the North; and if the Southern newspapers themselves did not advertise such happenings from one end of the South to the other, the negroes of the South would never know of them. In a word, it seems to me important to say (and I have tried to say it kindly), that fundamentally the North agrees with the South on the subject of race purity; but that it must be left at liberty to exercise the right to discriminate between an individual and his race, which is one of the incidents of the complete freedom from social danger that prevails here. For the South to demand the contrary would be to attempt to place upon the North "a yoke which neither our fathers nor we were able to bear."

I know that at this moment you are a candidate for Governor of the State of Georgia. I therefore enclose my public letter to you under this private cover, so that, if it would embarrass you in any way to print it at this time, you may return it to me, and I will then send it to some other newspaper. If it does not embarrass you to print it, there is no paper in the South in which I should be so glad to have it appear as in "The Atlanta Constitution."

Wishing you good luck in your campaign, I am, with kind regards, Yours sincerely,

[Seth Low]

TL Copy Con. 878 BTW Papers DLC.

From Hervey W. Laird

Montgomery, Ala., Sept. 1, 1905

Personal.

Dear Sir: It has been in my mind for some days to write you about the unfortunate Wanamaker affair but have been out of the city and saw the press stories while on my way to Virginia for a short vacation. Nothing has happened for some time that has given me so much cause for regret and I feel that the betterment of the negro has had a very serious set back. Heretofore attacks on you have emanated from a class of men who really have little force, but this event has been followed by condemnation from sources that will be bound to result in trouble for you and the institution. I have heard criticism from men who have always stood to you and who are representatives of the best thought of the State and section.

I have no idea in the world that you desire social equality. In fact I have never been able to bring my mind to any conception of such a thing. I am sure you realize it as well as I do. I know further that in the East all men ask you to lunch or dinner to talk business, and this, I believe, accounts entirely for the Saratoga meeting, but we have to deal with a condition here in the South. It is not what should be or what many would call justice or injustice, but what is, that all friends of the negro have to meet, and to gain an end these very conditions *must be met.* I would not argue that the position of the dominant element in the South is the right one, nor attempt to show that the contrary is true, but I would urge that all who desire the best for the negro and the section meet the conditions in every way, that good may come of it.

I would not have you think that I have any condemnation for you personally, nor do I feel that there was the least intention in your heart to violate the sentiments so long held in the South, but write that I may give you some idea of the way the matter appeals to me, a well wisher in every sense of the negro and a sincere friend of yourself in a personal way. The elements of ability to do great good that you have shown are so many sacred talents in your hands and God and a great people will hold you responsible for the reckoning day.

I am sure you will understand that I am telling you personally my opinion of the matter and assuring you of my sympathy rather than go into the press at a time when anything will only add to the flame. I feel sure the trouble will blow over and that there will be no disposition to cripple you in any way by the responsible men of the State, though I feel that if a session of the legislature should come along now it would take hard work to keep the appropriation from being taken away, which would mean a hard blow. I am also afraid of what might be done by irresponsible persons which, I fear, might in extreme cases, go to the point of doing you bodily harm or the destruction of your property.

I shall be glad to have anything from you that you may desire to give the press, but if you will pardon a suggestion my advice would be to say nothing unless it becomes more necessary than at this time.

With assurances of sympathy and regards, I am Very truly,

H W Laird

P.S. You fully understand that this kind of a letter is of the most confidential nature.

H. W. L.

TLS Con. 29 BTW Papers DLC.

To Roscoe Conkling Bruce

[South Weymouth, Mass.] September 4, 1905

Dear Mr. Bruce: I have your letter of August 26th, regarding the possibility of you being appointed as Principal of the Armstrong Manual and Training school. Permit me to say in reply that I should regret, more than I can express, to have you leave Tuskegee, especially at the present time or until the end of the next school year. I take into consideration that it is natural for you to look upon this in the light of a promotion, and a promotion is something every man should crave or value. Again I always consider that when a teacher of ours receives an offer in the direction of a promotion, it is a compliment to our work at Tuskegee.

What I am trying to say is this, that while I consider there is an opportunity for greater service at Tuskegee, the reasons you give for considering the matter favorably are strong and natural, yet I can but express the wish that if the offer comes to you in a definite way that you will see your way clear to remain with us this year, or until after the time of the Twenty-fifth Anniversary. Very truly yours,

[Booker T. Washington]

TLc Con. 565 BTW Papers DLC.

Emmett Jay Scott to the Editor of the Montgomery *Advertiser*

Montgomery, Ala., Sept. 6/05

Editor, The Advertiser: You prate much of Anglo-Saxon superiority & recently printed in your columns Tom Watson's vicious attack on Booker Washington & the Negro,[1] but your sense of fairness will not permit I am sure the exhibition of even partial justice to these helpless people by publishing what Negroes have had to say in reply to the attacks of the Watsons & Dixons.[2]

I hand you herewith two clippings from the New York Age, a Negro newspaper, with articles by Negroes who are as able to speak for themselves as you are to speak for your boasted civilization. Do these Negroes a little fairness by publishing the clippings I enclose. Do you dare to treat Negroes fairly? Do you dare to allow them to speak through the same columns in which they are traduced & villified. I await answer.

Fairness

ALd Con. 330 BTW Papers DLC.

1 The Montgomery *Advertiser*, July 23, 1905, 3, reprinted an article from the June 1905 issue of *Tom Watson's Magazine* which accused BTW of preaching that blacks were superior to whites and asserted that blacks were merely imitators of the white race who had made no contribution to civilization.

2 Thomas Dixon, Jr., had recently attacked BTW in an incendiary article, "Booker T. Washington and the Negro: Some Dangerous Aspects of the Work of Tuskegee," *Saturday Evening Post*, 178 (Aug. 19, 1905), 1–2. Dixon claimed that since the basic

race problem was that blacks were naturally inferior, BTW's efforts to improve their education, character, and material position would "only intensify that problem's dangerous features." He predicted that if blacks provided "direct economic competition rather than service," whites would kill them.

From John Wesley Edward Bowen

Atlanta, Ga. Sept. 12, 1905

Dear Mr. Washington: I recognize that you are passing through a stormy period at this time. I write to say that the bitter and senseless attack upon you by the press serves only to deepen the respect of your many friends for you. Do not apologize for anything. Your greatest victories were won in the past by your prudence, wisdom, hard work, and by your silence when attacked. God has called you to a great work and you are doing it. I pray for you. Yours sincerely,

J. W. E. Bowen

TLS Con. 27 BTW Papers DLC.

To John Wesley Edward Bowen

[Tuskegee, Ala.] September 13, 1905

Personal

My dear Dr. Bowen: Your kind letter of the 12th has just been received, and though I have received several letters bearing upon the subject, I wish to assure you that I have received none which have given me more consolation and satisfaction than the receipt of yours. What you say is most satisfactory and just in line with my own thoughts.

You need not be afraid that I shall make any apology or further explanation. I should not have spoken a single word bearing upon the subject but for the fact that the man who quipped up the dispatch in New York tried to make a fool of me. For me to have permitted myself to be left in the position of ostentatiously parading through the dining room with a woman on my arm, a thing that nobody else did in the hotel, would not have helped the race either North or South, and in my statement I simply meant to stand by the facts. Great pressure has been brought to bear upon me to get me to make some kind of other statement or apology, but that part of the matter is closed so far as I am concerned.

I have just said to my secretary, Mr. Scott, that which I am sure you will appreciate, that all progress is marked by suffering on somebody's part, and if this event will mark a single upward step on the part of the race I am willing to be placed in the position of what the world calls a sufferer. Heretofore others have fought our battles and have borne the suffering. The time is come when we in a larger degree must suffer in the interest of progress and civilization. For my part, I am prepared for my share of it. It is not at me that our enemies are aiming, it is the race and its civilization and progress.

I confess that one feature in connection with this whole matter that has disappointed me is to see that in a crisis like this when the very manhood life of the race is at stake, that we have deserters and enemies in the camp among our own race. Not a white paper in the South, however vile, has attempted to lead on this fight against me in any more bitter manner than such papers as the Boston Guardian, and in fact all those controlled by the Niagara Movement, and I am sorry that in this connection your own associate[1] seems to be placed in this awkward position. It does seem that there would be a point at which these men would stop. I see only yesterday that two of their papers, one published in Alexandria and another in Washington, have gone so far as to make the statement that my house has been shot into. In this connection permit me to say that while they have been doing all they can to incite violence and to damn me, that the white people of this community among whom I have lived for twenty-five years, have stood up manfully against powerful influences to get them to do our property or myself bodily harm or to enter into any unseemly conduct.

But the hearts of our people are all right. I can trust them notwithstanding a few mistaken individuals. A great test, however, is to come in the next few months. These Southern white papers with their united effort for the time being have been trying to turn a large element of the Southern white people from me. Their great effort from now on will be to alienate the colored people, and if they can accomplish that, they will feel that no Negro in the future will ever attempt to step beyond the narrow and limited bounds which they have set for him. My conduct in this as in other matters, has been perfectly simple and consistent. I have always obeyed every reasonable custom obtaining here in the South, but now for the South to go beyond the Mason and Dixon Line and attempt to control my actions is something unreasonable, and I would be a traitor to my own race as well as to other friends if I were to yield to this unreasonable attempt to limit our growth.

As you may well imagine, all kinds of threats, both public and private, have been made to prevent my coming South, but I was determined to be here on the opening day of school at any cost, and I will remain here until I find it necessary to leave on business.

For your own personal information I want to say that there has been no violence or attempt at it in this community. While there are evidently white people in Tuskegee and in this county who have questioned the wisdom of my action, they have done so in a calm and sensible matter.

Of course you will understand this as being in every respect perfectly confidential. Yours very truly,

Booker T. Washington

TLpS Con. 27 BTW Papers DLC.

[1] Jesse Max Barber.

To Charles William Anderson

[Tuskegee, Ala.] September 13, 1905

Personal

My dear Mr. Anderson: I wish you would let our friend at 57 Broadway[1] know how very satisfactory his man served me on the way South.[2] He is not only a careful man but a gentleman. I am also grateful to you for your help and interest.

I wish you would convey this message to Mr. Pinkerton because, for certain reasons, I do not want to send a letter out from here directly to him at present. You might tell Mr. Pinkerton in your own way that without knowing it was against the rules of the company to do so, I offered Mr. Osler a personal donation, but he promptly refused, saying it was against the rules of the company for any of their men to accept fees. I thought this spoke very highly for him.

I find matters in good shape here at the school. Yours truly,

Booker T. Washington

TLpS Con. 5 BTW Papers DLC.

[1] David C. Thornhill, superintendent in New York of the Pinkerton National Detective Agency.

[2] Scott had written to BTW Sept. 7, 1905: "I think that you can come to Tuskegee without delay, taking, of course, the precautions I have already mentioned en route. If there is any trouble, it is more likely to manifest itself on the train than at Tuskegee. We have had feelers out in all directions, and there is abundant evidence that they are not feeling quite as bitterly as they have been feeling." (Con. 557, BTW Papers, DLC.)

E. V. Osler, a Pinkerton detective hired to guard Washington during his return to Tuskegee, reported that "I was to note any assault, hisses or jeers made at Mr. Washington en route. . . . I did not hear anybody comment on Mr. Washington." BTW stayed in his drawing room, and the agent reported that the other passengers were unaware that Washington was aboard the train. (Pinkerton's National Detective Agency, four reports, Sept. 10–13, 1905, Con. 30, BTW Papers, DLC.)

To George H. Woodson

[Tuskegee, Ala.] September 13, 1905

Personal

Dear Mr. Woodson: When we had our last conference you were in some doubt as to the policy of the organization that you are connected with. You stated that you were not fully convinced that their object was a personal one.

I wonder if you have been reading the chief organ of that organization during the last three weeks, and if you are still convinced that the leaders have an unselfish and patriotic ambition, or if their only object is to try to accomplish the downfall of one individual? I am sure you are too broad and sensible a man to be deceived. You know that incident which is made the basis of the most vile attacks on me is simply another way certain people in the South say to the

Negro that he must go so high and no higher, and that the South wants to control the Negro not only in the South but out of the South. When they attack me, it is not B. T. Washington who is attacked, but the race. If these men had an iota of manhood in them and were not controlled by petty spite, now is the time when they would come out and stand up for the race, but you know what they are doing. I should like very much to hear from you on this subject. Yours very truly,

Booker T. Washington

TLpS Con. 309 BTW Papers DLC.

From Francis Herbert Warren[1]

Detroit, Mich., Sept. 14th. 1905

My Dear Mr. Washington, Your valued favor dated Sept. 5th. has been received and contents carefully noted. In reply I would say that I have seen nothing in the associated press reports of the Wanamaker-Washington dinner that placed you "in a ridiculous and foolish attitude" nor have I seen where you have been charged with any act, in connection with the affair, that was not clearly within your social and constitutional rights.

I look upon your statement as an attempt to modify Southern criticism for acts upon your part that were clearly within your rights whether they were true or false. The incident charged to you (of walking with Mr. Wanamaker's daughter) whether true or not furnished an answer from the white North to the white South that no such fears are entertained in this part of the country that Thomas Dixon Jr. credits the South with. Had your critics been permitted to do their worst about the incident it must have resulted in bringing hosts of white support to the position the Wanamaker family had assumed in relation to such matters. Let me ask, did not Mrs Warburton dine at the table with yourself and Mr. Wanamaker? And if she did what essential difference was there in that conduct and in walking to the dining room with the guest of the family?

Now, my dear Professor I want to say, that I fully appreciate the delicate position in which you find yourself for on two occasions I have felt the physical force of the damnable Southern prejudice. Once for resenting an insult at the hands of the Governor of Louisiana at which time I narrowly escaped lynching, and another time in the semi-southern city of Pittsburgh recently.

As I see the situation, the time has come when we cannot safely yield one iota of our rights either social or civil or political in whatever part of the country they are gained. The South is forcing the fighting and if we stand squarely and firmly upon our rights, especially such of our leaders as have the full confidence of the best white people of the whole country, Southern prejudice will only succeed in digging its own grave and the great Southern conspiracy to reduce the Negroes of this country to a degraded peasantry, or what is worse, to re-enslave them, will surely fail.

With highest personal regards, believe me, Sir, Yours most faithfully,

Francis H Warren

TLS Con. 309 BTW Papers DLC.

[1] Francis Herbert Warren (b. 1864) was a Detroit journalist and lawyer, and one of black Detroit's leading entrepreneurs. Born in Sarina, Ontario, Warren moved as a youth to Detroit, where he graduated from the Detroit College of Law and was admitted to the bar in 1903. After two years as a clerk in the Wayne County treasurer's office, he purchased and became managing editor of the Detroit *Informer* in 1905. He used it for the next seven years as a means of promoting his favorite causes, including the single tax and Bishop Henry M. Turner's African colonization movement. He hoped to combine these two interests by promoting a single-tax colony in Liberia. Like Turner, however, he had too large a stake in America to emigrate. He became an attorney for the Detroit branch of the NAACP. Among his business enterprises was a silver-mining company and a life insurance firm. (Katzman, *Before the Ghetto*, 204–5.)

To Essie Smith[1]

[Tuskegee, Ala.] September 15, 1905

Dear Madam: Your kind letter of August 17th has been received, and your suggestion that I make a contribution for a Confederate monument, to be erected on Court House Square of the County seat of Franklin, I confess touches me most deeply.

I should have answered your letter long ago, but for the fact that

I have been away from home, and in order to get a little rest, asked that no mail be sent me.

I am deeply interested in the erection of the monument, and would like to make a contribution, with the understanding that it is to be received in the same spirit in which it is asked.

Before determining just what I can and ought to do will you be kind enough to let me know the cost, or probable cost, and how much has been received towards its erection? With these facts in mind, I can reach a decision.

I have never visited the country of my birth since I left there when a very small boy, though I have been hoping to do so for some time. It seems that my life is crowded so full to the very brim, that I find time to do only a very small proportion of what I really want to accomplish. I shall still hope however, to have the pleasure of visiting Franklin at some time in the future.

In one way or another, by letter or otherwise, I have kept some what in touch with the members of the Burroughs family, to which I belonged during the days of slavery.

Your letter reminds me that I recall that one of the young white men who seemed to be very fond of me when I was a child, lost his life during the Civil War, and this makes your suggestion all the more interesting to me.

Hoping to hear from you soon, I am, Very truly yours,

[Booker T. Washington]

TL Copy Con. 255 BTW Papers DLC.

[1] Essie (Mrs. Cabell) Smith was president of the Jubal Early chapter of the United Daughters of the Confederacy in Rocky Mount, Va.

To Seth Low

Tuskegee Institute, Alabama. September 15, 1905

Personal

My dear Mr. Low: Copies of the communications which you sent to Mr. Howell and the Atlanta Constitution are received, and I am very grateful for what you have done. The Constitution so far does not seem to have given the matter any attention. Perhaps you have heard directly from Mr. Howell. I am not surprised at this, because I have been reading the Constitution since I have been home and I find that the feeling between Mr. Howell and Mr. Hoke Smith is stronger and more silly than I supposed it was. For example, a whole editorial column was recently devoted in the Constitution to proving the fact that Mr. Smith had at one time when he was Secretary of the Interior, appointed a Negro as a messenger at a salary that was $200 higher than some white employee received. That will give you some idea of the character of the contest. I am quite sure that Mr. Howell felt that if he published your letter it would give Mr. Smith some kind of advantage over him.

The discussion of the whole matter, however, is disappearing, and has disappeared to such an extent that I hardly believe it would be worth while to raise the question now by having your letter published.

I am glad to say that the white people in our immediate community for the most part have taken a very sensible view of the whole matter. Yours very truly,

Booker T. Washington

TLS Seth Low Papers NNC.

To George Bruce Cortelyou

[Tuskegee, Ala.] September 15, 1905

Personal

My dear Mr. Cortelyou: I see by the papers that the Tuskegee Institute post office has been put into the Presidential class of offices.

The individual who has served as postmaster at this institution for fifteen years beginning at a period before it was made a United States office, is named James B. Washington, and he is holding the same position, but *he is no relation of mine*. I want you to have this information because I do not want you or the President to feel that I would recommend one of my relatives for such a position. Yours truly,

Booker T. Washington

TLpS Con. 875 BTW Papers DLC.

From Essie Smith

Rocky Mount, Virginia, Sept. 18, 1905

My dear Sir, Your very kind letter of Sept. 17[1] was read with great interest and pleasure. I appreciate beyond words the cordial way that you received my request, and know that the spirit of any gift of yours would be the right one.

The County of Franklin is not a progressive one. The old Court House stands — the same that was here when you were a boy. The monument which we hope to build will cost about eighteen hundred dollars.

The County will give about six hundred. There have been several small contributions, but the Daughters of the Confederacy have not had the encouragement they hoped was expected. Personally, your letter was a great comfort to me, for it proved that I had made no mistake in writing to you.

I suppose that the young man to whom you referred was the one familiarly known as "Billy" Burroughs who was killed at Kelly's Ford, March 17, 1862. He was a member of the 2nd Virginia Cavalry, Co C.

The family is much scattered, but I recall several friends among their descendants.

I realize how full of work, and hope, and honor your life must be, but could not be if it were not for the sentiments of affection for your birthplace, and remembrance of earlier years which you must cherish.

Once more thanking you for your letter, and hoping sincerely to see you should you ever revisit the scenes of your earlier youth, and to show you, conspicuous among old land marks, the monument I am working so hard to build.

It has just occurred to me that you might be willing, for the sake of lang syne, to come to the unveiling and speak to these people. Why not? It is your County, as well as mine, and no honor is too great to confer on the people among whom one has been born. Pardon me, if I have allowed my pen to run away temporarily. I do think this would be an appropriate time and place for you to meet the men and women of Franklin, and help to show them what progress and the twentieth century means.

Again I thank you, Very sincerely yours,

Mrs. Cabell Smith

ALS Con. 810 BTW Papers DLC. BTW sent copies to W. H. Page and O. G. Villard.

1 BTW's letter was actually dated Sept. 15, 1905. See above.

From Whitefield McKinlay

Washington, D.C., Sept 20/05

Dr Mr Washington I have delayed thus long answering your letter of this week in order to learn from several of *our* friends who are in close touch with the "Antis" what are their comments etc. They tell me what I naturally conclude, that it has done the Guardian more harm than good. One of the Antis frankly told me that he didnt approve of their methods.

In my neighborhood a sample copy was left at each house and I presume the same thing was done thro out the City. Aside from a few narrow minded people who have no decided views or convictions on any subject, I feel certain that the bulk of the people who read the issue sympathize with you in the Wannamaker affair. In fact I think for every friend you may lose you gain two from them. Only this week one of their most intelligent followers told me that the more he has studied you, the more he realized that he had misunderstood you.

I am about to praise A. Grimke on his last letter but he will find as I constantly pointed out to him that there [are] a number of would be leaders that were formerly associated with him that are beyond reason & cant be brought into any movement that has your name attached thereto — hence I waste but very little efforts on them. Never the less the article is very timely & I think will do much good. I always told him & his brother Frank that they would rue the day that their names were associated [with] the Guardian, because he is downright crazy. Dubois is the Iago.

Yr hold on the colored people of this City is such that in order for that gang to weaken it they would have to prove to their satisfaction that you are a criminal. Very truly

W McKinlay

ALS Con. 4 BTW Papers DLC.

From Julio Despaigne[1]

Tuskegee Inst. Sep. 22, 1905

Mr. Washington, During the last term I have been observing the progress of the Institute and I have seen that there are yet many things to do.

The students have the habit of making their beds at the morning good for when the inspector comes that he can find it well, and in the after noon they disorder them and put clean and dirty clothes on them. The clean and dirty clothes are supposed to be in the closet and the beds should be made all the time.

Many of them have had one year here already and have not learned to do anything about the duty of the room.

The Barracks are very very dirty: I do not believe that in the walls of the Institute of Tuskegee ought to have dirty buildings like those.

I have learned that you send to room in those buildings the dirtiest students.

Almost every day the Captain Austin[2] and Major[3] excuse students from the dining room because they do not do their duty in their rooms. They do not gain the end that they wish because the students do not blush for the excuses from the dining room.

The teacher that was correcting my mistakes told me that she have no time for that, so you will excuse the mistakes you will find in my letter.

It will be good that change this proceding for demeriots warning and suspensions from the school.

I tell that because many of they do not go to dining room and those that not go no give these excuses any importance.

The inspector must not see only if the floor is clean, he must to see if the bed, the book-case, the washtand, the closet and the centre table is right. Many of them do no do their work good as they must to talk with the students in the room.

Almost every student of Tuskegee smokes; some of them smoke in the street of the school.

There is a very large number of students that use the tooth brush only to adorn the wash-stand, also there is a very large number of students that like to beat work; you must to try stop that.

I have hear that only the cleanest students can live in Rockefeller Hall.

In the last term were living there students so dirty as those that room in the Barracks.

Rockefeller Hall is a beautiful building but, the halls are too dark.

If you send to build another dormitory like it it will be good to put windows in front of it halls.

Some students have told that in the last June the white from Tennessee wanted to kill you, that is true?

Months ago, I read in the Tuskegee Student that the King of Belguin invited you to go to the exposition, are you going?

The students complain with reason for the clothes that they send to Laundry.

Sometimes they recieve the clothes dirtiest than when th[e]y sent them and many times they lose them. The girls breaks the clothes washing it.

For that trouble many of them prefer to send to wash their clothes away and pay for them.

The paper racks that is in the Library need fixing because always when the students take some paper some of them fall and make much noise.

During the last term students that almost never went to Chapel their names were present on the card every night.

I am going to call your attention about the Cubans that are in this institution. These people have much liberty here.

During the last term were here two of those people that were learning music not because they like it but to work less hours in the day.

They had excuses to get two hours in the day to learn and were supposed to work seven hours and a haf. At first they observed this rule correctly but, later they beat work every day and worked only two or three hours in the day.

Every body knew that and nobody told them nothing.

One of them that remained to pass the vacation here wrote in a written lesson "Tuskegee is good for the laze." If when they came here they were oblige to come in the rule he had not told that.

I have hear some of them to say that nobody tells they nothing because do not know English. They do not know English but they know when they do wrong and when they do right.

They says that all those try to be right all the time are slaves of you and of Tuskegee.

I will be very much obliged to you if you do not put them to room together any more.

When they come here none of them know the American costoms. It is impossible for them to learn their instruction with their Cuban costoms.

Neither is it best to put the new to live with the old because they steal their money and that makes that the new break the rule.

Next time when you are going to get a teacher for the Cubans do not put any Cuban to teach them, an American is always best.

At the beginning of the last term the Porto Rican Eugene Lecompte was teaching us and he was angry and le[f]t the class because he knew that Alfredo P. Encinosa was trying to take the class. We did not get any thing with the change of teachers because in all the time that he was occupping the place we did not learn anything.

One night Mrs. Washington went to visit the class and she asked us if we were satisfied with the teacher and the most answered "no." She attributed our dissatisfaction to the dificulty that is in the English.

So the summer before the last the Cuban and Porto Rican students did not come to class every day, excuse was that the teacher did not teach. Many of them tried to make me not went to class.

They told me that I was not going to learn anything.

I have observed that for those people a teacher is good at the beginning days.

In the last summer some of them went to class two times in the week; nobody told them anithing for that.

Their father or those incha[r]ge are working to get money to send them and to play their school. Every day they are thinking that their sons are getting instruction here. It will be very lamentable that at the end of three or four years when they go home their fathers does not see their improvement.

Days ago all the Cuban – all except me – asked Major for room in Rockfeller Hall and he did not want to give them rooms in it. Their for revenge were breaking the glass of the windows.

In the school there are some students that got condition in the last term and told that the condition did not make they any troubre because they had promove in their classes. It will be good make that all those students that do not do good work during the term repeat their classes.

In the last term when the member of the assambly that Tuskegee celebrate avery year came he[re] the officers went with them to ask to the students their rooms for them and of [if] they did not want to give their rooms others gave it wi[t]h bad will.

My room mates were compeled me that no sweep nor make my [bed?] because I did not sleep in the room.

I wish you make they understand the importance of the work that those people come to do here. Yours sincerly,

Julio Despaigne

ALS Con. 561 BTW Papers DLC.

[1] Julio Despaigne, of Guantánamo, Cuba, was in the B preparatory class during the 1905–6 school year. He remained at Tuskegee until 1908, when he was in the junior class.

[2] George A. Austin was assistant commandant at Tuskegee Institute from 1900 to 1912.

[3] Julius B. Ramsey, to whom BTW sent this letter, saying: "It contains many matters that it will be valuable to keep in mind." (Sept. 30, 1905, Con. 561, BTW Papers, DLC.)

To J. Douglas Wetmore

[Tuskegee, Ala.] Sept. 23, 1905

Personal

Dear Mr. Wetmore: One other suggestion: there are any number of opportunities in Alabama and other states, where some colored man charged with crime, might serve as a test case for not putting of colored people on the juries. That could be done without a great deal of expense, and a white lawyer could be hired to lead the way, if necessary. Very truly

Booker T. Washington

TLpS Con. 249 BTW Papers DLC.

To Robert Russa Moton

[Tuskegee, Ala.] Sept. 23, 1905

Personal

My dear Major Moton: I have yours of September 20th.

Regarding Mr. Ogden, would state that I had two or three long conferences with him while in New York, and also with Dr. Buttrick and Mr. Walter Page on the same subject.

After we had thrashed matters out privately, or individually, we all went as Mr. Ogden's guests, to the Union League Club for dinner, where we talked for four hours.

I am glad to say that the Saratoga matter, in my opinion, has strengthened the back bone of all of these people. Especially is this evident in reference to Mr. Ogden.

I should like to hear your opinion.

What Mr. Peabody will say, I do not know.

The discussion of the matter seems to have disappeared for the present, at least in the South. I suppose there is no more material left with which to feed the flames. Very truly yours,

Booker T. Washington

TLpS Con. 4 BTW Papers DLC.

From Thomas L. Leatherwood[1]

Washington, D.C., Sept. 23, 1905

Dear Sir: I received your letter saying that you had referred my letter written several weeks ago to you upon the subject securing your indorsement and support in my undertaking here in this city.[2] Mr. Dancy informed me the other day, that you referred it to him. I am sure you could not have referred to a better friend of yours. He is also a friend to the Enterprise.

Now Mr. Washington, I can say that I am sure that there is not a city in the United States that need[s] your influence more than this one. I have toiled hard day and night to espouse your doctrin[e] and defend your cause, and, that, too, without the assistance of any body. I am now closing six months hard work on the Enterprise and can say that I have met with great success, because of the fact, I have been able to secure 1800 subscribers and please the public. I began the publication without money, among a class of people whos[e] confidence was lost so far as Negro News papers are concern[ed]. All I had, was credit, and that is what is bothering me just at this time.

I need some financial aid to meet some pressing obligations and to place the paper on a better financial footing. My plans are to incorporate the paper under the management of a company, to be known as the Industrial Enterprise Publishing Company, with a capital stock of $5000, divided into 500 shares par value $10.00. Do you think this would be the best and safest plan? I have some parties figuring with me, but none of them are able to finance the company. It would take $500 to get incorporated here in the D.C.

I have the paper on very good footing, but cannot continue without financial aid from some source, and feeling that you were friendly toward the paper, I thought probably you would help me to make the paper a strong one. Should you decide to aid me, I assure you that I will highly appreciate what you may do and I will pledge to you, earnest, honest hard work, such as I am now doing.

Please let me hear from you on return mail as I am compelled to do something tangible by the first of Oct. and I don't want to loose controle of the policy of the paper if I can help it.

I send you marked copies of my two last issues. They are not what I would like for them to be, but as I am editor, solicitor, collector[,] general manager, pressman and every thing else connected with such work, I did not have time even to read proof after the compositors.

Thanking you for past favors, an[d] in advance for future ones, I remain obediently yours,

Thos. L. Leatherwood

ALS Con. 877 BTW Papers DLC.

[1] Thomas L. Leatherwood was editor and publisher of the Washington *Industrial Enterprise.*

[2] BTW had written Leatherwood on Sept. 15 thanking him for his strong support of the NNBL and saying that he had referred his letter to "some of my friends in Washington." (Con. 877, BTW Papers, DLC.)

From David C. Thornhill

New York, Sept. 23rd, 1905

Dear Sir: This will acknowledge the call of your Secretary, John R. Cox.[1] The matter as outlined by he is fully understood, and we will arrange to send forward a suitable representative on Friday, Oct. 20th so that he will arrive in Tuskegee on the night of October 21st, and will report to him. In matters of this kind, however, it is not customary to send one man, generally two. There is no telling the number of people who will be in attendance and about the College Grounds on October 23rd, and I further understand there are to be some excursions over the various roads, therefore recommend the sending of two men. If this meets with your approval, kindly advise me. Yours truly,

Pinkerton's National Detective Agency, by,
D C Thornhill
Superintendent

TLS Con. 5 BTW Papers DLC. Docketed in E. J. Scott's hand: "Hide motive someway."

[1] Julius R. Cox.

From Francis Jackson Garrison

Boston, Sept. 25, 1905

My dear friend: I have received & thank you for the James G. Birney pamphlet which you have returned to me. I shall be glad to read the Douglass proofs when they are ready.

I came back from Europe a fortnight ago, after nine weeks' absence. I was three weeks on the water, one in Italy, two in Switzerland, a couple of days in Paris, & the rest of the time in England & Ireland, where I saw our friends Fisher Unwin, the Clarks at Street, the Sturges at Birmingham, & Mr. Steinthal[1] in Manchester, as well as the Webbs (whom you did not see) in Dublin. Wherever I went, you & your work were asked about, & everything that I could tell was listened to with deepest interest.

While I was away I saw the declaration issued by the Niagara Falls Conference, & on the whole it seemed to me a very able & forcible presentation, & one to which I could heartily subscribe. Of course I recognized the personal animus of the clause about the need of leaders, but this seemed to me the only fly in the ointment, & as a general proposition, the race of course does need many leaders, & is gradually getting them. I recognized also that your address at the Business Men's Conference was a pointed rejoinder to several declarations in the Niagara document. Like everything that you write, it was admirable & forcible, & presented your point of view, with which I so largely sympathize, but I was sorry to see its implication that enunciations of fundamental principles & rights by those who do not stand in the firing line, or work in the enemy's country, are so much idle talk & unworthy of attention. The same sneer & taunt used to be thrown at the abolitionists who did not go south, but merely staid up north & passed resolutions & hurled denunciations. Now practical work is all important, but enunciation of fundamental principles & assertion of equal & inalienable rights are equally vital, & should not be sneered at or discouraged. I have always defended you against charges & criticisms on this point, & have maintained that you again & again declare the duty of imposing no restrictions on blacks that do not apply equally to whites in the same category, & that in every case where disfranchising amendments have been proposed, you have labored both privately

& publicly to defeat them; but I confess that I was utterly dashed when, on my return home, I read in the N.Y. Age your personal explanation about the Wanamaker dinner at Saratoga. Speaking with the frankness which I have ever exercised with you, I must say that in tone and substance it seemed to me unworthy of you, & calculated to delight equally your white detractors at the South & your colored critics & opponents at the North. To the former it will seem an apology for your mingling with whites at the North, & that you do it with reluctance & only in furtherance of your work, & your utterly unnecessary statement that you were staying at a colored hotel in Saratoga implies that you seek such wherever you can, which of course is not the case. I know how carefully you have to tread, how many different elements you have to face, north & south, what a volcano underlies the race in the South still, but this statement has a subservient sound which I am sure you could not have realized when you wrote it, and the Trotter crowd could have asked nothing better to substantiate their accusations against you. I cannot see why you should have taken any notice of the howl of the southern press because you dined with the Wanamakers, or hastened to explain that you did not escort any of the ladies to the dining-room. There is no reason why you should not escort any lady, white or colored to a dinner-table, lecture, concert or theatre, & I am sure that none of the Wanamakers themselves care a rap about the "horrible" accusation. The statement about your going to a colored hotel was quite gratuitous, as I have said, as if you wished the South to understand that you "know your place," as they would express it. If such were your real attitude it would weaken & not strengthen the position of the race in the South in these days of reaction & great proscription.

I know you will not misunderstand me, & will appreciate the spirit in which I make the above criticism.

I am sending you by this mail two copies of the *Words of Garrison*, a little volume which my brother Wendell & I are just publishing to commemorate the centennial of our father's birth. Please accept one, with our compliments, and place the other in your school library. You can read the whole book in half an hour, & I think you will find it refreshing & inspiring.

I hope you have got some measure of rest & renewed strength

this summer, in spite of the hot weather & your labors at the Business Men's gathering. With kind regards to Mrs. Washington, I am Yours faithfully,

Francis J. Garrison

P.S. Our venerable friend Mrs. Mawson,[2] of Newcastle on Tyne died just before I reached England.

ALS Con. 876 BTW Papers DLC.

[1] The Rev. S. Alfred Steinthal, a Unitarian of Manchester, was a correspondent of *The Liberator* and an old friend of William Lloyd Garrison, who visited him in 1867 and 1877. (Garrison and Garrison, eds., *William Lloyd Garrison*, 4:218, 273.)

[2] Presumably the widow of John Mawson of Newcastle-on-Tyne, whom William Lloyd Garrison had visited in 1867. Mawson died later that year, but members of his family were Garrison's hosts again in 1877. (Garrison and Garrison, eds., *William Lloyd Garrison*, 4:219, 235, 282.)

To Harry Scythe Cummings

[Tuskegee, Ala.] Sept. 26, 1905

Personal

My dear Mr. Cummings: Mr. Browne, our secretary, will send you 4,000 copies of the circular[1] that we discussed within the next few days. You can use them as was outlined in New York, of course keeping my name out of the whole matter.

I will let you hear from me in regard to another matter very soon. Yours truly,

Booker T. Washington

TLpS BTW Papers ATT.

[1] In the meeting of the Committee of Twelve on Aug. 3, 1905, BTW moved that the committee "furnish such assistance as it may find practicable to the Suffrage League of Maryland in its efforts to defeat the amendments pertaining to voting in the new constitution which will be voted on in Maryland, November this year." The committee prepared 5,000 copies of an article by Archibald H. Grimké entitled "Why Disfranchisement Is Bad." (Minutes of the Committee of Twelve on Aug. 3, 1905, copy dated Sept. 23, 1905, BTW Papers, ATT.)

From Charles William Anderson

New York, N.Y., September 26, 1905

Private.

My dear Doctor: This, in strictest confidence. Moore called upon me today, and advised me of an interview which he had with Mr. Milholland; and strange to say, Moore seemed to agree with him on many points. The tale is entirely too long to relate in detail, but the sum total of it was, that Milholland has some property in Brooklyn which he desires to place in the hands of the Realty Company to be sold to coloured tenants, on the easy payment plan. Moore evidently sees a dollar or two in it, and appears to be quite impressed with the importance of Milholland. After discussing the Realty proposition, they fell to discussing you. Brother Milholland maintained that you had been standing in the way of the suffrage movement, and would have to stop it. He said that he was your friend, but he felt that you ought to talk straight, and not attempt to play with him. He also said that Du Bois was a very strong character, and that he had been told that he would be a very useful man to the suffrage movement. He further stated that the Southern people were not your friends, and if you did not look out, you would get into trouble. He reflected in many ways upon you, and made some rather sharp comment on your attitude on the race question. The upshot of it all was that it is plain that he is very mad at you, and is starting another one of his "bluff" games. His threat to take up Du Bois and thereby furnish the Niagara movement with funds, is, in my judgment, only hot air. It would not be worth repeating except for the fact that in some mysterious way he seems to have half way convinced Moore. Privately, I am afraid that Fred thinks that there is a little money in sight, and is ready and willing to cultivate Milholland on that account. I told Moore that he was a very dangerous man to tie up with, and that I would advise caution. I am going to see Milholland myself this afternoon and find out just what it all means. In the meantime, please keep this strictly confidential, and do not let Moore know that I have mentioned the matter to you. How quickly these fellows will run after strange Gods when there is a little "graft" in sight. I have always felt that

Moore's one redeeming quality was his loyalty, but I am afraid I had my faith shaken in him today. Of course he did not take sides against you, but he assumed the familiar attitude of feeling that there was much to be said on both sides of the proposition.

I pass this on with strictest confidence for your private advisement. I will let you hear from me when I have learned more about it.

I leave for Adirondack (Warren County) New York, tomorrow, and will return not later than October 5th. Yours truly,

C. W. A.

P.S. Humphreys has just been in & he too intimated that you were unsound on the suffrage question — I gave him to understand that you were my friend. He then said "so am I, Dr Washington's friend." He has been over "hobnobbing" with Trotter in Boston.

TLI Con. 261 BTW Papers DLC. Postscript in Anderson's hand.

From Charles William Anderson

New York, N.Y., September 27, 1905

Private and confidential.

My dear Doctor: I called on Milholland late yesterday evening, and had a long talk with him. He did not make many severe criticisms to me on your action, and I am quite certain he felt that it would be indiscreet to tell all he thought to me. He started in by telling me that a movement was on foot to petition Congress for legislation with reference to the protection of the ballot, and said that he intended to start a great agitation which would be taken up by many of the Republican clubs throughout the country. In fact, he said the movement was already on foot, and that he wanted me to get hold of you and advise you not to oppose it in any way. I told him that you were very busy with your own affairs, and had never thought of opposing it, in my judgment. He then slopped over a little, and told me that wherever they went to help the suffrage movement, they met the objection that "Booker Washington was against it." He said that Congress, the President, and the leading members of strong Republican clubs, all make the same reply, and he therefore wanted to have me get in communication with you and advise you not to oppose this movement when it gets in operation. I talked a long while with him, and let him know in the beginning, that I was your personal friend, and that anybody who did not feel kindly toward you would be apt to be regarded by me with some suspicion. He told me that he liked to hear me talk up for my friend, and said "why, he is a particular personal friend of mine also." Boiled down, the result of my interview was that this movement is on foot, and that the leaders of it are Milholland, A. B. Humphreys, General Clarkson, Warren [Warner] Miller, and General Tremaine.[1] I don't think it amounts to much, and I don't think you need bother your head very much about the men who are at the head of it. The only significant thing about it is, that they have all been dickering with Trotter. Humphreys came to see me yesterday to see if I would not furnish Trotter with some names of prominent Republicans of this city, among whom he might distribute his paper. I told him very frankly that Mr. Trotter was a scoundrel, and that he would not get any favour from me of any sort. In fact, I would hate to repeat to you in a letter what I really said to Humphreys. When he left my office he knew exactly where I stood, and he also knew what I thought of Trotter, and what I thought of any white man who would fraternize with him. When I reached Milholland's office, the first thing that caught my eye was a copy of "The Guardian" lying on his desk. Hence, you see, they all are trying to play with Trotter, and this is the only important feature of the movement. These men may be able to give Trotter some money, and thereby keep that old paper alive. This is the only danger that I can see. Milholland did not talk to me about the real estate deal. He spent his time professing to be your friend, and yet complaining that you were in the way of what he chooses to regard as a great movement in behalf of the negro race. He also told me that he thought your secretary had some undesirable people calling to see him at the Manhattan. He said that he had noticed two or three men around who were poorly dressed, and who did not behave themselves with much decorum, and had concluded that they had called on your secretary, for he felt quite certain that you would not have invited any such persons to the hotel. It is the old dodge of trying to find some fault. I don't think he ever noticed any such persons; and I don't think he intended me to believe that he considered their presence due to your secretary. He really was afraid to talk to me about *you*, so he discussed your secretary. Hence, in my judgment, the whole thing is due to that little Business League matter. He is probably mad over his failure to get that tall speech of his into the papers, and is displaying a tendency to be annoying to you. I gave him no comfort, and he seemed to take an entirely different tack with me from the one taken with Moore. The way to stop these fellows is always to stand right up for your man, and not agree with them on any point. It is the safest policy always. However, in summing up, I do not think that I would lose any sleep over these little fellows. The only damage they can do is to furnish funds for that vile Boston sheet. Hower, I will keep my eyes on the whole crowd.

I leave for Adirondack tonight, I hope, and will by there until October 5th. Yours truly,

Charles W. Anderson

P.S. The Attorney General[2] has definitely promised me that he would designate Wilford Smith as one counsel to examine into and prosecute election frauds at the coming election. This will throw a few hundred dollars in his way. I have resigned from the Realty Co. Moore wants me to wait awhile, but I told him I wouldn't. I've got a public trust confided to me, and cannot afford to have my name stained by irregular methods in the Realty Co. There is nothing really bad yet discovered, but I thought I would be on the safe side & resign. Moore is a bit selfish. He wants to stay in & wants me to take a chance on my good *business* name, to keep his company. I told him "no" — emphatically.

C. W. A.

TLS Con. 27 BTW Papers DLC. Postscript in Anderson's hand.

[1] Henry Edwin Tremain (1840–1910), a Civil War hero and president of the Republican Club of New York City from 1901 to 1906.

[2] Julius M. Mayer, attorney general of New York.

To David C. Thornhill

[Tuskegee, Ala.] Sept. 28, 1905

Dear Sir: I take it that the men whom you send here in line with the suggestion of my stenographer, Mr. Cox, will in some way mask the nature of their errand. This I wish done. It will be entirely satisfactory for you to send two men instead of one. Please have these men report to my secretary, Mr. Emmett J. Scott, who will have full instructions for them. Yours truly,

[Booker T. Washington]

TLc Con. 5 BTW Papers DLC.

To Robert Ezra Park

[Tuskegee, Ala.] Sept. 28, 1905

Dear Dr. Park: The suggestion of an article, bearing upon the Congo conditions, and recommending an international conference strikes me favorably. I shall be glad to see the matter when you have been able to assemble it.

The book by Mark Twain, "King Leopold's Soliloquy" should reach me very soon. It has not yet come to hand. Very truly yours,

Booker T. Washington

TLpS Con. 30 BTW Papers DLC.

From Frederick Randolph Moore

New York, September 28th, 1905

My dear Mr. Washington: Mr. John E. Milholland telephoned me to call on him Monday last, which I did, ostensibly to talk about some lots he owns in East New York, Brooklyn, but really to talk over the matter of the suffrage question. He did the talking and I did the listening, and he is very emphatic in his determination to bring that question to an issue this fall, and says that your stand is the only hindrance, but intimated that they were determined to take the "bull by the horns," and force the issue.

I suggested that he see you when next you come to the city, and talk over the matter with you before deciding on a definite plan of operation. I mentioned the fact that I had noted Mr. Humphrey's visit to Boston and his agitation there, and he replied, that they were sending Mr. Humphrey about to focus attention on the question, and that they had secured Mr. Du Bois, whom he had been told was a strong man and would be most helpful to the cause.

If Du Bois and those with him get an idea that they are regarded as helpful agents by Mr. Milholland and those with him, and realize that funds are at hand to wage a battle, it seems to me that they can make a deal of trouble, and it will be just what they are looking for, "the necessary implements of war."

I told Charlie Anderson of my conversation, and he has called on Mr. Milholland, and has perhaps advised you of his conversation. I have not seen him since, but would say, that while Mr. Milholland is very very friendly to you, he thinks that you should stand "from under" or talk frankly with him over the matter. I told him that I would talk with you and arrange to have you see him when next you are in the city, and that Anderson and I would come with you if agreeable.

He seems quieted down over the Business League incident, and says that is a small matter; he understands your position thoroughly, but that the Republican Club is in thorough accord with him, and that there are many others who will assist him in the matter. Very sincerely yours,

Fred R Moore

Ad you speak of appeared in the Outlook Aug 19. Did not repeat it for it was in an obscure place.

TLS Con. 3 BTW Papers DLC.

To Charles William Anderson

[Tuskegee, Ala.] Sept. 29, 1905

Personal

My dear Mr. Anderson: I have your letter of September 26th, and of course shall treat the whole matter in the strictest confidence. I am not at all surprised to hear of the attitude of Milholland and Humphrey, in fact, I have been expecting it. I noted that Humphrey attended some suffrage meeting in Boston some days ago. The more experience I have, the more I think of your remarks to the effect that a professional friend of the Negro is a man to be watched. Both of those parties have it in for me because, in the first place, they hold me responsible for defeating their plans with the President. I have been perfectly frank with Milholland all along. I told him in the first place that while I had my views on the matter of cutting down Southern representation I should not give them to the public or any one else unless compelled to. Immediately after President Roosevelt was reelected he sent for me to come to the White House and give him my views concerning the policy of cutting down Southern representation, and that was a command which I could not dodge. I had to tell him frankly that I could see no good to come from the move to the colored people. I wrote Milholland and told him frankly as the enclosed copy of letter will show my attitude so that he could see personally that I was not trying to tote water on two shoulders. Very soon after I had seen the President, Milholland, Harry Cummings and ex-Senator Warner Miller called to see him, and the President gave them the cold shoulder, telling them I was opposed to the movement. Ever since then, they have had it in for me. Milholland and Humphrey have in turn taken up Hayes and Cummings, and I suppose they will in turn take up Trotter and Du Bois. They have already dropped Hayes, and I suppose they will drop the other fellows in turn.

It is rather strange as well as interesting to note that these people have just become alarmed on account of my unpopularity with the Southern white people and also fear that I am likely to get into trouble with this same element. Heretofore their complaint was to the effect that I was too popular with the Southern white people and was seeking to cultivate their friendship at the expense of the race.

It is very interesting to note that Vardaman, of Mississippi, has just come out in favor of cutting down Southern representation; in fact, he stands exactly on the same platform as Milholland and Humphrey.

I shall hope to see you soon and talk the whole matter over with you. When it comes to expending money, I really do not think that Milholland or Humphrey have much to spend on any movement. I know the principal sources from which they get their money and can come pretty near closing up these sources at any time. We must not fail, however, to let men like Humphrey and Milholland understand that if they are to take up such scoundrels as Trotter and Du Bois that we can have nothing to do with them. Yours truly,

Booker T. Washington

TLpS Con. 5 BTW Papers DLC.

To Andrew B. Humphrey

[Tuskegee, Ala.] Sept. 29, 1905

Personal

My dear Mr. Humphrey: I am wondering if it is not possible for the Constitutional League to help out somewhat in the Maryland contest? As you know, there is a desperate battle on in the state and the chances are our side will win. If you wish to help, I wish you would have direct correspondence with Mr. Harry S. Cummings, 225 N. Calvert St., Baltimore, whom I think you know. Cummings is a fine fellow and can be depended upon.

Enclosed I send you a sample of some literature that the Committee of Twelve is having widely distributed through the state among the white people; I also send you another pamphlet containing a brief of all the requirements for voting in the Southern States which the same committee is circulating. Yours truly,

Booker T. Washington

TLpS Con. 876 BTW Papers DLC.

Emmett Jay Scott to Clifford H. Plummer

[Tuskegee, Ala.] September 29, 1905

Personal.

My dear Mr. Plummer: Our friend will be glad to hear from you fully, outlining what takes place in the matter mentioned in your letter of September 23rd.[1] Very truly yours,

Emmett J. Scott

TLpS Con. 305 BTW Papers DLC.

[1] Plummer had written to BTW, actually on Sept. 25, 1905, offering to spy upon the annual meeting of the New England Suffrage League. He wrote: "I think they will try to talk and work along the lines of the so called Niagara Conference." (Con. 305, BTW Papers, DLC.)

A Draft of an Editorial for the New York *Age*

[Tuskegee, Ala., ca. September 1905][1]

TROTTER AND TROTTERISM

The New York Age has, up to this time, been silent concerning the so-called Niagara Movement, for the reason that we did not want to prejudge the movement, nor seek to influence the utterances of other journals upon this subject. From the first we have had our suspicions about the original objects of the organization, but we wanted to wait to have these suspicions confirmed, as we knew they would be, by the main mover in the organization. The head and front of this organization has now revealed himself and his objects, and the move, which he has now made, shows that he has not wisdom enough to protect his friends, when such wisdom might help his cause. The mainspring and moving spirit in this organization is none other than Monroe Trotter of Boston, Mass. In a recent issue of his paper he reveals the plot and plan of "The Niagara Movement." Since this meeting was held on foreign shores, in Canada, Monroe Trotter has celebrated the anniversary of the famous Boston Church Riot. Two years ago the editor of *The Age* happened to be present at the meeting which it was attempted to be broken up by the mob tactics directed by Trotter and his gang. In connection with the celebration of this riot he comes out boldly and frankly says that the "Church Riot Movement" and the "Niagara Movement" are one and the same thing, he says that the Niagara Movement is the outgrowth of the Church riot. That is, he claims the two are one and inseparable, and on this basis he asks for the support and confidence of the race. Further, in a recent magazine article, Dr. Du Bois himself says that Trotter is the "backbone," whatever that means, of the Niagara Movement.

In order that our readers and the members of the race generally may not now lose sight of the connection of the two movements we must remind them that a meeting was planned to take place in the Columbus Avenue Zion Church, Boston, in 1903, and a regular program had been planned. A few hours before the meeting was to be held (1) Monroe Trotter, or some of his fellow-conspirators, went into the church and scattered pepper in and around the sacred chancel; (2) Monroe Trotter and his gang of fellow-conspirators were instrumental in bringing into the church a gang of dissolute and drunken women from the streets; (3) they then stationed others of their conspirators in various parts of the church so that they might create a disturbance and drown the speakers' voices; (4) notwithstanding the presence of refined women and many children, a deliberate crime and insult to the race was planned and partly carried out (if Trotter had been truly brave he would have selected a white church to perpetrate this crime); (5) after Trotter and his main followers were arrested they tried, in the courts and in every conceivable manner and by all kinds of falsehoods to get out of the difficulty, but he and his ignorant followers were compelled to serve time in jail.

In order to show that the real object of the Niagara Movement is not to help the race but to break down the helpful influence of one member of the race, we have but to mention one or two facts.

First, there is not a plank in their address to the country but what has been sent out in almost the identical words time and again during the last thirty years.

Second, throughout the platform they say they are in existence mainly to bring about free discussion of all subjects, and yet Trotter was not invited to the Columbus Avenue Church meeting, he was not on the program to speak, and it was not presumed that he would speak. And then, besides, the meeting in Zion Church was called for the very purpose of hearing free speech and the main mover in the opposition to prevent free speech and free discussion, through the medium of a mob, was Monroe Trotter. One of the professed objects of the new "movement" was to secure personal liberty, freedom of action. In accepting the invitation to dine with a distinguished merchant outside of the South, in the way he has been doing for fifteen years, Dr. Washington was doing the very thing which the Niagara Movement professes to be in favor of; but Trotter, the real leader of this movement, was so narrow and evil-minded that he could not even keep silent and could not refrain from putting all of his friends in an awkward position because of his personal malice.

But this is not all: we give to the public now, what we should never have divulged, and what has not been published before, had not Monroe Trotter boldly said the Church riot and the Niagara Movement are one and the same thing. Since this is proclaimed to be true, we must let the race understand about another outrage in which Trotter was concerned. Immediately after the Church riot a number of Cambridge citizens, in order to show their disgust, invited Dr. Washington to speak at a reception given in his honor. Although Monroe Trotter and some of his followers were under indictment to keep the peace, they also planned to break up this Cambridge meeting. Several preparatory meetings were held and it was finally decided in Trotter's house that when the meeting should be in full sway one of their number would light a bonfire in a near-by vacant lot, that another in the church should yell "fire," and that a third should cut the electric wire, thereby throwing the church into darkness and confusion. This program of wrath, disorder and possibly murder, which Trotter and his gang had planned, came near succeeding. At their final meeting to perfect their arrangements ~~a colored~~ an Afro-American attorney of Boston,[2] who had learned of their scheme, threw open the door, walked into the midst of the band and gave them to understand in no Sunday-School language that he had the names of every man and knew all the details of their plans. He further told them that if a single one of them attempted to carry out the plan, he would have them all in jail in a few hours. At this revelation the little gang was thunderstruck and scattered in every direction; not one of them dared to show his face at the meeting. This is another sample of their bravery. It was whispered by many and believed at the time by not a few that Du Bois had a hand in these Church riots, and now lo and behold Trotter, himself, has boldly declared that the church riots and the Niagara Movement are connected.

Now, according to Trotter, the Niagara Movement sympathizes with and expects to pursue the same policy adopted by him as regards these two meetings. Still more recently, and still more to the point in the direction of proving that the men connected with this "movement" have nothing in view but to exhibit their personal dislike and jealousy toward one individual of the race, we call attention of the Afro-American public to the recent disgraceful alliance of Mr. Trotter through his paper with the vilest character of Southern newspapers in trying to breed a spirit among the Southern white people in the South that would result in the intimidation or assassination of Dr. Washington himself or in the burning of the property of the Tuskegee school. No Southern paper, however vile, has gone further than Trotter in this respect; in fact, no one could read Trotter's vile sheet without seeing that he has seconded every move and every suggestion that the lowest type of Southern white papers have made. Not a single one of the Southern papers which abused Dr. Washington for accepting Mr. Wanamaker's invitation at Saratoga printed as much abusive matter, or put it in such disgusting form, as did Trotter's paper, the organ of the Niagara Movement.

Another disgraceful feature, in connection with this recent outbreak of Trotter in connection with the vile portion of the Southern press, consists in the fact that Dr. Du Bois himself, has been in Boston during the greater part of the summer, and that he and Trotter have worked hand in glove in connection with the carrying out of all of these plans. The race, as we know it, is not yet ready to follow the criminal and inciter to riots in churches nor to follow the vilest portion of the press of the South in abetting assassination and destruction of school property. If Trotter had at least common sense, notwithstanding his own personal dislikes and his own personal mental weakness, he would at least protect his friends that are trying to work with and use him, by ceasing to put them in awkward positions, as he is constantly doing.

In saying what we have, we do not overlook the fact that good and well-meaning individuals are interested in this so-called new movement, but we again assert that the race will not have confidence in any set of men who select a man like Trotter for their leader and guide.

As disagreeable as the task is, we give the bare facts to our readers and to the race. Trotter is using, or is trying to use, the names of a few respectable men behind whom to hide his criminal and riotous record and disposition. Those connected with his movement must now reaffirm their allegiance to Trotter and his methods or throw him overboard. There is no middle ground. They ask the race to follow them, on which platform do they ask it?

We have said their program is insincere and that petty spite against one individual of the race actuates them. We repeat it.

In this editorial we do not, in proof of this assertion, elaborate the fact that Trotter's chief aide is Dr. Du Bois, who does not vote anywhere in this country and who plays no part in the politics of the race. They consider themselves, for the most part, too high to to break down the influence of one individual of the race.

Another one of the aides of Trotter is the owner of one of the largest barber shops in Atlanta, where no Afro-American need ask for accommodation. We refer to Mr. A. F. Herndon.[3] Monroe Trotter's followers in this movement are with one or two exceptions men who never attend the gatherings of the race and are rarely found in meetings wherein the interests of the race are concerned, and who have not contributed to legal contests for the rights of the race. They consider themselves, for the most part, too high to mingle with the race; too intelligent and "refined" to come into bodies where so-called common individuals are.

There is hardly a person connected with the Niagara Movement who can be pointed to as having taken the lead in a single movement for the betterment of the race. The only service they perform in behalf of the race is the making of speeches and the passing of resolutions. They are rarely seen in Negro churches or Sunday Schools where they could be of service to the race and community. We repeat, the race will not follow such leadership, it will not exalt or follow criminal characters.

In justice to several well-intentioned men, whose names were connected with the Niagara movement, we ought to say that they were innocent of many facts before they attended the meeting. In the future we shall hold to a strict account those who have respect for Trotter and Trotterism, quibble as they may. The fact remains that they must stand by or tear themselves away from such influences. *The Age* has always stood by and supported every effort in behalf of the race, whether it agreed with it or not. We stand ready to help the Niagara movement whenever it can be shown that it has unselfish and worthy motives.

TMd Con. 308 BTW Papers DLC. Of the many editorial corrections of the original in E. J. Scott's hand, only a few have been included for improvements of grammar or clarity.

1 Though this typescript is undated, internal evidence establishes that it was written after the first Niagara Movement meeting in July 1905 and the Wanamaker dinner incident in August 1905.

2 William Henry Lewis.

3 Alonzo F. Herndon (1858–1927) was for many years the proprietor of the most elegant barbershop in Atlanta. He also founded the Atlanta Life Insurance Co.

To John C. Asbury

[Tuskegee, Ala.] October 2, 1905

Personal and Confidential

My dear Mr. Asbury: I have read with interest your editorial concerning the Dixon article in the Evening Post. I ought to say, perhaps, in justice to the Post people, that the next week after publishing the Dixon article they wrote me and said their columns were open for reply at any time I chose to make it. I have not replied to the article and shall perhaps not make a "reply" as I have made it a rule from which I have very seldom departed, not to get in a direct controversy with either colored or white persons in newspapers, but I think at a little later date I shall write an article for the Post refuting the main points urged by Mr. Dixon in an indirect rather than a direct way. I have never felt that we could gain a great deal by being put upon the defensive, that, it seems to me, is an element of weakness. I want to write an article that will show constructive, progressive effort rather than defending the race against senseless attacks of a man like Dixon. The work here has stood for twenty-five years and is its own defense.

What you say about Du Bois offering to reply to the article is very interesting and amusing. I cannot conceive in my own mind what kind of reply Du Bois could make. Certainly Dixon or no other white man has ever attempted to damage and discredit the work of this institution and my own efforts more than Du Bois has done, and you will note that during the past summer that Du Bois and Trotter have been in Boston editing the Guardian, and they have outdone even the South in their attempts to villify me for exercising my rights in dining with Mr. Wanamaker. They have joined hands with the vilest element of the South and have scattered more broadcast than any Southern paper has done the vilest language used about me. Under the circumstances, I repeat, it would be interesting to note what kind of reply Du Bois could make. These men seem to forget that Dixon and the lower element of the Southern press are not aiming at me as an individual but at the race, and that when these men join Dixon and Tillman and Tom Watson in condemning me, they are condemning at the same time the race to which they belong. Yours very truly,

Booker T. Washington

TLpS Con. 5 BTW Papers DLC.

To Francis Jackson Garrison

Tuskegee Institute, Alabama. October 2, 1905

My dear Mr. Garrison: I note that December 10th will mark the one hundredth anniversary of the birth of your father, and I am very anxious that the members of our race see that the event be marked by some fitting celebration, something that shall be simple, helpful and uniform as far as possible throughout the country.

I am writing especially to know if you have any special suggestion that you would like to make on this point.

I have already taken measures to put the matter before the colored people in a way to get suggestions from them. Yours very truly,

Booker T. Washington

TLS James Weldon Johnson Collection CtY.

From Hightower T. Kealing

Philadelphia. Oct. 2, 1905

My dear Friend: I am moved to address you in a more intimate and confidential way than usual because there are some disturbing indications in the ranks of your supporters which I think ought to be considered. You have doubtless noticed the surprising attitude taken by Mr. Alexander in discussing your "mistake," as he calls your published statement regarding the Wanamaker affair. I am told that there are similar utterances from one or two other sources always previously supposed to be friendly. But, to my mind, the most serious of all is the mood in which I find Mr. Fortune. In a conversation last week, he seemed to think that the tide was setting against your cause and attributed it largely to the fact that you were over-cautious about coming out in the interest of your friends and against the plans of your opposers. It is my own opinion that we suffer by being deprived of your direct leadership in many public movements which have your sympathy, but fail in effectiveness because they have not your central figure to rally around.

On the other side, they have their leadership actively and openly with them and are not careful of the feelings and opinions of your friends. This undoubtedly is all to their advantage. I feel that some steps must be taken to strengthen your own ranks and weaken those of the opposition. The fight cannot be made any more bitter by an aggressive course against the enemy, for he is already using every means, fair and unfair, to injure you; the only question now is, How far will you play into his hands by forbearing to bring all of your strength against him?

Permit me to say that I think several mistakes have been made on our side, the main one being in dissipating our agencies of defence by giving insufficient aid to several different publications, when it would have counted for more had this aid been concentrated on one great paper capable of commanding respect by reason of its excellence. I think the Boston newspaper venture, for instance, was a mistake in that it took the New England field away from the Age and when it failed, the Age was unable to win them back. The result is that the Guardian holds it almost unchallenged to-day. This will illustrate what I mean by the mistake of not concentrating.

Another mistake that is being made, in my opinion, is your too great generosity in failing to use your great influence with the President to place your own friends on guard in positions of prominence occupied by those who are not in sympathy with you and have not bitten their tongues about saying so. If self-preservation is justifiable, then unhorsing the foe to put your own friends in the saddle is the best instance of it, I am sure.

I cannot go into details in a letter, but I feel that you ought to take this whole matter up in a personal conference with one or two of your most trustworthy friends at a very early date, and see if some effective and aggressive policy cannot be outlined before the President decides upon the changes it is wise to make in his administrative household.

I have written to you with perfect freedom, feeling that my uniform position towards you and your cause warrants candor, and that you will not misunderstand my motives. Very respectfully,

H. T. Kealing

TLS Con. 29 BTW Papers DLC.

From Sumner Alexander Furniss

Indianapolis, October 3rd, 1905

Dear Dr. Washington, I am in receipt of your telegram of this date. I had already taken up the matter in an indirect way with the party.[1] He is rather a hard proposition to handle. If he feels that any one really wants the property he immediately soars sky high in price. After receiving your telegram today, for fear that there might be some negotiation about which I knew nothing, I decided to speak to him personally. I approached him in the interest of "a young man friend of mine," and while I gleaned from what he said that he wanted to sell, the price about which he talked was absurd — four or five thousand dollars. He promised to consider the matter and to let me know in a few days the least amount that he would take for it.

Another party that had approached him for me had about got him to agree to take in the neighborhood of $1000. I think this price is about right. Anything more than this would be exorbitant. From what I can glean from inside information there is no one negotiating for the property.

If I can get him tied up in some sort of an option I will then be in a position to interest some one in the property with me. I have not the time to devote to it myself and could not afford at this time to invest even this much in it unless I could interest some one [in] it with me and could secure the services of someone to take charge of it and run it. Some little time ago Bishop Grant and some other gentlemen expressed a willingness to go into the enterprise provided the property could be bought at what I considered a reasonable figure. I believe it could be made to pay if purchased for a thousand dollars but I do not think it would pay to invest much more than that. I am satisfied that it is just about paying expenses, if that, at this time.

I shall keep in touch with the proposition, and shall do everything in my power to prevent it from falling into adverse hands. I realize, however, that I have something of a "Shylock" to deal with and of necessity negotiations will be slow for as I said before, as soon as he realizes that any one really wants the property, his idea of the value is instantly inflated, although the next minute he is brought face to face with the knowledge that sooner or later it will have to be disposed of to some one. Very truly yours,

S. A. Furniss

TLS Con. 3 BTW Papers DLC.

1 George L. Knox, owner of the Indianapolis *Freeman*.

From Charles William Anderson

Adirondack, N.Y. Oct 3 1905

Private

Dear Doctor: Your wire was answered today stating I could meet Scott on Friday, & requesting you to answer whether or not that was satisfactory.

As to Milholland, he wants to be nasty. I dont think he cares a fig for either the negro or the suffrage question. He is trying to rescue himself from approaching oblivion. His associates are activated by the same motive, in my judgment. When I saw him, he did not breathe fire and brimstone, nor did he make any threats. In his talk to me, he rather assented "with civil leer and without sneering," tried to "teach the rest to sneer." Do you see the point? He didn't dare to criticise you to me, so he contented himself with *deprecating* your unfortunate attitude. He seems to have indulged in outspoken criticism to Moore, but Moore did not assume a combative attitude with him. He opened with Moore by showing him a chance to make some money by giving him the tip about wanting to place some building lots in his charge to be sold to Colored people. This, of course, was only moonshine, but it doesn't require much bait to catch the average Colored man who wants to make "easy money." This gang – Milholland, Humphreys & the General are working for themselves. They are "grafters" in my opinion, and can be easily exposed. Milholland intimated that the President was also unsound on the suffrage question. So you see, you are in good company. I will take off my coat immediately on my return to the city, and will "get busy" watching those fellows. They are not dangerous. I am sure they mean to push Trotter as an offset to you, but they will soon drop him. He is too much like them for harmonious work. I hope to see you soon. I return on Thursday. Keep everything confidential. Mrs Anderson will write Mrs. Washington today. Yours Truly,

Anderson

ALS Con. 27 BTW Papers DLC.

To Timothy Thomas Fortune

[Tuskegee, Ala.] October 4, 1905

Personal

Dear Mr. Fortune: I want to urge upon you the importance of using your influence in the Council to have conservative, sensible action. I mean both in resolutions and in speech. I cannot see that any good will be accomplished by rash, unwise utterances. Such utterances will lose us friends at the North and will do no good in the South. You can help greatly in this matter. In thus advising, I do not mean to say that we should not be courageous and let the world know what we think, but it can be done both in speech and in resolutions in such a manner to attract friends rather than to repel them. Yours truly,

Booker T. Washington

TLpS Con. 261 BTW Papers DLC.

To Frederick Randolph Moore

[Tuskegee, Ala.] October 5, 1905

Personal

My dear Mr. Moore: I have read your letter of September 28th with interest and profit. These same two gentlemen, I mean Milholland and Humphries, have taken up at various times several different colored men, but they did not seem to hold on to them very long. They took up Cummings of Maryland, and Hayes, and now I presume they will try some others.

You state that Mr. Milholland says I must be frank with him. Enclosed I send you copy of a letter I wrote him some months ago. I do not see how anything could be more frank than this letter is.

The fact is, there are a number of "professional" friends of the colored people who use the colored people to keep themselves in prominence, and those are the kind of people that are always going to give us a certain amount of trouble. I think, however, on every occasion when it is proper for you to do so, you should give men like Milholland and Humphries to understand personally that the people of New York are not going to have any Trotter and Du Bois nonsense in that city. Yours very truly,

Booker T. Washington

TLpS Con. 4 BTW Papers DLC.

To Francis Jackson Garrison

[Tuskegee, Ala.] October 5, 1905

My dear Mr. Garrison: When I wrote you a few days ago regarding the centennial of your father, I had not noticed that the book which you sent me was meant to commemorate that event.

I am very much interested in what you say regarding your visit to Europe, and especially am I glad to hear through you from our mutual friends. I have thought of Mr. Webb, of Dublin, a good many times, and have always regretted that I did not get the opportunity of meeting him. I am very sorry to hear of the death of Mrs. Mawson. When I see you I shall hope to hear in a direct way more about our friends.

I am very sorry that you got the impression that my Business League address was meant as a rejoinder or reply to the Niagara Movement. I went over that address carefully with several colored people of different temperaments, some radical and some conservative, with a view of letting nothing appear in it that might give the impression of being a reply to anything that was said by the Niagara people. I think you misunderstood the meaning and spirit of what I said in regard to people who are at work in the South. I meant to condemn any effort on the part of people living out of the South who condemned those who are working in the South doing the best they could. I do not believe that your father would have condemned any man who, while living in the South, was working in the best manner that he could to bring about the same results that he was seeking to bring about yet by different methods. I do not claim that it would be proper for all persons who are working for the elevation of our race to live or work in the South, but I do think it an error for those who do not work in the South to condemn the men and women who are trying to do the best they can in the field.

In regard to the Wanamaker dinner. I have read carefully what you say and appreciate it thoroughly, as your words are always wise and frank. I do not believe that you can appreciate my statement unless you saw the full reports of the falsehood that were sent to the Southern press. In the case of my dining with the President, notwithstanding for months I was condemned in the most outrageous manner by the entire Southern press, I did not utter a word of reply or explanation, I kept silent because the facts as they took place at the White House were given to the public; in the case of the Saratoga matter I made a statement because the most outrageous falsehoods were stated and stated in a manner to make a fool of me before the public. If the statements which were used in the South had gotten lodgment in the North they would have proved as injurious there as in the South. I always go on the principle that it is safe to stand by the facts. In all my public work I very seldom, as you know, ever deny an untruth or make an explanation but in this case I made a statement after consultation with friends who thought that the falsehoods had been so widely spread and put in such a way as to do permanent harm. In a word, I was represented by the dispatch which was published most widely as having thrown aside my life work and gone to Saratoga for the purpose of entering into society and was spending money given by Carnegie and others in a way to make a fool of myself. There was much else of the same character. I made the statement that I was a guest at a colored hotel for the reason that there is an element of colored people and white people who are constantly finding fault with me; they say I go to a white hotel whenever I can instead of going to a colored hotel that is just as convenient and well kept. I do not know as you saw any of the editorials published by Southern papers on the subject, but for days and weeks they were as bitter as it was possible to make them. Several of them openly advocated my assassination and the destruction of our school property. I received of course, any number of threatening letters, some of which I wish you could have the opportunity of reading. Through it all it is a great satisfaction for me to know that for the most part the white people who live in our vicinity acted in a very sensible way, notwithstanding all kinds of influence was brought to bear on them to get them to do something violent.

I think that we have got to make up our minds that a large element of the South is fast reaching the position where it is determined that the education of the colored people shall go no further, and that as Tuskegee seems in a way to represent the highest point of success reached by a certain kind of institution, that as soon as possible they mean to make an example of it and stay its progress. Secondly, I think that in the future it will be found that the main opposition is going to be concentrated against industrial and technical education rather than mere literary training. The explanation of this is that the colored contractor or architect or carpenter or brickmason comes into competition with the white man while the Negro teacher and minister does not. I merely mention these matters as indicating the work that is before us. I am not, however, disheartened or discouraged. We are going to win and win magnificently, but it is going to require hard battling.

The visit of President Roosevelt is detaining me in the South quite late this year, and I am not quite sure whether I shall be able to get to Boston before Christmas or not. Yours very truly,

Booker T. Washington

TLpS Con. 876 BTW Papers DLC.

To Walter L. Cohen

[Tuskegee, Ala.] October 5, 1905

Personal

My dear Mr. Cohen: I am wondering if you would be willing to write an article which might be used in some colored paper, the name of which we would decide on later, showing in a general way what I have tried to accomplish in the direction of securing opportunities for our race and protecting their interests. In case you write the article, I am rather anxious that you not attempt to defend me, that is, put me on the defensive. There are certain elements of colored people who are all the time trying to show that I take no interest in the political welfare of the colored people and have done nothing in that regard. You are in a position to know what I have done in this respect, and I will repeat to you that which I have never done before, and that is this: what I have attempted to do in Louisiana I have attempted to do in nearly every one of the Southern States, as you and others are in position to know, and but for my action, as feeble as it was, the colored people would have been completely overthrown and the Lily Whites would have been in complete control in every Southern state. I think you have an idea of what I did in Alabama. Of course, but for the stand I took, I do not believe that either you or Col. Lewis would be in office and the race would be practically unrecognized in your state. You know how I have been jumped on by the Southern press and white politicians for standing up for you, Crum, and others. In a diplomatic way I should like for you to bring this in. Of course I should like for you to send me the article here, and we could discuss then its use after I have gone over it.

I am glad to see that there are signs of the disappearance of the yellow fever. I sympathize with you and your family in what you have gone through with during the last few months.

I hope that the arrangements are such that the President will have an opportunity to see and speak to the colored people while in New Orleans. Yours truly,

Booker T. Washington

TLpS Con. 28 BTW Papers DLC.

An Article in *Charities*

[Oct. 7, 1905]

WHY SHOULD NEGRO BUSINESS MEN GO SOUTH?

In a recent address to the members of the National Negro Business League, at their sixth annual meeting in New York, I said: "In commending opportunities for progress in business and commerce we should not disregard the fact that of the ten million members of our race, the great masses are in the South, and there, in my opinion, they will remain. While there are evils of which no one should lose sight — in creating and securing labor, in conducting business enterprises, and in securing homes — there is no other part of the United States that begins to offer a field more inviting than the South. We should see to it that we do not lose in the South that which we now possess. We should not grasp at a shadow, and lose the substance. If we neglect to occupy the field that is now before us in the South, it will become there as it is in the North — we will be excluded by those who are strangers to our tongue and customs."

In seeking to answer briefly the question that has been proposed to me, "Why should the Negro business man go South?" I believe I cannot do better than enlarge somewhat and make more specific the statement I have just quoted.

Emphasis should be put on the fact that the masses of the Negro people are now, and are likely to be for all time, in the South, for the most part on the farms and in the small towns, rather than the large cities.

They were born there, bred there, and even were it possible to remove them in any great numbers, I believe they are better fitted to live there than elsewhere, either on this continent or in Africa.

I saw the statement recently that until the beginning of the nineteenth century, no city has ever increased in size by the natural growth of its native population. Where great cities sprang up, they grew and maintained their population by constant accessions from the country districts. In other words, the population produced in the country went to the city only to die. It was not bad sanitary conditions alone that brought this about. The same causes which operated to destroy the population of the cities a hundred years ago, are still operating to-day, though to a less degree, no doubt, in the crowded city districts which most of the colored people usually live in, in the North.

I do not believe the masses of colored people are yet fitted to survive and prosper in the great northern cities to which so many of them are crowding. The temptations are too great, and the competition with the foreign population, with which they there come in contact, is too fierce.

I am convinced that for a long time to come the great mass of the prosperous, successful colored people will be found on the farms and in the small towns of the South.

But where the great masses of the Negro population are, there are the best opportunities for Negro business men. Experience has shown, I believe, even in the North, that the largest opportunities for the Negro in business are in providing for those needs of other members of his race, which the white business man, either through neglect, or lack of knowledge, has failed, or been unable to provide. The Negro knows the members of his own race. He knows the Negro people of his neighborhood, in their church, and in their family life, and is able to discriminate in his dealings with them. This superiority in the matter of credits is in itself a business advantage, of which competition cannot easily deprive the Negro, and one which, with the extension of the modern methods of business, is likely to become of increasing importance.

Every condition which favors the Negro in the South, the cheapness of land, of the cost of living, opportunities for work, and his natural adaptation to the soil, favor also the Negro in business in the South. Indeed the great need of the masses of the Negro people for direction in the matter of buying and selling, saving and investing, makes opportunities for the Negro who possesses training in business affairs.

But there are other reasons which must appeal more and more to one who considers the matter thoughtfully. Money earned by the Negro in the way of business in the South is ordinarily worth more than money earned in the same way in the North. It is worth more, not merely because it goes further, but because the business man, in earning it, can be of more service to his race. The Negro banker who, in the course of his business, finds it necessary to encourage thrift and industry among his people, the Negro tradesman, who, for his own protection, must constantly discriminate between the honest and industrious members of his race, is at the same time performing a service to his people and the community as a whole, which should and does give a dignity to his work and a significance to his whole life.

The Negro who, in the course of his own business, is doing something which at the same time makes the world better, will in the long run stand higher in the community among his neighbors of both races, than he who, making more, and spending more, spends it, as he is tempted to do, for the superficial things which make life in the great nothern cities so attractive to large numbers of the people of my race.

Charities, 15 (Oct. 7, 1905), 17–19.

To the Editor of the Boston *Herald*

[Tuskegee, Ala.] Oct. 11, 1905

Editor Boston Herald: The one hundredth anniversary of the birth of William Lloyd Garrison, which occurs on December 10, it seems to me, is an event which should not only deeply stir and interest the colored people throughout the country, but one which should not pass without proper recognition on the part of the white people.

Steps are being taken by the colored people to have the event celebrated by members of their race throughout the country, but all of us now recognize more and more the fact that the work of Mr. Garrison and his co-laborers not only freed the black race, but was equally important in emancipating a large part of the white people of the United States. It is also true, it will be conceded, that to Mr. Garrison and his co-workers we owe, in large part, the fact that we now have a united country.

As the national, and even internation[al], character and value of Mr. Garrison's services are now so widely recognized, I cannot, as a member of the race which he most served, refrain from urging upon the public the importance of seeing that the celebration of his one hundredth anniversary shall be of such a character as to do credit to our entire country. More and more, as the years pass by, all of us are enjoying the fruits of Garrison's work, and we should not fail to keep before this and coming generations the heroic and far-reaching nature of his services to mankind and the Republic. Yours truly,

[Booker T. Washington]

TLd Con. 330 BTW Papers DLC.

To Edward Augustus Johnson

[Tuskegee, Ala.] Oct. 12, 1905

Dear Mr. Johnson: Your letter of Oct. 9th contains the following sentence:

"I therefore wrote to Mr. Lankford[1] at Washington to hold up the deal for the Enterprise tentatively until I could perhaps reach you on your way North at some other Pt. than Tuskegee."

I write to ask if it is really true that you apprised Mr. Leatherwood or Mr. Lankford either of my correspondence with you with reference to the Industrial Enterprise property. Yours truly,

Booker T. Washington

TLpS Con. 877 BTW Papers DLC.

1 John Anderson Lankford (1874–1946) attended Tuskegee Institute from 1896 to 1898, then taught at several black colleges. Although he studied law and was admitted to the Washington, D.C., bar, Lankford worked primarily as an architect in the nation's capital. He served as a consultant on government buildings and as the official architect of the A.M.E. Church.

From Theodore Roosevelt

The White House Washington October 12, 1905

Personal.

My dear Mr. Washington: Here is a rough draft of my speech at Tuskegee. Will you please send it to me at St. Augustine, Fla., with any suggestions or corrections you may care to make, if you are not able to get it back here by Tuesday evening next, which of course would be much perferable![1] Sincerely yours,

Theodore Roosevelt

TLS Con. 7 BTW Papers DLC.

1 No copy of BTW's reply is in the papers of either BTW or Roosevelt.

From Francis Jackson Garrison

Boston Oct. 12, 1905

My dear Friend: I am just in receipt of your letter of the 5th inst. in reply to what I wrote you in regard to your explanation of the Wanamaker matter, and thank you for it. I have not seen any of the outpourings of the Southern press in regard to the matter, but can readily understand that they have been unscrupulous and calumnious to the last degree, and I am not surprised by what you tell me of the threats of personal violence and assassination and of the destruction of your school property. I have no doubt that this is not the first occasion that you received such anonymous and villainous threats through the mail. Indeed, I have long felt, as I have told you, the possibility of the torch being applied even to Tuskegee in some sudden whirlwind of passion such as may at any time sweep through the Black Belt, and my heart aches to think of the strain to which you are constantly subjected by these and a multitude of other things that would discourage and break down anyone less sane, well balanced and optimistic than yourself. As I said in my letter, too, I know how many elements both North and South you have to consider in anything which you may say or write, and I was only concerned that you should avoid anything that seemed in the least like truckling or apology, which I knew was farthest from your own mind, but which it seemed to me might easily be read into the statement which you printed with regard to the Wanamaker dinner.

I am waiting with deep interest, as doubtless multitudes more are, the visit of the President to Tuskegee, and I do hope that he will be more flat-footed and outspoken in his remarks than was McKinley, although the latter's bearing was certainly not discreditable in any way; but because of the White House dinner the South will be on tiptoe to see if the President says anything that could be twisted into a qualification or limitation, and I am hoping that what he says will ring true and will reiterate his demand for "a square deal" for everyone, regardless of race or color.[1] It is reported in the papers here that he or his secretary requested the mayor of Tuskegee to coöperate with you in the reception there, and that the mayor refused to do so, whereupon it was intimated that the town would have only a brief part in the President's day there, and that his time would chiefly be spent at the Institute, as very naturally it would be any way, since the town has nothing else to offer of interest to visitors. What, indeed, would be Tuskegee without the Institute! I hope that we shall see you in Boston before the end of the year, and that you will be able to come out to us at Lexington when you are again in this neighborhood. Yours faithfully,

Francis J. Garrison

TLS Con. 876 BTW Papers DLC.

1 Garrison forwarded his correspondence with BTW to O. G. Villard, who commented: "I am glad that you wrote to Booker Washington as you did, yet I pity him for he is truly in a desperate position and may yet prove a martyr to his cause. I am very hopeful that the President's visit to Tuskegee will put an end to the idle clamor against the work there. When I was in Washington on Sunday I found that the negro people had their hearts in their mouths in fear lest the President slop over or say some indiscreet thing on this trip. I should forgive Mr. Roosevelt for a great deal if he would only lunch with Washington while at Tuskegee, but both he and Washington are too much cowed now to look for that." (Villard to Garrison, Oct. 19, 1905, Oswald Garrison Villard Papers, MH.)

From Charles William Anderson

New York, N.Y. October 12, 1905

Personal.

My dear Doctor: You may be interested to know that I have caused the manager of the "Devan Shop," to have those Boston papers removed from his window. Some time ago I spoke to the proprietor in relation to the matter, but he did not act. The other day, I called upon Mr. Turner, the manager, and told him plainly that if these papers were not removed, I should take my patronage elsewhere. He immediately summoned the porter and instructed him to take them out of the case. I shall follow this matter up, and see to it that they are not replaced.[1]

The information about Du Bois, rather confirms my suspicion that Humphreys and his associates are bent upon taking up these fellows. I am to see Governor Odell this afternoon, when I shall tell him with all possible emphasis that these men ought not to be permitted to make trouble in this way. I feel reasonably confident that Odell will act in the premises.

You may be interested to know that Attorney General Mayer has designated Wilford H. Smith as a Special Deputy Attorney General, to assist in the prosecution of election fraud cases. You will recall that I told you some time ago that the Attorney General had made me this promise. Thus, you see, I am landing a little something for our friends all the while. I want to get around to Moore's case by the first of the month, but I wish you would be sure to tell him that he will have to devote his time and energy to the work of the Department, from 9 A.M. until 4.30 P.M. He is still connected with the realty company, and interested in many other ventures, and does not seem inclined to lay down any of them. So, I think it would be well to remind him of my position in the matter. You will recall that I made this statement to him in your presence at the Stevens House during your last visit. Of course the local leaders here will be angry over the removal of one of their men, but it shall be done right away.

Let me hear from you at your early convenience. Yours truly,

Charles W. Anderson

TLS Con. 27 BTW Papers DLC.

[1] Anderson wrote BTW on Oct. 16, 1905, that he had caused the Boston *Guardian* to be removed from two other shops in the city. (Con. 27, BTW Papers, DLC.)

To Hightower T. Kealing

[Tuskegee, Ala.] October 13, 1905

PERSONAL AND CONFIDENTIAL

Dear Mr. Kealing: I trust you will pardon me for so long delaying answering your letter. I write now only in answer to one part of same, and will take up the other matters later.

I thank you very much for writing me in the frank and confidential manner that you have. My reply is only to the part that concerns our friend.[1] His present mood is not new by any means, but nevertheless his conversation with you brings to the surface the pathetic aspect of his case. The fact is, he is deserving of recognition and help, and his present state of mind is simply resentment of the fact that his work and ability are not recognized by appointment to some public office. He is deserving of recognition, but no one can help him in that regard, because he will not help himself, and this, I have had to tell him frankly, more than once. Every time he is placed in position of responsibility, he lets himself down, and injures his friends. I have talked with the President frankly regarding his condition, more than once, and he is just as anxious to help him as I am, but he is afraid to do so.

After a good deal of persuasion on the part of friends, the President did give him an opportunity. He left under the most strict promise to keep entirely sober, and I think he did so for the most part, but before finishing the work he got intoxicated and left a bad odor behind him.

If he were sent to Haiti, or given any important position in Washington, it would only be a matter of a few weeks or months before he would get intoxicated and disgrace the President and his friends. That is the whole case in a nut-shell, and it has been my painful duty, more than once, to tell him so. He cried like a baby sometime ago when I told him frankly that the President had said that he had gone as far as he could go in his case.

Under the circumstances, I feel the best help any of us can render him is to assist him in making the paper a great national newspaper, which it is capable of becoming, and in fact is to a large degree. If we could just persuade him that his real work is in this direction, we can help him, and our friends will be helped at the same time.

For a number of months he will take this view of the case, and work very hard to make the paper a strong paper, then the old longing for public office gets possession of him and he finds himself in the same mood that he was when he talked with you.

Another phase of the case, which I presume he did not mention to you is that all through the campaign he took a weekly stipend from the National Committee, and of course, those in authority feel that there is something in the future in the way of public office for him, while I try to tell him the real truth.

If he were to go to Haiti, for example, I do not believe he would be there many months before he would be sent for on account of some difficulty.

I really wish there were some way to help him to what he wants, but the case in my opinion is not bright at present.

I shall write you about the other points mentioned in your letter soon. Very truly yours,

Booker T. Washington

TLpS Con. 261 BTW Papers DLC.

[1] T. Thomas Fortune.

From Napoleon Bonaparte Marshall

Boston, Mass. Oct. 14–1905

Dear sir: Although I am numbered among those who have radically opposed your attitude on certain public questions pertaining to the political and civic status of our people in this country; I feel that I ought to express to you my commendation of your timely letter on Common Schools which appeared in the New York Age of Oct. 12th inst. The Committee on National Aid to Education, of the New England Suffrage League has designated me to prepare for presentation in the next Congress a bill similar in its import to the old Blair Educational Bill which passed the Senate in 1886. Congressman Wm. C. Greene[1] of this State has consented to introduce this bill in the next Congress. In a recent speech at New Bedford I said, among other things: Confident that here is a measure that will, at least, solve the educational problem in the Southland, the problem which has engendered so much interracial discord and hatred between the radical and conservative elements of our people, we unreservedly invite the cooperation of all our people in all sections of our country, and urge them to bring what pressure they can upon their representatives in Congress in behalf of this measure. Your aforesaid letter in the New York Age, while it does not commit you on the question of national aid to the several States in the establishment and maintenance of common schools gives me the hope that you would gladly welcome such aid, provided the bill asking such aid were so framed as not to arouse the sovereign sensibilities of the Southern States. In my draft of the bill I have set apart a certain proportion of each State's donation say one-third for agricultural and industrial institutions. This idea although not incorporated in the final Blair Educational Bill was favorably considered by many Senators and representatives during the several years of its discussion in Congress. The bill bases its apportionment on illiteracy and not population and is non-sectional. Personally I should like your assistance and cooperation not only in the preparation of said bill; but also in its advocacy before the Congressional committee to which it shall be referred; and I am authorized to state that whatever information you can give in the way of statistical data or other useful information will be gratefully received by the Committee. I am, with much respect Very truly yours

N. B. Marshall

ALS Con. 29 BTW Papers DLC.

1 William Stedman Greene.

From Edward Augustus Johnson

Raleigh, N.C., Oct. 14, 1905

Dear Dr. Washington: Replying to yours of the 12th in which you inquire "if it is really true that you apprised Mr. Leatherwood or Mr. Lankford either of my correspondence with you with reference to the Industrial Enterprise property," will say that you misinterpret the words you quote from my letter, of course unintentionally. I did not mean to say that I had written Mr. Lankford or Mr. Leatherwood that you were in this deal. All these parties know is that I am trying to get you to interest some friend of yours to help *me* by taking some stock in the company. I am not sure that Leatherwood knows this even. I have tried to be very careful in this matter and avoid bringing you into it personally, but I have told these parties that the paper if started would be pro-Booker Washington in policy, and they agreed with me as to this.

I think I understand your position in the matter and shall keep the whole matter in confidence regardless of whether the deal goes through or not.

If you will read the sentence you quote from my letter you will see that what I said about reaching you was what I wrote you, and was in my *mind* at the time I wrote Lankford, *but not what I wrote him.*

Hoping to hear from you further in the matter, I am, Very truly,

E. A. Johnson

TLS Con. 877 BTW Papers DLC.

From Thomas L. Leatherwood

Washington, D.C., Oct. 15 1905

Dear Sir: No doubt, you have learned of my misfortune in the publication of the Industrial Enterprise; therefore you are not surprised at my seemingly negligence in not publishing your letter to the colored citizens of the South.

For fear you have not heard of my misfortune, I will tell you. Two weeks ago, a Negro printer while working for me wilfully pied and destroyed over two hundred pounds of my type that was set up in adds and reading matter, thereby damaging my office and business about $500, puting temporarily out of business. After he did his wilful deed, seeing that he had committed a deed that would land him in prison for ten years, left, and has not been heard of since. At the time it was done, I was out in the city attending to business, and when I returned to my office, I was shocked to find my office recked. What pussels me most, is, that I can't find any reasons signed as to why he did it. When he began work Monday a m, I owed him 60¢ only, and up to the hour, Wednesday, when he recked my place I had paid him $3.75 on that weeks work. There has been a sertain amount of prejudice against the Enterprise every since I took up the work here, and the only way I can figure the cause leading up to the act, is conspirricy to put the Enterprise out of business. The blow came just at the time I was strugling to reach the season of prosperity.

Having written you some time ago in behalf of the Enterprise, I decided to write you again. I don't know, but I am almost sure that I have done more actial work along the lines that you are map[p]ing out than any Negro paper existing in this country under like circumstances. You wrote me that you had referred the matter to your friends here, who would probably call to see me. Mr. Dancy informed me that you had called his attention to the matter, and that he had written to you relative to the same. Prof. E. A. Johnson of N.C. seemed, a few weeks ago, to have the matter under advisement, and was here for the purpose of perfecting an organization to be incorporated with a capital stock of $5000. These, however were ideas of my own, whereby I hoped to develop the Enterprise into a strong Educational and Industrial Home and fire side paper. All seems to have failed for the need of financial backing with which to finance the corporation. I am not out for graft, but would like to have the Industrial Enterprise live, and serve the mission for which I launched it. With a little assistence, I could continue the publication, and in the near future, it would pave its own way as a defender of the industrial rights of the great mass of colored citizens who need our incouragements.

I find that it is going to be impossible for me to repare my office without the aid of some body, and I thought if you entertained the least idea of helping a cause of this kind here, you could do nothing that would be more acceptable to my 1800 subscribers, than to assist the Enterprise.

Dr. Lampton, financial secretary of the A. M. E. church, who owns the Record here is anxious to form a combine of the two papers, but I don't see that to do so would build up the work of The Enterprise. There are other agents at work to get the Enterprise, but none of them su[i]ts me — yet I may be forced to surrender it, or suspend for good. I am willing to sell the paper or I am willing to continue the publication even at a sacrifice for the good I might do. If you have decided to help continue the publication, please wire me at my expence, that I may be able to proceed upon sertain lines, this week. I hope to get ready to resume work by the first week in Nov.

Thanking you for past favors and in advance for future ones, I beg to remain obediently Yours,

Thos. L. Leatherwood

ALS Con. 877 BTW Papers DLC.

Richard W. Thompson to Emmett Jay Scott

New Albany, Ind., 10/15, '05

Dear Mr. Scott: Yours under date of 12th came duly to hand, but was addressed "526 Culbertson street, Jeffersonville, Ind." Ordinarily, I will get anything in this vicinity addressed "any old way," but it might be well to call the attention of your secretary to the error, as it might some time cause an embarrassing delay in delivery when a green clerk would be "on."

I have copied the letter of the "prominent educator," and sent it to The Freeman, stating that it came to me from a well-known educator in the South, who wanted to say a word for Dr. Washington before a sympathetic audience, which, for obvious reasons, might not be secured in his immediate environment. I followed it with a brief comment, and suggested that the whole thing be used as an editorial to give it the best effectiveness.

Here is the way the Freeman's condition stands: G. L. and Elwood C. Knox[1] own two-thirds and G. W. Cable owns the remaining third. Cable is employed by the corporation as editor at a salary of $6.00 per week. Elwood runs the business end and Cable handles the literary end, the latter vising all copy that has to do with the policy of the paper upon public matters. As the Knoxes care for nothing but the monetary side of the business and know nothing of the weight or effect of an attitude one way or another upon a current issue, it would seem to be the part of wisdom to conduct any business negotiation through them — or at least in such a way that they would know that something was coming their way. Knox is a fiend for money. Cable is just the other way. He is honest and conscientious to the last degree. He is a dreamer as a newspaper man, as far as the cash-drawer is concerned, and wants to run The Freeman on as independent a basis as if it were backed by unlimited capital. I do not say his ambition is not worthy, but you know there is not a Negro paper in this country that can be sustained without doing some "propaganding" — being useful to some person, party or plan, supporting its best side and confounding the opposition. Cable objects to being an "organ," politically or otherwise. As a result, the paper is losing the support of several forces that contributed to its coffers, as well as being without a certain class of rather questionable, but paying advertising, which Wood accepted without hesitation, and wants to continue doing so. The paper is not making any money, and there is no harmony in the camp. Cable has spoken and written to me very candidly about the condition of affairs, for two reasons: first, to get me to stay with the paper at a meager compensation until better times should come; second to explain why that during the past year I have received only the princely sum of $8.00 in salary – part of that in trade. I exact a small salary, even if I do not get it, to ward off suspicion or at least confirmation that I am being subsidized by outsiders. For what they pay me, I could not remain two weeks. Frankly, I am only continuing with a view of being helpful to you folks. I get considerable latitude, as you see, but since Cable has been on, I must be more careful than before, to avoid being *trimmed* by his keener scrutiny. Yet he is a good friend of mine, and I can talk pretty straight to him on any matter that can be made to appeal to his judgment. In short, there is no *actual control* about The Freeman. In my opinion, however, since Cable is the brains of the concern and does the writing, it is essential that his good will be secured. Hence, it might be well to let a cautious proposition, looking to the extension of some favor, moral or material, filter through Cable to the Knoxes. Business matters, I understand, are gone over in conference, and policies are argued out with the three in meeting, if a difference arises. In the case of the Wizard, there would be no serious trouble, as all are friendly to him. The difficulty lies in Cable's fits of *independence*, at critical moments, and his aversion to dealing out body blows to the malevolent opposition. It may be that the paper has a goodly number of subscribers among the Niagara element, and he doesn't want to alienate them. It has been intimated to me that the combination might not last long as it stands. Cable says he wants more control, or he may have less. It would be a pity to let such a splendid property go down from sheer domestic infelicity. Well financed, as the Age appears to be, and in the proper hands, The Freeman would be invincible in the West and South. Cable was taken in because of dire financial necessity. From these voluminous facts, you may find an answer to your question.

You have doubtless noticed that I am pushing the Garrison memorial. From the Alexandria Home News, there seems to be an informer in the Tuskegee camp. See this week's issue on the rumored assault on Dr. Washington's home.

So Furniss goes to Haiti. He is able and competent, and the promotion is made upon pure merit, but the appointment will arouse no enthusiasm in Indiana, where Harry has scarcely lived a day in fifteen years, and never enjoyed an ounce of popularity. The country at large would have preferred a more representative appointment. However, I presume no kick will be made of any formidable nature. I give you the facts for your information solely.

While waiting for the return of Secretary Taft, to take up the matter of my transfer, I received a proposition from a watchman in the Pension Office, looking to an exchange. I wrote that I would be willing to consider the deal, and asked some questions. I am expecting an answer not later than this week. Pending that, I have done nothing, as I want to formulate a definite policy before asking my friends to help. Since I can get only a third-grade appointment on a transfer, and to ask the Department to find a vacancy might take a great deal of time, it is my opinion that if this exchange can be made, it will take me to Washington at a salary of $60 or more per month and give me a leverage from which I can work for something better. I can't get hold of my influences in this locality nor benefit myself politically, save by holding a nominal residence and voting-place in Indiana. The thought occurred to me that a dash might be made for the Furniss succession at Bahia, but it is doubtful if so good a place will now go to an Indiana Negro after the promotion of Furniss to Minister to Haiti. I would be very glad to have your opinion as to what I had best do relative to my entire case, as you see it. I shall advise you further as to the proposed exchange as soon as I hear from Morgan. If it is a go, it will involve a transfer from the War Department to the Interior. At any rate, I am sure if I can get to Washington, we can work more effectively along all lines than here, for we can get the advantage of frequent personal contact, which is everything — as you have found — in conducting diplomatic negotiations.

I am glad to know that Fortune is with you recuperating. He is a splendid man and I hope he will long be spared to us. Walters is in line and I believe he will "tote squar" from this on, if he has not done so in the past. He wanted Fortune for Haiti. Walters will be here on the 23d and will be my guest on the evening of the 27th, together with Mrs. Walters and baby.

It is a blessed thing that Cromwell is off the Record. Walters may be very little improvement, but his heart is in the right place — and that will help *some*. I gave Lampton a "hand" in The Freeman this week. Dr. Hall, of Chicago,[2] is going South shortly, and expects to visit Tuskegee. He is *all right*.

Let me hear from you when you can. I know you are in a stew now getting ready for Roosevelt. I noticed you were in Washington the other day arranging the details.

Wishing you abundant success in all things, I am Faithfully yours,

R. W. Thompson

TLS Con. 3 BTW Papers DLC.

1 The son of George L. Knox.

2 George Cleveland Hall (1864–1930) was one of BTW's chief supporters in Chicago and, during BTW's last years, his personal physician. Hall moved to Chicago from Michigan in the late 1880s and studied medicine at Bennett College, an Eclectic institution. His lifelong personal feud with Dr. Daniel Hale Williams began when Hall overcame Williams's objections to his Eclectic training and secured a position at Provident Hospital. Hall charged that Williams preferred white doctors to black ones, and the two men lined up much of black Chicago behind them. Their wives joined in the dispute that pitted the old professional-class elite behind Williams and the rising business class behind Hall. Hall was a member of the executive committee of the National Negro Business League, and urged black solidarity through support of black business, newspapers, and professionals. Though a personal friend of Washington, Hall was not an accommodationist. He was active in the early work of the NAACP and the Urban League. In the social politics of black Chicago, Hall had a great advantage over the aloof Williams. He was active in the black Hyde Park Republican Club, while Williams kept out of politics. Hall was dark and gregarious, while Williams was light-skinned and aristocratic in manner. So in the community, at Provident Hospital, and in the graces of BTW, Hall was able to keep the upper hand.

From Theodore Roosevelt

The White House, Washington. October 16, 1905

Personal

My dear Mr. Washington: I have at once struck out that sentence to which you object. The only reason I put it in was because you had put it into the draft you sent me. Did you remember that it was your own sentence? In the same way I shall change the term "black" to "colored" people. I used the term "black" because you used it in the memorandum you sent me. Sincerely yours,

Theodore Roosevelt

TLS Con. 7 BTW Papers DLC.

From Whitefield McKinlay

Washington, D.C. Oct. 16, 1905

Dear Mr. Washington: I delayed thus long answering your very kind letter concerning the President's speech as I wanted to get the opinions of both Terrell and Cobb. They join me in saying that there is nothing in it to invite criticism, and I venture to predict that if the Southern papers should publish it word for word it will do us more good not only in the South but throughout the country than any other speech that I can recall. It completely answers Dixon and those of his ilk.

I am very glad to see that Dixon was hissed in Columbia, and it looks to me as if South Carolina is coming back to her senses as she is trying to throw off the yoke of Tillman and hisses a fakir like Dixon. Very truly,

DICTATED

W McKinlay

TLS Con. 4 BTW Papers DLC.

To Thomas L. Leatherwood

[Tuskegee, Ala.] Oct. 20, 1905

Personal

My dear Sir: Replying to yours of October 15th, I beg to say that while I am deeply interested in the success of all enterprises among our people, including newspapers, it has never been my policy, as it could not in reason be, to take any prominent part in the publication of newspapers. In an entirely legitimate way, from time to time, this institution carries advertising, but beyond this, it is not possible for me to go.

I hope for your enterprise all the success it merits, and thank you especially for the kindly consideration you have shown me personally, and the institution as well. Very truly yours,

Booker T. Washington

TLpS Con. 877 BTW Papers DLC.

To Francis Jackson Garrison

[Tuskegee, Ala.] Oct. 20, 1905

Personal

My dear Mr. Garrison: I am writing you just a line to acknowledge the receipt of your letter and to say that we share, of course, your anxiety regarding the outcome of the visit of the President. It is not so much what the President may say or leave unsaid here that is of interest just now as the mere fact of his coming.

In my former letter to you I meant to have stated that all through the Wanamaker dinner excitement people from the outside attempted to bring all kinds of influence to bear on the white people living in the immediate vicinity and county to do something violent, but they resisted every such influence. This feature of the matter has given me more encouragement than anything else.

In regard to the little flurry created by the actions of the young hot-headed mayor of Tuskegee, it amounted to nothing. It was wholly at my request and suggestion that the President consented to spend thirty minutes in the town of Tuskegee on his way to the school. The young mayor hoped to get some cheap advertising out of parading the fact that he wanted to arrange the town program without consultation with me. But the solid people of the town are manifesting every day by their actions that they have little sympathy with such folly. One of the most interesting outcomes of the matter in relation to the President's visit is a request which I have just received from a party of 24 white women in the town of Tuskegee to be provided with some kind of accommodations in order to see and hear the President at the school. This, in view of the noise that they have made for three years, is rather interesting. At least a car load of white people from Montgomery will be here to see the President, notwithstanding the President goes to Montgomery on the same day.

The attached picture which appeared in the Atlanta Constitution during the discussion of the matter may interest you. Yours truly,

Booker T. Washington

TLpS Con. 876 BTW Papers DLC.

To Napoleon Bonaparte Marshall

[Tuskegee, Ala., ca. Oct. 20, 1905]

Personal

My dear Sir: Please forgive me for my tardiness in replying to your letter. I have been so engaged with perfecting details with reference to the President's visit to our institute next week, that I have not had the time to reply earlier.

Let me say that I am deeply interested in any scheme that has for its object the furtherance of education among our people here in the South. I am convinced that this is a subject to which we have got to give more serious attention in the future than we have in the past. I refer especially to the education of the children of the rural districts. 85% of the colored children live outside of the larger cities and towns, and the race is increasing faster than the educational facilities, and besides, in some quarters there seems to be a determined purpose to hinder rather than promote the black children's education. Of course the great body of our children will never pass beyond the public schools, and if they fail to receive training there, they grow up in the darkest ignorance.

I thank you very much for what you say regarding my open letter relating to the public schools. Now, of course, I could not give my endorsement to any special measure for public schools until I had had opportunity to examine the bill in detail.

There is one other point that I ought to put before you: sometime ago, I promised President Eliot that I would join him in an effort to get a bill through Congress for aiding education in the South, along definite lines. As yet, I do not know just what his plan is in detail, but he did outline it to me verbally. Perhaps what he has in mind, and what you have in mind might be condensed into one effort. It will require harder and more persistent work on the part of all, to get the country aroused to this subject. You will agree with me, I am sure, in saying that it is very seldom that the American people retrace their steps. They have passed judgment on the effort to give federal money for education in the South, and it is going to require harder effort to arouse interest now than if the subject had not been passed upon once.

You are very kind to refer in the first part of your letter to the fact that you have differed from me in the past on some subjects. Please permit me to say that I do not hold any ill feeling against any one who differs from me on matters of public policy. Some of my very best personal friends are those who differ absolutely from me on many essential points. No man ever gets my ill will by merely opposing my policies in a high and lofty manner. Personal abuse, blackguarding, and riotous conduct, however, are altogether another matter. I appreciate fully that no man can be of the highest service to his fellows unless he is willing to hear all sides of a subject; to hear from those who differ from him as well as those who agree with him. I have gotten as much benefit from those who have criticized my policies adversely, as from those who agree with me, so always feel free in the future to differ from me if you wish, and it will not interfere in the least with any personal feeling I may have. Sincerely yours,

Booker T. Washington

TLpS Con. 4 BTW Papers DLC.

Three Reports of Pinkerton Detectives

Tuskegee, Ala. Sunday, October 22nd, 1905

#58 reports: In company with #22,[1] I called at the Tuskegee Normal School, where I met Mr. Scott, Secretary to the President, Booker T. Washington. After reading my letter of introduction to him, Mr. Scott stated that on account of numerous letters of a threatening nature having been received at the school, addressed to Dr. Washington, he desired to know the feeling and sentiment of the people in Tuskegee and vicinity, and also to learn whether any party or parties in outlying towns or districts had any evil designs upon Dr. Washington, which would mar the ceremonies to take place on the occasion of the visit of the President of the U.S. to Tuskegee on the 24th day of October, 1905.

Mr. Scott mentioned a small settlement about seven miles from Tuskegee, named Tallassee, which is inhabited by a vicious class of white men. He also called to my attention the arrival of a white man in the vicinity of the school, who had acted rather strangely, and had later proceeded in the direction of Tallassee.

I informed Mr. Scott that Dr. Washington would be carefully guarded from any violence on the part of people who may come there for that purpose, and all suspicious characters would be closely watched and made to give a satisfactory account of themselves or be ejected from the grounds.

During the day #22 and myself patroled the grounds, and made observations. Upon investigating I learned that there was no foundation in the suspicion attached to the man who had presumably come from the direction of Tallassee and acted rather strangely. From all indications he was merely curious to see and observe the preparations being made for the reception of President Roosevelt.

I also proceeded to Chehaw, Ala., accompanied by #22, and mingled with people in and about the railroad station to learn their sentiments towards Dr. Washington and his school, which we found to be for, rather than against Dr. Washington and his institution, although several very threatening remarks were made by young men who were apparently of a disreputable character.

During the evening #22 and myself were seated in the public room of the Wade Hotel at Tuskegee. A man named Von Grabill spoke very disparagingly of the efforts Dr. Washington is using to elevate the colored race. Grabill stated that Dr. Washington advocated social equality and endeavored to impress upon the colored people the idea that they do not need to indulge in manual labor in order to live. Grabill further stated that Dr. Washington was doing harm rather than good to both races.

Report of #22 incorporated in the above.

Tuskegee, Ala., Monday, October 23rd, 1905

#58 reports: In company with # 22, I proceeded to Chehaw at 7:20 A.M. Upon our arrival there we met several people about the station, and learned that they were residents of the surrounding country. Persons arriving on the train were closely scrutinized, and spoken to by #22 and myself when any doubt existed in our minds as to their intentions.

One young man who said he belonged to the military company which intended to escort President Roosevelt on his arrival in Tuskegee, stated that he would like to exterminate Dr. Washington and his people; that they were a menace to the community, and he advocated their destruction. I learned that the fellow's name was "Bob," and was apparently not well thought of by the rest of the people there, as they did not seem to appreciate his remarks concerning the colored race.

Upon our return to Tuskegee, we proceeded to the Normal School, and met Dr. Washington, who spoke of the preparations being made for the reception of President Roosevelt. Dr. Washington expressed his wishes to me, and I assured him that #22 and myself would pay strict attention to them, and see that no opportunity was afforded any one to assault either the President or Dr. Washington before or after the ceremonies.

After discussing the matter thoroughly with Dr. Washington, #22 and myself made careful observation of all persons in the grounds and vicinity of same. No suspicious characters were found. Those whom we met and found to be strangers were questioned as to their presence, and after giving a good account of themselves, they were permitted to go.

Another trip was made to Chehaw by #22 and myself, as a number of strangers were arriving there from Atlanta.

After ascertaining that everything was well at Chehaw and Tallassee, we again proceeded to Tuskegee, and mingled with the citizens and strangers who were continually arriving in vehicles of all descriptions.

Some of the young men were disposed to "rail" about Dr. Washington and his school, but the best and most reputable citizens of the town spoke very highly of Dr. Washington and his work.

He is evidently well thought of by the best people of Alabama.

At 2:30 A.M., Tuesday, we discontinued.

Report of #22 incorporated in the above.

Tuskegee, Ala., Tuesday, October 24th, 1905

#58 reports: In company with #22 I proceeded to the grounds of the Tuskegee Normal School at 6:00 A.M., and later proceeded to Chehaw, returning with the first train load of people to Tuskegee.

At 8:15 A.M. I met Mr. Scott and perfected arrangements for the guarding of the President and Dr. Washington upon the arrival of the President's party.

The grounds and vicinity of Dr. Washington's residence were thoroughly covered by #22 and myself in order to determine whether any suspicious persons were about.

Upon the arrival of the President's party, #22 and myself met them at the train with Dr. Washington, and then drove to the Grand-Stand near the Executive Building of the school, where the President viewed the parade of the students, etc.

We then accompanied the President's party with Dr. Washington on a drive around the grounds for the purpose of viewing the buildings, etc.

A stop was then made at the Normal School Chapel, where the President was introduced by Dr. Washington, and made a speech.

#22 and myself co-operated with the secret service men or officers who accompanied the President.

Afterwards the President and his party were driven to the train, which they boarded for Montgomery, Ala.

#22 and myself then accompanied Dr. Washington and Mr. Scott to his office, and later to his residence, where we were introduced to Mrs. Washington.

Dr. Washington and Mr. Scott expressed satisfaction for the manner in which everything had been conducted by #22 and myself.

We then took our departure, and at 2:00 P.M. boarded train for

Chehaw, later boarded train for Atlanta, where we arrived at 1:00 A.M., Wednesday, October 25th, 1905.

Report of #22 incorporated in the above.

TL Con. 5 BTW Papers DLC.

1 Pinkerton agents #58 and #22 were probably the Captain Rutledge and Mr. Fitzpatrick whom BTW praised as "helpful to us in many ways." (BTW to Thornhill, Oct. 25, 1905, Con. 5, BTW Papers, DLC.)

A Press Release

Tuskegee Institute, Ala., Oct. 24 [1905]

VISIT OF THE PRESIDENT OF THE UNITED STATES TO TUSKEGEE INSTITUTE

President Roosevelt reached the grounds of the Tuskegee Normal and Industrial Institute at 8:30 o'clock this morning and after a brief stop in the Town of Tuskegee, where he was received by the Mayor and other distinguished citizens of Alabama, he spoke warmly and felicitously from a platform in the grounds of the Girls' College located here. The President's train was then carried directly into the grounds of the Institute, over its private track which connects with the main line.

From 12 o'clock last night until morning great crowds of country people, white and black, have been coming from all sections of the surrounding territory to Tuskegee. A variegated assortment of nondescript vehicles, of many kinds, were cared for by the Institute in an immense enclosure. The President was driven by this motley collection and seemed to greatly enjoy the sight.

The President's party consisted of: Secretary William Loeb, Jr.; Surgeon General Rixey, U.S. Navy; Hon. John McIlhenny of Louisiana; Hon. John C. Greenway of Michigan; M. C. Latta and J. L. McGrew, stenographers; H. A. Coleman, representing the Associated Press; R. H. Hazzard, representing the Publishers' and Scripps-McRae Press Association; Walter E. Clark, representing the New York Sun Press Association; H. A. Strohmeyer, photographer; Col. L. S. Brown, general agent of the Southern Railway

Company; and Judge Thomas G. Jones of the Federal Court of Alabama, and Hon. J. O. Thompson, Collector of Internal Revenue, Birmingham, Ala., who joined the Presidential party at Montgomery.

The President was received by Principal Booker T. Washington and members of the Institute Board of Trustees and Faculty. He then entered a finely built carriage, made by students of the school, drawn by horses raised at the school, and driven by a student in the school's uniform. Four other carriages, also made by the students, in which members of the Presidential party were seated, followed. The party at once proceeded to an elaborately decorated reviewing stand, erected in front of the Office Building, surmounted by the President's Flag. Immediately the Educational and Industrial parade, upon which the students and teachers have for several weeks been at work, started. First came the Institute Band, led by Elbert B. Williams, Bandmaster, member of the 9th Cavalry, U.S. Army — which saw service with the President's Rough Riders at Santiago — who is detailed by the War Department to Tuskegee, followed by the nearly 1,500 students of the school in two divisions; the young men uniformed in blue suits, with brass buttons, white gloves, and cadet caps, led by Major J. B. Ramsey, and then the young women, uniformed in blue dresses trimmed with red braid, and wearing blue straw braid hats, led by Miss Jane E. Clark, Dean of the Woman's Department, each bearing a stalk of sugar cane, tipped with a cotton boll, both raised in the school's Agricultural Experiment Stations. Immediately behind the student body came a series of 61 floats, representing the various phases of the work of the Academic Department and the 37 Industrial divisions of the school. The school was able to put in evidence, in this way, examples of the work being carried on in all the departments. Of the floats representing the Academic, Agricultural, Mechanical, and the Girls' industries, the most striking, perhaps, were the following:

The BROOMMAKING AND BASKETRY float displayed girls at work winding straw on broom handles by hand machinery, also pressing and sewing brooms and cleaning off old broom handles for the purpose of putting on new straw. The decorations on this float represented the basketry work. The roof was thatched with pine straw; draperies of corn, sweet gum balls, and China berries were used and the sides below the floor were covered with broom straw. Unique also was the exhibition of Indian baskets, reed baskets, pine, shuck and raffia baskets, raffia, head and shuck belts, brooms, bead purses, African purses, raffia hats, etc.

The MILLINERY float showed the making of uniform hats used by the girls in the school; four girls were at work, trimming, draping and trying on hats. The new shade of silk, the "Alice" blue was exhibited made up into a girdle and collar. A large arch of autumn leaves with the word "Millinery" woven in foliage erected on the float was a striking feature.

On the BLACKSMITHS' float there were in operation, a heating forge, a large drill press, and a thread cutter. Four boys were at work heating and forging, and bending tires. The float was decorated with specimens of shop work consisting of forgings, horse shoes, and fancy designed iron railings, etc.

SHOEMAKING was represented by a float containing six boys who were making shoes, repairing, cutting out and fitting uppers and making uppers by machinery. Leather decorations showing specimens of all kinds of shop work were in evidence.

The ELECTRICAL DIVISION presented a float rigged with a pole at either end with boys near the top, dressed with climbers and safety belt, carrying pliers, fastening wires to the regulation cross arms. A steam engine, an electrical dynamo and switch board were in full operation; a great number of electric lamps were burning as the float passed.

The MACHINE DIVISION float was remarkable in that all the machinery on it was built by students. There were in operation a drill press, one 7 H.P. Engine driving the machinery, and machine vises. Boys were handling all the machinery, performing their tasks in realistic fashion. The decorations included blue-prints showing the course of study as used in industrial classes. A steam boiler, mounted on a large wagon, with hose connections with the machine float followed, furnishing the power for the operation of the engine.

On the PRINTING float five boys were at work, setting type, imposing "forms," operating a printing press and a stapling machine, also binding books. The float was trimmed with specimens of the work done by the students. The wheels were decorated with scrap paper.

The BRICKMASONRY AND PLASTERING float carried six boys doing progressive work, building piers, turning arches, showing the three steps in plastering. Two finished arches were exhibited. The sides of the float were built to represent the primitive level. A transit was in place showing modern methods.

ARCHITECTURAL DRAWING was represented by a float carrying two students working at a table, drawing. The float, in general outline, represented a Gothic structure. Drawings were exhibited, showing the five orders of Architecture, and specimens of detail and design work as done by the students.

The EXPERIMENT STATION and the Experiment Teaching Division floats, represented cotton ginning and baling, cotton breeding, and analysis of soil and plants; showing how worn out soils are reclaimed. This was illustrated with sections of washed land, filled land, terracing and other operations incident to building up soils, also sections showing crops for three years rotation and soil inoculation.

One Hambletonian stallion, 5 high grade brood mares accompanied by their colts, a pedigreed Jack and five high grade mule colts were in the parade to represent the Live Stock Division.

The DAIRY DIVISION was represented by 50 head of cows including Jerseys, Guernseys and Holsteins, accompanied by their sires, 25 yearlings and calves. On the CREAMERY float were three girls and two boys making butter by the old and new method, running a separator, bottling milk and testing same for butter fat and acidity. An elaborate exhibit of butter, cheese, etc., made by the students was shown.

The float representing the TRUCK GARDEN DIVISION was loaded with turnips, collards, lettuce, pumpkins, squash, butter beans, snap beans, peas, carrots, cabbage, onions, okra and other vegetables, raised in the Institute Truck Garden; boys were showing the methods employed in preparing and selecting for market.

The NURSE TRAINING float represented the interior of a sick room. Girl nurses were in charge of a "fever patient" giving him a sponge bath, taking his temperature, administering nourishments and stimulants and recording symptoms on a chart as is done in the Institute Hospital wards. Another division on the same float showed a young woman and a young man in an operating room, preparing surgical supplies. Decorations were white with the Red Cross, also evergreens.

The PHYSICS float carried two tables with students demonstrating the properties of the permanent bar-magnet and constructing an electric bell connection; they were also showing mehanical experiments — the relation of mass, density and volume. Two students were operating a telephone line, and two sending telegraph messages to each other. Mechanical and electrical apparati were displayed.

The HISTORY float showed a class room with girls and boys reciting. By the time the float reached the President's stand the recitation was on the recent Peace Conference at Portsmouth. Students were costumed in the dress of different periods of the Nation's history.

The LIBRARY float represented a corner in the Carnegie Library. Students were looking up references in connection with their trades and academic classes, reading papers and magazines and drawing books from the Library. A class in United States History was looking up reference matter found in President Roosevelt's "Winning of the West." The book shelves were filled with books classified under History, Natural Science, Useful Arts and Domestic Science, and Literature.

The float representing CHEMISTRY AND DOMESTIC SCIENCE carried a group testing the local water supply for potable and laundry purposes; samples collected from all wells, taps, reservoirs, branches and every known source of supply. Students were testing samples for such foreign substances as lead, phosphates and chlorides, and suspicious amounts of iron and organic matter. Waters were being examined for hardness, degree of hardness and number of grains to the gallon. How hard water wastes soap; how to soften by boiling and how by chemicals was illustrated; also how to clarify muddy water by filtration, and by chemicals.

The TRAINING SCHOOL GARDENING float showed children working in a plot already set out with cabbage, strawberries, and onions; one part represented the soil prepared and the children setting out plants, and still another section showed the children preparing the soil. This float was decorated with green vines and foliage, and had a number of small children on it.

The AGRICULTURAL DEPARTMENT, more than any other, was very largely represented in the parade. The Tuskgeee Institute recognizes the fact that 85% of the Negroes of the South are engaged in some form of agriculture and places great stress upon agricultural training. As evidence of this fact it may be stated that the school owns between 2,300 and 2,400 acres of land of which about 1,200 acres are under cultivation. The main crops cultivated are corn for ensilage and stover, oats, native hay, cowpeas, vetch, sugar cane and teosinte. Other crops, of course, are raised on a smaller scale for experimental and instruction purposes, including several varieties of cotton in the Experiment Station. Over 500 tons of silage have been stored away in four large silos for winter feeding and the forage is to be fed as roughage. The farm has over 160 acres in sweet potatoes. The large truck garden of some 98 acres raises vegetables not only to supply the school's needs but to send out daily two wagons to supply the teachers and families living near the school and to citizens in the town of Tuskegee. The dairy also sends out two wagons through the same communities, morning and afternoon, to supply milk and butter. There is an orchard of 7,000 trees and a canning factory operated by the students in which they put up much of the fruit raised for use in the boarding department of the Institute. In the dairy herd, cows, yearlings and calves total 430; the beef raising herd 305; horses, mules, etc., 133; hogs number 1,000, and the chickens, geese and ducks make up a total of 809 fowls.

After the parade had passed and the students and teachers and the crowd were repairing to the Chapel, the Presidential Party was driven hurriedly about the grounds, so as to afford some idea as to the extent and scope of same; then to the Chapel, where the students sang a number of plantation melodies. The singing was led by the Institute choir composed of 150 voices and heartily joined in by the whole student and teaching body. The President is a great lover of the old-time plantation melodies, and Tuskegee Institute has made a great feature of preserving these old-time folk-songs.

Principal Booker T. Washington presented the President in the following words:

"This is a great day for the Tuskegee Normal and Industrial Institute; too great to be described by words. We have gathered to hear but one voice; to see but one face.

"In presenting our guest to the students, teachers, and citizens, I must not omit to express the gratitude felt by the people of the

Tuskegee Institute, and by the people of both races in this section of Alabama, for the honor which has been conferred upon them.

"That the Chief Magistrate of our beloved Republic of 80,000,000 people deemed it good and wise to include Tuskegee Institute in his trip through the South, and spend a few hours in seeing the work we are doing here, brings to the heart of every man and woman of our race in this country, a degree of encouragement and inspiration which it is impossible for any American citizen, not of our race, fully to appreciate.

"My friends, without further words of mine, I have the pleasure and the honor of presenting to you the President of the United States, Hon. Theodore Roosevelt."

The President spoke as follows:

[The President's Speech will be supplied by the Associated Press, Scripps-McRae, and the New York Sun Press Associations on the morning of October 24, 1905.]

All of the main buildings of the school were decorated with the American and Institute colors — the latter, old gold and crimson — and various native grasses and vines intertwined. The decorations were a departure from the usual thing of the sort and attracted much attention. A series of arches, decorated with agricultural products raised by the school, studded the way beginning at the main entrance of the grounds to the Chapel, and under these arches the President and parade passed. From the reviewing stand the President was able to see five hundred yards away, the Chapel where he afterward spoke and the extensive sloping lawn in front of the building into which the Floricultural students had planted a bed of Coleus plants shaped to form a huge anchor and above it the name "Roosevelt" in different shades of the same plant.

From Montgomery, Mobile, and Opelika in Alabama; Columbus, Newnan, West Point, and La Grange in Georgia, and all nearby, hundreds of white and colored citizens came to see the parade and hear the President's address; after the visit to the town of Tuskegee most of those who had gathered there followed the President's Party to the Institute school grounds. On every side the President was greeted most enthusiastically.

PD Con. 16 BTW Papers DLC. This was an advance report prepared by E. J. Scott on Oct. 22, 1905, for release on Oct. 24.

An Address by Theodore Roosevelt[1]

[Tuskegee, Ala., Oct. 24, 1905]

To the white population as well as to the black, it is of the utmost importance that the Negro be encouraged to make himself a citizen of the highest type of usefulness. It is to the interest of the white people that this policy be conscientiously pursued, and to the interest of the colored people that they clearly realize that they have opportunities for economic development here in the South not now offered elsewhere. Within the last twenty years the industrial operations of the South have increased so tremendously that there is a scarcity of labor almost everywhere; so that it is the part of wisdom for all who wish the prosperity of the South to help the Negro to become in the highest degree useful to himself, and therefore to the community in which he lives. The South has always depended, and now depends, chiefly upon her own sons for her work. Therefore in view of the scarcity not only of common labor, but of skilled labor, it becomes doubly important to train every available man to be of the utmost use, by developing his intelligence, his skill, and his capacity for conscientious effort. Hence the work of the Tuskegee Normal and Industrial Institute is a matter of the highest practical importance to both the white man and the black man, and well worth the support of both races alike in the South and in the North. Your fifteen hundred students are not only being educated in head and heart, but also trained to industrial efficiency; for from the beginning Tuskegee has placed especial emphasis upon the training of men and women in agriculture, mechanics, and household duties. Training in these three fundamental directions does not embrace all that the Negro, or any other race, needs, but it does cover in a very large degree the field in which the Negro can at present do most for himself and be most helpful to his neighbors. Every black man who leaves this Institute better able to do mechanical or industrial work, adds so much to the wealth of the whole community, and benefits all people in the community. I am pleased, but not in the least surprised, to learn that many among the men and women trained at Tuskegee find immediate employment as leaders and workers among their own people, and that their services are eagerly sought by white people for various kinds of industrial work, the demand being much greater than the supply. Viewed from any angle, ignorance is the costliest crop that can be raised in any part of this Union. Every dollar put into the education of either white man or black man, in head, in hand, and in heart, yields rich dividends to the entire community. Merely from the economic standpoint it is of the utmost consequence to all our citizens that institutions such as this at Tuskegee should be a success. But there are other and even higher reasons that entitle it to our support.

In the interest of humanity, of justice, and of self-protection, every white man in America, no matter where he lives, should try to help the Negro to help himself. It is in the interest, and for the protection of the white man to see that the Negro is educated. It is not only the duty of the white man, but it is to his interest, to see that the Negro is protected in property, in life, and in all his legal rights. Every time a law is broken, every individual has the moral tone of his life lowered. Lawlessness in the United States is not confined to any one section; lynching is not confined to any one section; and there is perhaps no body of American citizens who have deserved well of the entire American people as the public men, the publicists, the clergymen, the countless thousands of high-minded private citizens, who have done such heroic work in the South in arousing public opinion against lawlessness in all its forms, and especially against lynchings. I very earnestly hope that their example will count in the North as well as in the South, for there are just as many great evils to be warred against in one region of the country as in another, though they are not in all places the same evils. And when any body of men in any community stands bravely for what is right, these men not merely serve a useful purpose in doing the particular task to which they set themselves, but give a lift to the cause of good citizenship throughout the Union. I heartily appreciate what you have done at Tuskegee; and I am sure you will not grudge my saying that it could not possibly have been done save for the loyal support you have received from the white people round about; for during the twenty-five years of effort to educate the black man here, in the midst of a white community of intelligence and culture, there has never been an outbreak between the races, or any difficulty of any kind. All honor is due to the white men of Alabama, to the white men of Tuskegee, for what they have done.

Hitherto I have spoken chiefly of the obligations existing on the part of the white man. Now let you remember on the other hand that no help can permanently avail you save as you yourselves develop capacity for self-help. You young colored men and women educated at Tuskegee must by precept and example lead your fellows toward sober, industrious, law-abiding lives. You are in honor bound to join hands in favor of law and order and to war against all crime, and especially against all crime by men of your own race; for the heaviest wrong done by the criminal is the wrong to his own race. If you save money, secure homes, become tax-payers, and lead clean, decent, modest lives, you will win the respect of your neighbors of both races. Let each man strive to excel his fellows, only by rendering substantial service to the community in which he lives. The colored people have many difficulties to pass through, but these difficulties will be surmounted if only the policy of reason and common sense is pursued. You have made real and great progress. According to the census the colored people of this country own and pay taxes upon something like three hundred million dollars worth of property, and have blotted out over fifty per cent. of their illiteracy. What you have done in the past is an indication of what you will be able to accomplish in the future under wise leadership. Moral and industrial education is what is most needed, in order that this progress may continue. The race cannot expect to get everything at once. It must learn to wait and bide its time; to prove itself worthy by showing its possession of perseverance, of thrift, of self-control. The destiny of the race is chiefly in its own hands, and must be worked out patiently and persistently along these lines. Remember also that the white man who can be of most use to the black man is that black man's neighbor. It is the southern people themselves who must and can solve the difficulties that exist in the South; of course what help the people of the rest of the Union can give them, must and will be cheerfully given. The hope of advancement for the colored man in the South lies in his steady, common sense effort to improve his moral and material condition, and to work in harmony with the white man in upbuilding the commonwealth. The future of the South now depends upon the people of both races living up to the spirit and letter of the laws of their several states, and working out the destinies of both races, not as races, but as law-abiding American citizens.

Tuskegee Student, 17 (Oct. 28, 1905), 1–2.

[1] Before Roosevelt began his formal address his preliminary remarks were stenographically recorded. He said: "Mr. Washington, and you, students and graduates of Tuskegee: You can't be as much inspired by any thing I may say as I have been inspired by what I have seen here.

"Mr. Washington, it is a liberal education just to come here and see this great focus of civilization. Now, I had read a good deal of your work. I believed in it with all my heart. I would not call myself a good American if I did not. I was prepared to see what would impress me and please me, but I had no idea that I would be so deeply impressed; so deeply pleased as I have been. I did not realize the extent of your work. I did not realize how much you were doing. I wish I had the time not merely to go around and see the buildings and the grounds, but to see the finished product outside as well. I would like to go around and see the homes that are being built up by those who leave this institution. I would like to see the effect in actual life, of the training here, and I do wish that some man with the gift of description, would come here and go out from here and visit the graduates in their homes, and see what they are doing, and describe it all. I think there could not be anything better than that, so as to show what is being done.

"And, as I say, Mr. Washington, while I have always stood for this institution, now that I have seen it, and realize as I never had realized by the descriptions of it, all that it means, I will stand for it more than ever.

"And, of course, Gentlemen, I would not come here today if Tuskegee only trained its citizens in intelligence, without morality: only trained them to be, or tried to train them to industrial efficiency without a corresponding training of character. It is because Tuskegee stands for the moral, as well as the mental and physical side of training, that I will do all I can to help Tuskegee. It is for that reason I have the right to appeal to every white man to stand by this institution." (*Tuskegee Student*, 17 [Oct. 28, 1905], 1.)

From Francis Jackson Garrison

Boston Oct. 24, 1905

Dear Mr. Washington: I am indebted to you for your several notes and enclosures. How in the world do you find time to keep hot so many irons in the fire, and with so many people and so many things to consider? The President's visit to Tuskegee would alone seem enough to keep you busy for weeks and here you are trying to ensure celebrations of the W. L. G. Centennial all over the country, and abroad as well. With reference to Great Britain, I doubt very much whether anyone there is likely to take it up. Of course, my father's contemporaries and co-workers are pretty much all gone, and the two or three survivors are too old to take the initiative in such matters. During his lifetime he was almost better known on the other side than here, and I presume that even to-day there are as many persons who have intelligent knowledge of him there as here. Still, there are no longer groups of such people, as there used to be in the old days, in different parts of the Kingdom.

I am glad to receive the copy of the speech which the President is to deliver this morning at Tuskegee, but must confess that it is just about what I expected of him. He seems to be a "past master" in uttering platitudes, and in trying to avoid expressing what is really in his thought. Instead of "white" and "black" he says "rich" and "poor," and he deals most carefully in generalities, without having the courage to say the specific word and dare the direct and searching rebuke. I say this, knowing, as I have said again and again, that you are on the crust of a seething volcano; and it is going to be a long time before the situation will be otherwise; but with all his boasted courage, and his exhortations to everyone to be brave and daring and "strenuous," we have had no man in public life more ready to make terms with the bosses, and give them the patronage which is the breath of life and sinews of war to them. It seems to me that the speech at Richmond, which I liked none too well, was better than the one at Tuskegee.

The confusion of the Philadelphia Press about the date of my father's birth is a natural one, since it so happens that for a short time he himself was confused by the erroneous entry in the Town Records of Newburyport, where the date is given as Dec. 12, 1804, but we have convincing evidence, in letters and the testimony of those who knew, that the real date was 1805, and Dec. 10 has always been celebrated as the day. Such biographical sketches as were written for cyclopaedias, etc. during the period of doubt and hesitation give the wrong date, and many accept it without referring to the authentic biographies. Mr. Grimké came to see me the other day about the selections, and I have a half-tone portrait of my father which he can use on the broadside if he makes it up in that form. I am returning the clippings you sent, and am, always, Faithfully and heartily yours,

F. J. Garrison

P.S. Of course it is a great thing to have had two Presidents of the U.S. visit Tuskegee, & such marks of personal & official interest count for much, & probably make the ground firmer for you.

TLS Con. 302 BTW Papers DLC.

From Francis Jackson Garrison

Boston Oct. 25, 1905

My dear Friend: This morning's paper gives the report of the President's impromptu speech at Tuskegee before he delivered his set address, and I wish to tell you that I am very glad he gave this heartfelt utterance, after seeing the notable display which you gave him in the industrial procession. Please understand, too, that I have no fault to find with the truisms which he uttered in his carefully prepared address, but what annoys me is that the outcries of the South about the White House incident have made him so timid that he could not break bread under your roof, and that he refrained from saying as warm a word of you personally as he ought to, and as he cherishes in his heart. He is too politic, and I for one cannot "carry water on both shoulders," and laud the captain of the privateering Alabama as equally worthy of glorification and admiration with Farragut and the heroes of the Union navy. His repetition of the cant assertion that the South must be left to solve the "problem" is already interpreted by the Southern press as a conversion to their claim that they must be let alone to disfranchise or do whatever they choose. See enclosed editorial from to-day's Boston *Herald*. Yours ever truly,

Francis J. Garrison

TLS Con. 302 BTW Papers DLC.

Samuel Laing Williams to Emmett Jay Scott

Chicago, Oct 31–1905

My Dear Scott Dr Washington with Fortune and Cox reached Chicago Eight Oclock Saturday night – about 4 hours late. I met them and after locating at the Palmer House we hurried to the 1st Armory where fully 5000 people were eagerly waiting. His entrance into the hall was the occasion of a most dramatic demonstration. The president could scarcely have evoked such enthusiasm. The vast concourse of people were fully repaid for their waiting. He never spoke more effectively, and I never saw an audience more responsive. At the conclusion the people surged forward and for nearly an hour he pumped his arms in shaking hands. No man in America has ever had such a hold on these people as B. T. The big men of the convention as well as the obscure layman alike joined in the demonstration of respect and honor.

On Sunday afternoon he spoke again in the same place to an audience quite as large. This was a new speech, bristling with new thoughts and new inspirations. The people acted as if they had not heard him the night before. After the address the people rose en masse – followed him to the door, with demonstrations of joy and pride and pursued him to the carriage that waited to hurry him away and showered up[on] him "God bless you" etc. It was all quite wonderful and unlike any thing I had ever seen before, though as you know I have seen and known much about the man. We spent the rest of the afternoon and until late at night at Dr Halls where we had an elaborate luncheon, conference and smoke.

Yesterday, we, that is B. T.[,] Fortune, Manning and I spent the day at Zion City. I cannot begin to convey to you how profitable and interesting this visit was. The presence of Dr W. on the grounds was soon noised about and he had the freedom of the City. We got back to the city about 6 p m. and they left for N.Y. about midnight. I have said this much about the Dr's visit because I am quite certain you would be pleased to have an outline of what was done.

Referring to the B. L. report, I got Davis report. It is the most complete thing I ever saw. Of course I shall have to cut it down about one half to keep our report from being too bulky. I shall send the matter to Mr Alexander this week. You can hold the membership list until the last and then send it direct to him. I have not yet received the Treasurer's report.

Max Barber spoke last night to about 30 people on the Sovereignty of Ideals. He must have felt some what disappointed because when it came to discussing his paper nearly everybody insisted that Industrial Education was the primal necessity. Truly yours

S Laing Williams

ALS Con. 31 BTW Papers DLC.

From Abram L. Grant

Kansas City, Kans. Nov. 1, 1905

My dear Friend: I have just reached Kansas City from Indianapolis and I write to say that it is believed there that the "Freeman" can be purchased for from $1000 to $1200.

I discussed the matter pretty thoroughly with Dr. Furniss and we have decided that if we can get four men to place $250 or $300 each, as the case may be, that we would purchase it provided we can get Prof. H. T. Kealing to edit it.

Dr. Furniss as well as myself, feels as if he would like to be a silent partner and I thought that you might desire to be a member, as we discussed the matter some time ago.[1]

I think that Prof. Kealing would join the number and that would make Dr. Furniss, Prof. Kealing, you, and myself.

Kindly inform me at an early date what you think of it. Faithfully,

A. Grant

TLS Con. 3 BTW Papers DLC.

1 BTW's reply, if any, was not found in the BTW Papers, and there is no evidence that he owned stock in the Indianapolis *Freeman*, either directly or indirectly.

From Harry Scythe Cummings

[Baltimore] Nov 8/05

Dear Dr Washington: Maryland has done herself proud.

The Poe Amendment has been defeated by nearly 25,000 majority and in the landslide we have elected our local ticket. We will control sufficient votes and more – in the legislature – to prevent the presentation of any peculiar measure to the people for at least two years.

Our colored voters did nobly all over the state. The work of the Suffrage League and its friends has borne good fruit. I cannot thank you too much for your interest in us and your practical assistance.[1]

I hope to see you soon when I can explain more fully the fight and its results.

With kindest wishes I am Sincerely Yours

Harry S. Cummings

ALS Con. 2 BTW Papers DLC.

[1] BTW had sent a small amount to aid the Maryland campaign against disfranchisement, in addition to an earlier sum toward printing and distributing pamphlets for the cause. (BTW to Cummings, Nov. 3, 1905, Con. 2, BTW Papers, DLC.)

An Item in the Washington *Post*

[Washington, D.C., Nov. 13, 1905]

BOOKER WASHINGTON'S OVERCOAT

Far be it from us to tamper with Secretary Loeb's delicate yet trenchant witticism in connection with the Hengelmuller-Washington incident. We leave that gem to sparkle by itself, and even our admiration is leveled at it from a carefully and reverently measured distance, but the Hengelmuller-Washington incident may still be discussed from another point of view, and a very important one, without invading the hallowed arena of jeu d'esprit aphorism, and all that sort of thing. On this understanding, and with all rights reserved, we gently but firmly bulge in.

The matter of chief interest with us is the rabbit's foot which the Austrian Ambassador found in the pocket of Hon. Booker Washington's overcoat. Everybody knows, of course, so it need not be explained at length, that his excellency, Mr. Hengelmuller, and Prof. Booker Washington, head of the famous negro college at Tuskegee, Ala., happened to visit President Roosevelt on the same day and at about the same hour. The Ambassador escaped first and, in the hurry of his craving for fresh air, took Prof. Booker Washington's overcoat in mistake for his own. As he passed down the asphalt semi-circle, reveling in the peace and the serenity of the surroundings, he reached for a pair of gloves and, after dragging the deep Charybdis of the pocket, rose to the surface with a rabbit's foot. No gloves — just the left hind foot of a graveyard rabbit, killed in the dark of the moon.

Evidently the overcoat was not his. There had been a mistake. The garment was fine, expensive, fashionable, as became a wearer who moved in the very highest and most exclusive circles. It distilled the unmistakable aroma of the select. It fairly smelled of aristocracy. Nevertheless, it did not belong to Mr. Hengelmuller, so he turned back to the White House, made the exchange, got his own clothes, and heroically relinquished the rabbit's foot. The episode has terminated without international heartburnings or forebodings. The Austrian Ambassador recovers his overcoat and gloves, while the Hon. Booker Washington does not know — at least, until this moment — that he was ever in danger of losing his rabbit's foot.[1]

All's well that ends well. The cloud has passed, and the orb of glory follows its bright pathway unobscured by envy and contention.

Washington *Post*, Nov. 13, 1905, 6.

1 The rabbit's foot may have been an invention of the *Post* reporter, for some other newspaper accounts did not mention it. The Detroit *Journal* commented: "The Austrian ambassador may have made off with Booker T. Washington's coat at the White House, but he'd have a bad time trying to fill his shoes." (Nov. 14, 1905, Clipping, Con. 1042, BTW Papers, DLC.)

A Report of Pinkerton's National Detective Agency

St. Louis, Mo., Tuesday, Nov. 14, 1905

Dear Sir: Operative J. F. P. reports:

At 6:20 P.M. accompanied by Supt. H. W. M.[1] I went to Union Station for the purpose of meeting Mr. Booker T. Washington and party; said party was supposed to be due in St. Louis at 6:40 P.M. arriving on Big Four Ry. I was instructed by Supt. H. W. M. to accompany Mr. Washington on tour through the south and west for the purpose of protecting him from deeds of violence, should any such things occur.

Supt. H. W. M. and I met the 6:40 P.M. Big Four train; the 7:10 Vandalia train; the 9:40 P.M. Vandalia train and the 9:45 Big Four train, which was late and arrived at 11:05 P.M. Mr. Washington and party did not arrive on any of above named trains.

At 10:30 P.M. while in Union Station we observed two colored gentlemen enter station who appeared to be men of refinement and education and we thought probably one of Mr. Washington's party. Supt. H. W. M. followed the two gentlemen into the Union Station dining room and quietly interviewed one of them who stated that he was Bishop Grant of Kansas City. Mr. Grant stated that the Washington party had arrived in St. Louis at 2:00 P.M. to-day and had left for Little Rock at 8:40 P.M. via the St. L. I. M. & S. Ry; that he had met Mr. Washington and party in St. Louis during the afternoon.

Supt. H. W. M. then instructed me to take the first train to Little Rock and report to Mr. Cox, Secretary to Mr. Washington.

The mistake in our not meeting said party was due to an improperly sent telegram from New York; this telegram advised the St. Louis office to look out for a second telegram which would follow.

In addition to meeting trains mentioned we made one trip at 7:30 P.M. to the Western Union and Postal Telegraph offices to inquire for telegrams also called up telegraph offices at 10:00 P.M. but no wire had arrived.

I then purchased ticket via St. L. I. M. & S. Ry. for Little Rock and procuring a sleeper berth retired at 11:30 P.M. This train due to leave for Little Rock at 3:00 A.M. in the morning.[2] Yours respectfully,

Pinkerton's National Detective Agency,
By Wm. A. Pinkerton

TLSr Con. 4 BTW Papers DLC.

[1] H. W. Minster, resident superintendent in St. Louis.

[2] In subsequent reports, operative J. F. P. described his joining BTW's party in Little Rock; the journey to Pine Bluff, where BTW made three speeches; an address at the Overholser Opera House in Oklahoma City, and opera houses in Guthrie and South McAlester, Okla.; a reception and banquet given by the black citizens of Muskogee, Okla.; a speech at the Grand Opera House and a banquet at Joshenberger Hall in Fort Smith, Ark.; and accompanying BTW as far as Birmingham. He reported no unusual behavior. (Reports dated Nov. 16, 18, 19, 20, 21, 22, 23, 24, 25, 1905, Con. 4, BTW Papers, DLC.)

To Theodore Roosevelt

[Little Rock, Ark.] November 15, 1905

My dear Mr. President: This note will be handed you by Mr. S. Laing Williams of Chicago.

I find that Mr. Williams hesitates to accept the Consulship at Bahia which you have so kindly offered him, because of financial reasons and because he thinks he can be of much more service in this country. He does not wish to accept the place unless you are perfectly sure he cannot receive the Registership, or some similar place in the near future.

I really wish you could see your way clear to give him a position in Washington, that no colored man has before held, if you cannot give him the Registership.

This would help matters much at this time. Under President Garfield, Major John R. Lynch was Fourth Auditor of the Treasury.

But the main thing I want to urge you to consider is that Mr. Williams is one of the few colored men I have relied on to help create public sentiment among the colored people in the direction you and I believe in. It would be of immense benefit if Williams could be placed in Washington, where he could mold sentiment in the Negro press in the direction of holding up our hands. The Fortune Editorial shows how it is possible for matters to go wrong when wise men are not on guard. Very truly yours,

Booker T. Washington

TLdSr Con. 5 BTW Papers DLC.

An Account by Emmett Jay Scott of a Speech in Little Rock

Little Rock, Ark., Nov. 15. [1905]

Booker T. Washington spoke in the Opera House here this afternoon to an audience of three thousand people, composed of whites and blacks. In many respects it was one of the most remarkable meetings of colored and white people ever held in the South. The meeting had been widely advertised and people from the whole countryside had come into town to see and hear "the Sage of Tuskegee," as the colored orators love to call him. His visit was made the occasion of a public holiday by the Negro people of this region. Thousands of them tried in vain to get into the theatre this afternoon.

The meeting today was the first of a series of such meetings which Mr. Washington expects to hold in the interest of Negro people during the next ten days. During his trip, which covers Arkansas, Oklahoma and Indian territories, Mr. Washington will visit a region in which it is said the Negro people have made more progress in securing social and economic independence than they have anywhere else in this country. It is Mr. Washington's first visit to this region. He has come here upon the urgent request of the local Business League, of which Hon. John E. Bush,[1] receiver of United States lands, is the head.

According to the last census, Little Rock had a population of 38,000, of which 13,000 were colored. A recent article in the Arkansas Democrat says that 1300 Negro citizens of Little Rock own their homes. They pay taxes on $1,600,000 worth of property. Three years ago there was established in this city the first Negro bank in this part of the country, the Capitol City Savings Bank. The president of this bank is Hon. Mifflin Wistar Gibbs, formerly a judge in the Municipal Court here. Mr. Gibbs was born in Philadelphia, was a friend of Garrison, and played a prominent part in the anti-slavery agitation of half a century ago. In 1850 he went to California, was engaged for a time in mining in British America, where he studied law under an English barrister, returned to the United States and was admitted to practice at the bar. His last public office was that of United States consul to Tamatave, Madagascar. Mr. Gibbs is one of the wealthy men of the city. He owns several brick blocks in the heart of the city and other real estate. He has recently written an autobiography which gives many interesting details in the history of the Negro people, both before and after the war of secession.

In the schools of this city the colored people seem to be exceptionally well cared for. There are twenty-nine colored teachers in the schools here and four institutions of higher learning conducted by the Baptist and Methodist denominations. One of these schools, the Williams Industrial School, is conducted by the Southern Methodist Church. That and Shorter College, which Mr. Washington and his party visited this afternoon, were established two years ago. In addition to these there is the Arkansas Baptist College, supported by the colored Baptists, and the Philander Smith College which is supported by the Methodist Church North. These latter two colleges were established some twenty years ago.

In the course of his address this afternoon Mr. Washington said:

"A people without food must be taught how to grow food; a people without homes must be taught how to build homes, and a people without the proper method of living must be taught how to live. In the matter of labor, there is little or no opposition of prejudice to the Negro laborer in the South, and it is my greatest concern that the people take advantage of their opportunities. November and December are particularly the months of danger for a large number of our people in the South. These are the months when we are tempted to scatter to the winds, for gewgaws and things we can do without, the hard earnings we have gathered during the year. The money which will be thrown away during the next few months would keep a family in comfort for many, many months.

"It should be so that no matter how much property or how much education one may have, unless there is beneath it all a strong moral structure, all the property and education will avail nothing. We must learn to draw the line between the good and the bad, between the virtuous and the vicious. We should set such a high standard of living that no matter whether it be a teacher, minister or any leader of our people, if they led an immoral life they should not have the esteem and confidence of our people. We should lay especial emphasis upon the protection of the purity and uprightness of our women. In too many communities the idea prevails that our people mingle together, whether they be proper or improper persons. The standard should be set high, and these opinions corrected.

"We sometimes grow discouraged and despondent because of our condition in this country. In Russia there are one-half as many Jews as there are Negroes in this country, and yet I feel sure that within a month more Jews have been persecuted and killed than the whole number of our people who have been lynched during the past forty years, but this, of course, is no excuse for lynching.

"I have always, in every part of this country, North and South, in all my utterances tried to convince all that it is to the best interests of our race that we continually cultivate the spirit of friendship between the races here in the South. I repeat here what I have said, that we should secure and hold in every honorable way the friendship of the man who is to live by our side.

"Ignorance and race hatred never solved a single problem, or helped forward the interests of a race anywhere in the world. The best and most useful colored men are those who cherish the least racial hatred. The white man who is most esteemed and most respected in his community is the one who is broad and generous to all races.

"A spirit of race hatred will degrade and narrow us as a people. The spirit of love, sympathy and helpfulness strengthens and promotes lasting peace and prosperity between both races, both here and throughout the country."

At the conclusion of the address there was a remarkable demonstration. The things which Mr. Washington said, familiar as they are in general to most people in the North, were new here, and made a great impression. Whites and blacks crowded indiscriminately to the platform to press the speaker's hand, and to express their appreciation of his words.

E. J. S.

Boston *Evening Transcript,* Dec. 4, 1905, 5.

[1] John E. Bush (b. 1858) was apprenticed to a brickmaker at the age of fifteen, taught a country school briefly, and from 1875 to 1882 was a postal clerk. With C. W. Keatts he founded the National Order of Mosaic Templars of America in 1882. The benevolent and fraternal order spread throughout the South, attaining a membership of 20,000 in 1907. This organization enhanced Bush's influence among blacks all over the country. From 1898 to 1913 he was receiver of public monies in the U.S. Land Office in Little Rock. He was elected vice-president of the NNBL in 1913, and was the principal lieutenant of the Tuskegee Machine for Arkansas.

To Robert Curtis Ogden

[Pine Bluff, Ark.] November 16, 1905

Dear Mr. Ogden: I am sending you marked copies of Little Rock, Ark. papers giving an account of my first meeting. I have never had, anywhere in the South, such a cordial reception from whites and blacks as I have had in this state.

I witnessed the rather unique sight of the colored people refusing seats, for the want of room, to white people. The meeting was held in the Opera House and besides it being filled, several thousand were turned away.

The main thing I am writing to say is the more I come into contact with the people of the South, the more I am convinced, judging by my experience here, that the demagogue, like Jeff Davis[1] and the radical press are fast losing their hold upon a certain class of the Southern white people. And the character of the work which you are doing has helped the situation very much.

I am to deliver two addresses in state then I go to the Indian and Oklahoma Territories for two more meetings in each Territory.

I am using some portion of the money given me by the Southern Education Board in connection with the trip, though the railroads have been most kind in providing transportation and a special coach for part of the way. Very truly yours,

[Booker T. Washington]

TLc Con. 30 BTW Papers DLC.

[1] Jeff Davis (1862–1913) was the governor of Arkansas from 1901 to 1906. He was U.S. senator from 1907 until his death.

From Wilford H. Smith

New York November 18th, 1905

My dear Mr. Washington: I am writing you at the suggestion of Mr. Fortune, to say that he is very anxious to dispose of his interest in the New York Age. He has plans, he says, to take up farming in Florida, and wishes to get his matters in shape as early as possible so that he can leave the metropolis. He feels that he ought to realize about $6,000 for his interest. He wishes me to offer it to you first, and if you cannot arrange some way to purchase it, he will then seek a purchaser elsewhere, and hints that the other party might be unfriendly to your interests. You know Mr. Fortune very well, and can understand what all of this means. I promised him that I would lay the matter before you, and I am keeping my promise.

If you conclude to enter into any negotiations for his interest, I will be very glad to conduct the same for you.

I am corresponding with the Commissioner of Corporations at Washington, with a view of ascertaining whether or not we can incorporate the National Negro Business League through this Department.

As soon as I get definite information, I will inform you. Very truly yours,

Wilford H. Smith

P.S. Mr Moore suggests that you should not correspond with Mr F. about the matter but attend to it when you come.

S.

TLS Con. 881 BTW Papers DLC.

November · 1905

An Article in *The Independent*

[Nov. 23, 1905]

Negro Self-Help

From time to time in the past a great deal of matter has been furnished to the public, with the praiseworthy purpose of portraying the individual struggles and sacrifices of colored youths to secure an education. These efforts of struggling young men and women, with no inspiration in family tradition and fortune, and with little or no money with which to secure the knowledge they crave, is one of the most encouraging as well as pathetic features I have come across in my educational work during the past twenty years. As a hopeful indication of race character, and I may safely so describe it, it must be of peculiar interest to the average American interested in the Negro people.

On the other hand, much matter has also been furnished the public concerning the aid given the Negro race by philanthropic white people; attention is also frequently directed to the volume of money expended for the education of the Negro by State and municipal governments, the proceeds of land grants funds and of common taxation.

I do not think that the public has been sufficiently informed of what the Negro himself has been doing during the past forty years, and is doing now, toward his own education thru the religious organizations controlled by him.

Before dwelling upon this principal point, however, I wish to direct attention here to several minor ways of more or less importance in which the Negro is constantly displaying the quality of self-help — the most important and significant force in the uplift of any person or race, the absence of which must always be regarded as a fatal defect of character.

First, then, it is well to say that there are very few orphan asylums anywhere for Negro children. Possibly in nine or ten cases Negro families care for the orphans of their race in the neighborhoods where they reside. A child is not left many hours without parents before it strays into some family, or, more often, is sought out by some friend, and, without legal formality, soon becomes a real part of the family. Because of this custom one finds very little suffering among Negro children. In the Southern States the masses know little about hospitals. The sick and unfortunate are cared for by secret and fraternal societies, by the churches or by individuals. A second form of self-help, which is increasing year by year, is the voluntary taxation of Negro communities for the purpose of extending the public school term, often from one to three months; that is, these months are added to the regular public school term.

I could name other forms of self-help that are equally significant and praiseworthy.

But to return to the main point. Of the more than eight millions of colored people in the United States, it is estimated that two-thirds of the adults are members of some church. The great body of them are either members of the Baptist Church, or of some branch of the Methodist Church. The Methodists are divided into four groups or branches, namely: the African Methodist Episcopal, the A. M. E. Zion, the Colored Methodist, and those belonging to the main body of the Northern Methodist Church. Besides, in all the Southern States, and in some States outside of the South, there are Presbyterian, Congregational and Episcopal churches, and a few other denominations — including Catholics — not under the Methodist or Baptist groups, all contributing something toward the expenses of the schools and colleges.

The plan for securing money from the colored people thru their churches varies according to the location and conditions surrounding the people, as well as the customs and laws of the church. For example, in the case of the Baptists, there is at least one institution, usually called college or university, in each Southern State, supported in part or in whole by the pennies and dollars of the masses. In Alabama, for illustration, there is what is known as the Alabama Baptist Colored University, at Selma. Last year the colored people in Alabama contributed to the work of this institution $9,441.93, exclusive of student board and tuition. The property is owned by colored people; their money created it, with the exception of a few gifts from outside sources. There is at least one such school in each of the Southern States. The detailed circumstances surrounding them may vary, but the general plan is the same.

In the case of the African Methodist Episcopal Church, there are institutions that owe their existence almost wholly to the small gifts of the churches and individuals of the denomination. Last year $51,601.86 was raised by this denomination for the purposes of education. The oldest and largest of these institutions is the Wilberforce University, at Wilberforce, O. Altho this institution is now somewhat generously assisted by the State of Ohio, it was for years supported almost wholly by the colored people.

Let me use another illustration as showing what the African Methodist Episcopal Church is doing in the South. There is a school in Atlanta, Ga., called Morris Brown College, that was organized only a few years ago. It now owns a very valuable property and has a large student body. The college was built and is supported, to a large extent, by money raised by the church membership. For 1904 the institution received from all sources for running expenses, $15,985.58, of which the churches in that connection in the State of Georgia contributed $6,200, the third Sunday in September being set apart for the taking of offerings for the educational work; and $850.50 was raised thru the industrial department. The remainder was contributed thru other channels of the church, and mostly all of it by Negro people.

The African Methodist Episcopal Zion Church has ten institutions of learning, of which Livingstone College, at Salisbury, N.C., is the most important. The Corresponding Secretary of Education of the Zion Church reports that the money collected last year amounted to $20,706.54, which went to all the schools of the church to supplement their other revenues for running purposes.

Thru the Freedmen's Aid and Southern Education Society of the Methodist Episcopal Church, the colored membership contributed for education for the current year, $19,251.73. For the ten years, 1896–1905, inclusive, $79,228.13 was contributed.

The Negro Baptists support quite a number of educational institutions, and to carry on the work the churches raised during the past year $85,888.18.

To sum up, we find that the A. M. E. Church contributed $51,601.86 for educational purposes last year; the A. M. E. Zion Church, $20,706.54; the Colored Methodist Episcopal Church, $45,000; the Methodist Episcopal, $15,926.40; the Baptists, $85,-888.18; making the total, $218,622.98, for only two branches of the Christian Church. If the contributions of the Negro Congregationalists, Presbyterians and Espiscopalians, etc., be approximated, we should have probably an annual contribution for educational purposes by the Negro Christians of $250,000.

Within the past ten years, it is safe to say, according to these figures, that the Negro in America has contributed at least $2,000,000 thru his churches toward his own education. This, I think, all fair-minded people will agree, is a pretty good record for a race of people which was in slavery forty years ago. And these figures, of course, do not include the amounts which colored people are contributing constantly to local and independent institutions. The Tuskegee Institute, for example, receives contributions from colored people annually, and the same is true of other institutions which have no direct church connection.

Independent, 59 (Nov. 23, 1905), 1207–8.

To Wilford H. Smith

[Tuskegee, Ala.] Nov. 25, 1905

My dear Mr. Smith: I have your letter. Permit me to say that I do not own a single dollar's worth of interest in any colored publication in this country. It has been my uniform practice not to invest a dollar in such enterprises and I can see no reason for departing from my rule in the case you mention; neither should I do so under a threat, either implied or direct, that the interest would pass into unfriendly hands.

I hope by the time I reach New York, which will be early in December, that you and Mr. Moore will have the matter of the incorporation of the League well worked out. Also tell Mr. Moore to have plans laid out for work as we must begin active operations in December or January 1st. Yours truly,

Booker T. Washington

TLpS Con. 881 BTW Papers DLC.

To Francis Jackson Garrison

Tuskegee Institute, Alabama. Nov. 25, 1905

My dear Mr. Garrison: I have just returned from a two weeks trip through the state of Arkansas, Indian Territory and Oklahoma. I went to the latter two territories especially with a view of looking into the condition of our people who have recently moved there from the South, and also to see something of the condition of the colored people in the Indian Territory who were classed as Indians, or who were at one time slaves of the Indians.

At every point where I spoke, the meetings were large and most enthusiastic. I am not writing, however, to tell you about the meetings except in one direction. The more I have actual contact with the masses of the white people in the South, the more I am seeing that the graphical newspapers and the demagogues are losing their hold of a large element of Southern white men and women. As you know, there has been a good deal of bitterness heard of Arkansas of recent years. In spite of the fact that Gov. Jeff Davis has done everything in his power to keep the feeling of race hatred stirred up, and I understand on several occasions he has spoken of me in the most bitter terms, the white people came out to the meetings in such large numbers at the three points where I spoke, Little Rock, Pine Bluff and Fort Smith, that the colored people had to refuse in two cases admission to a large number of white people on account of saving space for the colored people for whom the meetings, of course, were held. Two points confirm the view of the case that I have expressed. In Little Rock the man[1] who is opposing Jeff Davis for the office of governor and U.S. senator came aboard my train and in full view of a large number of people who stood upon the platform, cordially shook hands with me and thanked me for coming into the state and for what I said. In Pine Bluff, in the heart of the Black Belt of Arkansas, one daily newspaper said the day previous to my going there that no white man who respected himself ought to attend the meeting, and threatened to see that any white man who did attend the meeting was ostracized. I spoke about two o'clock in the afternoon. I gave out copies of my address to the newspapers as I usually do. Both newspapers gave practically no attention to the meeting in the afternoon; one told the man who took my speech to him that he did not expect to give the meeting any notice until he found out how public sentiment was going. The next afternoon the paper that was most bitter published an account of the meeting occupying four columns.

At the Pine Bluff meeting the mayor of the city presided, and I think spoke as well and as boldly as any man would have done in Boston. He pointed to a prominent colored man who sat upon the platform while he was introducing me, and said to the audience that though he might be criticised by the newspapers, he wanted to say that he would rather see that colored man U.S. Marshal for Arkansas than the majority of the white men who are applying for that position.

Another element in the trip that surprised me was the courteous manner in which the railroads treated me and the party of seven or eight colored men who were with me. They furnished us special coaches and free transportation from beginning to end.

I shall hope to see you when I am in Boston in December. Yours very truly,

Booker T. Washington

TLS Francis Jackson Garrison Papers NN-Sc. A press copy is in Con. 876, BTW Papers, DLC.

[1] James Henderson Berry (1841–1913) ran against Jeff Davis in the Democratic primary of March 1906 for the nomination to the U.S. Senate.

A Statement for *The Voice of the Negro*

[Tuskegee, Ala., Nov. 27, 1905]

During President Roosevelt's visit to the South he did not change his position on a single vital question in reference to our race or in reference to the North. Notwithstanding he made no change in the South, he was received most enthusiastically, even more so than was President McKinley, by all in the South.

The great lesson, it seems to me, to be learned from this incident is that if an individual maps out his course and sticks to it when he is right, the people will come to him. The rebuke that [the] President gave a certain governor who attempted to defend lynching was worth his whole Southern trip. No other President has ever spoken so bravely and strongly while in the South.

At Tuskegee he uttered the following words: "In the interest of humanity, of justice, and of self-protection, every white man in America, no matter where he lives, should try to help the Negro to help himself. It is in the interest, and for the protection of the white man to see that the Negro is educated. It is not only the duty of the white man, but it is to his interest to see that the Negro is protected in property, in life, and in all his legal rights."

At Little Rock he said: "The horrible effects of lynch law are shown in the fact that three-fourths of the lynchings are not for that crime at all, but for other crimes. And above all other men, Governor, you and I, and all who are exponents and representatives of the law, owe it to our people, owe it to the cause of civilization and humanity, to do everything in our power, officially and unofficially, directly and indirectly, to free the United States from the menace and reproach of lynch law."

These words should leave no doubt as to where the President stands on the question of the Negro's legal rights and as to the question of lynching.

TM Con. 27 BTW Papers DLC. Enclosed in a letter to J. Max Barber, Nov. 27, 1905.

To George Eastman

[Tuskegee, Ala.] Nov. 28, 1905

My dear Sir: You do not know how very grateful we are to you for your generous and unexpected gift to the school. You cannot realize how much it helps us and how much additional good it will permit us to accomplish.

In regard to the photographic outfit, I will say that we shall write you in a few days as soon as we get a little more definite information in regard to what we desire.

In a general way I would say that I very much wish we could have a department at this school for teaching photography. We could not only use the department in much of our work here to advantage, but we could train students who would go out and establish galleries in different parts of the South. While there is prejudice in many directions in the matter of photography, strange to say, a colored man would have almost as good opportunity to succeed as a white man; in fact, there are a number of colored men in the South who are succeeding in photography. Yours truly,

Booker T. Washington

TLpS Con. 716 BTW Papers DLC.

To Charles Allmond Wickersham[1]

[Tuskegee, Ala.] Nov. 29, 1905

Personal and Confidential

My dear Sir: There is a matter that I have for some time hesitated to speak to you about. I am doing so now because I feel that you will not misunderstand me.

I am not by any means foolishly sensitive over conditions so far as they relate to my race in the South. There are certain conditions that we cannot change by complaint, but I feel that you will agree with me that wherever matters can be improved that it is the best for both races that it be done.

I am referring especially to the conditions under which colored people have to ride on your road, and of course yours is not the only one of which this is true.

One point of constant complaint and source of bitterness on the part of a good many colored people is in the way the colored car is arranged. For example, at Montgomery a colored woman has to pass through the smoking car occupied by white men, which is disagreeable to many colored women. Aside from this, the door between the smoking car and the colored people's car is frequently open and makes one feel that he is riding in the end of a smoking car instead of in the regular coach.

Another source of complaint is in the fact that the newsboy has all of his things in the colored car, and sometimes occupies as many as four seats, as was true when I came from Montgomery only a few days ago.

I wonder if it would be possible, without extra cost to the railroads, to provide a coach for colored people with a small smoking room in it and the same thing for white people? That would get rid, I think of all complaints. I do not, however, want you to understand that I am making any complaint against the conductors or any one connected with your road, because in all my travel I have never seen a more kindly and obliging set of conductors than you have on your road.

I hope you will at least, give the matter whatever attention you feel that it calls for. Yours very truly,

Booker T. Washington

TLpS Con. 880 BTW Papers DLC.

[1] Charles Allmond Wickersham (1860–1949) rose from telegraph operator and dispatcher to become president and general manager of the Atlanta and West Point Railroad Co. and the Western Railway of Alabama by 1900. In 1913 he was also the general manager of the Georgia Railroad. These three positions Wickersham held continuously until his retirement in 1947. He was, in addition, the president and director of several smaller roads: the Augusta & Summerville, the Augusta Belt, the Milledgeville, the Monroe, the Lexington Terminal, and the Elberton & Eastern. Beginning in the 1920s, Wickersham broadened his business interests to include directorships of the Coca Cola Co., the Coca Cola International Corp., the Trust Company of Georgia, and the Atlantic Steel Co. In the 1940s he served as a trustee of Tuskegee Institute.

From Jesse Max Barber

Atlanta, Ga. November 29, 1905

Dear Dr. Washington: Your kind communication of November 27th with your statement of opinion concerning the President's Southern trip is to hand. I wish to thank you for your kindness.

I regret very much that you cannot find time to prepare an article for the January issue of our Magazine. As I wrote Mr. Scott sometime ago, we are getting up a special issue of the Magazine for January on several subjects that bear vitally upon the race question in the South. For instance, there will be articles on "The Negro's Attitude towards Social Equality"; "By What Name shall we call Our Race"; "The Negro's Progress for 1905" and "The Negro's Program for 1906." Prof. Wm. Pickens and Mr. Charles W. Chesnutt are to write on Social Equality. Dr. Bowen will give us a contributed article on what name the Negro race should be called. Professors W. S. Scarborough and Kelly Miller will write on "The Negro's Program for 1906." Dr. W. E. B. Du Bois is to write on the Niagara Movement. He will recommend that the united support of the race be given to this Movement. We are very anxious to have a consensus of opinion from the leading thinkers of the race on the proper attitude the Negro should exercise towards educational questions, towards property getting, towards political affairs and towards national racial organizations. We want to give all sides free scope in our Magazine to discuss the questions we have just named. It is not our desire — and never has been — to appear one-sided and narrow. Of course, if the press of business is so great that you will not have time to prepare the article, we will have to state to the public that you were invited, but were not able to give us the article because of pressing duties, but we very much prefer that you give us an article, although it be ever so brief. Yours very truly,

J. Max Barber

TLS Con. 27 BTW Papers DLC.

To Jesse Max Barber

[Tuskegee, Ala.] Dec. 1, 1905

Dear Mr. Barber: Your letter has been received. I regret very much that I was not able to send you more than an appreciative statement regarding the President's visit. The fact is that I must fulfill some of my back promises in the way of articles before I attempt to make new pledges. I am under obligation for articles long since promised to several magazines, and besides, am under promise to write one or two books which have not been finished. Aside from all this, I have to raise money each month to pay the salaries of 151 officers and teachers. Aside from looking after the executive work of this institution, I have to raise over $200,000 each year. This, with the numerous calls to serve the public in any number of ways, makes it almost impossible for me to do all that my heart would lead me to do in the way of furnishing contributions to such publications as yours. Yours truly,

Booker T. Washington

P.S. You speak of making some statements regarding my not writing an article; this, it seems to me is unusual for a magazine of your character. It is perfectly right to discuss an article that I have written but quite unusual to discuss an article that I have not written.

B. T. W.

TLpS Con. 27 BTW Papers DLC.

To Francis Jackson Garrison

[Tuskegee, Ala.] Dec. 2, 1905

Dear Mr. Garrison: Yours of November 28th is received. I am very glad indeed that you are pleased with the preparations now going forward for the celebration of your father's anniversary. As I wrote you this morning, I am now more and more encouraged at the new evidences of interest not only on the part of colored people but on the part of the whites. I know of few churches anywhere in the country among our people where they are not going to observe the anniversary. I had no idea that it would be so uniformly taken up.

In regard to Mr. Trotter, I would say that his case is almost a pathetic one. I have refused to give him any attention whatever. How any man with even common decency could attempt to drag such a sacred cause as the celebration of your father's anniversary into the mire and mud as he is trying to do is past my understanding. Certainly there was no excuse for anybody trying to create a disturbance or differ over such a matter. However much we may differ about means and methods of work, there was no excuse for any difference on this topic. Trotter's case, however, is not the saddest; I am more and more convinced that Du Bois is behind him and using him as a tool to keep up this dirty work. But the main thing is the proper celebration, and that I am sure will be successful. Yours truly,

Booker T. Washington

TLpS Con. 876 BTW Papers DLC.

A Sunday Evening Talk

Tuskegee Institute, Alabama, December 2, 1905

The Survival of the Fittest

You will recall that Mr. Fortune, in speaking to you a few evenings ago, quoted the passage of Scripture which runs something like this: "To him that hath shall be given, and from him that hath not shall be taken even that which he hath." Now, that suggests a principle which I am very anxious to have all of you seize hold upon, and not only get it into your minds and hearts, but to have you as far as possible, carry with you into your actual, practical lives, after you leave Tuskegee. You will have to realize, more and more, that neither our previous condition, attracting, as it may have, sympathy and pity in the past, nor our color, will help us forward in any appreciable degree. We must appreciate the fact that we must face real life, and that we are to rise or fall, succeed or fail, just in proportion as we show ourselves worthy, and in life's contest sympathy is going to play a very minor part. Let us take an example in the physical world: you will learn as you go out into life that people must either develop the territory that they occupy or move on and let some other more thrifty portion of the human family enter into and occupy that territory. I repeat that unless the people have within themselves the ability to get all there is out of the territory they are occupying; unless they have the ability to get out of the soil the most there is in it, they have got to move on and somebody else, more thrifty, more provident, will come forward to occupy their land, whether it happens to be large or small; and you will find that no law, whether passed by local, state, or Federal authority, can help any people that does not have within itself the power of self-help; the power to incorporate itself into the civilization about it, and go forward. Let me illustrate: you will find that if a weak man, or a number of weak people, own a piece of land, however small, in a growing town or city, unless these petty landowners (and you have seen it illustrated over and over again) have within themselves the power to get something out of that little piece of land; unless they have intelligence enough to keep up with the growth and progress of civilization about them, they will find that in a few months or years at most, they will have to give up their land; will have to give up the town lot, for example, because they have not shown the ability to get enough out of the land to pay the increasing taxes, and compete with the life that is about them. The same truth will hold with regard to farm land, whether it be in Mississippi, Alabama, or elsewhere, the people — their color matters not — who occupy the farm land of Alabama today, unless they are able to get the very most out of the land they may hold, will have to yield to others, perhaps to people from a foreign land, who possess greater capacity and skill, and the land they have occupied will pass into the hands of those who have more ability to get out of the soil more than the people who held it formerly. Let me repeat, no part of the earth will remain idle: the present progressing, pushing stage of civilization demands that no part of the earth shall remain for any length of time idle, or only partially worked; it demands that every inch of land shall be brought to the very highest degree of development.

A few days ago a number of us were out in the Indian Territories, a country which a number of years ago was set aside for the Indians. All kinds of stringent laws were passed for the protection of the land and the tribes, and if it had been possible for law of any kind to protect people; if law could insure growth the Indians would have remained in possession of the rich territory, into possession of which they were placed some fifty or sixty years ago. They squatted upon that land, were given possession of it, but were not able to develop it; they did not appreciate its mineral or agricultural resources, or use the streams of water to any extent; the result was that civilization has forced these people to the rear. More enterprising spirits have gone into that rich but undeveloped country and the Indian has been left behind, notwithstanding the numerous laws that were passed for his protection. And so it will always be: the people who own land must bring it to its highest development, or they must move on and let others possess themselves of their territory.

We have the same truth illustrated in the case of San Domingo. If you have not studied the history and present condition of San Domingo, I wish very much you would do so as soon as possible. There is one of the richest countries in the world, rich in agricultural, mineral and water resources; rich in everything that is essential to the maintenance of a high degree of civilization. Today San Domingo, with all its wealth, and the freedom that exists there — and we sometimes say that the colored man in this country is in his present condition because he has not freedom — with all the freedom any people can possess, all the political power that can be given to a people is, notwithstanding political and social freedom, in a deplorable condition today. That country is practically in the hands of the United States. The United States collects its revenues, pays out its revenues. The country has practically lost its civilization, because the people have failed to get anything out of the soil — have failed to develop its mineral resources: failed to work its iron and gold mines. The result is that the country has been spending every year more than it has been earning. It has been paying out more for imports than it has been receiving for exports, and the same is true with a nation as with an individual, when spending power exceeds earning power the individual or nation goes into bankruptcy. Unless the educated men of San Domingo are wise enough to put their education into agricultural, mining and other fundamental industries, you will find that San Domingo with all its wealth will lose its hold on its island just as the Indian's country has passed from the jurisdiction of the red man.

The same condition holds for Liberia. A number of colored people from the United States and numerous aborigines are occupying this Republic, whose area is not greater than the state of Alabama. Within the last few days, I have been reading the message of President Barclay[1] of that country. It is a most informing document, but all through that message you will find the same truth which I am trying to bring to your minds tonight. A number of people have squatted on this territory, and you will find that unless there is a great change in the government, in the control and development of the natural resources of Liberia, it is a matter of a few months before that magnificent territory will pass from the hands of those black people, into the hands of European nations. I made a little comparative study of their revenues. I find in the first place, that most of their revenue comes from customs, and articles from which the money is drawn are mainly supplied by the natives in the black districts in what they call the hinterland. To give you some idea of the condition existing there, (and this is taken from the report of the Postmaster General) you will find that the receipts for the past year were very much the same as the receipts of the Postoffice here in our Institute last year. There is practically very little difference, and the resources from the entire development of Liberia were less than the receipts of this institution last year, and so, you will see that these people cannot longer be permitted to squat upon this big territory unless they are going to get out of it a much larger measure of the treasure which it is capable of yielding. The same thing is true in South Africa where millions of our people occupy land emboweled with diamonds and gold and have occupied these lands for centuries, but the time came when other peoples, alert, progressive, said, "you have not developed the proper intelligence and skill to get down into the soil and get out this — gold and diamond ore, civilization will not longer allow you to hold this territory," and so Englishmen and Germans and other nations are today in possession of the whole of South Africa.

I want you as students who are going out from Tuskegee, to have it firmly fixed in your minds that wherever you go, however small the piece of land you occupy you have got to get the most out of the soil; or somebody else will crowd you out. The same is true in regard to labor, commercial business and education. If we do not develop the talents in these respects to the very highest degree, somebody else, some other nation will crowd in upon us and we shall not be able to hold our own. Civilization demands from every individual the very utmost the Creator has placed at his command, and we must live up to its demands or go to the wall. I want you to spread these truths among every people wherever you may have an opportunity to exert an influence.

Tuskegee Student, 17 (Dec. 2, 1905), 1, 3. Stenographically reported.

[1] Arthur Barclay (1854–1938), a West Indian immigrant to Liberia in 1865, was the fifteenth president of Liberia, serving from 1904 to 1912. His administration was distinguished for its reform efforts and for being the first to acknowledge tribal people as citizens. In 1924 Barclay became a supporter of Marcus Garvey.

Emmett Jay Scott to James Griswold Merrill

[Tuskegee, Ala.] Dec. 4, 1905

Dear Dr. Merrill: Mr. Washington is on the eve of going North, and asks me to take care of the correspondence that he has been having with you with reference to his speaking at your coming anniversary.

Your first letter to him stated that you expected to have two principal speakers, one a representative of the A. M. A., and one a colored man, Mr. Washington, to represent the colored people.

Your recent letter states that you are planning to have Dr. Du Bois also speak. Mr. Washington is of the opinion that since Dr. Du Bois is an alumnus of Fisk that he would perhaps give a much more satisfactory address for the university than he could give. He also asks me to state that since the point of view of himself and Dr. Du Bois might differ, he does not think that it will be wise to have anything in the way of a seeming controversy, that more good would be accomplished by having one distinct impression left. With these facts in view, it would seem wiser for him to defer going to Fisk until some other occasion.[1] Yours truly,

[Emmett J. Scott]

TLp Con. 806 BTW Papers DLC.

[1] Merrill replied that Du Bois was not coming, and BTW agreed to speak. (Merrill to Scott, Dec. [6], and BTW to Merrill, Dec. 14, 1905, Con. 806, BTW Papers, DLC.)

From Charles William Anderson

New York, N.Y., December 4, 1905

Personal.
My dear Doctor: Yours of the 1st instant is at hand and carefully noted. I shall call Mr. James W. Johnson's attention to the life membership for which I presented his name. He will remit in the near future.

Relative to the last paragraph in your letter, I beg to say that the first information I had of the fact that brother Lyons was my guest, I got from the columns of "The New York Age." Mr. Lyons was in town two or three days during the week before last, and called in to see me Friday as I was preparing to go up town. He rode up with me as far as 53rd Street, and then went to the Hotel Marshall. This ride from my office to 53rd Street constituted all of the "homulgation" [homologation] that was done with me. So you see that the Cedar Street organ is still sustaining its reputation for accuracy. I tried to find out what the good brother was doing in town, but could not. W. H. Ellis[1] called me up on the phone and told me that the gentleman was at his office and was coming to see me. Evidently he had some business with Ellis and brother Clarkson, the nature of which he very carefully concealed.

I am privately advised that the "Age" is on the market, and has been offered to the "Niagara gentlemen." What do you hear about it? In my judgment it is the last play in the Cedar Street scheme of coercion.

Hoping to see you soon, Yours truly,

Charles W. Anderson

TLS Con. 27 BTW Papers DLC.

1 William Henry Ellis (1864–1923), a mulatto entrepreneur who often claimed Cuban and Mexican origins, was born on a small farm near Victoria, Tex. Ellis quickly advanced from working as a cowboy to employment as an agent for a San Antonio leather and hide merchant, who sent him on business trips to Mexico. There Ellis thought he saw a large and profitable market for cotton. After some successful sales in Mexico of cotton from his own Texas plantation, Ellis undertook to resettle 100 southern black families, experienced cotton-growers, on the Durango estates of the British Agricultural, Industrial and Colonization Co. of Tlahualilo in December 1894. Soon about 816 persons came from Alabama and Georgia. Bad organization, cultural conflict, and diseases doomed the project. By the end of July 1895, only about

sixty American blacks were still in residence. Eventually the U.S. government subsidized the return of approximately 660 disgruntled colonists.

The undaunted Ellis served as a customs inspector in Brownsville, Tex., ventured into real estate in Chicago, and embarked on a career as a world traveler, visiting Asia and Central and South America, and making several trips to Europe. In 1896 Ellis arrived in New York City, an utter stranger equipped only with a reference somehow obtained from Collis P. Huntington. With characteristic bravado Ellis invaded Wall Street, becoming its first Negro broker and renting offices in the Drexel building just above those of J. P. Morgan and Co. His clearest source of dependable revenue was his service as business agent for the Hotchkiss estate.

When in London for Edward VII's coronation, Ellis met Ras Makonnen, who invited him to visit Ethiopia. Ellis did so in October 1903 and discovered a whole world of commercial possibilities — plantations, banking, railroads, and mining.

Ellis was followed to Addis Ababa in November 1903 by U.S. Consul-General Robert P. Skinner. A French promoter in Abyssinia later alleged that Ellis claimed all the credit for arranging the commercial treaty which Skinner negotiated with Menelik II. When the State Department's representative, Frederick Kent Loomis, set out from New York in June 1905 to bring the signed treaty back to Menelik, Ellis accompanied him. Loomis disappeared mysteriously while on board ship, and it was Ellis who ultimately delivered the official document. Menelik in gratitude made Ellis Duke of Harrar, an Ethiopian province, and bestowed upon him two million acres of its land. An investigation by the State Department cleared Ellis of any wrongdoing in Loomis's death.

Ellis seems to have continued working as a broker in New York, with a branch office in Mexico City. His one newsworthy deal was the sale to the city of the New York and Westchester Water Co., from which Ellis made a half-million-dollar profit. In 1912 Charles W. Anderson believed Ellis was interested in heading the Negro Bureau of the Republican party, but no political career materialized. Ellis died in Mexico City while on a business trip.

To Whitefield McKinlay

N.Y. [City] Dec 9 [190]5

Personal.

You and Governor[1] meet me at depot eight thirty tonight. Let no one know I am to be there. Important.

B. T. W.

HWcIr Con. 4 BTW Papers DLC.

1 P. B. S. Pinchback.

From Pinckney Benton Stewart Pinchback

Washington Dec 10 – 05

Dear Doctor, I enclose clipping from this mornings Star.[1]

You will see by it how difficult it is for you to come here and see the President without the public knowing it.

This stuff was in private before McKinlay & I left you last night. We did not part until 12.35 o'clock.

Trust you had a pleasant trip.

Went to Grimke's Church to hear him on Garrison. He dwelt on the necessity of organization and unity and spoke of Du Bois as a fighter etc. Nothing objectionable in his paper from our point of view.

Will attend another meeting at Grimke's Church this afternoon and hear Miss Cooper Mr. Cooke & Tunnell & Miller. Yours very truly

Pinchback

Post says you are supposed to have endorsed Vernon, but you have stated you do not endorse persons for office.

ALS Con. 880 BTW Papers DLC.

[1] The Washington *Star*, Dec. 10, 1905, 1, reported that BTW had conferred with the President for more than an hour regarding the appointment of the register of the treasury. The *Star* stated that BTW endorsed S. Laing Williams for the position.

To Cyrus Field Adams

New York, N.Y. December 11, 1905

Personal & Confidential.

Dear Mr. Adams: It is reported in important circles that you are spending most of your time getting up opposition to Mr. S. Laing Williams, the candidate for Register of the Treasury. If this is true, I want to say you are endangering your own position.

I have been frank with you in the past and have stood by you and I think I ought to be equally frank with you now. Very truly yours,

[Booker T. Washington]

TLc Con. 2 BTW Papers DLC.

From Oscar R. Hundley

Huntsville, Ala. Dec. 14th, 1905

Confidential.

My Dear Doctor: The establishment of the new Federal Judge is now it seems an established fact. I write to ask if you will not give me the benefit of your valuable aid in securing this position. Among those who are seeking the appointment, I am the *only one who has stood squarely with the President and the policies of his administration*, especially as to his position with regard to your people. I have very fixed ideas as to the treatment that should be accorded to your people. Not only should they be accorded and protected in every right guaranteed them under the constitution and laws of our country, but they should be treated kindly and encouraged in their efforts to build themselves up as a lawabiding, God-fearing people. It is an unequal match with them at best, and our sympathy should not be extended them grudgingly. I have not been afraid to express my convictions on this and all other subjects of importance as my speeches in the East during the recent campaign will demonstrate. After the lynching of Maples, I was instrumental in calling a meeting of our citizens to condemn this inhuman and lawless act, and wrote the resolutions which were adopted by the meeting, and which put in motion the subsequent efforts of the courts to punish the criminals engaged in that inhuman affair. Now, Doctor, you can aid me greatly in this my only ambition. Will you do it? With grateful appreciation of anything you may do, I remain, Very truly yours,

Oscar R. Hundley

TLS Con. 3 BTW Papers DLC.

From Emmett Jay Scott

Tuskegee Institute, Alabama. Dec. 15, 1905

Dear Mr. Washington: The extraordinary thing to me in the Williams matter is that the President should summarily dismiss Williams from consideration, on letters received from Morris, and Jones,[1] without knowing either of them, and certainly without being advised as to the character of the two men.

Your high recommendation of Williams should certainly outweigh everything said by these other two fellows.

Here is necessity, it seems to me, for plain talk on your part. If your recommendations are to be treated in this light manner, perhaps it is just as well for you to let him assume the full responsibility of selecting these men. Very truly,

Emmett J. Scott

TLS Con. 556 BTW Papers DLC.

[1] Edward H. Morris and John G. Jones of Chicago, whose letters opposing S. Laing Williams were sent to Albert Jarvis Hopkins, U.S. senator from Illinois, and forwarded to BTW presumably by Roosevelt. Jones, a Republican legislator, asserted that Williams was not a Republican and was vacillating and incompetent. Morris wrote of Williams: "Until very recently he was a democrat, then an Independent, and in the past year or two a Republican. . . . Booker T. Washington most likely favors Williams, but we do not need any advice from Alabama, when it comes to putting colored men in office from Illinois." (Jones to Hopkins, Dec. 9, and Morris to Hopkins, Dec. 9, 1905, Copies, Con. 31, BTW Papers, DLC.)

From Emmett Jay Scott

Tuskegee Institute, Alabama. Dec. 15, 1905

Dear Mr. Washington: I send you herewith copy of the Guardian, Conservator and Bee under separate cover. The especial reason for bringing the Guardian to your attention is an editorial therein in which Charles Morris makes the statement on the editorial page to the effect that the President's speech was written here and manifold copies sent out from here all over the country to different papers. It occurs to me that a serious leak has happened if it is possible for anybody to make a statement of this kind with so much positiveness and defiance. It shows that even the best of our friends are not as true as they should be. Of course it is a serious indictment to bring, and it may be that you can in some way develop how this thing happened.

The other editorials are of usual tenor, but show that the enemy is still active.

Everything here proceeds as usual. Yours truly,

Emmett J. Scott

TLS Con. 556 BTW Papers DLC.

From Charles Allmond Wickersham

Atlanta, Ga. Dec. 16, 1905

Principal: Replying to your letter Nov. 29th:

There is no reason why colored people cannot enter their car from the front end without passing through smoker and I have instructed that trainmen direct all colored people to enter train accordingly, which will eliminate any complaint of having to pass through smoker.

As to the door being open between the compartments; we have directed that previous instructions be rigidly enforced to keep this door closed, except when members of the crew have occasion to pass through same. With the entrance of colored people through the smoker eliminated, the door should be opened but rarely.

The newsboys have no right to occupy more than one seat, and the Conductors have again been instructed to see to it in all cases that newsboys do not encroach on other seats. If their stock is too large for one seat they will have to reduce it. As you are aware, however, it is not often that the colored travel is sufficient to require anything like all the seats in the coach.

I think the above action will eliminate all causes for complaint as enumerated by you. It is our desire to give the negroes good service and I will be only too glad to handle any individual case brought to my notice which would indicate that they have not been properly treated. Yours truly,

Charles A. Wickersham

TLS Con. 880 BTW Papers DLC.

Emmett Jay Scott to W. Allison Sweeney

[Tuskegee, Ala.] December 18, 1905

Dear Mr. Sweeney: I have your letters of December 15th[1] and 16th[2] and am sorry to learn that it is your purpose very soon to cease the publishing of the Leader. If the Doctor's response to your suggestion was not as hearty as you had hoped, it is traceable only to the fact of his tremendous responsibilities. His resources are comparatively limited in view of the help he tries to render his friends. No man is more willing than he to help out when possible. But to carry the whole burden is more than he or any one man in his circumstances can do.

With sincere regards, I am, as ever, Yours truly,

Emmett J. Scott

TLpS Con. 881 BTW Papers DLC.

1 Sweeney complained that he had needed $200, asked BTW for $175, and received only $50. "You, I think, cannot recall," he wrote Scott, "a request, suggestion, or Tuskegee inspired editorial sent to or made upon me that did not at once engage my attention and service, and in my statement to subscribers, advertisers and the public, which will appear in the next issue of The Conservator, I cannot if I would spare my self, The Leader, and those I deem have deserted me. . . ." (Dec. 15, 1905, Con. 881, BTW Papers, DLC.)

2 Sweeney enclosed an editorial from the Chicago *Conservator* accusing BTW of buying "crippled newspapers" such as the *Leader* and using them to attack the Niagara Movement and its supporters. (Sweeney to Scott, Dec. 16, 1905, Con. 881, BTW Papers, DLC.)

A Statement on William Lloyd Garrison[1]

Tuskegee Institute, Ala., December 20, 1905

William Lloyd Garrison

Mr. Garrison was one of those rare men who saw clearly in his own generation, the direction in which he could best consecrate his life, and having chosen what his work should be, let nothing swerve him from his purpose. Through Winter and Summer, cloud and sunshine, discouragement and encouragement, he steadfastly clung to his purpose. He not only led the way in the freeing of the black slave, but in a larger and equally important sense, he led the way in freeing from the influence of slavery a large element of American white people.

It was true of Mr. Garrison as of many reformers, during the immediate period in which he lived, that many persons did not appreciate the high and far-sighted character of his work, but as time passes, more and more they are beginning to see what magnificant results were brought about by his courage and fidelity.

Booker T. Washington

TMpSr Con. 299 BTW Papers DLC.

1 Signed in Scott's hand, and enclosed in a letter from Scott to William R. Carter, principal of the Topeka Industrial Institute, Topeka, Kan. Carter was a Tuskegee graduate of 1893.

From W. Allison Sweeney

Chicago, Ill. Dec. 25 1905

Dear Doctor and Friend: Please accept acknowledgment and thanks for your's under date of Dec 22.

I regret very much Doctor that an unexpected exiengency compelled me to appear in the attitude of "riding a free horse to death" for I *shall* not forget and will *always* remember with gratitude your consideration as expressed by your acts in the past.

I am your debtor. Very Truly and very Faithfully

W Allison Sweeney

ALS Con. 881 BTW Papers DLC.

From Charles William Anderson

New York, N.Y., December 27, 1905

Personal.

My dear Doctor: This is to advise you that Fortune has informed me that the proper financial arrangements have been effected between himself and Mr. Peterson, and I have therefore concluded to appoint Mr. Peterson on January 1st. Moore has tendered his resignation, and Peterson will take charge on January 1st. If you cause this information to be handed out to any of the newspapers of the country, I think you had better refrain from mentioning the fact that Moore has resigned. Make the announcement of the Peterson appointment without any reference to Moore's resignation. This will make our Boston friends mad enough to stand on their heads and spit backward. I think, also, it will be advisable for you to write a letter to Fortune and remind him that in making this appointment I am helping him out financially, and he, in turn, ought to see to it that the columns of the "Age" are not open to these little inch high politicians around here, who think they are plotting against me. It seems to me that I am entitled to this much consideration from Mr. Fortune. Therefore, I would suggest that you drop him a hint along this line, and remind him that as I am doing him a favour in this matter, he ought at least to see to it that the columns of his paper are not used by my enemies.

I shall leave here for Augusta at 3.25 P.M. on Friday, December 29th, over the Southern Railroad. I shall probably remain in Augusta until midnight on January 2nd, or the morning of January 3rd. You can communicate with me C/o Dr. C. T. Walker, Tabernacle Baptist Church, or C/o Mr. Henry C. Young,[1] Corner of Gwinnett & Marbury streets.

Hoping you are very well, I remain Yours truly,

Charles W. Anderson

TLS Con. 27 BTW Papers DLC.

[1] Henry C. Young (1864–1917), a grocer and president of the Pilgrim Health and Life Insurance Co., headed the Augusta branch of the NNBL.

To W. Allison Sweeney

[Tuskegee, Ala.] December 30, 1905

Personal.

Dear Mr. Sweeney: We shall be sending you within the next few days an advertisement to help out in some degree in the matter about which you wired Mr. Scott. Yours truly,

Booker T. Washington

Your paper appears far from dead or dying.

B. T. W.

TLpS Con. 881 BTW Papers DLC. Postscript in BTW's hand.

To Timothy Thomas Fortune

[Tuskegee, Ala.] December 30, 1905

Personal.

My dear Mr. Fortune: I am glad to learn from letter just received that the arrangement we have discussed is about to be consummated for January 1st. As I have talked this matter over with Mr.

Anderson, I think he seems as much interested in looking after this arrangement to help you as well as Peterson. If anything, he is more disposed to give you free leeway in developing the Age into a great property. Under the circumstances I wonder if you will not feel that this is his attitude, and that you will not feel disposed to open the columns of your paper to those who are disposed to assail him. This matter appears a little thing, but yet I am quite sure in the end it is really a big thing. I pass the suggestion on for whatever you may think it is worth. Yours truly,

Booker T. Washington

TLpS Con. 1 BTW Papers DLC.

To Charles William Anderson

[Tuskegee, Ala.] Dec. 30, 1905

Personal

Dear Mr. Anderson: Could you not secure a man in New York who would get right into the inner circles of the Niagara movement through the Brooklyn crowd and keep us informed, as [to] their operations and plans? Yours truly,

Booker T. Washington

TLpS Con. 27 BTW Papers DLC.

An Article in the *Congregationalist and Christian World*

Dec. 30, 1905

THE NEGRO IN THE NEW SOUTHWEST

At the present time I am inclined to believe there is no other place in this country where one can study the race problem to a greater advantage than in the Indian and Oklahoma Territories. I visited this region recently, upon the invitation of Hon. J. E. Bush and the members of the Negro Business League, at Little Rock, Ark., and spent about ten days in different parts of Arkansas and of the territories seeing and talking to the people of both races.

Although I had known something of this Western country before, I was not prepared for the manifestations of energy, forethought and substantial achievement which I encountered there, particularly in Oklahoma Territory. Standing in the midst of the magnificent brick and stone buildings of Oklahoma City, it was hard to comprehend that sixteen years before this busy marketplace had been a vacant prairie.

Into this new country the colored people from the South have come in considerable numbers. While I was pleased to learn that an unusually large number of these black immigrants had become owners of land in the city and in the country, I was not surprised to see that in the cities at least, except in Muskogee, I.T., they did not seem to have prospered in the same degree as have their white neighbors. Considering the conditions out of which most of them came and the habits and traditions they brought with them, nothing else could have been expected of them.

It became clear to me, in looking over this territory and its people, that it was less what they found here than it was what they brought with them that accounted for the rapid improvement the people have made. It is, in other words, not so much the soil as the ideas and ambitions that these people brought to the soil that accounts for their success.

A story which I heard on the train while passing through Oklahoma will illustrate what I mean. During the "boom" in Oklahoma a man came into the hotel, flinging himself into a chair and wiping his brow, exclaiming, "Well, I got 'em!" "Got what?" asked his neighbor. "Why, those lots out there," naming the street. "Why," said his neighbor, "that is 'way out on the prairie." "I know it," was the reply, "but in three or four years that land will be covered with brick blocks." "Well," concluded his friend in telling the story afterward, "I could not see it then, but they are there today."

This will illustrate what I mean when I say the people who came out there to settle have found pretty much what they brought with them. The Northern white man saw here, on this vacant soil, brick buildings, railways, the telegraph and all the machinery of the civilization he had left behind him. The black man brought no such vision in most cases with him. He had no training in business, no capital and no confidence in his ability to form corporations or share in those enterprises by which cities are built up and communities enriched. Often the colored immigrant came to this part of the country merely because he was discontented where he was; perhaps the notion that he could vote or would in some way have more freedom or respect here than he had at home was the inducement that brought him.

Whatever other special difficulties the Negro immigrant may have encountered, it is the white man's possession of a clear and definite purpose, and the Negro's lack of it, which has been his greatest handicap. In one direction, however, the Negro in Oklahoma seems to have shown superiority; that has been in the raising of cotton. The white man who came into the territory saw the fields here sown with wheat and corn, such as he had been accustomed to raise in the North. The Negro saw only cotton. Thus it has come about that the raising of cotton in this territory is, I am informed, almost wholly in the hands of Negroes. At the World's Fair at Paris in 1900, it was a Negro Oklahoman who took the prize for the best cotton.

Nothing illustrates better, perhaps, than the facts I have just stated, the nature of the problem of Negro education. The Negro, in order to make rapid or real progress, must get this vision and insight that the white man has. He cannot get it from books alone. He must get it by doing things that the white man has done. He must begin in the soil and in the industries and learn, by doing, until all the details and all the machinery of modern civilization are familiar to him. While he is getting this training he will necessarily acquire habits of thrift, foresight, temperance and all the other elements of that moral training that goes with and is a necessary part of these things and this civilization.

In certain parts of the Indian Territory where they have been longer settled and have had special opportunities, I found the Negro people had made considerable progress in the line I have indicated. There are a number of Negro towns in Indian Territory where colored men have had an opportunity to experiment and learn something about business administration and self-government in a way they do not have where these affairs are in control of the white race. Particularly in the Creek nation, where the Negroes who came out to this territory in 1838, as the slaves of the Indians, are largely in control, has the colored population prospered. There are two Negro banks, a fire insurance company and a considerable number of stores in Muskogee, the principal town of that nation.

The most interesting and significant thing I had an opportunity to observe on my visit to the Indian Territory was the way in which the different characters of the two races, the Indian and the Negro, have manifested themselves. I had for a time, while a teacher at Hampton, charge of the Indian students, and had learned to have a high degree of respect for their character and abilities. I was naturally anxious to learn, during my stay here, as much as I could in regard to them. It struck me, therefore, as at once sad and ominous, upon entering Indian Territory, that there were no Indians anywhere visible. I was told that they had gone back from the railways. When I reached the towns I was told again that the Indians had gone back from the town. They had retired to the hills. One old colored man told me very solemnly that he had observed that the Indian objected to whitewashed fences. As soon as civilization got far enough along that the people began to whitewash their fences, the Indian "went back."

The Negro, however, was everywhere in evidence. He was working on the streets and in the mines, side by side with Polish and Italian laborers. I noticed that white women had taken the places of the Negro in the hotels and occasionally in the barber shop. But on the other hand I found a considerable number of colored men in business of some kind or other, and many of them doing quite as well as the white man beside them. On the whole, I came away from this new Southwestern country with the feeling that the Negro people in this region were making real and rapid progress and doing as well as any one could possibly expect of them.

Congregationalist and Christian World, 90 (Dec. 30, 1905), 979.

1905

The Tenth Annual Report of the Tuskegee Woman's Club

[Tuskegee, Ala., 1905]

Tuskegee Woman's Club

The Tuskegee Woman's Club closes the tenth year of its work in sober retrospection of the days that have closed in upon it since its organization in March 1895. Of the thirteen charter members five remain; Mrs. Booker T. Washington, Mrs. J. B. Washington, Miss S. H. Porter, Mrs. Logan and Miss E. E. Lane.

The first club year ended with a membership of thirty five. This tenth year closes with a broken membership of seventy four – one, Mrs. J. N. Calloway has passed on to the great beyond. Conscious of our loss, but of her great gain, we close our ranks and look for the golden summer of doing, of helping and fulfilling.

Among the various topics discussed in the semi-weekly meetings of the club this year have been the works of leading colored musicians, the value of the X Ray, Wireless Telegraphy, Famous Women of the hour, and reviews of current articles. These with debates, musical numbers and readings have formed the literary programs for 1905. Dr. Kenney and Mr. Wood have added to the enjoyment of two evenings of the year; the first with a lecture on the Value of Electricity and Medical Science; the latter with pleasing dramatic numbers.

During the year, the club has contributed Four dollars quarterly toward the support of Beatrice Reynolds, a waif from Thompson's Quarters who has been placed in Mrs. Pace's[1] Orphanage in Covington, Ga., Five dollars toward Mr. Moses C. Purifoy's[2] school work and a balance of Sixteen dollars and forty cents is on hand in the treasury. The ladies of the club contributed liberally toward several barrels that have been sent to destitute people. In March when the club undertook to assume the responsibility of finding the means to provide a suitable home for a small baby in unwholesome surroundings, the gentlemen of the faculty kindly contributed twenty five dollars, sixty five cents, toward the expenses, and thus helped most successfully in giving the boy a fair start in life, and the club work a very substantial help in time of need.

As the club membership has grown, subdivisions have been organized, and during the current year, ten of these have been represented by club members who have reported monthly the work accomplished: Mrs. Washington, the Mothers' Meeting in the town of Tuskegee, Miss Smith[3] the E. A. Russell Settlement Work, Miss Spears,[4] the Margaret Murray Washington Club, Miss Lawrence,[5] the Ednah D. Cheney Circle, Miss Edwards[6] the Vesta Club, Mrs. J. B. Washington the Humane Society, Miss Porter the W. C. T. U., and Mrs. Penney the Out of Door Mission School; Mrs. Matthews[7] the Prison work.

REPORT OF JAIL WORK

Thirty visits have been made to the prisoners in the jail of the town of Tuskegee. Religious services have been held at each visit. Fruit and clean clothing have been given to the prisoners who have expressed their gratitude and have made strong efforts to present a tidy appearance during our visits. Four small boys imprisoned for robbery were with four men who could not read or write. All were given their first lessons by a fellow prisoner who had better advantages. The Christmas was made brighter by a gift to each, a few additions to make palatable their dinner, and some picture magazines that were left to amuse them. Four Bible students and several teachers have given much time to help better the work for these unfortunates. We are grateful, too, for the considerate help of the jailor who has exerted every effort to make our work tell for good.

E. A. RUSSELL SETTLEMENT WORK

The work at the Settlement has been carried on, as formerly, by the resident worker, Miss Annie Davis, who for the first time in the seven years' history of the Settlement has received recognition from the county authorities. The cooking, sewing classes and Mothers' Organization have been conducted by Miss Davis, the pupils of the Day School have put in the crop on the ten acre lot; but the visiting workers Misses Vanderzee[8] and C. C. Smith have assisted in the Sunday School work which was interrupted by the smallpox scare for several weeks. The Christmas tree exercises long looked forward to by old and young were not carried out as elaborately as hoped because of this, and it was a sore disappointment. Santa Claus was liberal; and those able to be out were made happy and grateful.

The Easter service of the children was simple, but helpful and touching and in marked improvement over the past years. The two room model house of a widow of the people has been painted during the year. She has shown the other cottagers by precept and example how to keep her house and family neat and clean and has watched and tended her small ten acre farm with good results.

The year ends with an average attendance of fifty three in the school, twenty four women in the Mothers' Meetings and one hundred thirty men, women and children in the Sunday School.

Thompson's Quarters

After more than three years Sunday School work in Thompson's Quarters, we find the interest increasing and the attendance larger this past winter and spring than in previous years. The average attendance has been thirty five, mostly children, occasionally four or five adults have been present. The rent is still paid by the Bible students. Two loads of wood were given us this winter.

We have not confined ourselves to Sunday School work alone. Along with the Bible teaching we lend a hand wherever it is needed, visiting the sick and adding somewhat to the comfort of the afflicted. In one home of eight children, we were enabled through kindness of teachers and Bible students to assist in giving a child a respectable burial. This was a great consolation to the parents who had recently come into this vicinity.

We encourage the children to attend day school, and help pay tuition for some. Along with the Bible instruction and food for the soul, we occasionally have simple parties with very light refreshments, such as a stick of candy for each child, or a small cake, or iced lemonade. On warm days, we find that these parties have a wholesome effect. The tempers are sweetened for the time being, and fights are less frequent.

Our Christmas tree was the delight and joy of every child, for it was one that our small boys had cut and put up themselves. It was loaded with gifts such as dolls, stockings and candy which were donated by friends of one of our teachers.

Through the kindness of the school, we were able to give the children a rare treat in the form of a May picnic on the school grounds. Some of the young women of the Missionary Society pleasantly entertained the little ones and furnished the refreshments.

At Easter time the children received colored eggs which were given by some of the Y. W. C. A. members. Four children of the Quarters have been sent away to better homes. One is at Miss Wright's school, Denmark, S.C. and the other three are at the Reed Home, Covington, Georgia, conducted by Mrs. Pace. We feel encouraged to carry on this work, realizing as we do more and more the need of it.

THE TEMPERANCE DIVISION

Vigorous efforts have been made during this year as has been true in past years, to keep the work of the temperance cause fresh in the minds of the students and the children of the neighboring vicinity, and to impress them with the importance of the work which is being done throughout the world by prominent citizens and organizations, to suppress the use of alcohol as a beverage, and its associated evils.

The subject has been presented during the year as follows: (1) All of the young men of the school have been addressed, the subject having been considered from a social, economic and hygienic, as well as moral standpoint. (2) The entire company of young women of the school was given a thorough review of the work of the Women's Christian Temperance Union and also a full report or statement of the life and work of Frances E. Willard. (3) On "Temperance Sunday" a talk was made before the Young People's Society of Christian Endeavor an earnest plea being made for each one who listened to the talk there, and Christians everywhere, to use their influence always in favor of the suppression of the liquor traffic. (4) A talk was made on the subject "Intemperance and Its Effects" to a rural school, composed of seventy five or more children who repeated the pledge against the use of alcohol as a beverage, the use of tobacco and profanity. (5) Many private talks to individuals and special classes have been given during the year.

Judging from various expressions of students who have manifested an interest in the work of the temperance cause, we believe that the effort to create a sentiment against the destructive "King Alcohol" will prove effective and that a large number of our young people, fourteen hundred students, will be active in the work, endeavoring to establish in themselves and those with whom they will be associated, habits of purity, temperance and total abstinence.

Ednah Cheney Club

The Ednah Cheney Club at Tuskegee Institute was founded several years ago in honor of the noble Mrs. Cheney who died at her home in Jamaica Plain, Massachusetts, November 18th, 1904.

Since Mrs. Cheney was a friend of the weak and a champion of woman's cause, the Club has been impressed that its highest aim must be that of service if it is at all to emulate the virtues of so useful a life.

Tuskegee's Ednah Cheney Club is composed of the young women of the Senior Class. This year's membership is twenty five. The young women give expression to their desire to be of service in interesting themselves in the poor and unfortunate in the neighborhood of the school. The "poor house" occupants and many others know of the joy experienced when a crowd of these young people visit them, bringing food, clothing and cheer.

The young women this year have also endeavored to acquaint themselves with the things that women are doing as set forth in the current literature of the day.

Though not known to the present members of the club, Mrs. Cheney's spirit has taken that hold upon them that means a broadening and strengthening to them all.

The Vesta Club

The Vesta Club, composed of the girls in town but attend[ing] school at the institution, at one of their meetings decided to make a small contribution to an old lady in town. One dollar was collected and given to sister Emily Jordan for a Christmas dinner. These girls are supposed to meet at the odd hours when they are on the institute grounds and are not otherwise employed. They read good books and papers and discuss subjects pertaining to home life, such as will aid in their progress and culture.

Department of Woman Suffrage

There has been greater interest in the study of the suffrage movement during the past year than ever before. The Woman's Journal which is the official organ of the suffragists has been more generally read than heretofore. This Journal has been issued for 35 years from 3 Park St., Boston. A few months ago the price was reduced from $2.50 to $1.50. The National Headquarters at Warren, Ohio, send helpful and encouraging propaganda from which our department has gathered help and hope. Great gains have been made for the cause since the international meeting at Berlin in 1904. The leader of the suffrage department of the Tuskegee Woman's Club is sincere and enthusiastic. She does not, however, claim that the ballot in the hands of women will usher in the millennium at once. Neither does she see the near approach of the right of the elective franchise for her sex in the South; hence, the study with us has been rather more academic than practical. The minutes of each meeting during the past year have been devoted to this study under the leadership of Mrs. Logan whose excellent library on the subject has also been placed at the service of all interested members of the club. The Peace Arbitration movement has been greatly promoted by suffragists of the United States.

Mothers' Meetings

For a number of years we have carried on the Mothers' Meetings in the town of Tuskegee. The object of these meetings is to create an interest amongst the women in general for self improvement, for the general development of their homes and for their children. We believe that we are accomplishing this condition even though we are doing it slowly. We have held twenty eight meetings this year, beginning Saturday at two o'clock and closing at five. There have been on an average fifty women in attendance at each meeting. Many of the Saturdays we have had from sixty five to seventy five present. The meetings are always opened with devotional exercises.

We have no Treasurer and no President. In fact we have no officers at all; it is simply a gathering of women who want to be helped and who want to help. We have discussed the following subjects: "The Part a Woman should take in Buying Land and in Building a House," "The care of children which includes dressing, feeding, sleeping, teaching et cetera," "The boys place in the home,"

"The importance of close confidence between mother and daughter, father and son," "How to teach children reverence for parents and for that which is sacred," "The kind of a teacher to have in a community — one who will not only teach what is in the book, but will teach cooking, sewing, sweeping, dusting and all forms of house work."

The mothers have also been urged to plant and to raise all sorts of vegetables in order to improve the physical life of themselves and of their families. Once during the year we had a very fine exhibit of turnips, peas, beans, potatoes, rice, butter, eggs, fowls etc. and you would have been very much pleased to have seen the interest these women took in bringing together this exhibit. The women are also taught how to buy and what to buy, not only for eating purposes, but for wearing purposes. Some of the women have gone so far as to ask us to select their dress goods and to select a pattern by which to make their dresses and to select their hats and their jackets. This has been a task which we have not enjoyed doing, but we thought it best to do it for the time being. Many of the women who belong to these Mothers' Meetings are themselves engaged in other Saturday meetings throughout the country. At Little Texas, Sweet Gum, Howard Chapel and some other points, Mothers' Meetings are carried on and in this way we have extended the influence of the Tuskegee Mothers' Meetings more than we had dared hope for.

During the year the Mothers' Meeting gave a dinner for all of the people in town and in the vicinity of the town who were sixty years of age and over. At the time there were thirty five old people present. Some of them were so old they could scarcely get up and down the steps. This has been done in order to encourage the mothers to think of some one else outside of themselves. I believe that almost anyone who saw these mothers some years ago on the streets and who sees them now would concur with us in saying that there has been a marked improvement in their manners and conduct in general on the streets; there being less familiarity than ever before between the men and women. There is not such a tendency now on the part of the women to sit around in front of the stores on the street, talking and laughing loudly. There is also a great improvement in the matter of dress on the part of the women. We seldom see a woman in town now who has not on a neat calico dress and sailor hat. In the creation of these Mothers' Meetings, we hope to improve not only the town of Tuskegee and the women who live in it, but also the vicinity about us.

TM Con. 560 BTW Papers DLC.

[1] Dina Pace, an 1883 graduate of Atlanta University, founded Reed Home, an orphanage and school, in 1884.

[2] Moses Charles Franklin Purifoy of Brewton, Ala., graduated from Tuskegee Institute in 1895 and then taught in Conecuh and Escambia counties.

[3] Caroline (Carrie) C. Smith taught basketry and broom-making at Tuskegee Institute.

[4] Edna Amelia Spears (Landers after 1908) taught history and geography at Tuskegee Institute from 1903 until after BTW's death. An 1898 graduate of Tuskegee, she studied at Teachers College, Columbia, in 1901–2.

[5] Dora Mayo Lawrence, a 1903 Tuskegee graduate, was a stenographer and then filing clerk in the administration department at Tuskegee Institute.

[6] Susie E. Edwards Palmer taught English at Tuskegee Institute. In 1905 she married the school's registrar, John H. Palmer.

[7] Minnie L. Matthews was a matron in the housekeeping division of Tuskegee Institute.

[8] Anna R. Vanderzee was a matron in the housekeeping division at Tuskegee Institute.

From Thomas Seymour Barbour

Boston, Mass. January 3, 1906

My dear Mr. Washington: I am almost ashamed to bring to you a suggestion involving any cost in time and strength, as I know your burdens are multitudinous. But I write of a need whose urgent and pitiful claim I know you recognize and the service required is one which no other can render as you can. You know well the situation in the movement for Congo relief. I send you a copy of a letter which within a few days will be in the hands of 25,000 pastors. We are hoping for a great outbreaking of interest and active effort over the entire country. Among other plans Mr. and Mrs. Harris,[1] English missionaries from Baringa, Africa, who have been in the heart of the horrors and gave testimony at hearings of the Commission, have been invited to come to this country. They will reach here probably about the 20th inst. They will speak widely. We wish to secure particularly for Mr. Harris the largest possible hearing and are anxious to have meetings in four centers, Boston, New York, Philadelphia and Washington, which shall call out a great and influential company. Nothing could secure this so surely as your presence, together with that of Mr. Clemens. I proposed the Washington meeting to Mr. Clemens a couple of weeks ago and he agreed to the appointment. I did not then introduce the suggestion as to the other three cities as Mr. Harris's coming was not certain. I will write to him of this within a day or two and his interest is so intense that I feel sure he will endeavor to comply with the suggestion. How much it will mean to our cause throughout the country and with Congress if we announce Mr. Clemens and yourself, with Mr. Harris, for the meetings in these four great centers, I need not say. I told Senator Spooner[2] of the proposed meeting for Washington and he was greatly interested, believing that it will count immensely as, of course, it cannot fail to do. Will you not write me that you will give this help and let me know the earliest dates open to you after the 22nd inst.? I know of your meeting on that date in New York City and of your great kindness in arranging for the service by Mr. Clemens in connection with the Congo State. This will give a strong impetus and I hope will serve also the more immediate aim of the meeting. If followed up by a meeting devoted distinctively to the appalling situation in the Congo State, the result will be immense.

I wish to ask also regarding your meeting on the 22nd inst. We have literature we are anxious to get into circulation. Would you feel any objection to the sale of Mark Twain's pamphlet, "King Leopold's Soliloquy," on the street before the hall as the meeting closes?[3] Would any use of literature inside the hall be practicable? We have small leaflets that could be distributed freely. You will understand that I am far from wishing that even this cause shall intrude in a way to divert attention from the great work for which specifically the meeting is held. I believe, indeed, that the two movements, in God's good providence, shall reach on to one great end but there are proprieties which, of course, should be observed.

With great appreciation of the spirit and power for service in you which lead to this request and inquiry, Very sincerely yours,

Thomas S. Barbour

TLS Con. 808 BTW Papers DLC.

[1] John Hobbis Harris (1874–1940) and his wife, Alice, were English Baptist missionaries at the Congo Balolo Mission. BTW probably met them when they toured the United States in the spring of 1906 in behalf of the Congo Reform Association, of which John Harris became organizing secretary. In 1910, when BTW toured England, the Harrises were organizing secretaries of the Anti-Slavery and Aborigines Protection Society in London. John Harris organized a luncheon in London for BTW under the society's auspices and arranged for his lectures in other cities. He kept BTW posted on news of the Universal Races Congress in London in 1911 and planned BTW's tour of Europe in the interest of black Africans in 1915, which was cut short by the outbreak of war. John Harris was a Liberal member of Parliament in 1923–24. He wrote several books on African affairs and was knighted in 1933.

[2] John Coit Spooner (1834–1919), a Republican U.S. senator from Wisconsin from 1885 to 1891 and from 1897 to 1907.

[3] BTW agreed to speak at the meeting but said of Twain's pamphlet: "I very much fear that this would greatly divert attention from the purpose of that meeting and might serve to confuse the people with regard thereto." (BTW to Barbour, Jan. 9, 1906, Con. 808, BTW Papers, DLC.)

From George Wiley Clinton

Charlotte N.C. Jan 3, 1906

My Dear Dr. Washington: Your letter of recent date has been received and perused with care. I had just returned from Anniston Ala. where I delivered the Emancipation address on Monday. I mailed a letter to you relative to our forthcoming meeting as a Board of Bishops at Tuskegee on the 17th inst.

I[t] gives me pleasure to promptly answer yours which is now before me.

First of all I want to congratulate you for the good results following the literary campaign of the "Com. of 12" in Maryland. I have been that way twice since the Election and many believe that the literature sent out by the "Com. of 12" did much toward bringing about the defeat of Gorman & the "Poe" Amendment.[1] I feel greatly encouraged and more hopeful than ever. I heartily acquiesce in the plan to meet at Washington in connection with the Executive

Com. of the Young Peoples religious Congress on the plan suggested by your letter. I shall be present, therefore will not have to [incur?] any additional expense to make the trip to the meeting. I shall not be able to have that little pamphlet on the sanitary needs of our people in readiness. I have selected as a title for it, "Health, Home and Happiness." I see that it is not your purpose to have a meeting, but merely to bring the work of the "Com of 12" before the other body. I think that a good plan. I am preparing a list of Presiding Elders throughout our church to send to Mr. Hugh Brown[e]. I began to prepare a list of all the preachers, but I found that to be too voluminous & I thought unnecessary. I think the latter list will suffice. I hope you can be at Tuskegee when we meet. I am, Yours very respectfully,

Geo. W. Clinton

ALS Con. 318 BTW Papers DLC.

1 Charles W. Chesnutt also wrote to BTW praising the Committee of Twelve for its contribution to the defeat of disfranchisement in Maryland. (Jan. 8, 1906, BTW Papers, ATT.)

Emmett Jay Scott to James Carroll Napier

[Tuskegee, Ala.] January 3, 1905[6]

Personal and Confidential.

My dear Mr. Napier: I am very glad that you have been able to arrange satisfactorily and definitely the matter of the engagement at McKendree Methodist Church.[1] This meeting ought to be a satisfactory one and should be a big step in advance for us. I wish to ask that you on your own personal responsibility and without seriously considering whether discretion suggests that we take measures to see that some dare-devil crank does not at the church Sunday morning, either as Mr. Washington enters or comes out, offer him an indignity or violence. Of course, my fears may be ill-advised in these matters but it seems better to be on the alert than to allow such a thing to pass without mention. You can have two or three good strong persons upon whom you absolutely depend either accompany him to the church or stand about the door so as to offer him complete protection. This letter is for the eyes of *no one but yourself*. Faithfully, and sincerely yours,

Emmett J. Scott

TLpS Con. 879 BTW Papers DLC.

[1] BTW visited Nashville to deliver the fortieth anniversary address at Fisk, and on Sunday, Jan. 7, 1906, he addressed the congregation of the McKendree Methodist Church. It was an unprecedented occasion in Nashville for a black man to speak in a southern Methodist church. The crowd filled not only the main auditorium but the adjoining halls and rooms, and more than 500 persons were denied admission. BTW spoke for more than an hour to an enthusiastic audience, and at the end the dean of the theology school of Vanderbilt University extended BTW an invitation to give a lecture there in the spring. (Typescript press release, Jan. 9, 1906, Con. 329, BTW Papers, DLC.)

To Theodore Roosevelt

Tuskegee, Alabama, January 4, 1906

Dear Mr. President: I think I ought to say to you that I find the colored people throughout the country are very sensitive on the subject of your making any move in the direction of reducing the number of colored people holding office in the South. When I see you I shall talk the matter over with you more in detail. Yours very truly,

Booker T. Washington

TLS Theodore Roosevelt Papers DLC.

To John Wanamaker

[Tuskegee, Ala.] January 8, 1906

Personal

My dear Mr. Wanamaker: I have not forgotten the subject of our conversation last summer; in fact I have thought about it a great deal. I do not know if I am not inclined to change my view that I expressed to you last summer. The Negro population of Philadelphia is so large and is growing so fast that I believe the effort ought to be made to reach and help them right in Philadelphia. Of course something done on the outside of the city would reach a few but not those, perhaps, in most need of help. I believe that if the buildings to which you referred when I saw you could be made the center of such work that it would succeed.

I have been thinking over the matter of a proper minister to take the lead, but have not as yet settled in my own mind who would be the best person. Rev. Mr. Creditt,[1] of your city, is a good man, one of the best that I know of.

I suppose you saw something of the newspaper excitement and flurry on account of my dining with you at Saratoga. The whole matter has passed away and I believe that good will come out of it all. I am satisfied that we are getting to the point in the South where there is a large and growing element of Southern white people who cannot be deceived by the radical newspapers and the demagogues. I have been holding meetings recently in Arkansas and Alabama where I have spoken to large audiences of both white and colored people, and I find that a large element of the white people cannot be deceived any longer and the number is increasing. In the last analysis I believe that they respect men like yourself who stand up for principle and do the right thing regardless of public clamor. Yours very truly,

Booker T. Washington

Since the above letter was dictated, I have been in Nashville, Tenn., and last Sunday afternoon was invited to speak in the largest and most wealthy white Methodist church in the city. The audience room was simply packed with the best men and women of Nashville, and they seemed just as enthusiastic and interested as any audience I ever addressed in the north.

B. T. W.

TLpS Con. 339 BTW Papers DLC.

[1] William Abraham Creditt was the pastor of the Cherry Memorial (First African Baptist) Church, the most prominent black Baptist church in Philadelphia.

From Charles William Anderson

New York, N.Y., January 8, 1906

Confidential.

My dear Doctor: Doubtless Mr. Scott has given you all the details of our most satisfactory interview with the President on Saturday last. I am sure you will be pleased with the nature of it. "Our friend" did not hesitate a moment, but plainly announced his intention not to allow appointments of coloured men to be made in such a way as to give anybody the impression that your influence was not entirely potent in such matters. Of course he put it in his own straightforward way, and it was positive, and satisfactory.

Mr. Scott has probably also advised you about the Fortune matter. Mr. Loeb told us that Senator Kean[1] of New Jersey had brought a letter to the White House, written by Fortune to some New Jersey coloured man, informing him that for a certain monetary consideration, he could have him placed by you in any one of a number of places, which were enumerated. What do you think of this for effrontery and idiocy? It seems absolutely impossible to make Fortune play with his friends, and prevent him from damaging himself. Mr. Scott, doubtless, has given you the story in detail. Mr. Loeb informed us that a list of the places — Consulates and other places — was enclosed in the letter.

I have just been advised that Du Bois' speech here last night, in Charlie Morris' church, was a failure. My Deputy, Harry Middleton, was on the ground to take notes, as was also Fred Moore. Morris announced himself as being heart and soul with the Niagara movement, and called upon his friends to stand by him. He asked all those who were willing to follow him in this direction, to stand up, and, while quite a few stood up, they were composed almost entirely of women and boys. Middleton informs me that not more than twenty men were in the audience. Gilchrist Stewart was one of these.

I will send the list for the Carnegie Hall Meeting another day.

Before closing, I want to congratulate you on "our friend's" determination to name Williams if the charges against Vernon are true, and to give Williams another place even if Vernon is appointed to the Registership. This helps matters along wonderfully, in my judgment. I would suggest, however, that in the event of Napier's refusal to accept the place at Bahia, that no other man be recommended until it has been discovered whether or not he will accept it. If Napier refuses, this will make the third refusal of this particular place, and will look as though we are trying to play foot ball with someone. Knowing Secretary Root as well as I do, I am confident that he will fill this place without consultation with anybody if we don't hurry up and find somebody who really wants it. This permitting of a lot of little "two-by-four-men" to refuse a place which they would have been seeking had they not had your influence to support them, is not much to my liking. Any one of these men would have gladly accepted Bahia had not he felt that you could get him something a great deal better. Hence, I do not think they are treating you quite fairly in playing tag with this post.

Relative to the Stewart charges, I am very strongly convinced that they should be forwarded at once. Yours truly,

Charles W. Anderson

TLS Con. 27 BTW Papers DLC.

[1] John Kean (1852–1914), a Republican, was U.S. senator from New Jersey from 1899 to 1911.

From Samuel Langhorne Clemens

[New York City] Jan. 8/06

Dear Mr. Washington: *That* suits me exactly: I will choose my subject *to suit myself;* & shall probably choose it *that night,* (22d) *on the platform.*[1]

Therefore, if any one asks you what it is going to be, you can answer with truth that you don't know & that *I* don't know. Sincerely Yours

S. L. Clemens

ALS Con. 318 BTW Papers DLC.

[1] Clemens spoke on Jan. 22, 1906, at Tuskegee's Silver Jubilee meeting held in Carnegie Hall for the purpose of raising funds for the school. (New York *Times*, Jan. 23, 1906, 1, 2.)

To Portia Marshall Washington

[Tuskegee, Ala.] January 9, 1906

My dear Portia: I have not heard from you for several weeks. I hope however, that you are well and happy. Miss Clark read to me last evening a very interesting letter from you which I was very glad to hear.

I sent you a Christmas present which I hope reached you by the 25th.

Your mamma and Davidson are now in Colorado. They are going to spend a few days in Colorado Springs and then go on to California and Mexico before returning.

I am very glad that you continue to be satisfied and make a good record in your studies. We shall expect great things from you when you return.

As you know, we are planning to celebrate the Twenty-fifth Anniversary of the founding of the school in April. A good many important people are to be [here], including Mr. Carnegie, President Eliot and Secretary Taft. Your papa,

B. T. W.

TLpI Con. 17 BTW Papers DLC.

To Morris Ketchum Jesup

[Tuskegee, Ala.] Jan. 9, 1906

My dear Mr. Jesup: I had a rather remarkable and interesting experience in Nashville last Sunday. I was invited to speak in the largest and most aristocratic white Methodist church in the city. There was considerable nervousness on the part of those who invited me as to how the meeting would turn out. I am glad to say, however, that the audience room was completely packed with white men and women, and I was told that over five hundred were turned away who could not get into the room. I was never more kindly treated nor were my words more sympathetically received in Boston than in Nashville before that white audience.

It may interest you further to know that the dean of the theological department of Vanderbilt University,[1] who was present, has invited me to deliver a lecture before the theological students of Vanderbilt on the subject, "How can the young Southern man help in the lifting up of the Negro race?" Yours very truly,

[Booker T. Washington]

TLp Con. 324 BTW Papers DLC. BTW sent the same letter to Robert C. Ogden, Jan. 9, 1906, Con. 991, BTW Papers, DLC.

1 Wilbur Fisk Tillett (b. 1854), a Methodist Episcopal clergyman, was dean of the theology school of Vanderbilt University beginning in 1886.

To Francis Jackson Garrison

Tuskegee Institute, Alabama. Jan. 10, 1906

Dear Mr. Garrison: I had a most remarkable experience in Nashville last Sunday afternoon. I went to Nashville to deliver an address at Fisk University in connection with the celebration of the fortieth anniversary of that institution. When it was found I was to be there, an invitation was extended me to deliver an address at three o'clock in the afternoon in the most wealthy and aristocratic white Methodist church in the city. All of us had a good deal of anxiety as to the outcome. To the surprise and gratification of all, the church was simply packed with men and women, and I was told that five hundred white people were turned away. To illustrate the nervousness and anxiety in connection with the meeting, just before I left the university to drive to the church, one of the men in charge telephoned that it would not be wise for President Merrill to ride down with me in the carriage to the church as that might tend to hurt the meeting. I at once told President Merrill that I would not consent to any such arrangement and that he must go with me, which he did. There was not a single incident in connection with the meeting that would have indicated that the meeting was not being held in Boston. It was the general understanding, I think, that only white people were to attend the meeting, but a good many colored people did come in and I notice[d] they were treated with as much consideration as the white people. After I had spoken for an hour, and, by the way, notwithstanding it was a Sunday, the audience cheered my address more than a dozen times, men and women crowded up to shake my hand, and a number of Southern white women brought their children up to have them do the same thing. At the close of my address, the dean of the theological department of Vanderbilt University came up to me and extended an invitation to deliver a lecture before the theological students of Vanderbilt University during the spring on the subject, "What can the young Southern white man do to help in the elevation of the Negro?" I have accepted the invitation, and look forward to going with a good deal of interest.

The more I get about among the people, the more I am convinced that a large element of Southern white people are simply sick of the slavery in which they have been held by the radical newspapers and political demagogues. Of course this class is far from being in the majority just now, but I do believe it is growing in number.

On the evening when I spoke at Fisk University I should say that at least a third of the audience were white people, and I was told by President Merrill that most of them live in Nashville. I saw the curious spectacle of white women sitting down on the floor in the aisle in order to hear. They tried in a good many ways to have seats reserved, but President Merrill's invariable reply to them through the telephone was that those who came first would be first served. Yours very truly,

Booker T. Washington

TLS Francis Jackson Garrison Papers NN-Sc. Copies are in Con. 32, BTW Papers, DLC, and the Oswald Garrison Villard Papers, MH. The same letter was sent to William J. Schieffelin on Jan. 13, 1906, Con. 334, BTW Papers, DLC.

To William Dudley Sprague[1]

[Tuskegee, Ala.] Jan. 10, 1906

Dear Mr. Sprague: I telegraphed you yesterday that Booker had not returned to school for the reason that the doctor was undecided what was best for him. For several days we have been going over the matter very carefully, and the doctor now advises that owing to Booker's physical condition that he drop out of school for the remainder of this school year and that he work on the farm in the open air, or without taxing his mind as to studies. In this way the doctor advises that his body will be built up in his opinion to the point where he can buckle down to work in the fall and accomplish better results. Booker himself is very anxious to do this, especially to work on the farm in the air.

I think the suggestion which you made at the bottom of his last monthly statement regarding a change in his studies is a very wise one.

Just as soon as his body gets into condition for some study, I shall let him take one or two lessons a day under a private instructor and in this way gradually by fall we hope to prepare him for better work. I want, however, to have it understood that he can enter Dummer again at your opening in September if his health permits.

I have just received the enclosed statements and am not quite sure, under the circumstances, that on account of his not returning what his financial obligations are. I want to do whatever is necessary in this regard. Yours very truly,

Booker T. Washington

TLpS Con. 17 BTW Papers DLC.

1 William Dudley Sprague (1871–1947) was headmaster of Dummer Academy, South Byfield, Mass., from 1904 to 1906.

To Ralph Waldo Tyler

[Tuskegee, Ala.] Jan. 10, 1906

Personal and Confidential

Dear Mr. Tyler: Your very kind letter has been received and I have read it with deep interest and appreciation. I thank you very earnestly for writing me so frankly and fully.

I want to say in the first place, that anything bordering upon politics is entirely foreign to my nature and wholly distasteful to me. In consenting to work with the President in the way that I am trying to do, I had to decide the question as to whether or not I should do the duty that seems to have been forced upon me, or whether I should shirk because the work is not to my liking. Just now I labor under this disadvantage: my relations with the President are such that persons can put any words into my mouth or any interpretation upon my actions that they desire without my having liberty to make reply.

I am going to tell you that which I have told very few people, and that is this: When the President went into the White House he asked me not to make special and specific endorsements to him of individuals for any office, and he has repeated the same request within a few days. He asked me to hold myself in readiness to be of help concerning the ability and character of any colored persons whom he was considering for office. Of course you can easily understand that [if] I was to become a special endorser of any individual, I would in that case be a special pleader in behalf of A. or B., and my usefulness to the President would be at an end. This is the position I have occupied all along, and the position I now occupy.

The sand storm that some people have kicked up regarding Mr. Williams has arisen in this way. Soon after Mr. Roosevelt succeeded President McKinley, he asked me to give him the names of a number of colored people of ability and high character whom he might consider from time to time for positions under the government, and among those names I gave that of Mr. S. Laing Williams, feeling then, as I do now, that he was a person who would reflect credit and honor on the race in any position that he might occupy. The President understands perfectly well the position that I occupy.

To carry out the specific suggestion which you make in your letter, while it might be wise and relieve me of embarrassment, would be belieing the attitude which I have all along sustained to the President. Of course, should he ask me to help him out by suggesting another candidate, that would be quite a different matter, but to take before him unasked a new candidate would be to place myself in the position of making true just what some of the enemies are stating is already true.

Now to another subject which is wholly confidential. Sometime ago you said that you thought that you would like to get out of the country for a few years. It is possible that the President may ask me to give him the names of two or three people who would be able to fill the consulship at Bahia, Brazil. In case you were offered this position, could you accept it? Yours very truly,

Booker T. Washington

TLpS Con. 336 BTW Papers DLC.

From Archibald Henry Grimké

Washington, Jan. 10/06

Dear Mr. Washington: Your letter of the 4th inst. was duly rec'd. Since its receipt I have read Du Bois' article in The Voice,[1] & agree with you that it is full of false statements touching The Committee of Twelve & his relations to it. I have seen Kelly Miller & asked him to reply to it in The Voice. He had not at the time seen the article, & so could not say that he would comply with my request. It seems to me that Kelly is the best member of the Committee to make the answer, which it appears to me the time has come to make once for all. Will you not write Kelly & second my request? That is of course if you think a reply is called for on the part of our Committee. Du Bois & The Guardian people would like to involve us in a controversy, at least they would like nothing better than to involve you & me, for against us they are especially bitter.

With best regards, I am Cordially yours,

Archibald H. Grimké

ALS Con. 322 BTW Papers DLC.

1 W. E. B. Du Bois, "The Growth of the Niagara Movement," *Voice of the Negro*, 3 (Jan. 1906), 43–45. Du Bois declared that the Afro-American Council was a failure and that the best people in that organization had switched to the Niagara Movement. Du Bois took credit for founding the NNBL, which was based on his studies at Atlanta University, but said that he did not take part in its activities "because I'm a teacher, not a businessman." Du Bois also claimed that it was his plan that led to the establishment of the Committee of Twelve, but he was forced to resign because he did not approve of the membership or the dictatorial power and secret funds of the "one man" who controlled the committee.

To William Dudley Sprague

[Tuskegee, Ala.] January 11, 1906

My dear Mr. Sprague: In writing you a few days ago about Booker, I meant to have expressed my deep sense of satisfaction because of the many evidences which show that Booker went forward very fast in the matter of forming strong substantial character while he was with you. He is now at work on the farm. Yours very truly,

Booker T. Washington

TLpS Con. 17 BTW Papers DLC.

To Samuel Sidney McClure

[Tuskegee, Ala.] January 11, 1906

Personal

My dear Sir: Several days ago, while in conference with a friend, opportunity was provided for me to review a most valuable work, in manuscript, by one of the bravest and truest of Southern white men, Rev. Quincy Ewing,[1] of Birmingham, Alabama, entitled, "The Criminality of the Negro."[2] In the article, he expresses his disapprobation of that part of the Southern press, Southern orators, who unfairly magnify the criminal propensities of the Negro race. He quotes freely from Southern papers, to show how outrageous are many of the sentences imposed for trifling offenses. He convincingly maintains that the Negroes are less criminal than the whites, and in every way stoutly defends and vindicates them from the atrocious charge made against the race by men who now control the shaping of Southern opinion, and the political machinery of this section.

McClure's Magazine has proved such an effective medium for reaching the public that it has occurred to me you might care to consider for serial publication, and afterwards in book form, the manuscript of this work.

I am led to write you this personal letter on the ground simply that it is an extremely valuable contribution, as the voluntary testimony of a white Southerner of recognized character and position, and so calculated to attract attention and discussion.

I am writing this letter absolutely without the knowledge of Mr. Ewing.

I shall be very glad to hear from you with any suggestions you may care to submit in the matter. Very truly,

Booker T. Washington

TLpS Con. 328 BTW Papers DLC.

[1] Quincy Ewing (1867–1939), an Episcopal clergyman, was one of the "forgotten voices" of southern liberalism in the Progressive era. Both his academic and theological training were at the University of the South. He was the rector of churches in Cleveland, Ohio (1890–91), New Orleans (1891–93), Greenville, Miss. (1895–1903), Birmingham (1903–5), Napoleonville, La. (1906–29), and Lindsay, Calif. (1929–35). Perhaps one reason for Ewing's exile of almost a quarter-century in the Cajun country was his performance of the marriage of a divorced fellow-Episcopal clergyman. Another factor, undoubtedly, was his outspoken advocacy of equal justice for blacks. His best-known published work was "The Heart of the Race Problem," *Atlantic Monthly,* 103 (Mar. 1909), 389–97. (Wynes, *Forgotten Voices,* 119–35.)

BTW two days later invited Ewing to preach Tuskegee's commencement sermon, but Ewing declined, saying: "It is probable that, within a few months, I shall be vigorously condemned in certain quarters for my attitude toward the Negroes of the South, and I am not willing that Tuskegee should be put in the position of honoring a Southern white man who may be at the time of its Commencement under considerable fire as a 'traitor to the traditions of his race, a slanderer of the Southern people, etc., etc.' " (BTW to Ewing, Jan. 13, and Ewing to BTW, Jan. 15, 1906, Con. 321, BTW Papers, DLC.)

[2] The manuscript apparently was never published.

To Ernest Davidson Washington

[Tuskegee, Ala.] January 12, 1906

Dear Davidson: Booker worked on the farm yesterday, and was engaged in plowing a mule. He seems to enjoy it very much. Your papa,

B. T. W.

TLpI Con. 17 BTW Papers DLC.

From Charles William Anderson

New York, N.Y., January 12, 1906

My dear Doctor: Replying more fully to your telegram relative to the Bahia Consulate, I beg to advise you that after looking the entire matter over, I have concluded that Mr. James W. Johnson of this city, is by all odds the very best man for the place. With him as a candidate, we cannot possibly be placed on the defensive; but, on the contrary, we shall be supporting a man against whom nothing can possibly be said, except that he is a member of "Ethiopia's blameless race." You know as well as I do that he is a man of sound judgment, ripe scholarship, and possesses a character free from every stain. He is a graduate of Atlanta University, and is now taking a post-graduate degree at Columbia. More than this, he has splendid working knowledge of Spanish, and is also very familiar with French. Thus, you see, he will measure up to the very high standard prescribed by Secretary Root in the matter of consular appointments. As President of the Coloured Republican Club of the City of New York, he has rendered much valuable service to the cause and candidates of our party, and has contributed to our victories both in time and treasure. Mr. Johnson is, in my judgment, a thoroughly unexceptionable candidate, and one with whom we can win. Let us both get behind him at once, and push him with all the strength at our command. If we do, we shall win.

In this connection, perhaps it may not be amiss to say that his appointment would confuse the opposition greatly, as they could not be so blind as not to see the influences which brought it about. Therefore, I hope you will communicate at once with the President, and state the case with that strength of language which is yours — and only yours. Yours respectfully,

Charles W. Anderson

TLS Con. 27 BTW Papers DLC.

Tuskegee Institute in 1906

A SELECTION OF PHOTOGRAPHS BY
FRANCES BENJAMIN JOHNSTON

FROM THE
FRANCES BENJAMIN JOHNSTON COLLECTION
LIBRARY OF CONGRESS

Booker T. Washington.

Booker T. Washington and his children Ernest Davidson Washington (standing left), Booker T. Washington, Jr., and niece Laura Murray Washington.

Margaret M. Washington.

Emmett J. Scott.

Emmett J. Scott and family.

Booker T. Washington and Emmett J. Scott.

Robert R. Taylor.

George Washington Carver.

Jane E. Clark.

Robert E. Park.

Home of John H. Washington and family.

John H. Washington and family.

Margaret M. Washington (seated) and faculty of the industries for girls department.

Faculty of the academic department.

Chaplain Edgar J. Penney and his wife,
Estelle C. Penney.

Chaplain Edgar J. Penney (seated center)
and the senior Bible class.

The Lincoln Gates with the Tuskegee Chapel in the background.

Slater-Armstrong Memorial Trades Building.

Carnegie Library.

Charles Winter Wood, librarian, and Florence E. Sewell, cataloger, in the Carnegie Library.

Road work near Douglass Hall.

Student military corps.

Band concert.

The commandant of cadets, Major Julius B. Ramsey (seated center), and battalion officers.

Tuskegee Institute baseball team.

Tennis game.

Physical education class.

Graduate nurses.

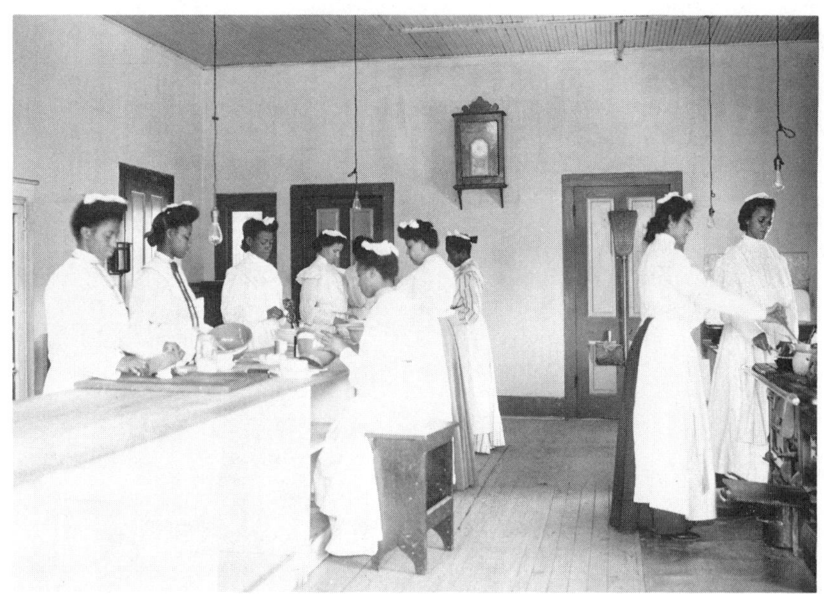

Cooking class.

Wheelwright division class.

Woodworking shop.

Basket-weaving.

Millinery class.

Electric generator.

Oiling a milk separator.

Ploughing on the Tuskegee farm.

Planting sugar cane.

Cultivating onions.

Silos at Tuskegee Institute.

Music class.

The 1906 senior class.

Geography class.

Students studying a loaf of bread.

Dignitaries on reviewing stand during twenty-fifth anniversary ceremonies. Front row from left: (3rd) Charles W. Eliot; (5th) Hollis B. Frissell; (7th) Lyman Abbott; (8th) Wallace Buttrick; (9th) Robert C. Ogden; (10th) Andrew Carnegie.

Group of faculty and guests at twenty-fifth aniversary celebration. Seated left to right: Robert C. Ogden, Margaret M. Washington, Booker T. Washington, Andrew Carnegie.

Replicas of Tuskegee Institute's first buildings.

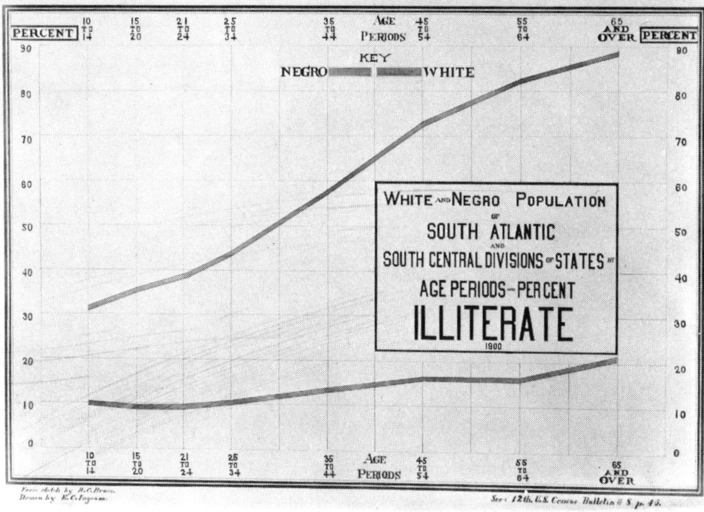

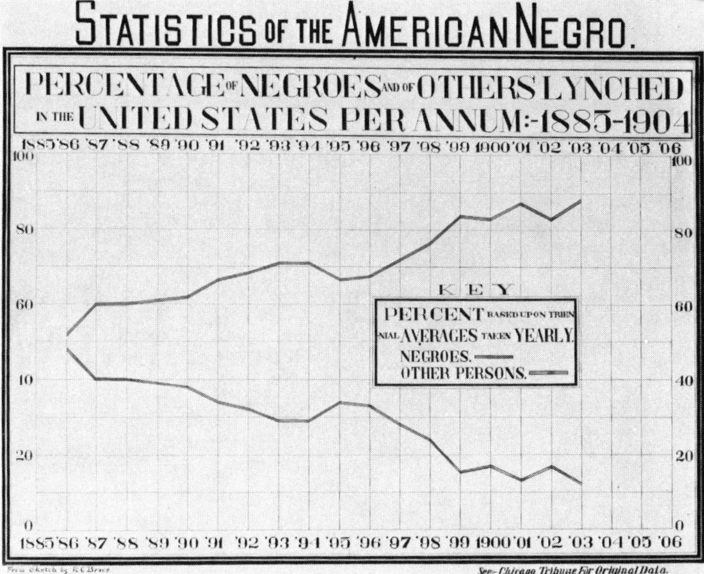

Two charts prepared at Tuskegee Institute.

Booker T. Washington.

Booker T. Washington, Jr.

From Ralph Waldo Tyler

Columbus, Ohio. January 12, 1906

My Dear Mr. Washington: Your very kind letter of the 10th. at hand. I appreciate fully the position you occupy, and though I had not before received from you personally a statement of the position you occupy with the President, bearing on appointments, I was perfectly satisfied that that position was in perfect accord with your life's work — laboring for your race.

I really could not conceive of any other motive that could actuate your recommendations, for to me you are the embodiment of unselfish devotion to race interests.

I know Mr. Williams, and know him to be fitted for the work, and I know that he is a man of honor, a high-souled generous fellow.

I know that Prof. Vernon, his opponent for the position, is the especial protege of the A. M. E. Church, which organization is moving heaven and earth to discredit you in the eyes of not only your own people, but in the eyes of the whites. His appointment would strengthen the Methodist Bishops who held high carnival under the McKinley administration, and who bartered offices for a consideration.

I felt that Mr. Williams' selection at this time, would only tend to make the fight on you more acute, and for that reason thought it wise that a "brand new" man be chosen. I still feel that the man selected should be the man of your choice — a Negro who is in sympathy with your grand work. This is a Republic, you know, and Republics are ungrateful — they say. At any rate, a man today may ride upon the crest of the waves, applauded by his people, and tomorrow be relegated to obscurity by his people whom he benefited.

Your work is of too great importance to the whole race to be relieved of the position, exalted position you now occupy, and for that reason I believed you should hedge yourself about with strong, loyal, constant friends in every department of life.

Relative to the question you ask — would I accept appointment to fill a consulship at Bahia, Brazil, in case I were offered the position, my answer is that I would esteem it such an honor to be the object of Dr. Washington's recommendation that I could not refuse.

even if at a sacrifice. I have never held office, never sought office, and would not seek today, though if one came to me, purely at the suggestion of you, I would accept. And whether or not you should suggest me, you can always rely upon it that I stand unequivocally, firmly and unyielding in support of you and your wise administration of the trust it seems that God has placed in your keeping — the interests and advancement of our race.

For this world, at least, I can change the words "Lead Kindly Light," to Lead Booker T. Washington.

The President did right to call you into his confidence. I admire him for it. Very sincerely yours,

Ralph W Tyler

TLS Con. 336 BTW Papers DLC.

To Jesse Lawson

[Tuskegee, Ala.] Jan. 13, 1906

Personal

My dear Mr. Lawson: I have your letter stating that the New Jersey congressmen are urging your claims for recognition at the hands of the President. No one is more cognizant of what you have done for the race and all that is highest and best than I am, and I made known my faith in you when Mr. Roosevelt first became President and suggested to me that he would like to get the names of several colored people to be considered for appointment to the position of magistrates in the District of Columbia. Your name was among the first that I suggested, but found out afterward that you were ineligible owing to the fact that you were living in New Jersey.

My position in connection with the President is rather a peculiar one. We had an understanding when he first went into the Presidential office, and he has repeated the same request within the last few days, that I not make specific recommendations or give specific endorsements to him of persons for positions under him, but that I hold myself in readiness to answer any questions that he may ask or give my opinion concerning the fitness of men he is considering for office. The minute that I become a special endorser of individuals then I become a special pleader in their behalf and my opinion ceases to be a disinterested one and becomes a personal and party opinion. I should be placed in a much stronger position to help you if pressure were brought to bear through your congressmen and others so that the President would speak to me concerning your fitness for office. I could then speak in a way that would be of real service; in fact this is the way that I have been able to help friends to whom I have been of some slight assistance in the past. I am quite sure you can understand the wisdom of this course. In many cases he has asked me, as in the case of the consulship at Bahia, to give him the names of several colored men that might be considered. I have done that in that case, and have in several other cases given him the names of three or four colored men who might fill well the position designated and have left him to make his own selection out of the several names submitted to him.

When I see you I shall talk this matter over more fully with you. Yours very truly,

Booker T. Washington

TLpS Con. 3 BTW Papers DLC.

To Theodore Roosevelt

[Tuskegee, Ala.] January 13, 1906

Personal

My dear Mr. President: I have received the enclosed newspaper article from Mr. Loeb. I had already seen it.

Of course you will have to bear in mind that you are doing something that no other President has done, and that is making an effort to put into office a number of intelligent, conscientious and first class colored men, and this class of colored men are not the ones, who, as a rule, have the political backing and political following that the old school colored politicians had. It is almost impossible to combine the two elements, except in a few cases like that of Anderson in New York.

The man who wrote this editorial is E. H. Wright, and if you will look at the files in your office you will find he is an applicant for the position of Register of the Treasury and that is the animus of the editorial. Wright writes most of the editorials for this paper. I ought to say, however, that while Wright opposes Williams' appointment, he is a higher class of man than E. H. Morris or J. G. Jones who wrote you protesting against Williams sometime ago. S. B. Turner,[1] whose name is signed to this letter, himself amounts to very little and his paper has a circulation of only a few hundred and that mainly in Chicago. I think, however, Turner stands well with Governor Deneen.

Judging by what I know of conditions among the colored people in Chicago, I would state that it is a safe conclusion that 80 per cent perhaps, of the active colored politicians are either indifferent toward Williams or opposed to him. On the other hand, I should say that at least 85 per cent of the masses of the people, including the best element, favor his recognition at your hands. Much of the opposition among the politicians has been worked up by Cyrus Field Adams, the present Assistant Register of the Treasury, who fears that if Williams is made Register he will be displaced. Yours truly,

Booker T. Washington

TLpS BTW Papers ATT.

1 Sheadrick Bond Turner (1869?–1927) was a lawyer and editor of a small Negro newspaper who also served in the Illinois Senate from 1914 to 1916 and from 1918 to 1927. Born in Louisiana, Turner moved to Springfield, Ill., where he began publishing the *State Capital* in 1889. Later he moved to Chicago and renamed the paper the *Illinois Idea*.

From Ralph Waldo Tyler

Columbus, Ohio. [ca. Jan. 15, 1906][1]

My Dear Mr. Washington: About 115 or 120 years ago, a beautiful young girl was abducted at Bahia, and brought to America, abandoned and sold into slavery, becoming the property of a white family named Seymour, in Connecticut — that was when slaves were held in the nutmeg state.

In course of time the family moved to York state, and to this girl was born children, one Ann, also a pretty girl and resembling her mother, was taken when but 5 years old by Alfred Kelley,[2] father of the Ohio Canal system, who had just married,[3] and brought with them to Columbus, Ohio in 1817,[4] where she continued to reside, for seventy-odd years, until her death at the age of 91 years. She was educated by the Kelleys and married, in their home in this city, to a William McAfee, a mulatto, and this union was blessed by several children, among whom was my mother.

I did not think to mention this to you in my letter the other day. The Bahia girl never again saw home or parents. Her daughter Ann, my grandmother, likewise, after being brought to Ohio, never again saw her old home or mother. It is a rather pathetic story, and it occurred to me, after you mentioned the Bahia matter to me, that it would be rather a sort of "eternal fitness of things," if I should be the fortunate man selected, that a lineal descendent of the unfortunate native Bahia girl should be sent to represent the country from whence she was stolen, by the country she was unwillingly brought to. This incident alone would make that appointment a pleasant one to me, though, of course, I am not building any hopes upon it, being content just to permit the matter [to] rest with you.

Like all those unfortunates of our race whose foreparents were slaves, we cannot trace our genealogy any further back than the great-grandmother.

Frequently, when I stop to think of this, it makes me inexpressably sad to think that while the proud caucasians can trace their lineage back as far as the mind of man runneth — back to the first bit of recorded history, we can go no further than a great-grandmother — more frequently no further back than our mothers. Very sincerely yours,

Ralph W Tyler

TLS Con. 336 BTW Papers DLC.

1 Scott docketed the letter on Jan. 17 with the remark: "In many respects very interesting! Said sent to you."

2 Alfred Kelley (1789–1859), the first lawyer in Cleveland in 1810, was county prosecuting attorney from 1810 to 1822, and a banker and businessman. Kelly promoted canal-building in Ohio as canal commissioner from 1822 to 1834, and later was a railroad entrepreneur.

3 Kelley married Mary Seymour Welles of Lowville, N.Y., in 1817.

4 Kelley did not move to Columbus until 1830.

To Kelly Miller

N.Y. [City] Jan 18 [190]6

Personal –
Hope you – McKinley[1] and others will watch closely progress of Inter State Commerce bill bearing on Sleeping Cars for our people.[2]

Booker T. Washington

HWcSr Con. 328 BTW Papers DLC.

[1] Whitefield McKinlay.

[2] For a full discussion of the lobbying efforts of BTW and his associates, see Crofts, "The Warner-Foraker Amendment," 341–58.

From Albert G. Davis

Birmingham Ala. Jan. 18th 1906

Dear Prof: I have a request to make of you and one that I sincerely trust that you will see your way clear to grant. For the past 17 years you have consistently and persistently been unable to comply with any of my beseeching supplications. I am hopeful that the auspicious year of 1906 will effect a change of heart.

My enemies have seemingly placed a brick wall between us, almost making an insuperable barrier. Not wishing to monopolize your time, I shall state my request briefly. I am anxious to have my disabilities removed and desire your coöperation. I am one of your early graduates as well as my wife and any assistance that you render me will be given her as well.

I desire you to write two letters for me and in my behalf. One to Hon I. W. Hill[1] at Montgomery State Supt. of Education requesting him to restore my life certificate, and another letter to Hon. Jos. O. Thompson at Birmingham Ala. requesting him to take my case up with the authorities at Washington. I am guilty of no crime, and have endeavored to support my wife and *six* children as best I can. No graduate of Tuskegee has excelled or approximated me in my efforts to demonstrate the literary work that is done at Tuskegee and I cannot believe that you would have the heart to deny this request.

It is foreign to my intention to claim that I am blameless, still I do think that my punishment has been adequate for all of my shortcomings. I am 35 years of age, and am vigorous in body and mind; right now I am at my best intellectually, and am striving to startle all Alabama shortly. For more than a year I have been studying law without a tutor, and within twelve months, will make application for examination before the Ala. Supreme Court.

I am striving with might and main to put up the best examination Alabama has ever known and I will be a much disappointed man should I receive anything short of 95%. Whenever I demonstrate my fitness in this manner "all the animals in the menagerie" are stirred up and abuse, contumely and etc are resorted to. I am called everything and every crime in the calendar is laid at my door. Somehow I thrive off of abuse and such only increases my ambition to make greater efforts.

Hoping to hear from you at once, I am Yours gratefully

Albert G. Davis

ALS Con. 3 BTW Papers DLC.

[1] Isaac W. Hill (b. 1861) was Alabama state superintendent of schools from 1902 to 1907.

An Item in the Denver *Rocky Mountain News*

Washington Jan. 19 [1906]

B. T. WASHINGTON
OCCUPIES BERTH
OF MORTAL ENEMY

Representative James Heflin of Alabama, who, in a campaign speech two years ago, said that if an anarchist had thrown a bomb under the table at which President Roosevelt and Booker T. Washington dined "no harm would have been done," is a victim of retributive justice, as well as of the chaffings of his colleagues.

When returning to Washington from Alabama this week Mr.

Heflin is reported to have engaged a sleeping car berth, which, upon entering the train, he found occupied by Mr. Washington. The colored educator is said to have slept peacefully throughout the night, while Mr. Heflin sat up until his wrath cooled sufficiently for him to climb to an upper berth.[1]

Denver *Rocky Mountain News*, Jan. 20, 1906, 3.

1 For another account of the incident see Julius R. Cox to Emmett J. Scott, Jan. 24, 1906, below.

An Item in the New York *World*[1]

[Jan. 19, 1906]

BOOKER T. WASHINGTON'S DENIAL

Booker T. Washington, yesterday, when shown the statement published recently to the effect that he had advised the President to remove all colored office-holders in the South from office said: "I have given no such advice; the statement is false."

New York *World*, Jan. 19, 1906, 1.

1 E. J. Scott wired BTW on Jan. 18: "Information reaching me is to effect that our people in all quarters are greatly stirred regarding false statements sent out as to Negro office holders in South. You may care to consider meeting this criticism with disavowal." BTW replied by wire from New York on Jan. 19: "Flat denial to Associated Press last night. Practically all New York papers have it this morning." (Con. 566, BTW Papers, DLC.)

To Emmett Jay Scott

[New York City] January 20, 1906

Dear Mr. Scott: I cannot understand the working of the head of many of our educated people. What in the world Mr. Hill hoped to accomplish by that poem[1] in this week's Independent I cannot understand.

The last two lines, of course, gives the point to the whole of it. The expression of such sentiment will accomplish no good in the South and is calculated to do much harm in the North.

If we, who are on the ground, do not have confidence in the future and permanency of our own work we certainly cannot expect others to have it. Very truly yours,

Booker T. Washington

TLS Con. 2 BTW Papers DLC.

[1] In his poem "Tuskegee," Leslie Pinckney Hill began with the question, "Wherefore this busy labor without rest?" He found himself unable to answer, because of his awareness that an envious white South might "root out the seed we sow." (*Independent*, 60 [Jan. 18, 1906], 142.)

To Samuel Laing Williams

[New York City] January 22, 1906

Personal & Confidential.

My dear Mr. Williams: I have received your letter of January 15th. I do not think you ought to feel too much discouraged or too hopeless. At the time Mr. Scott and Mr. Anderson saw the President two weeks ago he told them most emphatically that either you or Vernon would be appointed and if it was Vernon your name would be sent in at the same time for some important place. He made this distinct and plain to both of them. I can only take him at his word.

In the case of Vernon, you will have to bear in mind that with the President just now, when he is trying to get important matters through the Senate that politics count for much. Vernon, it appears, had the entire Kansas, Missouri and Colorado delegation behind him, while in your case none of the Illinois delegation supported you, but on the other hand were luke-warm or opposed you. Added to this there was an active element of Illinois colored office-holders in the District and in Chicago who opposed you. These are the facts with which we have had to deal.

Any man who aspires to political preferment has to pass through what you are now passing through. One other thing you should remember the President has done that which no other President has done in the appointing you as Consul to Bahia. I shall hope to have a talk with you soon. Very truly yours,

[Booker T. Washington]

TLc Con. 34 BTW Papers DLC.

From Thomas Dixon, Jr.[1]

New York Jan. 22, 1906

Sir: In response to your appeal for funds I hereby offer to contribute $10,000 from the profits of "The Clansman" to Tuskegee Institute provided you give complete and satisfactory proof that you do not desire Social Equality for the Negro and that your School is opposed to the Amalgamation of the races. Sincerely,

Thomas Dixon Jr

TLS Con. 320 BTW Papers DLC.

1 BTW spoke at a fund-raising meeting in Carnegie Hall with Mark Twain, R. C. Ogden, and others on Jan. 22, 1906, the Silver Jubilee of Tuskegee Institute. Just before BTW entered the hall, a messenger boy handed him Dixon's note. When asked what he had to say on the subject, BTW replied: "I will make no answer whatever. I have nothing to say." (New York *Times*, Jan. 23, 1906, 2.)

From Thomas Dixon, Jr.

New York [Jan. 23, 1906]

I invite you to debate with me in the largest Hall available in New York the question of "The Future of the Negro in America."

The entire proceeds may go to your school and I will agree not to refer to my play "The Clansman." The issue of Social Equality and Race Amalgamation which I asked you to meet last night in your address at Carnegie Hall is one which the American people will demand that you face squarely sooner or later. Sincerely

Thomas Dixon Jr

TLS Con. 320 BTW Papers DLC.

From Charles Betts Galloway

Jackson, Mississippi Jan. 23d, 1906

My Dear Sir: Many thanks for your kind letter and your kindly interest in our library enterprise. The schedule received has been filled out and forwarded according to instructions. Now a word more. You know what I have stood for in education, good government and the elevation of *all* the people. Of course I ask no recognition of such service, but I would appreciate larger facilities in order to more efficiently continue it. This gift from Mr. Carnegie would greatly strengthen the hands of some of us who are trying to serve our country in a much needed way. The prejudice against the education of our colored youth, as you know, comes largely from those who are uneducated themselves. So to multiply the real, helpful friends of the colored people we must educate the whites, *and in an atmosphere of sympathy with the largest and best things.*

Your kindly assistance in this matter is deeply appreciated. And now as the papers have gone on, a few words more from you may secure immediate consideration. If he could give us now $25,000.00 for that library building, while certain agitations are on, it would be of immense service. Of course you understand all the reasons for this seeming urgency.

Again thanking you for your kindly interest and wishing for you and the work you represent, every possible success, I am Yours very truly

Chas. B. Galloway

ALS Con. 322 BTW Papers DLC.

Julius Robert Cox to Emmett Jay Scott

[New York City] January 24, 1906

Dear Mr. Scott: On the account of the reaction that the attached[1] may have it is unfortunate that it appeared, but it is the gospel truth in almost every detail. Conductor Pusey does not like Heflin and told me all these facts as soon as the train left Opelika, with the additional wish that he hoped nothing would be on the Bir. sleeper so the ——— (you can guess) would have to stay in the day coach where he belonged. Heflin fumed and swore, but it only made matters worse for himself, as he could have secured a lower in Atlanta had he acted nice, but Pusey made him take the choice between an upper or the coach.

The story first appeared in the Washington Post and I have a suspicion that Pusey is responsible for it as the story comes too straight in detail for an outsider to hit on. Yours,

J. R. Cox

TLS Con. 565 BTW Papers DLC.

[1] The attached newspaper clipping from the Montgomery *Times* reported that Congressman J. Thomas Heflin sat up all night in a day coach while his constituent, BTW, slept in a Pullman berth he had bought at Chehaw, Ala., before the congressman had asked for a reservation. See another account, An Item in the Denver *Rocky Mountain News*, Jan. 19, 1906, above.

To Thomas Dixon, Jr.

[New York City] January 25, 1906

Personal.

Dear Sir: Replying to your communications permit me to say I have expressed myself fully on all the subjects you touch upon, in my various speeches and publications, and I cannot feel that any good can be accomplished at this time by taking up the subjects in the manner your communications suggest. Very truly yours,

[Booker T. Washington]

TLc Con. 320 BTW Papers DLC.

From Charles Alexander

Boston, Massachusetts January 25, 1906

My dear Dr. Washington: The backbone of the Guardian is at last broken on account of my vigorous protest. The manager of the New England Newspaper Union had quite a quarrel with Trotter last week which resulted in Trotter's taking his work to another office. I made personal complaint of the outrageous manner [in] which Trotter had been allowed to attack you. I characterized the edition last week as the most villainous, as well as vicious attack that has appeared for some time and to my surprise, the manager had not seen the paper up to that time. As soon as he examined it, he became violently angry, and when Trotter put in appearance, he went for him without gloves. Trotter threatened to take the paper away from the office and the manager said that he would be very glad if he would, that he could not stand for the kind of libelous matter that Trotter was publishing.

I felt very proud this morning when the manager called at my office in person and gave me some of the secrets of the Guardian dealings and if you will let me know when you are in the city, I will tell you the whole story.

The office where Trotter has selected to have his paper published for the future is not well equipped and the paper will cost considerably more in that office than in the office of the N. E. Newspaper Union. This new place has no facilities for furnishing ready print and at best, he will get very poor service. The manager of the Union said to me this morning that if I would have my lawyer write to this new printer and warn him against printing libelous matter in the paper, that he would frighten him so that he would go through every bit of the reading matter published and would cut out any damaging or libelous paragraphs. I am inclined to do this, but I do not wish to go ahead until I hear from you. The fact of the matter is, I believe that I could get close enough to the new printer who is known to me to get him to stop the paper altogether so far as he is concerned. This printer publishes a paper for the Mayor[1] of the city of Boston and out of fear of affecting the appearance of the Mayor's paper, I am sure that he would not undertake anything so treacherous as the publication of the Guardian.

Please let me know at once when I shall see you and go through this matter. Sincerely yours,

Charles Alexander

TLS Con. 32 BTW Papers DLC.

[1] John Francis (Honey Fitz) Fitzgerald (1863–1950) was mayor from 1906 to 1907, and again from 1910 until 1914.

From Ralph Waldo Tyler

Columbus, Ohio. January 27/06

My Dear Dr. Washington: The "Clansman" opened a three-performance engagement here last evening at our leading theatre, and I thought you might be interested in seeing our criticism on the play.[1] For two weeks the advance press agent has been appealing to prejudice here in order to attract a large crowd. Dixon's challenge to you to discuss the social equality question (which was but a scheme to advertise his book and play) was used for all it was worth. This "hot roast" which we hand the play, and incidentally the book, this morning will have the effect of reducing the attendance this afternoon and this evening to an unprofitable minimum, as The State Journal is regarded as the most influential newspaper in Ohio, and any criticism we make of dramatic attractions are accepted as gospel truth by the public.

The applause bestowed upon it last evening was such as the gallery always bestows upon the blood and thunder scenes in a melodrama at cheap theatres, and it in no wise bespoke a sympathy, on the part of the audience, for the desired aim of the book and play. The applause was just such applause as follows the exciting, spectacular racing of a band of cowboys and bedizzoned [bedizened] Indians around the ring in a Buffalo Bill Wild West Show. I think I have contributed a mite to seriously "knock" the "Clansman" in Columbus. Sincerely yours,

Ralph W Tyler

TLS Con. 336 BTW Papers DLC. On stationery of the *Ohio State Journal.*

[1] The attached review from the *Ohio State Journal* concluded: "The play is lib-

erally supplied with gun play, violent assaults, meetings in caves by green moon light, and negro characterizations which are a libel on the race. In short, if 'The Clansman' did not play upon the prejudices it would not play at all."

From Booker Taliaferro Washington, Jr.

Tuskegee Institute, Alabama. Sunday Jan. 28th, 1906

My dear Papa; I received your telegram and I suppose that when you sent it you had not then received my letter.

I received the things that you sent me, the skates, the basket ball, and the fruit. I thank you very much for them.

To-day has been such a lovely day. I have been to every thing to-day. I got up early this morning and went to Christian Endeavor, went to church and sat in our seats, and after dinner went to the Y. M. C. A. So to-night I am staying away from Chapel to write to you and Mamma.

Last night I attended the Natural History Debating Club. Prof Carver spoke to that club which meets in the Agricultural Building. He gave a very interesting talk. Mrs. B. K. Bruce spoke to the Y. M. C. A. to-day. She gave a very good talk. Mr. Whittaker preached an extra fine sermon to-day also.

The weather here has been very changeable. It has been quite cold up [to] to-day. We really had snow one or two nights ago. But it did not last long as it melted almost as soon as it fell on the ground.

That was a great meeting that was held in Carnegie Hall. I saw a short account of it in one of the N.Y. papers, and also a picture of you taken when you were addressing the large audience.

I still continue to get on all right on the farm, and I think that Mr. Green[e] will have a very good report to give you of me when you return.

With lots of love, I remain Your loving son,

Booker

P.S. Papa the Sugar of Milk is all out.

ALS Con. 17 BTW Papers DLC.

From Emmett Jay Scott

Tuskegee Institute, Alabama. January 31, 1906

Dear Mr. Washington: I sent you a Conservator a day or two ago. I notice that much of the stuff which appears in that issue is a matrix of the matter that appeared in the Guardian the week before. I notice also that the same stuff appears in the Broadax of Chicago. This fellow is industrially doing whatever his resources will permit him to do in the way of being nasty. It is only such creatures as Wilkins and Broadax-Taylor,[1] however, that can be used by him.

I note your letter with regard to Mr. Alexander's telephone message.[2] The Guardian came out last week with a good deal less matter but as slanderous as ever. I trust that the newspaper Union will hold out against further printing this defamatory sheet. Yours truly,

E J Scott

TLS Con. 566 BTW Papers DLC.

[1] Julius F. Taylor, BTW's severest critic in Chicago, was editor of the Chicago *Broad Ax* from 1899, when he moved the newspaper to Chicago from Salt Lake City, until 1931. A Democrat and supporter of William Jennings Bryan, Taylor often bitterly denounced black Republicans. He frequently assailed BTW as "the greatest white man's 'Nigger' in the world," and "the Great Beggar of Tuskegee." After 1910, however, Taylor moderated his views of BTW and even printed news releases from Tuskegee. He argued that his change of heart was due to the fact that BTW was less active in politics and was devoting more time to purely educational work. (Spear, *Black Chicago*, 82–83.)

[2] This exchange contained the same information as the letter from Charles Alexander, Jan. 25, 1906, above.

To Booker Taliaferro Washington, Jr.

[New York City] February 1, 1906

Dear Booker: I have received your letter of the 28th and I am glad indeed to hear from you. I am especially glad to know that you are getting on so well and making such a good record for yourself. It is very pleasing to know you enjoy your work on the farm so much. Work on the farm or out in the open air will help you regain your health and strength and prepare you for hard study.

I sent you this morning one box of sugar of milk and by express I am sending you six boxes. I guess your Mama and Davidson will be home within a few days. I shall be starting South before very long.

I hope you are doing some systematic and regular reading, in addition to that you ought to keep up with the current news. Mr. Wood will help you in this. I sent you papers containing an account of the big meeting here, it was a great success and very interesting.

I was especially glad to know that you attended so many meetings Sunday, I hope that you will keep it up. Your papa.

[Booker T. Washington]

TLc Con. 17 BTW Papers DLC.

Frederick Randolph Moore to Samuel Laing Williams

[New York City] Feb. 2–[190]6

If possible be in New York Sunday morning to confer with friends Stevens House[1] – all expenses paid. Get full information where stock of Conservator is and what can buy it. You can return Sunday. Answer.

Fred R. Moore

HWcSr Con. 34 BTW Papers DLC.

1 BTW's hotel.

Charles William Anderson to Emmett Jay Scott

New York, N.Y., February 3, 1906

Confidential.

My dear Emmett: Yours of the 29th ultimo has been received, and receipt forwarded to Mr. Belmont. The Doctor wrote Mr. Belmont a very handsome letter, a copy of which he was kind enough to send me.[1] Hence, you see, we are all happy. You may be interested to know that Mr. Belmont promised to do something more later on.

Doubtless you are aware that a white man, evidently a Hebrew, has been appointed to Bahia. You will recall that I told you at our last meeting that, in my judgment, if Napier refused the place, it would be given out without consultation with the Doctor or his friends. Thus, you see, I am either "a prophet, or the son of a prophet." I hope this continual dropping of our men, will not go much further. Remember, we have lost three good places in the consular service alone – the consulship at Santo Domingo, the one at Vladivostok, and Bahia. These, together with the loss of the naval officer at New Orleans, the Postmaster at Athens Georgia, and the office held by Postmaster Vick in North Carolina, and the Collectorship of the Port at Wilmington, North Carolina, and a Receivership of Public Moneys in Alabama, make a very serious loss to the race under this administration. I am advising the Doctor to put "our friend" in immediate possession of these facts, and to advise him that our quota ought not to be in any way diminished. I am quite sure that our "great and good friend" at the White House does not realize how much the race has really lost. The process has been gradual, and he has possibly not noticed it. One by one, at considerable intervals of time, offices held by coloured men have been given to "whites"; and I am fearful that before the President has time to make up for the loss (which he surely will do), some enemy may get hold of these facts and exploit them in the newspapers. Hence, I feel that it is important to call this condition to the Presidential attention at once. Don't you? Of course we have my own appointment, and Crum, and Lewis, to offset these losses, but when you consider the salary of the Athens Post Office, that of the naval officer at New Orleans, and those of Postmaster Vick, and the Collector at Wilmington, North Carolina, as against the combined salaries of myself, Lewis, Terrell, and Crum, you will discover that we are on the bad side of the ledger. If Rucker and Deveaux are added to this list, the loss will be very great indeed. I need not waste any words in attempting to convince you that something ought to be done to stop this persistent falling off in our representation.[2]

Let me have your views on this matter. Yours truly,

Charles

TLS Con. 261 BTW Papers DLC.

1 BTW wrote August Belmont thanking him for a gift of $5,000 after the Tuskegee Silver Jubilee meeting at Carnegie Hall to appeal for endowment funds. BTW called the gift through Charles Anderson "one of the most pleasant surprises I have ever experienced." (Jan. 26, 1906, Con. 719, BTW Papers, DLC.)

2 Scott wrote to Anderson Feb. 6, 1906, commenting on this decline in the number of officeholders: "Personally, I feel that these things ought to be looked after, but, as I say, I have lost heart and am not so 'pushing' as I have been in these matters. I feel considerably annoyed that the Doctor should carry so much of the burden and reap so little of encouragement. Of course, he does not feel as I do in the matter, being of a temperament more optimistic." (Con. 27, BTW Papers, DLC.)

From Kelly Miller

[Washington, D.C.] Feb. 6, 1906

My dear Dr. Washington: According to arrangement of last Friday, Mr. Grimke and myself have engaged the services of Hon. H. W. Blair as "Counsel" to look after the interests of the colored race as they might be affected by the Railroad Rates Bill. We gave him to understand that he would be expected to watch every move in connection with this measure, ferret out the secret plans of Southern Senators and members, and to keep us fully advised. This he is willing to do, and will accept a fee of three hundred dollars ($300.00), one half to be paid at once, and the rest at our convenience. It is understood, however, that at the close of the session or upon the passage of the measure, we may offer additional compensation according to the estimate we may place upon the character and value of the service rendered. We should like to have a check for $150.00 in hand by Saturday to enable us to fulfill our promise to him.

He went at once to the capitol to look into the matter, and promises to keep us in close touch with the drift of things. Both Mr. Grimke and myself are much pleased with the interest which he manifests in the matter, and with his adroit suggestions as to methods of procedure. Yours truly,

Kelly Miller

TLSr Copy BTW Papers ATT.

To Kelly Miller

[New York City] February 10, 1906

My dear Mr. Miller: Just sent you a telegram reading as follows, "Blair money is being sent you today. Tell him now is time to watch matters closely as bill is being considered by Senate Committee."

In accordance with the above telegram, enclosed you will find money order for one hundred and fifty dollars.[1] Very truly yours,

[Booker T. Washington]

TLc BTW Papers ATT.

[1] BTW wrote Miller on the same day that he was disturbed that no definite fee had been specified. "If anything else is expected," BTW wrote, "an indefinite or implied promise most always brings trouble or friction." He told Miller that he believed $300 was an adequate amount. (BTW Papers, ATT.)

Francis Jackson Garrison to Oswald Garrison Villard

The Cedars [Lexington, Mass.] Febry 11, 1906

Dear Oswald: If I were to speak at Tuskegee, I should be moved, as you are, to make my talk more or less personal to B. T. W. & on the signal ability & wisdom with which he has built up his great institution. I should quote from Walter Page's tribute in 1899, when he wrote me, "Washington is by far the greatest constructive mind his race has produced, & one of the most useful men now alive. *His institution could be spared less well than any university or school of any sort that we have in America. Harvard would not be so missed when the final & correct measurement of things is made.*" (Eliot of course would not admit that!) I should allude to the incalculable benefit it has been to all sections & to B. T. W. himself that he has gone so widely up & down the country, coming in contact with the best men & minds & impressing his rare personality upon them, but should remind people that this cannot continue indefinitely, & that now is the time for the philanthropy of the country to adequately endow Tuskegee & lift the burden of the annual expenses from his shoulders, giving him time for further constructive & developing work. I am deeply impressed by the stories of the graduates told in "Tuskegee & its People," & by the extraordinary work accomplished in three years by Holtzclaw[1] in Mississippi, as proving how thoroughly B. T. W. inspires his boys & girls with his own spirit of consecration, & shows how to build on the (apparently) most hopeless foundations. Two hundred Tuskegees would not be too many in the South to-day.

I am sorry to see that the Virginia House has passed the Jim Crow extension bill, but I hope the reaction against Dixonism & Vardamanism is setting in, nevertheless. Good for your Jewish friends!

B. T. W. has the *spirit* of the old abolitionists, in his resolute adherences to counsels of peace, love, faith in the sure victory of right & justice, & the patience that comes from that faith. This is crudely stated, but I write in tearing haste for the mail. Affectly

Uncle Frank

Love to Julia.

ALS Oswald Garrison Villard Papers MH.

1 William Henry Holtzclaw, born in the log cabin of a sharecropping family near Roanoke, Ala., in 1874 or 1876, was the perfect disciple of the founder of Tuskegee. A regular field hand at the age of nine, he was determined to improve his education and his lot. Beginning in 1890 in the A preparatory class of the Tuskegee night school, he worked his way through to graduation in 1898, working as a printer as soon as he had learned the trade in the Tuskegee shop. A brother and sister followed him to the institute. After his father's death midway through his course, Holtzclaw taught school for a time to support the family, but returned to complete his education. Turning down an offer to teach at Tuskegee, he taught for four years at Snow Hill Industrial

Institute in Alabama and then founded his own school in Mississippi, Utica Normal and Industrial Institute, on the Tuskegee model. Beginning in a brush arbor in 1902, he gradually built a school with aid from the Slater Fund and northern donors. Most of his teachers were Tuskegee graduates, as was his wife, who had charge of the girls' industries. Utica was a mirror of Tuskegee both on campus and in its extension services to the surrounding black rural people. Continuing his self-improvement, Holtzclaw earned a master's degree at the Alabama Agricultural and Mechanical College in 1908 and attended Harvard summer sessions for a decade. In 1915 he wrote an autobiography, *The Black Man's Burden,* which emphasized his civilizing mission in "darkest Mississippi."

From Nine [Melvin Jack Chisum]

[New York City] Sunday night Feb 11th, 06

Dear Dr. Washington: As result of a bit of getting about, it is my good fortune to be in pos[s]ession of a couple of facts that are I believe, worth while.

Mr. Hump[h]rey was sent to Phil., on Wednesday and is back – informs me that the Philadelphia meeting was about to fall through – the League has "staked" them (the Philadelphians) and the meet will take place Feb 21st.

The Niagara people will attend tomorrow night, but not in a body or as an organization.

You will find me waiting at the Stevens House at 1 p.m. tomorrow (Monday). Will wait there until 2:30, later if necessary. I am, Your obedient humble servant.

Nine

P.S. I got copy of program from – Dr Gilbert today and will get same printed tomorrow *by all means.*

ALS Con. 318 BTW Papers DLC.

Lewis Garnett Jordan[1] to Emmett Jay Scott

Louisville, Ky. Feb. 12, 1906

My dear Sir & Bro: This comes to you strictly private. I want your advice and if you think well of it suggest it to Mr. Washington. It is this — "The Moon" now being published by Mr. Du Bois is the supposed mouthpiece of the Niagara Movement and will in time doubtless become very readable. As you know the Niagara Movement is chiefly to overthrow what they call the Booker Washington idea. The only charge that has been made against the Afro-American Council is, that it was domineered by Booker T. Washington. A little semi-monthly paper in the interest of the Council is almost a necessity.

Mr. Cary Lewis,[2] a rising young man could be utilized as managing editor of something of the kind. I would take the editorship of it or get Rev. Dr. Frank[3] of this city to do so and in a private way you and Thompson could largely edit it. I have some ideas about a journal along this line that would appeal to readers white and black, north and south. Now I feel sure that such a paper can be gotten out for six or seven hundred dollars a year and a part of this can be had from subscriptions and with a little effort after a year could be made self-supporting. What do you think of it and could you suggest the feasibility of Mr. Washington taking any interest in such a journal.

God bless you. Write me at 2121-12th St. N.W. Washington D.C. as I will be there until Saturday or Monday. I shall not mention this to Mr. Washington but shall expect to hear from you and will be guided by your advice in the matter. Yours for the uplift of the race,

L. G. Jordan

TLS Con. 324 BTW Papers DLC.

[1] Lewis Garnett Jordan (1852–1940) was a Baptist minister and missionary who was born in slavery in Meridian, Miss. In 1896 Jordan became corresponding secretary of the Foreign Mission Board of the National Baptist Convention, a post which he held for twenty-five years. Jordan wrote several books on missionary work and edited the *Mission Herald*. He was a life member of the NNBL, and active in the National Prohibition party.

[2] Cary B. Lewis was an active member of the Afro-American Council in Louisville in 1906–7. Later, as publicity agent for the black Anderson-Watkins Film Co. in Chicago, he promoted the feature film *A Day at Tuskegee* in 1913.

[3] John H. Frank, born in Louisville in 1859, was a Baptist minister and editor who preached at the Fifth Street Baptist Church from 1877 until 1936. He was also director of the Colored Orphans Home of Louisville.

From Melvin Jack Chisum

Washington, D.C. Feb 16th 06

Dear Doctor: Most of the day has been spent with my newly made cantankerous friend.[1] The cat got clear out of the bag today. He is "busted."

In a discussion of the dinner last night, he said that "the niggers ought to have the thing published in the Bee." My reply was, "Get Busy Man."

He told me that he had an agreement with Messrs Terrell and Dancy, but they had failed to make good, and, that if I could, without embarrassment, he wished me to urge the thing along.

I told him that I would gladly do anything that would lead to his obtaining the business – if he really wanted to publish it. He assured me that I would be doing him a special favor and confided to me that his finances were in a most precarious condition.

He assured me that I will be doing him a very great personal favor by prevailing upon Judge Terrell to have the entire meeting's reproduced with pictures.

Mr. Terrell and I will take it up tomorrow morning and I expect to follow this report with a positive statement that the thing is done. The way seems clear to the result we so much need.

If I find it a *wise*, and the *necessary* thing to do my plan is to pay myself and get the work done. But, rest perfectly sure, that my plan is so surely carefully lain that he will not see.

The "Guardian Crowd" to the contrary notwithstanding, I have him Doctor, I have him. He explained to me that on the strength of what I have said to him that he is going to support Mr. Vernon without reserve, but – without harming his friend, Mr Lyons, that he believed my line of procedure to be the best yet advanced to him.

What he proposes to do, is this. Reproduce the speech made before the Manassas meeting on Wednesday evening, give a picture of the banquet as it was at True Reformer's Hall last night, reproduce the speeches made there and yours in particular.

He plans to get one hundred dollars from Mr. Dancy and Terrell – 50 dollars from each man. I am going to do my best to get them to take him up.

But will in no way connect your Excellence with my plans. For I do not trust a soul with any real fact that touches my visit here.

I am your obedient humble servant,

Chisum

ALS Con. 2 BTW Papers DLC.

[1] W. Calvin Chase.

From Melvin Jack Chisum

Washington, D.C. Feb 17th, 06

Dear Doctor: Enclosed you will find cuttings which prove one thing is at least accomplished, that of getting Chase in favor of Mr. Vernon — may I suggest that this cutting be, through some agency of your Emeinence sent to Mr. Vernon with instruction that he send Chase 5 cash subscriptions which will be 10 dollars as a mark of appreciation of his "most valuable" paper.

I have spent about 4 hours today with Judge Terrell he (the Judge) and I were for an hour of the time, with Recorder Dancy, and I tried my best to get them to arrange a deffinite program with Chase to publish the matter mentioned in last night's report, agreeing to pay one third of the expense myself.

The brethren would not do it, on the ground that they thought Mr Chase charged too much for his space. *I have not given up.*

I will not leave here until I accomplish the very thing I came here to accomplish, it is near completion. I have a way to get at him concerning the reproduction of the speech that appeared in the Star on Thursday he wants $15.00 to publish it with picture. May I have it done? If so wire me the one word, *Yes*, if not, wire me *No*. Rest assured I will not pay him the money with my own hands, nor will I get caught.

If I dared trust any of these folks I could get the other thing done but I can not trust them that far. I have the smaller matter in hand for I do not need to so nearly show my hand in it, I mean the matter of reproduction of speech and picture's appearance in the Bee.

Please send me 20 dollars to this address — if I am to manage the other business — then please send $35.00. I am, Your obedient humble servant, Chisum, your own property, to use as your Eminence desires, Absolutely.

[Melvin J. Chisum]

ALS Con. 2 BTW Papers DLC.

From Samuel Laing Williams

Chicago, Ill., Feb. 17 1906

Dear Dr. Washington — Your telegram of even date asking for answer to your letter of the 4th inst. is just received. When I received your letter I confess to some feeling of surprise, because in your letter of the 22d of Jan it is stated that the president expressed his intention to send in my "name at the same time for some important place." It occurred to me that in making this promise to Anderson and Scott so definite and positive that he had some place in mind.

You will appreciate how almost impossible it is for me to select a place when the status and present term of the places held are almost past finding out. There are only three positions in Washington ever held by colored men. Two of these have already been filled and the other is the 4th Auditor of the Treasury. There might be a possible chance for a place in the Department of Justice and that of Commerce and Labor. The president is probably unwilling to create a vacancy in any of these or other places to accommodate a colored man. Usually there seems to be nothing outside of the Civil service list.

The president's positive promise to consider me for some appointment in the District if I would decline Bahia I have always cherished as something quite certain. It now seems that this promise had in it the element of some contingency. Of course I am quite anxious to do any and every thing possible to aid the president in a fulfillment of his promise.

Did you get my letter sent to Hotel Manhattan about the Conservator? I have met the stockholders twice since I saw you. They are not ready yet to go in for a receiver, but are quite anxious to sell. I inquired into the condition find that they are about $900 in debt. The assets are some what uncertain – probably $600. They dislike Wilkins, opposed to his policy in reference to you and your work, but they have no back bone. They can put him out at any time but they are without courage. The capital stock $2500, all paid up except the 1/4 owned by Wilkins. In other words the present status of the property is such that it cannot be bought before there is a liquidation of debts by some form of judicial sale. Sincerely yours

S Laing Williams

ALS Con. 34 BTW Papers DLC.

To Robert Heberton Terrell

[Tuskegee, Ala.] Feb. 19, 1906

My dear Judge Terrell: I am writing for three purposes. First: I want to thank you and my other friends there for your great kindness to me while I was in your city lately.

Second: to explain the full nature and intent of my remarks before the Business League concerning the banking business in Washington. I do not know as I made it clear to the audience, but what I had in mind was to urge that another bank or banks be started as soon as possible, not only on account of the good that these institutions would accomplish, but for the further and equally important reasons that I feel perfectly sure that so long as other cities are establishing banks and there are none in Washington, month after month and year after year the old whine and criticism against some of my dearest friends in Washington will be kept up, but as soon as a new bank or banks are organized they will have something else to discuss and the interest in the new institution will soon absorb the feeling of disappointment and bitterness that has sprung up because of the failure of the former bank. I believe in the end that nothing would accomplish more good for our friends who were in any way connected with the old bank than for a new bank to be organized and succeed in Washington as I am quite sure it would.

Third: I am willing to undertake, and I believe I can succeed, the task of raising the money to clear off the mortgage on Cedar Hill, provided you will secure for me the full authority from Mr. Grimke and his co-trustees as well as from any other organizations that have been instituted in Washington for the purpose of carrying out Mrs. Douglass' ideas in connection with the home. I should also like to have the full and hearty consent of the Douglass family. In carrying out this plan, however, I should have to feel free to pursue my own methods and not be hampered by committees and other machinery. I believe, however, that if I am left free that I could get the money in two or three months, but I do not want to act without authority.

Please remember me kindly to Mrs. Terrell. Tell her that I note that the North Carolina papers say she made a very conservative speech in Charlotte. It is curious that our friends instinctively make radical speeches in the North and conservative speeches in the South. I presume, however, they are unconscious of doing so. Yours very truly,

Booker T. Washington

TLpS Con. 336 BTW Papers DLC.

From Melvin Jack Chisum

Washington, D.C. Feb. 19th, 1906

My dear Dr Washington: Have accomplished my best days work. Mr. Chase is printing your Manassas meeting speech, the Business Leag[u]e speech and writing a favorable editorial, such an one as will bring the break we want.

After all, I find him a rather tame – though dangerous I'm sure – proposition. I have found a way to stave off any probable loss of his confidence to a most remote date.

Now! The Bee will be a surprise to everybody that knows it the forthcoming week and the war is on between his highness bub Trotter and bub Chase. Are you willing that I remain here for a couple of weeks and make shure of Chase's broadsides being properly directed so as to part them beyond the point of repair, or reconnection? I know Trotter will fire on the Bee, and think I ought to be in the con[n]ing tower with Chase when he does.

This is about the toughest proposition I've tackled, but up to the present point all is safe and sure. This man is at heart, a vile, malicious, jealous — heartless "cuss."

He said to me today, "Chisum you and I are going to make some headway together, what I need is a fellow like you who has sense enough not to let his hatred of men run away with his common sense, this paper has an editorial that expresses my contempt for Booker W—— and his bread and butter brigade, but as you say, for my own good I might just as well to keep that sort of thing to myself, etc." [I enclose the editorial he refers to.]

To him I proclaim no love of you, only I am careful as to whom I express my self. To him I am constantly pounding you, but always with the added "confidential," "Mr Chase, I would let no one but you hear me say this."

He is very jealous of you and your power with the President. And says to me that he would give anything if only he could undermine that confidence. I advise him to steady himself and study a new method. He invites me to put my mind with his and help, to which I have very properly agreed and "we" Chase and "I" — I dont think — are going to figure it out between now and the Business Leag[u]e Convention, (which he and I will attend to gether, as he says,) just how to make you make some move that will break you up with the President. I have asked him if he believes that he will then be able to get anything under Mr. Roosevelt, he says no, but if he can discredit you now, he will have a better chance with the next president. I am Faithfully your humble servant,

Chisum

ALS Con. 2 BTW Papers DLC. Brackets in original. No enclosure attached.

To Charles William Anderson

[Tuskegee, Ala.] February 20, 1906

Dear Mr. Anderson: Please note the enclosed list of Consular places attached. This list has been made up by Mr. Scott, but I want to be very sure in taking up the matter with Secretary Root that I give a correct list.

I trust that you will return list with any suggestion you may care to make. Very truly yours,

Booker T. Washington

[Enclosure]

Colored men: Consular Service

Gained

Colored man from Iowa; don't recall post.

Lost

J. N. Ruffin, Asuncion, Paraguay.
Richard T. Greener, Vladivostok.
J. B. Peterson, resigned, Puerto Cabello, Venezuela.
White man at Bahia.
White consul at point in San Domingo.

TLpS Con. 2 BTW Papers DLC.

To Nicholas Chiles[1]

[Tuskegee, Ala.] Feb. 20, 1906

Personal

My dear Mr. Chiles: I have read carefully what you say regarding the Business League meeting in Atlanta. There are several points that I want to put before you.

1st, granting for the minute, for the sake of argument, that all you say is true regarding conditions at Atlanta, is there not another point of view to be considered? Do you not think that the bringing of a large number of intelligent, prosperous and cultured class of colored people from all over the country into such a city as Atlanta will tend to shame the class of white people who inflict indignities upon us and will open their eyes to the fact that colored people are making such tremendous progress that the South cannot afford to attempt to humiliate them much longer?

Second, ought not our Northern and Western brethren bear in mind that if many of us who live in the South can endure these afflictions during ten or twelve months in the year, they might share them for a few days in the year.

Third, I believe that in going to Atlanta we will be doing real missionary work, not only among the colored people but among the white people.

Fourth, many of the conditions described in your letter are much exaggerated. I really feel that when we get to Atlanta that the main humiliation that we are going to rest with will be in the separate entrance to the depot, that is the crux of the whole matter. The accommodations for the colored passengers, as I understand it, are in every way satisfactory, including restaurant arrangements, but I confess that the separate entrance is a disgrace and a humiliation. I am going to use my utmost endeavor between now and the meeting of the League to have this distinction done away with, and I want to say to you that if you will get as many people to write me letters as possible protesting against the humiliation it will help. I very much hope, however, that nothing will prevent Kansas coming in large numbers to the Atlanta meeting. You will remember at one time when Mr. Douglass was forced to ride in a cattle car, somebody tried to cheer him up by telling him that it was a disgrace for him to be humiliated in that manner. Mr. Douglass replied that it was impossible for him to be humiliated. We must take something of the same attitude when fighting the kind of battles and passing through the kind of difficulties that we are now waging war against. You of the North and West must come to our rescue, and you do not know what a great encouragement it will be to us to know that our brethren from a distance are at least willing to share our troubles for a few days in each year. Yours truly,

Booker T. Washington

TLpS Con. 329 BTW Papers DLC.

1 Nicholas (Nick) Chiles (1869?–1929), active in black Republican politics in Kansas, was editor of the Topeka *Plaindealer* for thirty years.

From Melvin Jack Chisum

Washington, D.C. Feb 20th, 06

Dear Dr. Washington: On my return tonight I find your telegram and shall go to New York on the first train tomorrow morning. It is very good of you to say that I have done well, this is a statement which I hope always to deserve from your lips, and I thank you for it.

I confess that I am not satisfied with the job, I so wish to complete it, and I am sure I can, but I must obey orders, you are my general — I go to New York tomorrow morning as you command.

It was my good fortune to attend The Metropolitan Literary Society's meeting tonight. Miss Nan[n]ie Burroughs,[1] spoke and in her speech she raked you mercilessly, before she got through she raked also Bishop Turner, Prof Du Bois, Mr Kelly Miller and *"all"* the colored men in Washington D.C. This gave me a chance and I brought the house down by flaying her in a nice sort of a way and closing with the statement that while we were at a loss we would be glad to have her find us, especially so, since we were informed (by her) that she had more brains than Profs. Washington, Kelly Miller, Du Bois, Bishop Turner and all the men in Washington rooled into one.

She is a dangerous little tramp, as is also that Rev Jordan — the missionary man, who also spoke. Please accept enclosed cutting and a page of statistics that I thought might interest you. Possibly you may slip in a few while this mixup is on.

I am also sending you a couple more of the 'stution Leag[u]e circulars. Please send me to New York a small sum of money as I am all in. I am, Your obedient humble servant,

Chisum

ALS Con. 2 BTW Papers DLC. No enclosures attached.

1 Nannie Helen Burroughs (1879–1961), active in the black women's club movement and in the education of black women, was a bookkeeper and stenographer for the Foreign Mission Board of the National Baptist Convention in Washington, D.C., from 1898 to 1908. She was founder and president of the National Training School for Women and Girls (beginning in 1907), secretary of the Douglass Improvement Co. (beginning in 1909), and a life member of the NNBL.

To Timothy Thomas Fortune

[Tuskegee, Ala.] February 21, 1906

Dear Mr. Fortune: I can vouch for all the facts stated in this editorial,[1] and I hope you will use it. Du Bois in his new role of an agitator is fast making a fool of himself through his little paper. When he stuck to the business of scientific investigation he was a success, but he is going to prove a failure as an agitator following in the wake of a crazy man like Trotter. I have refrained from mentioning his name in the editorial and hope you will not put it in the paper as I do not want to give him any free advertising.

I had a great time with the Pen and Pencil Club in Washington. They are a fine set and give you credit for the organization of the club. I think Washington City is pretty thorougly captured. The Niagara people seem down at the heels. Yours truly,

Booker T. Washington

TLpS Con. 261 BTW Papers DLC.

1 No editorial is attached.

From Archibald Henry Grimké

Washington, Feb. 21/06

Dear Mr. Washington: Mr. McKinlay has just shown me the copy of a letter written by you to Judge Terrell relative to Cedar Hill, etc., and of your willingness to undertake to raise the money necessary to meet the needs of Cedar Hill, provided you received full authority to do so in your own way from me & my co-trustees, unhampered by "committees & other machinery."

From the Trustees, as president of the board, I will see that you have what you desire, viz. full authority to act in the premises in your own way.

The Frederick Douglass Memorial & Historical Association is the only body of people that has any legal connection with Cedar Hill.

It is incorporated by act of Congress, & holds[,] under the will of Mr. Douglass[,] Cedar Hill in fee simple.

As to your obtaining the "full & hearty consent of the Douglass family" I do not think that you will find any difficulty now. For Mr. Chas. Douglass assured me before he left the dining hall on the night of the banquet of the Pen & Pencil Club that he would give me his cooperation & subscription later, & assured me of the same for his brother Lewis.

I wish & in this wish my brother & McKinlay join, that you would consent to serve as a trustee of the Frederick Douglass Mem. & His. Association. The Board will be glad to elect you just as soon as you signify to me your willingness so to serve.

You have, dear friend, my deep & hearty thanks for the timely and valuable aid which you are willing to give this noble memorial to a great & good man. You are certainly a brick & a gold brick at that! Ever cordially yours,

Archibald H. Grimké

P.S. I have just finished a couple of articles for The Age along lines of your suggestion in the Terrell letter about starting new banks etc. etc.

A. H. G.

ALS Con. 322 BTW Papers DLC.

To Elihu Root

[Tuskegee, Ala.] February 23, 1906

Personal

Dear Secretary Root: Mr. S. Laing Williams is not willing to go to Vladivostok in case the position should be offered him on account of the severe climate. If you still have in mind putting a colored man in the position, I feel quite sure that Mr. Cummings, of Baltimore, whom Secretary Bonaparte has recommended, or Mr. J. W. Johnson, of New York, whom Mr. Anderson and I spoke to you about, would prove first class men. If neither of these men are available, I think Mr. Anderson and I could recommend several other persons to fill this or any other position with credit. Yours very truly,

Booker T. Washington

TLpS Con. 4 BTW Papers DLC.

From Albert G. Davis

Birmingham Ala. Feb. 23rd 1906

Dear Prof. I wrote you a day or two ago stating my troubles in detail.[1] You know that I have never received a particle of aid from you since graduating from your institution 17 years ago. Heaven and earth are being brought together to convict me on perjured testimony. No graduate of your school is a convict, and I cannot bring myself to believe that you will instead of helping to get me out of jail write me a nice unctious letter with sugar-coated words. The reputation of your institution is at stake placed there by the wretches your recommendation is reputed to have placed in office.

I am as innocent of the charge of impersonating colored men on Nov. 18th last as you. I am too well known in Birmingham to be allowed to perpetrate a crime like that. The men whom you have taken to be your friends have undertaken to get rid of me at all hazards through the perjury route and for you to stand by and see the nefarious work accomplished would be ———.

Please write to Messrs. Burkhart and Pratt, Attorneys at Law, Lyon and Terry Building Birmingham Ala at once if you do not care for my case to go by default. Do not write me as I am in jail there to remain unless your heart is in the right place. Hoping to hear from you at once through those attorneys I am Your friend,

Albert G. Davis
County jail

ALS Con. 3 BTW Papers DLC.

[1] Davis wrote on Feb. 21, 1906, that he had been charged with impersonating a letter carrier at a civil service examination. He claimed that he had an alibi and that the testimony against him was perjured. He urged BTW to lend him money and legal assistance. (Con. 3, BTW Papers, DLC.)

BTW did nothing for Davis, however, probably because of the advice of his nephew, G. W. A. Johnston, who wrote from Birmingham on Feb. 28, 1906: "I fear that if you try to help Davis he will use the effort to the detriment of all concerned, this is the reason I feared to go to the jail and let him talk to me." (Con. 3, BTW Papers, DLC.)

To Melvin Jack Chisum

[Tuskegee, Ala.] Feb. 24, 1906

My dear Mr. Chisum: I have received both of your letters and am most grateful to you for what you have done. It seems that you have accomplished good results. I shall be in New York in March and shall see you. Yours truly,

Booker T. Washington

TLpS Con. 2 BTW Papers DLC.

To Albert G. Davis

[Tuskegee, Ala.] 2-26-1906

Dear Mr. Davis: I am getting in communication with influences in Birmingham and shall see what can be done in the matter to which you refer. Very truly,

Booker T. Washington

TLpSr Con. 3 BTW Papers DLC.

From Melvin Jack Chisum

New York, N.Y. Feb 26th, 06

My dear Dr Washington: I am sending you by this same post a copy of the Bee. If there is anything further you want done I am willing to tackle it, so long as I live.

Chase *is to get* his pay from Messrs Lankford, Dancy and Terrell. Am so glad you are pleased with my efforts. I am, Your obedient humble servant

Chisum

P.S. Thanks for letter — which has just arrived.

ALS Con. 318 BTW Papers DLC.

To Alexander Walters

[Tuskegee, Ala.] March 1, 1906

My dear Bishop: I send you my personal check for Twenty-five Dollars, to be used in connection with the work of keeping some one in the field, to do the work of the Afro-American Council.

I hope others may also respond to your appeal, so that you may keep up this important work. Very truly,

Booker T. Washington

TLpS Con. 339 BTW Papers DLC.

To Harry C. Smith

[Tuskegee, Ala.] March 2, 1906

PERSONAL

Dear Mr. Smith: I have your letter of recent date, and appreciate your kindness in writing me so fully and frankly.

The more you come into contact with Trotter and his immediate followers, the more you will find that they have but one object in view, and they will soon part company with anybody who does not follow them in that respect. Their object is to try to tear down individual members of the race through misrepresentation, and personal abuse.

You, on many occasions have disagreed with me on matters of public policy. I have never fallen out with you for this. I always recognize the fact that any man has the right to criticise the public acts and works of another public man.

You have indulged in argument, instead of abuse, hence my high regard for you.

If more of our journalists would learn that personal abuse does not pay, we would have a stronger and much more influential press.

You are entirely mistaken about Whitefield McKinlay. I cannot recall that he has ever spoken to me disparagingly in any respect of you.

In order that you may see for yourself just who Trotter and his immediate followers are, enclosed, I send you a report, which I have never let go out of my hands before, by a detective. Same shows up their intention of cutting the electric light wires in a church, and their attempt to create a stampede and riot while I was speaking in a church in Cambridge sometime ago.

Please return it when you have read it.

I am sorry about the unpleasant occurrences at Springfield, Ohio. Such outrages in the North, do much to encourage the bad element in the South.

I hope at some time you may be able to see for yourself, the work we are trying to do here. Very truly yours,

Booker T. Washington

TLpS Con. 334 BTW Papers DLC.

To Whitefield McKinlay

[Tuskegee, Ala.] March 3, 1906

Strictly Confidential

Dear Mr. McKinlay: I presume you have seen the printed charges gotten up by people in Kansas against Vernon. They seem to be making a persistent effort to defeat him.

What I want you to do is this. While I shall of course take no part in the controversy, I do want to be kept informed as to what is going on; especially I want to know in advance if Vernon is going to be defeated so that we can have plenty of time to be sure that Williams is placed. Please see Senator Blair at once and arrange with him, in your own name, to keep you closely informed in advance what is to be done in Vernon's case so we will have time to act with the President before a decision is announced by the Senate. I will pay Senator Blair whatever is necessary to secure this result. You can communicate with me by telegram any information that Senator Blair may give you.

You will have noted that the special committee appointed to investigate Vernon's case is composed of Senators Burroughs,[1] Spooner and Bailey.[2] Yours truly,

Booker T. Washington

TLpS Con. 261 BTW Papers DLC.

[1] Julius Caesar Burrows (1837–1915) was a U.S. senator from Michigan from 1895 to 1911.

[2] Joseph Weldon Bailey (1862–1929) was a U.S. senator from Texas from 1901 to 1913.

To William Howard Taft

[Tuskegee, Ala.] March 3, 1906

Personal

Sir: If not inconsistent with the rules of your Department, I wonder if you would inform me if it is legal for any states to refuse to give the colored people any recognition whatever in the state militia and still draw their quota from the public fund toward the support of the state militia.

Several of the Southern states have recently mustered out all of the colored companies, and I should like to know what the ruling of the Department is on the subject mentioned. Yours truly,

Booker T. Washington

TLpS Con. 336 BTW Papers DLC.

From Charles William Anderson

New York, N.Y., March 5, 1906

My dear Doctor: Relative to your telegrams and letter concerning the appointment of Mr. Johnson to the post of Puerto Cabello, I regret to say that I have been unable to see Mr. Johnson, owing to his serious illness. He is confined to his bed, and is under the care of a trained nurse, with what seems to be pneumonia. I expect, however, to see him in a day or two, and impart the news. I have informed his brother of our success in his behalf, but he has not felt it advisable to give James W. the news in his present condition.

I shall pass the circular along concerning our Washington man.[1] This is really a very unpleasant case, and the end of it is not yet. I had hoped all along that inasmuch as "no marks were left," the man was safe; but it appears now that some marks were really left. Hence, the matter has taken a serious turn. But we shall see what we shall see.

Relative to our man Chisum, I want to advise you that you have left an awful load on my hands. He has been to me for money five times since you left the city, and got it four times. On the fifth visit I informed him that I could not meet his wishes. The trouble with him is that he has made up his mind not to work, and expects to live by borrowing. I think I shall have to fall out with him before you come back, so be prepared to hear of a break. He is a much too expensive luxury for me. I will, however, try to grin and bear it, but if I break down before you return here, don't be surprised.

Please let me know just when you expect to be in this city again. Yours truly,

Charles W. Anderson

TLS Con. 2 BTW Papers DLC.

[1] Probably W. T. Vernon. See BTW to Whitefield McKinlay, Mar. 3, 1906, above.

From Charles William Anderson

New York, N.Y., March 6, 1906

My dear Doctor: I came upon Ex-Congressman Rowland B. Mahany,[1] of Buffalo, last night in the Waldorf-Astoria Hotel, and during the conversation discovered that he had addressed the two suffrage meetings of the Constitution League, recently held at Philadelphia, and Washington D.C. Almost his first words related to you and your supposed attitude toward the suffrage movement. He criticised you very freely for not supporting the Constitution League program, and seemed to be more anxious to destroy your influence than he was to promote the cause of the suffrage league. I immediately told him that you were not only my trusted leader, but my personal friend, and that I agreed with you fully about the remedy for the suffrage evil, and, at the same time, reminded him that even if I did not agree with you, I at least would give you credit for purposes as honourable as my own, and felt that he and his associates ought to do likewise. I told him very plainly that you and I, and the other men who think as we do, have the same right to our opinion that he has to his, and ought not to be accused of unsteadiness of purpose, or indifference to the best interests of the race, or lack of personal courage. Whereupon, he started in to prove that your work was very much over-rated, and that the coloured people ought to wake up to the fact that they were sadly in need of a leader who did not have to solicit funds, or hold political office. I then sailed into him, and made the fur fly for about ten or fifteen minutes. I told him that I loathed those white men who were going about the country trying to induce the coloured people to destroy their leaders. I reminded him that the men engaged in this work were all men who had no status of any kind among their own race. It then came out that he had had several long talks with Milholland concerning me, and that Milholland had convinced him that I had been conspiring with you to defeat his plans. It did not take long for me to let him know that neither you nor I cared a continental about Milholland, or any of his brood, and I said some things to this young Irish Ex-Congressman, that I would not dare to commit to paper. The strangest part of it all is that these fellows are much more anxious to secure the undoing of you and myself, than they are to promote the cause of an honest ballot, which they profess to have so much at heart. Of course Mahany got all of his opinions from Milholland. Thus, you see, that this scoundrel is going to and fro in the country, and exerting his poor abilities to the job of destroying certain coloured men. Mahany told me of Mrs. Terrell's attending the Philadelphia meeting, and attending the conference held at the close of the meeting. He said that she joined in both functions with her whole heart and zeal. He spoke of her in the highest terms, and said he wished we had a few men as brave as Mrs. Terrell. It seems to me, Doctor, that it is high time that this woman should be called down a little.

This is a long letter to be wasted on so insignificant a proposition as the suffrage league, but I thought you ought to know just what these scamps are attempting to do. Yours truly,

Charles W. Anderson

P.S. Mahany ran for congress on an Independent ticket & was defeated, (in Buffalo) and afterwards supported a Democrat for mayor. He is a bright fellow, but utterly devoid of party standing. He is cordially hated by the leading Repubs. of Buffalo, and is regarded as an Irish agitator.

C. W. A.

P.P.S. I forgot to say that Mahany said, during our colloquy, that he was confident that your influence at the White House was about dead. So you see, the destruction of your influence with the President is a part of their programme.

C. A.

TLS Con. 2 BTW Papers DLC. Postscripts in Anderson's hand.

[1] Rowland Blennerhassett Mahany (1864–1937), a Republican congressman from New York from 1895 to 1899, was harbor commissioner of Buffalo, N.Y., from 1899 to 1906. Later he was editor of the Buffalo *Enquirer* (1910–11), and held several federal appointments from 1914 to 1921.

To Charles William Anderson

[Tuskegee, Ala.] March 8, 1906

Personal

My dear Mr. Anderson: I received both of your last letters and also your telegram. They contain very interesting information. I am exceedingly glad to hear that our friend Johnson has been placed, and equally pleased to know that he will not be among the "decliners" because certainly if another person recommended by us were to decline, we should find ourselves statesmen without a job.

There is only one weak point to Johnson's appointment, and that is the Atlanta University crowd will try to claim it as a recognition of their faction, but of course we must not make Johnson suffer on account of a few fools. Johnson is a first class man, and I have rarely met an individual whom I have learned to like better on so short acquaintance.

What you say about Mahany and Milholland is very interesting though not surprising. Milholland belongs to that class of white men who cannot bear to see a colored man reach any degree of prominence or influence, and I shall not be surprised if he continues his fight against you and me through the guise of the Business League[1] until those fellows sap his purse. I am quite sure he is a dangerous man from every point of view.

Enclosed I send you a marked portion of a letter relating to the Washington meeting, which shows that they did not guard all the points in their program. The newspapers, however, I notice, are giving the League very little attention. The Washington Post did not even mention the meeting being held, and I was told by several parties that were present that not a single white man except the speakers was in the house. I have not heard about the Philadelphia meeting.

I hope you will not worry with Brother Chisum. I hope that he will be fat and with a full purse by the time I reach New York City. Seriously, I had to telegraph him to leave Washington because I found him entirely too expensive.

It is my present plan to be in New York on the 14th to stay a few days. Don't tell Chisum.[2]

I wish very much that you and Mrs. Anderson might be present at our Anniversary celebration. It now looks as if it were going to be quite an affair.

Enclosed I send you a copy of a letter bearing upon Bishop Turner which came this week from Mr. Loeb. Turner is coming out with a statement denying that he made any such speech.[3]

I shall bear in mind what you say concerning Mrs. Terrell and act on it. Yours very truly,

[Booker T. Washington]

TLp Con. 249 BTW Papers DLC.

[1] BTW meant to write "Constitution League."

[2] This sentence added in BTW's hand.

[3] Newspaper accounts of Bishop Turner's speech in Macon, Ga., in February 1906 reported that he had called the American flag a "dirty and contemptible rag." Turner denied the charge, stating that he was quoted out of context. He did say, however, that because of the denial of civil rights to blacks they were, in effect, not citizens of the United States. (Atlanta *Constitution*, Feb. 24, 1906, Clipping, Con. 336, BTW Papers, DLC.) On Mar. 9, 1906, BTW wrote to Turner informing him that President Roosevelt had expressed "considerable chagrin" over the alleged remarks. BTW told Turner that he had "written the President fully about the misrepresentation practiced upon you." Roosevelt had apparently received several letters demanding that Turner be indicted for treason. (Con. 336, BTW Papers, DLC.)

To Whitefield McKinlay

[Tuskegee, Ala.] March 8, 1906

Personal

My dear Mr. McKinlay: Your letter is received. I am extremely fearful of your doing anything that might be interpreted in the direction of opposing Vernon's confirmation. Of course anything that you do owing to your relations with me, will be interpreted as representing my attitude. I want to be perfectly square with the President while I hold my present relations with him and I will oppose nothing that he wants done and will help forward all that he desires to have done. The point of my letter was for you to keep me informed as to the exact facts. Yours truly,

Booker T. Washington

TLpS Con. 261 BTW Papers DLC.

From Robert Heberton Terrell

Washington, D.C. March 8, 1906

My dear Mr. Washington, I am sending to you the letters written me by the children of Frederick Douglass. As you will see they do not breathe the spirit of enthusiasm relative to the preservation and consecration of Cedar Hill that we should like to find in them. Yet neither the sons nor the daughter objects to any effort you may make to lift the indebtedness on this sacred property. My advice to you is to go on with your plans and purposes. The Douglasses will fall in line. I have endeavored to see Mr. Grimke and have him arrange it so that one of the sons of Mr. Douglass be put on the board of trustees. This act would harmonize matters and make your work pleasant in every way.

I have secured a copy of the act of Congress by which the Association was incorporated. I enclose it herewith. The Pen and Pencil Club will collect the money subscribed at its banquet. It would be well for Mr. Grimke and his associates to see to it that one of the members of this club is made a trustee, if there is a vacancy on the board. Such a thing would help matters along. It is often necessary to cater to the selfishness of people, if one would have things done. Of course it goes without saying that you ought to have a high place among the officials of the corporation.

I am glad that Johnson has been appointed in Peterson's place. He is altogether the man for the place. The attack upon Mr. Vernon is severe and nasty. I am sorry for it. Such exhibitions do us no good. There is a woman in the case and she has camped here with an armful of charges. She swears all kinds of vengeance against Mr. Vernon because of an alleged wrong to her ten years ago. I am informed that she is stopping with Mr. George W. Lee, a well known and prominent Baptist preacher who has become interested in her cause. She haunts the capitol day after day and has succeeded in getting interviews with members of the committee before whom Vernon's case must come. The matter has been referred to a sub committee for investigation. I cannot tell, of course, what effect this woman's attack will finally have on the case. The 'hold up,' however, is unfortunate, to say the least.

The echoes of your last visit to us have not yet died away.

With best wishes for you and Mrs. Washington, I am, yours faithfully,

Robert H. Terrell

ALS Con. 336 BTW Papers DLC.

From William Howard Taft

Washington, March 10, 1906

Dear Sir: I have the honor to acknowledge the receipt of your inquiry in the matter of the disbandment of companies of militia which are composed exclusively of colored men. I have called upon the Judge-Advocate General for his views as to the law applicable to the case and I inclose a copy of his opinion for your information. I think his idea is the correct one, that it is beyond the power of the United States Government to prescribe the composition of regiments or companies of the organized militia in time of peace, a function which is expressly vested in the States by the Federal Constitution.

But are you quite sure that the cases which have been brought to your attention indicate a tendency to arbitrary action on the part of the State authorities? The general militia law requires the War Department to cause the organized militia to be annually inspected. If the reports of inspection are unfavorable, in respect to the material equipment of the command for active duty in the field, the allotment which would otherwise become available for encampment purposes is diminished to that extent; there is a similar deduction when the reports show a failure to conform to the requirements of Section 18 in respect to drill and instruction.

In many of the States companies are disbanded upon the unfavorable reports of inspectors, and this quite without regard to whether they are composed of white or colored men. Very truly yours,

Wm H Taft
Secretary of War

TLS Con. 336 BTW Papers DLC.

From Henry McNeal Turner

Atlanta, Ga. March 10th, 1906

Dear Doctor: Yours of the 9th inst before me. Very much oblige[d] to you for your voluntary explanation to the President U.S.A. But if they do go far enough to arrest me for Treason, I know they will have to give me an opportunity to defend myself. And I think I shall be able to prove forty times more treason perpetrated against my race, under the shadow of the United States flag, than they can establish against me. Hundreds of the most barbarous and inhuman so-called laws have been enacted, under this same flag, and nothing has been said or done about it. They are welcome to arrest me as soon as they like, if they will allow me to defend my self, and show what brutal laws the flag sanctions, or is as silent as death about. I have gone through thirteen bloody battles, and twenty-four bloody skirmishes to protect the good name of the stars and stripes. And my speeches have enlisted the best end of ten thousand men, as soldiers to fight and die against the disintegration of this country. And under the decision of the United States Supreme Court Oct. 15th 1883 and May 18th 1896, alienating the Black man from the protection of Civil liberty, the Negro is not a citizen of the United States any way, and I doubt its power to try me for treason or any other colored man. At all events, should it come, I will try and be ready.

I send you a few clippings from the Atlanta Constitution, of what I did say and can say more if necessary. Yours with high Esteem,

H. M. Turner

ALSr Con. 336 BTW Papers DLC.

From Herbert George Wells[1]

[London?] 10 iii–06

Dear Sir: I am an English writer whose name may or may not be known to you & I am coming out to the U.S.A. in April. I purpose to write some articles on *The Future in America* and I am very anxious to meet & talk with one or two representative educated men of colour, upon the colour question.

I had hoped to come to you at Tuskegee but I find that my time & the distances I have to traverse render this nearly impossible. My own opinions (expressed pretty freely in *A Modern Utopia*) are against insurmountable colour separations & I am happy to find my own preconceptions sustained by the experience of my friend, Mr. Sidney Olivier, who was recently acting governor of Jamacia. There many of the worst features of the race conflict in the U.S.A. do not arise.

I shall be very glad indeed if you can put me in the way of any typical presentation of the negro view. I shall be in New York (Century Club 7 West 43d Street) during the first week in April, thence I shall go via Boston (1 week) Chicago (1 week) Springfield (?) Pittsburgh & one or two other intermediate places to Washington (first or second week in May). If there is any good typical negro quarter or community in Va within an easy run of Washington I shall go to see it.[2] Yours very sincerely

H. G. Wells

ALS Con. 388 BTW Papers DLC.

1 The novelist H. G. Wells (1866–1946).

2 BTW expressed regret that Wells did not plan to see the Negro in the South, "where the whole problem of his future is to be worked out." (BTW to Wells, Mar. 24, 1906, Con. 338, BTW Papers, DLC.)

From Charles William Anderson

New York, N.Y., March 12, 1906

My dear Doctor: Both your favours of recent date received. I note what you say about the reference to Johnson as a graduate of Atlanta. Like you, I feel that it would have been much better to have omitted the reference, yet in view of the fact that Johnson some time ago wrote a letter to Du Bois, refusing to have anything to do with the Niagara movement, and the further fact that it is announced that his appointment was secured through me, and that he is at present the president of the "objectionable" Coloured Republican Club of the City of New York, will prevent the enemy from finding any comfort in his appointment, and from exploiting it in any way. Relative to the letters which have been sent to the President, concerning Bishop Turner's alleged "dirty rag" speech, permit me to say that "The Boston Guardian" of March 3rd contains a New York letter from the pen of John E. Bruce, which supports Bishop Turner's statement that the American flag is but a dirty rag, and reiterates it. If the President were advised that the author of this article is a federal office holder under General Clarkson, I am confident that there would be some interesting developments. The same article also stands up stoutly for the Constitution League movement and accuses you of never having exercised the right of franchise. Thus, you see, there is an opportunity for some reprisals.

Mr. Johnson sat up yesterday for the first time in ten days. He expects to be out and around in two or three days. I have written to Assistant Secretary Bacon[1] asking him to postpone the date of Mr. Johnson's examination for one week. The original date set for it was March 13th, but he will not be able to take the trip by that time. His contract here called for forty weeks at $100 a week. Thus, you see, his action has been very manly in making this sacrifice to stand by us.

I forgot to say that the "Age" article was written by Stokes. I furnished the facts. The Wibecan forces are as mad as they can be. Wibecan himself is said to be shedding tears copiously over Johnson's appointment.

Let me hear from you at your earliest convenience. Yours truly,

Charles W. Anderson

TLS Con. 2 BTW Papers DLC.

[1] Robert Bacon (1860–1919), formerly a banker with J. P. Morgan and Co., was Assistant Secretary of State from 1905 to 1909, Secretary of State briefly in 1909, and U.S. ambassador to France from 1909 to 1912.

An Article in *The Independent*

[Mar. 15, 1906]

INDUSTRIAL EDUCATION IN AFRICA

Some months ago there was printed in one of the more prominent magazines an appeal addressed to the civilized world by a young African prince, Momolu Massaquoi,[1] of Gallinas, in the British Protectorate of Sierra Leone, West Africa. This brilliant and enlightened young negro, altho he was born in Africa, was educated at the Central Tennessee College at Nashville. In 1893 he represented Africa at the World's Parliament of Religions at Chicago. At present he is the hereditary ruler of a small African tribe in the hinterland of Sierra Leone, which he is earnestly seeking to bring under the influence of Western and Christian civilization.

In order to accomplish this purpose he had established at Ghendiman, the capital of his country, an industrial school, where he is teaching his people, among other things, the arts and trades of civilized life. He became deeply impressed, during his visit to the World's Fair, with the achievements of the Western peoples, and was inspired with an ambition to give his people the benefit of sciences and arts of which his observation had taught him the importance and value.

Much as he desired for his people the benefits of a larger knowledge of, and closer intercourse with, Christian peoples, he had not failed to recognize that contact with the white race often brought with it more of evil than of good. In his appeal, to which I have referred, he urges the calling together in an international council, "the friends of Africa."

One of the purposes of this international council would be the formation of a permanent society, which should stand, in its relation to the civilized world, as a sort of guardian of the native peoples of Africa, a friendly power, an influence with the public and in the councils where so often, without their presence or knowledge, the destinies of the African peoples and of their territories are discussed and decided.

There is more than one reason why I am disposed at this time to support the appeal of this young African prince. It has often seemed to me a sad and mistaken policy that in making their disposition of

Africa the Powers have not given more attention to the permanent interests of the native peoples. It has been unfortunate that at the councils which settled the fate of vast territories, and of millions of peoples, neither these people themselves nor any one who could adequately represent them has been present.

In framing the policies which involve the permanent happiness and welfare of native peoples I believe that the missionary, whose relations with the natives is more intimate and more disinterested than most others, is often a wiser councilor than the trader, or the soldier, and that, in the long run, the policy which seems to protect and educate the native will pay better than that which, in seeking to subjugate and exploit, has so often destroyed him.

There is, perhaps, no place where we need wisdom more than on the frontiers of civilization. It has always been so, but it is particularly true today. A wide view of the world's economy demands that we protect from destruction not only the forests, and the beasts that live in them, but the indigenous races to whom they by all human right belong. In the final organization of the world's work, I believe all the peoples of the earth may hope to find their task and place. They should be preserved, if for no other reason, for the special service they are able to perform. Particularly is this true of West and Central Africa, where as yet the white man has never been a laborer or settler, but merely a sojourner, and where the future development of the country is wholly dependent upon the labor of black men.

A permanent international society, which should number among its members scientists, explorers, missionaries and all those who are engaged, directly or indirectly, in constructive work in Africa, could exercise a wise and liberal influence upon the colonial policy of the European nations. By its influence upon international opinion, which has often been the only power in which the natives have found protection, it could powerfully aid in securing the success of those policies which aim at the permanent interests of Africa and its people.

My own experience has led me to doubt the value of criticism which does not proceed from some positive and constructive notion as to how the evils of which complaint is made can be remedied.

I have discovered that it is often more profitable to encourage those you come in contact with in the direction in which they are right than it is to oppose them in the direction in which they seem to be wrong. It often happens that in the end more will be accomplished by doing some positive good than by opposing many actual or seeming evils.

It has seemed to me, therefore, that at the present moment, when the atrocities in the French Kongo have apparently aroused the people of France, and an active agitation is being carried on in Europe and America for the intervention of the Powers in the Kongo Free State, and it would perhaps aid in bringing about a change in conditions if the "friends of Africa," those who have the permanent interests of the people and their country most sincerely at heart, would unite to promote some definite measure of positive improvement for the people.

My own knowledge of the needs of native African people is, I confess, not extensive. It has largely been gathered from reports of missionaries and travelers, from the experiments of Tuskegee students in Togo and other parts of Africa in cotton culture, and their experience in teaching the natives American methods. Recently I have had an opportunity to hear indirectly in regard to the present situation from a large number of missionaries on the West Coast. From all that I am able to learn from these sources and others I am disposed to believe that no single measure would do more to improve the character and condition of the native peoples and prepare the way for the permanent establishment of Christian religion and Christian civilization than the introduction and wide extension of industrial schools.

It should be remembered that the industrial school is no new thing in Africa. Long before Hampton Institute was founded there was a flourishing industrial school at Lovedale, in South Africa. In the whole history of what is known in Africa as the "native question," I doubt if there is any more interesting or more encouraging incident than those related in the story of this institution and of the other industrial schools in Africa that have grown out of this original experiment. At the present time there seems to be a very general conviction among the missionaries in Africa that an industrial education is a necessary part of their work.

The demand for industrial teachers, in connection with mission work is, as I have reason to know, beyond the ability of our schools to supply.

This is in part due to the keen demand for industrial teachers in the colored schools in our own country. A teacher who has industrial training, I have been informed, can frequently obtain almost twice the salary that is paid a colored teacher trained in the best Northern university. While industrial teachers are in such request at home it will always be difficult to obtain them for the foreign mission schools. Another fact that enters into the situation is the constantly increasing demand for trained men and teachers of the negro race from colonial governments and from great private enterprises like the British Cotton Growing Association and others, which are seeking to fit the native peoples to meet the new demands of the world's industry and commerce. All of these things indicate, I am inclined to believe, a growing impression among practical administrators of colonial affairs, as well as among students and missionaries, that the problem of dealing with the weaker races is fundamentally one of industrial education.

The surest way of preserving these more primitive people from the evils which the higher civilization invariably brings in its train, is to develop in them talents which will make them useful and inculcate those habits of life which will cause them to be respected.

I believe that an international council of the "Friends of Africa" could do much to encourage the work already begun in this direction and greatly aid in overcoming the obstacles to its further extension.

While I have no definite suggestions as to what measures should or could be taken by such an international council, either for the protection of the natives from the evils that now threaten them or for encouragement of the work of their betterment, there are certain things which I believe my experience justifies me in laying down as fundamental to any effort in these directions.

I have very little faith in the success of any effort to educate or to increase the economic value of the native Africans that is not conducted by those who have confidence in and a disinterested desire to improve the condition of the people intrusted to their care. Any experiment which seeks to encourage native industry by force or merely by an appeal to his "enlightened self-interest" will fail. An enlightened self interest which divorces itself from all social and sentimental interests and is not stimulated either by religious feelings or a sense of personal pride is one of the latest products of civilization. With the African people, as I have known them, feeling, and particularly religious and social feelings, enter more or less into everything that they do. Experience in the Southern States has proved that experiments that do not reckon with this fact will not succeed.

For this reason, if for no other, I am disposed to believe that no attempt to educate the native peoples of Africa or to lift them to a higher plane of industrial efficiency, will have any permanent success that does not go hand in hand with the teaching of the Christian religion, or at least with a devotion and desire to help the people similar to that which has inspired the work of the missionaries in Africa.

I believe it is a wise policy which induced the English Government in South Africa and in India to give substantial aid without reference to the sect or creed they represented, to those mission schools where industrial training was taught.

But without reference to any specific measures that could or should be taken for the betterment of the native peoples of Africa, it seems to me it is a seasonable time for the friends of Africa to come together. An international council, should it do no more than outline in opposition to the policy of forced labor and ruthless commercial exploitation, some plan for the encouragement and further extension of industrial education in Africa, would have done much to secure the future of what is, whatever its faults, one of the most useful races the world has ever known.

Independent, 60 (Mar. 15, 1906), 616–19. Copy in Con. 969, BTW Papers, DLC.

[1] Momolu Massaquoi was the author of *The Republic of Liberia* (1926). His was a ruling family of Sierra Leone who for several centuries supplied slaves to European traders.

To Henry A. Rucker

[Tuskegee, Ala.] March 20, 1906

Confidential

My dear Mr. Rucker: Without letting any one know who wants the information, will you be kind enough to find out for me, if it is not too much trouble, who of the persons on the enclosed list voted at the last Presidential election, and indicate also which of them have met the conditions for voting in the way of paying poll taxes, etc. Yours truly,

Booker T. Washington

Bishop Turner
Bishop Gaines
Dr. Bowen
Mr. I. Garland Penn
Prof. Hope[1]
Prof. Towns
Dr. DuBois
Prof. Crogman
Dr. Flipper[2]
J. Max Barber
Mr. Herndon

TLpS Con. 4 BTW Papers DLC.

[1] John Hope (1868–1936) was the son of a white man and a black woman of Augusta, Ga. He graduated from Worcester, Mass., Academy and Brown University (B.A., 1894). He taught at Roger Williams University (1894–98) and then at Atlanta Baptist College (later Morehouse College) after 1898. He was president of Morehouse from 1906 to 1931 and led in the merger of the several Atlanta black colleges into a new Atlanta University, of which he was president from 1931 until his death. Hope's membership in the Niagara Movement alienated BTW and his philanthropist friends, until R. R. Moton, a friend of both, restored a measure of mutual respect. In 1909 BTW aided Hope's effort to secure money from Andrew Carnegie. Hope joined the NAACP and served on its advisory board. He was a close friend of Du Bois and offered him employment at Atlanta University when Du Bois broke his connection with the NAACP. (Torrence, *John Hope;* Meier, *Negro Thought,* 114.)

[2] Joseph Simeon Flipper (1859?–1944), an A.M.E. clergyman, was president of Morris Brown College in Atlanta from 1904 to 1908. He was a bishop of the A.M.E. Church beginning in 1908.

To Henry Smith Pritchett[1]

[Tuskegee, Ala.] March 21, 1906

Dear Dr. Pritchett: I am in entire ignorance concerning the conditions under which persons can receive help from the Carnegie Foundation. I have in mind one of my old teachers,[2] a man now perhaps 65 or 70 years old, who has been teaching for 40 or 50 years. He is now connected with the Virginia Union University at Richmond, but is really unable to do effective work and ought to retire. Can you tell me what ought to be done? Yours truly,

Booker T. Washington

TLpS Con. 331 BTW Papers DLC.

1 Henry Smith Pritchett (1857–1939), an astronomer, was director of the U.S. Coast and Geodetic Survey (1897–1900) and president of Massachusetts Institute of Technology (1900–1906). In 1906 he became president of the Carnegie Foundation for the Advancement of Teaching, serving until 1930.

2 George Mellen Prentiss King, a teacher at Virginia Union University and former president of Wayland Seminary, which BTW had attended about 1877, wrote to BTW on Feb. 27, 1906, asking if he were eligible for a Carnegie pension, as he had taught since 1867 and was seventy-three years old. BTW undertook to help him, and at first the signs were favorable. Pritchett found King ineligible, however, because he was a Baptist connected with a Baptist institution. King protested that he was never sectarian in his teachings or in his interest in black education. He tried again in 1908 with the encouragement of BTW and Charles W. Eliot, and in an interview with Pritchett asked to be made an exception to the ban on sectarian teachers. Pritchett was noncommital, however, and the Carnegie Foundation board rejected the request. Undaunted or desperate, King applied a third time. Early in 1913 BTW wrote King in a "wholly confidential" letter that, while the Carnegie Foundation could not break its rule, Carnegie's secretary, James Bertram, had over the years become personally interested in King's case, and at Bertram's suggestion BTW wrote Carnegie asking him to add King's name to his private pension list. Carnegie was now so old, however, that BTW's letter had to wait for many days in his office before it was placed before him. "The suspense has been rather trying to my worn nerves," King commented. Finally, on Jan. 31, 1913, came word that Carnegie had settled a pension of $70 a month on King. (King to BTW, Feb. 27, Mar. 31, 1906, Con. 325; BTW to King, Feb. 22, 1908, Con. 375; King to BTW, July 7, 1908, Con. 375; King to BTW, Jan. 1, Jan. 28, Feb. 1, 1913, Con. 480; BTW to King, Jan. 2, 1913, Con. 480, BTW Papers, DLC.)

To Everett William Lord[1]

[Tuskegee, Ala.] March 21, 1906

My dear Sir: I am glad that you have written as you have in regard to the Porto Rican students. I have taken up the matter with Major Ramsey who is in charge of the young men, and Miss Jane E. Clark who is in charge of the girls, and Miss Clark has already written you. Enclosed I send you Major Ramsey's report.

From the first I have given a great deal of personal attention to the care of these Porto Rican students. I have done it mainly because I have been anxious that they be not spoiled. It is very difficult, as you know, for a student to receive aid from any source without being weakened, and especially is it difficult for one to be helped from a government without his getting the feeling that he must lie down upon the government and be treated as a hot house plant. These students are much better dressed both in comfort and in appearance than the average student at Tuskegee, and you can always rest assured that we never let them suffer for anything that is absolutely necessary for their comfort. We do try, however, to teach them to be sensible and economical, and this I am quite sure is what you want. Our experience on the whole with the Porto Rican students has been satisfactory. We find that while at first they grumble and complain a good deal, before they leave us they settle down to sensible ideas of life. Yours truly,

Booker T. Washington

I believe that we could inflict no greater wrong upon these students than to yield in any measure to their whims and to have everything they want simply because the money comes from the government.

TLpS Con. 315 BTW Papers DLC.

1 Everett William Lord (b. 1871) was assistant commissioner of education in Puerto Rico from 1902 to 1908. He was secretary of the National Child Labor Committee from 1908 to 1910, executive secretary of Boston University from 1910 to 1913, and dean of the college of business administration at Boston University beginning in 1913.

From Melvin Jack Chisum

New York, N.Y. Mch 21st, 1906

Dear Dr. Washington: I have been thinking of a plan that will give me the freest possible movement and yet keep the name Chisum out of the papers, in case you decide to send me to do the Chicago work.

My plan: I will assume an other name; get about with all the people; give my business as a waiter and get a *dinner job* to prove the claim.

Dinner men, in the large restaurants and cafes work from 11 to 3 p.m. each day and some work from 3 p.m. to 12 midnight – I will get on the 11 a.m. to 3 p.m. job for that will allow me sufficient time to do my work.

I am certain I can do this work in that way for I am not known in Chicago.

No one would have any interest in Jack Cameron a waiter, just doing what he could to move in decent society and keep soul and body together with the aid of a pan.

I will observe your instruction and keep my name out of the papers and will, I assure you, get all the information you need. I remain Faithfully yours

Melvin Chisum,
x
Jack Cameron

Unless you suggest a different name, which I will be glad to have you do if you like.

ALS Con. 32 BTW Papers DLC.

From Melvin Jack Chisum

New York, N.Y. Mch 28th, 1906

My dear Dr. Washington: Allow me to thank you again and again for the ten dollars which you ordered sent me, it helped some and I am grateful.

Enclosed please find advertisement of a colored gentleman who is going to "get *the world right,*" he may have the job.

The Telegraph which he quotes is not only "yellow" but a paper without either clean clothes or character and most often utterly untruthful.

Accept my sincere congratulations upon the anniversary of a quarter of a century's unequaled achievement for a grateful nation and a preaching praying, but not perhaps an entirely thankful race.

The race however – in the main – dear Doctor, love and worship you, the hearts of the masses of us are yours.

From one who will always deem it a very great honor to serve you in the ways that please your Eminence most.

Melvin J Chisum

ALS Con. 2 BTW Papers DLC.

To Leslie Pinckney Hill

[Tuskegee, Ala.] March 29, 1906

Mr. Hill: My after-thoughts are always, I suppose, better than my first thoughts. What I had in mind when I spoke of my wish that teachers would not think of themselves as in classes was this: For example, I do not know today, notwithstanding all of my association with him, whether Dr. Park is a graduate of any college or what college. I know absolutely nothing about the kind of preparation that he has had for his present work, except I have incidentally heard him remark that he has spent some years in Germany. The only classification I make of Dr. Park in my mind is that he is a broad, sympathetic, strong, helpful man, and that is the kind of classification I like to see our men lend themselves to as fast as possible. The best educated man is the one who is wholly unconscious of the fact that he is educated at all, this means that his mind dwells upon the objective rather than the subjective side of life. I should think of Jenkin Lloyd Jones in the same way. I know absolutely nothing about the educational opportunities that he has had.

Since turning over in my mind one other point which you suggested, the only case where I can remember of making the kind of comparison that you feared I sometimes might make was, in speaking to the students one night when I made remarks to the effect that so far our well educated men, referring perhaps directly to the college men, had not in any degree shown themselves successful in economic, constructive work. I make that statement, first, because I consider it a fact, and, second, because I hope to spur that class of men on to that kind of endeavor. If I am mistaken in this regard, I shall be very glad to be corrected.

These are the two points on which I do not think I made myself clear in our conversation which I was very glad to have had.

Booker T. Washington

TLpS Con. 3 BTW Papers DLC.

From Roscoe Conkling Bruce

Tuskegee, Alabama. March 30, 1906

Dear Mr. Washington: Thanks heartily for the opportunity of reading the editorial in "The Montgomery Advertiser."[1] When I read the editorial in the "New York Age," I felt at once that it issued from your pen.

Now my personal opinion is that for me to vote down town would be nothing more than a joke. There is neither rhyme nor reason in voting for a candidate and programme to which you are opposed; the alternative is to throw your vote away. A man doesn't want merely to go through the motions of voting. I don't see, therefore, why you should criticize the college man on such grounds as the editorial selects! Very respectfully yours,

Roscoe C. Bruce

TLS Con. 571 BTW Papers DLC.

[1] An editorial in the Montgomery *Advertiser*, Mar. 24, 1906, 4, quoted approvingly a paragraph of a New York *Age* editorial asserting that many more southern blacks could vote if they would only pay their poll taxes and register, and taking to task the black college men, "who rejoice in advising the people to stand up for their political rights" and then fail to "qualify and exercise the primary and necessary function of voting." The *Advertiser* added: "There are negroes in Alabama who could qualify themselves and vote if they would. The fact that they fail to do so is a sufficient answer to the charge of universal disfranchisement so often made by extremists."

To Roscoe Conkling Bruce

[Tuskegee, Ala., ca. Mar. 31, 1906]

Mr. Bruce: I am glad to read yours of March 30th. In my opinion, however, the house which you would erect, is built very largely on the sand.

Leaving aside, for the present, the individual reasons — which each one must settle for himself — as to where and when he should vote, and considering the broader proposition, I would state, that I have never advised, and do not now do so, to any voting colored man, whether educated or not, to go into politics for a livelihood. In the present condition of things, there is no field of employment where the rewards would be so unsatisfactory as in politics; neither would I have insisted eight or ten years ago, that the educated man of our race give attention to voting, in the same way that I now do, for the reason that their example would have perhaps led the masses, who are largely unprepared, to try to follow their course. Now that such restrictions have been thrown around the ballot in the Southern states as to insure the educated colored men a reasonable opportunity of voting, I think that this class should set the example for the less fortunate ones and at the same time, the educated class being small in numbers, can thus pave the way for the gradual introduction of a larger voting population as the years pass by.

I do not remember the ground covered in The Age editorial, but [what] I do attempt to emphasize is the following point: with few exceptions, the intelligent men of our race do not, in a practical way, show an interest in the ballot. For the average man, there is no deep philosophical problem underlying the process of voting. It is simply the paying of one's taxes, and the casting of one's vote, a very simple process.

If you cared to undertake the investigation for your amusement, and perhaps for your instruction, I think you will find that very few of the men on our teachers' list, of voting age, are prepared to vote anywhere, or actually did vote during the last presidential election, either North or South.

I referred a minute ago to your house being built on the sand. I mean this: the Democrat living in Vermont would have the same reason for not voting because he felt sure that the Republican candidate would be elected on each occasion, that you suggest for not voting in this county.

Aside from that, again within the past few months, two elections have taken place in this county; at the first election, the opposing forces a Democrat and Republican President, and a Democrat and Republican candidate for members of Congress, and in this case each party was credited with the exact number of votes cast. Does your argument hold in that case?

Again, there was an election in this county within the last ten days, where the subject to be voted upon was purely economical. Hedge the question around in any way you choose, I do not believe that you can get rid of the plain, hard, unvarnished fact that the intelligent young colored man ought to see to it that he prepares himself to vote, and actually does vote somewhere in the country, and if this class is not careless and indifferent in regard to performing its duty in this respect, I stand open for speedy conversion. Yours truly

Booker T. Washington

TLpS Con. 571 BTW Papers DLC.

From Charles William Anderson

New York, N.Y., April 3, 1906

My dear Doctor: Enclosed please find a letter from Mr. Harry S. Cummings of Baltimore. As you will note, he has added his name to the long list now looking for the Registership of the Treasury. What do you hear of Vernon's case? I am answering Cummings this day that, while I know that you are anxious to serve him in any way you can, I am rather of the opinion that the President himself has a man in view for the position he is seeking, in case Mr. Vernon is not confirmed. I advised Cummings to write to you if he felt like doing so, but, at the same time, informed him that I was strongly of the opinion that the matter of Vernon's successor, in case of his rejection by the Senate, had already been settled, and settled by the chief executive himself.

I am afraid our friends at Washington (the judge and his wife)[1] are playing a big game. Somehow or other, everything that they know about our program, has already reached the enemy. I would respectfully admonish you to be careful what you say to, or in the presence of, either of these people. The friendship of almost a life-time, between Governor P. and myself has been severely strained of late, if not entirely broken, and I believe much of it is due to the influence of this pair. They have called the Governor's attention to my failure to inform him of the matters which have been calling me to Washington from time to time, and aroused his suspicion. I have had a letter from him within the past few days, and after reading it, became convinced that this family had much to do with the old gentleman's present unhappy state of mind.

However, these are not the days for any such considerations, and I therefore wish you a grandly successful celebration of the Twenty-fifth Anniversary of Tuskegee.

Let me know your movements, and when you will be in this neck of the woods. Yours truly,

Charles W. Anderson

TLS Con. 2 BTW Papers DLC. No enclosure found.

[1] Robert H. Terrell and Mary Church Terrell.

An Address on the Twenty-fifth Anniversary of Tuskegee Institute[1]

[Tuskegee, Ala., April 4, 1906]

"And Jesus said, I will make you fishers of men."

In the spirit of these words, the foundation of this institution was laid in 1881, through a gift from the State of Alabama.

For twenty-five years, then, the Tuskegee Normal and Industrial Institute has been fishing for men. What of it, and with what results? In our quest we have used land, houses, henneries, shops, laundries, kitchens, class-rooms, the Bible, arithmetic, the saw, the trowel, and *money* — all these and more we have used in our efforts to fish for men.

A span of five and twenty years in the life of a nation, race or institution, means little as the Great Law-giver reckons time. This is not a sufficient lapse of time in which to conceive and execute a fundamental plan for the redemption of a people, and yet it is ample time in which to note *tendencies* and define *possibilities.*

Pause

Primarily, I believe that my race has found itself, so far as its permanent location is concerned. When this institution began its mission there was uncertainty, lack of faith, halting, and speculation as to our permanent abiding place. As to what degree the influence of the Tuskegee Institute has contributed to this end I will venture no assertion, except to state that, so far as I can interpret the present ambitions and the activities of my people, the main body of the race has decided to remain permanently in the heart of the South, or in what is known as the Black Belt. Fortunately for this institution, it has its location right in the midst of a black population of 215,000 within a radius of 50 miles, and surrounded by states that contain additional millions whose lives it seeks to inspire and guide.

In a little building loaned us for the occasion by the African Methodist Episcopal Zion Church, the school had its birth. It began with one teacher and thirty pupils. From this it has extended its material foundation to 2300 acres of land, 900 of which are cultivated. It has 86 buildings, some small, others large, and real and personal property to the value of $874,943. If we add to this the productive endowment fund of $1,228,458 in the hands of the Trustees, it will be seen that the total material resources of the institution now amount to $2,103,401. For operating expenses we had at first only the $2,000 annually granted us by the State of Alabama. The present cost of operating is about $182,000 annually. A large proportion of this sum we have to secure from the public each year. So much for the physical side of our institution.

The student body is now composed of over 1400 students instead of 30 pupils. Besides the 176 in the Training School, or Children's House, there are half a hundred in the town night schools. The first students came from the counties immediately around the school.

Now students come to us mainly from the lower South, but in all 36 states and territories and 12 foreign countries are represented. A circumstance which adds to the expense and complication of our efforts is that 90 per cent of the student body board and sleep upon our grounds, this being necessary in order that we may impart correct habits of home life. With the number of students named, it is safe to say that we refuse admission, for lack of room and means, each year to as many girls as we enroll.

Counting those who have finished the full course, together with those who have taken a partial course to the extent of fitting them to do reasonably efficient work, we have sent out into the world quite 6,000 men and women who are now largely engaged as workers in agriculture and mechanics, as housekeepers and teachers of both industrial and academic branches throughout the South as well as in Africa and one or two other foreign countries.

Pause

Within a few generations the American Negro has passed through three distinct and momentous transitions. The first of these crises came when he was torn from the primitive civilization which he had created in Africa. While this was not a European or American civilization, it was nevertheless a civilization in some degree creditable.

The second came when he was introduced into a wholly new condition, that of American Slavery.

The third when, slavery ended, he found himself facing the new life of freedom and citizenship.

Perhaps I will not be far out of the way if I add to those a fourth and fifth transition. The fourth when for years he was used in the game of battle-dore and shuttle-cock between the contending political forces of the North and the South. That brings us down to the present time in which, in my opinion, the race in this country has entered upon a wholly new period — a period in which emphasis is being placed upon a side of life not covered in any of the previous experiences of my people. I mean the era of free, independent and intelligent economic and industrial development, accompanied with a growing sense of the worth and value of their own qualities and a desire to make the most of them, under God, for their own good and the welfare of the world. Having to some extent become conscious of the great task imposed on them as a people, they are seeking to lay the foundation deep in the essentials of life. But in this task they often meet many and sometimes needless obstacles.

Pause

If this country is to continue to be a Republic, its task will never be completed as long as seven or eight millions of its people are in a large degree regarded as aliens and are without voice or interest in the welfare of the Government. Such a course will not merely inflict great injustice upon these millions of people, but the nation will pay the price of finding the genius and form of its government changed, not perhaps in name, but certainly in reality, and because of this the world will say that free government is a failure.

Pause

In the relation to our government, then, what is the fundamental mission and what should be the spirit of such an institution as the Tuskegee Institute? As I conceive it, a part of the mission of this school is expressed in the purpose and determination to assist the race in laying such a gradual and permanent foundation in right living, through the accumulation of property, industry, thrift, skill, education of all characters, moral and religious habits and all that which means our usefulness to the community in which we abide, that *naturally, logically, sympathetically* we shall make ourselves grow into full and rightful *enjoyment* and intelligent *use* of the privileges and rewards of citizenship.

Is not this a worthy end? Is not this a mission in which every lover of righteousness, North and South, can unite? Any less ambition would be unworthy of *us*, unworthy of *you*. Any less ambition would make us *perpetual drags, instead of potential forces for good.*

Wherever a Negro touches the life of any community he weakens or he strengthens it; he helps to corrupt it, or helps to purify it. Which, which shall it be?

Weakness invites injustice, and just so long as any portion of the human family is weak, the strong will be tempted to actions which blacken their character and debase the morals of the community. It requires no courage to inflict injustice upon the unprotected. The lifting up of the black man will be a double *blessing* — a *blessing to the weak*, a *blessing to the strong*. If one drop of ink changes the physical condition of many gallons of pure water, how much more is it true that one act of injustice inflicted upon a weak member poisons the life of the whole community.

Pause

Any race suddenly thrown into the midst of a high civilization of which it has not been a voluntary and intelligent creator is likely to mistake the *superficial* signs of civilization for the *reality*, the fuller possession of which can come only to those who have grown with it and who have *re*created it in their own experience and by their own acts.

The main work, then, with which the education of the Negro has to concern itself has constituted a double problem. In most cases where one deals with a backward race, the problem is simple, plain, direct education. In the case of the American Negro, because of his peculiar history and present environment, education has had to concern itself in the past, and should do so in the future, with the problem of teaching the Negro to stand on his own feet. As Carlyle says — "Let us stand on our own basis, at any rate! On such shoes as we ourselves can get. On frost, mud if you will, but honestly on that — on the reality and substance which Nature gives us, not on the semblance, on the thing she has given another than us." I add, with such a spirit, on such a foundation let the Negro seek to gradually build himself into his own glory, rather than to be a weak imitation of others.

The black man has peculiar and original qualities of his own which he should never discard or be ashamed of, and in the development of these he has a field where there are few rivals.

Pause

The second function with which education is concerned is to help the Negro to so articulate while raising his life into that of his white neighbor in a manner that shall mean peace, mutual helpfulness and absolute justice practiced in all the relations of life.

To accomplish these two ends what better tools or mediums could be employed than those which the Tuskegee Institute recognizes — the primary elements of nature — soil, animals, wood, iron, leather, cloth, food — things that bring the student into contact with, and help him to study not merely about the world through the medium of books, but to study things themselves through nature's text book. In following this course we do not wish to limit the growth of any human being.

The methods suggested have another value. Any means of developing the Negro masses, that fails to strengthen his ability and his determination to hold on to his share of the fundamental industries of the South — such as work in agriculture, mechanics, household duties, is weak and mistaken. These are our birthrights, and they should not be sold for a mess of pottage. Without industrial opportunity and efficiency the Negro in the South will find himself in the same condition as many Negroes in the North and the Jews in Russia. Within the industrial and economic opportunity afforded us in the South, education, whatever may be its character, will mean little.

Pause

As we close the first quarter of a century of our efforts here and enter upon a new period, may I be forgiven one personal word.

Pause

First, to the citizens of both races in Tuskegee and Macon County: From the time I came into your midst in 1881 alone and a stranger, I have been the constant recipient of kindness and marked evidences of friendship, and during all these years never have I received one personal indignity in the form of word or act, nor have I asked anything of a black or white citizen that was in his power to grant that I have not received.

Nor can I forbear to refer to the unfailing thoughtfulness, unselfish interest and support during all these years by the Board of *Trustees*, the *teachers*, *graduates* and *students*. Your loyalty and trust have given me *strength* when I have been *weak*, *courage* when I have been *faint*, *faith* when I have been *doubtful*.

In referring to the living I must not forget the dead, but dead only in the flesh. For the spirit and influence of George W. Campbell, Lewis Adams, William H. Baldwin, Jr., and the departed teachers whose life blood has enriched this work, live now at Tuskegee, and will live evermore.

Any discussion of the subject should not fail to give proper credit to the helpful, sagacious, and delicate efforts of Southern white men, of whom the late Chancellor Walter B. Hill of Georgia was a type, for what they have done and are doing in the interest of the elevation of both races in the South and the adjustment of their relations.

To the generous supporters and donors, not forgetting the State of Alabama, from our largest *single* giver, to the friend who has given us annually his twenty-five cents, and there are many such, my heart goes out in deepest gratitude for your faith in me and your support during many trying ordeals.

Pause

Armstrong—Hampton—Frissell, what familiar and sacred names — what they have always meant to us at Tuskegee in gratitude, in love, in helpfulness, no words of mine can describe.

Now as to the future of this institution. Let its past be its best guarantee. I can add no other word in this regard except that I have complete faith in the permanency of this work and in our ability to grow in the direction of increasing usefulness to our race, the South, our whole country. My own part in this work has not been free from error, from shortcomings, but when I have stumbled it has not been from lack of desire to see and to do the right. I trust that upheld by a higher Power and inspired by your confidence, my part in this institution may be more acceptably rendered in coming years than in the past.

Pause

If the friends gathered here, and the absent hundreds, were to ask me in what manner they could best assist us to strengthen and make more useful this plant and the idea and spirit for which it stands, I would say, we need a considerable sum of money that might be used at the discretion of the Trustees and Principal, in *rounding* out the *rough edges* and *strengthening many little weak points* which no one can see and appreciate except those who live in the midst of *needs* of a large institution *from day to day*. Then, in order that so large a proportion of thought, time and bodily strength of the Principal may not be given to the securing of the funds for our daily bread, our endowment should be speedily increased to three or five million dollars.

Pause

And now may I close? If I am asked in what direction, in my opinion, the Tuskegee Institute has been most helpful during the twenty-five years of its life, I should refer to its ownership of land, buildings, endowment, industries, class-room work, to its graduates, to what this school has done in pointing the masses of our people to the importance of getting homes, bank accounts, skill, education and high moral and religious standards — all this has been helpful and valuable, but over and above all this and to *sum the whole,* I should say we have done thus far our greater work in putting a new spirit into the people, a spirit that makes them feel that they have friends right about them, a spirit that has filled them with the idea that they *can* make progress, that they *will* make progress, and fulfill their mission *in this republic.*

TM Con. 311 BTW Papers DLC. Pauses and underlining in BTW's hand.

[1] The twenty-fifth anniversary of the founding of Tuskegee Institute brought together a crowd of the school's supporters and well-wishers. Among the principal speakers were Secretary of War William Howard Taft, Charles W. Eliot, Lyman Abbott, Oswald Garrison Villard, and Andrew Carnegie, as well as a number of Tuskegee graduates and prominent black figures. Speaking for the white South were President John W. Abercrombie of the University of Alabama and the Southern Methodist bishop Charles B. Galloway of Mississippi. Robert C. Ogden introduced BTW for his address, remarking that he had known him since BTW was a student at Hampton, but had no idea then that he would become "a statesman in the solution of one of our most important questions." The principal addresses of the occasion were stenographically reported in a special 44-page edition of the *Tuskegee Student,* 18 (Apr. 28, 1906).

Timothy Thomas Fortune to Jesse Max Barber

New York, April 5, 1906

Dear Mr. Barber, After reading the April number of the Voice of the Negro and being shocked by the brutal coarseness and vulgarity of your treatment of the question of those who think differently from you on the question of the reduction of Southern representation, with the very coarse cartoon accompanying the editorial[1] I decided at the last moment not to use the enclosed article and cut. If Dr. Washington's mouth is padlocked on the question of Southern Representation, it was padlocked by me, as he came over to my view of the matter reluctantly after I had shown him the danger which lurked in that proposition.

I have come to the conclusion that we can do nothing with you Niagara people because you appear to me naturally to run to coarseness and vulgarity in your treatment of men who differ from you, and in criminal practices, as in the case of Trotter, and in under hand throat cutting as in the case of a great many of those who write for the press but don't sign their names from this territory.

I very much regret this, because I thought you a man of broader mind and of more delicate sensibilities than your editorials and cartoons in the April number of the Voice of the Negro appear to show you to be, and, because the best interest of the race cannot be served in the manner in which you treat the matter there and in which it is generally treated by the intelligent men of the Niagara Movement, who simply appear to run riot in defamation of character and misrepresentation of fact. Yours truly,

T T F

TLIr Copy Con. 3 BTW Papers DLC.

[1] It was the cartoon that Fortune found objectionable, for the editorial was a straightforward argument that reduction of representation in Congress of states that disfranchised blacks would mean that "fifty men who are now in Congress at the expense of the public, and whose chief occupation is the belittlement of the Negro, would be sent back to the farms." The cartoon caricatured BTW with a lock on his lips labeled "Southern Representation." (*Voice of the Negro*, 3 [Apr. 1906], 242–43.)

From Jesse Max Barber

Atlanta, Ga. April 6, 1906

My dear Sir: I have arranged with Mr. Hill of your school to have him furnish me an article on the Twenty-fifth Anniversary of Tuskegee Institute, which article we expect to illustrate rather copiously with pictures made by Underwood & Underwood.

Although there were great crowds at Tuskegee when I was there and everything was show and excitement, still I had the opportunity of making a careful study of some of the features of your school, and am delighted to say that my impression was not unfavorable.

I wish to thank you for the many courtesies shown me while at your school. You have a magnificent opportunity. Practically, the Nation comes at your beck and call. As a Negro, and as one vitally interested in all that pertains to the uplift of my race, I trust you may make no mistake in using these opportunities, and that truly you may justify the magnificent expressions that were heard of you on every hand.

With best wishes, I am Yours very truly,

J. Max Barber

TLS Con. 32 BTW Papers DLC.

To William Howard Taft

Tuskegee Institute, Alabama April 9, 1906

My dear Secretary Taft: This is the very earliest moment in which I could find time to thank you from all my heart for the magnificent address which you delivered during our Anniversary. Every one spoke of it as being a statesman-like deliverance in the very highest sense. I cannot refrain from repeating what I said to you when you were here, first, I could not see how you could find time to prepare such an address, and second, it is hard for me to realize how you can see so clearly into the actual conditions existing here at the South. The average man coming into this section speaks from the outside rather than from the inside.

I sent the President the following telegram the day after you left: "The speech of Secretary Taft yesterday was simply immense. It more than met the highest expectations of everyone and we are most grateful to you and to him."

One other point. Will you be kind enough to send me a memorandum containing all of your expenses, and I shall be very glad to see that a check is sent to cover the whole.

I am more chagrined than I can express over the fact that the Pullman car people made such a blunder in not reserving your stateroom. I not only had a letter from them stating that it would be reserved, but had a man go to the office in New Orleans in person and see to it.

You have helped us by your presence and by your words more than it is possible for you to understand. Yours very truly,

Booker T. Washington

TLS William Howard Taft Papers DLC.

To Frederick Randolph Moore

[Tuskegee, Ala.] April 9, 1906

My dear Mr. Moore: From time to time I have expressed to you my gratification at the improved condition of your magazine and at the strong features of it that now and then appear.

I think I ought to say to you that which many of your best friends are constantly expressing, however, and that is that for the same money and strength you can get out a magazine that in dignity and power will be quite different from the one which you are now publishing. I do not believe that it will cost you a single dollar more to get out a really high toned magazine than the one now being issued. In magazine breadth, dignity and form, your best friends will tell you that it does not come up to the Voice of the Negro. I understand, of course, that you cannot work a revolution at once, but it ought not to stop short of being the best. Yours very truly,

Booker T. Washington

TLpS Con. 33 BTW Papers DLC.

To John Wesley Edward Bowen

[Tuskegee, Ala.] April 9, 1906

Dear Dr. Bowen: Enclosed I send you copy of letters which I have written at your suggestion to both the trustees of Gammon and the Freedmen's Aid Board of Trustees.[1]

In this connection I cannot refrain from enclosing a vicious cartoon which appears in the last issue of your magazine.

In this letter I have expressed the feeling I have toward you in my heart, and I presume the cartoon expresses your feeling toward me. Yours very truly,

Booker T. Washington

TLpS Con. 315 BTW Papers DLC.

1 BTW in both enclosed letters recommended Bowen for the presidency of Gammon Theological Seminary, praising his ability and integrity. Bowen became president of Gammon in 1906.

To Andrew Carnegie

[Tuskegee, Ala.] April 9, 1906

Dear Mr. Carnegie: You were good enough, while at Tuskegee, to inquire with regard to the school from which my Secretary, Mr. Scott comes. He attended Wiley University, at Marshall, Texas, one of the schools under the supervision and direction of The Freedmen's Aid.

You have recently offered to give this school Fifteen Thousand Dollars, for a library, provided they raise Fifteen Thousand Dollars additional, for its maintenance.

Mr. Scott is very anxious that this school, from which he comes, secure one of your libraries. It has done a magnificent work in its chosen field, and is entitled to encouragement. To raise Fifteen Thousand Dollars, however, is something of a hardship, the officers of the school feel.

The Board of Trustees of the school pledge Five Hundred Dollars a year, for the keeping of the library, and this sum will be guaranteed by the Freedmen's Aid and Southern Educational Society, Cincinnati, if this latter proposition meets your approval.[1]

You gave, as you may recall, in the case of Livingstone College, a library without any reservations.

If you can consider the matter, it will be greatly appreciated. Very truly yours,

Booker T. Washington

TLpS Con. 318 BTW Papers DLC.

[1] Carnegie approved of the grant of $15,000 to Wiley University without the usual reservation of matching funds. James Bertram wrote BTW that Carnegie did so "principally on account of Mr. Scott. . . ." Bertram urged BTW not to publicize the arrangement in order to keep other schools from getting the idea that Wiley was a precedent.

To Theodore Wellington Jones

[Tuskegee, Ala.] April 10, 1906

My dear Mr. Jones: Enclosed I send you a copy of a speech delivered by William Lloyd Garrison during our Anniversary.

I notice that the Conservator states that I am responsible for Mr. Taft's speech. I wonder if you would not write the Conservator a letter and ask them if I am not also responsible for Mr. Garrison's speech. Both men spoke from the same platform at my invitation. I think it well to make him print Garrison's speech. One of the points that I have been striving to attain to at Tuskegee for years is to have a platform where we could have free discussion, something rather unknown in the South until recent years. Yours truly,

Booker T. Washington

TLpS Con. 324 BTW Papers DLC.

To Francis Jackson Garrison

Tuskegee Institute, Alabama. April 10, 1906

My dear Mr. Garrison: I wish you could have been here last week to have witnessed the magnificent reception given your brother; it is hard to describe it in words. But my especial point in writing you is to send you a copy of the Montgomery Advertiser, the leading Democratic paper in this state, which contains a description of the tilt between President John W. Abercrombie, of the University of Alabama, and your brother.[1] The mere fact that we have gotten to the point where in the heart of the South we can have men disagree on so vital a question on the same platform and not offer threats of lynching and shot guns in my opinion indicates great progress. One of the points that I have been trying to reach at Tuskegee for years is to get to the place where we could have free discussion on our platform whether we agree or not with those who speak, and that place we are fast reaching. Yours very truly,

Booker T. Washington

TLS James Weldon Johnson Collection CtY. A press copy is in Con. 322, BTW Papers, DLC.

1 Under the title "Abercrombie and Garrison Have Views at Variance," the Montgomery *Advertiser*, Apr. 7, 1906, 5, gave the complete text of Abercrombie's address

at the Tuskegee twenty-fifth anniversary celebration and paraphrased the impromptu reply of William Lloyd Garrison, Jr. After pronouncing slavery of greater benefit to the slaves than to the owners, Abercrombie called the enfranchisement of blacks "the colossal mistake" of Reconstruction. As for universal education, he said: "If the continued inaction of the national government renders it necessary for one of the races to receive meager educational advantages, it is best for the negro, that for a season, the advantages should go to the dominant race." Garrison said that he spoke as a member not of a superior race, but of the human race. As a white man, he felt humiliation because of the wrong of slavery. On the voting rights issue he said the only way to learn was by doing, not by instruction from the outside. The black journalist J. Max Barber declared Garrison's reply to Abercrombie the high point of the anniversary, and reported that the audience "broke loose in thunderous handclapping and shouting." (*Voice of the Negro*, 3 [May 1906], 321.)

To Charles William Anderson

[Tuskegee, Ala.] April 10, 1906

Personal

My dear Mr. Anderson: I have yours of April 3d which came in the midst of our Anniversary season. I am planning to pass through New York sometime between the 18th and 24th. I shall not be in your city, however, to remain, I fear, until towards the last of the month.

One point raised in your letter troubles me a good deal, and that is the possibility of some break between you and Gov. Pinchback. If I may be allowed to advise or even suggest, I want to urge you to take into consideration the fact of the Governor's age, and the further fact because of his unfortunate financial condition he is more likely to be more sensitive than a man in another condition would be. In a word, when a man is on the upward grade, sure of success, he has a different spirit than he has when placed in an opposite condition, and for that reason I think you can afford to go very much out of your way to conciliate him and retain his friendship.

I confess that until you called it to my attention recently I had not scented the danger lurking among those Washington parties to the extent that I have, and I shall be more careful with my words and actions in the future.

I can do nothing regarding Cummings unless the President calls the matter to my attention. It is likely I shall have an interview with the President on the 21st, and most likely he will raise a number of questions, at any rate I can find out then where we are.

Enclosed I send you a letter received from Bush which shows that another friend is on the border of trouble because he seems to have gotten a "refusing" favor.

Our Anniversary was a magnificent success from every point of view, as far as my judgement goes. Yours very truly,

Booker T. Washington

TLSr Copy Con. 2 BTW Papers DLC. No enclosure found.

From William Howard Taft

[Washington, D.C.] April 12, 1906

My dear Mr. Washington: I have your letter of April 9th, and thank you very sincerely for your warm words of approval of my speech. I enjoyed my visit to Tuskegee very much, both because of the company, and of your great work which I saw there in substantial form.

I shall not send any bill for my expenses because of the pleasure I had in going, and I make that as a contribution to your work. I wish I had the means to make a substantial one.

I have already sent you a revised copy of the address which I delivered.

With very warm regards and highest respect, believe me, Sincerely yours,

Wm H Taft

TLpS William Howard Taft Papers DLC.

Emmett Jay Scott to John Anderson Lankford

[Tuskegee, Ala.] April 12, 1906

Personal and Confidential.

My dear Mr. Lankford: I am sending the enclosed, which I wish you to treat as confidential. It has occurred to me that you could accomplish much good by getting it into The Bee.

I take it that you have your own method of approaching the Editor of that paper. Of course it is my desire that you treat the whole matter as emanating[?] from you, and as if an Atlanta friend sent it to you with the hope that you could get it in The Bee.

After you have read the matter over, I would be glad to hear what you think about it. Very truly yours,

Emmett J. Scott

TLpS Con. 3 BTW Papers DLC.

From Charles William Anderson

New York, N.Y., April 13, 1906

Dear Doctor: Note this editorial from the Boston "Pilate" – the leading Roman Catholic paper of the country. Someone of my Catholic friends sent it to me.

I hope you will move in Bush's[1] interest at once. Although I have seen but little of him, he strikes me as being genuine. He seems to be the kind that deserves help.

I fear Cummings is shooting too high. That Chicago convention speech has fired his ambition.

Moore is here working at his old trade of visiting from house to house and talking "small beer." He is still the first to bring bad news, and still believes every other friend false. He is like a Summer coon – neither fit for fur or meat.

I am pleased to say that my annual (not quarterly) examination has been concluded, and the office remains rated at No 1. Thus it has been rated higher every day since I have been here, than it has when Treat[2] held it. Yours,

Anderson

ALS Con. 2 BTW Papers DLC.

[1] John E. Bush.

[2] Charles H. Treat (1841–1910) was Treasurer of the United States (1905–9). He had been Anderson's immediate predecessor as collector of internal revenue in the Wall Street district (1897–1905).

From William G. Willcox

New York, April 13, 1906

Dear Mr. Washington; In connection with the enclosed letter, I cannot refrain from expressing my regret that some of the speakers indulged in quite so much personal praise for your own part in the great work which Tuskegee is doing. I fully appreciate your own evident dislike of any such personal adulation, for to my mind the realization of the great opportunity which has fallen to your lot and of the extent to which the efforts and hopes of both races for the uplifting of your people are centered in you, must bring such a sense of responsibility and consecration that any fulsome personal praise must be well-nigh intolerable.

I should not mention this matter, however, but for the fact that I believe it for the best interest of your work that such expressions should be discouraged as far as possible. There are plenty of critics North and South, who are watching for any evidence of the personal pride and vanity which they consider the inevitable result of your success, and few things could hurt your influence more than any impression that this expectation had been realized. I have no fear that you, yourself, will ever give any occasion for such an impression, but I cannot help fearing that such expressions as were used by some of the speakers, may tend in that direction and so do positive harm. It is difficult for you to discourage such public expressions out of deference to your personal wishes, but if you feel as I do, that such expressions are really against the interest of your work, any such suggestion from you to future speakers would of course be heeded. Your work speaks for itself and has nothing to gain, I think, from any public personal praise. On the contrary, I am decidedly of the opinion that in keeping your own personality in the background, as you always have done, you really strengthen your personal influence and your hold upon the confidence and support of the friends of the negro race. Very truly yours,

William G. Willcox

TLS Con. 339 BTW Papers DLC. No enclosure found.

To Jesse Max Barber

[Tuskegee, Ala.] April 14, 1906

Personal

My dear Sir: I thank you very much for your kind letter of April 6th. I am very much interested in the article which you are going to use in your magazine, bearing upon our work here, and I thank you for telling me about it.

I was very sorry that I could not give you more personal attention, and extend more in the way of personal courtesy to you while you were here, but you know how great the crowd was and that the consequent demands upon my time made it impossible for me to do much in that direction.

One of the achievements that I hope to see brought about at Tuskegee is to get to the point where there shall be freedom of discussion; to have a platform where persons of any race or section of the country can have his say. In pursuing this policy, however, I am not unmindful of the fact that in this critical period we shall have to be very careful to guard against expressions that might prove harmful, by placing the race in a false position, and making its upward march the more difficult.

As one example of what I am constantly doing, wherever opportunity presents itself, I send you for your own eye, copy of a letter which I wrote to President Eliot, who was kind enough to give me an outline of his address at Tuskegee.

You will note that the address which he delivered was quite different from the one which he had planned to deliver.

I shall be glad to have you come here again in the future, whenever you can do so. Very truly yours,

Booker T. Washington

TLpS Con. 32 BTW Papers DLC.

From Francis Jackson Garrison

Lexington, Mass. April 14, 1906

My dear Friend: I thank you for the three Montgomery papers which you have kindly sent me, the last of which has the best account I have seen of my brother's little speech, & of Prest. Abercrombie's address which called forth his protest & testimony. I am very glad that you introduced my dear brother at the "psychological moment," & that his unpremeditated remarks went straight to the heart of the question. Evidently they went to the hearts of the great majority of his hearers as well, as he put his foot at once on the assumption that the whites are a "superior race," & virtually echoed the words of our father to the free colored people in 1831, "I never rise to address a colored audience without feeling ashamed of my own color; ashamed of being identified with a race of men who have done you so much injustice," &c. What a monstrous perversion of words & facts was Abercrombie's when he talked of the negroes, under slavery, getting "release from barbarism," "the foundation of the home, the introduction to civilization, & the elevating influences of the Christian religion!" Such cant sickens me.

I am glad that you find encouragement in the fact that this exchange of diametrically opposite opinions could take place without threats of lynching & shooting, & I dare say you are right, but the Southern press has been quick to seize upon the matter, & some of them, like the Vicksburg *Herald* (which I am told had three columns of denunciation & abuse) have shown the cloven hoof as of old. Doubtless you are better able than me to guage the value or consequence of these utterances, & to make the proper discount for political fustian, but some of your northern visitors, like President Eliot, came back enthusiastic over Tuskegee but disheartened (or depressed) by the implacable, unyielding attitude of the southern whites.

I was delighted with your address, & do not see how it could have been bettered, & you have certainly planted the banner on the outer wall now. The Boston *Herald*'s characterization of two paragraphs as worthy of Lincoln was no empty compliment or exaggeration. I congratulate you with all my heart on the wisdom that guided your utterance, and on the splendid success of the celebration. I don't see how Carnegie can resist the temptation to invest two or three, or five millions in the Institute at once! I find the volume on "Tuskegee & its People" most fascinating & inspiring, & have read & re-read it, & read it aloud to others. I wonder how many years you will have to wait for the Dotger legacy.[1] I dare say that if you could cash at once all the legacies which have been written into wills, but await the decease of the donors, your endowment would not fall very far short of the $3,000,000 mark. I saw you had a small plum of $10,000 from Mrs. Boardman[2] of New Haven, the other day. Always gratefully & faithfully yours,

Francis J. Garrison

ALS Con. 322 BTW Papers DLC.

1 Andrew J. Dotger of South Orange, N.J., died Dec. 30, 1905, leaving Tuskegee a bequest first estimated at $500,000, but later scaled to not less than $100,000, to go to the institution at the death of his wife, Clara L. Dotger. Born in Philadelphia in 1841, Dotger had retired from the New York Stock Exchange some thirty years earlier. He had no connection with Tuskegee and had never visited it. BTW said in his annual report: "In expressing our deep gratitude for this unexpected and very generous remembrance, I want to say that during the brief and only interview that I ever had with Mr. Dotger he informed me that he was planning to remember the school in his will because he had studied its policies and methods and believed thoroughly in both. It was found later that he first became interested through a summer meeting held at Poland Springs Hotel, Maine." (*Twenty-fifth Annual Report of the Principal of Tuskegee Normal and Industrial Institute*, May 31, 1906, 7, Con. 580, BTW Papers, DLC.)

2 Probably Lucy Hall Boardman of New Haven, widow of the wealthy lawyer and businessman William W. Boardman.

John Anderson Lankford to Emmett Jay Scott

Washington, D.C., April 14th, 1906

My Dear Friend Scott: Yours of the 12th, inst. at hand contents duly noted, I read the matter over with care and it expressed my sentiments. I made the occasion to see the Editor of the Bee, and after we had discussed the political atmosphere of Washington and the country at large, I told him that I had a letter from one of my Atlanta friends, which I would like for him to publish. He read it and we discussed it pro and con, and he promised me that he would publish it in the next week's issue of the Bee. He said my friend would have to send me a small check, I asked him how large it would have to be, he told me that he would leave that to his discretion. You know a great deal about these matters and about what he should have, or what would make him publish about, what we would have him publish. I have found it a great help to me since I have been in this city to make friends with the Bee, and to do that, as you know, somewhat, the temperament of the man, about what I had to do.

He is under some obligations to me and I feel sure that he will publish the article in a prominent place in the paper. I am respectfully yours,

J. A. Lankford

TLS Con. 326 BTW Papers DLC.

To William G. Willcox

[Tuskegee, Ala.] April 16, 1906

My dear Mr. Willcox: You do not know how very much I thank you for the two letters which have just been received. The suggestions you make and the advice which you give concerning the development of our work and the improvement of our race are admirable from every point of view.

I hope I did not take an unwarranted liberty, but I did have both of your letters read to our teachers and students last night in the Chapel.

I was especially pleased with what you said concerning the frequent mention of myself in connection with this work by the speakers. Your letter expresses my own views and wishes so fully and in a way that would have been awkward to have done so myself, that I took the liberty of having it read, and I feel quite sure that the suggestion will spread from the teachers and students among others. This frequent praise of myself by speakers is always a matter of great distaste to me, but I presume it is one of the inflictions that one has to bear up under as best he can.

We are very grateful to you for your increased subscription to the school. Yours very truly,

Booker T. Washington

TLpS Con. 339 BTW Papers DLC.

From Isabel Hayes Chapin Barrows

N.Y. [City] April 16, 1906

My dear Dr. Washington, Now that I am back again in New York and can look back upon the Tuskegee celebration from a little distance I want to congratulate you on the grand occasion. You will find my reports in the Outlook and in the Christian Register, with a paragraph in the Woman's Journal. It was a pleasure to be able to use my pen once more in behalf of a work that has always so deeply interested me.

I also want to thank you for allowing the Kowaliga school to be represented in your exhibit of the work of your graduates. On my homeward way I stopped a day and visited the school and the turpentine works of the Dixie Co. and the saw mill and found to my surprise that a classmate of my son in law is the cashier of that company! He is a splendid man, an honor to the colored race.

And now once more, Mr. Washington, I want to ask you if the time has not come when you can take the Kowaliga school into your favor? Your influence against it is an adamantine wall that I find everywhere. I cannot quite understand it all. I do understand perfectly that you have not time *personally* to visit it, to act as trustee, or to be in any way sponsor for it. It is natural and necessary that you should stand loyally by your own graduates. It seems to me that you can do that and at the same time cheerfully acknowledge when other schools are doing well. If they are *not* doing well at Kowaliga I am sure Mr. Benson and Mr. Strothers would be grateful to you for any suggestions as to improvement in their work. But if you have no desire to do that, can you not at least take away the ban that you have placed on their work and which makes it ten times as hard for them as it ought to be?

I think if you could have been behind a screen the other night at Kowaliga, and heard William Benson, at evening prayers in the school, pray for Tuskegee and *for you personally*, in tender, grateful words, your heart would have been touched as mine was. I think you would have felt that he was trying to do his best and deserved the sympathy of the greater and stronger men who are working for their people.

I need hardly say that Mr. Benson knows nothing of my writing to you. I simply could not resist it, having known and honored you so long. I felt that a direct appeal to you might secure for William Benson your old-time confidence in him that I cannot believe he has ever forfeited.[1]

I was sorry not to see Mrs. Washington in Tuskegee, but there were so many who had a greater claim on her that I did not call upon her. Yours sincerely,

Isabel C. Barrows

TLS Con. 315 BTW Papers DLC.

1 BTW in reply promised vaguely to discuss the Benson matter sometime when in New York. (Ca. Apr. 18, 1906, Con. 316, BTW Papers, DLC.)

Emmett Jay Scott to John Anderson Lankford

[Tuskegee, Ala.] April 16, 1906

My dear Sir: I want to suggest that you meet your friend's expectations in the matter of the remuneration, advising me as to what you do and I shall be glad at once to reimburse you.

Of course you can give your friend your check, stating that you had cashed the money order which came to you and give your check instead.

I am, with sincere regards and deep appreciation of your letter, Yours very truly,

Emmett J. Scott

TLpS Con. 326 BTW Papers DLC.

From John Wesley Edward Bowen

Atlanta, Ga., April 16th. 1906

Personal

Dear Mr. Washington: I acknowledge with a sense of gratitude and appreciation the receipt of your letter containing a copy of your recommendation to our Board of Trustees with reference to the Presidency of our Seminary. Your putting of the case is in courteous, strong, dignified and convincing language. I thank you for the same. But beyond the language and the fact of your appeal for me, I appreciate the spirit of friendliness you so strongly manifest toward me.

Let me say with reference to the cartoon that appears in our Magazine, that it is a great surprise and a distasteful thing to me. I knew nothing of its appearance until your letter came, I had been in the West. It does not represent my feelings towards you in the least, on the contrary, speaking personally it is not only distasteful but offensive, for I regard you as a man of highest character and farthest-removed from the suggestion made in that cartoon. I have already spoken my feeling to a part of the management of our Magazine in stronger language than I here write to you. You may rely implicitly upon my esteem, respect and high course toward you and also upon my influence as far as I can render it to do the right thing by you.

I hope the celebration came up to your high ideals. With sentiments of profound respect and pure friendship, I am, Yours Sincerely,

J. W. E. Bowen

TLS Con. 315 BTW Papers DLC.

To Oswald Garrison Villard

Tuskegee Institute, Alabama. Apr. 19, 1906

Dear Mr. Villard: Let me thank you for your kind letter conveying to us a lock of John Brown's hair and the interesting and significant letter which accompanies same. All of these, including the letter from his son will be placed in the historical room of the library. Yours truly,

Booker T. Washington

TLS Oswald Garrison Villard Papers MH.

From Jesse Max Barber

Atlanta, Ga. April 23, 1906

My dear Sir: I thank you very much for your favor of April 14th. You need give yourself no uneasiness regarding the attentions shown me while at Tuskegee. Everyone was very courteous and I did not suffer at all for lack of attention. I understood that the great crowds prevented you from showing anyone any personal attention.

Your desire to make Tuskegee a place where we may have freedom of discussion on all the vital problems affecting the country is a worthy ambition and should receive the encouragement of all well-wishers of the race. If we can get free and untrammeled speech in this section of the country, conditions will right themselves very speedily.

I am glad to have had the opportunity of reading this letter which you wrote President Eliot. Evidently, Mr. Eliot was going to make a speech that would have done us a great deal of harm, and I am glad you influenced him not to deliver the address that he had in mind. In doing so, you have rendered the race a valuable service.

The article we intended to publish in the May number of our Magazine did not arrive. Somehow or other Mr. Hill was not able to prepare it on time, and, therefore, we had to go to press without it. However, I am giving the occasion an extended editorial write-up.[1] You will, of course, see from some of the things I have said that

I do not reverence Tuskegee without reservation, but still I have found many good things about the school, and have taken occasion to say as much.

I shall be glad to visit Tuskegee again when occasion offers. Yours very truly,

J. Max Barber

TLS Con. 32 BTW Papers DLC.

1 "Tuskegee's Twenty-fifth Aniversary," *Voice of the Negro*, 3 (May 1906), 315–22. See vol. 9.

From Margaret James Murray Washington

[Tuskegee, Ala.] April 24—1906

Mr. Washington: I think you will find that there are some lady teachers visiting with gentlemen teachers in the different offices. I do not write you about this because I have any special lack of confidence in these ladies and in these gentlemen, but simply because it is a bad example for students. Yesterday morning, Sunday, during church services, Miss Thompson[1] and Mr. Pitt[2] were in the office where Mr. Pitt works. It does seem to me that any young person would see the impropriety of waiting until the people go to church and until a building is vacated to do a thing of this kind.

Miss Dotson[3] also visits with Captain Austin in his office. All of these young men go to Major Ramsey's office and it seems to me that Captain Austin and Miss Dotson should see this is not the proper thing to do, not because the thing in itself is bad, but because it looks badly to the average student and to the average grown-up person, for I have heard both of these young women criticised about this sort of thing, not by students only, but by our teachers. Yours very truly,

Mrs W

TLI Con. 255 BTW Papers DLC.

1 Fannie Thompson was an assistant in the cooking division at Tuskegee Institute from 1903 to 1906.

2 Claudius N. Pitt was assistant bookkeeper at Tuskegee Institute from about 1903 to 1911.

3 Mary Louise Dotson, a former Tuskegee student who received a cooking certificate in 1900, was an assistant in the cooking and laundry divisions at Tuskegee Institute from 1903 to 1906.

A Bill from Pinkerton's National Detective Agency

New York, April 25th, 1906

For Services and Expenses
In case of
Protecting Visitors

		To Services of Opt. G. A. F.	
Apr.	2	A.M. to Apr. 7th, P.M., 5½ days $8.00	44.00
		Expenses of same:	
	2	To Apr. 7th, car fares and incidental expenses while with parties on train, including tips to waiters and porters	14.95
			58.95

TD Con. 4 BTW Papers DLC.

To Charles Patrick Joseph Mooney

[Tuskegee, Ala., ca. Apr. 30, 1906]

Personal

My dear Mr. Mooney: I remember you very well, and especially our pleasant journey from Washington Southward. I have thought about you a good many times since and wondered where you were located, and for this reason I am especially glad to have your letter showing that you are in a place of such use and power.

Now, regarding the Negro and the Panama Canal.[1] What I am now stating of course is strictly confidential. The suggestion to take any large number of colored people from the Southern States to dig the Panama Canal is not practical for this reason — labor is very scarce in the South, and the minute any effort is made on the part of the government officials to secure colored labor from the Southern States to go to Panama, that minute will the Southern congressmen refuse to vote appropriations to build the canal, that is the whole story in a nutshell. In fact, on several occasions the Southern papers have taken this matter up and have warned their congressmen to permit nothing to be done in the direction of enticing colored people to go from the South to Panama. The President I am quite sure understands this phase of the question fully. The American Negro is by far the best workman for that kind of work in the world in my opinion, and it is a pity that he cannot have a larger hand in the digging of the canal.

When I am again in Chicago I shall hope to call to see you. In the meantime, if I can serve you in any manner, please do not hesitate to let me know. It is probable that a friend of mine, Mr. S. Laing Williams, will call to see you in a few days. He is a fine fellow, and you can depend upon him for any service you may have in connection with our people in Chicago. Yours very truly,

Booker T. Washington

TLpS Con. 328 BTW Papers DLC.

[1] Mooney, an editor for the Chicago *American*, wrote BTW that he believed that blacks would be well suited to work on the Panama Canal, and that he planned to take up the idea with Secretary William H. Taft after consulting with BTW. (Apr. 25, 1906, Con. 34, BTW Papers, DLC.)

BIBLIOGRAPHY

This bibliography gives fuller information on works cited in the annotations and endnotes. It is not intended to be comprehensive of works on the subjects dealt with in the volume or of works consulted in the process of annotation.

Contee, Clarence G. "Butler R. Wilson and the Boston NAACP Branch," *Crisis*, 81 (Dec. 1974), 346–48.

Crofts, Daniel W. "The Warner-Foraker Amendment to the Hepburn Bill: Friend or Foe of Jim Crow?" *Journal of Southern History*, 39 (Aug. 1973), 341–58.

Daniel, Pete. *The Shadow of Slavery: Peonage in the South, 1901–1969*. Urbana: University of Illinois Press, 1972.

Fehnstoke, Ruperth [S. Becker von Grabill]. *Letters from Tuskegee, Being the Confessions of a Yankee*. Birmingham, Ala.: Roberts and Son, 1905.

Fox, Stephen R. *The Guardian of Boston: William Monroe Trotter*. New York: Atheneum Publishers, 1970.

Garrison, Wendell Phillips, and Francis Jackson Garrison, eds. *William Lloyd Garrison, 1805–1879: The Story of His Life Told by His Children*. 4 vols. Boston: Houghton Mifflin and Company, 1894.

Harlan, Louis R. "The Secret Life of Booker T. Washington," *Journal of Southern History*, 37 (Aug. 1971), 393–416.

Holmes, William F. "Whitecapping: Agrarian Violence in Mississippi, 1902–1906," *Journal of Southern History*, 35 (May 1969), 165–85.

Katzman, David M. *Before the Ghetto: Black Detroit in the Nineteenth Century.* Urbana: University of Illinois Press, 1973.

Lamon, Lester C. *Black Tennesseans, 1900–1930.* Knoxville: University of Tennessee Press, 1977.

Levy, Eugene. *James Weldon Johnson: Black Leader, Black Voice.* Chicago: University of Chicago Press, 1973.

Matthews, Fred H. *Quest for an American Sociology: Robert E. Park and the Chicago School.* Montreal and London: McGill-Queen's University Press, 1977.

Meier, August. "Booker T. Washington and the Negro Press: With Special Reference to the *Colored American Magazine,*" *Journal of Negro History,* 38 (Jan. 1953), 67–90.

———. *Negro Thought in America, 1880–1915: Racial Ideologies in the Age of Booker T. Washington.* Ann Arbor: University of Michigan Press, 1963.

Smith, Edwin W. *Aggrey of Africa: A Study in Black and White.* New York: Richard R. Smith, Inc., 1930.

Spear, Allan H. *Black Chicago: The Making of a Negro Ghetto, 1890–1920.* Chicago: University of Chicago Press, 1967.

Torrence, Frederic Ridgely. *The Story of John Hope.* New York: Macmillan Company, 1948.

Wynes, Charles E., ed. *Forgotten Voices: Dissenting Southerners in an Age of Conformity.* Baton Rouge: Louisiana State University Press, 1967.

INDEX

NOTE: The asterisk indicates the location of detailed information. This index, while not cumulative, does include the major identifications of persons annotated in earlier volumes of the series who are mentioned in this volume. References to earlier volumes will appear first and will be preceded by the volume number followed by a colon. Lyman Abbott's annotation, for example, will appear as *3:43-44. Occasionally a name will have more than one entry with an asterisk when new information or further biographical detail is presented.

Index